George W. Clark

The Gospel of John

a popular commentary upon a critical basis, especialy designed for pastors and

Sunday schools - Vol. 4

George W. Clark

The Gospel of John
a popular commentary upon a critical basis, especialy designed for pastors and Sunday schools - Vol. 4

ISBN/EAN: 9783337285449

Printed in Europe, USA, Canada, Australia, Japan

Cover: Foto ©Lupo / pixelio.de

More available books at **www.hansebooks.com**

THIS VOLUME

IS

AFFECTIONATELY INSCRIBED BY THE AUTHOR

TO THE MEMORY OF THE LATE

HENRY C. FISH, D.D.,

TO WHOSE PLANS AND EFFORTS IT OWES ITS EARLY ISSUE,
AS A TOKEN OF MUTUAL FRIENDSHIP AND LOVE, AND
AN EXPRESSION OF GRATEFUL REMEMBRANCE
OF HIS AID, ENCOURAGEMENT, AND
HELPFUL INTEREST DURING
YEARS OF TOIL UPON

THE FOUR GOSPELS

THE FOUR GOSPELS.

"WE have the gospel proclamation of Christ before us in a fourfold form. The different books do not offer different doctrines. They teach historically, and preach for instruction, one and the same Christ; only each has his own method. These various methods of preaching and teaching Christ are founded not in different conceptions, in progressive knowledge, and the like. They are determined by the form of the scope and of the historical stage within which, and in relation to which, Christ is made known. For the first church of Christ, within the bounds of Israel, the method of the first Gospel was the right form for preaching Christ. Hence Matthew used a definite material, exactly fitted for this design. The next two Gospels show us what shape the same material takes when it is made known to Gentile Christian churches. These Gospels confine themselves to the same material, because they are neither apostolical, nor yet original, but of a secondary origin. Then something else came to be needed. The commonwealth of Israel fell to ruin, and the distinction between the Gentile and Jewish Christians within the Christian church lost its earlier meaning, so that it was no longer to be considered in the evangelical teaching concerning Christ. At this time, in opposition to the general enmity against belief in Christ, they needed the general proof of the necessity, possibility, and nature of belief. And against the reviling of Christ they needed the most general declaration of him. The fourth Gospel supplies this want. It presents the person and life of Christ in its most essential and most comprehensive significance for a church which by this time was simply the church of Christ united in one."—CHRISTIAN E. LUTHARDT, *Bibliotheca Sacra*, Jan., 1873, p. 13.

PREFACE.

A TRADITION is related most fully by Theodore of Mopsuestia, who lived in the latter part of the fourth century, that while the apostle John was residing at Ephesus the Christians of Asia laid before him the Gospels of Matthew, Mark, and Luke, and asked his opinion of them. He testified to their truthfulness, but added that they who discourse on the coming of Christ in the flesh ought not to omit speaking of his divinity, lest in after time they who were accustomed to such discourse might suppose that Christ was only what he appeared to be. The brethren having exhorted him to write such things as seemed to him the most important, he at length complied, and at the very beginning discoursed upon the divinity of Christ, judging this to be the necessary commencement of the Gospel, and then went on to the incarnation. That there may be substantial truth in this tradition is not at all improbable, and accords well with the nature and later date of the fourth Gospel. Being occupied with the deep things of God, and containing the sublimest discourses of our Saviour, its exposition is more difficult than that of the other Gospels. This difficulty, however, is lessened by the clearness, simplicity, and beauty of its language. In dealing with its lofty themes the expositor is tempted to a diffuseness which is not best suited to either the common reader or to the ordinary Sunday-school teacher. It has therefore been the aim in these Notes to avoid such prolixity, yet to present such comments on *every* verse as will lead to the apprehension of its true meaning. Such a course is also believed to accord best with the simplicity of the Gospel itself.

In its plan this work is similar to those previously issued on the Gospels of Matthew, Mark, and Luke. The Scripture text is given in paragraph form. Carefully-selected Scripture references have been placed in the margin, besides those given in the notes and remarks. To make everything as clear as possible to the eye, different kinds of type are used. Approved readings of the original are noted; more exact translations are given whenever they will throw light on any passage; words, idioms, and phrases of the original are explained; the latest results of exegetical and textual criticism and of recent discovery are presented; and the drift and object of the discourse or narrative are exhibited. At the end of each chapter nearly as many remarks or suggestions are added as there are verses, the whole forming a brief practical and doctrinal commentary on the Gospel. The aim has been to give a popular commentary on a critical basis, suited to the wants of Sunday-schools and families, and helpful also to many pastors and preachers.

The chronology and harmony of the Gospels are kept in view, and thus the individuality of John is the more clearly seen while catching glimpses of the other three sides of the sacred narrative. The work is so prepared as to be used in connection with the author's *Harmony*, and his *Notes* on the other Gospels, and at the same time is entirely independent of them.

This volume is now sent forth by the author with gratitude to God that he has been enabled to complete the task which he originally undertook—to present a series of Notes on the four Gospels. It is a cheering fact that the former volumes have met with such a favorable reception, and the author hopes that this last of the series may meet as cordial a welcome.

SOMERVILLE, N. J., March, 1879.

REVISED EDITION.

This volume has been revised, and such changes, corrections, and additions have been made as seemed to be demanded under the present state of exegetical learning and textual criticism. An Index is added.

HIGHTSTOWN, N. J., March, 1896.

INTRODUCTORY REMARKS.

THE FOURTH GOSPEL.

FOR general observations on all the four Gospels the reader is referred to the author's Introduction to his *Commentary on the Gospel by Matthew*, pp. v.-viii., and his *Harmony of the Gospels*, pp. 224, 225. Compare quotation from Luthardt on preceding page.

THE WRITER OF THIS GOSPEL.

By almost universal consent the fourth Gospel has been ascribed to the apostle John. The evidence that it was written by him is—

1. The apostle's own testimony in chapter 21 : 24: "This is the disciple which testifieth of these things, and wrote these things: and we know that his testimony is true." By comparing this statement with verse 20 and the following, it appears that "this disciple" is "the disciple whom Jesus loved," and there can be no reasonable doubt that the apostle uses these words modestly to designate himself. Attempts have been made to disprove the genuineness of this passage, and even of the whole chapter. But, aside from the fact that the chapter is plainly Johannean in style, "it is contained," as Alford states, "*in all the principal MSS.*"

2. The testimony of early ecclesiastical writers. Recent investigations of manuscripts in the Vatican Library have brought to light the fact that Papias, a disciple of John, who lived in the first part of the second century, was acquainted with this Gospel, and that he attributed it to the apostle John. (See note by Dr. Schaff in Lange's *Introduction to Gospel of John*, p. 26.) Ignatius refers to it, as seems plain from a correspondence between his words and certain passages in the Gospel. The same remark may be made of Justin Martyr (A. D. 150), who quotes John 1 : 13; 3 : 3, 5. Tatian (A. D. 170), who prepared a harmony of *the four* Gospels, quotes from the fourth as that of John, and so do Apollinaris and Athenagoras, A. D. 178. Theophilus (A. D. 181) expressly ascribes this Gospel to John. Writers of the third century are equally decided in their testimony that this Gospel is the production of John.

The nineteenth century has given rise to a class of critics, chiefly in Germany, who have disputed the genuineness of this Gospel, and indeed of every inspired writing. But as they agree not among themselves as to the grounds of their objections, and as their arguments have been ably refuted by both German and English writers, we may dismiss them with only this brief allusion; and the more readily as it belongs not to the practical character of this Commentary to enter minutely into an examination of the fanciful and speculative theories of the modern school of doubt.

SKETCH OF THE WRITER.

John was the son of Zebedee and Salome. Zebedee was a fisherman, and resided on the shore of the Sea of Galilee. From incidental allusions to him in the Gospels, he appears to have been prosperous in his calling, having hired servants and owning his house, Mark 1 : 20; John 19 : 27. John is supposed to have become a disciple of John the Baptist, and to have been one of the two disciples to whom the Baptist said, in Bethany beyond Jordan, "Behold the Lamb of God!" John 1 : 35, 36. From this time John appears to have been recognized as one of the disciples of our Lord. He was evidently an eye-witness of the events recorded in the second, third, and fourth chapters of his Gospel. But at the time of our Lord's meeting him at Bethany he did not cease his occupation; for, some time subsequent to this, while Jesus was walking by the Sea of Galilee, "he saw James the son of Zebedee and John his brother in a ship with Zebedee their father, mending their nets; and he called them. And they immediately left the ship and their father, and followed him," Matt. 4 : 21, 22; Mark 1 : 19, 20. At this time must be dated the formal and solemn call of both James and John to be the constant attendants of our Lord. Zebedee appears to have consented to the withdrawal of his sons from his occupation, and to their following the Lord that henceforth they might be "fishers of men," Matt. 4 : 19. There is reason to believe that both he and his wife Salome were among the devout ones who had waited for the "Consolation of Israel." After the calling of his son his name drops from the historical records, and we hear no more of him. It is probable that he soon died. Salome, believing in the Messiahship of Jesus, with motherly pride and ambition seized an opportunity for uniting with her sons in the request that they might have the pre-eminent distinction of sitting, "the one on thy right hand, the other on thy left, in thy kingdom," Matt. 20 : 21; Mark 10 : 37. There is reason to believe that at a much earlier period of his ministry she connected herself with those women who followed him and ministered to him of their substance, Luke 8 : 2; compare Luke 23 : 55 and Matt. 27 : 55. We find her present with them at the crucifixion and at his burial—"they beheld the sepulchre and how his body was laid"—and with them she united in preparing spices and ointments for embalming his body, Luke 23 : 55, 56. She was, moreover, with the women and Mary the mother of Jesus, and with his brethren, who after the ascension accompanied the apostles to the upper room at Jerusalem, and there "continued with one accord in prayer and supplication," "waiting for the promise of the Father," Acts 1 : 14, compared with Luke 23 : 55.

John was probably younger than his brother James, the name of the latter being generally placed before that of John. Both were selected among the twelve apostles (Mark 3 : 17), and both were surnamed by the Lord Boanerges, or Sons of Thunder. The reason of their being so designated does not plainly appear. It is scarcely conceivable that the appellation conveyed the idea of censure or reproof. It was more probably descriptive of the power and energy of their ministry and of the vehemency of their spirit, and also of the profound nature of their utterances, especially after they were endued with power from on high. While we associate with John all that was mild and gentle in spirit, we must not fall into the error of supposing he was deficient in positive elements of character, in courage and daring, in sternness, and even severity. His Epistles, while they breathe forth gentleness and love, are yet marked here and there by great severity of expression. (See 1 John 1 : 6 ; 2 : 4, 22 ; 3 : 8, 17, etc.) "The youthful, womanly form which art has assigned to John has served to remove from our minds the stronger features of his nature. Yet these may not be forgotten, for even in this aspect the eagle is his true symbol. His love was no soft feeling, but a living principle, an absolute devotion to truth as he had seen and known it in the person of his Lord. He stands forth as the ideal of a thoughtful Christian, relentless against evil, and yet patient with the doubting."—WESTCOTT, *Introduction*, p. 304.

This appellative name does not occur again in the New Testament, which may be accounted for by the fact that it was a collective name of both brothers. John speaks of himself—and the Christian world now almost instinctively so speaks of him—as "the disciple whom Jesus loved," but we are not to infer that his fellow-disciples, in their times, ever so designated him. Nor does John use the expression till he relates the account of the last passover and the betrayal by Judas. That he was greatly beloved and admitted to peculiar intimacy with our Lord is unquestionable. He lay upon his bosom at the Supper. Hence the Fathers spoke of him as the *episteethios*, the bosom-friend. He and Peter and James were selected from the Twelve to witness the miracle of the calling from death to life of the daughter of Jairus, Mark 5 : 37 ; Luke 8 : 51 ; to be "eye-witnesses of his majesty" when "transfigured before them," and to hear "the voice which came to him from the excellent glory, This is my beloved Son, in whom I am well pleased," Matt. 17 : 1 ; 2 Pet. 1 : 16, 17 ; to accompany him to Gethsemane and behold his agony, and render the sympathy of chosen friends, Matt. 26 : 37 ; Mark 14 : 33. To John alone Jesus from the cross committed the care of his mother in those memorable words: "Behold thy mother! Woman, behold thy son!" "And from that hour that disciple took her to his own home," doubtless to be her guardian and to perform all filial duties toward her while she lived, John 19 : 26, 27. If at that very hour John bore the anguished mother to his home, he must have hastened back to the scene of the crucifixion, for he calls special attention to the fact that he saw one of the soldiers pierce the side of Jesus and blood and water issue therefrom, ch. 19 : 34, 35. We find him among the first at the sepulchre when told of the resurrection, and again returning to his home, as if to await full confirmation of what he already believed from circumstantial evidence rather than from the teaching of Scripture—namely, that Jesus had risen from the dead, John 20 : 1–10. The confirmation soon came, the Lord appearing to the eleven before the close of the day, ch. 20 : 19, 20. After this, when on the shore of the Sea of Galilee, there occurs another and last recorded instance of our Lord's distinguished regard for the apostle, the language used seeming to indicate for him a protracted life and service, ch. 21 : 20–23.

In the book of Acts John is not brought before us with marked prominence, and, as Alford remarks, "always in connection with, and thrown into the background by, Peter." For some years he appears to have remained at Jerusalem. He, with Peter, was sent to Samaria to visit and instruct those who had received the word of God under the preaching of Philip, Acts 8 : 14. He returned to Jerusalem, and was there at the time of the Council in regard to circumcision, about A. D. 50, Acts 15 : 1, 2; compare Gal. 2 : 9. Henceforth, the historian being silent as to John's subsequent life, we have to resort to tradition, which, however, in his case is entitled to consideration, if not to our fullest credence.

Polycrates of the second century relates that John died in Ephesus; and Irenæus, a disciple of Polycarp, who was himself a disciple of John, relates that John lived there till the time of Trajan, or to A. D. 98. But neither of them, nor any other writer, states at what time he came there. There is plausibility in the conjecture of Lücke and Neander that he did not come to Ephesus till after the death of Paul, about A. D. 68, and then in order to strengthen the disciples in the faith and to guard them against certain errors and corruptions which, through the efforts of false teachers, had found their way into the Asiatic churches. That while at Ephesus he was banished to the Isle of Patmos there is no reason to doubt, but the time cannot be determined. From Patmos he returned to Ephesus, at what date is not known, and there, after living to an advanced age—probably till he was nearly a hundred years old—he died a natural death, about A. D. 98. The many legends respecting his sufferings and his miraculous deliverance from them, such as his being cast into a caldron of burning oil and coming out unhurt, etc., are wholly untrustworthy, and therefore not deserving of consideration.

TIME AND PLACE OF WRITING THE FOURTH GOSPEL.

According to the testimony of ancient writers, this Gospel was the last written of the four. Irenæus, Clement, and Origen are explicit on this point. But there is no way of determining the precise date. Professor Plumptre (*Smith's Dictionary*) thinks it was written midway between A. D. 62, date of the Epistle to the Ephesians, and A. D. 95, at which time, according to Eusebius, the apostle was banished to Patmos—that is, about A. D. 78. Alford also inclines to a date somewhere between A. D. 70 and A. D. 85.

As to the place where it was written, the ancient testimony decidedly preponderates in favor of Ephesus. Irenæus, as cited by Euseb., *H. E.*, ver. 8, states that John published his Gospel while he dwelt in Ephesus of Asia. Jerome makes the same statement. This is confirmed by John's explanations of Jewish terms, customs, and localities, showing that he wrote at a distance from Palestine, after the destruction of Jerusalem and the overthrow of Jewish polity and worship, when Gentile believers had become numerous. Thus he speaks of "the feast of the Jews" (ch. 5:1; 6:4); explains that the Sea of Galilee is the Sea of Tiberias (ch. 6:1); says that rabbi means teacher, and Messiah, Christ, ch. 1:38, 41; and relates that "the Jews had no dealings with the Samaritans," ch. 4:9. There is no contradictory testimony, save from one or two anonymous writers, who assert that the apostle wrote his Gospel in Patmos, but published it in Ephesus. But as they furnish no proof of this statement, and as it is evidently inconsistent with the apostle's testimony in the Apocalypse that he had before borne record of the word of God (Rev. 1:2), we may regard their statements as wholly unreliable.

SOURCES OF THE FOURTH GOSPEL.

John had been, as has already been noticed, the bosom-friend and constant companion of our Lord throughout his ministry. He was therefore familiar with his discourses and deeds, and that these had been impressed upon his mind with great power the Gospel gives clear evidence. It is not necessary to infer that he must at once have committed them to writing in order to keep them in memory, for, according to the Lord's promise to his disciples, whenever his words should be needed the Paraclete, the Holy Spirit, would bring all things whatsoever he had said unto them to their remembrance, John 14:26. The apostle was, therefore, by virtue of inspiration, endowed with ability to write this Gospel. Knowing this, it would profit us nothing to inquire whether he might not have drawn some of his materials from human sources. Lange suggests that as Mary, to whom he sustained the relation of a son, lived with him, "this little family, formed under the cross, could have had no more engaging matter of conversation than the memory of the Lord, and that we may doubtless ascribe to Mary a mental share in the gradual formation of this slowly-maturing Gospel." It would indeed be unnatural to suppose that "this little family" did not frequently converse together about the sayings and doings of the Lord, but surely it is only a pleasing fancy that Mary contributed in any way to the formation of this wonderful Gospel; while to suppose that the apostle was under the necessity of depending upon any uninspired sources for the subject-matter thereof would be a reflection upon his inspiration.

DESIGN OF THE FOURTH GOSPEL.

The opinion is widely prevalent that John wrote his Gospel as a supplement to the other three; in other words, that his purpose was to record such discourses of the Master, and present such aspects of his person, life, and teaching, as the other evangelists had failed to present. The apostle has indeed done this—has given to the world a more spiritual delineation of the doctrine and life of Christ than either one of the synoptic Gospels—a Gospel that is unique in substance, style, and scope. If Matthew presents him as King, Mark as Servant or Mighty Worker, and Luke as man, John presents him as the Son of God. John was doubtless acquainted with the other Gospels. He writes as one who supposes his readers to be informed of the chief events of our Lord's life. Compare chs. 1 : 32; 3 : 24; 11 : 2, etc. Two-thirds of his Gospel is new, and matter found elsewhere is given with important additions and in a new light. That he really supplements in some respects is one thing—that this was his object in writing is quite another. But that this Gospel is supplementary in the sense of its supplying deficiencies or of meeting failures in the other three, or that the apostle wrote at the instigation of others in order to provide for these alleged deficiencies,—of this there is no evidence whatever. Certain ancient writers, as Clement of Alexandria, Jerome, etc., are cited in support of the opinion that John wrote with such intent; but they, as Alford says, "appeal to no historical or traditional fact as the ground of their own statements." The opinion ought, therefore, to be dismissed as a mere legend, the whole scope of the Gospel showing that the writer was controlled by the profounder purpose of setting forth, as has just been stated, the Godhead of our Lord Jesus Christ, and thus grounding and confirming the faith of Christians.

In proof of this we have, first, the formal statement of the writer in ch. 20 : 31 : "These are written, that ye might believe that Jesus is the Christ, the Son of God; and that believing ye might have life through his name." Thus was it intended for Christian readers, to establish them in the fundamental truths of the gospel, and to set forth Jesus as the Christ, the eternal Son of God, in all his offices and relations to the believer. And, secondly, the subject-matter of the Gospel, between which and this statement there is throughout entire agreement. To present Christ as the Son of God, his equality with the Father, his divine, essential, inherent character,—this is the thought ever before the writer. And this he does, not, as do the synoptic writers, by narrating the acts and deeds of our Lord, but rather by recording his discourses on different occasions, his profound utterances respecting his person, and his true relation to the Father. Everywhere he is the Word of God, the Life and Light of men, the Only-Begotten Son in the bosom of the Father, the Way and the Truth and the Life, the Resurrection and the Life, the Bread of Life, the Living Water, the Door, the Good Shepherd, etc. These terms and expressions convey nothing less than the thought that creative and sustaining power resides in him—that he is the Source of life, the Quickener of the dead, and the Fountain of all comfort and refreshing to the soul. And thus they harmonize with the declaration that "the Word," or Logos, "was God," that "all things were made by him, and without him was not any thing made that was made," while at the same time they indicate the distinctive character of this Gospel, its marked individuality in contrast with the synoptic Gospels.

INTRODUCTORY REMARKS.

To the objection that the Jesus of the fourth Gospel is entirely different from the Jesus of the other Gospels, Dr. A. P. Peabody has well answered as follows: "So far, however, is this from being the case that the most we can say is that he is all of their Jesus, and more. The human traits are the same in the four. The narrative, so far as it is parallel, is coincident, the only difference being that the fourth Gospel bears the marks of a closer intimacy, a more realizing sympathy, with its subject, as must have been the case if the author held that peculiar relation of Christ's confidential friend in which he professes to stand. But is Jesus even more or greater in the fourth Gospel than in the other three? Have we not in them intimations of all that is more fully developed in the fourth? As regards outward incident, the raising of Lazarus seems to us unique, from the intense vividness and lifelikeness of the narrative. But can it have presented a grander spectacle, or implied a more godlike sympathy or a more sovereign power in the Conqueror of death, than the scene at the gate of Nain, when Jesus meets the funeral procession, sees the widow in her desolate agony following her only son to the grave, arrests the bier, raises the lifeless form, and gives the youth to his mother's embrace, while for the wild wail of the mourners rises the glad shout, 'God hath visited and redeemed his people'? Then as to the alleged peculiarities in John's representations of the exalted personality of Jesus, are they peculiar to him? Have we not as full and emphatic, though generally less detailed, indications of them in the synoptics? Nay, one of the loftiest of these representations is drawn out by Matthew with an amplitude far transcending that of the fourth Gospel. In the latter Jesus repeatedly speaks of himself as the Judge of the world. But what are these dogmatic statements compared with the discourse recorded by Matthew, in which the Son of man sits on the throne of his glory, and all nations are gathered before him, and divided as a shepherd divides the sheep from the goats, the sheep on his right hand, the goats on his left? What higher claims does Jesus make for himself in the fourth Gospel than when he says, 'All things are delivered unto me of my Father;' 'All power is given unto me in heaven and on earth;' 'Hereafter shall ye see the Son of man sitting on the right hand of power, and coming in the clouds of heaven;' 'Lo, I am with you alway, unto the end of the world'? Nor is the promise of the Holy Spirit, which fills so large a space in the fourth Gospel, wanting in the synoptics: 'Take no thought how or what ye shall speak; for it shall be given you in the same hour what ye shall speak; for it is not ye that speak, but the Spirit of your Father that speaketh in you;' and again, 'Tarry ye in the city of Jerusalem until ye be endued with power from on high.'"—*Christianity and Science*, pp. 85-87.

Evidence at any length of the distinctive character of the fourth Gospel cannot here be given, except in so far as it bears upon the question of design. Notice the manner in which the apostle introduces his Gospel to the world, the first sentence reminding us of the first verse of Genesis announcing the creation of the heavens and the earth: "In the beginning," before the foundation of the world, in the depths of eternity past, "was the Word (the Logos), and the Word was with God, and the Word was God." How different this from the manner in which the synoptists begin their Gospels! Then, looking at the whole preface covering the first fourteen verses, what profound thought lies wrapped up in it! This Divine Logos, who is eternal with God and of his essence, is the Maker of all things, the Source of life and light, and therefore the Life and Light in himself. This Light dwells in darkness, but the darkness comprehends it not. He is in the world made by him, but the world knows him not. He is made flesh and dwells among men, yet is he in the bosom of the Father. His humanity is perfect, yet his equally perfect Deity manifests itself to his "chosen," who behold his glory, the glory as of the only-begotten of the Father, full of grace and truth, and who receive of the infinite fulness dwelling in him, and grace for grace. "The theme is the eternal Logos or personal Word that was with God and of divine essence from the beginning of beginnings, and at last became incarnate for the salvation of the world. The leading ideas are life and light, grace and truth, as emanating from and centring in the Logos. Starting with the divine genealogy, or eternal divinity, of Christ, the evangelist presents, in a few bold outlines, the progress of revelation from the creation to the incarnation, a sort of miniature photograph of the history of preparation for Christ's coming in the flesh, and states the impression which his workings and personal appearance made upon the unbelieving world and the believing disciples." [DR. SCHAFF, *in Lange on John*, p. 51.] If, now, the whole structure of the Gospel that follows be examined, it will be seen that the same underlying thought, the divinity of Christ, pervades it throughout. It is truly the divine Gospel, the apt and expressive symbol of which is the eagle soaring aloft and gazing heavenward.

It has been thought that the evangelist had also in view the errors of Cerinthus, of the Gnostics, of the Ebionites, etc., and that his object in writing this Gospel was to show their falsity. It would, perhaps, be rash to assert that these errors were not in his mind. Certain it is that the subject-matter of this Gospel bears against and utterly refutes them, and, as well, the heresies of our own time. What a deadly blow it gives to the theories and speculations of the humanitarians of this and every age! If life is only in Christ, if we partake of this life only by virtue of a personal belief in him, an eating of his flesh and drinking of his blood, how vain are the hopes of all who look for salvation by virtue of an inherent or acquired righteousness! "Thus we see the striking agreement between the writings of John and Paul, to say nothing of other New Testament writers. For instance, 'righteousness' is the form of expression peculiar to the first Epistle. But where Paul says, 'The righteousness of God without the law was manifested' (Rom. 3:21), John, still in character, says, 'The life was manifested.' (1 John 1:2; compare John 1:4.) Where Paul comes to 'declare God's righteousness, that he might be just and yet a justifier'

INTRODUCTORY REMARKS. 15

(Rom. 3 : 26), John comes to 'bear witness, and show unto you that eternal life, which was with the Father, and was manifested to us.' (1 John 1 : 2; compare John 3 : 36, etc.)"—JUKES.

PECULIARITIES OF THE FOURTH GOSPEL.

The limits assigned to this Introduction forbid more than a brief and imperfect consideration of this subject.

1. As to its *style*. It is characterized by great minuteness of description, clearness of expression, and a charming simplicity. "It is artless and colloquial. The language is Hellenistic, but the thought Hebraistic."—ELLICOTT. The Gospel is also noted for its small vocabulary, no book of equal size in the New Testament making use of so few words. At times it exhibits a peculiar use of tenses, but there is no evidence that John uses one tense for another. In every instance the careful student will discover that the tense was selected for a definite and fitting purpose.

2. Its matter is so profound that no human mind has ever sounded its depths. Devout scholars in every age have dug into this mine of truth and brought forth much precious ore, but they have confessed, as all who follow them must confess, that there are riches lying deeper down than any mortal can reach. "John excels," says Jerome, "in the depth of divine mysteries." "No writing combines greater simplicity with more profound depths. At first all seems clear in the childlike language which is so often the chosen vehicle of the treasures of Eastern meditation; and then again the utmost subtlety of Western thought is found to lie under abrupt and apparently fragmentary utterances. St. John wrote the Gospel of the world, resolving reason into intuition and faith into sight."—B. Foss WESTCOTT.

3. This Gospel, as compared with the synoptic Gospels, is remarkable for its omissions. We have no account of the earthly parentage and birth of Christ, of his lying in a manger, of his circumcision, of the flight of his parents to Egypt and their return, of his baptism and introduction into the ministry. It contains but few allusions to John the Baptist, and these relate chiefly to the fact of his baptizing in Enon, to the testimony he bore to Christ as the Lamb of God, to himself as the friend of the Bridegroom, and to the "joy" felt by him in decreasing while Christ increases, chs. 1 and 3. It is silent as to our Lord's transfiguration on the holy mount, his apprehensions of the cross, and his sufferings of soul in Gethsemane, not even an allusion being made to the agony and bloody sweat. When he is apprehended we see no manifestation of bodily weakness or of inward sorrow, but only of power, before which his adversaries fall prostrate and they are made willing to let his disciples go unharmed. At his trial, on his way to Calvary, and when suspended on the cross we mark the absence of any expression of human sympathy. There is no warning of Pilate by his troubled wife. No daughters of Israel bewail his sad fate. There is no confession from a dying malefactor, "This man hath

done nothing amiss;" no admission from a Roman centurion, "Truly, this was the Son of God." We read of no rending rocks, of no quaking earth, of no darkness covering the land. No voice comes from the cross, "My God! my God! why hast thou forsaken me?" And, last of all, he omits the ascension. We can account for these omissions only on the ground that the evangelist is portraying neither the King, nor the Servant, nor the Son of man, but the Divine Man, the Son of God, who, as such, needs no human sympathy, no testimony from man, no ministry of angels, no help or sympathy from Nature. "All this," as Jukes remarks, "could have no place in the laying down of his life by the Eternal Son. Even in dying he need not 'commend' himself to God (Luke 23:46). He said, 'It is finished,' and he bowed his head and gave up his spirit, ch. 19:30. 'It is finished' seals with a sufficient witness the full accomplishment of his own perfect work."

4. This Gospel is remarkable for its *additions* as well as for its omissions, While it records but eight miracles, only two of which are in the other Gospels, and there is not a parable in it—the Good Shepherd being an allegory—it relates lengthy conversational discourses by our Lord to the Jews which are not even adverted to by the synoptists, yet contributing to the general design of setting forth the divine nature of Christ. While only touching upon our Lord's Galilean ministry, he brings to view his early Judæan ministry, and his later teaching and contact with the Jews at Jerusalem, showing how he met their unbelief and how their opposition was brought to its height. Moreover, we have a valedictory discourse, addressed by our Lord to his disciples (chs. xiv.-xvi.), which teaches, among other things, the oneness between himself and his people, his unchangeable love for them, the office of the Paraclete or Comforter, the expediency of his return to the Father, and the promise of his coming again to receive them unto himself; and, most wonderful of all, the intercessory prayer in the seventeenth chapter, which reads as if it might have been offered in heaven, and is too rich and profound in thought to admit of any adequate exposition. Space will not admit further allusion to matter peculiar to this Gospel. Enough has been said to show that it is emphatically the divine Gospel, that it was written for Christians of all time, that in a peculiar sense it is supplementary to all time, meeting the error and scepticism of every age concerning the person and work of Christ and the relation he sustains to God and his people.

The following glowing words from Rev. Dr. A. P. Peabody are appropriate here:

"This Gospel is the most remarkable book in the world. . . . . There is in all human literature no narrative which so blends majesty and tenderness, sublimity and pathos, as that of the raising of Lazarus. The discourses ascribed to Jesus in controversy with his Jewish adversaries manifest as much dialectic skill as moral energy, and are on a level, both in their intellectual and their spiritual aspects, with the highest Messianic conceptions of the Christian Church. The communings and intercessions at the paschal table are an unexhausted treasury of holy thought and heavenward aspiration, the loss of which would bereave Christendom more sorely than the extinction of all that has been written in a similar vein for the last seventeen centuries, and especially would rob the dying, and those who survive them in sorrow, of peace, consolation, and hope, which not even the glowing words of hallowed genius and poetry to which they have given tone and spirit could begin to replace. Even in the working up of materials common to the four there is, if you will pardon the word for the thought, an *interiorness*, a vividness of realization, not manifested by the synoptics; in fine, that closest approach of biography to autobiography which occurs only when the biographer and his subject are associated by a spiritual twinship, in which the author of the fourth Gospel may be contrasted rather than compared with the other evangelists. As a single instance out of several which might be selected, I will refer you to the narratives of our Saviour's resurrection. . . . . The spirit of the risen Jesus so throbs in every trait of the successive acts of that sublime drama as portrayed in the fourth Gospel that the sacred volume contains no words more congenial than the very words of that narrative with the moment when kindred are gathered for the last time around the lifeless body from which the soul has passed on to its Redeemer."—*Christianity and Science*, pp. 80-82.

ARRANGEMENT AND ANALYSIS.

In carrying out his great design John makes a selection from the materials he possessed, ch. 20 : 30; 21 : 25. He evidently follows the order of time, but the Gospel may also be arranged as follows:

i. The Introduction, displaying the glory of the Son of God, ch. 1 : 1-14.
ii. Some events connected with his public life manifesting this glory, ch. 1 : 15-12 : 50.
iii. Events preparatory to and connected with his death, further showing forth his glory, ch. 13 : 1-19 : 42.
iv. His resurrection and several appearances to his disciples, manifesting the power and glory of his risen life, and thereby confirming and completing their faith, ch. 20 : 1 ; 21 : 25.

The Gospel may also be analyzed as follows:
i. The Prologue or Introduction, ch. 1 : 1-14.
 1. The Word in his essential nature, as Maker of all things, and the Source of life—the Light of men, vers. 1-9.
 2. John's witness of the true Light, vers. 6-8.
 3. The fact and purpose of the incarnation, vers. 10-14.
ii. The proofs of the divine mission and ministry of the Incarnate Word, ch. 1 : 15–ch. 11 : 46.
 1. The testimony of John the Baptist—

(1.) To the pre-eminence of Jesus, vers. 15-28.
(2.) To Jesus as the Lamb of God, vers. 29, 36.
(3.) To the descent of the Spirit upon Jesus, ver. 32.
2. The power of Jesus to detach the human heart from the world and attach it to himself, as evinced in the call of his disciples, vers. 37-46.
3. His omniscience, ver. 48.
4. "The series of glories to be unfolded in his Person and Work" (ALFORD), vers. 50, 51.
5. The miracle of turning water into wine, ch. 2 : 1-11.
6. His authority and power as Teacher:
   (1.) He expels the traders from the temple, ch. 2 : 13-17.
   (2.) Declares his power to raise up the temple of his body, vers. 18-22.
   (3.) Expounds the new birth. Its connection with him as the Antitype of the serpent lifted up in the wilderness. The cross the evidence of God's infinite love, ch. 3 : 1-17.
   (4.) Explains why man is under condemnation, vers. 18-21.
   (5.) Before him the greatest of the prophets must wane, according to the Baptist's last testimony, vers. 22-30.
   (6.) He is above all, and all things are given into his hands by the Father, vers. 31-37.
   (7.) He is the source of living water, ch. 4 : 1-15.
   (8.) He discerns the hidden life and social relations of the Samaritan woman, and expounds the character of true worship, vers. 16-26.
   (9.) His self-consuming zeal in doing the will of his Father, vers. 31-38.
   (10.) At Cana he heals the nobleman's son at Capernaum, vers. 43-54.
7. His replies to the cavillings of the Jews, and his mighty works, chs. 5-11. Further proofs:
   (1.) Heals the impotent man, ch. 5 : 1-16.
   (2.) The Mighty Quickener, vers. 17-29.
   (3.) Has authority to execute judgment, ver. 22.
   (4.) Witness borne to him by John the Baptist, by his own works, and by the Scriptures, vers. 30-47.
   (5.) He feeds the multitudes and declares himself to be the Bread of Life, ch. 6 : 1-58.
   (6.) He walks on the sea, vers. 15-21.
   (7.) He reveals the true character of Judas, vers. 70, 71.
   (8.) He vindicates his divine mission and again proclaims himself the source of living water, ch. 7.
   (9.) By his teaching he appals the officers who had been sent to take him, ch. 7 : 43-53.
   (10.) He is the Light of the world, the Guide to truth, ch. 8.
   (11.) Heals the man born blind, ch. 9.
   (12.) He is the Door of the sheep, the Good Shepherd, ch. 10 : 1-21.

INTRODUCTORY REMARKS.

(13.) He teaches his oneness with the Father, vers. 22-42.
(14.) He raises Lazarus; "the Resurrection and the Life," ch. 11 : 1-46
iii. Signs that his ministry draws to an end, chs. 12, 13.
  1. The anointing, 12 : 1-9.
  2. Increasing anger and plottings of the Jews, vers. 10, 11, 19.
  3. The triumphal entry into Jerusalem, vers. 12-16.
  4. The corn of wheat falling into the ground, vers. 20-26.
  5. Jesus, troubled in soul, prays to the Father, vers. 27-30.
  6. Announces the speedy casting out of the prince of this world; his lifting up and drawing all men unto him, vers. 31-33.
  7. The light is with the people "yet a little while," vers. 34-36.
  8. Judicial blindness of unbelievers, vers. 37-42.
  9. Jesus washes his disciples' feet, ch. 13 : 1-17.
  10. He announces by sign his betrayer, vers. 18-30.
  11. He exhorts his disciples to love one another, and warns Peter, vers. 31-38.
iv. The valedictory address to his disciples, chs. 14-16.
v. The intercessory prayer, ch. 17.
vi. The closing scenes, chs. 18, 19.
  1. The betrayal and the binding, 18 : 1-12.
  2. Before Annas and Caiaphas, vers. 15-24.
  3. Peter's denial, vers. 25-27.
  4. Before Pilate, ver. 28.
    (1.) The accusation, ver. 30.
    (2.) The kingship and the kingdom, vers. 33-37.
    (3.) What is truth? ver. 38.
    (4.) The scourging and the surrender of Jesus to be crucified, ch. 19 : 1-16.
  5. The crucifixion, vers. 17-37.
    (1.) The title on the cross, ver. 19.
    (2.) The parting of the garments, vers. 23, 24.
    (3.) The saying of Jesus to his mother and "the disciple whom he loved," vers. 26, 27.
    (4.) The thirst, vers. 28, 29.
    (5.) "It is finished," ver. 30.
    (6.) The death, ver. 30.
    (7.) The burial, vers. 38-42.
vii. The Resurrection, or the New Life, ch. 20 : 1-29.
  1. His appearances to Mary Magdalene and his disciples, vers. 11-20.
  2. The impartation of the Holy Spirit, vers. 21, 22.
  3. The blessing, vers. 24-29.
  4. Conclusion: the design of this Gospel, vers. 30, 31.

viii. The epilogue, ch. 21.
  1. The draught of fishes, "the sign of the future" (WESTCOTT), vers. 1–11
  2. The thrice-repeated question put to Simon, vers. 15–17.
  3. Simon Peter's manner of death foretold, vers. 18, 19.
  4. Saying regarding the beloved disciple and the "report," vers. 21–23.
  5. The conclusion, vers. 24, 25.

NOTE TO THE REVISED EDITION.

The discoveries and investigation of recent years have brought to light much to confirm the general belief of centuries that the Apostle John wrote the fourth Gospel, and nothing against it. The date of the martyrdom of Polycarp has been pushed back ten years to A. D. 155. As he was eighty-six years old at his death, he was born in A. D. 69. He had thus abundant time and opportunity to be a hearer and disciple of the Apostle John, according to Irenæus, of Lyons, who had been a disciple of Polycarp. John died about A. D. 100, and it is now generally admitted that Polycarp made use of the first Epistle of John, which cannot well be separated from his Gospel, whether considered in respect to its style or its doctrine.

The "Diatessaron," a Harmony of the four Gospels, by Tatian, has recently been discovered, in which we find the fourth Gospel with the three others. Now Tatian was born A. D. 110–120, and died about 170. He was the pupil of Justin Martyr. Now the Gospels of Tatian's Harmony appear to have been those of Justin. And so through Tatian and Justin we learn that the four Gospels, as we now have them, were generally known among Christians as early as A. D. 140–150. Papias, of Hierapolis, born about A. D. 70, was, according to Irenæus, a "hearer of John and a companion of Polycarp," and in common with the latter made use of the first Epistle of John, which presupposes the fourth Gospel. Indeed it is evident that the views of Papias were formed under the influence of John's Gospel.

To these must be added the recently discovered fragment of the "Gospel of St. Peter," which bears testimony that the four Gospels, including that of John, were generally accepted and circulated early in the second century. Since time is required for such works to get into circulation and gain acceptance, we very naturally put back the date of this Gospel to the latter part of the first century.

SYNOPTICAL VIEW OF THE FOUR GOSPELS.

THE chronology of the Gospels is in many respects undetermined. The duration of Christ's ministry is much disputed. It continued at least two and one half years; for John in his Gospel mentions three Passovers, John 2 : 13; 6 : 4; 13 : 1. If the feast (or "a feast of the Jews") mentioned in John 5 : 1 be also regarded as a Passover, then his public ministry continued about three years and a half. But if the feast was that of Purim (Esther 9 : 26), as many suppose, occurring a month before the Passover of John 6 : 4, then must we assign the shorter term to his public ministry. Although certainty may not be attained, yet the amount of labor that Jesus performed, and the time required for his three preaching tours throughout Galilee, before the Passover mentioned in John 6 : 4, incline us to regard the feast of John 5 : 1 as also a Passover. In accordance with this view the following table is arranged, and the probable chronological order and harmony given; but where either is quite doubtful, or beset with special difficulty, the references are printed in **heavy** type. The reasons for the arrangement are given by the author in his HARMONY OF THE GOSPELS.

I. EVENTS CONNECTED WITH THE BIRTH AND CHILDHOOD OF JESUS.

A period of about thirteen and a half years, from B.C. 6 to A.D. 8.

SECT.	SUBJECT.	MATT.	MARK.	LUKE.	JOHN.
1.	Luke's Preface....................	....	....	1 : 1–4	....
2.	John's Introduction................	....	....	....	1 : 1–14
3.	The Genealogies....................	1 : 1–17	....	3 : 23–38	....
4.	Annunciation of John's Birth........	....	....	1 : 5–25	....
5.	Annunciation of the Birth of Jesus...	....	....	1 : 26–38	....
6.	Mary visits Elizabeth..............	....	....	1 : 39–56	....
7.	The Birth of John the Baptist.......	....	....	1 : 57–80	....
8.	An Angel appears to Joseph..........	1 : 18–23	....	....	....
9.	Birth of Jesus......................	1 : 24, 25	....	2 : 1–7	....
10.	The Visit of the Shepherds..........	....	....	2 : 8–20	....
11.	The Circumcision....................	....	....	2 : 21	....
12.	Presentation in the Temple..........	....	....	2 : 22–38	....
13.	Temporary Return to Nazareth........	....	....	2 : 39	....
14.	Again at Bethlehem; Visit of the Magi.	2 : 1–12	....	....	....
15.	Flight into Egypt...................	2 : 13–15	....	....	....
16.	Herod's Massacre of the Children....	2 : 16–18	....	....	....
17.	Return and Residence at Nazareth....	2 : 19–23	....	2 : 40	....
18.	Childhood of Jesus..................	....	....	2 : 41–52	....

II. ANNOUNCEMENT AND INTRODUCTION OF CHRIST'S PUBLIC MINISTRY.

About one year, from the spring of A.D. 26 to that of A.D. 27.

19.	The Ministry of John the Baptist.....	3 : 1–12	1 : 1–8	3 : 1–18	....
20.	The Baptism of Jesus.................	3 : 13–17	1 : 9–11	3 : 21–23	....
21.	The Temptation.......................	4 : 1–11	1 : 12, 13	4 : 1–13	....
22.	Testimony of John to Jesus...........	....	....	....	1 : 15–34

SYNOPTICAL VIEW OF THE GOSPELS.

SECT.	SUBJECT.	MATT.	MARK.	LUKE.	JOHN.
23.	Jesus gains Disciples; returns to Galilee				1 : 35-51
24.	The Marriage at Cana				2 : 1-11
25.	Visits Capernaum				2 : 12

III. FROM THE FIRST PASSOVER OF CHRIST'S PUBLIC MINISTRY UNTIL THE SECOND.

One year, from April, A.D. 27, to April, A.D. 28.

SECT.	SUBJECT.	MATT.	MARK.	LUKE.	JOHN.
26.	At the Passover; the Traders expelled				2 : 13-25
27.	Visit of Nicodemus				3 : 1-21
28.	Jesus remains in Judea				3 : 22-24
29.	Further Testimony of John the Baptist				3 : 25-36
30.	John Imprisoned			3 : 19, 20	
31.	Jesus departs for Galilee	4 : 12	1 : 14	4 : 14	4 : 1-4
32.	Discourses with the Woman of Sychar				4 : 5-42
33.	Teaches publicly in Galilee	4 : 17	1 : 14, 15	4 : 14, 15	4 : 43-46
34.	Heals a Nobleman's Son				4 : 46-54
35.	Rejected at Nazareth	4 : 13		4 : 16-30	
36.	Makes Capernaum his Residence	4 : 13-16		4 : 31	
37.	Four called as Constant Attendants	4 : 18-22	1 : 16-20		
38.	A Demoniac healed in the Synagogue		1 : 21-28	4 : 31-37	
39.	Heals Peter's Wife's Mother	8 : 14-17	1 : 29-34	4 : 38-41	
40.	First Preaching Tour throughout Galilee	4 : 23-25	1 : 35-39	4 : 42-44	
41.	The Miraculous Draught of Fishes			5 : 1-11	
42.	Sermon on the Mount	5 : 1-7 : 29			
43.	A Leper healed	8 : 1-4	1 : 40-45	5 : 12-16	
44.	Heals a Paralytic	9 : 2-8	2 : 1-12	5 : 17-26	
45.	The Call of Matthew	9 : 9	2 : 13, 14	5 : 27, 28	

IV. FROM THE SECOND PASSOVER UNTIL THE THIRD.

From April, A.D. 28, to April, A.D. 29.

SECT.	SUBJECT.	MATT.	MARK.	LUKE.	JOHN.
46.	At the Passover; Heals the Impotent Man				5 : 1-47
47.	Plucking the Ears of Grain	12 : 1-8	2 : 23-28	6 : 1-5	
48.	Healing the Withered Hand	12 : 9-14	3 : 1-6	6 : 6-11	
49.	Withdraws to the Sea of Galilee	12 : 15-21	3 : 7-12		
50.	The Twelve Apostles chosen		3 : 13-19	6 : 12-16	
51.	The Sermon in the Plain			6 : 17-49	
52.	Healing of the Centurion's Servant	8 : 5-13		7 : 1-10	
53.	Raises a Widow's Son at Nain			7 : 11-17	
54.	John's Message to Jesus	11 : 2-19		7 : 18-35	
55.	Upbraiding the Cities of Galilee	11 : 20-30			
56.	Anointed by a Penitent Woman			7 : 36-50	
57.	Second Circuit of Galilee			8 : 1-3	
58.	A Blind and Dumb Demoniac healed	12 : 22-37	3 : 19-30		
59.	A Sign demanded of Jesus	12 : 38-45			
60.	Christ's Mother and Brethren	12 : 46-50	3 : 31-35	8 : 19-21	
61.	Parable of the Sower	13 : 1-23	4 : 1-25	8 : 4-18	
62.	Other Parables spoken to the Multitude	13 : 24-35	4 : 26-34		
63.	Wheat and Tares explained; and other Parables to the Disciples	13 : 36-53			
64.	The Tempest stilled	8 : 18, 23-27	4 : 35-41	8 : 22-25	
65.	The Two Demoniacs of Gadara	8 : 28-9 : 1	5 : 1-21	8 : 26-40	
66.	Matthew's Feast	9 : 10-13	2 : 15-17	5 : 29-32	
67.	Discourse on Fasting	9 : 14-17	2 : 18-22	5 : 33-39	
68.	Jairus's Daughter; the Bloody Issue	9 : 18-26	5 : 22-43	8 : 41-56	
69.	Healing of the Blind and Dumb	9 : 27-34			
70.	Second Rejection at Nazareth	13 : 54-58	6 : 1-6		

SYNOPTICAL VIEW OF THE GOSPELS.

SECT.	SUBJECT.	MATT.	MARK.	LUKE.	JOHN.
75.	Return of the Twelve...............	....	6 : 30, 31	9 : 10	....
76.	Feeding the Five Thousand.........	14 : 13-21	6 : 32-44	9 : 10-17	6 : 1-14
77.	Jesus walks on the Sea.............	14 : 22-36	6 : 45-56	....	6 : 15-21
78.	Discourse at Capernaum............	....	....	....	6 : 22-71

V. FROM THE THIRD PASSOVER UNTIL THE ENSUING FEAST OF TABERNACLES.

Six months, from April to October, A.D. 29.

79.	Jesus continues in Galilee.........	....	....	....	7 : 1
80.	Traditions of the Elders............	15 : 1-20	7 : 1-23	....	....
81.	The Canaanitish Woman...........	15 : 21-28	7 : 24-30	....	....
82.	Deaf and Dumb Man, etc., healed...	15 : 29-31	7 : 31-37	....	....
83.	Feeds the Four Thousand...........	15 : 32-39	8 : 1-9	....	....
84.	A Sign again demanded............	15 : 39-16 : 4	8 : 10-12	....	....
85.	The Leaven of the Pharisees........	16 : 4-12	8 : 13-21	....	....
86.	Blind Man healed..................	....	8 : 22-26	....	....
87.	Visit to the region of Cæsarea Philippi.	16 : 13-20	8 : 27-30	9 : 18-21	....
88.	Jesus foretells his Death............	16 : 21-28	8 : 31-9 : 1	9 : 22-27	....
89.	The Transfiguration...............	17 : 1-13	9 : 2-13	9 : 28-36	....
90.	Healing the Dumb Demoniac......	17 : 14-21	9 : 14-29	9 : 37-43	....
91.	Jesus again foretells his Death......	17 : 22, 23	9 : 30-32	9 : 43-45	....
92.	The Sacred Tribute................	17 : 24-27	9 : 33	....	....
93.	Contention among the Disciples....	18 : 1-14	9 : 33-50	9 : 46-50	....
94.	Dealing with an Offended Brother, etc.	18 : 15-20	....	....	....
95.	On Forgiveness....................	18 : 21-35	....	....	....
96.	Still continues in Galilee...........	....	....	....	7 : 2-9
97.	Goes to the Feast of Tabernacles....	....	....	9 : 51-56	7 : 10
98.	Concerning following Jesus.........	8 : 19-22	....	9 : 57-62	....

VI. FROM THE FEAST OF TABERNACLES TILL CHRIST'S ARRIVAL AT BETHANY, SIX DAYS BEFORE THE FOURTH PASSOVER.

Six months, less six days.

99.	Jesus at the Feast; teaches publicly..	....	....	....	7 : 11-8. 1
100.	The Woman taken in Adultery.....	....	....	....	8 : 2-11
101.	Further Public Teaching...........	....	....	....	8 : 12-59
102.	Seventy instructed and sent forth....	....	....	10 : 1-16	....
103.	Return of the Seventy.............	....	....	10 : 17-24	....
104.	Reply to a Lawyer; Good Samaritan.	....	....	10 : 25-37	....
105.	Jesus at the House of Martha and Mary.	....	....	10 : 38-42	....
106.	How to pray......................	....	....	11 : 1-13	....
107.	Heals a Dumb Demoniac..........	....	....	11 : 14-36	....
108.	Jesus Dines with a Pharisee........	....	....	11 : 37-54	....
109.	On Hypocrisy, Worldliness, etc.....	....	....	12 : 1-59	....
110.	Slaughter of Certain Galileans......	....	....	13 : 1-9	....
111.	A Blind Man healed on the Sabbath..	....	....	....	9 : 1-41
112.	The Good Shepherd................	....	....	....	10 : 1-21
113.	Jesus at the Feast of Dedication.....	....	....	....	10 : 22-39
114.	Retires beyond Jordan.............	....	....	....	10 : 40-42
115.	Heals an Infirm Woman on the Sabbath	....	....	13 : 10-21	....
116.	Journeying and Teaching; warned against Herod.................	....	....	13 : 22-35	....
117.	Jesus hears of Lazarus' Sickness.....	....	....	....	11 : 1-6
118.	Dines with a Chief Pharisee........	....	....	14 : 1-24	....
119.	Requirements of Discipleship.......	....	....	14 : 25-35	....
120.	Lost Sheep, Lost Silver, Prodigal Son..	....	....	15 : 1-32	....
121.	Parable of the Unjust Judge.........	....	....	16 : 1-13	....
122.	The Rich Man and Lazarus.........	....	....	16 : 14-31	....
123.	Teaches Forbearance, Faith, etc.....	....	....	17 : 1-10	....
124.	Goes to Bethany and Raises Lazarus...	....	....	....	11 : 7-46
125.	Retires to Ephraim................	....	....	....	11 : 47-54
126.	Passes through Samaria and Galilee...	....	....	17 : 11-19	....
127.	On the Coming of the Kingdom of God.	....	....	17 : 20-37	....
128.	The Importunate Widow, etc.......	....	....	18 : 1-14	....
129.	Finally leaves Galilee; on Divorce....	19 : 1-12	10 : 1-12	....	....
130.	Blesses Little Children.............	19 : 13-15	10 : 13-16	18 : 15-17	....
131.	The Rich Young Ruler............	19 : 16-30	10 : 17-31	18 : 18-30	....

SECT.	SUBJECT.	MATT.	MARK.	LUKE.	JOHN.
132.	Laborers in the Vineyard.............	20 : 1-16	....	....	....
133.	Third Time foretells his Death........	20 : 17-19	10 : 32-34	18 : 31-34	....
134.	The Ambitious Request of James and John...........................	20 : 20-28	10 : 35-45	....	....
135.	Healing Two Blind Men near Jericho..	20 : 29-34	10 : 46-52	18 : 35-43	....
136.	Zaccheus; the Ten Pounds............	....	....	19 : 1-28	....
137.	Jesus sought at Jerusalem............	....	....	....	11 : 55-57
138.	Arrives at Bethany Six Days before the Passover...........................	....	....	19 : 28	12 : 1, 9-11

VII. THE LAST PASSOVER WEEK.

Seven days, April 2nd to April 8th, A.D. 30.

SECT.	SUBJECT.	MATT.	MARK.	LUKE.	JOHN.
139.	*First Day of the Week.* Public Entry into Jerusalem...	21 : 1-11	11 : 1-11	19 : 29-44	12 : 12-19
140.	Certain Greeks desire to see Jesus	21 : 17	11 : 11	....	12 : 20-36
141.	*Second Day of the Week.* The Barren Fig-tree.............................	21 : 18, 19	11 : 12-14	....	....
142.	The Temple Cleansed................	21 : 12-16	11 : 15-19	19:45-46; 37, 38	....
143.	*Third Day of the Week.* Withered Fig-tree...................................	21 : 20-22	11 : 20-26	....	....
144.	In the Temple; the Two Sons........	21 : 23-32	11 : 27-33	20 : 1-8	....
145.	The Wicked Husbandmen............	21 : 33-46	12 : 1-12	20 : 9-19	....
146.	Marriage of the King's Son..........	22 : 1-14	....	....	....
147.	Tribute to Cæsar...................	22 : 15-22	12 : 13-17	20 : 20-26	....
148.	Concerning the Resurrection.........	22 : 23-33	12 : 18-27	20 : 27-40	....
149.	The Great Commandment...........	22 : 34-40	12 : 28-34	....	....
150.	Christ the Son of David	22 : 41-46	12 : 35-37	20 : 41-44	....
151.	Last Discourse to the Jews..........	23 : 1-39	12 : 38-40	20 : 45-47	....
152.	The Widow's Mite..................	....	12 : 41-44	21 : 1-4	....
153.	Reflections on the Unbelief of the Jews	....	....	....	12 : 37-50
154.	Discourse on the Mount of Olives.....	24 : 1-51	13 : 1-37	21 : 5-36	....
155.	The Ten Virgins; the Talents........	25 : 1-30	....	....	....
156.	Graphic Scene of the Judgment......	25 : 31-46	....	....	....
157.	*Fourth Day of the Week.* The Rulers conspire.............................	26 : 1-5	14 : 1, 2	22 : 1, 2	....
158.	The Supper and Anointing at Bethany	26 : 6-16	14 : 3-11	22 : 3-6	12 : 2-9
159.	*Fifth Day of the Week.* Preparation for the Passover...................	26 : 17-19	14 : 12-16	22 : 7-13	....
160.	*Sixth Day of the Week.* The Passover ; Contention of the Twelve.........	26 : 20	14 : 17	22 : 14-18. 24-30	....
161.	Washing the Disciples' Feet.........	....	....	....	13 : 1-20
162.	The Traitor pointed out; Judas withdraws..............................	26 : 21-25	14 : 18-21	22 : 21-23	13 : 21-30
163.	Jesus foretells the Fall of Peter......	....	....	22 : 31-38	13 : 31-38
164.	Institutes the Lord's Supper (1 Cor. 11 : 23-26)........................	26 : 26-29	14 : 22-25	22 : 19, 20	....
165.	Valedictory Discourse..............	....	....	....	14 : 1-31
166.	" " Continued......	....	....	....	15 : 1-27
167.	" " Concluded.....	....	....	....	16 : 1-33
168.	Christ's Intercessory Prayer.........	....	....	....	17 : 1-26
169.	Again foretells the Fall of Peter......	26 : 30-35	14 : 26-31	22 : 39	18 : 1
170.	The Agony in Gethsemane...........	26 : 36-46	14 : 32-42	22 : 40-46	18 : 1
171.	Betrayal and Apprehension..........	26 : 47-56	14 : 43-52	22 : 47-53	18 : 2-11
172.	Jesus before Annas	....	....	....	18 : 12-14, 19-23
173.	Peter thrice denies Christ	26 : 58,69-75	14 : 54,66-72	22 : 54-62	18 : 15-18, 25-27
174.	Jesus before Caiaphas..............	26 : 57,59-68	14 : 53,55-65	22 : 54,63-65	18 : 24
175.	The final Formal Examination........	27 : 1	15 : 1	22 : 66-71	....
176.	Jesus led to Pilate.................	27 : 2	15 : 1	23 : 1	18 : 28
177.	Remorse and Suicide of Judas (Acts 1 : 18, 19)........................	27 : 3-10	....	....	....
178.	Jesus before Pilate..................	27 : 11-14	15 : 2-5	23 : 2-5	18 : 28-38
179.	Jesus before Herod.................	....	....	23 : 6-12	....
180.	Again before Pilate; Barabbas........	27 : 15-26	15 : 6-15	23 : 13-25	18 : 39, 40

SYNOPTICAL VIEW OF THE GOSPELS.

SECT.	SUBJECT.	MATT.	MARK.	LUKE.	JOHN.
181.	Scourged and delivered to be crucified.	27 : 26–30	15 : 16-19	23 : 25	19 : 1–16
182.	Led away to be crucified	27 : 31–34	15 : 20–23	23 : 26–33	19 : 16, 17
183.	The Crucifixion	27 : 35–44	15 : 24–32	23 : 33–43	19 : 18–27
184.	Phenomena attending his Death	27 : 45–56	15 : 33–41	23 : 44–49	19 : 28–30
185.	The Burial	27 : 57–61	15 : 42–47	23 : 50–56	19 : 31–42
186.	*The Seventh Day of the Week.* Sepulchre sealed and guarded	27 : 62–66	....	....	....

VIII. FROM CHRIST'S RESURRECTION TILL HIS ASCENSION.

Forty days, April to May, A.D. 30.

SECT.	SUBJECT.	MATT.	MARK.	LUKE.	JOHN.
187.	*The First Day of the Week.* The Resurrection	28 : 2–4	....	....	....
188.	Women visit the Sepulchre	28 : 1	16 : 1–4	24 : 1, 2	20 : 1, 2
189.	Vision of Angels	28 : 5–8	16 : 5–8	24 : 3–8	....
190.	Peter and John at the Sepulchre	....	....	24 : 12	20 : 3–10
191.	Jesus appears to Mary Magdalene	....	16 : 9	....	20 : 11–17
192.	Meets the Other Women	28 : 9, 10	....	....	....
193.	Report of the Women	....	16 : 10, 11	24 : 9–11	20 : 18
194.	Report of the Watch	28 : 11–15	....	....	....
195.	Appears to Two Disciples and to Peter (1 Cor. 15 : 5)	....	16 : 12, 13	24 : 13–35	....
196.	*Evening at the Close of the First Day of the Week.* Appears to Ten Apostles (1 Cor. 15 : 5)	....	16 : 14	24 : 36–49	20 : 19–25
197.	*Evening at the Close of the First Day of the Next Week.* Appears to Eleven Apostles	....	....	....	20 . 26–29
198.	Appears to Seven Apostles	28 : 16	....	....	21 : 1–23
199.	Appears to above Five Hundred (1 Cor. 15 : 6)	28 : 16–20	16 : 15–18	....	....
200.	He is seen of James; then of all the Apostles, 1 Cor 15 : 7 ; Acts 1 : 3–8	....	....	....	....
201.	The Ascension (Acts 1 : 9–12)	....	16 : 19, 20	24 : 50–53	....
202.	John's Conclusion of his Gospel	....	....	....	20 : 30,31; 21 : 24, 25

NOTE TO THE REVISED EDITION.

Every attentive reader of the Gospels must have noticed how different are the words of Jesus in John from those in the synoptics. How shall we explain this? Shall we, with Weiss, Sanday, and some others, suppose our Lord's words to have been transformed under the receptive activity of the inspired apostle's mind? Or shall we rather regard John himself as largely transformed in thought and expression to Jesus? I incline to the latter. John's receptive and deeply spiritual mind had in a high degree taken in the hidden human and Divine Christ, while with him on earth. For fifty years he had made him the subject of his contemplation, and had gone over and over the words of his higher teachings, until he was thoroughly imbued with them. In common with the aged he lived largely in the past, and so the words of Jesus were vividly before him, affecting even his own thoughts and style. The promised Spirit too was with him (ch. 16 : 13) to guide him in narrating the truth. John was thus truly himself in writing, and at the same time faithful to the rarest sayings of Jesus. We catch occasional glimpses of John's peculiar style of Christ in the other Gospels. Matt. 11 : 27; Luke 10 : 22.

A FEW WORKS REFERRED TO IN THESE NOTES,
AND ACCESSIBLE TO GENERAL READERS.

ALFORD, DR. HENRY. Critical Commentary.
BENGEL, DR. J. A. Gnomon of New Testament. A New Translation by Professor C. T. Lewis and M. R. Vincent.
BOWEN, REV. G. Love Revealed. On John, chs. xiii.-xvii.
CAMPBELL, DR. GEORGE. The Four Gospels.
CONANT, DR. T. J. The Meaning and Use of *Baptizein*, Philologically and Historically Investigated.
ELLICOTT, DR. C. J. Historical Lectures on the Life of Christ.
FARRAR, DR. F. W. Life of Christ.
FISH, DR. H. C. Bible Lands. Illustrated.
GODET, DR. F. Commentary on John. Translated from the French.
HACKETT, DR. H. B. Illustrations of Scripture.
HANNA, DR. WM. Life of Christ.
HOVEY, DR. A. Miracles.
KITTO, DR. J. Cyclopædia of Biblical Literature. Third Edition. Edited by Dr W. L. Alexander.
LANGE, DR. J. P. Commentary on the Gospel according to John. Translated from the German.
MEYER, DR. H. A. W. Critical and Exegetical Commentary. Translated from the German.
NEWMAN, DR. J. P. From Dan to Beersheba.
OLSHAUSEN, DR. H. Commentary. Dr. A. C. Kendrick's Revision.
ROBINSON, DR. E. Biblical Researches in Palestine, etc.
RYLE, J. C. Expository Thoughts on John.
SMITH, DR. W. Dictionary of the Bible. American Edition; revised and edited by Professor H. B. Hackett, D.D.
STANLEY, DEAN A. P. Sinai and Palestine.
STIER, DR. R. Words of the Lord Jesus. Revised American Edition.
THOLUCK, DR. A. Commentary on John. Translated from the German.
THOMSON, DR. W. M. The Land and the Book.
TRENCH, PROF. R. C. Notes on Parables; on Miracles.
VAN LENNEP, DR. H. J. Bible Lands; their Modern Customs and Manners.
WESTCOTT, B. F. Introduction to the Study of the Gospels.
WILSON, CAPT. C. W. Recovery of Jerusalem.
WORDSWORTH, DR. C. The New Testament, with Notes.

THE GOSPEL ACCORDING TO JOHN.

CHAPTER I.

Introduction.—The eternal existence and divine attributes of the Word.

1 *IN the beginning was the Word, and the Word ^{*Gen. 1. 1 · Prov. 8. 22, 23, etc.; 1 John 1. 1; Rev. 19. 13.}

THE TITLE is not claimed as a part of the inspired text. In the two oldest Greek manuscripts it is simply *according to* or *by John*. But many ancient manuscripts have *The Gospel according to John*—that is, as written and delivered by him. The four Gospels present only one divine record, but form four points of view. That of John is about to be given. The word *saint*, so often applied to John and other writers in the New Testament, is an addition of late date, and inconsistent with the style and simplicity of God's word. *Gospel* means *good news*, and is applied to the four inspired narratives of the life and teachings of Christ. They contain the good news of a Saviour and his salvation.

The four Gospels furnish us with four pictures of Christ's life and teachings, all taken from different points of view. Matthew sees in him chiefly the royal Lawgiver; Mark, the mighty Worker; Luke, the Friend of man; but John, the Son of God. In accordance with their several aims, Matthew traces back the Saviour's lineage to Abraham, the father of the nation; Luke, to Adam, the father of the race; John, to the reaches of past eternity, when the eternal Word dwelt with the Father, Matt. 1:1; Luke 3:38.

CHAPTER I.

John begins his Gospel by setting forth the Word, in his pre-existent nature, as partaking of the Godhead (vers. 1, 2); in his acts as Creator (3); in his earlier relations to men as the Author of life and truth (4, 5); which,

however, men had not received (6-13) * and in his last manifestation to man, as incarnate (14). John's testimony is now brought forward (15-18); his answer to the priests who were commissioned to investigate his pretensions (19-28); then, on the next day, he presents Jesus as the divinely-promised Lamb of God (29-34); on the day following he repeats his testimony, and two of his disciples followed Jesus as their Master (35-39). The new disciples in turn bring their friends to Jesus (40-51).

1-14. CHRIST THE WORD.— *The original condition and dignity of Jesus Christ. Christ the true light; What he gives to believers; his incarnation.*

In the beginning, before time, before creation; for time, properly speaking, began with creation. The history of the new creation opens with an allusion to the history of the old creation. See Gen. 1:1. The phrase signifies "before creation had begun" (see ver. 3); "before the mountains were brought forth" (Ps. 90:2); "in the depths of past eternity." See Prov. 8:22, 23. The Word, therefore, was himself uncreated and eternal. **Was the Word**, not *was made*, but *was*— that is, the Word existed. Thus Christ was before time, and uncreated. The name "Word" is applied to Jesus Christ only twice in the New Testament outside of this passage, and then only in the writings of John—viz., 1 John 1:1 and Rev. 19:12, 13. In the last of these passages the name of the incarnate and victorious "Word" is referred to as a name which no man

27

2 was ᵇwith God, ᶜand the Word was God. The same ᵇ ch. 16. 28.
ᶜ ch. 10. 30; Ps.
45. 6; Isa. 7. 14; Matt. 1. 23; Phil. 2. 6; 2 Pet. 1. 1; 1 John 5. 7.

knew—*i. e.*, whose meaning no man could fully comprehend. Whatever explanation we give of it must be based upon the office which *words* perform among men. Now, words are the means by which we express what is in us and make ourselves known to others. A single word—how perfectly it may reveal character! (See Matt. 5 : 22; 12 : 36.) How completely it may put two souls in communication with each other! (See John 20 : 16.) So it is most probable that Jesus Christ is called the Word of God because it is through him that God expresses himself in creation, in providence, and in redemption. In fine, the Word is the Revealer of God (see verse 18; Col. 1 : 15; Heb. 1 : 1-3). **And the Word was with God,** not identical, but in a sense distinct. It is intimated that the Word and God were from eternity distinct persons, John 16 : 28; 17 : 5. It was the Word to whom the Father said, "Let us make man in our image," Gen. 1 : 26. **The Word was God,** though distinct, yet in a sense one. While there is a distinction of personality between the Father and the Word, they are yet one in essence. The Word is not inferior to the Father, but as the Father is God, so the Son is God, and equally possessed of all divine attributes and powers.

It is an interesting question to inquire into the origin of the term LOGOS in Greek (properly translated WORD in English), as used by John at the beginning of his Gospel. In a well-prepared article on this subject (*Baptist Quarterly*, April, 1876, p. 140), Dr. N. M. Williams thus concludes: "Our conclusion, then, is this, that John was not indebted to Philo, or to the Targumists, or to the Apocrypha, or to Proverbs, or to any other part of the Old Testament, for the Logos doctrine, for in not one of these quarters is the doctrine to be found; but that the term itself, which clearly was not *coined* by the evangelists, was already in existence, and therefore was not drawn directly and consciously from the Gnosticism of Alexandria. As *logos* had come to be well known, partly through the Septuagint and partly through Philo, John deemed it a suitable word for the expression of his views. But whence the doctrine? This we believe to have been suggested by the Old Testament, and to have been drawn directly in part from the teachings of Christ, and in part from what John saw of Christ himself. The illuminating influence of the Holy Spirit must, of course, be presupposed. That Jesus called himself the Logos is more than can be shown, but the Logos *idea* was clearly taught. The description found in the prologue is to be found, also, in a scattered form in the body of the Gospel. In the prologue John says: 'In the beginning was the Word;' and Jesus himself had said, 'Before Abraham became, I am.' John says, 'And the Word was with God;' and Jesus himself had said, 'With the glory which I had with thee before the world was.' John says: 'And the Word was God;' and Jesus had said: 'I and my Father are one.' John says: 'All things were made by him;' and Jesus had said : 'My Father worketh hitherto, and I work.' John says: 'In him was life;' and Jesus himself had said: 'I am the bread of life.' John says: 'And the life was the light of men;' and Jesus had already said: 'I am the light of the world.' . . . Thus it appears that instead of weaving out of his own intellect that sublime description of the pre-existing Son of God which we find in his prologue, John took the thoughts, and almost the very words, from the Saviour himself. He arranged the thoughts; he gave them a compact form; he threw over the whole a rich, truthful coloring, drawn from what has been called his *experience* of the Logos doctrine; and so we have the most unique composition and the most profound thought to be found in human language."

2. **In the beginning with God.** There never was a time when this distinction of personality in the nature of the one God did not exist. With this thought of eternal existence is connected that of creation. Only by virtue of his eternal existence could the Word create the world, vers. 3, 10. Hence the importance of this foundation-truth, as stated in vers. 1, 2, preparatory to the statement in the next verse.

3 was in the beginning with God. ᵈ All things were made by him, and without him was not anything
4 made that was made. ᵉ In him was life, and ᶠ the life
5 was ᵍ the light of men. And ʰ the light shineth in darkness, and the darkness comprehended it not.

ᵈ Gen. 1.1, 26; Eph 3. 9; Heb. 1. 2, 10-12; 3. 3-6.
ᵉ ch. 11. 25.
ᶠ Isa. 49. 6.
ᵍ Isa. 9. 2.
ʰ ch. 3. 19, 20; 12. 36-40; 1 Cor. 2. 14.

The manifestation and work of the divine Word; the testimony of John the Baptist.

6 ᶦ There was a man, sent from God, whose name was

ᶦ Matt. 3. 1, 3.

3. The Creation of the Universe. All things were made ; sun, moon, and stars, heaven and earth, all the forces of nature, angels, and men (see Col. 1 : 16 ; Heb. 1 : 10). **By him** means " through him." God creates (see Gen. 1 : 1), but he creates through the Son (see Heb. 1 : 2 ; John 5 : 19), not as through a blind instrument, but as through One in living union with himself (John 10 : 30 ; Rom. 11 : 36.) "This form of expression is used in speaking of a divine agent in Rom. 11 : 36 ; 1 Cor. 1 : 9 ; Gal. 1 : 1. It seems to intimate that the Son does not act apart from the Father (see ch. 5 : 19-23). Nor does the Father act apart from the Son ; 'for without him was not even one thing made which has been made.' "—*Annotated Paragraph Bible.* **And without him,** etc. Sin came after the original creation—came not from God, but from man (see Rom. 5 : 12), and indeed was not a creation. **That was made.** More nearly, *that has been made ;* all that ever has been made.

4. Verses 4-13 treat not of the teachings of Christ in the flesh, but of his earlier revelations. **In him was life ;** the source of all intellectual, moral, and spiritual life, as he had been the source of all physical life. Ver. 3. **The life was the light of men ;** the living presence and working of Christ in the world was the source from which men derived all they had of spiritual light ; that is, of spiritual knowledge, purity, and blessedness (see Ps. 36 : 9). It was Christ who talked with Adam in the garden and appeared in human form to the patriarchs. He gave the law amid thunderings and lightnings on Mount Sinai, and manifested himself in a cloud of glory in the Tabernacle. He spoke as the Angel of Jehovah, and as the Captain of Israel. By dreams and visions, by secret whispers to men's consciences, by the manifold voices of nature and of providence, Christ enlightened to some degree every human soul, Ps. 85 : 8 ; Rom. 1 : 19 ; John 1 : 9.

5. The insufficiency of these earlier manifestations to give men spiritual life and to bring them to God is now declared. **The light shineth in darkness,** rather *the darkness ;* the light has been and is shining, through the whole series of divine revelations, in a world where every heart is darkened by sin (see Eph. 5 : 8). **The darkness comprehended it not ;** wilful blindness prevented men from seeing the heavenly sunlight that shone everywhere around, and so the world remained ignorant, degraded, and unholy. Compare ch. 3 : 19 ; Matt. 23 : 37.

6. A man sent from ; commissioned from above. Matt. 3 : 1-3 ; Luke 1 : 11-17. A prophet and more than a prophet, Matt. 11 : 9, 10. Compare Nicodemus's words to Jesus, ch. 3 : 2. **John.** This name in Hebrew means *one whom God has graciously given*—an appropriate name for the child given in answer to prayer, and who was to be the forerunner of Christ. A gracious gift, not only to his parents, but also to the Jewish people and to the world. Luke (ch. 1) as an historian gives an account of his birth. His parents were both of the priestly race. He was born in the south of Judea, some suppose Hebron, others Jutta, and lived a Nazarite (Luke 1 : 15 ; Num. 6 : 1-3) in that wild and thinly-settled region till he began his ministry, Luke 1 : 80. He commenced his ministry in the fifteenth year of Tiberius Cæsar, which was the 779th year of Rome, or A. D. 25, probably in the spring or summer. In the autumn commenced a sabbatical year, the year of our Saviour's baptism and the beginning of his ministry, as well as of a good portion of John's ministry. The evangelist here, like Mark

JOHN I.   A. D. 25.

7 John. ᵏThe same came for a witness, to bear witness of the Light, that all *men* through him might believe.
8 ˡHe was not that Light, but *was sent* to bear witness of that Light.
9 ᵐ*That* was the true Light, which lighteth every
10 man that cometh into the world. He was in the world, and ⁿthe world was made by him, and ᵒthe
11 world knew him not. ᵖHe came unto his own, and
12 his own received him not. But ᑫas many as received him, to them gave he power to become the sons of
13 God, *even* to them that believe on his name; which

ᵏ ch. 3. 26–36.
ˡ ver. 20; ch. 3. 28.
ᵐ Isa. 49. 6; 1 John 2. 8.
ⁿ Heb. 1. 2; 11. 3.
ᵒ ch. 17. 25.
ᵖ Isa. 53. 1–3; Luke 19. 14; 20. 13–15; Acts 13. 46.
ᑫ Isa. 56. 5; Jer. 3. 19; Rom. 8. 14, 15; Gal. 3. 26; 1 John 3. 1.

---

and Matthew, introduces John abruptly, as one demanding notice only in his official work as the forerunner of Jesus. Verses 6–13 may be considered a subordinate and parenthetical passage, more fully detailing the thought of verse 5.

7. **The same came for a witness.** John the Baptist, "burning and shining light" as he was, was only a reflector and witness of Him who was the true, original, real source of light for all the world. **That all men.** Omit *men*. **Through him,** through John, **might believe** on Jesus as the Light. We have here the aim of John's testimony. He was the harbinger of Jesus and the leader of the faith of Israel to Christ. The apostles and others came from his disciples, but not only by his testimony as still left us in the Gospels, but also through them, John still points and leads to Christ, vers. 29–36.

8. **He was not that Light,** rather, *the Light,* emphatic, *the* light of the world, as some of the disciples of John and some Jews might suppose, ver. 20; 3 : 28; 5 : 25. Some looked no further than John, instead of looking through him and his testimony to Christ. **Was sent.** Not in the original. Some supply *he was;* better, however, to supply *he came.* **To bear witness,** etc. His whole mission, baptism, and preaching were a testimony to **that,** rather, *the* Light, Jesus Christ.

9. A difficult passage. The most natural rendering is the preferable one. **That was the true Light,** etc. Some translate, "The true light which lighteth every man, was [now] coming into the world." Others, "The true light was that which, coming into the world, lighteth every man." Either of these is grammatically allowable. The Bible Union rendering I think is better:

"There was the true light, which lights every man that comes into the world." A fact is stated. Jesus was the Christ, and was already in the world (next verse). Christ was the *true light,* the Sun of righteousness and the source of truth. *True* means *real, original,* in opposition to *representative,* and hence permanent and universal. **That cometh,** etc. It is more natural and more in accordance with the arrangement of the sentence in the original to refer this to "every man," rather than to "the true light." Every one, directly or indirectly, comes under the influence of Christ.

10. **He was in the world,** etc. The reference is to mankind in general. Though coming with such powerful witness to the world he had made, and to the people he had chosen for his inheritance, both the world at large and the Jewish people rejected Christ's light and remained in the darkness of their sin. **Knew him not;** did not recognize him.

11. **Unto his own;** possession or inheritance. **His own;** his chosen people, Israel. If any distinction is to be made between the two expressions, it is that the former *his own* refers more to the land of Palestine, and the latter to the Jewish people. **Received him not.** Notice, this is stronger than what was said of the world in the preceding verse. The Jews did not receive the Christ of their own Scriptures; they rejected him.

12. **As many as received him.** A hearty act of faith. **Gave he power;** empowered them; a glorious fact and a happy realization. **Sons of God;** rather *children of God.* **To them that believe.** Salvation through faith is thus brought to view at

were born, ʳnot of blood, ˢnor of the will of the flesh, 14 nor of the will of man, ᵗbut of God. And the Word ᵘwas made flesh, and dwelt among us (and ˣwe beheld his glory, the glory as of ʸthe only-begotten of the Father), ᶻfull of grace and truth.

ʳ ch. 8. 33–41
ˢ Rom. 9. 10–16.
ᵗ ch 3. 3–8.
ᵘ Matt. 1. 16, 20–23; 1 Tim. 3. 16; Rom. 1. 3; Heb. 2. 14–17.
ˣ ch. 2. 11; 11. 40; Matt, 17. 1–5.

The testimony of John the Baptist to Jesus; Jesus gains disciples.

ʸ Ps. 2. 7.
ᶻ 2 Cor. 12. 9; Col. 1. 19; 2. 3, 9.

15 John bare witness of him, and cried, saying, This was he of whom I spake, ᵃHe that cometh after me is preferred before me, ᵇfor he was before me.

ᵃ ch. 3. 31; Matt. 3. 11.
ᵇ ch.8. 58; Mic. 5.2.

the beginning of this Gospel. None ever received Christ or believed in him except as the result of a special divine energy recreating their natures and making them children of God—a change which neither holy parentage and bloody sacrifices, nor fleshly birth into any chosen nation, nor even the strongest effort of the unassisted human will could ever accomplish, vers. 12, 13. Thus the evangelist, like Paul in Rom. 1–3, prepares the way for the glorious announcement of the gospel by showing how hopelessly dark and lost the world was without it. 13. **Born, not of blood;** literally, *of bloods.* The plural here is the same as the singular in its meaning: Not by natural generation. They were possessed of the privileges and blessings of being "children of God," not in consequence of noble lineage, of being descended from the loins of holy patriarchs and prophets. Perhaps some reference may also be made to bloody sacrifices and rites. **Nor of the will of the flesh.** Not by the desire and power of the natural and physical in human nature. The idea is lower than that of the next phrase, "will of man." The contrast to born "of God" suggests the additional idea of corrupt nature (ch. 3 : 6); not by any wisdom or power of corrupt human nature. **Nor of the will of man;** pointing to the noblest and wisest powers of man: not by or in consequence of the advice, wisdom, or highest power of man, or anything that man by wisdom and intellect could do. **But of God;** the Author of regeneration, ch. 3 : 5, 6; Eph. 1 : 5. This does not exclude the instrumentality of the word, James 1 : 18.

14. The last and highest manifestation of Jesus Christ in becoming man. The **Word was made,** *became,* **flesh;** took to himself human nature in both its parts, body and soul, 1 Tim. 3 : 16; Rom. 1 : 3; Heb. 2 : 14–17. He had a real human body which could suffer and die, John 19 : 28. He had a real human soul also, John 12 : 27. But though the Word united humanity to himself, he did not cease to be God. **Dwelt among us;** tabernacled among us, as the divine glory of old shone in and upon the tabernacle, John 2 : 19, 21; Col. 2 : 9. **Beheld his glory;** manifested in his miracles, his transfiguration, his teaching, and his whole life, John 2 : 11; 11 : 4; 2 Pet. 1 : 16. "One remarkable peculiarity of this evangelist is the reference which he constantly makes to what he and his colleagues had 'seen and heard,' as affording indisputable evidence of the truth of his testimony." **The glory as of the only-begotten of the Father,** such as became One of his dignity. Here the term "only-begotten" intimates a relationship between Christ and the Father such as no earthly "children of God" can ever boast; **full of grace and truth;** of grace, as revealing the pardoning mercy and adopting love of God; of truth, as being in his own person the reality which the ceremonies and prophecies of the Old Testament foreshadowed.

15–34. THE TESTIMONY OF JOHN THE BAPTIST TO JESUS.—Recorded only by John.

15. This verse may be regarded as a parenthesis, confirming what has been said of Christ's glory by John the Baptist's testimony to the Saviour's pre-existent dignity and glory, and the three verses that follow as a confirmatory statement by the apostle John, the writer of this Gospel. This is the view of many

16 And of his °fulness have all we received, ᵈ and grace ° ch. 3.31; Col. 1.19.
17 for grace. For ᵉ the law was given by Moses, but ᵈ Matt. 13.12; Eph. 4. 7.
° Ex. 20. 1, etc.

eminent expositors, among them Olshausen and Tholuck. I prefer, however, with Origen, Chrysostom, Erasmus, Lange, and others, to regard John the Baptist as continuing his testimony in the succeeding verses. In this and the following verses he rises into a high prophetic strain, taking the past and future into one view.

This was he of whom I spake, or, some occasion, such as that referred to in ver. 19 or in Luke 3 : 15. The expression is similar to that in ver. 30. **He that cometh.** The language is vivid, and therefore the present is used. **After me ;** in time. The birth of Jesus was six months after John's, and so the beginning of his ministry was about as much later. **Is preferred before me ;** in dignity and honor. **For he was before me ;** having existed from eternity with the Father. Compare ch. 8 : 58.
16. **And of his fulness.** According to the highest critical authorities, *For out of his fulness ;* of grace and truth (ver. 14) of which he is the embodiment; of moral beauty and excellence. **All we received.** This is generally referred to believers, and hence upon this expression is built the argument that the apostle John, and not John the Baptist, speaks in this and the two following verses. See on ver. 15. It seems better to regard John the Baptist, with one sweep of prophetic vision, taking in the Old Testament saints and prophets, himself and his discipleship, and those who should believe on Jesus, as alike dependent on the Messiah and recipients of his fulness. All were as present before him. **And,** here equivalent to *namely.* **Grace for grace,** *grace in the place of grace* or *upon grace;* favor upon favor; continually new and larger accessions of grace; successive communications of ever-increasing blessings; grace uninterrupted, unceasingly renewed. The expression in the original is unusual and difficult. It may be literally translated, *Grace over against grace.* Hence the view that it means " grace or *excellence of character* received by the Christian corresponding to each grace or excellence in Christ," is possible. Believers are like Christ, and are growing into his likeness; and all this from and through him. (See this view discussed in *Baptist Quarterly,* Jan., 1871, pp. 79-86.)
17. **For the law,** which utters condemnation and death rather than mercy and divine favor, and which also in itself was unable to produce in sinful man a single moral excellence, or a single beauty of character, **was given by** (*through*) **Moses.** The law was not his; it was *given* through him. Its office was rather restraint and conviction of sin, and by its types and shadows pointed to Christ, Rom. 3 : 20 ; Gal. 3 : 19. **Grace and truth.** *Grace* stands forth prominently in ver. 16, *truth* in ver. 17. Both are in contrast to the law. The gospel indeed embodies all the grace and truth of the law, and reveals them in full measure. **Came by.** Not "given through," as with Moses; but *came through.* Grace and truth were in Christ and through Christ. They are his, and manifested and brought to man through his appearing in humanity. **Jesus.** The personal name of our Lord, the Greek form of Joshua, meaning *Jehovah his help* or *Saviour,* and given him by command of the angel of the Lord, because he should " save his people from their sins." Matt. 1 : 21. **Christ.** His official name, meaning *anointed,* corresponding to the Hebrew Messiah. Ps. 2 : 2 ; Dan. 9 : 24, 25 ; John 1 : 41 ; 4 : 25. He was the anointed Prophet, Priest, and King of spiritual Israel, of the kingdom of God. "The antithesis which is made in this place by John, as in Paul too, between *law* and *grace,* is worthy of remark. The *grace* is the leading idea, but the *truth* also forms an antithesis to *law.* By the legal relation condemnation falls upon men. The law indeed, in its sacrifices and ceremonies, had grace also, but only *symbolically* (Col. 2 : 17 ; Heb. 10 : 1), as opposed to which, the unveiled, absolute truth now appears. For *came* John could not well have written *was given ;* it is the historical fact of the appearing of Christ in humanity by which *grace* and *truth* have become the portion of mankind."—THOLUCK. Compare 1 Cor. 1 : 30.

18 ᶠgrace and ᵍtruth came by Jesus Christ. ʰNo man hath seen God at any time; ⁱthe only-begotten Son, which is in the bosom of the Father, ᵏhe hath declared *him*.
19 And this is ˡthe record of John, when the Jews sent priests and Levites from Jerusalem to ask him,

ᶠ Rom. 3. 24.
ᵍ ch. 14. 6; Rom. 15. 8.
ʰ ch. 6. 46; Ex. 33. 20.
ⁱ ch. 3. 16, 18.
ᵏ ch. 17. 6; Matt 11. 27.
ˡ ch. 5. 33.

"The inferior economy might be entrusted to the hands of a servant (Heb. 3 : 2-6); the realization of all its foreshadowed blessings, and especially the exercise of the highest divine prerogative of sovereign mercy, could be committed only to One whose intimacy with the Father, such as no mere man could pretend to, would enable him to make the fullest revelation of God (ver. 18)."
—*Annotated Parag. Bible.*
18. **No man hath seen God at any time,** rather, *No one has ever seen God;* he is incorporeal, and hence invisible to human sight. Moses had a glimpse of him, saw his back part (Ex. 33 : 20-23); but no one has seen him in his essential essence and glory. "A decided distinction is supposed (ch. 6 : 45, 46) between hearing God and seeing him, and the first is attributed to men in general, the second to the Son alone. Hearing causes us to have perception of the object in *motion*, consequently in *communication* with us; vision perceives the object in the condition of rest, and is consequently better adapted to express that knowledge which springs from perfect unity with God. The sole absolute knowledge of God Christ also claims for himself in Matt. 11 : 27."—THOLUCK.

The only-begotten Son, the Logos united with humanity, ver. 14. Many ancient authorities read *the only-begotten God,* clearly indicating that he is the only-begotten, as he is God. It is difficult to decide between these two readings. But the preponderance of external and internal evidence seems to be on the side of *God only begotten* (without the article). Both readings present truth. The former the Divine Sonship; the latter, Christ as both God (ver. 1) and begotten (ver. 14) from the Father. He was indeed the God-man, but back of this was his Divine relation in the Godhead. Yet in this Gospel Sonship is uniformly applied to Christ's incarnate state. (See Abbott, *Bibliotheca Sacra,* 1861, p. 859, and Hort, "Two Dissertations," Cambridge, 1877.) **Who is in the bosom of the Father.** The highest unity and most intimate knowledge are denoted. According to Oriental custom, the best beloved lies in the bosom of his host and holds the most intimate and confidential converse, ch. 13 : 23. **He hath declared him.** Literally, *He declared him,* proclaimed and revealed him by his words and appearance. All Old Testament revelation came through the Son; so also the New Testament.

19–28. JOHN DECLARES TO THE PRIESTS THAT HE IS NOT THE MESSIAH, BUT HIS FORERUNNER.—After the general mention of the Baptist's testimony (ver. 15) the evangelist proceeds to enumerate several particular occasions on which this testimony was given. It is probable that on the last day of the temptation the deputation from the priests and Levites came to John (ver. 19); and on the day following Jesus returned from the wilderness, and was saluted by John as the Lamb of God, ver. 29. Some, however, suppose that Jesus had already returned, and that his personal presence is implied in ver. 26. 19. **The record,** rather *the witness,* or testimony. **When the Jews.** In this Gospel the phrase "the Jews" commonly signifies the Jewish authorities as distinguished from the "people" and as hostile to the Saviour. John the Evangelist wrote after Jerusalem had been destroyed and the Jews had ceased to be a nation. He no longer considered himself as belonging to a community that had "killed the Lord Jesus" and had "persecuted his apostles," 1 Thess. 2 : 15. "The Jews," here, were doubtless the members of the Sanhedrim, the highest civil and ecclesiastical tribunal of the nation. These sent to John the Baptist a deputation of priests, with Levites, who acted as servants for the priests in the ministrations of the temple, Num. 1 : 47-54. **Priests** were of the tribe of Levi and of the family of Aaron,

84   JOHN I.   A. D. 27.

20 Who art thou? And ᵐ he confessed, and denied not; 21 but confessed, I am not the Christ. And they asked him, what then? Art thou ⁿ Elias? And he saith, I am not. Art thou ᵒ that prophet? And he an-

ᵐ ch. 3. 28; Matt. 3. 11; Luke 3. 15; Acts 13. 25.
ⁿ Mal. 4. 5.
ᵒ Deut. 18. 15, 18.

Levites were the descendants of Gershom, Kohath, and Merari, the sons of Levi, who assisted the priests in sacrifices and other services and guarded the temple, Num. 3 : 17 ; 8 : 5–22. **Jerusalem**, the capital and most noted city of Palestine; mentioned much more frequently by Luke than by the other evangelists. Jerusalem signifies dwelling or foundation of peace. It was once called Salem, and was the abode of Melchizedek (Gen. 14 : 18 ; Ps. 76 : 2), but afterward Jebus, Judg. 19 : 10. The latter name was probably applied specially to the hill Zion, which when reduced by David was also called the city of David, 2 Sam. 5 : 6, 9. After it came into the possession of the Israelites the sacred writers apply Jerusalem to the whole city as its common name. It was built on four hills: Zion on the south, which was the highest, and contained the citadel and palace ; Moriah, on the east, on which stood the temple ; and Acra and Bezetha, north of Zion and covered with the largest portion of the city. Jerusalem is near the middle of Palestine, about thirty-five miles from the Mediterranean, and about twenty-five miles from the Jordan and the Dead Sea. Its elevation is 2610 feet above the former sea, and 3927 feet above the latter. It has been taken and pillaged many times, so that ancient Jerusalem is really a buried city, the surface of the ground at present being from fifty to a hundred feet above what it was in the time of David or of Christ. The valleys have been filled by the destruction of buildings and bridges, and by other rubbish, mostly during the last eighteen centuries, since the destruction of the city by the Romans, A. D. 70, though doubtless in part by the sieges and sacks of the six centuries before the Christian era. The modern city is called by the Arabs *El Khuds*, " the holy," and contains about fifteen thousand inhabitants, mostly poor and degraded. **Who art thou?** It was considered a duty of the Sanhedrim, as supervisors of the religious affairs of the nation, to prevent the preaching of false prophets. The universal excitement which the Baptist's work had caused, together with the growing suspicion in many minds that he might be the Messiah, compelled the rulers of the Jews to investigate his claims and inform themselves with regard to his movements (see Matt. 21 : 23). John had never consulted them, and his denunciations of their Pharisaic pride and formalism (Matt. 3 : 7) had not prepossessed them in his favor. These priests and Levites evidently came with an unbelieving and inquisitorial spirit to put his pretensions to a rigid test, and if possible to find matter of accusation against him.

20. **He confessed and denied not,** etc. John's temptation was almost simultaneous with that of Jesus. Thousands would have followed him if he had declared himself the Christ. But, like his Master, he put away all worldly ambition. In his humility he shrank from the very thought of being considered the Messiah. **I am not the Christ.** The order of the words is emphatic in the original, *I indeed, I for my part*. The expression is suggestive of the fact that he knew of One who was the Christ. There was thus not only a confession of his own true character, but an implied confession of another as the Christ. To have confessed himself the Christ would have been to deny Jesus as the Christ.

21. **Art thou Elias?** " John came indeed ' in the spirit and power of Elijah ' (Luke 1 : 17), and therefore was called Elijah by Christ (Matt. 11 : 14; 17 : 11), as well as by the prophet Malachi (Mal. 4 : 5), but in the sense in which the Jews used the word he was not Elias. They expected Elijah to return in person (Matt. 17 : 10)." Many of them believed in a sort of transmigration of souls, so that they afterward fancied Jesus to be John the Baptist risen from the dead (Luke 9 : 7). The Talmud tells of opening a door and setting a chair for Elijah at feasts, if perchance the old prophet at some unexpected moment should come in. **I am not.** It was necessary for John to negative all these superstitious expectations of Elijah's bodily return to earth.

22 swered, No. Then said they unto him, Who art thou? that we may give an answer to them that sent us.
23 What sayest thou of thyself? ᵛ He said, I *am* the voice of one crying in the wilderness, Make straight the way of the Lord [Isa. xl. 3], as said the prophet Esaias.
24 And they which were sent were of the Pharisees.

ᵛ ch. 3. 28; Matt. 3. 3.

Art thou that prophet? The absence of any name makes it clear that they meant the prophet foretold by Moses in Deut. 18:15. Although this prediction really referred to Christ (see Acts 8:22; 7:37), many of the Jews believed that it referred to some prophet who should rise to prepare the way of the Messiah (see Matt. 16:14). With strict truthfulness and humility, he **answered, No.** He would only appear as the harbinger of Christ, ver. 23.
22. **Then.** *Therefore they said.* Since they failed to designate the right one. **Who art thou?** John had answered, thus far, by brief and sharp negations. The formalists were bent only on asking "Who?" John could not give them a full account of himself, nor point out Jesus to them, because they, looking only to externals, and having no sense of their own needs, were in no state to receive his testimony. **To them that sent us.** The Sanhedrim, ver. 19. "They ever ask about his *person;* he ever refers them to his *office.* He is no one—a voice merely; it is the work of God, the testimony to Christ, which is everything. So the formalist ever in the church asks, *Who* is he? while the witness for Christ only exalts, only cares for, Christ's work."—ALFORD. (See next verse.)
23. So he only repeated what he had often said to others. **I am the voice of one crying.** It is not himself, but his preaching and mission that John makes prominent. His whole public life was as a sermon. His preaching was indeed a *voice* of one *crying aloud,* of short duration, but by its great earnestness exciting attention, and the place of his preaching was the **wilderness.** Wilderness denotes an unenclosed, untilled, and thinly-inhabited district. The word was applied to mountainous regions, to districts fitted only for pasture, and to tracts of country remote from towns and sparsely settled. The *wilderness* in which John preached was a striking emblem of the spiritual desolation of Israel at that time. **Make straight the way.** Make a direct road and level it, referring to the custom of levelling and straightening the roads before Oriental monarchs on their journeys and marches. The custom still prevails in the East. **Of the Lord,** of the Messiah. **As said the prophet Esaias,** *Isaiah.* The prophecy is briefly quoted according to its sense, and points to the ministry of John as preparatory, and to him as the precursor of Christ. He went before, rebuking the proud, exposing hypocrites, calling men to repentance, directing their minds to the Messiah, and making ready a people prepared for the Lord, Luke 1: 16, 17. The other evangelists quote the prophecy, Matt. 3:3; Mark 1:3; Luke 3:4, 5.
24. **Were of the Pharisees.** The *Pharisees* were a religious party or sect which originated about one hundred and fifty years before Christ. Their name means *separatists;* they were those who separated themselves from Levitical and traditional impurity. To become a member of the Pharisaic association one must agree to set apart all the sacred tithes, and refrain from eating anything that had not been tithed or about the tithing of which there was any doubt. As the tithes were regarded as holy, so the eating and enjoying them were regarded as a deadly sin. A Pharisee must ascertain whether the articles which he purchased had been duly tithed, and have the same certainty in regard to the food he ate both in his own house and in the houses of others. As publicans and sinners were not careful about this, Pharisees would, of course, not eat with them, for in so doing it was assumed that they partook of food which had not been duly tithed, Luke 5:30. Neither would they associate with them, for, as excommunicated persons, they regarded them as very heathen, Matt 18.

25 And they asked him and said unto him, why baptizest thou then, if thou be not that Christ, nor Elias, 26 neither that prophet? John answered them, saying, ⁿ I baptize with water; ʳ but there standeth one among

ⁿ Matt. 3. 11.
ʳ Mal. 3. 1.

17. It was also binding on them to observe strictly the laws of purity, according to the Mosaic ritual and the traditions of the elders, Mark 7 : 3. They held strictly to their oral law or traditions, attaching more importance to them than even to their written law, Matt. 15 : 1–6. They were the formalists of their age and nation, and were too often characterized for their ostentation, self-righteousness, and hypocrisy. They were the most numerous sect among the Jews, and had great influence with the people.

25. Since the Pharisees paid so great regard to outward observances, they were particularly troubled about the new rite of baptism which John had instituted, and they ask him, **Why baptizest thou, then?** The word *baptize* is the Greek word *baptizo* transferred into our language and the termination altered, and means, literally, *to immerse*. This has been the meaning of the verb in the original in every stage of the Greek language, and it is still its meaning in the modern Greek. In this all lexicographers are agreed. In accordance with this meaning, the Greek Church in all of its branches has uniformly practised immersion from the earliest period to the present. Its figurative meaning is based on this ground-meaning, and always expresses an idea of immersion. But it is only with the literal meaning that we have here to do. The baptism of John was a new rite. It was not founded on the immersions of the old dispensation, under which persons performed the ceremony of bathing or immersing the whole body—not on others, but on themselves, Lev. 15 : 6; 16 : 4. The immersion of one person by another, as a divinely-appointed act, is peculiar to Christianity, and was first introduced in connection with it. It was practised neither among Jews nor heathen. Some, indeed, would found it on proselyte baptism among the Jews, but this appears not to have been known till long after John. Indeed, the earliest mention of proselyte baptism is found in the Babylonish Talmud, a Jewish commentary of the sixth century. John himself declared that he received his commission to baptize directly from God (ver. 33), and Jesus intimated that the rite was revealed to John from heaven, Luke 20 : 4. As a new rite it was a distinguishing feature of his ministry, and he is called *The Baptist*, Mark 6 : 25; Luke 7 : 20. Compare the author's *Notes on Matthew*, ch. 3 : 6, and his *Notes on Mark*, ch. 1 : 4: also see Dr. Conant's *Baptizein*, Carson *On Baptism*, and kindred works.

26. **I baptize with water,** rather, "*in* water," according to the original. The Greek preposition *en* with *baptizo*, in connection with the immersing substance, never means *with*, but always *in*. See Conant's *Baptizein*, sec. 3, 2. Meyer says on this phrase in Matt. 3 : 11: "*En* (*in*) is, in accordance with the meaning of *baptizo* (immerse), not to be understood instrumentally, but, on the contrary, as *in*, in the element wherein the immersion takes place." So also the very learned Presbyterian scholar, Dr. George Campbell, comments on the same passage: "The word *baptizein* (baptize) both in sacred authors and in classical signifies *to dip, to plunge, to immerse*, and was rendered by Tertullian, the oldest of the Latin Fathers, *tingere*, the term used for dyeing cloth, which was by immersion. It is always construed suitably to this meaning. Thus it is *in water, in Jordan*." "When the Greek word *baptizo* is adopted, I may say, rather than translated, into modern languages, the mode of construction ought to be preserved, so far as may conduce to suggest its original import. It is to be regretted that we have so much evidence that even good and learned men allow their judgments to be warped by the sentiments and customs of the sect which they prefer. The true partisan, of whatever denomination, always inclines to correct the diction of the Spirit by that of the party."—*The Four Gospels*, Boston edition, vol. iv., pp. 23, 24.

John afterward (ver. 33) 'old his disciples that his authority for administering the ordinance was directly from God.

27 you, ⁑whom ye know not; ᵗhe it is, who coming after   ⁑ vers. 10, 11.
me is preferred before me, whose shoe's latchet I am   ᵗ vers. 15, 30; Acts 19. 4.
28 not worthy to unloose. These things were done ᵘ in   ᵘ ch. 10. 40; Judg 7. 24.
Bethabara, beyond Jordan, where John was baptizing.

But when these Pharisees demanded his authority he gave them no answer. It was enough for them to know that his baptism and work were insignificant in importance, compared with those of the Messiah who was already at the doors. **There standeth one among you whom ye know not.** Possibly, as John looked upon the multitude, his eyes rested upon Jesus, who had but just now returned from his temptation in the wilderness, and who stood there in the crowd unnoticed and unknown. Yet this supposition is not necessary. He had been among them in his baptism. His ministry began then, and he was now among the Jewish nation, known by John as the Messiah, though unrecognized by them.

27. Omit the words, **Is preferred before me,** according to the correct text. **Whose shoe's latchet;** the strap of whose *shoe* or *sandal.* "The shoe itself, if we may so call it, consists of a piece of a strong, untanned skin; ... this is cut somewhat larger than the sole of the foot, and is made fast by means of strings or thongs of leather, which gather the edges and are tied around the foot very much like the ancient sandals. This kind of shoe is used not only by shepherds, but by the inhabitants of all the remote villages. ... It seems to have been used by the poorer classes in ancient times."—DR. H. J. VAN LENNEP, *Bible Lands,* p. 186.

28. **In Bethabara.** According to the best manuscripts, *In Bethany beyond Jordan.* The precise spot is unknown, but it was doubtless in the immediate vicinity of the river. **Where John,** etc. John was baptizing in the Jordan, Matt. 3 : 5, 13; Mark 1 : 5, 9. This Bethany must have been upon or near the eastern bank of the river. (See the latter part of the quotation below.) The deputation from Jerusalem got so little satisfaction from John that they did not care to inquire about this greater One to whom he pointed them. "So the day passed and Jesus remained unknown; assuming, saying, doing, nothing by which he could be recognized." The people did not know him, for only John and himself had seen the dove and heard the voice at his baptism. Jesus would not bear witness of himself; he left this to John, whose appointed office it was to make him known. **Where John was baptizing.** "An hour and a half's gallop across the plain takes one from Jericho to *the Jordan.* The Latin bathing-place is seven miles from the Dead Sea. That of the Greeks is some two miles farther north. There is a lower pilgrims' ford, two and a half miles from the Dead Sea, used by modern pilgrims and travellers between Jerusalem and Moab. The first-named of these, which we visited, is generally accepted as the place of our Lord's baptism, as it was of Israel's crossing and other great events. The ford we had hoped to cross, but the water was too swift and deep. Although the dry season was upon us (it was April 22d), we found the river at least one hundred feet wide and apparently from eight to twelve feet deep in different places. No Arab would venture to attempt to swim across. In bathing we were obliged to keep near the bank. The water was of a milky color, and not uncomfortably cold. ... This would seem to be a fitting place for Christ's baptism. The river a little above darts from a ravine thickly studded with green trees, and being arrested by headlands, here sets back, apparently clasping a wooded islet in its shining arms, and forming by the graceful curve of its refluent waves quite a handsome little lakelet, around which thousands of spectators could be congregated, as when of old there went out to John the Baptist 'Jerusalem and all Judea, and all the region round about Jordan, and were baptized of him in Jordan confessing their sins,' Matt. 3 : 5, 6. ... The *Bethabara,* beyond Jordan, near where John baptized (John 1 : 28), was not far off, but is yet unidentified. The word means 'house of passage,' indicating a ford. But all the best manuscripts read *Bethany* ('place of dates') *beyond Jor-*

29 The next day John seeth Jesus coming unto him, and saith, Behold ᵃ the Lamb of God, ʸ which taketh 30 ᵃ away the sin of the world! ᵃ This is he of whom I said, After me cometh a man which is preferred before me; for he was before me. And ᵇ I knew him

1. 3; 2. 17; 1 John 2. 2; 3. 5; 4. 10; Rev. 1. 5.   ᵃ Lev. 16. 21, 22.
ᵃ vers. 15. 27.   ᵇ Luke 1. 80.

ᵃ Gen. 22. 8; Ex. 12. 3-10; 29. 38, 39; Isa. 53. 7; Acts 8. 32.
ʸ Isa. 53. 4-6, 11; 2 Cor. 5. 15; Gal. 1. 4; 3. 13; Heb.

dan. Lieut. Conder thinks he has identified the place, some twenty-five miles from Nazareth, in a ford called by the natives 'Ford of Crossing.' But he is probably misled by the wrong reading of the text. The idea of a *ford* is not in it."—DR. FISH, *Bible Lands Illustrated*, pp. 261, 264–266.

29–34. JOHN POINTS OUT JESUS TO HIS DISCIPLES AS THE LAMB OF SACRIFICE WHO IS TO EXPIATE HUMAN GUILT. In regard to the sacrificial symbols of the Old Testament, there can be no doubt that the idea conveyed to the Hebrew mind by the sin-offerings of the old dispensation was that of satisfaction to a justly-offended Deity. There was an instinct of justice that approved of this demand for satisfaction. This satisfaction, moreover, was rendered by substitution. The sinner substituted the life of another for his own life, and himself went free. Satisfaction by substitution was God's method of salvation. The work of Christ for us must be interpreted in accordance with these ideas of sacrifice into which God educated the race. To call the sacrificial language of the New Testament a mere accommodation to Jewish notions is to deny the foresight and design of God in the institution of the Old Testament types, and to put the Mosaic system on a level with the heathen religions.

29. **The next day,** after the deputation had come and gone, **John seeth Jesus coming unto him,** doubtless for the very purpose of receiving John's testimony. John could now point out Jesus to his own disciples, who would accept his witness as final and authoritative. **Behold the Lamb of God.** Jesus is called a lamb, not simply because of the purity of his personal character, or his meekness and patience under suffering, but because he was the Lamb of Sacrifice, destined by God and accepted by God as a propitiation for the sins of the world. **Which taketh away the sin of the world.** No Jew could hear of a "lamb that taketh away sin" without being instantly reminded of the sacrifices of the temple, in which the death of an animal victim was accepted in place of the sinner's death, and satisfaction was rendered to the offended holiness of God. Isaiah, in foretelling the sufferings of the Messiah and his propitiatory work, had made use of this same figure (see Isa. 53: 7). When the Baptist called Jesus by this name, he meant that Jesus was the divinely-appointed victim, on whom the Lord would "lay the iniquity of us all," who should be "brought as a lamb to the slaughter" and be "wounded for our transgressions," that "by his stripes we might be healed." Jesus was the Lamb of God in whom all the sacrificial types of the old dispensation and all the prophecies of a suffering Messiah should be fulfilled. In taking human nature he had taken upon him "the sin of the world." In that nature he would bear the suffering and death which were the penalty of sin, and thereby bring to men deliverance from its dominion and power. This was a redemption not for the Jews only, but for all mankind (1 John 2 : 2).

30. **This is he of whom I said.** John points to Jesus as the personage to whom all his former announcements referred. The expression is the same as in verse 15. **After me,** in time. **Is preferred before me,** in dignity and honor; **for he was before me,** referring to Christ's eternal pre-existence with the Father.

31. **And I knew him not.** There is a pathos in this regretful utterance of the Baptist. It seemed strange to him now that, with all his personal knowledge of Jesus' holy character, he should not earlier have recognized him as the Messiah. Yet **that he should be made manifest to Israel, therefore am I come,** etc.; this making known of Jesus was the great object

A. D. 27. JOHN I. 39

not; but that he should be made manifest to Israel, ^c therefore am I come baptizing with water.
32 ^d And John bare record, saying, I saw the Spirit descending from heaven like a dove, and it abode
33 upon him. And I knew him not; but he that sent me to baptize with water, the same said unto me, Upon whom thou shalt see the Spirit descending, and remaining on him, ^e the same is he which bap-
34 tizeth with the Holy Ghost. And I saw, and bare record, ^f that this is the Son of God.

^c ver. 7; Mal. 3. 1; Matt. 3. 6: Luke 1. 17, 76–79; 3. 3, 4; Acts 19. 4.
^d ch. 5. 32; Matt. 3. 15, 16.
^e Mal. 3. 2; Matt. 3. 11; Acts 1. 5; 2. 2–4, 10, 44; 19. 6.
^f Matt. 3. 17.

of John's mission. **Baptizing with water,** rather, according to the original, *baptizing in water.* See notes on vers. 26, 33.

32. **John bare record;** *bore testimony, witness.* **I saw,** at his baptism, **the Spirit descending.** This descending and abiding of the Spirit was the appointed sign (ver. 33) by which John was to recognize Jesus as him **which baptizeth with the Holy Ghost,** as an all-encompassing purifying element, just as John's baptism is said to be a baptism not "*with,*" but "*in* water." **Like a dove,** *As a dove,* which may refer either to the *shape* or *manner* in which the Spirit descended; probably the former, for Luke (3 : 22) says "in a bodily shape like (as) a dove." It was something also that could be seen. John saw it. The dove was a fit emblem of the pure, gentle, and peaceful character of Jesus and his work, Isa. 61 : 1–3; Matt. 10 : 16; 11 : 29; 12 : 19–21. John adds: **And it abode upon him.** Thus John received the promised token of the Messiah, and Jesus received the heavenly anointing; and here the active and official ministry of Jesus begins. Ps. 45 : 7; Isa. 11 : 2; 42 : 1.

33. **Baptize with water ... baptizeth with the Holy Ghost.** That the former of these phrases ought not to be translated "with water" is evident from the words "in Jordan" (Matt. 3 : 6), where we cannot possibly say "were baptized of him with Jordan." The preposition in both these cases is the same, as also in the phrase "baptizeth with the Holy Ghost," which ought to be rendered "baptizeth in the Holy Ghost." Cyril, Bishop of Jerusalem A. D. 350, who wrote while Greek was a living language, gives us his understanding of this phrase as follows: "For the Lord saith, 'Ye shall be immersed in the Holy Spirit not many days after this.' Not in part the grace, but all-sufficing the power! For as he who sinks down in the waters, and is immersed, is surrounded on all sides by the waters, so also they were completely immersed by the Spirit." Wherever this baptism of the Holy Spirit is mentioned, it is always said to be "*in* the Holy Spirit," as the element in which the baptism is performed. Archbishop Tillotson has seized upon the essential idea of this baptism in his exposition of Acts 2 : 1–4: "'*It filled all the house.*' This is that which our Saviour calls baptizing the apostles with the Holy Ghost, as they who sat in the house were, as it were, immersed in the Holy Ghost; as they who were baptized with water were overwhelmed and covered all over with water, which is the proper notion of baptism." John, by contrasting his baptism in water with that in the Holy Spirit and fire, showed the very great superiority of Christ's office, work, and power. As spirit and fire are more powerful, penetrating, and subtle than water, so Christ's work would be higher, more spiritual and profoundly searching than his, consuming the dross and producing a higher spiritual life, with all the attendant fruits and blessings.

34. **And I saw and bare record,** or *witness.* John had heard the voice at the baptism proclaiming Jesus to be Son of God, Matt. 3 : 17. What he says in vers. 15 and 18 of Christ's pre-existence and intimate association with God shows that he understood by this title a dignity such as no mere man could lay claim to. Though John may not have fully comprehended its meaning, the Spirit, who spoke through him, meant it as a testimony, not only to Jesus' Messiahship, but to his original divine dignity and equality with the Father.

35 Again, the next day after, John stood, and two of 36 his disciples; and looking upon Jesus as he walked, 37 he saith, ᵍ Behold the Lamb of God! And the two disciples heard him speak, and they followed Jesus. ᵍ ver. 29; Isa. 45. 22; Heb. 12. 2.

The Jews did not expect the Messiah to be a divine person, any more than they expected him to be a Lamb of sacrifice. It was surely nothing but the teaching of the Spirit that led John, in these two testimonies, to utter nothing that might flatter the common Jewish expectations of a human conqueror or king, but to introduce the Saviour to the world by expressions which imply the two great essential truths of Christianity; namely, the divinity of Christ and his atoning death for the sins of the world. **That this is the Son of God.** "Jesus Christ is not the only person who is called the Son of God in the Scriptures. Angels (Job 1 : 6; 38 : 7), kings and rulers (2 Sam. 7 : 14; Ps. 82 : 6), the righteous and their families (Gen. 6 : 2, 4), and especially believers in Jesus (1 John 3 : 2), are all so called to express their high rank or relation and resemblance to the Most High. But Christ calls himself, and is called by the sacred writers, not *a* son of God, but THE *Son of God* (John 1 : 34; 11 : 4), and what is, if possible, still more distinctive and complete, THE SON. (The absence of the article in some cases can be easily explained grammatically. G. W. C.) In most of the passages in which the title is applied to others it occurs in the plural number, or, if in the singular number, without the article, as when God says to Solomon, 'I will be his father, and he shall be my son,' 2 Sam. 7 : 14. The passages in which magistrates and angels are called sons of God are not only plural and indefinite, but they are found only in such poetical books as Job and the Psalms, and are manifestly the language of poetry. Moreover, these, and also those in which the title is applied to Adam (Luke 3 : 38) and Solomon, are solitary passages, not only peculiar to certain writers, but occurring only once or twice in those writers. Christ, on the other hand, calls himself the Son of God, or the Son, habitually in the Gospel of John, and is frequently called by this distinctive name in all the writers, historical, doctrinal, and poetical, in the New Testament. Furthermore, these casual applications of the titles to men and angels in the Old Testament are often alluded to in the New as justifying and *foreshadowing* the appropriation of the name as the proper prerogative of him who was the King of kings and the Lord of men and angels. The occasional use of the titles 'Son of man' and 'Son of God' in a subordinate sense in the Old Testament, therefore, so far from militating against their appropriation in a peculiar and far higher sense in the New, was, in fact, only the *preparation of suitable language* to express that high peculiarity — only the type and prophecy of the coming of him who *was* truly and emphatically THE SON OF MAN and THE SON OF GOD, and so was a fit Mediator between God and man, even the God-man Christ Jesus."—Dr. W. S. TYLER, Amherst College, in *Bibliotheca Sacra*, Oct., 1865, p. 621.

35–42. THE BAPTIST'S TESTIMONY LEADS JOHN, ANDREW, AND PETER TO FOLLOW JESUS.

35. **The next day,** after his first testimony, related in verse 39, **John stood,** or *was standing,* at his customary place of preaching, **and two of his disciples.** One was Andrew (see on ver. 40), and the other was doubtless John, the author of this Gospel, who from modesty always abstained from mentioning his own name. On **John,** see INTRODUCTORY REMARKS.

36. **And looking,** with fixed and reverent gaze, **upon Jesus as he walked,** without followers and in dignified silence. It would seem that Jesus avoided all private intercourse with the Baptist, in order that there might be no suspicion of collusion between them; **he saith, Behold the Lamb of God!** John and Andrew could hardly have understood this if they had not heard the day before those other words that explained it: "that taketh away the sin of the world," ver. 29. That public witness of the Baptist had produced little immediate effect; this private testimony to the two disciples fixed all their Messianic hopes on Jesus.

37. **And the two ... heard . . and**

38 Then Jesus turned and saw them following, and saith unto them, What seek ye? They said unto him, Rabbi (which is to say, being interpreted, Master), 39 ʰ where dwellest thou? He saith unto them, ⁱ Come and see. They came and saw where he dwelt, and abode with him that day; for it was about the tenth hour.
40 One of the two which heard John *speak* and followed him, was ᵏ Andrew, Simon Peter's brother.

ʰ ch. 12. 21; 1 Kings 10. 8; Ps. 27. 4; Prov. 8. 34; Song Sol. 1. 7.
ⁱ ch. 6. 37; Prov. 3. 17; Matt. 11. 28; Rev. 3. 20.
ᵏ Matt. 4. 18.

followed Jesus. They walked after Jesus, as if to overtake and converse with him. It was leaving their old master to return no more. Yet they went with John's full knowledge and approbation. A great part of the Baptist's work had been accomplished when once he had prepared these first followers for Jesus.
38. **Then Jesus turned.** Rather, *And Jesus turned.* **Saw them following.** His heart was drawn out toward these first representatives of his future church. With a kind word he relieved their timidity and embarrassment, and opened the way for the expression of their heart's desire. **What seek ye?** He asks for their good. He would draw out their secret faith and the desire of their heart. **Rabbi.** The Hebrew *Rab* means *great*, great one. Applied sometimes to kings, judges, or noblemen, it afterward became a title of honor in the Jewish schools, in the sense of *master, teacher*, doctor. *Rabbi* means *my master*, being a highly honorable term. See on ch. 20 : 16. **Where dwellest, abidest, thou?** Jesus' question was one of encouragement, and yet of admonition to self-examination. It was an intimation that he was no temporal prince, but that, such as he was, he might be found of those who truly sought him. Their answer implies that they did not desire a merely casual conversation, but longed to abide with him, and to receive continuous instruction from him. By calling him "Rabbi" they recognized him as their proper "master," or teacher.
39. **Come and see.** According to the highest critical authorities, *Come and ye shall see.* They accepted this friendly invitation. **Abode with him that day,** probably in some humble inn or tent which Jesus had chosen for a lodging-place. **About the tenth hour;** according to the Jewish method of reckoning time, four o'clock in the afternoon; but more probably John followed the Roman method, according to which the day began at midnight, and thus it was ten o'clock in the morning. There seems to be internal evidence in John's Gospel that he adopted the common Roman reckoning. Thus, here, "the tenth hour" accords better with ten o'clock A. M. than four P. M. The introduction of the two disciples "on the morrow" (ver. 35), and the statement, "they abode with him that day," accord better with the morning hour. So also in chapter 4 : 6, "the sixth hour," six P. M. (numbering the hours from midday as well as from midnight, and not exceeding the number twelve), agrees remarkably with our Lord's weariness from his journey, and the time, instead of noon, when the woman would naturally come forth to draw water. So also in chapter 4 : 52, seven P. M. may be said to agree better with the circumstances and probable distance between Cana and Capernaum. This view also accords with the fact that John wrote for the people (primarily for the Christians) of Asia Minor, and that they were largely unacquainted with, and unaccustomed to, the Jewish mode of reckoning. Compare Author's Harmony, § 181. Matthew, Mark, and Luke follow the Jewish method, by which the day began at 6 A. M. This long day of converse with the Saviour established their faith that he was the Messiah, and determined their future course as his disciples. It was the first teaching of Jesus, and the beginning of his church. John considered it "the birth-hour of his higher life," and this minute mention of days and hours shows how deeply every incident was impressed upon his memory.
40. **Andrew** was a name of Greek origin, and was in use among the Jews. It is derived from a word that means *man*,

41 He first findeth his own brother Simon, and saith unto him, We have found the Messias, which is, **42** being interpreted, the Christ.ᵐ And he brought him to Jesus; and when Jesus beheld him, he said, ⁿThou art Simon, ᵒthe son of Jona; ᵖthou shalt be called Cephas (which is by interpretation, ᑫa stone).

ˡ Dan. 9. 25, 26.
ᵐ Ps. 2. 2.
ⁿ ch. 6. 70, 71.
ᵒ Matt. 16. 17, *Bar-jona.*
ᵖ Matt. 16. 18; 1 Cor. 1. 12; Gal. 2. 9.
ᑫ ch. 21. 2; Matt. 10. 2.

and may have been applied to him on account of his manly spirit. He belonged to Bethsaida (ver. 44), and was a disciple of John the Baptist, and had the honor of leading his brother Peter to Christ, ver. 41. He resided afterward at Capernaum, Mark 1 : 29. He appears in connection with feeding the five thousand (ch. 6 : 8), afterward as the introducer of certain Greeks to Jesus (ch. 12 : 22), and also, with Peter, James, and John, asking concerning the destruction of the temple, Mark 13 : 3. Of his subsequent history and labors nothing is certainly known. Tradition assigns Scythia, Greece, and Thrace as the scenes of his ministry. He is said to have been crucified at Patræ, in Achaia, on a cross in the shape of X, which is therefore called St. Andrew's cross.

Simon Peter. Jesus surnamed him Peter, ver. 42; Mark 3 : 16. Simon is contracted from Simeon, and means *hearkening;* Peter signifies *a piece of rock, a stone,* equivalent to the Aramaic *Cephas,* first given him as a surname at his introduction to Jesus, ver. 42. Peter was the name by which he was generally, though not always (Acts 15 : 14), designated as an apostle. It was given him in allusion to his hardy character, noted for decision and boldness, and to the conspicuous position he should hold among the apostles, in subordination to Christ, as one of the great foundations of the church, Eph. 2 : 20; Rev. 21 : 14. Not only is the name significant, but also its position at the head of the four catalogues of the apostles, Matt. 10 : 2; Mark 3 : 16; Luke 6 : 14; Acts 1 : 13. He was among the first who recognized Jesus as the Messiah, and with Andrew, his brother, the first called to be a constant attendant of Jesus, Mark 1 : 16-18. He was spokesman of the apostles, as in Matt. 16 : 16, and the chief speaker on the day of Pentecost. He was also the first to carry the gospel to the Gentiles, Acts 10. Thus Peter may be said to have opened the kingdom of heaven to both Jews and Gentiles. But though prominent and foremost among the apostles, he was not *over* them nor *above* them. That he had no superiority of rank is evident from 1 Pet. 5 : 1, where he describes himself as a fellow-elder, and from the fact that Paul in Gal. 2 : 7-9 speaks of him as one of the "pillars" together with James and John, compares him as an apostle to the circumcision to himself as an apostle to the uncircumcision, and rebukes him as an equal. That the apostles were all equal in rank appears from Matt. 18 : 18; 19 : 27, 28; 20 : 25, 26, 28; 23 : 8; John 20 : 21-23; Acts 1 : 8. The most we know of Peter is derived from the Gospels and the Acts of the Apostles. The latter book traces him to the Council at Jerusalem. After this he was with Paul at Antioch (Gal. 2 : 11), labored at Corinth (1 Cor. 1 : 12; 3 : 22), and at Babylon, where he wrote his first Epistle, 1 Pet. 5 : 13. According to a tradition which may be considered in the main reliable, he visited Rome in the last year of his life, and suffered martyrdom by crucifixion, under the reign of Nero.

41. He first findeth his own brother Simon. See preceding verse. Andrew was the first one who found his brother. The evangelist implies that he himself also sought and found *his* brother James, although not so quickly as Andrew. See Matt. 10 : 2. **We have found the Messiah.** The Hebrew *Messiah* is equivalent to *Christ* in Greek, and both mean *anointed.* All these disciples had been taught by the Baptist that God's Anointed One was near at hand, and had been longing and looking for his appearance.

42. When Jesus beheld him, rather, *Jesus beholding him,* casting a piercing glance into his inmost heart, **he said, Thou art Simon the son of Jona,** *Jonah.* Very likely Jesus saluted Simon thus, without having heard his name, in order to convince him of his Messiahship. It was also to be a

43 The day following, Jesus would go forth into Galilee. ʳAnd [he] findeth Philip, and saith unto him, ʳ 1 John 4. 19.

reminder that he was but a frail man, notwithstanding the honor he should confer upon him. Instead of *Jona* the best manuscripts read *John*, here and also in ch. 21 : 15, 16, 17. The difference, however, is not of great importance, since either form would be equivalent to the same name in Hebrew. Jesus saw all Simon's natural generosity, boldness, courage, but with these his instability and self-confidence. **Thou shalt be called Cephas.** Cephas was the Hebrew or Aramaic word for *Peter (rock)* in Greek. (See on ver. 40.) See note on Matt. 16 : 18. Grace should work a change by which he should become firm as a rock. By being planted in faith upon the Rock Christ Jesus, Peter should become himself a foundation-stone of Christ's church. Jesus here showed divine knowledge of Peter's character and future service, and marked his entrance upon a new life by giving to him a new name.

43-51.—JESUS CALLS PHILIP, AND PHILIP BRINGS NATHANAEL.

43. The day following Jesus would go forth, he had not yet set forth. **Into Galilee.** Galilee was a Hebrew name, meaning a *ring* or *circle*, and was probably first given to a small "circuit" among the mountains of Naphtali (Josh. 20 : 7), where were situated the twenty towns given by Solomon to Hiram, king of Tyre, 1 Kings 9 : 11. The name may contain an allusion to one or more of the circular plains of those mountains. It came afterward to be applied to the whole northern province of the land of Israel between Phœnicia and Samaria, the Jordan and the Mediterranean. It was divided into two parts—upper or northern, lower or southern. The northern portion was designated "Galilee of the Gentiles," because it bordered on territories inhabited by Gentiles, and especially because it was itself inhabited by a mixed population. According to the testimony of Strabo and others, it was inhabited by Egyptians, Arabians, and Phœnicians. It was near to Tyre and Sidon. According to Josephus, who knew the country well, Galilee contained two hundred and four cities and villages, the smallest of which numbered above fifteen thousand inhabitants, which would raise the population to upward of three millions, or about fifteen hundred to the square mile. "After the careful review now closed, we feel justified in saying that Galilee at the time of Christ was one of the finest and most fertile portions of the earth. . . . Abounding in springs, rivers, and lakes ; . . . possessing a rare and delightful climate, and scenery of great variety and beauty ; its surface never dull or monotonous, but infinitely varied by plains and valleys, gentle slopes and terraced hills, deep ravines and bold peaks, naturally-fortified eminences and giant mountains ; its soil naturally fertile, but forced by skilful husbandry to the highest state of productiveness, until this province was noted for the perfection and abundance of its fruits,—Galilee thus possessed features of richness and beauty rarely if ever combined in so small a country. . . . Its agriculture and fisheries, wine and oil trade, and other industries were in the most flourishing condition. . . . Its synagogues and other public buildings were built often in splendid style and at great expense. . . . We find the Galileans to have been a moral, intelligent, industrious, and enterprising people, possessed of vigorous minds and healthy bodies, . . . familiar with their own law and history, and not wanting in the finest poetical spirit ; with the disposition and ability to appreciate in the main the teachings of Christ ; a people among whom were found the most devoted men, 'Israelites indeed ;' both country and people, one may say with truth, fitly chosen of God as the training-place of those men—Master and disciples—who were to move the world ; the proper soil in which first to plant the seeds of that truth which was destined, ere long, to be spoken by eloquent lips in the pulpits of Cæsarea, Antioch, Constantinople, and Rome."—*Bibliotheca Sacra*, April, 1874, pp. 263, 264. South of Galilee lay Samaria, and south of Samaria, Judæa. **Findeth Philip.** Andrew and Peter had probably told Philip of Jesus, but it was Jesus' own call that determined his decision. *Philip* is a name of Greek origin,

44 Follow me. Now *Philip was of Bethsaida, the city *ch. 12. 21. of Andrew and Peter.

45 Philip findeth ᵗNathanael, and saith unto him, We have found him, of whom ᵘMoses in the law, and the ᵗch. 21. 2. ᵘDan. 8. 18; Luke 24. 27, 44.

meaning *lover of horses*. He was a native of Bethsaida, a disciple of John the Baptist, and called by our Lord the day after the naming of Peter. He is mentioned in connection with feeding the five thousand, as introducing, with Andrew, certain Greeks to Jesus, and as asking, after the Last Supper, "Lord, show us the Father and it sufficeth us," ch. 6 : 5–7; 12 : 21; 14 : 8–10. Of the labors and death of Philip nothing is certainly known. A tradition says that he preached the gospel in Phrygia and suffered martyrdom. He doubtless had also a Hebrew name. **Follow me.** This did not, until later, involve a giving up of all other occupations. The disciples were now private learners and followers. Jesus afterward ordained them as preachers and apostles, Luke 6 : 13.

44. **Bethsaida,** a little town on the Sea of Galilee, about a mile north of Capernaum. *Bethsaida* is supposed to be the name of two towns, one on the east and the other on the west of the lake. The name, which means *a house of fishing* or *fishery*, could easily be applied to more than one place, especially where fishing was so common a business. The Bethsaida on the north-eastern border of the lake is referred to in Luke 9 : 10; Mark 6 : 32; 8 : 22. The one mentioned here was on the west side, near Capernaum, the birthplace of Andrew, Peter, and Philip. Luke 10 : 13. Jerome and Eusebius mention together Bethsaida and Capernaum as lying on the shore of the lake; and Epiphanius speaks of them as being not far distant from each other. Willibald (A. D. 722), who visited this region, went from Magdala to Capernaum; thence to Bethsaida, where there was "a church on the site of the house" of Andrew and Peter; and then to Chorazin. These historical references confirm the conclusion that Bethsaida of Galilee, the birthplace of Andrew, Peter, and Philip (John 1 : 44), lay upon the western shore of the lake.

"About half a mile north of Capernaum (*Khan Minyeh*) is a beautiful little bay, with a broad margin of pearly sand. At its northern extremity are fountains, aqueducts, and half-ruined mills; and scattered round them are the remains of an old town called Tabighah. There is every reason to believe that this is the site of Bethsaida. (Robinson, *Bib. Res.*, iii. 358, ff.) No site along the whole shore seems so admirably adapted for a fishing town. Here is a bay sheltered by hills behind and projecting bluffs on each side; and here is a smooth, sandy beach, such as fishermen delight to ground their boats upon. The strand forms a pleasant promenade, and so far answers the description in Mark 1 : 16–20."—Prof. J. L. Porter, *Alexander's Kitto's Cyclo.*, vol. i. p. 357. Compare on Mark 6 : 45. **The city of Andrew and Peter.** This makes it probable that both were friends of Philip, and had imparted to him what they had seen and heard of Jesus.

45. **Philip findeth Nathanael,** a friend of Philip's, with whom he had had earnest talk about the expected Messiah. **Nathanael** (meaning *gift of God*), supposed to be the same as Bartholomew. He was a native of Cana of Galilee (ch. 21 : 2), and noted for his simple, truthful character, ver. 47. In the first three Gospels, Philip and Bartholomew are constantly named together, and Nathanael is never mentioned; while in the fourth Gospel, Philip and Nathanael are similarly combined, but nothing is said of Bartholomew, ch. 1 : 45; 21 : 2. According to tradition, he labored in India (Arabia Felix is sometimes called India by the ancients), and was crucified either in Armenia or Cilicia. **We have found him,** mark the warm and frank relation of personal experience. **Of whom Moses in the law,** the Pentateuch, the five books of Moses, thus distinguished from the other books of the Old Testament. See Gen. 49 : 10; Num. 24 : 17–19; Deut. 18 : 15. **And the prophets did write,** Isa. 7 : 14; 9 : 6; 52 : 13; Ez. 34 : 23–31. **Jesus of Nazareth, the son of Joseph,** literally, *Jesus the son of Joseph of Nazareth*. According to custom, he names his reputed father first, and then his residence. **Nazareth,** according to some, means

A. D. 27. JOHN I. 45

ᵛprophets did write, Jesus ʷof Nazareth, ˣthe son of 46 Joseph. And Nathanael said unto him, ʸCan there any good thing come out of Nazareth? Philip saith unto him, Come and see.

ᵛ Isa. 4. 2; 7. 14; 9. 6; 53. 2; Mic. 5. 2; Zech. 6. 12; 9. 9.
ʷ Matt. 2. 23; Luke 2. 4; John 18. 5.   ˣ Matt. 1. 16.   ʸ ch. 7. 41, 42, 52.

a branch—a fit name of the place where the Branch (Isa. 11 : 1; Zech. 3 : 8; 6 : 12) should live and grow up. I have, however, been led to think that it signifies the *one guarding* or *guarded*, from the hill on whose sides it was built (Luke 4 : 29), which, rising to the height of four hundred or five hundred feet, overlooked a vast region, land and sea, and thus guarded it. New Testament writers

NAZARETH.

always speak of it as *a city*, and never as a village, and hence it was a place of some size and importance. It was finely located in Lower Galilee, about seventy miles north of Jerusalem, and nearly halfway from the Jordan to the Mediterranean. According to Josephus (referred to above on *Galilee*), its population reached fifteen, perhaps twenty, thousand. It is not named, however, in the Old Testament, nor by Josephus. But Josephus names very few of the cities of Galilee. It seems not to have been held in very good repute—more, perhaps, on account of the rude and refractory temper of its inhabitants than for any gross immorality, Luke 4 : 16, 29; ver. 46. Modern Nazareth belongs to the better class of Eastern villages, and has a population of nearly three thousand. Its location makes it very secluded, being situated on the edge of a beautiful little valley, which is itself enclosed by an amphitheatre of hills that rise around it into fourteen distinct peaks. From one of these can be obtained one of the finest views in Palestine. It is altogether probable, as Olshausen suggests, that Mary or Joseph had property here; Nazareth is called "their own city," Luke 2 : 39.

46. **Can there any good thing,** any eminent personage, with special reference to the Messiah, **come out of Nazareth?** A question implying surprise, modesty, and caution. Nathanael was a Galilean (ch. 21 : 2), and this speech of his shows that Nazareth was in ill-repute even among Galileans. The cause was probably not so much

JOHN I.

47 Jesus saw Nathanael coming to him, and saith of him, Behold ᵃan Israelite, indeed, in whom is no guile!
48 Nathanael saith unto him, Whence knowest thou me? Jesus answered and said unto him, Before that Philip called thee, ᵃwhen thou wast under the fig tree, I saw thee.
49 Nathanael answered and saith unto him, Rabbi, ᵇthou art the Son of God; thou art ᶜthe King of Israel.
50 Jesus answered and said unto him, Because I said unto thee, I saw thee under the fig tree, believest thou? thou shalt see greater things than these.
51 And he saith unto him, Verily, verily, I say unto you, Hereafter ye shall see ᵈheaven open, ᵉand the angels of God ᶠascending and descending upon the Son of man.

ᵃ ch. 8. 39; Gen. 32. 28; Ps. 32. 2; 73. 1; Rom. 2. 28, 29; 9. 6–8; 1 Pet. 2. 1.
ᵇ Matt. 6. 6; Acts 10. 4.
ᵇ Matt. 14. 33.
ᶜ ch. 12. 13–15; 18. 37; 19. 3; Jer. 23. 5, 6; Ezek. 37. 21–25; Hos. 3. 5; Matt. 2. 2; 27. 11, 42.
ᵈ Ezek. 1. 1.
ᵉ Gen. 28. 12; Matt. 4. 11; Mark 1. 13; Luke 2. 9, 13; 24. 4; Acts 1. 10; 2 Thess. 1. 7.
ᶠ Luke 22. 43; 24. 51; Heb. 1. 14.

---

any gross immorality of the place, as the rude and refractory character of the people. See Luke 4 : 29. **Philip saith unto him, Come and see,** "the best remedy for preconceived opinions."— BENGEL. Personal acquaintance with Jesus will do more to convince the sceptical than any amount cf argument or theorizing. Nathanael, fortunately, was docile enough to fall in with Philip's suggestion.

47. Jesus . . . saith of him. To those standing by, but so that Nathanael heard it. **Behold an Israelite indeed.** Not outwardly, but inwardly; one answering to the true idea of an Israelite, as contrasted with the prevalent formalism and hypocrisy of the time; a true, prayerful servant of God. See Gen. 32 : 28; Ps. 15. **In whom is no guile.** Not that Nathanael was free from all sin, but that he was one who sought the Lord in sincerity. See Ps. 32 : 2.

48. Whence knowest thou me? Nathanael gave a proof of his guilelessness by acknowledging Jesus' description of his character to be correct. A man of guile would have deprecated such praise. **When thou wast under the fig tree, I saw thee.** It was the custom of the Jews to use the shelter of the fig tree, with its shade and seclusion, for reading the Scriptures and prayer. Jesus referred to some recent experience of Nathanael's, which he had thought hidden from all the world. He had, perhaps, been praying, like Simeon (Luke 2 : 25, 26), that he might see the Messiah. Jesus showed him that he not only had divine knowledge of his past history, but that he had perfect insight into his heart. It was this reading of his heart which surprised Nathanael, and led him to the exclamation that follows.

49. Rabbi. See on ver. 38. **Thou art the Son of God.** See on ver. 34. Nathanael adopted for his own the words of John the Baptist (ver. 34)— words which went beyond the common belief of the Jews, and implied the divine nature of the Saviour. See Ps. 2 : 7; ch. 11 : 27. **Thou art the King of Israel.** So the Messiah is represented in Ps. 2 : 6; compare Ps. 72 : 1. Both of these confessions involved faith in Jesus as the true Messiah. The confession of Nathanael implies his deep conviction that no human eye could have witnessed his retirement.

50. Believest thou? Though to Nathaniel so great a thing, it was comparatively a small thing to Jesus. **Thou shalt see greater things than these,** greater proofs of my Messiahship. As he is supposed to be one of the apostles (see on ver. 45), he did see greater things in the miracles and discourses of Jesus, in his resurrection, ascension, and in the descent of the Spirit on the day of Pentecost. It was a joy to Jesus that Nathanael so soon believed. He would reward this faith by strengthening and confirming it. "To him that hath shall be given."

51. Verily, verily, *truly, truly*. The use of this word twice is peculiar to John, and gives intensity to the expression, calling special attention to what follows. **I say unto you,** answers to "Thus saith the Lord," used by the prophets. **Hereafter,** *henceforth, from this time,* **ye shall see heaven open;** the heavens had been shut by Adam's sin. **The angels . . . ascending and descending,** etc. This is not a prediction of special angelic appearances, like those mentioned in Matt. 4 : 11; 26 : 53; Luke 22 : 43, but rather a figurative description of Jesus' whole mediatorial work, and its results to men. There is evidently an allusion to Jacob's dream of the heavenly ladder, and the angels ascending and descending upon it. See Gen. 28 : 12. Jacob saw in this heavenly ladder a symbol of unity restored between heaven and earth; the angels carried up his prayers and brought down messages of mercy and forgiveness and providential blessing. But what Jacob could not see, Jesus here fully revealed—namely, that he was *himself* the heavenly ladder, the medium of recognition and intercourse between heaven and earth. "And this, the glory of Christ, they (his disciples) should behold, and should understand that they too, children of men, were by him, the Son of man, made citizens of a kingdom which, not excluding earth, embraced also heaven, . . . Jesus of Nazareth being the central point in which these kingdoms met, the golden clasp which bound them indissolubly together."

The Son of man. A favorite name with Jesus, yet, with the exception of the expression of the martyr Stephen, who beheld his glorified humanity at the right hand of God (Acts 7 : 56), the name is never applied to him, but by himself. It is never applied to any one but Christ in the New Testament. It designates him, of course, in his human nature, as the term "Son of God" does in his divine nature. Two things are noticeable about the term: First, that it seems to presuppose the divine nature, for one who was merely man would scarcely use this term in such connections and with such frequency as Christ does merely as a distinctive appellation. But one who was conscious of a divine nature would naturally use this as he does to denote the state into which he has come, in places where that new state has a special significance. Second, that Christ calls himself, not *a* son of man, but *the* Son of man; he is not merely one among many, but *the* one among them all. He was the Son of man in the highest sense (Ps. 8 : 3-5; Heb. 2 : 6-9), possessed of all the attributes and characteristics of our common humanity, a perfect and model man, the representative of the race, the second Adam from heaven, 1 Cor. 15 : 45, 47, In the first three Gospels, where the external life of Jesus is narrated and his human nature brought out prominently, he more frequently calls himself "the Son of man;" but in the fourth Gospel, where his inner life and divine being are specially brought to view, he styles himself more frequently "the Son of God," or simply "the Son." Daniel (7 : 13), in foretelling Christ's coming with the clouds of heaven, implies that, notwithstanding his exaltation and glory, he would come in the form and likeness of men, for he says that he saw "one like the Son of man." See also Rev. 1 : 13; 14 : 14. It was a title of humiliation, though an honor to our race. Jesus applied it pre-eminently to himself as the Messiah, "as God manifested in the flesh," indicating, notwithstanding his divinity, his *true humanity* and his oneness with the human race. The Jews rightly understood it to mean the Messiah (John 12 : 34), though they did not enter into the fulness of its meaning. It has been asked, What relation does the calling of the disciples here narrated bear to the calling of the same persons recorded by the other evangelists? This was in Judea several months earlier. We must distinguish between their call to discipleship, as related in this chapter; their call to be constant attendants, preachers, or evangelists, recorded in Matt. 4 : 18 : 22; Mark 1 : 16-20; and their selection as apostles, related in Mark 3 : 13-19; Luke 6 : 12-16. After this they were miraculously endowed, and sent out on a mission to the Jews, Matt. 10 : 1-4; Mark 6 : 7-11; Luke 9 : 1-5. Compare *Author's Harmony,* §§ 23, 37, 54, 72.

PRACTICAL REMARKS.

1. There is a foreshadowing of the doctrine of the Trinity in the Old Testament, ver. 1; Gen. 1 : 26; 3 : 22; 11 : 7; Isa. 6 : 8; Dan. 4 : 17.

2. That God took upon himself our

human nature lies at the foundation of the gospel. "That One who, before the creation of the world, dwelt in the bosom (ver. 18) of God, himself also God, who created all things, and is the source of all life and all blessedness, took upon himself human nature, becoming the divine man Jesus Christ, and by his life and death procured salvation for us, is asserted with all the directness and force of which language is capable. That it involves mystery is no obstacle to our faith, but should rather confirm it. Our own being, comprising in it two natures wholly unlike, is a mystery. How much more that of the eternal Son of God!" vers. 1–5; 14.

3. Jesus Christ has a distinct personal existence, inseparable from, yet associated with the Godhead, vers. 1–5; ch. 6 : 38; 10 : 36; Col. 1 : 15, 16, 17; Phil. 2 : 6.

4. Christ is the organ of external revelation. The Holy Spirit gives us an inward apprehension of the truth, vers. 4, 5; ch. 14 : 26; 15 : 26; 16 : 13; Rom. 8 : 16; 1 Cor. 2 : 10.

5. The Creator must be greater than the created. With what believing and obedient spirits should we receive his Word! vers. 1–5; 1 Chron. 29 : 11; Ps. 145 : 3; Isa. 1 : 19, 20; Mark 16 : 16; Acts 5 : 29; Heb. 5 : 9.

6. How wonderful that the Maker of worlds should become the life and light of men! vers. 6–8; Matt. 4 : 16; Luke 2 : 32; John 6 : 35; 8 : 12; 9 : 5; 1 John 5 : 12.

7. We should pray earnestly that God by his Spirit would take away our blindness, so that we may receive the light which is in Jesus, ver. 9; Hos. 14 : 2; John 3 : 19; Acts 26 : 17, 18; Eph. 4 : 18; James 1 : 5.

8. The sinner's course consists in rejecting the light which is given to illumine his moral darkness, vers. 10, 11; John 3 : 19, 20; 9 : 41; Heb. 10 : 26, 27; James 4 : 17.

9. John is sent to introduce a Saviour in whom there are grace to pardon all our sins, and power to keep us after we are pardoned, vers. 12–14, 17; Matt. 1 : 21; John 17 : 15; Heb. 7 : 25; Jude 24.

10. Only through believing in Jesus do we find pardoning grace and real salvation, ver. 12; Acts 4 : 12; Gal. 2 . 16; Eph. 2 : 8; 1 John 1 : 7; 5 : 1.

11. To accept the true light is to give in our allegiance to God; to reject it is to turn our backs on God, vers. 10–12; Luke 11 : 35, 36; John 3 : 17, 18–20, 21; 8 : 12; 2 Cor. 4 : 4.

12. How sublime is our privilege! We may become the sons of God, ver. 12; Rom. 8 : 14; Gal. 3 : 26; 2 Pet. 1 : 4; 1 John 3 : 1.

13. Every lover of Jesus ought to be ready to witness for the Master, ver. 15; Isa. 43 : 10; Matt. 10 : 32; Mark 5 : 19, 20; 8 : 38; Rom. 10 : 9, 10.

14. He who has found the Saviour longs to make others partakers of the great salvation, vers. 15, 26, 27, 29; 1 Sam. 12 : 23; Acts 5 : 42; 6 : 4; 19 : 8; 1 Cor. 9 : 16.

15. Those who would prepare the way for Christ in the hearts of others must be content to hide themselves behind their message, that the Redeemer alone may be exalted, vers. 19–29; Matt. 3 : 1–4; John 1 : 36; 1 Cor. 1 : 17; 2 : 2; Gal. 6 : 14.

16. In taking the place of the lowest servant before Christ, we are only putting ourselves where we properly belong, vers. 20, 26, 27; Job 22 : 29; Ps. 138 : 6; Matt. 5 : 3; Luke 18 : 14; James 4 : 6, 10.

17. The Lamb of God has taken our sins upon him, and has borne them away for ever, ver. 29; Isa. 53 : 4–11; Matt. 26 : 28; Heb. 2 : 17; 9 : 28; 1 Pet. 3 : 18.

18. Personal effort on the part of every Christian will speedily be followed by the conversion of the world to God, vers. 29, 35, 41; Eccles. 9 : 10; Matt. 9 : 38; 21 : 28; Luke 14 : 23; John 9 : 4.

19. We know Jesus better than John did. We ought to improve every opportunity of saying to sinners, "Behold the Lamb of God!" vers. 29–36; Matt. 10 : 27; 25 : 40; Mark 16 : 15; Luke 10 : 37; Rev. 22 : 17.

20. We need not only to be baptized in water, but to be born of the Spirit, vers. 31–33; ch. 3 : 5; 1 Cor. 6 : 11.

21. Jesus undertakes the humble work of teaching us our real needs and revealing to us his power to save, vers. 35–38; Matt. 4 : 23; 18 : 11; Acts 10 : 38; 2 Cor. 8 : 9; Rev. 3 : 17.

22. Jesus encourages our earliest efforts to find him, vers. 37–39; Deut. 4 : 29; 1 Chron. 28 : 9; Matt. 7 : 7; James 4 : 3–5.

The Marriage at Cana of Galilee; miracle of turning water into wine.

II. AND the third day there was a marriage in ᵉCana ᵉJosh. 19. 28.

23. Christ dwells not only in the heavens, but in the believer's heart, vers. 38, 39; John 14 : 17; 1 Cor. 3 : 16; 1 John 2 : 5; Rev. 3 : 20.
24. Let us also be followers of Jesus, and receive the blessings he has promised, vers. 37, 43; Matt. 10 : 22; 21 : 22; John 3 : 16; 20 : 7; 1 Pet. 1 : 4; Rev. 2 : 10; 21 : 7.
25. All we need, in order to be delivered from the penalty and power of sin, is to accept of Christ and his finished work by faith, vers. 42–45; Matt. 21 : 21; John 8 : 24; Acts 16 : 31; Heb. 11 : 6; 1 John 5 : 4.
26. Christ is only found of those by whom he is sought, vers. 42, 45; 1 Chron. 28 : 9; Isa. 55 : 6; Jer. 29 : 13; Matt. 16 : 24; John 6 : 37.
27. We are prepared to bring others to the cross when we have been there ourselves, vers. 41, 45; Acts 4 : 13; 6 : 15; 2 Pet. 1 : 18.
28. It is our duty to respond instantly to the divine command, "Follow me," ver. 43; Job 22 : 21; Ps. 95 : 7–9; Prov. 27 : 1; 2 Cor. 6 : 2.
29. There is no teacher like Jesus, vers. 45–51; Matt. 22 : 46; Luke 21 : 15; John 3 : 2; 7 : 46.
30. As kindly as Christ welcomed his disciples will he receive us if we ask, vers. 39 : 47; Matt. 21 : 22; Luke 11 : 13; 2 Pet. 3 : 9; Rev. 22 : 17.
31. Men may talk to us of a Saviour, but we can never know him unless we come to him ourselves, ver. 49; Matt. 13 : 11; John 4 : 42; 7 : 17; 1 Cor. 2 : 14; Eph. 3 : 17–19.
32. Love rather than duty should prompt us to serve God, vers. 47–50; Deut 6 : 5; Prov. 8 : 17; Mark 10 : 29, 30; John 14 : 23; 1 John 4 : 19.
33. We should cautiously guard against popular prejudices, ver. 46; Lev. 25 : 35; Prov. 19 : 17; Matt. 5 : 7; James 2 : 1–4; John 3 : 17.

CHAPTER II.

This chapter begins with an account of our Lord's first miracle, the turning of water into wine at a marriage-feast, vers. 1–11. After this Jesus visits Capernaum (12), then g ᵉs up to the Passover at Jerusalem, where he cleanses the temple of the traders, and incidentally predicts his own resurrection (13–2²); also works miracles, 23–25.

1–11. THE MARRIAGE AT CANA OF GALILEE. CHRIST'S FIRST MIRACLE; WATER CHANGED INTO WINE. Jesus declares himself independent of Mary's control. After this he visits Capernaum. Latter part of winter or spring of A. D. 27.

1. **The third day,** may refer back to ch. 1 : 43 (after starting for Galilee the journey could be made in two days), or to the calling of Nathanael (ch. 1 : 46); or it may have been the third day after the arrival in Galilee. It seems best to regard it as the third day after the incident related in ch. 1 : 44–51. **There was a marriage.** The most natural sense of the language is that *the third day* was the day of the marriage. (See last paragraph on ver. 2.) **Cana of Galilee,** a village eight miles north of Nazareth, according to some, but according to others, a village about four miles north. "A *Kenna*, three and half miles north of Nazareth, on the road to Tiberias, is likely the Cana referred to. The tradition connecting this spot with Cana of Galilee is a very ancient one, and until recently it has generally been accepted as correct. It existed as far back as the latter half of the eighth century, when St. Wilibald visited the place. Dr. Robinson heard the name *El-Falil* applied to the Kenna four miles farther north, and accepted *that* as the true Cana of Galilee. From his time, until lately, it has generally been located there. Recently, however, Kefr Kenna, the first mentioned, is fast coming to be the universally-accepted place. Osborne found *El-Feil* (Galilee) applied to *this* spot; but Dr. Thompson is doubtful whether any such designation distinguishes the one from the other, and I could discover no trace of that name as applied to either of the two situations. I found Kefr Kenna to be a small, neat village, delightfully situated on a hillside looking south-east, and embosomed in vineyards and trees of olive, fig, pomegranate, and other varieties. There

2 of Galilee; and the mother of Jesus was there; and
both Jesus was called and his disciples to the mar-
3 riage. And when they wanted wine, the mother of

---

are thirty or forty houses, besides a plain little synagogue. The church edifice is said to stand over the site of the miracle, and on the floor (simply smooth and level ground) I was shown the reputed big earthen jars that held the wine. Near by is a large fountain enclosed by a wall, from which the water for the miracle may have been taken. I drank of it, and found it excellent."—Dr. Fish, *Bible Lands Illus.*, pp. 534, 535.

Concerning the northern *Kenna*, Dr. Robinson says: "It is situated on the left side of the wady if coming down from Jefat, just where the latter enters the plain *El Buttauf*, on the southern declivity of a projecting tell, and overlooking the plain. The situation is fine. It was once a considerable village of well-built houses, now all *deserted*. Many of the dwellings are in ruins. There are also several arches belonging to modern houses, but we could discover no traces of antiquity." Either of these places satisfies the conditions of the narrative. All we know from Scripture is, that it was the scene of this and a subsequent miracle (ch. 4: 46, 54); that it was not far from Capernaum (ch. 2 : 12; 4 : 46), and on higher ground (ch. 2 : 12); and that it was the home of Nathanael, ch. 1. **The mother of Jesus was there.** There seems to have been some relationship between the family in Cana and that of Mary. On Galilee, see note on ch. 1 : 43.

2. And both Jesus was called, *invited*, **and his disciples, to the marriage.** He who had left Galilee a few weeks before, the unnoted son of Joseph, had now returned with five disciples, ch. 1 : 40-51. They probably went first to Nazareth, but finding the whole household absent in Cana, they proceeded thither, arriving there on the day of the marriage. This they did all the more readily because Nathanael resided there, 21 : 2. The families were so intimate that not only Jesus, but his disciples, though most of these were strangers in Cana, were invited to the wedding. Their coming may have been unexpected, and the invitation given upon their arrival. Wedding-feasts often lasted several days (Gen. 29 : 27; Judg. 14 : 12), and Jesus and his disciples may possibly have arrived on the third day of the feast; but ver. 10 would seem to indicate that the feast had not been prolonged beyond one day. So Tholuck.

3. When they wanted wine, *wine having failed.* Wine was thought, in those days, to be a necessary provision for a joyous occasion like a wedding. But the family of Cana was in humble circumstances, and this unexpected addition to the number of guests made the supply run short. "None but those who know how sacred in the East is the duty of lavish hospitality, and how passionately the obligation to exercise it to the utmost is felt, can realize the gloom which this incident would have thrown over the occasion, or the misery and mortification which it would have caused to the wedded pair. They would have felt it to be, as in the East it would still be felt to be, a bitter and indelible disgrace."—Dr. F. W. Farrar, *Life of Christ,* p. 162.

The mother of Jesus saith unto him, They have no wine. Mary, as a relative of the family, busied herself about the entertainment, and was distressed lest this lack of wine should become apparent to the guests and cause mortification to the host. She had been long expecting Jesus to manifest his power and fulfil the promise of his birth. He had reached the age when public teachers entered on their work. He had come to Cana attended by disciples who recognized him as Messiah. These disciples informed her that the Baptist had pointed him out as the long-promised Deliverer. Though he had as yet done no miracles (ver. 11), it was the universal belief that the Messiah's entrance upon his work would be accompanied with such signs, ver. 18. Since his coming to the marriage had been the occasion of the lack of wine, what better opportunity to show that he had a power never yet suspected by the world? Mary tells him of the need, but leaves him to supply it in his own way.

4 Jesus saith unto him, They have no wine. Jesus
saith unto her, ʰ Woman, ⁱ what have I to do with
5 thee? ʲ mine hour is not yet come. His mother saith
unto the servants, Whatsoever he saith unto you, do
6 *it.* And there were set there six water-pots of stone,
ᵏ after the manner of the purifying of the Jews, con-
7 taining two or three firkins apiece. Jesus saith unto

ʰ ch. 19. 26.
ⁱ so 2 Sam. 16. 10; 19. 22.
ʲ ch. 7. 6.
ᵏ Mark 7. 2–4; Luke 11. 38.

---

4. Woman; in itself a respectful and even solemn address. (See 19: 26.) **What have I to do with thee?** *What to me and thee* is common? My relations and business are wholly different from thine. Why, then, interfere? This form of expression occurs several times in the New Testament, Matt. 8: 29; Mark 1: 24; Luke 4: 34. The phrase is common to the Hebrew and the later Greek, 2 Sam. 16: 10; 19: 22; 1 Kings 17: 18; Ezra 4: 3. It always implies disapprobation, though sometimes employed in friendly reproof. There is a tone of rebuke in these words which shows that Mary, with all her consideration for the wedding-party, had something of impatience and motherly vanity in her request. It was necessary at the very outset of Jesus' ministry that she should learn a great lesson—namely, that in his new work he must be wholly independent of her control, and free in all things to do the will of God. "It was not for her to dictate, or even to suggest, what he should do." **Mine hour is not yet come.** My time for manifesting my power and glory, ver. 11. Elsewhere, John uses this phrase in reference to the time of his death and glorification, ch. 7: 30; 12: 23, 27; 13: 1. Mary had doubtless many erroneous notions with regard to the nature of Jesus' work. Perhaps she expected some immediate setting up of his Messianic kingdom. Jesus answered not only her words, but the thought that prompted them.

5. His mother saith unto the servants, evidently as one entrusted with the arrangements of the feast, **Whatsoever he saith, . . . do it.** Mary's faith outlived the apparent repulse. Either the manner of Jesus' answer, or his known sympathy with all human wants, led her to believe that he would yet interpose and relieve the bridal pair from their embarrassment and anxiety.

6. And, or *now,* **there were set,** er, according to some, simply, *there were,* **six water-pots,** not wine-jars, **of stone**—that is, stone jars or vessels—**after the manner of the purifying of the Jews.** Used to hold the large supplies of water needed in their various ablutions. See Mark 7: 1–8. So many guests had come that the water-pots were now empty. **Containing two or three firkins, apiece.** A firkin contained 9 gallons; each water-pot therefore contained from 18 to 27 gallons. Together, they all held from 120 to 162 gallons. Each pot held over a half barrel.

7. Jesus saith unto them, Fill the water-pots with water. There must be obedience. The pots being full, excludes the possibility of adding wine, or of a mixture. **And they filled them up to the brim.** Such a quantity made the miracle that followed more indubitable and wonderful. Somewhere just after this point the miracle occurred. Some suppose that the whole amount of water was turned into wine, others that only so much as was drawn by the servants. This is not exactly stated; so we must leave it where we find it. The more natural supposition, however, seems to be that the whole was turned into wine. Why fill so many water-pots if only a portion—perhaps a small portion—was made wine? The large amount best accords with the object of the miracle, the manifestation of Christ's power and glory, and with the greatness and richness of God's gifts displayed everywhere in nature.

At marriage-feasts at the present day in the East, "all of the guests are expected to drink at least to the health of the bride and the bridegroom. . . . This large quantity of wine would provide but little for each guest, considering the habits of the people, who crowd into the house to partake of the feast as long as the provisions last, being pressed

them, Fill the water-pots with water. And they
8 filled them up to the brim. And he saith unto them,
Draw out now and bear unto the governor of the
9 feast. And they bare *it*. When the ruler of the
feast had tasted ¹the water that was made wine, and   ¹ ch. 4. 46.
knew not whence it was, (but the servants which
drew the water knew,) the governor of the feast
10 called the bridegroom, and saith unto him, Every
man at the beginning doth set forth good wine; and
when men have well drunk, then that which is
worse; *but* thou hast kept the good wine until now.

to do so by their hospitable host or master of the feast, who also urges, and sometimes compels, even the passers-by to come in and drink to the health of the bridegroom and bride. The number of guests must have far exceeded what had been anticipated, otherwise the provision would have proved sufficient."—DR. H. J. VAN LENNEP, *Bible Lands*, pp. 122, 603, 604.

8. The governor of the feast. The word thus translated is of rare occurrence, and means literally *the ruler of the dining-room and tables with three couches*, or sets of cushions. Sophocles defines it, *the president of a banquet.* He was characterized by the Athenians as "one who superintends the tables and preserves order." He was himself one of the guests, who by general consent or the selection of the host was set to preside over the banquet. It was his place first to taste each new lot of wine and test the food. There is no evidence from the narrative that he was one of the servants, but seems to have been on intimate terms with the bridegroom, and in his stead presided at the table. Compare Apocrypha, Ecclesiasticus 35:1, 2. The Greeks and Romans had a similar practice.

9. Had tasted the water that was made wine; that is, the wine made from the water. The water was changed into real wine, both in form and substance. It looked and tasted like wine, and in every respect was wine. Hence the Romanists can draw no argument from this miracle in favor of transubstantiation. Their pretended change of bread and wine contradicts the senses. **The servants which drew the water knew.** From this expression an argument may be drawn for the view that what the servants drew from the vessel was water, and

the change into wine was made while bearing it to the ruler of the feast. The language is parenthetical and somewhat indefinite, and the drawing may refer to that in filling the jars, ver. 7. It seems, therefore, that the argument, though possible, is not decisive. As a matter of *principle* it makes no difference whether Jesus made a great quantity or little. **Called the bridegroom,** perhaps across the table or across the room. The wedding took place in the house of the bridegroom, and he gave the feast. Hence the ruler thought the bridegroom had provided the wine.

10. Every man at the beginning, when the taste is most sensitive and the guests would be the most critical, and when there would be a desire to make a good impression. This remark was one of surprise, rather than of pleasantry. **Doth set forth good wine,** that which was held in the highest esteem. He states what was customary, and intimates that what the bridegroom had done was contrary to custom. **Well drunk.** The word thus translated means *to become drunk* in Luke 12:45; Eph 5:18; Rev. 17:2. If this be the meaning here, then it may be said that "this allusion to drunkenness, as perhaps not uncommon at such feasts, does not imply that it had been or was likely to be seen at the marriage at Cana." But this verb also means to *drink freely*, and does not necessarily imply intoxication. Such is its meaning in Gen. 43:34; Hag. 1:6 (Septuagint), and this is its probable meaning here. Compare also Cant. 5:1. In the East at the present day "intoxication from too liberal a supply of wine on such occasions cannot be said to be frequent, the number of guests that must share in the distribution of the beverage serving to obviate riotous

A. D. 27.   JOHN II.   53

11   This beginning of miracles did Jesus in Cana of Galilee, ᵐ and manifested forth his glory; and his disciples believed on him.   ▪ ch. 1. 14; 11. 4, 40; Acts 2. 22.

consequences; besides, all desire . . . to take part in the interesting processions with which the ceremony closes." DR. H. J. VAN LENNEP, *Bible Lands*, p. 603.
That which is worse. Poor, inferior wine. It is not necessary to suppose that the good was the stronger, and that which was worse the weaker, though the latter would include a sour wine. Philo (On Drunkenness, sec. 53) speaks of the votaries of wine going from one kind to another, till they have finished with large drinks of the unmixed and strongest sorts. **But.** Omit, according to the best authorities. **Thou hast kept the good wine until now,** till this late hour or period of the feast. The phrase *until now* naturally indicates that this want occurred toward the end of the feast, and in connection with ver. 1 seems to show, as Tholuck remarks, "That the celebration could not have been prolonged, as some suppose, beyond one day." The *good wine* was doubtless pure and good in the proper sense of the term; not necessarily strong, but rather mellow, rich, and fragrant. Dr. H. C. Fish and his son both informed me that the best wine they found in Palestine was at Hebron. This was in May, 1874. The wine was about seven months old, very rich and fragrant, and so mellow and mild that a large quantity could be drunk without intoxication. Compare a brief reference in *Bible Lands Illustrated*, p. 537.

In this wonderful miracle we cannot for a moment suppose that Jesus would minister to intemperance, either in that age or in any other. In regard to the present aspect of the temperance question, the following from Dr. Arnott is in place: "It is of the utmost importance to observe and remember the difference between wine-growing countries in ancient times and our own northern land now. The main points of distinction are these two: 1. The chief agent of intoxication among us is not wine at all, but a much more potent draught, which was entirely unknown to antiquity. 2. Even the wines which we use, partly imported from abroad and partly manufactured at home, are, by admixture of spirits and other materials, much more powerful as intoxicants than the wines ordinarily used of old on the soil which produced them. I adjure all, as they fear God and regard man, as they would save themselves and their brethren, not to overlook these distinctions. I entertain a sorrowful and solemn conviction, which I have often spoken before, and speak now again weeping, that many among us wrest to their own destruction those Scriptures which commend the use of wine. To quote these expressions, and apply them without abatement to the liquors now ordinarily used in this country, is logically incorrect and practically most dangerous. It is quite true that wines capable of producing intoxication were made and used in those days. It is also quite true that there were both drunkards and isolated acts of inebriation in those days; yet it is neither just nor safe to assume that what is said in the Scriptures of wine is applicable, without restriction, to our intoxicants. As to the measure of the difference, exact knowledge is probably not attainable, and it does not become any one to dogmatize; but if al were induced to acknowledge that there is a difference, and stirred up to seek direction for themselves from him who gives the word, as to how far a scriptural commendation of the weaker may be transferred also to the stronger stimulant, our object would be obtained, for they who seek shall find, the meek he will guide."

11. **This beginning of miracles,** *of his signs,* a wonderful series. As this is not only the first miracle of Jesus, but also the first recorded by John, a few thoughts on the MIRACLES OF CHRIST will be in place. He performed them in proof of his divine mission, ch. 2: 22; 9:3-5; 10: 25, 37. The Jews expected the Messiah would work miracles, ch. 7 : 31; Matt. 12 : 38; Luke 16, 17; so also did John the Baptist, Matt. 11 : 3. The miracles of Christ were variously designated. When they were specially regarded as evidences of his divine mission, they were called

semeia, signs, Mark 8 : 11; when as the manifestation of supernatural power, they were called *dunameis, mighty works,* corresponding more strictly to the word *miracle* in common English usage, Mark 6 : 2; 9 : 39; when as extraordinary and portending phenomena exciting astonishment or terror, they were called *terata, wonders,* ch. 4 : 48; Acts 2 : 22; compare Mark 13 : 22; and when viewed still more generally and comprehensively, as something completed and to be reflected on—the natural acts and products of his being—they were called *erga, works,* ch. 7 : 3, 21. In our common version the first of these is translated *signs, miracles, wonders;* the second, *mighty works, mighty deeds, wonderful works, miracles;* the third, *wonders;* and the fourth, *deeds.*

To get a full and correct conception of Christ's miracles, they should be viewed in all these aspects. They were not simply the manifestations of a supernatural power, but also the product of that power inherent in our Lord, the natural fruits, the outworkings, of his own divine nature; they were not merely adapted to impress the mind deeply and excite astonishment or terror, but they were also the signs, the evidences, of himself and of the truth of which he was the embodiment. They were, in fine, the supernatural phenomena produced by his own power in proof of his divine nature and work. They were not in violation of Nature nor necessarily a suspension of its laws, but rather above Nature, so far as we know, or in accordance with laws and principles unknown to us. It is indeed in accordance with Nature to expect miracles in connection with a new dispensation. "All the great chapters of Nature's history," says Prof. Hitchcock, "begin with them; and if the Christian dispensation were destitute of them, it would be out of harmony with the course of things in the natural world." —*Bibl. Sac.,* July, 1863, p. 552. **Did Jesus,** or *Jesus wrought,* **in Cana of Galilee.** See on ch. 1 : 43. **Manifested forth,** simply *manifested,* **his glory,** his Messianic glory, implying also his divinity. See ch. 1 : 14. **His disciples believed on him.** Though they had faith before, that faith was greatly increased. Jesus' Messiahship had been demonstrated before this by his teaching and his insight into human hearts, ch. 1 : 48–50. It was now demonstrated by a work of divine and creative power. The details of this miracle are so minute and vivid as to reveal the hand of an eye-witness. John had already become a disciple of Jesus, and was doubtless present at the wedding, being one of those whose faith was confirmed. "Apart from all that is local and temporary, this miracle may be taken as the sign and symbol of all which Christ is evermore doing in the world, ennobling all that he touches, making saints out of sinners, angels out of men, and, in the end, heaven out of earth—a new paradise of God out of the old wilderness of the world. For the prophecy of the world's regeneration, of the day in which his disciples shall drink of the fruit of the vine new in his kingdom, is eminently here. In this humble feast the rudiments of the great festival which shall be at the open setting-up of his kingdom—that marriage festival in which he shall be himself the Bridegroom and his church the bride—that season when his hour shall have indeed come."—TRENCH on *Miracles.*

In addition to this, two other points may be noted:

1. THE EVIDENCE OF THIS FIRST MIRACLE. Every care seems to have been taken that there might be no charge of deception or collusion. It was necessary that the first miracle of Jesus should be one which none could with any fairness deny. Hence "the quantity of wine produced was so great that it could not by any possibility have been introduced into the vessels unobserved. The vessels were water-pots, not wine-jars, that no one might think some sediment of wine remaining in them had given a flavor to the water afterward poured in, and so had caused it to be mistaken for a thin and diluted wine. The servants were witnesses that the water-pots were at first empty, had then been filled with water, and in the next moment were found full of wine, so that it is plain the wine came from no other quarter. Last of all, there was the testimony of the ruler of the feast, who, knowing nothing of the history of this wine, pronounced it not only real wine, but good wine. In this evidence the keenest eye can discover

12 After this he went down to Capernaum, he, and his mother, and ⁿhis brethren, and his disciples; and they continued there not many days.

ⁿ Matt. 12. 46; 13. 55, 56.

no flaw."—KITTO, *Life of Christ*, p. 203.

2. THE CREDIBILITY OF THE MIRACLES IN GENERAL. A miracle is an event palpable to the senses—an event which, though not contravening any law of Nature, the laws of Nature, if fully known, would not be sufficient to explain—an event produced in the realm of second causes by a supernatural agent outside that realm; namely, by the First Great Cause. It is not a suspension or violation of natural laws, but the result of the divine will acting upon Nature in a manner analogous to the action of the human will on Nature. Hence, "if God be possible, miracles are possible," and that possibility can be denied only upon principles of atheism or pantheism. Nature is not an end in itself, but exists for great moral purposes. Let the free will of man introduce discord in the moral universe, and the Author of Nature is justified in interposing a miraculous exercise of his power to secure the accomplishment of the normal end for which Nature was created. Hence belief in miracles is exactly proportioned to men's conviction of sin and need. Once allow that the race is ruined by transgression, and the presumption against miracles is changed to a presumption in their favor. The Scripture miracles have then only to present their overwhelming weight of evidence to the candid mind, in order to be received as realities. All our hope of heaven stands or falls with our acceptance of the miracles; for if the greatest miracle of all be not a reality, if the resurrection of Christ be a delusion, then our faith is vain and we are yet in our sins. But once grant the resurrection of the Lord Jesus, and all the other miracles, from first to last, form only its natural accompaniments.

12. **After this.** An indefinite interval of several days, or even two or three weeks. Jesus probably spent a portion of March, and possibly of February, at Capernaum. **He went down to Capernaum**, about 25 miles northeast of Cana, on the north-west shore of the Sea of Galilee. The expression *went down* accords with the fact that Cana was on elevated ground, and Capernaum was about 600 feet below the Mediterranean. Peter was afterward, and perhaps now, a householder in Capernaum. As Jesus went to the home of Nathanael to cement the friendship of his disciple, so now he may have gone to the home of Peter. *Capernaum* was the name of a fountain (Josephus, *Jew. War*, iii. 10, 8) and a town situated on the borders of the tribes of Zebulun and Naphtali. It was a thriving commercial place on the road from Damascus to the Mediterranean, and a central position for travelling and performing missionary-tours into Lower and Upper Galilee, Perea, and Judea. It was thus peculiarly fitted as the principal residence of Jesus during the three years of his ministry. It is called "his own city," Matt. 9 : 1. Its name was appropriate for his dwelling-place, meaning *village of Nahum*, or *consolation*. It was also the residence of Andrew, Peter, James, and John, who were natives of Bethsaida (ch. 1: 44), and probably of Matthew. Its present complete desolation forcibly illustrates our Lord's denunciation in Matt. 11 : 23. Its name is lost and its exact site is still in doubt. The most probable spots are: (1) Dr. Robinson supposes it to have been at *Khan Minyeh*, on the northern borders of the fine plain of Gennesaret, about five miles from the Jordan, where there is the copious fountain of *Ain et-Tin*, and ruins of some extent still remain. See Robinson, *Bib. Researches*, ii. 403, 404, iii. 344-358. (2) Mr. Tristram maintains that its site is at the Round Fountain, three miles farther south, near the south end of the plain of Gennesaret, where is found the catfish which Josephus states the fountain of Capernaum produced. A considerable stream also flows from it to the lake, which also answers to Josephus's description. *Land of Israel*, p. 442. (3) But Dr. Thompson and the majority of later travellers place the site near the head of the lake at *Tell Hum*, about three miles north of *Khan Minyeh*, and about the same distance from the point where the Jordan enters the lake. It is argued that *Hum* is the

Jesus goes up to the Passover at Jerusalem, cleanses the temple, and performs miracles. • ver. 23; ch. 5. 1; 6. 4; 11. 55; Luke 2. 41; Ex. 12. 14; Deut. 16. 1, 16.

13 ° And the Jews' passover was at hand; and Jesus

closing syllable of Capernaum, and that its first part, *Caphar*, which signifies a village, has given place to *Tell*, meaning a site or ancient ruin. But no fountain is found nearer than two miles. "I incline to the view that the first of these sites is Capernaum, and that *Tell Hum* is Chorazin. I believe the three cities of Capernaum, Bethsaida, and Chorazin extended up the shore from the plain of Gennesaret in the order named. During our stay in this region we carefully examined each Scripture reference in the light of the conjectural localities, and at least my own mind reached a tolerably satisfactory view as to where these cities stood. *Capernaum*, in this case, was on the northern boundary of the plain of Gennesaret, extending to the 'Round Fountain.' The site is closer marked by *Ain et-Tin*, the '*Spring of the Fig tree.*' The spring rises under a larger fig tree, and falls into the lake by a high projecting rock which overhangs the ruins of a *khan* (hence Khan Minyeh), another name for the site. The rocky promontory is deeply cut in every direction, probably for aqueducts. I rode over the hill and down its sides, and scanned every object. Bits of pottery, and fragments of stone-work, and dim traces of foundations may be detected, and one sees from here that it is by far the highest near elevation on the west of the lake, and involuntarily feels that the biblical intimations all harmonize with this spot. . . . It may be a small thing upon which to construct a theory, but certainly it is a fact of interest, that if these locations be accepted as the right ones, there is a beautiful *order* in Christ's enumeration of the three cities named. And we can fancy him uttering, with the finger pointing toward each in succession down along the lake, the denunciation upon Chorazin, Bethsaida, Capernaum. And perhaps the *elevation* of the last-named place above the others gave point to the expressions 'exalted to heaven' and 'cast down to hell.'"—DR. FISH, *Bible Lands Illustrated*, pp. 568, 571.

He, and his mother, and his brethren, better, *brothers*, as *brethren* is generally used in a spiritual sense. These brothers were still unbelievers, and continued to be such till after his resurrection, ch. 7 : 5; Acts 1 : 14. They were probably younger sons of Mary the mother of Jesus. Their knowledge of the quiet and unostentatious life he had led in Nazareth made it hard for them to recognize his glory, even after he began to work miracles. Still, they saw that a turning-point in his history had come, and they followed his steps to observe, and possibly to restrain him. And they continued there not many days. Their stay was short, on account of their shortly going up to the passover, ver. 13. As yet Jesus had taken no step that made known to the people at large his entrance upon a public career. This he must first proclaim at Jerusalem, the head-quarters of the nation, ver. 15. The miracle in Cana appears to have been performed with special reference to confirming the faith of his new disciples. The private manifestation of his Messiahship went before the public offering of himself to the nation at Jerusalem.

13-25. JESUS CASTS OUT THE TRADERS FROM THE TEMPLE. This very probably occurred early in the day, on the fourteenth of Nisan, the sacrificial victims being slain in the afternoon. See on ver. 23. Recorded only by John. Matthew (21 : 12, 13), Mark (11 : 15-19), and Luke (19 : 45-48) describe a similar cleansing of the temple which took place during the week preceding Jesus' crucifixion. John is the only evangelist who gives the account of this first cleansing. The circumstantial mention in the Gospels of the place and occasion of each of these cleansings forbids us to confound them, as some have done, or to say that there was but one. The one introduced, the other closed, his public life. The first was Jesus' warning to a nation that desecrated God's house and perverted his best gifts. This seems to have produced only a temporary effect: the traders, expelled for a day, soon came back again. The second cleansing was a symbolic declaration of the

A. D. 27. JOHN II. 57

14 went up to Jerusalem. ᵖ And found in the tem-   ᵖ Matt. 21. 12, 13.
ple those that sold oxen and sheep and doves, and
15 the changers of money sitting; and when he had
made a scourge of small cords, he drove them all out
of the temple, and the sheep, and the oxen; and
poured out the changers' money, and overthrew the

sentence of judgment against those who, once mercifully warned, had refused to put the offence away. The last cleansing of the temple presents Jesus as the same purifier and punisher that he had been in the beginning, making the same persistent claims, and acting with the same authority in the presence of the Jewish rulers and in prospect of death. So the beginning and the end are bound together as parts of one consistent plan.

13. **The Jews' passover.** This first passover of Jesus' ministry commenced April 9th, A. D. 27. Further on passover, see note on ver. 23. **Was at hand,** *was near,* within three or four days. **Jesus went up to Jerusalem,** from Capernaum, where he had been sojourning (ver. 12), and probably in company with some party of pilgrims going up to the feast from that city. His disciples, doubtless, accompanied him, ver. 22. Hitherto, he had not taught any but his disciples. He now went to the head-quarters of the nation to present himself before the rulers of the Jews as their promised Messiah. This he does, first of all, by a symbolic act asserting his authority over his Father's house, and his divine commission to cleanse it. On **Jerusalem,** see note on ch. 1 : 19.

14. **And found in the temple.** The temple enclosure was 1000 feet square, and along its sides ran the magnificent porticos or colonnades of Solomon and of Herod. Within this open space, which was called the Court of the Gentiles, was a second and smaller court, which only Jews could enter, and near the centre of this stood the temple-edifice proper. It was in the Court of the Gentiles, surrounding the sacred edifice, that Jesus found **those that sold oxen and sheep and doves.** All these were offered in sacrifice upon the temple altar, Ex. 20 : 24; Lev. 14 : 22. So many Jews came from a distance to the feasts that there was a large demand for sacrificial victims. It is probable that the traffic in these animals, which was once carried on outside the temple enclosure, had been gradually allowed to enter the Court of the Gentiles, partly on the plea or convenience, and partly from the cupidity of the priests, who cared more for the rents of the stalls than for the sanctity of God's house. So the clamor of avaricious traders rose on every side, disturbing the service of the inner court and distracting the minds of the worshippers. **The changers of money sitting.** Every adult male among the Jews was required to pay a yearly tax of half a shekel for the support of the temple-worship. It was not lawful to receive this tribute-money in Roman coin, stamped as it was with heathen symbols and inscriptions. "The moneychangers" were men who for a profit took this current Roman coin, and gave in return Hebrew shekels and half-shekels, minted in the times of the Maccabees. Jesus intimated, in Matt. 21 : 13, that these various kinds of traffic had become an occasion of fraud and extortion. "Sitting" was the common posture of tradesmen at their business.

15. **Made a scourge of small cords,** or rushes, probably strewn for the cattle to lie on. This scourge was not so much for actual use as for a symbol of authority. **Drove them all out of the temple.** As afterward in the garden (ch. 18 : 6), so now, there was such majesty in his look and such divine authority in his words that none could resist him. The manifestation of the Holy One, the Messiah, as a rebuker and punisher roused the slumbering consciences of the transgressors. Like the scribes and priests (Mark 11 : 18), they "feared him" and fled. **And the sheep, and the oxen,** these were what he drove out of the temple. **Poured out the changers' money and overthrew the tables.** These changed, at a premium—often a very exorbitant one—the current coin of the day for the Jewish **half-shekel,**

3 *

16 tables; and said unto them that sold doves, Take these things hence; ⁹make not ʳmy Father's house 17 an house of merchandise. And his disciples remembered that it was written, The zeal of thine house hath eaten me up.

18 Then answered the Jews and said unto him, ˢWhat sign showest thou unto us, seeing that thou doest

⁹ Jer. 7. 11.
ʳ ch. 5. 17, 18; 10 29, 30; Luke 2. 49

ˢ ch. 6. 30; Matt. 12. 38.

the yearly temple-tribute. See Matt. 17 : 24. Some made donations to the treasury Luke 21 : 1, 2; and others who came to the passover probably paid their tribute, which became due in the month Adar, answering to parts of February and March. These moneychangers were a convenience and a necessity, but they were dishonest in their exactions, practised extortion, and violated the law, Deut. 23 : 19, 20.

16. **Sold doves.** The poor were allowed to offer doves in sacrifice, instead of a lamb, Lev. 5 : 7; 12 : 8; 14 : 22; Luke 2 : 24. **Make not my Father's house,** etc. Jesus says not *our*, but *my*, Father, conscious of his own divinity and Messiahship. "My Father's house" is a phrase similar to that in Luke 2 : 49, and implies that he was Son of God and Lord of the temple. It was a declaration that in him the great prophecy of Malachi was beginning to be fulfilled (Mal. 3 : 1-3), and that the Lord (Messiah) whom the nation were seeking had "suddenly come to his temple." According to the prophecy of John the Baptist (Matt. 3 : 12), his fan was in his hand, and he wielded it in separating the precious from the vile, and in reforming the abuses of his house. Compare Isa. 4 : 2-4.

17. **The zeal of thine house;** zeal for its purity and honor. **Hath eaten me up;** according to the best manuscripts, *will consume me.* Tholuck and some others contend that the future here is used in the sense of the present : Absorbs all my energies and powers, and leads me utterly to disregard danger and death. The quotation is from Ps. 69 : 9. It well describes the spirit of Jesus' ministry. Human nature was God's defiled and desecrated temple. He would redeem and purify it, even at the cost of suffering and death.

This is a fitting place to notice the three divisions of Jesus' ministry. Jesus' plan was *first* "to present himself to the Jews as their Messiah. . . . Of his Messiahship he must give proof, first and chiefly, by his words, which should show him to be the Truth of God; and, secondly, by his works, which should show him to be the Power of God. . . . Thus presenting himself to the people, and especially to its ecclesiastical rulers, . . . he must await the action of the nation." He meets in Jerusalem, however, little but incredulity and hostility. About eight months of teaching and of miracles in Judæa under the eyes of the Jewish authorities resulted only in rousing them to plot against his life. "Forced to flee from Jerusalem, the Lord goes into Galilee. And now the *second* stage of his ministry begins. His work in Galilee had a twofold purpose; first, the gathering of disciples, that through their testimony, if not through his, the rulers of Jerusalem might be led to hearken and the nation be saved. But if this were vain, and nothing could convince them, these disciples might serve as the foundation of that new and universal church which God would build if the Jews rejected his Son." In the *third and last* stage of his ministry, when it became evident that nothing could convince his enemies, and that they were determined to destroy him, he once more made clear and prominent his Messianic claims, and went back into Judæa, into Peræa, and to Jerusalem, confessedly to meet his death, and in that death and the resurrection following to "open the kingdom of heaven to all believers."

18. HE PREDICTS THE RESURRECTION OF THE TEMPLE OF HIS BODY, vers. 18-22. 18. **Then answered the Jews,** rather, *The Jews therefore answered;* the members of the Sanhedrim, whose conduct in permitting the desecration of the temple Jesus had thus openly rebuked. **What sign showest thou?** They demanded the evidence of his authority, holding that the messenger of Jehovah must substantiate his

A. D. 27.   JOHN II.   59

19 these things? Jesus answered and said unto them, ᵗDestroy this temple, ᵘand in three days ᵛI will raise
20 it up. Then said the Jews, Forty and six years was this temple in building, and wilt thou rear it up in
21 three days? But he spake ʷof the temple of his
22 body. When therefore he was risen from the dead, ˣhis disciples remembered that he had said this unto them; and they believed the Scripture, and the word which Jesus had said.

ᵗMatt. 26. 61; 27 40; Mark 14. 58; 15. 29.
ᵘMatt.12.40;27.63.
ᵛch. 10. 17, 18; Mark 8. 31; 1 Cor. 15. 3, 4.
ʷch. 1. 14, Gr.; Col. 2. 9; Heb. 8. 2; so 1 Cor. 3. 16; 6. 19; 2 Cor. 6. 16.
ˣLuke 24. 8.

claims by "a sign from heaven." See Matt. 12 : 38; 16 : 1. "His life was indeed remarkable for such signs, but he would not sanction superstitious notions or gratify a cavilling temper, and he therefore refused the demand." In the next verse, however, he intimates an event which should be a sign to them and to all people.

19. **Destroy this temple,** etc; a purposely enigmatical saying, for the reason that he could not yet speak openly of his death. It may have been accompanied with a gesture implying that he was himself the temple of God of which he spake. None, however, understood it at the time, though it obtained wide circulation, and was urged as an accusation against him at his trial and crucifixion, Matt. 26 : 61; 27 : 40. **And in three days I will raise it up.** Notice that Jesus' part is not that of destruction; that belongs to the Jews. He will only raise up in glory that which has been previously destroyed. Compare the sign of the prophet Jonah, Matt. 12 : 39, 40.

20. **Forty and six years was this temple in building.** Herod began to rebuild the temple on a large and more splendid scale in the eighteenth year of his reign, in the 734th year of Rome. The temple proper was rebuilt in eighteen months; the surrounding galleries were completed in eight years; but the exterior structures and outbuildings were not entirely finished till about A. D. 64, in the reign of Nero. It was still going on in the time of our Saviour. Hence the Jews meant that the temple had already been in process of building forty-six years. No wonder they could not understand how he could **raise it up in three days.** See last paragraph of ver. 22.

21. **But he spake of the temple of his body.** The Godhead tabernacled in Jesus' flesh (ch. 1 : 14), and in it manifested its glory. The temple was only the symbol of him in and through whom God meets and dwells with men. As God dwells in him for ever, so the believer becomes a temple of God by being united to the Lord Jesus, 1 Cor. 3 : 16.

22. **When therefore he was risen,** or *had risen,* **from the dead, his disciples remembered.** Many of Jesus' words were thrown out as seed-thoughts, to be quickened into life only when the enlightening Spirit was bestowed, after Pentecost. See John 14 : 26. **Unto them,** should be omitted, according to the best authorities. **And they believed the Scripture;** that is, the Old Testament, which in several passages foretells the resurrection of Christ; *e. g.,* Ps. 16 : 9, 10; 68 : 18. The resurrection is included in all those prophecies which speak of the "sufferings of Christ and the glory that should follow," 1 Pet. 1 : 11. Compare ch. 20 : 9; Luke 24 : 26, 27. **And the word which Jesus had said,** better *which Jesus spoke.* The words of Jesus and of Scripture are of equal authority. The resurrection of Christ is a standing miracle and the conclusive argument of Christianity, confirming the faith of Christians in all ages, 1 Cor. 15 : 13-19. Perhaps the Jews remembered these words, and saw in them a deeper meaning. For after Jesus was buried they came to Pilate, saying, "Sir, we remember that that deceiver said while he was yet alive, After three days I will rise again," Matt. 27 : 63. "Now there is no trace that Jesus had *ever* uttered any such words distinctly to them; and unless they had heard the saying from Judas, or unless it had been repeated from common rumor derived from the apostles—*i. e.,* unless the 'we remember' was a distinct falsehood—they could have referred to no other occasion than this. And that they should have heard

23 Now when he was in Jerusalem at the passover in the feast-*day*, ʲmany believed in his name, when 24 they saw the miracles which he did. But Jesus ᵃdid not commit himself unto them, because he knew all 25 men, and needed not that any should testify of man; for ᵇhe knew what was in man.

ʳ ch. 7. 31; 8. 30
10. 42; 11. 45.
ᵃ ch. 6. 15.
ᵇ ch. 4. 17–19; 6.64, 16. 19, 30; 1 Sam. 16. 7; Mark 2. 8; Acts 1. 24; Rev. 2. 23.

it from any of the disciples was most unlikely, for over the slow hearts of the apostles these words of our Lord seemed to have passed like the idle wind."—DR. F. W. FARRAR, *Life of Christ*, vol. i. p. 193. With this saying the Jews also may have associated the sign of the prophet Jonah, Matt. 12 : 39, 40. Compare Matt. 27 : 63.

23. **At the passover.** The *passover* was instituted in commemoration of God's *passing over* (for this is the meaning of the word) or *sparing* the Hebrews when he destroyed the first-born of the Egyptians. The festival was celebrated eight days from the fifteenth of Nisan, the latter part of March or the first part of April (Ex. 12 : 1–11, 14–20), and was one of the three great festivals (Ex. 23 : 14–17) to be attended yearly at Jerusalem by all the males of the nation, except the sick, the aged, the blind, the deaf, and boys under twelve years of age. On the tenth day of the month Abib (Ex. 13 : 4)—or, as it was afterward called, Nisan (Esth. 3 : 7)—a male lamb or kid without blemish was selected. On the fourteenth day of Nisan it was slain in the temple, "between the two evenings" of three and six o'clock. In the evening, the beginning of the fifteenth day, the paschal supper was eaten by not less than ten nor more than twenty persons. Bitter herbs and unleavened bread were to be eaten with it, and all was done originally with haste, standing with loins girt, their feet shod, and their staff in hand. The standing posture and the apparent readiness for a journey were at length discontinued. The Jewish year was reckoned from this month, and John marks the various stages of Christ's public ministry by the passover, chs. 2 : 13, 23 ; 4 : 45; 5 : 1; 6 : 4; 11 : 55. The civil commencement of their year began six months later. **In the feast-day;** some would say, "during the feast," lasting, as it did, for eight days, but it is better to say, "*on the festival*" or "*feast-day*." The word *passover* above designates the whole feast, and this a particular day of the feast. This was not the time when he expelled the money-changers, but afterward, perhaps the next day. The fifteenth of Nisan, reckoned from six o'clock of the preceding evening, was the grand feast of the passover. The first and seventh days were peculiarly solemn, Lev. 23 : 5–8 ; Num. 28 : 18, 25; Matt. 26 : 17. **Many believed in his name;** *on his name;* that is, trusted in Christ himself as one sent of God. **When they saw the miracles,** the signs, which he did, or *wrought*. "These miracles are not recorded, but they were evidently remarkable." See ch. 3 : 2. Comp. ch. 4 : 45.

24. **But Jesus did not commit himself unto them.** For illustration compare ch. 6 : 15. "He did not entrust himself and the mysteries of his person and kingdom to all those who appeared disposed to regard him as a teacher sent from God." **Because he knew all men.**

25. **And needed not that any** *one* **should testify of, or concerning, man, for he himself knew what was in man.** He knew not only the secrets of each heart, but also the instability and depravity of human nature itself. Compare Rev. 2 : 23. John gives special prominence to our Lord's deep knowledge of men, ch. 5 : 42; 6 : 61, 64, etc. He saw that those who believed on him were influenced mainly by the transient impression of his miracles, and had most imperfect notions of his person and work. The fact that Jesus did not commit himself to *them* was only a sign that the Jews in positions of influence and authority did not commit themselves to *him.* He had offered himself as Messiah to the rulers of the nation, but they had virtually rejected him.

PRACTICAL REMARKS.

1. Jesus by his presence here, and by his teachings, always honored the insti-

JOHN III.

Nicodemus visits Jesus by night.

III. THERE was a man of the Pharisees, named ᵇ Nico-   ᵇ ch. 7. 45–52; 19.
2 demus, a ruler of the Jews: ᶜ the same came to Jesus   38, 40.
                                                                                                  ᶜ ch. 7.

tution of marriage, vers. 1–11; Matt. 5: 32; Heb. 13:4.
2. To know whether a party of pleasure is right, ask, "Can I consistently invoke the presence of Jesus there?" ver. 2; Ps. 139.
3. When perplexed, tell every want to Jesus, ver. 3; Phil. 4: 6, 7; Ps. 55: 22; 1 Pet. 5: 7.
4. Whoever assumes without special warrant to invoke the supernatural, plainly deserves reproof, ver. 4; Col. 2: 18; Matt. 12: 38, 39.
5. Jesus always heeds most the underlying thought of a prayer, ver. 4; Joel 2: 13; Isa. 29: 13; Ezek. 33: 31; Ps. 78: 35–37.
6. Steadfast faith persists, notwithstanding the first rebuff, ver. 5; Luke 11: 5–9 and 18: 1 ff.
7. Jesus is a large and liberal giver, ver. 6; Matt. 14: 20.
8. Full obedience brings a full blessing, ver. 7; 2 Kings 13: 19.
9. The world gives the best first; Jesus gives the best last, ver. 10; Matt. 1: 19; 28: 19; Luke 16: 25; Luke 6: 20–25. See *Spurgeon's Sermons*, fifth series, Nos. 17, 18.
10. The religion of Jesus turns even the water of purification into the wine of gladness, vers. 9–11.
11. The divine mission of Jesus is proved at the very outset of his ministry, ver. 11.
12. Jesus begins the miracles of redemption by ministering at a marriage. He will end redemption by ministering in the glorious festivities of the final marriage, ver. 11; Rev. 19: 7, 8; Luke 12: 37.
13. Jesus was obedient to every requirement of the Jewish religion, ver. 13; Ex. 23:17; Deut. 16:16. We should imitate him in our implicit obedience to every Christian ordinance, Matt. 3: 13–15; Mark 16: 15, 16.
14. Be sure all sin must be "found" out, even though entrenched in pious traffic, ver. 14; Mal. 3: 1–3.
15. Reformers, apt to be too severe, should study Christ with his scourge of small cords, ver. 15; Matt. 12: 19; 2 Pet. 2: 11; Jude 9.
16. Jesus cleanses not only the outward temple, but the nature of man—not only the outward life, but the inmost heart, ver. 16; 1 Cor. 3: 16, 17.
17. Jesus by his Spirit is now seeking to purify our hearts, his church, and the world, so that they may be fit abodes for God. At the judgment he will come to cast out all who do iniquity, and to make all things new, vers. 14–17; Matt. 13: 41, 42; Rev. 21: 5–8.
18. Jesus' zeal in purifying God's house ought to be in us, ver. 17; 2 Cor. 11: 2; Gal. 4: 16–18.
19. We should be specially zealous for personal purity, forbidding the world to intrude into either our worship or God's throne in our hearts, vers. 15–17; 1 John 3: 3; Ex. 20: 3.
20. Reformers must be prepared to answer opposition, vers. 19–20.
21. And must expect even the morning of their career to be overcast with the shade of suffering, ver. 21.
22. Prophecy is a most conclusive evidence, ver. 22; Luke 24: 25; 16: 31.
23. Then, as now, many are mentioned as believers, but few are trustworthy, few faithful, in the final test to fellowship, the cross, vers. 23, 24; Luke 23: 1, 25.
24. Jesus knows thoroughly *our* fidelity or our faithlessness, ver. 25; Rev. 2: 23.

CHAPTER III.

John begins this chapter with the account of the visit of Nicodemus to Jesus by night, vers. 1–21. After this, Jesus leaves Jerusalem, but remains in Judea exercising his ministry, vers. 12–24. During the same time John the Baptist baptizes in Ænon, and gives his final testimony regarding Jesus, vers. 25–36.

1–21. NICODEMUS VISITS JESUS BY NIGHT. THE DISCOURSE THAT ENSUES. This incident probably occurred during the passover festival, which lasted seven days. See on ch. 2: 23. In no other of Jesus' discourses have we so full and complete a summary of the whole scheme of human redemption as in this, which inaugurated his Messianic

by night, and said unto him, Rabbi, [d] we know that thou art a teacher come from God; for [e] no man can do these miracles that thou doest, except [f] God be with him.

[d] Matt. 22. 16.
[e] ch. 2. 23; 7. 31; 9. 16, 30–33; Acts 2. 22.
[f] Acts 10. 38.

teachings. Election, Atonement, Regeneration, Faith, Judgment, are all clearly presented. Those who suppose that Jesus' teachings changed their character with the increase of his experience, and those who believe that his rejection by the Jews and his final crucifixion were unforeseen and surprising contingencies to him, may see their views refuted here as well as in his baptism. There were abundant reasons why, at the beginning of his ministry, he should be silent in his *public* discourses with regard to his sufferings and death. But in this private interview with a susceptible hearer—an interview whose nature was not made known by Nicodemus until after Jesus' death—our Saviour might unfold the whole substance of his teaching and the whole nature of his Messianic work.

1. **Man of the Pharisees.** On Pharisees, see note on ch. 1 : 24. **Nicodemus** means *conqueror of the people;* mentioned only by John. "Nicodemus is called 'a ruler of the Jews' in John 3 : 1; and as that title is given in some passages (ch. 7 : 26 ; Acts 3 : 17, etc.) to members of the Sanhedrim, it has been inferred that he was one of that body. He was probably also a scribe, or teacher of the Law (*teacher of Israel,* John 3 : 10 = *teacher of the Law*), and hence belonged to that branch of the council which represented the learned class of the nation. Of the three occurrences—this and those in ch. 7 : 50 and in ch. 19 : 39—in which Nicodemus appears in the Gospel history, the second occupies an intermediate position between the first and the third as to the phase of character which they severally exhibit; and in this respect, as Tholuck suggests, the narrative is seen to be psychologically true. We have no means of deciding whether Nicodemus was present in the Sanhedrim at the time of the Saviour's arraignment and trial before that court. If he was present, he may have been too undecided to interpose any remonstrance (none is recorded), or may have deemed it unavailing amid so much violence and passion. Stier would find in

'*we know,*' as plural, a characteristic shrinking from anything like a direct personal avowal of his own belief; but more probably he meant in this way to recognize more strongly the ample evidence furnished by Christ's miracles that he was a teacher sent from God. In this confession perhaps he associates with himself some of his own rank who were already known to him as secret believers. See ch. 12 : 42; 19 : 38."— Prof. H. B. Hackett, D. D., in Dr. Smith's *Dictionary of the Bible,* Amer. ed. According to a very likely tradition, he became an open disciple of Christ after the resurrection, and was baptized, and was cruelly persecuted by the Jews.

Ruler of the Jews, a member of the Sanhedrim (see quotation above), the highest ecclesiastical tribunal of the nation. Tradition reports him to have been a man of great wealth and a rigid observer of the Pharisaic forms. These, however, did not give peace to his soul.

2. **The same came to Jesus,** according to the oldest manuscripts, *to him,* **by night,** through *fear,* as might be inferred from the manner in which his coming is afterward spoken of in contrast to his coming openly, ch. 19 : 39. Nicodemus felt assured that this Galilean young man, whom his associates so despised, was able to answer his questions and give him spiritual help. False shame kept him from coming openly to the Saviour. Such an interview, if generally known, would compromise his position and bring down upon him the hatred of the Jews. Yet, though he was too timid to come publicly, we must remember that he was the only one of the rulers to come at all. It was the first trembling step of a truly candid soul, and Jesus rewarded it by communicating to him truths never before or after so fully and nobly unfolded. **Rabbi.** See on ch. 1 : 38. **We know that thou art a teacher come from God.** More exactly, *Thou hast come a teacher.* Compare "sent from God," ch. 1 : 6. Nicodemus did not yet recognize Jesus as the Messiah, but only as a prophet who spoke with

3 Jesus answered and said unto him, Verily, verily, I say unto thee, *Except a man be born again, he cannot see the kingdom of God.

*Gal. 6. 15; Tit. 3. 5; James 1. 17, 18; 1 Pet. 1. 3, 23.

divine authority. The word "*we*" seems to show that Nicodemus knew of still others of the Sanhedrim (see 12 : 42) who were disposed to favor Jesus. **for no man can do these miracles, signs, that thou doest except God be with him.** "From what Jesus did he inferred the truth of what he taught." He alluded to the miracles mentioned in 2 : 23. Nicodemus doubtless thought that he made large concessions when he acknowledged Jesus to be a prophet, and expected that this confession would secure him any instruction he might need. He must learn that he had spoken only the smallest fragment of the truth. Jesus is a thousand-fold greater than he has ever imagined, and a knowledge of his truth is to be reached in no such easy way. The reply of Jesus in the next verse seems abrupt. But as Nicodemus came seeking instruction, Jesus at once gave him that which he most needed and was the most important for his spiritual good. He teaches him what is necessary to experience in order to become a member of his kingdom. This was the first truth Nicodemus needed to know.

3. **Verily,** *truly,* **I say unto thee.** Jesus thus authoritatively and solemnly introduces the necessity of the new birth. **Except a man,** *any one,* whether Jew or Gentile, **be born again.** Some translate *Born from above;* that is, of God or of the Spirit. In either translation it denotes the beginning of a new spiritual life. The reply of Nicodemus, however, in ver. 4, shows that it means *born again* or anew. Compare Tit. 3 : 5; Gal. 4 : 9. Proselytes from the heathen were said to be "born again" and to become "new men" when they entered the fold of Judaism. Nicodemus understood Jesus partially, and saw that he referred to the necessity of some radical change before he could be a subject of God's kingdom. "Paul calls the change a new birth, or re-generation (Tit. 3 : 5), and here in John it is presented as another than the natural birth ; and hence the fitness of the term 'new birth,' or 'regeneration,' is implied. The teaching here, and elsewhere, is,

that a change is to take place in man of which God is the Author, and which does not simply bring out what was already in man, but rather originates that which before had no existence. The doctrine that apart from grace all men are sinners, wholly destitute of true love to God, is plainly taught here, and as plainly, but far more fully, in many another place. See Rom. 3; 8 : 1-15. This is the doctrine of 'total depravity,' which it is so fashionable at present to ridicule. Let a man choose between God's word and human fancies, and either accept the doctrine or reject the Bible, and not try to ride two horses in opposite directions at one and the same time." **Kingdom of God.** This phrase occurs in this Gospel only here and in ver. 5. In ch. 18 : 36, Jesus speaks of his "kingdom," that it is not of this world. *Kingdom of God* is also used by Mark and Luke, but *kingdom of heaven* by Matthew (3 : 2, etc.), the former expression having special reference to its central locality, the latter to him whose it is. The same thing is expressed by "kingdom of Christ," or simply "kingdom," Eph. 5 : 5; Heb. 12 : 28. The prophets had represented the Messiah as a divine King (Ps. 2 : 6; Isa. 11 : 1; Jer. 23 : 5; Zech. 14 : 9; Mic. 4 : 1-4; 5 : 2), and especially Daniel (Dan. 2 : 44 ; 7 : 13, 14), who had spoken of a kingdom which the God of heaven would set up. Hence, *kingdom of heaven,* or *of God,* became common among the Jews to denote the kingdom or reign of the Messiah. Their own theocracy was also typical of it. They, indeed, perverted the meaning of prophecy, and expected an earthly and temporal kingdom, the restoration of the throne of David at Jerusalem, and the actual subjugation of all nations. John the Baptist, Jesus, and the apostles, however, rescued the phrase from error, and gave it its full and true meaning. This *kingdom, reign,* or *administration* of the Messiah is spiritual in its nature (John 18 : 36; Rom. 14 : 17), and is exercised over, and has its seat in, the hearts of believers, Luke 17 : 21. It exists on earth, Matt. 13 : 18, 19, 41, 47 ; extends

4 Nicodemus saith unto him, ᵇ How can a man be born when he is old? Can he enter the second time into his mother's womb, and be born?
5 Jesus answered, Verily, verily, I say unto thee, ⁱ Except a man be born of water ᵏ and *of* the Spirit,

ᵇ 1 Cor. 2. 14.
ⁱ Matt. 28. 19; Mark 16. 16; Eph. 5. 26, 27; 1 Pet. 3. 21.
ᵏ Rom. 8. 9; 1 Cor. 6. 11.

to another state of existence, Matt. 13 : 43, 26 : 29; Phil. 2 : 10, 11; and will be fully consummated in a state of glory, 1 Cor. 15 : 24; Matt. 8 : 11; 2 Pet. 1 : 11. It thus embraces the whole mediatorial reign or government of Christ on earth and in heaven, and includes in its subjects all the redeemed, or, as Paul expresses it (Eph. 3 : 15), "the whole family in heaven and earth." *Kingdom of God* and *church* are not identical, though inseparably and closely connected. The churches of Christ are the external manifestations of this kingdom in the world. **See,** to enjoy and have part in. Compare 1 Pet. 3 : 10.

4. How can a man be born when he is old? Nicodemus would seem to be advanced in life. This, and the phrase **the second time,** show that the translation, *born again,* or *anew,* in vers. 3 and 7, is preferable to *born from above.* Nicodemus's difficulty was in seeing how a Jew of the straitest sect, and scrupulous in his obedience for years, should need to undergo any such change as Jesus spoke of. His words are to be taken figuratively. "He had been once born a Jew and a child of promise; how could it be needful that he be born again?" He could see how a Gentile must undergo a great change in order to enjoy the blessings of Israel and of the Messiah, but that the Jews must also experience such a change was more than he could understand. It semed to him quite an impossibility, quite as difficult as a second natural birth. In his surprise, therefore, he gives vent to his thoughts by asking a question which will draw from Jesus an explanation.

The rabbinical idea of the new birth was quite superficial, having principal reference to the external change of a proselyte to Judaism. Yet we must not ascribe too low views to Nicodemus. He was a man of thought, and somewhat advanced in years, and had been deeply impressed with the miracles and words of Jesus. He felt a need of something deeper and more spiritual than he had yet found in his learned researches.

5. Verily, verily, etc. A solemn asseveration, as in ver. 3, giving weight to the words following. In this verse we find an advance upon ver. 3. Born in two respects. Instead of "*see,*" we have here "*enter into.*" **Except a man be born of water and of the Spirit.** Some hold *water* here to be used merely as a symbol of purification. Others refer it to baptism, which seems more natural, and makes the meaning of Tit. 3 : 5 fuller and more pertinent. Indeed, 1 John 5 : 6-8, in connection with the latter passage, shows very conclusively that the phrase "born of water" refers to the ordinance of baptism. Nicodemus had heard of John's baptism, for he was one of the body which had sent the deputation to John. His first thought would naturally be, that Jesus was referring to some outward ordinance, like John's baptism. Jesus, therefore, in mentioning the terms of discipleship, spoke of the baptism of water as necessary indeed, but as useless unless connected with, and symbolical of, another, grander work, the renewal by the Holy Spirit. It was hard for Nicodemus to acknowledge the necessity of being born of water. But Jesus told him that besides this he must be born of the Spirit, "born of water *and* the Spirit," made partaker of a new life by the inward work of the Spirit of God. "Born of water" comes before "born of the Spirit," only because the outward was present to the mind of Nicodemus, and so is laid hold of by Jesus as a means of illustrating the regeneration of the Spirit. It is most unreasonable to find in this order an argument for baptismal regeneration. Faith in Christ is required in order to baptism, and such faith as is a fruit of the Spirit and an evidence of regeneration, Acts 2 : 41. Compare Rom. 10 : 9, 10, where both orders are used successively. The kingdom of God in its completed form is external and visible, as well as internal

6 ¹he cannot enter into the kingdom of God. ᵐThat which is born of the flesh is flesh, and that which is born of the Spirit is spirit. Marvel not that I said
7
8 unto thee, Ye must be born again. ⁿThe wind bloweth where it listeth, and thou hearest the sound thereof, but canst not tell whence it cometh and whither it goeth; °so is every one that is born of the Spirit.

l Matt. 18. 3.
m Gen. 5. 3; Rom. 7. 18; 8. 5-8.
n Job 37. 10-13, 16, 17, 21, 22; 1 Cor. 2. 11.
o ch. 1. 13; Eccles. 11. 5.

---

and spiritual. As it includes the outward as well as the inward life, entrance into it is first by "being born of the Spirit," and secondly by "being born of water." Jesus does not say that baptism is necessary to regeneration, but that baptism and regeneration both are necessary to enter the kingdom of God; that is, in its complete form, as it reigns in the heart and is externally manifested through the church in the world.

The following, by Dr. D. D. Whedon, is worth pondering: "Those who refuse to perform and accept the sign do wilfully exclude themselves from the kingdom of God. Yet, although the conditional duty, it does not stand on the same ground of an absolute condition, without which salvation is itself impossible, as is the case in being born of the Spirit.... Baptism may in many cases be impossible. There are many, however, who by gross negligence or for other reasons *stay out of the Christian church*, abandoning thereby the ordinances of God, both of baptism and communion, and yet suppose themselves to be justified Christians. For aught they do, the ordinances of baptism and the Lord's Supper would die out. How they will answer this contempt of the solemn requirements of Christ at the judgment-day is for themselves to answer."

6. **That which is born of the flesh is flesh.** As often in Paul's writing, flesh is here used to designate human nature as fallen and depraved. Compare Rom. 8 : 1-15. Sinful human nature can only bring forth fruit after its kind. **That which is born of the Spirit,** the Holy Spirit, is Spirit, is Godlike, holy, and thus "a partaker of the divine nature," 2 Pet. 1 : 4. The contrast is between the natural and spiritual birth. All true spiritual life must come from him who created human nature at the first, and who alone can renew fallen human nature in his own image. See ver. 8.

7. **Marvel not,** etc., referring to the surprise of Nicodemus expressed in ver. 4. So extraordinary a change had seemed to him quite impossible. **Ye,** thou and all others. **Born again,** see ver. 4.

8. **The wind bloweth.** The same Greek word means both *wind* and *spirit*. This seems to have led Jesus to compare the operation of the Spirit with the movement of the wind. **Where it listeth,** *pleaseth*. In regeneration God acts as a sovereign with almighty power, and no one can control or bind him in his acting. Nicodemus had asked *how*, ver. 4. Jesus replies as to the *manner* of the Spirit's operation. There are three points of comparison: Freedom and independence; strength which none can resist; incomprehensibility as to its mode, origin, and termination. **Thou hearest,** though the eye sees it not, **the sound thereof;** so the Spirit works unseen, but produces changes which show its activity. **But canst not tell;** literally, *But knowest not*, etc. Though known, yet mysterious. **Whence it cometh and whither it goeth.** Though the wind may seem capricious, yet it is governed by fixed laws, which even now are but little understood. So the Spirit in his sovereign and mysterious action moves by the perfect law of divine wisdom. Physical changes are often produced by invisible agencies whose working we cannot comprehend. Marvel not, then, that God can secretly change the dispositions and aims of the soul. As the wind's action is mysterious, **so is every one that is born of the Spirit.** So is it with every one, etc. Thus Jesus did not say that the work of the Holy Spirit is lawless or arbitrary, but simply that we must not deny the possibility of the Spirit's work of new creation because we cannot observe its progress or comprehend its method.

9 Nicodemus answered and said unto him, p How can these things be?
10 Jesus answered and said unto him, q Art thou a master of Israel, and knowest not these things?
11 r Verily, verily, I say unto thee, We speak that we do know, and testify that we have seen; and s ye receive not our witness. If I have told you t earthly things, and ye believe not, how shall ye believe, if

p ch. 6. 52, 60.
q Isa. 9. 16; Heb. 5. 12.
r ch. 1. 18; 14. 24; Matt. 11. 27; 2 Pet. 1. 16–21; 1 John 1. 1–3.
s ch. 5. 38; 12. 37.
t 1 Cor. 3. 1, 2.

9. Jesus teaches (vers. 9–21) that there is no salvation unless we trust in a crucified Saviour. **How can these things be?** An interrogatory exclamation. It seemed incredible that such a change should be the indispensable condition for entrance into the kingdom of the Messiah, that God in his sovereignty would gather in his kingdom whom he would, and that Jews, no more than Gentiles, could expect to have place in that kingdom unwashed and unchanged. It thus made that kingdom spiritual, in opposition to the worldly views of the Jews. Nicodemus's former views were so completely overthrown by this humbling doctrine of Jesus that he broke out in incredulity and astonishment.

10. **Art thou a master,** rather, *the teacher,* **of Israel,** the teacher of the Israelites, known and distinguished by thy learning? He was eminent, perhaps, for his researches regarding the Messianic kingdom. **And knowest not these things?** Dost not comprehend them? This is not a rebuke, but a reminder that he should have known the great doctrine which Jesus had announced regarding his kingdom. The Old Testament should have given Nicodemus a more thorough knowledge (see Ps. 51 : 10; Ezek. 11 : 19, 20; 36 : 26), for it had often spoken of "the new heart" and "new spirit" which God would bestow. Compare Jer. 31 : 33. "Though giving prominence to national and ritual laws, yet everywhere and abundantly it insists that nothing but a right heart avails with God, and that all external obedience, without inward holiness, is abomination." The reason why Nicodemus and the rest of the Jews did not see and appreciate the spirituality of the Old Testament was their own lack of spirituality.

11. Nicodemus must receive the testimony of Jesus, apostles, and the prophets as matters which they know. For the third time Jesus uses the authoritative and solemn affirmation, **Verily, verily,** etc., vers. 3, 5. He is about to introduce the doctrine of his sufferings. **We speak,** referring principally to himself, but including with himself prophets and others who proclaim the same truth. Compare 1 Cor. 2 : 9, 10. **We do know,** no uncertain knowledge, ch. 1 : 1–3. **That we have seen.** See ch. 1 : 7, 8, 9, 14, 33, 34. The Jews would receive the testimony of men in respect to things which they had known and seen; how unreasonable, therefore, their unbelief of the testimony of Christ, the prophets, John the Baptist, and those disciples who were chosen witnesses! **And ye,** the Jews, especially the leaders, to whom Nicodemus belonged, **receive not our witness,** *testimony.* The testimony of Jesus was concerning things within his personal knowledge; and his knowledge was drawn from his own divine consciousness, and not merely from Scripture by inference and argument. How great the sin of rejecting such a witness! ver. 13.

12. **If I have told you earthly things;** literally, *the earthly things,* such as regeneration, by which one enters into the kingdom of God on earth, and which also is a change in man's conscious being on earth, the need of which can be felt and the effects of which can be observed. Baptism and those doctrines which are connected with human consciousness and the present world are also included in earthly things. **How shall ye believe?** "How can one read a language if he has not learned the alphabet?" **Of heavenly things,** literally, *the heavenly things;* of my divine origin and pre-existence; of the eternal counsels of God for human salvation; of the great work yet unexecuted; of suffering for the sins of the world; and of all this as flowing from the infinite love of God.

13 I tell you of *heavenly things? And *no man hath
ascended up to heaven, *but he that came down from
heaven, *even* the Son of man which is in heaven.
14 *And as Moses lifted up the serpent in the wilderness, even so *must the Son of man be lifted up;
15 *that whosoever believeth in him should *not perish, but have *eternal life.
16 *For God so loved the world, that *he gave his only-begotten Son, that whosoever believeth in him

*1 Cor. 2. 6, 7; 1 Tim. 3. 16.
*ch. 1. 18; Prov. 30. 4.
*ch. 6. 33, 51, 62; 8. 42; Eph 4. 9, 10.
*Num. 21. 7-9.
*ch. 8. 28; 12. 32-34.
*ch. 6. 40, 47; 11. 25, 26; Mark 16. 16; Rom. 5. 1, 2; 10. 9-13.

*ch. 10. 28; Matt. 18. 11.   *ch. 17. 3; 1 John 5. 20.   *2 Cor. 5. 19-21;
1 John 4. 9-11, 19.   *Rom. 5. 10; 8. 32.

This would include the hidden wisdom of God concerning human redemption, 1 Cor. 2 : 8-13. In contrast to these wonderful revelations of the gospel and the Spirit, the earthly things may include the revelations made in the Old Testament.

13. Of all these things Jesus is the only teacher, for he alone has come from heaven, and is, by virtue of his divine nature even now in heaven. **No man**, *no one*, **hath ascended**, etc. Human teachers, born on earth can be in **heaven** only as they ascend. But Christ, who is the Logos (ch. 1 : 1-3), was eternally there, and had his human life only as he **came down from heaven**, and by virtue of his divine nature **is in heaven**, and his proper dwelling-place is there. On **Son of man**, see note, ch. 1 : 51.

14. **And as.** Continuation of the thought from the last verse. Jesus does not seem to proceed here to the heavenly things, but continues to speak of those things which are to be enacted on the earth. **As Moses lifted up the serpent in the wilderness;** the image of a hated thing, yet bringing healing to all who looked to it in faith. See Num. 21 : 9. **Even so must the Son of man be lifted up**, upon the cross, in the likeness of sinful flesh, to make an atonement for sin, and so become a Saviour of the lost, 1 John 2 : 2.

15. **That whosoever,** any one, whether Jew or Gentile, **believeth in him.** Like the serpent, he was lifted up to heal those who looked to him in faith. Nicodemus is brought to see that while he is utterly dependent on God for regeneration, there is something, nevertheless, for him to do; namely, to believe on him who is "manifested to take away our sins." **Should not perish, but** should be

omitted, according to the highest authorities. The words are found in ver. 16. **Eternal life,** *everlasting life*, unending blessed existence—the whole being in spiritual harmony and intimate union with God for ever, with all of the blessed and glorious results. This life begins with regeneration, and goes on widening and deepening for ever. We have a glimpse here of the heavenly things. In these two verses (14, 15) we have an illustration of our Lord's interpretation of the Old Testament Scriptures in regard to himself, Luke 24 : 27. Justification by faith, and that in a crucified One, is brought to view, as typified in this incident in Jewish history. Many would trace out the type still further. "That which healed was (without poison, indeed) the same that had slain. The crucified One, who delivers, is likewise, in appearance only, a sinner and malefactor (Rom. 8 : 3); thus Luther, Bengel, Olshausen, Jacobi."—Tholuck. However this may be, Jesus did not here enter upon such minute analogies.

16. Many commentators suppose that our Lord's conversation with Nicodemus closed with the preceding verse, and that with this commence the words of the evangelist himself. It is more natural, however, to regard this and the five verses following as the words of Jesus. They fit in their place, and verses 20, 21 appropriately close such a conversational discourse. So Meyer, Alford, Lange, and others. **For.** This word looks forward as well as backward. Jesus is not only summing up what he had said in vers. 14, 15, but he continues to unfold and apply the truth. **God so loved.** Another glimpse of the heavenly things, ver. 12. **The world,** of sinful men. **Gave his only-begotten Son.** See on ch. 1 : 14. John

17 should not ^g perish, but have everlasting life. ^h For God sent not his Son into the world to condemn the world; ⁱ but that the world through him might be
18 saved. ^j He that believeth on him is not condemned; ^k but he that believeth not is condemned already, because he hath not believed in the name
19 of the only-begotten Son of God. And this is the condemnation, ^l that light is come into the world, ^m and men loved darkness rather than light, because
20 their deeds were evil. For ⁿ every one that doeth evil hateth the light, neither cometh to the light,

g 1 Cor. 1. 18; 2 Cor. 4. 3; 2 Pet 3. 9.
h ch. 12. 47.
i Isa. 53. 4–6, 10–12; 1 John 2. 2; 4. 14.
j ch. 5. 24; 6. 40, 47; 20. 31; Rom. 8. 1, 34–39; 1 John 5. 12.
k Heb. 2. 3; 12. 25.
l ch. 1. 4, 9–11; 8. 12.
m Isa. 30. 9–13; Prov. 1. 29–31; Rom. 1. 28.
n ch. 7. 7; Job 24. 13, 17; Amos 5. 10.

here learned the appellation, *only-begotten*, from Christ himself. God loves the world, and the measure of his love is the gift of his Son. **That whosoever believeth.** Only those who believe are saved. The object which his love seeks is the salvation of each one of us. **Perish**, in everlasting punishment, Matt. 25 : 46. In opposition to this is **everlasting life.** See on ver. 15. Faith is an earthly thing, ver. 12. Thus we find in the teaching of Jesus to Nicodemus a mingling of the heavenly and earthly things. It has been asked, How could Jesus speak to Nicodemus of "the heavenly things" when he seems to refuse to do so in ver. 12? In reply it may be said : (1) That ver. 12 is not to be taken as an absolute refusal, but rather as introductory to a further unfolding of truth, including something of the mysterious and heavenly. (2) Jesus could not well speak of salvation without mingling both earthly and heavenly things. (3) It would seem from the after-history of Nicodemus that his heart was now opening to the truth (ch. 7 : 51; 19 : 39), and his previous education and knowledge probably prepared him, as a sincere inquirer, to receive the mysteries of the kingdom.

17. **God sent not his Son . . . to condemn**, rather, *to judge*, **the world.** The Jews thought Messiah was coming to punish the Gentiles, while he saved Israel. **But that the world through him might be saved,** or *may be saved,* on complying with the conditions of salvation. God's provision of mercy includes not one nation only, but all nations and all ages. While it was not the purpose of God to send his Son to judge the world, yet, as a result of their unbelief, Christ is said to have come also for judgment, ch. 9 : 39.

18. **He that believeth on him is not condemned,** *is not judged*, being justified by faith, Gen. 15 : 6; Ezek. 28 : 16; Hab. 2 : 4; Rom. 5 : 1. **Is condemned already,** *has been judged already,* **because he hath not believed.** See on ver. 19. The great sin is rejection of the Saviour, ch. 16 : 9. It leaves the soul unsheltered under God's condemnation. The last day will be a "*revelation* of the righteous judgment of God" (Rom. 2 : 5), but the judgment itself is made up already.

19. **This is the condemnation,** rather, *the judgment;* the cause or reason of the judgment. "A highly-spiritual conception of the idea of the judgment, which also lies at the basis of the words in ch. 12 : 46–48. Compare Acts 13 : 46; Tit. 3 : 11 : John 9 : 41."—THOLUCK. He "proceeds to the immoral, damnable nature of unbelief, and to the intimation that the rulers of the Jews are already further gone in this unbelief than Nicodemus suspects. Thus they are already judged."—LANGE. **That light is come,** or, *That the light has come,* **into the world.** Christ is the Light (ch. 1 : 4, 5), and refusal to come to him shows deep-rooted hostility to God's holiness and love. **Men loved darkness,** *the darkness;* ignorance, sin, and Satan. **Rather than light,** truth, holiness, and Christ. The reason, **because their deeds were evil.** The bent of their lives and the product of their character were evil; they were bent on sin and wrought wickedness.

20. Further reason why men love the darkness rather than the light. **For every one that doeth evil hateth the light;** the heart, being depraved, is opposed to the truth and hates holiness, Rom. 8 : 7. **Neither cometh to**

A. D. 27.   JOHN III.   69

21 lest his deeds should be reproved. °But he that   • Ps. 139. 23, 24.
doeth truth cometh to the light, that his deeds may
be made manifest that they are wrought in God.

Jesus, leaving Jerusalem, teaches and baptizes in Judæa.
22   After these things came Jesus and his disciples into
the land of Judæa, and there he tarried with them,

the light; in his dislike and hatred keeps away from the light. Lest his deeds should be reproved, discovered as detestable and punishable. "The more man abandons himself to evil, the more does he regard it as his proper self, and loves it as himself. As that which is holy is in opposition to him, and reproves his evil works, he feels himself mortified in that character which is proper to him, and begins to hate what is holy. Christ presents this as the reason (ch. 7 : 7) why he was hated by the world."—THOLUCK. 21. But he that doeth truth, *the truth*, obeys it, acts uprightly, cometh to the light. He who loves holiness and loves God will infallibly be attracted to Jesus. These were fitting and encouraging words to Nicodemus. It would seem that he was attracted thus, and that these wonderful words, though not bringing forth immediate fruit, did afterward lead him to an open avowal of discipleship. See on ver. 1. That his deeds may be made manifest. God has designed that the works of his children should be seen and known, Matt. 5 : 14–16. Neither do they seek concealment and dread detection, like evil-doers, Prov. 28 : 1. The Christian desires also to let his light shine, ch. 11 : 9, 10; Rom. 13 : 12; 1 Thess. 5 : 8. That they are wrought in God, under the renewing and sanctifying influence of the Holy Spirit, and that the works have God as their source. Some translate, *For they are*, etc., assigning the reason for the intention expressed in the preceding clause; the ground of the moral boldness of him who comes to the light.

22–24. JESUS CONTINUES IN JUDÆA, TEACHING AND BAPTIZING. JOHN BAPTIZING AT ÆNON. 22. After these things, the conversation with Nicodemus (vers. 1–21), the preceding miracles (ch. 2 : 23), and the cleansing of the temple (ch. 2 : 15), all of which occurred in connection with the feast at Jerusalem. Jesus and his disciples, such as Andrew, Peter, Philip, Nathanael, John, mentioned in the first chapter, and perhaps others. Land of Judæa, the country as distinguished from the capital, and probably near the Jordan, north-east of Jerusalem. See ch. 4 : 3, 4. *Judæa* was south of Samaria, bounded by Jordan on the east, the Mediterranean on the west, and the territory of the Arabs on the south. The boundary of the province seems to have been often varied by the addition or abstraction of towns. Tarried with them, and baptized, administering the ordinance, not in person, but through his disciples, ch. 4 : 2. His miracles and teaching had called forth no response from the leaders of the people, whom it was his first aim to influence. The authorities at Jerusalem had virtually rejected him. But there "was still hope that their hostility might be removed by greater knowledge of his character and work. The Lord, therefore, still remaining in the province of Judæa, and thus directly under the eyes of the priests, began the work of baptizing." Here he appears to have remained for nearly eight months, or from April till the latter part of November or the first of December (ch. 4 : 3, 35), waiting for the recognition of the nation. His baptism was, like John's, a baptism of repentance, to prepare the people for the setting up of God's spiritual kingdom. See Matt. 4 : 17.

THE NATURE OF JESUS' BAPTISM. This was, like that of John, a baptism of repentance. "It was an indispensable condition to the reception of the Christ, the holy One of God, that sin should be repented of and put away. John had already baptized many into the hope of his coming, but others had equal need to be baptized into the reality of it. Thus Jesus began his work as the Baptizer with water unto repentance. It was this baptism that gave to

23 ᵖ and baptized. And John also was baptizing in   ᵖ ch. 4. 1, 2.
Ænon near to Salim, because there was much water
24 there; ᵠ and they came and were baptized. For   ᵠ Matt 3. 5, 6.
ʳ John was not yet cast into prison.   ʳ Matt. 14. 3.

The final testimony of John the Baptist to Jesus.
25   Then there arose a question between *some* of

---

nis Judæan ministry its distinctive character. It was an attempt to bring the nation, as headed by its ecclesiastical rulers, to repentance. But as they had frustrated the counsel of God within themselves, being not baptized of John, so they continued to frustrate it by rejecting the baptism of Jesus."

23. Ænon signifies *springs* or *fountains*. **Near to Salim.** The exact location of these places is unknown, but it is probable that they were situated in one of the lateral valleys running down to the valley of the Jordan from the west. In regard to it Dr. Hackett says: "The later observations tend to narrow the limits of the question; they indicate at least the region, if they do not fix the site, of Ænon. Jerome's testimony (RELAND'S *Palæstina*, p. 480), that it was eight miles south of Scythopolis, agrees with the ascertained condition of that neighborhood. Dr. Thomson (*Land and Book*, ii. 176), who visited *Beisan* (Scythopolis) and the neighborhood, represents the valley there as abounding in fountains and brooks, which make it one of the most fertile places in Palestine. Though finding no traces of the names still current, he says that Ænon and Salim were no doubt in this *Ghor Beisan*." But Robinson and Conder, with more probability, place it in the neighborhood of Salim, east of Nablous, the ancient Shechem. Prof. Wm. A. Stevens, of Rochester, visited this region in 1883, and found in the Wady Beiden, three or four miles north of Salim, a probable site of Ænon, with abundance of water and space for the multitude that gathered about John. Prof. McGarvey also visited this Wady, and found a stream, and mills, and though the season was very dry, pools abundant, well suited for baptizing. He also found "a beautiful valley among the mountains, about one mile wide and three miles long." Here herds of camels were grazing and drinking, and swarms of

boys were bathing at different places in the stream. The name Ænon, signifying *springs* and " much water" or "deep waters," are descriptive, and readily find identification in this region.—(DR. SMITH, *Bible Dictionary*, Amer. ed.) With the last view, Mr. Drake, who held the first rank in the English Palestine Expedition, substantially agrees. **Because there was much water,** or *many waters*, many springs or streams suitable for purposes of baptism. "*Much*, as the rite of immersion required."—BENGEL. The phrase *much water* has the idea of *an abundance of water*. Compare Rev. 1 : 15; 14 : 2; 17 : 1; 19 : 6, where the same words are used in the original. John continued his work for two reasons: first, because Jesus had not yet been openly received by the nation as the Messiah; and, secondly, because multitudes were yet unconscious of their spiritual needs, and unprepared to recognize him. The Baptist felt that his work of witnessing to Jesus was not done until the kingdom of Messiah was actually set up. **And they,** the people, **came and were baptized,** were still, as formerly (Matt. 3 : 5, 6), coming to John and submitting to his baptism.

24. **For,** introduces the reason of John baptizing at Ænon. He continued his ministry, though on a decreasing scale, till his imprisonment. **Not yet cast into prison,** Matt. 4 : 12; Mark 1 : 14. John's ministry probably lasted a number of months after this, when he was imprisoned by King Herod Antipas (see Mark 6 : 17) in the fortress of Machærus, on the eastern shore of the Dead Sea. (Josephus, *Antiq.*, xviii. 5, 2.) This occurred probably about November, A. D. 27, and about a year after our Saviour's baptism. John's ministry continued about eighteen months. He was beheaded probably in March, A. D. 29. Compare on Luke 9 : 9; also *Author's Harmony*, §§ 30, 31.

25. **Then there arose,** rather, *There arose, therefore,* in view of the fact just

A. D. 27.   JOHN III.   71

John's disciples and the Jews about purifying.
26 And they came unto John and said unto him, Rabbi, he that was with thee beyond Jordan, ᵃ to whom thou barest witness, behold, the same baptizeth, and all *men* come to him.
27 John answered and said, ᵗ A man can receive nothing, except it be given him from heaven. Ye
28 yourselves bear me witness that I said, ᵘ I am not the Christ, but ˣ that I am sent before him. ʸ He
29 that hath the bride is the bridegroom; but ᶻ the friend of the bridegroom, which standeth and heareth him, rejoiceth greatly because of the bride-

ˢ ch. 1. 7, 15, 26–36
ᵗ 1 Chron. 28. 4, 5
Amos 7. 15; 1
Cor. 4. 7; 12. 11
15. 10; Gal. 1. 1
Heb. 5. 4; James
1. 17.
ᵘ ch. 1. 20, 27.
ˣ ch. 1. 23; Mal. 3.1.
ʸ Ps. 45. 9–17; Song
Sol. 3. 11; 4. 10;
Matt. 22.2; 2 Cor.
11. 2; Eph. 5. 25–
27; Rev. 21. 9.
ᶻ Song Sol. 5. 1;
Matt. 9. 15.

stated that Jesus and John were both baptizing. **A question,** or *a dispute,* **between some of John's disciples;** better, *on the part of John's disciples.* They seem to be the most eager in the dispute. **And the Jews.** According to the best manuscripts, *with a Jew.* This "Jew" was probably an emissary and representative of the Jewish authorities, who sought in this way to sow dissension between Jesus and the Baptist, and thus bring both into contempt. **About purifying;** doubtless with regard to the respective values of Jesus' and John's baptisms. Baptism is a rite emblematic, among other things, of moral purification. It would seem that the Jew gave preference to the baptism of Jesus; possibly, had been baptized by one of Christ's disciples. The envy and excitement of John's disciples may be seen from their somewhat exaggerated statement in the next verse: "All men come to him." There is nothing here to show that John's baptism was in its nature distinct from Christ's. We merely have an account of a dispute between a Jew and certain disciples of John. Compare note on Matt. 28:19 regarding the institution and development of gospel baptism.

26. **Rabbi.** See on ch. 1:38. **He that was with thee.** They do not name Jesus; their jealousy will not permit them. **Beyond Jordan,** as one of the subjects of thy baptism, Matt. 3:13. **To whom thou barest witness;** more exactly, *hast borne witness,* who was dependent upon thee for his introduction to the people. **Behold, the same baptizeth;** mark the tone of disparagement. **All men come to him.** Thus the party hostile to Jesus sought to excite John's jealousy toward him. Jesus must have been carrying on his work for some time if such numbers had already flocked to him. It is evident that John's fame had reached its culmination, and was beginning to decline. Jesus was not only drawing John's disciples from him, but was gaining a wider influence than John had ever possessed. It is evident from this that John's disciples were really troubled with the fact that Jesus was now exerting the greater influence and was attracting the greater number of disciples. They failed to understand the relation subsisting between John and Jesus. John has an opportunity to instruct them, and he improves it in the remaining verses of this chapter.

27. **John answered** them that he could not go beyond the bound of his mission as appointed by God. **A man can receive nothing, except it be given him from heaven.** "All this happens by God's appointment. No man can go beyond the limits of his divine commission. I cannot arrogate to myself what God has not given me. The growing influence of Jesus proclaims his calling to be from God."

28. He reminds them that he had always said that he was not the Christ, but Christ's forerunner. **Ye yourselves bear me witness that I said,** etc. This testimony John had already given, 1:23–27. **I am sent before him,** before Jesus as his forerunner.

29. John unfolds the relation he sustains to Jesus, being similar to that which the bridegroom's friend holds to the bridegroom. **He that hath the bride is the bridegroom.** The relation between Jehovah and his covenant people is often illustrated by the

groom's voice; this my joy therefore is fulfilled.
30 ᵃ He must increase, but I *must* decrease.
31 He that cometh from above ᵇ is above all; ᶜ he that is of the earth is earthly, and speaketh of the earth; ᵈ he that cometh from heaven is above all.
32 And ᵉ what he hath seen and heard, that he testi-

Heb. 1. 3–8; Rev. 19. 16. ᶜ 1 Cor. 15. 47, 48. ᵈ ch. 6. 33; Eph. 1. 21; Phil. 2. 9–11. ᵉ ch. 8. 26; 15. 15.

ᵃ Ps. 72. 8–17; Isa. 9. 7; Dan. 2. 34, 35, 44, 45; Col. 1. 18; Rev. 11. 15.
ᵇ ch. 1. 15, 27; 5. 22, 23; Matt. 28. 18; Rom. 9. 5;

marriage-bond. See Isa. 54 : 5; Hos. 2 : 19. All this is applied to Christ and his church, Eph. 5 : 32; Rev. 21 : 9. John the Baptist was the **friend of the bridegroom**, whose duty was to negotiate the preliminaries and arrange the marriage-feast. The repentant and believing among the people constituted the bride whom John had been making ready for the wedding—a wedding which should be consummated when the kingdom of Messiah was established. Jesus was the bridegroom, and to him, not to John, belonged the bride. *Who* **standeth and heareth him,** the bridegroom. Notice the lower position of the friend of the bridegroom, who stands at the service of the bridegroom to do his bidding, and counts it his joy to hear his voice. **Rejoiceth greatly because of the bridegroom's voice.** John, with prophetic insight, saw in the flocking of the multitude to Jesus the pledge of the "gathering of the nations" unto him, and the evidence that his preparatory work had not been in vain. All thought of jealousy, or envy, or disappointment was absent from his mind. Even though Jesus' influence overshadowed and destroyed his own, his joy was **fulfilled,** or made complete, by the growing triumphs of the Messiah's kingdom.

30. **He must increase, but I must decrease.** John's light, which, like that of the morning star, had "shone out so brilliantly, enlightening for a season the whole Jewish heavens, must fade away and sink out of sight in the beams of the rising Sun of righteousness.

31. Olshausen, Tholuck, and others regard the rest of the chapter as the meditation of the evangelist, but Alford, Meyer, and Lange take it as a continuation of John's discourse. The latter view seems preferable, for the following reasons: (1) There is no break in the connection. (2) The present tense continues to be used in vers. 31, 32, thus referring to the time when John was speaking. (3) These closing verses expand the idea which John had just uttered, "He must increase, but I must decrease." (4) John is speaking as a prophet, and these sentences form a fitting close of his prophetic words. John declares Jesus to be the divine and only Saviour. **He that cometh from above,** from heaven (see ver. 13), **is above all,** in dignity and office (Rom. 9 : 5; Eph. 1 : 21, 22), for Jesus is God as well as man, and by his divine nature is lifted far above every son of Adam. He that is of, *from*, **the earth,** a mere ordinary man—John is here speaking of himself—**is earthly,** in mind and thought, **and speaketh of the earth.** All his teachings must be limited and fettered by the earthliness of his nature. Even his "prophetic illumination was but darkness compared with that of Christ, the Light of the world." **He that cometh from heaven is above all,** and therefore he is no retailer at second-hand of heavenly instructions.

32. **And** is omitted by the oldest and best manuscripts. **What he hath seen and heard,** directly and in his own person (ver. 11), **that he testifieth,** or bears witness to. "He is not like human ministers, who only declare what they have been taught by the Holy Spirit and are inspired to communicate to others. As God, he declares with authority truths which he has seen and heard and known from all eternity with the Father," John 5 : 19, 30; 8 : 38. **And no man,** *no one*, **receiveth his testimony;** that is, comparatively. There is no contradiction between this verse and verse 26. In the one we have the excited and exaggerated statement of John's jealous disciples; in the other is John's "hyperbole of deep pain" at the blindness of the people. A few disciples had been led to follow Jesus, and many had received his baptism, ver. 26. But John

33	fieth; ᶠ and no man receiveth his testimony. He that hath received his testimony ᵍ hath set to his	ᶠ Rom. 10. 16-21. ᵍ Rom. 3. 3, 4; 1 John 5. 9, 10.
34	seal that God is true. ʰ For he whom God hath sent speaketh the words of God, for God giveth not	ʰ ch. 7. 16; 8. 26-28. ⁱ ch. 1. 16; Col. 1. 19.
35	the Spirit ⁱ by measure *unto him.* ʲ The Father loveth the Son, ᵏ and hath given all things into his	ʲ Isa. 42. 1; Matt. 3. 17. ᵏ Matt. 11. 27.
36	hand. ˡ He that believeth on the Son hath everlasting life; and he that believeth not the Son shall not see life, but ᵐ the wrath of God abideth on him.	ˡ 1 John 5. 10-13. ᵐ Gal. 3. 10; Eph. 5. 6; Heb. 10. 29.

saw how far even the disciples were from appreciating the greatness of Christ, and how small the number of followers was compared with the multitude of unbelievers. "Do you say, 'All men come to him'? Where, then, are the priests and rulers? Nay, the nation still rejects him."

33. All who receive Christ's testimony attest God's truth. **He that hath received,** referring specially to such of John's disciples as had gone to Jesus and accepted his testimony, **hath set to his seal,** rather, *hath set his seal,* **that God is true,** that he is a God of truth, and that Christ is worthy of confidence. No document was held to be authentic in the East unless a seal was attached to it. Jesus was the ambassador and representative of God, and all were called to believe and follow him. This believing and following were like putting one's seal to the record or testimony of God, certifying that it was true.

34. **For he whom God hath sent speaketh the words of God;** not human words, like those of John and the prophets, but divine words, so that those who heard them heard the words of God himself. See Deut. 18 : 18. **For God giveth not the Spirit by measure unto him.** According to highest critical authorities, *For he giveth not the Spirit by measure,* without limit, thus making the expression general, having reference, however, to Christ, since the next verse is explanatory of this. It is a rabbinical saying that prophets received the Spirit by measure. Jesus had not the Holy Spirit as a partial, scanty, transient possession, but it "abode upon him" in inexhaustible and immeasurable abundance. "The Spirit dwelt in him, not as in a vessel, but as in a fountain, ay, as in a bottomless ocean."

35. **The Father loveth the Son, and hath given,** etc. The power of Christ is unlimited; nothing in heaven or earth is excepted from his control, Matt. 11 : 27; 28 : 18; John 13 : 3. This results from the eternal love of the Father for the Son, ch. 17 : 24. Both this love and this communication are perfect, because the Father and the Son are for ever one.

36. **He that believeth on the Son hath everlasting life.** See on vers. 15, 16. Since the relation of Jesus to the Father is so intimate and sublime, the consequences are unspeakably important. To believe on the divine Saviour, God manifest in the flesh, is to have everlasting life as a present possession, and heaven begun below. **And he that believeth not,** or, rather, *He that disbelieveth,* and hence disobeyeth **the Son,** including the idea not only of inward unbelief, but of outward insubordination. Unbelief implies disobedience, and disobedience unbelief. **Shall not see life,** the true freedom, harmony, intense activity, and satisfied existence of a soul that enjoys the favor of God, is filled with his Spirit, and lives in constant communion with him. Since it is only by union with Christ that man can come into this relation to God, it follows that "he that hath not the Son hath not life" (1 John 5 : 12), and if he remains in this state can never "see life." **But the wrath of God abideth on him.** How much this expression is like John the Baptist, who warned the people to flee from the coming wrath! Matt. 3 : 7-10; Mark 1 : 7-9; Luke 3 : 17. All men, being born destitute of love to God, are "by nature children of wrath," Eph. 2 : 3. Their only way of escape from this wrath of God is by believing on Christ. If they refuse to believe, the whole weight of God's righteous anger remains upon them. As eternal life is the present possession of all believers,

and only waits to be unfolded in this world and after death, so the wrath of God is the present possession of all who do not obey Christ—a wrath which only waits the day of its final revelation in their complete and awful destruction, Rom. 2 : 5; 2 Thess. 1 : 7-9. This testimony of John to the fearful consequences of rejecting Christ is like the " final peal of thunder from Mount Sinai." It shows that there is wrath under the gospel as well as under the law.

We are come to the close of our Lord's early ministry in Judæa. Let us glance a moment at his work there. "As he did not himself baptize, it is a question how his time was spent. Probably he taught the crowds that came to his baptism, but there is no hint that he healed the sick or wrought any miracles. We can scarce doubt that he went up to Jerusalem to attend the two great feasts during this period, that of pentecost and that of tabernacles, and here he must have come more or less into contact with priests and Pharisees. It does not appear, however, that he went about from place to place to teach, or that he taught in any of the synagogues. Still, it is not improbable that before he began to baptize, or at intervals during his labors, he may have visited many parts of Judæa, and have noted and tested the spiritual condition of the people. It may be, also, that at this time he formed those friendships of which we find later traces, as that with Joseph of Arimathea and that with Mary and Martha."

Practical Remarks.

1. Beware of coveting too eagerly to live much in the public eye; it greatly restrains any open and radical expression of the religious nature, vers. 1, 2; ch. 7 : 48; 1 Cor. 1 : 26-31.
2. Many, when at first convicted of sin and a need of a Saviour, would seek him without having others know it, ver. 2.
3. The true way to deal with inquirers is with the most incisive directness, ver. 3; Matt. 19 : 20, 21; Luke 9 : 57-62.
4. True spiritual life and religious experience begins with the new birth, ver. 3.
5. We are all by nature destitute of love to God, and consequently our perceptions of truth are blunted and our aims perverted and selfish, vers. 5, 6; John 6 : 63.
6. Mysteries in religion are to be expected, since we find them in all the works of God, vers. 4, 8; 1 Cor. 1 : 25.
7. No outward reformation or transient emotion can avail us without a radical change in the affections and disposition of the heart, vers. 5, 6.
8. Only the Holy Spirit can reach and turn back into their proper channels the deep currents that now flow toward selfishness and sin, vers. 5-7; ch. 1 : 13; Rom. 7 : 25.
9. Because God alone can regenerate the soul, it does not follow that there is nothing for us to do, vers. 5-7; ch. 6 : 29; 1 John 3 : 23; Phil. 2 : 12.
10. The work of the Holy Spirit is not arbitrary or lawless, any more than the blowing of the winds. Some things about the winds we know, so that we may voyage across the ocean by attending to them. Some things with regard to the work of the Spirit, God reveals to us, so that we may avail ourselves of his help. "Turn you at my reproof," says God; " behold, I will pour out my Spirit upon you," Prov. 1 : 23. God will give the Holy Spirit freely "to them that ask him," Luke 11 : 13. If we believe on Christ we shall be saved, vers. 15, 16. It is our immediate duty, therefore, to turn to God, to ask for the Spirit, to accept of Jesus as our Saviour, leaving the matter of our regeneration trustfully in the hands of God, ver. 8; Deut. 29 : 29.
11. A want of experimental knowledge of the things of the Spirit is an aggravated sin in those that are made heads over Israel, vers. 9, 10; Rom. 2 : 17-23; 1 Cor. 9 : 26, 27.
12. Since Jesus knew the truth he taught, all should believe it, vers. 11, 13.
13. A heavenly life here is the first and best evidence we can present to man of a heaven hereafter, vers. 12, 13.
14. There are two sides to truth, the earthly and the heavenly—one seen from the human point of view, the other from the divine. Both should be included, and neither one excluded, in our theology, ver. 12.
15. The cross the great central fact and truth in the scheme of redemption, ver. 14.
16. Pre-eminently here and every-

Jesus, on his way to Galilee, discourses with a Samaritan woman.

IV. WHEN, therefore, ^a the Lord knew how the Pharisees had heard that Jesus made and ^o baptized more

^a Luke 1.76; 2.11; 19.31; 1 Cor. 15. 47; 2 Cor. 4. 5.
^o ch. 3. 22, 26.

where how vital to salvation is this one thing—putting faith in Christ! vers. 15, 16, 18, 36.

17. If we reject the light and remain in our sins, we incur not only the guilt of reaffirming our past decision against God, but of refusing the only possible salvation. It is not the greatness of our sins that prevents our salvation—it is not any unwillingness of God to bestow his Spirit upon us; it is only our resistance to God's mercy and our refusal to accept of Christ, vers. 19-21.

18. The love of God is the great fountain from which came forth the purpose of salvation and all the blessings of the atonement, ver. 16.

19. The reason why sinners do not believe is that they love sin and do evil, and the truth condemns them, vers. 18-21.

20. The mission of Christ is not condemnation, but salvation, vers. 17, 18.

21. If we dislike the religion of Christ, the difficulty is in our own hearts; we are under the power of sin, vers. 19, 20.

22. A truly upright man does not dread examination, but rather seeks to compare his character with the tests of God's word, ver. 21.

23. Beware of those who would repress conscientious inquiry by saying, " The question of baptism is only a dispute about a little water." Real baptism has always required " much water," vers. 22, 23.

24. In John the Baptist we see how great the knowledge of Christ which God's Spirit can give. The same Spirit can enlighten our darkness and enable us to see the glory and power of Christ, vers. 25-29; ch. 15 : 13-15.

25. Men are often more ready to dispute about rites than to sit at the feet of Jesus and learn of him and follow his example, ver. 25.

26. Personal humiliation is a matter of rejoicing if Jesus be exalted thereby. A true knowledge of him will give us that unselfish devotion which was possessed by John, vers. 27-30; Phil. 1 : 29.

27. Contentment with our lot and faithful performance of duty will most contribute to our usefulness and our real honor, vers. 28-30.

28. We should rejoice when great numbers come to Jesus, though a less number may follow us, ver. 29.

29. To resign cherished plans, to renounce success, and to give place to others, form one of the severest tests of character, vers. 29, 30.

30. The truths of the gospel possess divine authority, vers. 31-36.

31. God demands that we confirm his testimony by accepting and following the Saviour, vers. 31-33; 1 John 5 : 10.

32. The most practical evidence of the truth of the gospel is found in the experience of its doctrines, ver. 33 ; ch. 7 : 17.

33. Christ alone is an absolutely perfect Teacher. His instructions are the instructions of God, vers. 33, 34.

34. Christ is the Lord and Lawgiver of the new dispensation, ver. 35 ; Matt. 11 : 27 ; Eph. 1 : 22.

35. Each one of us has either life or death as his present possession, vers. 18, 36 ; ch. 5 : 24.

CHAPTER IV.

It was a special design of John's Gospel to present some of the most remarkable discourses of our Lord, both public and private. In the preceding chapter we have his discourse to Nicodemus concerning the entrance into his kingdom. In this chapter we have that to the Samaritan woman, in which he presents his infinite grace as the Saviour of the world. Jesus leaves Judæa and returns to Galilee through Samaria (vers. 1-4), rests on his journey at Jacob's well near Shechem (5, 6), converses with a Samaritan woman (7-38), abides at the city two days, and many Samaritans believe on him (39-42). Jesus arrives in Galilee and teaches publicly (43-45), and heals, without seeing him, the son of a nobleman at Capernaum (46-54).

1-4. JESUS CLOSES HIS EARLY JUDÆAN MINISTRY, AND DEPARTS INTO

JOHN IV. A. D. 27

2 disciples than John (though Jesus himself baptized
3 not, but his disciples), he left Judæa, and departed
4 again into Galilee. And he must needs go through
5 Samaria. Then cometh he to a city of Samaria,
which is called Sychar, near to the parcel of ground

GALILEE THROUGH SAMARIA. The object of the Judæan ministry was not to gather crowds of disciples, but to bring the nation, *as represented by its rulers*, to repentance. Jesus' baptism was therefore a baptism of repentance, like that of John. Jesus continued this work of baptizing in Judæa until it was perfectly evident that the authorities had determined to be influenced as little by his success in winning disciples as they had been by his miracles and his cleansing of the temple. When he found that his success only increased their hostility, and threatened to draw down on him greater enmity than had been shown to John the Baptist, he retired to Galilee.

1. **When therefore the Lord knew how,** *that,* **the Pharisees,** the party most opposed to John the Baptist (Luke 7 : 30), **had heard that Jesus made and baptized more disciples than John;** literally, *makes and baptizes,* being the words of the report which the Pharisees heard. How Jesus knew we are not informed. His disciples may have told him, yet Jesus knew the hearts of men, and needed not any to tell him, ch. 2 : 25. This increase of disciples threatened to cause them more trouble than John had ever given.

2. **Though Jesus himself baptized not, but his disciples.** This being parenthetical, *Jesus* is used instead of *he*. Several reasons suggest themselves why Jesus *did not baptize:* (1) Baptism in water was a ministerial act to be performed by his followers, while baptism in the Holy Spirit he reserved for himself, Matt. 3 : 11 ; Mark 1 : 8 ; Luke 3 : 16 ; (2) As Jesus would have had to baptize unto himself, it was more fitting that his disciples should do it. Baptism was a work of the servants, not of the Master, and Jesus would not allow the minds of any to be diverted from his words by priding themselves upon being baptized by his hands, 1 Cor. 1 : 17.

3. **He left Judæa.** See on ch. 3 : 22. **Departed again into Galilee,** knowing that the enmity of the Jewish authorities would otherwise be too soon turned against him. This departure was all the more proper, as it was now at the end of November or in December (see ch. 4 : 35), and open-air gatherings of the people were rendered difficult on account of the season. **Galilee.** See on ch. 1 : 43. This verse corresponds with Matt. 4 : 12 ; Mark 1 : 14 ; Luke 4 : 14. Between the 11th and 12th verses of the 4th chapter of Matthew occurred the events related in John 1 : 15 to 4 : 1. Compare *Author's Harmony,* §§ 22-31.

4. **Samaria** took its name from its capital city, Samaria. According to Josephus (*Jewish War,* iii. 3, 4), it lay between Judæa and Galilee, commencing in the north at a village called Ginea, on the southern border of the plain of Esdraelon, and extending southward to the toparchy of Acrabatha, in the lower part of the territory of Ephraim. This Ginea, or En Gannim (meaning "the fountain of gardens"), has been properly conjectured as the village which rejected Jesus, Luke 9 : 53. **He must needs go through,** etc. There were three routes from Judæa to Galilee: first, a westerly route, along the coast of the Mediterranean ; secondly, an easterly route, the other side of Jordan through Peræa ; and thirdly, a central route, through Samaria. Scrupulous Jews, in order to avoid Samaria, used to take the second of these. Jesus, however, was above this prejudice, and took the third, as the most direct from the place of his last sojourn.

5-42. JESUS CONVERSES WITH A SAMARITAN WOMAN. Recorded only by John.

5. **Then cometh he to,** the neighborhood of, **a city of Samaria, which is called Sychar,** believed by many biblical scholars to be the ancient Shechem. See Gen. 33 : 18 ; but see below. It was beautifully situated at the highest point of the narrow valley (running east and west) that separates Mount Gerizim and Mount Ebal. It was about forty miles, or two days'

6 ᵖ that Jacob gave to his son, Joseph. Now Jacob's well was there. Jesus, therefore, being ᑫ wearied with *his* journey, sat thus on the well; *and* it was about the sixth hour.

ᵖ Gen. 33. 19; 48.
22; Josh. 24. 32.
ᑫ ch. 19. 28; Matt.
4. 2; Luke 9. 58;
2 Cor. 8. 9; Heb.
2. 17; 4. 15.

journey, from Jerusalem. See below. **Near to the parcel**, etc. See Gen. 33 : 19; 48 : 22; Josh. 24 : 32. "The position of Sychar is very clearly indicated in the Gospel of John. It was 'near to the parcel of ground that Jacob gave to his son Joseph.' And 'Jacob's well was there.' The well was in the 'parcel of ground,' and it exists to this day in the entrance of the valley of Nabulus, at the foot of Mount Gerizim. But the well is a mile and a half from the site of Shechem, now Nabulus, and the question arises, If Sychar and Shechem were identical, could it be described as *near* the well, while at such a distance? The word translated *near* is indefinite. It is difficult to say what distance would be called 'near.' It would appear, however, that the city must have been a good way off, for the disciples had gone there to buy bread, and they were absent some time. It has been said that, as the women came from the city to draw water at this well, Sychar could not have occupied the site of Nabulus, because in that town there are numerous fountains. To one conversant with Eastern life and habits, such an argument has no weight. The mere fact of the well having been Jacob's would have given it virtue in the estimation of the old Samaritans. And even independent of its associations, some little superiority in the quality of the water would have attracted people to it from a still greater distance. . . . Various theories have been advanced as to the origin and meaning of the name Sychar. It has been suggested that the Jews applied it as a by-name in scorn to the Samaritan capital."—J. L. PORTER, *Alexander's Kitto's Cyclopædia.*

But Thomson, and others, with good reason identify Sychar with the little village of Askar, on the south-eastern declivity of Mount Ebal, about a half mile north-east from Jacob's well. Our Lord was on his way to Galilee. The great road runs past the mouth of Wady Nabulus. Jacob's well is on the southern side of the opening and Askar about a half mile distant on the northern side. The main road passes quite close to both. Shechem was a mile and a half distant, and it is not very probable that the woman would have walked that distance from a city, where there was an abundance of water, to draw water from this deep well. It is said that the etymology is against Askar, but this objection is not of much weight, since in the Samaritan dialect there was a confusion of letters. But it is asked, why did not Jesus continue his journey a little farther to Askar, instead of sending his disciples to the city to buy? To this it may be replied, Jesus was weary, and besides he had a purpose, as the event showed, in the coming of the woman, and his conversation, which was more to him than food, ver. 6, 32.

6. **Now**, rather, *And*, **Jacob's well was there**, so called from the tradition mentioned in ver. 12. This well, now choked with stones and rubbish, is still visible—the only spot in Palestine where we can say with certainty, "Just here the feet of Jesus trod." The well is situated one and a half miles from the present town, "on the end of a low spur or swell running out from the northeastern base of Mount Gerizim, and is still fifteen or twenty feet above the level of the plain below."

"Jacob's well is six minutes' ride from Joseph's tomb. It is almost under Gerizim (but not in sight of Nabulus, though but fifteen minutes' ride from it). It is on a knoll—really a spur of Gerizim, eighteen feet high — shaped like a bowl bottom side up. A rickety lodge, or booth, was near by, which I at first took to mark the well, but there is absolutely nothing to mark it on approaching, and I did not discover its locality till quite upon it. The exact position and external appearance are often misrepresented. . . . Approaching, we find an irregular open space, or chamber, cut out some six feet in the ground, and walled up on the sides. It was originally nearly square—say 17 by 15 feet. An archway once spanned the chamber. Over, it, too, once stood a

7 There cometh a woman of Samaria to draw water:
8 Jesus saith unto her, Give me to drink. (For his disciples were gone away unto the city to buy meat.)
9 Then saith the woman of Samaria unto him, How is it that thou, being a Jew, askest drink of me, which

little chapel. In the centre of this chamber is the well. Heaps of rubbish and stones cover over and entirely conceal its mouth. Seeing this, most of our party rode on. I was not satisfied with a glance, and so, alighting, I sprang down into the chamber and began to uncover the well, lifting away stone after stone, until I was able to look down in. It is 9 feet in diameter, and for a distance of some 12 feet is carefully walled up. Thence downward it is solid rock. By dropping in pebbles I found it to be dry (there is water only in the wet months), and I judged by the time of the descent of the stones that it cannot be now over some 60 feet deep, perhaps less. Maundrell, in 1697, found it to be 105 feet deep. A dozen years ago an Arab was let down into the well, and by measuring the rope it was found to be 75 feet deep, and quite dry at the bottom. The same flutings which I had observed in the curbing of the well of Abraham at Beersheba are found here. They furrow the sides of the well for some feet, being, of course, more deeply cut at the lip. They give force to the saying of the woman, 'Thou hast *nothing to draw with, and the well is deep*,' John 4 : 11. And why was a woman from Sychar down here for water, when there was plenty of it *there?* Because it was cooler than the spring-water, and because (perhaps) a special sacredness was supposed to attach to this well of Jacob. Then, too, if she actually lived in the city, it may have been in that part extending farthest down in this direction. At most, it was near by—say a mile and a half off."—DR. FISH, *Bible Lands Illustrated*, pp. 454–457.

Jesus . . . wearied . . . sat thus; that is, just as he was, tired and hungry with the long day's travel. On the well, its curbstone, or projecting margin. About the sixth hour, *i. e.*, 6 P. M. John uniformly uses the Roman method of computation, according to which the day began, as with us, at midnight, and the hours were reckoned from midnight and noon, while the other evangelists adopt the Jewish method of reckoning from sunrise. See John 19 : 14 and Mark 15 : 25. The common time for drawing water was toward evening. See on ch. 1 : 39.

7. There cometh a woman of Samaria, not the city but the country of Samaria; her city was Sychar, vers. 5, 28, to draw water, probably after the Eastern custom, with a pitcher upon her head. Women were the water-carriers. It was a strange sight when the disciples saw a *man* bearing a pitcher of water, Mark 14 : 13; Luke 22 : 10. (See HACKETT'S *Illustrations*, p. 97; FISH'S *Bible Lands Illustrated*, p. 112.) Jesus watched her as she let down her vessel by a cord, and waited till the full pitcher rested upon the mouth of the well. Then he saith unto her, Give me to drink. Jesus knew that the asking of a favor like this would open her heart to receive his words. He was indeed thirsty, yet was more desirous of giving than receiving. He asks for water, that he may the better give the water of life, vers. 10–14. In regard to Oriental customs it is not considered "improper for a man though a stranger, to ask a woman to let down her pitcher and give him to drink." —DR. VAN LENNEP, *Bible Lands*, p. 44.

8. For his disciples were gone away unto the city to buy meat, rather *food*. The city, Sychar, was more than a mile away from the well, which was on the route. Jesus did not go with them to Sychar, because it lay to the westward of his course. His purpose was apparently to proceed directly northward after the return of the disciples. This verse is thrown in to explain why the disciples were not with Jesus. It is not necessary, however, to put it in a parenthesis.

9. How is it that thou, being a Jew, etc. She recognized him as a Jew either by his speech or his dress. There was a tone of surprise and triumph in her reply, for the Jews held the Samaritans as heretics and enemies, and abstained from all intercourse with them. The Samaritans, on their part,

am a woman of Samaria? (For ʳthe Jews have no ʳ 2 Kings 17. 24, etc.; Neh. 4. 1, 2; Luke 9. 52, 53; Acts 10. 28.
dealings with the Samaritans.)
10 Jesus answered and said unto her, ˢ If thou knewest
ᵗ the gift of God, ᵘ and who it is that saith to thee, ˢ Ps. 9. 10. ᵗ ch. 3. 16.
Give me to drink; ᵛ thou wouldest have asked of him, ᵘ vers. 25, 26; ch. 9.
35-37. ᵛ Ps. 10. 17; Luke 11. 9, 10; 23. 42, 43.

returned this hatred, Luke 9 : 53. "Necessity," she would say, "can compel this Jew to ask drink even of me, a Samaritan." **Have no dealings with**, rather, *do not associate with*, have no friendly intercourse with, *Samaritans*. "This ill-will, however, did not extend beyond familiar intercourse, for in such matters as buying and selling intercourse was allowed. This is manifest both from Jewish writers and from the conduct of our Lord's disciples on the present occasion."—C. C. TITTMANN, *Com. on John*. **Samaritans.** The Samaritans were the descendants of heathen colonists from Babylonia, Cuthah, Ava, Hamath, and Sepharvaim, whom Shalmanezer, king of Assyria, sent into the country after he had taken Samaria and carried away the better portion of the ten tribes, and of the remnant of Israelites left behind, with whom they intermarried. A mixed people, as well as a mixed religion, was the result, 2 Kings 17 : 24-41. On the return of the Jews from the Babylonish captivity the Samaritans requested permission to assist them in rebuilding the temple. This they were denied, after which they opposed the Jews and greatly retarded their work, Ezra 4 : 1-5; Neh. 2 : 10, 19; 4 : 1-3. Later still, Manasseh, son of the high priest, married the daughter of Sanballat, the governor of Samaria, and Nehemiah would not allow him to perform the functions of the priest's office, but drove him from the city, Neh. 13 : 28. Accordingly, the Samaritans, under Sanballat, reared a temple on Mount Gerizim, and Manasseh acted there as high priest. This served to deepen the hatred between the Jews and the Samaritans, and render it perpetual, John 4 : 9; 8 : 48. The temple on Mount Gerizim was destroyed by Hyrcanus about 129 B. C., but the Samaritans still regarded the place as sacred and as the proper place of national worship, John 4 : 20, 21. They rejected all the sacred books of the Jews except the Pentateuch. The feeling of the Jews toward them is illustrated by their answer to

the denunciation of Jesus against their formalism: "Thou art a Samaritan, and hast a devil," ch. 8 : 48. The Samaritans had given up the continuance of God's revelations in the prophets, and so God was no longer an object of true knowledge or worship. A few families of the Samaritans now remain at Nablous, the ancient Shechem. They have a very ancient manuscript of the Pentateuch, are strict observers of the Law, keeping the Sabbath and the ancient festivals, and are expecting the Messiah.
10. **If thou knewest the gift of God,** salvation, spiritual and eternal life, which comes through me, the Messiah (ver. 25), **thou wouldest have asked.** Jesus doubtless saw in her a certain readiness for the truth, which led him thus to converse with her. He drew her attention to the fact that he, the maker of a request, could *bestow* a far greater thing than he *asked*. **And he would have given thee living water,** life-giving water, signifying the blessings of divine grace, Ps. 36 : 8; Isa. 41, 17, 18; Jer. 2 : 13, etc.
"The expression *living water* sometimes means water that is alive, or fresh water, bubbling up from a fountain and flowing, in contrast to water which stands collected in cisterns. The corresponding Hebrew words are rendered by the Greek translators of the Old Testament sometimes *living water* sometimes *springing water*. In this sense the woman understood the term. But our Lord employed it differently, as meaning *life-giving water*, and he meant to convey a hint of something that could invigorate *the soul* and make it truly happy, as if he had said, 'Thou wouldest have asked of me that which would refresh and bless thy soul.' Living water here signifies the whole sum of blessings which Christ furnishes for renewing the souls of men and making them tranquil and happy. It also signifies the happiness itself which is bestowed.
"This explanation accords with the

JOHN IV. A. D. 27.

11 and he would have given thee ˣ living water. ʸ The
woman saith unto him, Sir, thou hast nothing to
draw with, and the well is deep; from whence then
12 hast thou that living water? ᶻ Art thou greater than
our father Jacob, which gave us the well, and drank
thereof himself, and his children, and his cattle?
13 Jesus answered and said unto her, ᵃ Whosoever

ˣ Jer. 2. 13; Zech. 13. 1; 14. 8.
ʸ 1 Cor. 2. 14.
ᶻ ch. 8. 53.
ᵃ ch. 6. 27, 49; Ps. 49. 16-20; Prov. 23. 5; Isa. 65. 13, 14; Col. 3. 2; 1 Tim. 6. 17.

---

universal usage of the sacred writers, and particularly of our Lord himself, . . . for in another conversation, recorded in John 7 : 38, . . . this figure obviously expresses both the abundance and perpetuity of the happiness which a believer enjoys, very nearly as in the fourteenth verse of this chapter he says the believer's happiness is like 'water springing up into everlasting life.' In Rev. 7 : 17 he is said to feed the blessed in the future life, and to lead them to *living fountains of waters;* that is, to furnish means of happiness—happiness most abundant and ever-enduring. In Rev. 21 : 6 and 22 : 17 he promises that he will give of *the fountain of the water of life,* and that the pious shall receive the water of life; that is, happiness, and whatever can make them day by day more and more happy. . . . God is called *the fountain of living waters* in contrast to idols, inasmuch as he is the Author and Giver of all bliss. See Jer. 2 : 13; 17 : 13. In the 36th Psalm David is admiring the immensity of God's kindness. 'They shall be abundantly satisfied,' he says, 'with the fatness [the rich bounties] of thy house; and thou shalt make them drink of the river of thy pleasures.' He then adds: 'For with thee is the fountain of life; in thy light shall we see light;' that is, thou art the Author and Giver of all happiness. From thee, most blessed One, there flows to us every kind of bliss. Hence men are said to 'draw water out of the wells [fountains] of salvation' (Isa. 12 : 3); that is, to seek and to receive from God happiness of all kinds. In Zech. 14 : 8 also is this promise: 'In that day living waters shall go out from Jerusalem;' that is, from Jerusalem there shall go forth over the whole earth every variety of blessings. Such being the usage in regard to this term, we think that by *living water* in the passage under consideration are meant all the advantages furnished by our Lord for attaining true happiness, and even that happiness itself."—C. C. TITTMANN.

11. **Sir, thou hast nothing to draw with.** Bucket and rope were not kept there for common use. Whoever would draw must bring them. **The well is deep.** See on ver. 6. The well was over a hundred feet deep. The woman knew that Jesus could not draw water from this well. She took his words literally, seeing in them only an unseemly depreciation of the well hallowed by ages, and concluded, perhaps, that he would give her water from some other source. **From whence then hast thou that,** rather *the,* **living water,** *the springing water,* bursting from the veins of the earth. *Whence,* if not here? None can be cooler, purer, or better than this.

12. **Art thou greater than our father Jacob,** etc. The Samaritans were in the habit of tracing back their race to Jacob; hence she speaks of him as *father.* She first speaks of the well as having been opened by Jacob. This well was good enough for Jacob. Dost thou make thyself greater than he? Next she hints at the abundance and excellence of the water, saying, Jacob **drank thereof himself, and his children, and his cattle.** To disesteem such a well and seek another would indeed seem impious to the mind of a Samaritan. The question suggests that the woman may have had in mind the One greater than Jacob, without suspecting that Jesus was he. This is in harmony with the fact that Jesus proceeds to expand the metaphor, that she might comprehend its spiritual meaning.

13. Jesus, perceiving that this woman was teachable, replies, contrasting the water of the well with that water which refreshes the soul, **Whosoever,** or *every one that,* **drinketh of this water shall thirst again.** The water of the well refreshes only for a time; it is the symbol of all earthly gifts.

A. D. 27.   JOHN IV.   81

14 drinketh of this water shall thirst again; but [b] whosoever drinketh of the water that I shall give him shall
never thirst; but the water that I shall give him [c] shall
be in him a well of water springing up into everlast-
15 ing life. [d] The woman saith unto him, Sir, give me
this water, that I thirst not, neither come hither to
draw.
16 Jesus saith unto her, Go, call thy husband, and
17 come hither. The woman answered and said, I have
no husband.

[b] ch. 6. 35, 58; 11. 26; Rev. 7. 16.
[c] ch. 7. 38; 14. 16–19; Rom. 8. 16, 17; 2 Cor. 1. 22; Eph. 4. 30.
[d] ch. 6. 34; 17. 2, 3; Ps. 4. 6; Rom. 6. 23; 8. 5; James 4. 3; 1 John 5. 20.

All temporal good gives but a temporary satisfaction. It should be noted that Jesus does not answer the woman directly whether he was greater than Jacob. She was not yet prepared for that. He did not undervalue that water, for he had asked for it himself. But he wished to show her that he had that to give which was worthy of still higher esteem. His words would soon reveal to her his greatness.

14. THE CONTRAST MORE CLEARLY PRESENTED. **Whosoever drinketh,** whosoever has tasted and got under the influence of this water, **shall never thirst.** Thirst often signifies a sense of need, a strong desire, *a longing for* real good and true happiness, Ps. 63 : 1; Matt. 5 : 6; ch. 6 : 35; 7 : 37. So, *not to thirst* is often spoken of that settled satisfaction which a person enjoys who is truly blessed, Isa. 49 : 10. To *drink this water* is to receive these blessings by faith, ch. 6 : 35. This water slakes the spirit's thirst, and slakes it for ever. Not of course as though one draught of it would do this; it is he who drinks, and who continues to drink, that shall not thirst any more. **Shall be in him a well,** or *shall become in him a fountain,* **of water, springing up into everlasting life**—a fountain so plentiful that it bursts forth and springs up on high, most abundant, most enduring, and most complete, filling the soul with present and enduring happiness. This life will be no mere external possession, but an inward and permanent one, making the soul itself a perpetual fountain. "Death not only will not interrupt this life, but will rather bring it to perfection." And this unspeakable blessing it belongs to Jesus only to bestow. "To take another image : the spark which goes forth from the fire of the Redeemer becomes in every human breast a self-existent flame.

After Christ has brought into being to individuals the communion with God, it advances in all these individuals to a consummation," ch. 8 : 12.—THOLUCK. *15.* **Sir, give me this water,** etc. She still seems to take our Lord's words literally, and misses their spiritual sense. But she is no longer indignant that Jacob's well, though so sacred to her, was undervalued; nor did she treat lightly the professions of Jesus, though a Jew. **That I thirst not, neither come hither,** *all this way hither,* half a mile, **to draw.** She would be free from thirst and the drudgery of her water-carrying. Compare the request in ch. 6 : 34. Perhaps her words meant more than they expressed. Yet the words of Jesus to her will be vain unless she be roused to see that her spiritual needs are far greater than her earthly needs. So the Saviour applies himself to awaken in her a deep sense of sin, and discourses to her as to one ready to receive the truth.

16. Jesus turns the conversation to another subject, thereby showing his divine knowledge and his skill in reaching and probing the heart. **Go, call thy husband,** etc. Jesus knew that she had not a husband, as appears from ver. 18. Why, then, the command? To prove to her his divine authority and arouse her conscience. The command brings up at once the shamefulness and guilt of her life. "Chrysostom notices with great propriety the modesty and wisdom of our Lord, in that he did not instantly expose to her view her whole life, but previously sought an occasion for doing so."—C. C. TITTMANN. At first he simply says, "Go, call thy husband," and by degrees he passes on, till she can say, He "told me all things that ever I did," ver. 29.

17. **I have no husband,** that is, no lawful husband. A frank and sad con-

4 *

18 Jesus said unto her, Thou hast well said, I have no husband: *for thou hast had five husbands; and he whom thou now hast is not thy husband: in that
19 saidst thou truly. The woman saith unto him, Sir,
20 ʲI perceive that thou art a prophet. Our fathers worshipped in ᵍthis mountain; and ye say, that in ʰJerusalem is the place where men ought to worship.
21 Jesus saith unto her, Woman, believe me, the hour cometh, ⁱwhen ye shall neither in this mountain, nor

* ch. 1. 42, 47, 48; 2. 24, 25.
ᶠ ch. 1. 49; 6. 14; 7. 40; 2 Kings 6. 12; Luke 7. 16, 39; 24. 19.
ᵍ Gen. 12. 6, 7; 33. 18-20; Judg. 9. 7.
ʰ Deut. 12. 5, 11; 1 Kings 9. 3; 2 Chron. 6. 6; 7. 12, 16; Ps. 132. 13, 14.

ⁱ Mal. 1. 11; 1 Tim. 2. 8.

---

fession of a troubled conscience, yet mingled with a desire to conceal her criminality. It showed her sincerity, that she would not call the man with whom she lived her husband. Jesus replies, **Thou hast well said,** her truthfulness and frankness were commendable, **I have no husband.** In quoting her reply the position of the words is changed in the original, so that the emphasis is on *husband.* He gently rebukes her life, and at the same time shows his omniscience.

18. **Thou hast had five husbands.** This is generally regarded as either an instance of the "degrading facility of divorce among the Samaritans as well as the Jews," or indicative of unfaithfulness and desertion on her own part. The five husbands, however, must be regarded as lawful husbands, and are here plainly distinguished from the sixth as unlawful. Some of these five may have died or been divorced. Still, it doubtless implied inordinate desire and undue haste. Yet the sin here emphasized is the fact that **he whom thou now hast is not thy husband.** She had not been lawfully married to him. Perhaps, also, she had deserted her last husband, or he had not been properly divorced from her. Dr. Van Lennep (*Bible Lands,* p. 557), referring to the terrible frequency of divorces among Jews and Muslims at the present day, says, "We have known a man not forty years of age who had successively married and put away a dozen wives. . . . Women, too, not far advanced in age, are sometimes met with who have been married to a dozen men in succession." Jesus showed her that all the incidents of her wicked life were perfectly known to him.

19. She is neither indignant nor irritated with his reply. Her estimation of his character is greatly raised, and she says, **Sir, I perceive that thou art a prophet.** This was really an admission of her guilt. She did not yet seem to suspect his true character as the Messiah, though the Samaritans viewed the Messiah mainly as a prophet, ver. 29. Feeling that such knowledge could come only from God, and probably too desiring to turn the conversation from so unpleasant a topic respecting herself, yet more especially with a hope that this divinely-commissioned prophet might teach her the true way back to God and to virtue, she referred to the great question at issue between the Jews and the Samaritans.

20. **Our fathers,** probably her Samaritan ancestors who erected a rival temple on Mount Gerizim in the time of Nehemiah. See on ver. 9. Although this had been destroyed B. C. 129 by John Hyrcanus, an altar still remained, and upon it they sacrificed. **Worshipped,** offered that homage which consists in sacrifices and public ceremonies. **In,** or *on,* **this mountain,** Mount Gerizim, which rose before them to a height of 800 feet. **Ye say, that in Jerusalem . . . men ought to worship.** God had chosen Jerusalem as the place of his sanctuary (see 1 Kings 8 : 48; 9 : 3; 11 : 13; Ps. 76 : 2), but the Samaritans, by falsely reading "Gerizim" instead of "Ebal" in Deut. 27 : 4, maintained that this mountain was the place appointed by Moses.

21. Our Lord so replies as to avoid any discussion. He teaches her that the place of worship need be no longer discussed; that a great change as to public worship was at hand; that while the Jews had the right in this controversy, for to them had been committed the "oracles of God," and the worship of the Samaritans was a mixture of error and superstition (ver. 22), yet this question, after all, was

22 yet at Jerusalem, worship the Father. Ye worship ye know not what; ¹ we know what we worship; for 23 ᵐ salvation is of the Jews. But the hour cometh, and now is, when the true worshippers shall worship the Father in ⁿ spirit ᵒ and in truth; ᵖ for the Father seek-

ᵏ 2 Kings 17. 27. 29, 41; Ezra 4 2. 3.
¹ 2 Chron. 13. 10-12; Ps. 147. 19; Rom. 3. 2.
ᵐ Gen. 49. 10; Isa. 2. 3; Zech. 8. 20-23; Luke 24. 47; Rom. 9. 4, 5. ⁿ Rom. 8. 15; Gal. 4. 6; Eph. 6. 18; Phil. 3. 3. ᵒ ch. 1. 17; Josh. 24. 14; 1 Sam. 12. 24; Ps. 17. 1. ᵖ Ps. 147. 11; Prov. 15. 8.

one of minor importance. The time had come when worship should not be confined to special places; when neither this mountain, Gerizim, nor yet Jerusalem should possess superior sanctity (ver. 20); when the truth should be fully made known that God is a Spirit, and that only such worship is accepted as corresponds to the spiritual nature of God, and is offered in the deepest sincerity of the heart, and in the way which he has appointed—namely, through Jesus Christ, vers. 23, 24. In this reply it seems evident that Jesus is addressing a sincere inquirer, and not one merely seeking controversy on an old subject of dispute between the Jews and Samaritans. **Woman, believe me,** as if introducing something which might seem improbable; a solemn and emphatic expression, used only in this place by our Lord. It is more familiar, condescending, and personally impressive than the usual "Verily, verily, I say unto you." **The hour cometh,** rather, *an hour is coming.* **Nor yet at Jerusalem,** better, *nor in Jerusalem.* **Ye shall ... worship the Father.** Thus he familiarly introduces her at once to the worship of God as the Father of all, Samaritans as well as Jews. Compare Acts 17 : 26-28.

22. **Ye worship ye know not what.** Ye are ignorantly incorrect as to your worship. The word *what* cannot refer to the object of worship, except so far as the Samaritans lost sight of the Messiah as more fully revealed in the prophecies which they rejected, for both Jews and Samaritans worshipped God. It rather refers to the *manner* of worship, and especially to the place, which was the topic of conversation. The Samaritans knew not what kind of worship they used, being in error regarding any command to worship on Gerizim. The Jews knew what their worship should be, and they had an appointed place and temple by divine command. For introduces the proof of what Jesus had just said. **Salvation,** literally, *the salvation,* the appointed salvation through the Messiah. The word *salvation* applies specially to Christ, who alone brings salvation. Thus the word is used in Luke 2 : 30; 3 : 6. Compare author's note on those passages. **Is of the Jews.** The Messiah was to come from the lineage of David, and David belonged to the Jewish nation. Salvation, therefore, was evidently of the Jews. The argument is as follows. The true worship would be in that nation from which God had ordained that the Messiah should come.

23. What Jesus had expressed negatively in regard to worship (vers. 21, 22) he now expresses positively and more fully. **The hour cometh**—it was future in its complete development —**and now is,** inasmuch as Christ had already come and was proclaiming the glad tidings, **when the true worshippers,** they who offer true and acceptable worship. Their worship is in accord with the nature of both God and man. **In spirit and in truth.** Some of the older expositors suppose that these words denote the Holy Spirit and Christ, the latter being the absolute Truth. But it is better to regard them as referring to the inner worship of the heart, since we are taught in the next verse that our worship must be spiritual, to correspond with the nature of God. The words *in spirit and in truth* may mean spiritually and truly. But more exactly they designate that worship which is offered in the mind and heart, as opposed to form and ceremonies, and which is conformed to the divine nature and to God's revealed truth. With the soul and sincerely, uprightly, in conformity to truth. "Dost thou wish to pray in a temple? Pray in thyself; but first become a temple of God."—AUGUSTINE. Compare Gal. 5 : 6; 6 : 15; Eph. 1 : 3, 17; 3 : 17. These words assured the woman convicted of

JOHN IV.
A. D. 27.

24 eth such to worship him. ^qGod *is* a Spirit; and they that worship him must worship *him* in spirit and in truth.
25 The woman saith unto him, I know that Messias cometh (which is called Christ); when he is come, he will tell us all things. Jesus saith unto her, ^sI that speak unto thee am *he.*

q Isa. 40. 18; Acts 7. 48; 2 Cor. 3. 17; 1 Tim. 1. 17.
r vers. 29,39; Deut. 18. 15-18.
s ch. 9. 37; Matt. 26. 63, 64; Mark 14. 61, 62.

her sins and longing for deliverance that, however unable she might be to settle in her own mind the controversy between Samaritans and Jews, there was a refuge for her in God, and that if she only possessed the spirit of true repentance and faith, she might be sure of acceptance. **For,** rather, *for also,* **the Father seeketh such to worship him.**

24. Jesus gives another reason for spiritual worship, drawn from the nature of God. **God is a Spirit,** rather *God is spirit;* not corporeal, but pure spirit, essentially and absolutely. This is not spoken of the Holy Spirit alone, but of the immaterial nature of God, comprehending all the persons of the Godhead. Compare *God is light,* 1 John 1 : 5; *God is love,* 1 John 4 : 8. He must therefore be worshipped *in spirit and in truth*—in our souls, thoughts, feelings, and desires, with a right knowledge of him, and in conformity to that knowledge. See preceding verse. This spiritual worship was indeed offered, in connection with rites and ceremonies, by the pious under the Old Dispensation. But now, under the gospel, this spiritual worship would be more eminent, more complete, and more comprehensive, not being restricted to any one time, place, or nation. Compare similar sentiments in Acts 17 : 22-31.

This answer of Jesus (vers. 21-24) suggested to the woman the glorious hope of the Messiah, and perhaps the half conviction that Jesus might be the great personage for whom the Samaritans, as well as the Jews, were waiting. Though they rejected the whole of the Old Testament, with the exception of the five books of Moses, they found prophecies of him even there. See Gen. 49 : 10; Num. 24 : 17; Deut. 18 : 15-20. They seem to have expected, not a temporal prince, but a teacher and prophet, and it was doubtless with eager desire that this woman, now conscious of her sins, looked for him who should reveal to her all that she needed to know.

25. The woman therefore accepts the words of Jesus as the truth, and specially applicable to the times of the Messiah. **I know that Messias cometh.** This is not an appeal to the Messiah, nor a continuation of a dispute, but the words of a full heart under the influence of the truth. See on ch. 1 : 17, 41 on *Messiah* and *Christ.* The Samaritans did not so call the Promised One; they regarded him as another Moses (Deut. 18 : 15), a prophet and teacher, the Restorer But she uses the Jewish appellation, perhaps in deference to Jesus and admiration of him. **Which,** *who,* **is called Christ.** This is probably an explanation of the evangelist similar to ch. 1 : 41, and hence parenthetical. Some, however, regard it as the words of the woman. **When he is come.** If everything is not made plain, it will be then. If she has to yield assent to things now which she cannot fully comprehend, she will understand it then. **He will tell us all things.** He will reveal to us the divine will and lead us into all truth. Perhaps she thought that he who now had told her all things that ever she did (ver. 29) could tell about that Promised One, or even that he might be the One for whom they looked. At least she seemed so teachable, her desire to know the truth was so strong, and her ideas of the Messiah so near the truth, that Jesus condescends to make himself known to her, as he could not to the Jews without encouraging them in error.

26. In answer, therefore, to her words, **When he is come, he will tell us all things,** Jesus said plainly, **I that speak unto thee am he,** the first and clearest declaration of his divine Messiahship. Sinful as her life had been, Jesus saw in her a hungering and thirsting after righteousness, and the fact that she was a member of an outcast and de-

27   And upon this came his disciples, and marvelled
that he talked with the woman; yet no man said,
What seekest thou? or, Why talkest thou with her?
28   The woman then left her water-pot, and went her way
29   into the city, and saith to the men, Come, see a man,
ᵗ which told me all things that ever I did; is not this   ᵗ ver. 25.
30   the Christ? Then they went out of the city, and
came unto him.
31   In the mean while his disciples prayed him, saying,

spised people only drew his heart out in deeper sympathy for her spiritual needs. The woman of Samaria was the first of those few outside the Jewish fold whom the Saviour drew in and saved as a pledge of his final gathering of all the nations under his sceptre.

27. Jesus forgets his hunger in doing the will of God. **And upon this,** as these words were spoken, **came his disciples,** from the city, where they had obtained food, vers. 8, 31. **And marvelled,** or, *wondered*, **that he talked with the woman,** rather, *a woman.* Oriental custom restricted intercourse with the female sex, and the rabbins thought women incapable of rabbinical instruction. They echoed Oriental contempt for women by such sayings as these: "No man salutes a woman;" "He who instructs his daughter in the law is as one who plays the fool." The disciples partook of this prejudice, and thought it strange that Jesus should take the trouble to talk to a woman at all. Influenced, no doubt, by reverence for their Master, **no man said, What seekest thou?** asking the woman what was her business, the object of the conversation, **or, Why talkest thou with her?** asking Jesus. Many, however, take it that they did not dare to ask *Jesus* either of these questions. Here, as at other times, many questions arose in their minds which they were too timid to express. Even thus early the disciples looked upon Jesus with a reverential awe which prevented any undue familiarity, ch. 21 : 12.

28. **The woman then left her water-pot,** her water-pitcher, **and went her way into the city.** She could go with more expedition without her pitcher. Besides, it might be of use to Jesus and his disciples at their meal. Yet these were but incidental reasons. Her admiration and joy filled her heart. Her water-pot and her work were as nothing to the revelation which Jesus had made to her soul, and to the glad news she wished to convey to the city. "The woman in *her* zeal forgot her occupation, as Jesus in *his* had forgotten his thirst."—THOLUCK.

29. **And saith to the men,** or *to the people,* **Come, see a man,** *who,* **told me all things that ever I did.** It is the testimony of an awakened conscience as well as the exaggerated language of enthusiastic feeling. She believed that he who had disclosed such guilty secrets (vers. 17, 18) could, if he would, reveal the whole course of her past life. In her ardor she sought to make the whole town partakers of the blessing she had herself received. **Is not this the Christ?** or rather, *Is this the Christ?* Though she believed this most firmly, she did not herself assert it. She thought it best to set them to inquiring for themselves. "A question often sets working a mind which would be utterly unmoved by an affirmation." Chrysostom praises both her zeal and her prudence. She does not say, "The Messiah is come; I have seen him;" but she invites them to come and see and judge for themselves. Nor does she say, "Come, see a prophet, or the Messiah;" but "Come, see a man," etc.

30. **Then,** omitted by some high critical authorities, **they went out of the city.** The woman's intense earnestness produced an effect on her townsmen, notwithstanding her past character and the smallness of her present knowledge of Christ. **And came unto him,** rather, *And were coming to him.* A crowd went with her, and while they were coming the following conversation took place. See on ver. 35.

31. **In the mean while,** while the woman had gone into the city and the people were coming to see Jesus, his

32 Master, eat. But he said unto them, ⁿ I have meat to
33 eat that ye know not of. Therefore said the disciples
one to another, Hath any man brought him *aught* to
eat?
34 Jesus saith unto them, ˣ My meat is to do the will
35 of him that sent me, and to finish his work. Say not
ye, There are yet four months, and *then* cometh harvest? Behold, I say unto you, Lift up your eyes, and
look on the fields; ʸ for they are white already to har-

ⁿ ver.34; Job 23.12

ˣ ch. 6. 38; 17. 4; 19. 30; Ps. 40. 8.

ʸ Matt. 9. 37, 38; Luke 10. 2.

disciples, who had brought food from the city (vers. 8, 27), **prayed him, saying, Master, eat,** more exactly, *Rabbi, eat.* Many hours had passed since they had partaken of food. He had become wearied in his journey (ver. 6), and was in need of food when he arrived at the well. Perhaps, too, they urged him because he seemed to be engrossed in his thoughts, putting off his meal and unwilling to partake of food.

32. As on many other occasions, Jesus seizes upon this opportunity of using natural objects in teaching spiritual truth. He makes known to his disciples the feelings of his heart in prosecuting his work, and thus by his example he would stimulate them in their spiritual labors. Jesus therefore said to them, **I have meat,** *food,* **that ye know not of,** ver. 32. While their weak minds were occupied with the idea of bodily sustenance, his heart was filled with the great object of his ministry—doing good to souls. The blessing he conferred upon this poor woman, and the prospect of a spiritual harvest among her despised people, so refreshed and strengthened him that it did away with his desire for food, as it had previously taken away his desire for water, ver. 9.

33. The disciples wonder at our Lord's reply, yet through reverence they did not ask nor urge him further, but said to one another, **Hath any man brought him aught,** *anything,* **to eat?** They thought that perhaps he had obtained food in some way during their absence, showing a greater incapacity for rising from the sensuous to the spiritual than even the woman had done. Jesus therefore explained his meaning.

34. Knowing that his disciples perceive not his meaning, he speaks more plainly. **My meat,** *food,* **is to do the will of him that sent me.** Jesus found his nourishment and refreshment in doing God's will. So great was his delight in performing his divine labors that he could forget his food and drink. It was his Father's will that salvation by faith in a Saviour should be proclaimed, and a door of mercy set wide open to the chief of sinners, ch. 6 : 39, 40. **And to finish his work.** The work of God which Jesus finished was the work of obedience, self-sacrifice, suffering, and death for the redemption of mankind, ch. 17 : 21-24. All this he so longed to have accomplished that every step toward the consummation gave him a joy immeasurably beyond the mere sensuous delight of the hungry man in food.

35. He would excite in his disciples the same disposition to do their work. This he does by a threefold encouragement: Large opportunity for work, abundant results of their toil, and great facility in accomplishing their labor. **Say not ye, There are yet four months, and then cometh harvest?** Some take this proverbially, referring to a similar saying in the Talmud. Tholuck thinks that our Lord pointed to the fields, and that it was just then seed-time, there being four months between seed-time and harvest. It was indeed suitable for Jesus to speak thus at that season of the year, and highly probable, too, from his custom of drawing illustrations from the objects of the natural world around him. The harvest began with the passover. On the second day of the festival the first fruits of the barley-harvest were presented. The wheat-harvest was two or three weeks later. The passover, A. D. 28, began on March 29th, and the four months before would be the latter part of November. This journey was therefore probably performed late in November or early

A. D. 27.   JOHN IV.   87

36 vest. ᵃ And he that reapeth receiveth wages, and gathereth fruit unto life eternal; that both he that soweth and he that reapeth may rejoice together.
37 And herein is that saying true, ᵃ One soweth, and an-
38 other reapeth. I sent you to reap that whereon ye bestowed no labor: ᵇ other men labored, and ye are entered into their labors.
39 And ᶜ many of the Samaritans of that city believed on him ᵈ for the saying of the woman, which testified,
40 He told me all that ever I did. So when the Samaritans were come unto him, they besought him that he

ᵃ Prov. 11. 30; Dan. 12. 3; Phil. 2. 15, 16; 1 Thess. 2. 19, 20; 2 Tim. 4. 7, 8.
ᵃ Judg. 6. 3; Mic. 6. 15.
ᵇ Jer. 44. 4; 1 Pet. 1. 12.
ᶜ Gen. 49. 10.
ᵈ ver 29.

---

in December. Perhaps at this time the fields were green with springing wheat, for the sowing took place in November. **Look on the fields, for they are white already to harvest.** Jesus pointed to the eager throng of Samaritans that came pouring forth from the city-gates. Perhaps they were coming through green fields, and he saw them ripe for gathering into the kingdom of God, and compared them to wheat, which grows white as it becomes ready for the sickle.

36. And he that reapeth receiveth wages ... unto life eternal. The reward of the reaper in spiritual things consists in this, that his harvest is one of immortal fruit—fruit that nevers withers or decays: he gathers men as grain into the granary of eternal life. **That both he that soweth and he that reapeth may rejoice together.** Another class has also a reward and equal joy in the harvest with the reapers—namely, the sowers—those who sowed in tears, and never saw even the springing of the seed they planted.

37. And herein, rather, *For herein,* **is that saying true.** Only in spiritual sowing and harvesting does this proverb prove true in the highest sense. **One soweth, and another reapeth.** It often happens that he who reaps the field is not the one who sowed the seed.

38. I sent you to reap that whereon ye bestowed no labor. This Jesus utters in anticipation of their mission as apostles. Their labors and success were present before his mind. And this visit of Jesus doubtless prepared the way for the spread of the gospel among the Samaritans, Acts 8: 5–17. These words, too, of Jesus must have risen into special importance in the minds of Peter and John when they were sent from Jerusalem into Samaria to assist in the work of the Lord, Acts 8: 14. **Other men labored,** *have labored,* **and ye are entered,** *have entered,* **into their labors.** Jesus beholds the future harvesting of souls by the apostles, and speaks of it as already being accomplished. Moses and the patriarchs had prepared the way for Christ, even among this people, whom the Jews looked upon as heretics and heathen. Had it not been for this sowing long ago, there could have been no reaping on the part of the apostles. Jesus, too, gathered but a small harvest in comparison to that gathered by them. But Jesus here is more properly the Lord of the harvest who sent them forth. Compare Matt. 23 : 34. The gathering in of the Samaritans at this time into God's kingdom is to Jesus' mind a type of all spiritual harvests. While he cheers the reapers in their toil by the thought of the grandeur of their work and the glorious fruit they gather in, he at the same time chastens their exultation by the thought that all their success is due to the labor of other patient souls who have prepared the way for them, and who now from happier climes look down upon the harvest as sharers in the praise and joy.

39. And many of the Samaritans ... believed on him for, *because of,* **the saying of the woman.** The fact that Jesus had exhibited such supernatural knowledge, and the magnetic power of this woman's personal conviction, moved many susceptible souls to believe that Jesus was the Messiah, even before they had seen him. Thus, while Jesus was instructing his disciples there was preparing an illustration of the whitening harvest of believing and inquiring souls.

40. So when the Samaritans were come, better, *when therefore*

41 would tarry with them; and he abode there two days. And many more believed because of his own 42 word; and said unto the woman, Now we believe, not because of thy saying; for *we have heard *him* ourselves, and ᶠknow that this is indeed the Christ, the Saviour of the world.

* ch. 17. 8 · 1 John 4. 14.
ᶠ Rom. 10. 11-13.

the Samaritans came. They showed the exalted opinion they had formed of Jesus in hastily coming out to see him, and their faith in that **they besought him that he would tarry with them,** both to receive their hospitality, and to be more fully instructed. With all Jesus' desire to instruct them, he waited for them to express their desire for instruction. This impulse to receive and trust the Saviour appeared in their subsequent treatment of the apostles, as well as in their present treatment of Christ, Acts 8:14. **And he abode there two days,** interrupting his northward journey and turning westward to Shechem, or rather northward to Askar, that he might teach them.

41. **And many more** than those who had believed because of her word **believed because of his own word,** or teaching; not on account of miracles, for there is no record of any miracles performed in Sychar.

42. **Now we believe,** rather, *we no longer believe because of thy saying,* or story. The word here translated *saying,* though often used contemptuously, is not so used by these Samaritans. Her report now seemed insignificant in comparison to our Lord's instructions. **For we have heard him ourselves.** They now have personal knowledge and experience, and needed not the report of another. "They seem to glory that their faith has now a firmer basis than a woman's tongue."—CALVIN. Yet our Lord's instructions had confirmed her report. **And know, a high order of faith, that this is indeed the Christ.** *The Christ* should be omitted, according to the most approved critical reading. **The Saviour of the world,** of the human race. Found only here and in 1 John 4:14. Why is it first heard from the lips of these Samaritan converts? Such language, with the mighty truth bound up in it, was still a long way off from Jewish thought—did not, indeed, arise in the minds of the apostles till after the resurrection. The Jew clung to his exclusive prerogatives, and passionately refused to forego them. These Samaritans were under no such temptation. Such exclusive prerogatives were not, and never had been, theirs. Having accepted the "salvation" which was primarily "of the Jews," they could rejoice that, although "of the Jews," it was not *for* the Jews alone. Having themselves received the Messiah, it was most natural for them to regard his work as without limitations of nation or race, and to call him, not "King of Israel," but "*Saviour* of the world." The Samaritans, with all their errors and superstitions, had in some respects a larger and freer notion of salvation than the Jews. While Jewish bigotry and exclusiveness would not recognize the Messiah, it is significant that this despised and outcast race received him. This was due, not to any special teaching granted them by Jesus, but to the sovereign grace of God, which so often chooses the weak and ignorant as heirs of salvation, while the strong and wise of this world reject the gospel and are lost. Notice that we have here THE FIRST CONTACT OF JESUS WITH THOSE OUTSIDE THE BOUNDS OF ISRAEL. There were four of these occasions. The persons were—first, these Samaritans; secondly, the Roman centurion; thirdly, the Syro-Phoenician woman; and fourthly, the Greeks at the feast. Though Jesus took a singular interest in all these, they were, notwithstanding, marked exceptions to the general course of his ministry. He undertook no mission to the Samaritans. "The law which he imposed on his disciples, 'and into any city of the Samaritans enter ye not' (Matt. 10:5), this, during the days of his flesh, he imposed on himself. He was 'not sent but unto the lost sheep of the house of Israel' (Matt. 15:24; Acts 13:46), and if any grace reached Samaritan or heathen, it was, so to speak, but by accident, a crumb falling from the children's table." His

A. D. 27. JOHN IV. 89

Jesus arrives in Galilee; heals a nobleman's son at Capernaum.

43 Now after two days he departed thence, and went
44 into Galilee. For ᵍJesus himself testified, that a
45 prophet hath no honor in his own country. Then
when he was come into Galilee, the Galileans received him, ʰ having seen all the things that he did
at Jerusalem at the feast; ⁱ for they also went unto
46 the feast. So Jesus came again into Cana of Galilee, ᵏ where he made the water wine.

ᵍ Matt.13.57; Mark 6. 4; Luke 4. 24.
ʰ ch. 2. 13-17, 23; 3. 2.
ⁱ Deut. 16. 16.
ᵏ ch. 2. 1, 11.

gospel was ultimately to be preached throughout the earth; and these four preludes of the coming mercy show that Jesus' plan comprehended the whole race of man. But for the very sake of the ultimate diffusion of the gospel it was important that his personal ministry should be confined to a people educated and prepared by past revelations, and should thus sum up and complete God's historic dealings with Israel.

43-46. JESUS DEPARTS FOR GALILEE, AND THERE TEACHES PUBLICLY, Matt. 4: 17; Mark 1: 14, 15; Luke 4: 14, 15. According to Luke, he teaches in the synagogues of Galilee. John records his coming to Cana. His visit to the latter place was probably during the month of December, A. D. 27. Compare *Author's Harmony*, ?? 33, 34.

43. **Now after two days**, rather, *the two days* mentioned in ver. 40. **He departed thence, and went into Galilee.** According to the majority of critical authorities, *He departed thence into Galilee.* On **Galilee**, see note on ch. 1 : 43. Perhaps, as Dr. Lange suggests, Galilee here may be used in the narrower and provincial sense of Upper Galilee, in distinction from Lower Galilee, including the region of Nazareth.

44. **For Jesus himself testified.** What is the force of the word *for?* How is the connection explained? Some would render **For,** *although*. Others think that our Lord's "own country" here means Judæa, though elsewhere it means Nazareth. Some, again, connect this verse with the following one. The Galileans did indeed receive him, but it was only on account of his miracles and fame at Jerusalem; for, as he had declared, a prophet has no honor, etc. It seems to me best to regard this as the reason for avoiding Nazareth, and perhaps the region of Lower Galilee. See on last verse. **A prophet hath no honor in his own country.** That the word "country" refers specially to Nazareth and its vicinity is rendered probable from its use in this sense by the other evangelists. See Matt. 13 : 54, 57; Mark 6 : 1-4; Luke 4 : 23, 24. Familiarity with the early life of Jesus had rendered his townsmen incredulous of his claims, ch. 7 : 5; Mark 6 : 3. He would not offer himself to them for their final acceptance or rejection until they had had greater opportunity to hear from other places of the mighty works he had done. Even when he came to Nazareth, a little later, his townsmen rose up to take his life, Luke 4 : 28, 29. Great privileges had hardened the hearts of the inhabitants of Nazareth, as well as the hearts of the rulers at Jerusalem. But it was otherwise with other parts of Galilee.

45. **Then when he was come,** rather, *when therefore he came,* **into Galilee. The Galileans received him,** with respect and reverence, but not necessarily with true faith in him as the Saviour. **Having seen all the things,** *the things* should be omitted, **that he did at Jerusalem at the feast,** ch. 2 : 23; 3 : 2. Notice, the Samaritans believed on him, not because of his miracles, but his teaching (ver. 42); the Galileans received him, not so much because of his teaching, but on account of his miracles. **For they also went unto the feast.** "Even those who lived farthest off from Jerusalem, in Galilee, made a point of going to the passover. This remark serves to show the publicity of our Lord's ministry both in life and death."

46-54. JESUS HEALS THE NOBLE-

And there was a certain nobleman, whose son
47 was sick at Capernaum. When he heard that Jesus
was come out of Judæa into Galilee, he went unto
him and besought him that he would come down,
and heal his son; for he was at the point of death.
48 Then said Jesus unto him, ¹Except ye see signs
49 and wonders, ye will not believe. The nobleman
saith unto him, Sir, come down ere my child die.

¹ ch. 2. 18; Num. 14. 11; Matt. 16. 1; 1 Cor. 1. 22.

MAN'S SON LYING ILL AT CAPERNAUM. AT CANA. Recorded only by John.

46. The first part of this verse is closely connected with the preceding verse. The last part naturally begins a new paragraph. **So Jesus,** according to the most approved reading, *So he,* **came again,** in the month of December, A. D. 27, **into Cana of Galilee,** a few miles north of Nazareth (see on ch. 2 : 1), **where,** about nine months before, **he made the water wine,** ch. 2 : 1-11. The word *so* points backward to verses 44, 45, and indicates that his repairing to Cana was due to the fact that the inhabitants of Cana and the Galileans generally were more favorably inclined toward him than his townsmen at Nazareth.

And there was a certain nobleman, a civil or military officer in the service of Herod Antipas, tetrarch of Galilee and Peræa. He was probably a Jew; possibly the "Chuza, Herod's steward," whose wife Joanna afterward ministered to Jesus, Luke 8:3. **Whose son was sick at Capernaum,** his residence, situated on the north-west shore of the Lake of Galilee and about fifteen miles from Cana. "Earthly greatness is no defence against afflictions." But afflictions do not always bring the powerful and rich, as they did this nobleman, to Jesus' feet.

47. **When he heard,** *he having heard.* **Judæa** (see on ch. 3 : 22) **into Galilee.** See on ch. 1 : 43. No long time could have passed since Jesus arrived in Cana, for the news of his movements spread rapidly. **He went ... besought ... come down.** Capernaum was much lower than Cana. "I passed over the ground between the two places, and found it to be, as would be expected from the well-known depression of the lake below the general level of the country, descending at almost every step."—DR. HACKETT, *Illustrations of Scripture,* p. 217. See on ch.

2:12. **Heal his son ... at the point of death.** It was the pressure of an outward necessity, rather than the impulse of a converted and submissive heart, that drove him to Jesus. Yet his faith in Jesus' power to work miracles was so strong that when every other resource had failed he made a day's journey to secure the Saviour's aid.

48. **Then Jesus,** better, *Jesus therefore,* in view of his imperfect faith, **said unto him, Except ye see signs and wonders** (see on ch. 2 : 11), **ye will not believe.** He had done no miracles in Sychar, yet the Samaritans had at once believed on him. He found in Galilee a sad contrast to all this. The nobleman and his countrymen would not believe in him as a Saviour unless they first witnessed surprising miracles. Even when he performed "signs and wonders" to win their faith, he deplored the lack of spiritual perception which made these necessary. So "he who spoke of his son's sickness heard of his own." He received a rebuke instead of the favorable answer he had expected. Instead of instantly going with him, Jesus pointed him to the state of his own heart. It would seem as if the nobleman, conscious that he could never pass the test, filled with anxiety lest further delay might be fatal, and more convinced than ever that his only hope lay in Jesus, now flung himself in earnest entreaty upon the undeserved mercy of the Saviour.

49. **Sir, come down ere my child die.** Notice the tender expression, *my child.* Here was an intense earnestness that showed the depth of a father's affliction. It showed that he had made the request, not because he wished to see a sign, but because he believed that Jesus could heal his son. He now left no room for debate or delay. He put the whole heart into one request. Yet how imperfect was the faith! It was

A. D. 27. JOHN IV. 91

50 Jesus saith unto him, Go thy way, thy son liveth.
51 ᵐAnd the man believed the word that Jesus had spoken unto him, and he went his way. And as he was now going down his servants met him, and told
52 him, saying, Thy son liveth. Then inquired he of them the hour when he began to amend. And they said unto him, Yesterday at the seventh hour the

ᵐ Rom. 4. 20, 21; Heb. 11. 19.

---

the faith of a man who never yet had become Jesus' disciple. "He said, 'Come down,' as if Jesus could not cure his son while absent, 'ere my child die,' as if Jesus could not raise him from the dead!"
50. Jesus answers his prayer by healing the son in a very unexpected way. **Jesus saith unto him, Go thy way, thy son liveth.** "Oh, the meekness and mercy of this Lamb of God! When we would have looked that he should have punished this suitor for not believing, he condescends to him that he may believe." Imperfect as his faith was, his prayer was answered, but answered in a way that would most humble him and most glorify Christ. Jesus answered this man of rank with the calmness of a superior dignity and authority. There was no obsequiousness and no flattery. He would not go with the nobleman, nor be moved from his appointed sphere of duty by any sudden influence from without. He would do God's work in God's own way. He would heal the sick boy without even seeing his face. Herod's officer received in answer to his prayer a greater blessing than he sought — an exercise of Christ's power which not only delivered his son from his malady of fever, but delivered his own heart also from its malady of unbelief. **The man believed, . . . went his way,** apparently so fully persuaded of Jesus' truth and power that he did not stop to ask how the cure should be wrought or whether it should be instantaneous or not.
Here it may be fitting to add a few words on miracles and faith. Jesus mourned that men were so little alive to the self-evidencing power of his character and words as to need the outward props and buttresses which miracles supplied. "There are two different kinds of faith — that which you put in what another is or in what another has said, because of your own personal knowledge of him, and your perception of the intrinsic truthfulness of his sayings; and that which you cherish because of certain external vouchers for his truthfulness that he presents. Jesus invites us to put both these kinds of faith in him, but the latter and the lower, in order to lead on to the former and the higher, the real, abiding, life-giving faith in him as the Saviour of souls." "Miracles are a species of proof inferior to moral evidence, and are due to the condescension of God, who affords an extraordinary prop, and one we have no right to demand, to that hesitating, incomplete faith which has been excited by the superior appeals" of the truth itself.
51. **And as he was now going down.** Cana among the hills was upon a much higher level than Capernaum on the seashore. See on ver. 49. **His servants met him, and told him, saying, Thy son,** rather, *child*, **liveth.** According to some of the best critical authority, *That his son liveth.* He had been given up for dead, ver. 47. The servants came to give their master the earliest news of the child's cure, and to tell him that there was no need of further seeking to bring Jesus.
52. **Then inquired he of them the hour,** etc. He wanted to confirm his own faith in Jesus' word by ascertaining the exact facts of the child's recovery. It is evident that he expected to hear only that the disease had turned, and that his son was out of danger. **Yesterday at the seventh hour,** probably at 7 P. M., the reckoning being according to the Roman method. See note on ver. 6, and *Author's Harmony,* ¿ 181, note. **The fever left him,** completely forsook him. The father received far more than his highest hopes had seemed to warrant. The child had grown worse until the hour named, but then had suddenly and completely recovered.

JOHN IV.   A. D. 27.

53 fever left him. So the father knew that *it was* at the same hour in the which Jesus said unto him, Thy son liveth: ⁿ and himself believed, and his whole house.
54 This *is* again ᵒ the second miracle *that* Jesus did, when he was come out of Judæa into Galilee.

ⁿ Acts 16. 15, 34; 18. 8.
ᵒ ch. 2. 1-11.

53. So the father knew that it was at the same hour in the which. The nobleman had reached Cana late on the same day that he started from Capernaum. Immediately seeking Jesus, he had found him at seven o'clock in the evening. In his eagerness to reach his home and see with his own eyes the answer to his prayer, he probably started back again at once, but was obliged to spend the night at some place on the way. Next day, when more than half his journey was completed, he met the servants, who had started the same morning to bring him the glad news that "yesterday at the seventh hour the fever had left" the child. **And himself believed, and his whole house.** He had believed before in Jesus' power to work miracles, but from this time he was attached to Christ as one of his true disciples. Hitherto he had regarded him as a prophet, now he accepted him as the Messiah. But he could not keep his faith and gratitude to himself. He told his son and his family of him who had wrought the marvellous cure. And thus Christ's dealing with him resulted in a treble blessing—first, the healing of his son; secondly, his own progress from an historical to a saving faith; and thirdly, the including of his whole household in the bond of a common discipleship and salvation.

54. This is again the second miracle, equivalent to, *This second miracle,* etc., John 21:16. It was the second miracle wrought in Galilee. During his first return to Galilee after his baptism Jesus appears to have wrought no miracle except that at Cana, ch. 2:11. It was also the second at Cana; that is, while Jesus was there, the miracle itself being wrought in Capernaum, vers. 46, 52. It also marked his second return from Judæa into Galilee. **Judæa,** see on ch. 3:22. **Galilee,** see on ch. 1:43.

PRACTICAL REMARKS.

1. Withdrawal from danger is sometimes as much due to Christ and the church as facing martyrdom, vers. 1-3; Matt. 10:23.
2. It is often wise to go from one place to another, in order to do the more good. Impatient reformers often defeat their own ends, vers. 1-3.
3. The rejection of the gospel by some often proves the occasion of its reception by others, vers. 1-3.
4. The path of duty is often the path of necessity. Duty itself makes a way necessary, ver. 4.
5. Weary as Jesus was, he forgot the wants of the body in ministering to a needy soul, vers. 5, 6.
6. The laboring and heavy-laden should remember that Jesus was often wearied in providing salvation. He can sympathize and give relief, ver. 6.
7. Like Jesus, we may be wearied *in* the work, but not *of* the work, ver. 6.
8. Jesus taught not only patiently, but revealed to the woman with wonderful fulness the sublimest truths of his kingdom, vers. 6-26.
9. Imitate the tact of Jesus. Get a sinner to do you a kindness, and you will make him kindly disposed to hear you, ver. 7; 1 Cor. 9:22.
10. The soul is of infinite worth. To teach even the lowest was the occupation of the Lord of angels, vers. 9-26.
11. Do not despair of the conversion even of one the most prejudiced, ver. 9; Isa. 32:20.
12. Let us magnify with our lives and lips the worth and sweetness of God's grace, and then will sinners cry aloud, Give me to drink, ver. 10; Ps. 51:12, 13.
13. The first need of a sinner is to feel his sinfulness, vers. 10-15; Matt. 9:13; Luke 15:17, 18.
14. The second need is to see and feel the freeness of God's love and grace, ver. 14.
15. The wants of the soul find their full supply only in Jesus, vers. 13-15.
16. All earthy joys are unable to satisfy the desire of an immortal nature, ver. 14.
17. "The Christian's happiness is unknown to the world, because it is

Jesus goes to Jerusalem to the passover; healing of the impotent man at the pool of Bethesda; the Jews seek to kill him.

V. AFTER ᵖ this there was a feast of the Jews, and ᵖ ch. 2. 13; Lev. 23. 2; Deut. 16. 1.

from within; it is to all but its possessor a spring shut up, a fountain sealed," ver. 14; Song Sol. 4 : 12.
18. Christ always answers true prayer, but often in a way the least expected, vers. 15, 16; 2 Cor. 12 : 9.
19. Christ is the great Touchstone and Revealer of human hearts, vers. 16-19; Luke 2 : 35.
20. Everywhere we may find God and worship him, vers. 20-23; Acts 7 : 48, 49.
21. Since God. is a Spirit, he marks every insincere word and every evil thought; yet, however imperfect the form may be, he loves the worship of those who come to him in spirit and in truth, ver. 24; Isa. 57 : 15, 16.
22. Jesus reveals himself to the sinner just at the right moment, vers. 25, 26.
23. The zeal of Jesus is reproduced in the converted soul, vers. 28, 29; 1 Pet. 4 : 10.
24. The professed followers often wonder at the ways and means of Christ's working, ver. 27.
25. The new-born soul feels the impulse to make the glad tidings known to others, vers. 28, 29; ch. 1 : 41.
26. Supreme joy consists in doing the will of God and finishing his work, vers. 31-34; Ps. 40 : 8; Col. 1 : 9-11.
27. It is always harvest-time while there is a single unsaved soul within sound of the gospel, ver. 35.
28. Reaping for the Saviour is better than earthly harvesting, for the fruits are immortal and the wages eternal joy, ver. 36.
29. Even if we are permitted only to scatter seed, often in tears, we may be assured that no seed shall be lost, vers. 36-38.
30. The testimony of new-born souls is often most effective, vers. 39, 40.
31. The conversion of one soul is generally followed by the conversion of others, vers. 41, 42.
32. Christ is no respecter of persons, having no sympathy with the prejudices of race and nation, ver. 40; ch. 8 : 48-58.
33. "The great days of grace in which the Lord visits us are numbered, and swiftly pass away," ver. 43.
34. The preacher is not to gauge duty or work by either honor or reproach, vers. 43-45.
35. Sickness teaches us our weakness and dependence, ver. 47.
36. Afflictions should lead us to Christ, vers. 46, 47.
37. Jesus loves to hear the prayers of a parent for a child, vers. 46, 47; Luke 18 : 15-17.
38. Jesus often tests the faith of those who seek him for their good, ver. 48.
39. Jesus answers petitions that are very defective, vers. 49, 50; 2 Cor. 12 : 7-10.
40. Sickness and death come to the young as well as to the old, vers. 47-49.
41. Jesus can save us by his word as easily as by his presence, ver. 50.
42. Jesus often so answers our prayers as to increase our faith. "The little spark of faith in the breast of the nobleman is lit by Jesus into a clear and enduring flame for the light and comfort of himself and his house," ver. 50.
43. Jesus will not "break the bruised reed, nor quench the smoking flax," but when he has performed his wonders of providence and grace he looks for their results in confirmed love to him and active labor in his service, vers. 50-53.
44. When Jesus answers our prayers, it is well to examine how and when he did it, vers. 51-53.
45. All of Christ's words and works, all his grace and providence, will bear the most careful scrutiny, vers. 51-53.
46. A careful examination of Christ's dealings with us will result in our increased faith and love, ver. 53.
47. Jesus gives exhibitions of his power, grace, and mercy just at the right time and place, ver. 54.

CHAPTER V.

This chapter is composed of the record of an incident and the discourse which it occasioned. John opens the

2 Jesus went up to Jerusalem. Now there is at Jerusalem, ᵠ by the sheep *market*, a pool, which is called ◆ Neh. 3. 1; 12. 39. in the Hebrew tongue Bethesda, having five porches.

chapter by narrating that Jesus went up to a feast at Jerusalem, ver. 1. Here occurred the third miracle that John records, the healing of the impotent man at the pool on the Sabbath, vers. 2-9. At this violation of their traditional punctiliousness in observing the Sabbath the Jews remonstrate with the man healed (10-12), but afterward turn their indignation against Jesus, 13-16. Jesus responds by claiming to be a co-worker' with the Father (17-19), by appealing also to works still greater (20-29), and to the witness of the Father, of John the Baptist, and of the Scriptures, 30-39. Yet he affirms that the Jews will still refuse him, and shows why (40-44); and he concludes by warning them that they will be unanswerably accused even by their own standard, the writings of Moses.

1-15. JESUS AT THE PASSOVER. HEALS THE IMPOTENT MAN ON THE SABBATH. Related only by John.

1. **After this,** *these things***,** the occurrences in Galilee related in ch. 4: 43-54. A period of about four months had elapsed, during which many events had occurred. Compare *Author's Harmony,* §§ 34-50. **There was a feast of the Jews.** There has been much controversy as to the feast meant here, for on it depends to a considerable degree the question of the length of our Lord's ministry. If this is the passover, then there are four passovers mentioned by John during Christ's ministry, and it must have lasted three years; otherwise there may have been only two years. The chief objection to the theory that a passover is meant here has been the omission of the article in the Greek text. The principal feast of the Jews would scarcely be called *a feast*, though perhaps under certain circumstances it might possibly be so styled. But almost equally decisive objection to the alternative adopted generally by recent scholars, that it is the feast of Purim, is, that that feast was not celebrated at Jerusalem, but by the Jews in their own homes. The Sinaitic manuscript, and many other ancient authorities, read *the feast of the Jews*, which meant almost certainly the passover.

If this is not the original reading here, it tends to show what was an early traditional view. The plucking of the ears of grain about this time (Luke 6: 1) rather marks this feast as a passover. Jesus goes up, according to his custom, both for the observance of a national custom and to avail himself of the great concourse of people gathered to the feast for the preaching of the kingdom. This was the passover of A. D. 28, and commenced March 29th. See *Author's Harmony,* § 46, note.

2. **Now there is,** or, *And there is*, from which some would infer that Jerusalem was standing when John wrote this Gospel. But not necessarily, for this pool remained after the destruction of the city, and was pointed out in the time of Tertullian and of Eusebius. Besides, John may use the present tense, as the scene was then vividly before his mind. Instead of **market** here it should probably read *gate*. This gate was near the temple, on the north-east side of the city (Neh. 3 : 1 ff.), and derived its name from the sale of sheep there for purposes of sacrifice. **Bethesda.** This pool or reservoir of water had a house built over it, probably for the accommodation of the sick who wished to avail themselves of the supposed healing properties of the water. About the name of the pool there is some doubt. Some read *Bethsaida*, which means *house of fishing*. instead of *Bethesda, house of mercy*. The latter is to be preferred; so called from the supposed curative properties of the water. The explanatory clause, **in the Hebrew tongue,** and in ver. 1 the designation of the feast as *the feast of the Jews*, are among the indications that this Gospel was written for Gentile readers. By *Hebrew* is meant the Aramaic, the language spoken by the Jews at the time of our Lord. **Having five porches,** porticos where the sick could be sheltered from the wind and rain. The pool to which the name of Bethesda is usually given is just within the walls, on the eastern side, near St. Stephen's Gate. It is 360 feet long, 130 feet wide, and 75 feet deep. Compare DR. HACKETT, *Illustrations of Scripture*,

A. D. 28. JOHN V. 95

3 In these lay a great multitude of ʳimpotent folk, of
blind, halt, withered, ˢwaiting for the moving of the
4 water. For an angel went down at a certain season
into the pool, and troubled the water; whosoever then
ᵗfirst after the troubling of the water stepped in ᵘwas
made whole of whatsoever disease he had.

ʳ Isa. 1. 6; 64. 6.
ˢ Prov. 8. 34; Lam. 3. 26.
ᵗ Eccles. 9. 10.
ᵘ Zech. 13. 1; 1 John 1. 7.

p. 291. But in 1888 there was discovered under the French church of St. Anne, on the right of St. Stephen's gate, a tank in the rock, and more recently a twin pool by its side, and the remains of the five porches still visible (Quarterly Statement of the Palestine Exploration).

POOL OF BETHESDA.

3, 4. **A great multitude.** *Great* should be omitted from this statement, according to the best text. **Impotent folk,** infirm people. **Halt,** the *lame* or crippled. The **withered** were those whose muscles had dwindled and who were more or less paralyzed. The last part of this verse, beginning with the word **waiting,** and all of ver. 4, are also rejected by the best authorities. They are not only wanting in the best manuscripts, but there are strong internal evidences of the spuriousness of the passage. In the first place, there is a number of words in it which are rare in New Testament Greek. And, more important still, the statement seems apocryphal. It was probably a marginal addition to some very ancient manuscript, giving a popular or traditional

5 And a certain man was there, which had an infirm-
6 ity thirty and eight years. When Jesus saw him lie,
 ˣ and knew that he had been now a long time *in that*   ˣ Heb. 4. 13, 15.
 case, he saith unto him, ʸ Wilt thou be made whole?   ʸ Isa. 65. 1; Luke
7 The impotent man answered him, Sir, I have no man,   18. 41.

explanation of the assemblage of the sick mentioned in ver. 3, and of the troubling of the waters in ver. 7. It is also probable, from ver. 7, that this pool derived its healing virtue from a gaseous spring that discharged its waters at intervals within it. At Kissingen, in Germany, a spring of this sort about the same time every day, after a rushing sound, commences to bubble, and is most efficacious at the very time when the gas is making its escape. Eusebius says that a pool named Bethesda was pointed out in his day whose waters would become red at times, which would indicate mineral properties. "Mineral springs are abundant in Western Asia, and most of them formerly had protecting structures built over them, some of whose remains are yet standing. . . . Ebbing and flowing are not at all uncommon. . . . Near Beirut is a fountain of this kind, gushing forth from the foot of Lebanon in so copious a flow that its waters are utilized as a mill-stream to supply flour for the city, yet it is periodically dry for hours at a time."—DR. H. J. VAN LENNEP, *Bible Lands*, p. 46. See further on ver. 7.

5. **A certain man was there,** etc. The statement of the time that this man had been subject to disease is characteristic of John's method in the selection and recital of Christ's miracles. He gives only a few, but they are striking and exceptionally wonderful. And John recounts them in such a way as to bring out their exceptional traits. He tells us the great quantity of water that the Lord changed into wine. This man whom Christ cured had been sick or *in his infirmity thirty-eight years;* and Lazarus was raised from the dead, not, as in the cases recorded in the other Gospels, before burial, but after he had been in the ground three days. His disease was probably the result of the sins of his youth, ver. 14. He was now an old man, just able to crawl from one place to another. He had come to this pool as the last hope of bettering his case, but, poor and friendless, his waiting only seemed to aggravate his misery, for while others were benefited, he had no strength to seize the blessing at the moment when it was within his reach.

6. The knowledge which Jesus possessed of the man's long sickness may have been supernatural, and the language, the words, **When Jesus saw him lie, and knew,** with his perception of the whole case, **that he had been . . . a long time in that case,** quite naturally suggests it. John also loves to present Jesus in his higher powers, manifesting his divine nature, ch. 1 : 47, 48; 2 : 11, 25. Yet there is no positive evidence from the language that he did not obtain it in the ordinary way, by inquiry. The peculiar character of the man's case excited Christ's sympathy. We may well suppose that Jesus saw not only the whole past history of the man, but the fact also that there was in his mind some sense of the connection between the outward malady and the sin which had caused it. This feeling, that he was justly deserted by God as well as by man, may have shown itself in the hopeless dejection of his countenance. It was this that attracted the compassion of Jesus. He singled out this man from the multitude of sick beneath the porches, because he saw that in this one case a true conviction of sin would enable him to link a spiritual blessing upon the act of physical cure. **Wilt thou,** *dost thou desire to,* **be made whole?** The question was designed to draw his attention and prepare the way for his cure. It was the magic of a kind word to a heart all unused to such. It was an assurance that some one pitied him and cared for him. It awakened the hope of healing that was wellnigh extinguished. "Jesus prepared him to believe in his might by leading him to believe in his love."

7. The man's complaint, that another gets precedence of him whenever the water is troubled, is not explained if we leave out the explanation of vers. 3 and 4. It was this which probably

when the water is troubled, to put me into the pool; but while I am coming, another steppeth down before 8 me. ⁴ Jesus saith unto him, ᵃ Rise, take up thy bed, 9 and walk. And immediately the man was made whole, and took up his bed and walked.

ᵇ Ps. 72. 12; Mark 1. 41.
ᵃ Matt. 9. 6; Mark 2. 11.

caused an explanation in the margin, which afterward found its way into the text. See on vers. 3, 4. **Sir, I have no man,** etc. Alone, friendless, helpless, yet not beneath Christ's notice. **When the water is troubled.** Intermittent springs of medicinal character are not uncommon, though such a one as this seems to have been is quite unknown. Dr. Brown regards the troubling of the water, and the efficacy thus imparted to it, as miraculous, and says: "Who ever heard of any water curing all, even the most diverse, diseases—blind, halt, withered—alike? Above all, who ever heard of such a thing being done 'only at a certain season,' and, most singularly of all, doing it only to the 'first person that stepped in after the moving of the waters'?" **To put me into,** etc. The virtue of the water disappeared so fast, or was so soon exhausted by the first comer; literally, *that he may cast me in,* thus picturing the extreme haste and rapidity with which the favorable opportunity was seized. There was a rush and scramble for the one chance, such as we have seen for choice seats in a car or a hall, or for the first deal at a strawberry festival. At the pool were many seekers for a single chance. In the gospel are places and healing for all. No jostling, no thrusting aside and down. This poor man was able to move, but only slowly, and so, however often he started, he failed. Hope flickered up again and again, only to flicker down. Yet against hope he hoped on, watching, waiting. His case was pitiable indeed—a strong appeal to the Lord's mercy.

8. **Jesus saith unto him.** His first word was a question; his second a command. The man had hoped that one would come and put him in the pool, but something better is in store for him. And now the tender sympathy of Jesus, his serene consciousness of power, the inspiring and cheering look he bent upon the sufferer, seem to have drawn forth absolute confidence, and to have prepared the impotent man for instant obedience. **Rise, take up thy bed, and walk.** "I observed in a house at Ramoth-Gilead the recesses on the elevation or platform for spreading the 'bed' (a thin quilting) so often spoken of in Scripture, and saw just how it could be 'taken up' and carried away, Mark 2 : 9."—DR. FISH, *Bible Lands Illustrated,* p. 313. It is customary in the East to roll them up. Mark the authority with which Jesus speaks, not merely to a man, but to disease, for the disease must flee the man before the man can rise and walk. This authority often struck men with astonishment. There was child-like simplicity, utter freedom from parade and ostentation, yet the sublime consciousness of divine power expressed in word, in tone, in bearing. These words have been called "three thunder-strokes of healing might," yet there was little of the thunder. There was the sudden outgo of restoring might, but quiet as the word of love spoken from friend to friend. The word translated *bed* here means originally a *poor man's bed,* then any small bed or couch, a light mattress or blanket. Here it seems to be used for the simple litter or stretcher such as a sick man would be carried round the streets in.

9. **And immediately the man was made whole.** The immediateness of the cure is almost always stated in the Gospels as the sign of its miraculousness. A gradual cure leaves room for the operation of natural laws. In this case, however, the disease was probably incurable, so that the instantaneousness of the healing process only adds to the miracle, but does not make it. The three classes of disease afflicting those gathered at the pool were blindness, lameness, and withered limbs; and, though it is not expressly mentioned, this case probably belonged to the second class. **Took up his bed and walked.** The man did not object that he *could not* rise and walk. He obeyed, and in so doing found his strength. In this he is our pattern and our encouragement. If we heartily set ourselves

10 And ^b on the same day was the sabbath. The Jews therefore said unto him that was cured, It is the sabbath day; ^c it is not lawful for thee to carry *thy*
11 bed. He answered them, ^d He that made me whole, the same said unto me, Take up thy bed and walk.
12 Then asked they him, ^e What man is that which said

^b ch. 7. 23; 9. 14 Matt. 12. 10-13.
^c Ex. 20. 10; Neh. 13. 19; Jer. 17. 21, etc.; Matt. 12. 2; Mark 2. 24; 3. 4; Luke 6. 2; 13. 14.

^d Mark 2. 9-11.   ^e Matt. 21. 23; Rom. 10. 2.

to do the Lord's bidding, there will be neither time nor need to parley about our power to do what is bidden. On **the same day was the sabbath,** the seventh day of the week, the Jewish Sabbath. This introduces a new paragraph, and on this fact turns the controversy that follows. There is little doubt that Jesus deliberately chose the Sabbath day for the performance of this miracle, in order to furnish occasion to clear away false views of that day, and show what was its true design and the proper principle of its observance. Christ is often represented (or *mis*-represented) as though he fell in with all the views and practices of the times, right or wrong, true or false. So far is this from true that we see him deliberately planning to force an issue between himself and the false teachers in this and many another matter. In fact, how else did it come to pass that he was in hatred hunted to the death? The allegation is a slander. He came to "bear witness to the truth" and against the false.

10. John uses the word **Jews** generally to describe, not the whole people, but the ruling class, which was specially hostile to Christ. The act which they condemned was in their view a violation, not only of the general law in regard to the Sabbath, but also of the special law against carrying burdens through the streets on that day. Compare Jer. 17 : 21, 22; Neh. 13 : 15-19. But evidently, as Christ shows in other places, such acts as this were no violation of the spirit of the law. **Therefore, since it was the Sabbath, said unto him that was cured.** Probably they knew that Jesus had cured him, for they ever were on the watch to catch him; but they speak to the man, as he is the actual transgressor, and hope through him to strike the Lord. **It is the sabbath,** etc. "Already the pharisaical Jews, starting from passages such as Ex. 23 : 12; 31 : 13-17; 35 : 2, 3; Num. 15 : 32-36; Neh. 13 : 15-22, had laid down such a multitude of prohibitions, and drawn so infinite a number of hair-splitting distinctions, that a plain and unlearned man could hardly come to know what was forbidden and what was permitted." Jesus taught that the Sabbath was made for man, and not man for the Sabbath; that on this principle was to be interpreted the law of the Sabbath, as of every other institution; and that to stand for the mere letter of the law, regardless of the design of that letter, and especially to proceed to add restrictions not involved in the original law and not added in the spirit of the law, was heresy and abomination. Unquestionably, this is the principle on which we are to interpret the law in respect to every divine institution for man; but one must take care not to subvert an institution on the plea of such interpretation. This has been done by some in respect to the ordinances of the gospel.

11. **He that made me whole, etc.** The man's answer shows the impression that his cure had made on him, for Christ's command was so contrary to the prevalent ideas of the Sabbath that in ordinary circumstances it would probably not have been obeyed. Almost any one would have feared to expose himself to the wrath of the rulers by a violation of their known construction of a law so strict as that of the Sabbath, the violation of which was punishable with death. But, as the healed man viewed it, one who could perform such a miracle was a prophet, and would not command anything wrong. This was correct reasoning, for God's word cannot be against itself. Perhaps also he may have thought that he who could control the laws of Nature could suspend the letter of an outward religious ordinance.

12. The form of their question, **What**

13 unto thee, Take up thy bed and walk? And he that was healed wist not who it was; for Jesus had conveyed himself away, a multitude being in *that* place.
14 Afterward Jesus findeth him ᶠ in the temple, and said unto him, Behold, thou art made whole; ᵍ sin no
15 more, lest a worse thing come unto thee. The man departed, ʰ and told the Jews that it was Jesus which
16 had made him whole. And therefore did the Jews persecute Jesus, and sought to slay him, because he had done these things on the sabbath day.
17 But Jesus answered them, ⁱ My Father worketh

ᶠ Ps. 66. 13–15; 116. 12–19.
ᵍ ch. 8. 11; Ezra 9. 14; 1 Pet. 4. 3.
ʰ Matt. 10. 32, 33.

ⁱ ch. 9. 14; 14. 10.

man is that, is contemptuous. The miracle is nothing to them. The petty violation of the letter of a command was everything.
13. Wist not, knew not. Jesus had conveyed himself away, rather, *Jesus avoided him, there being a crowd in the place.* There were several reasons why Jesus avoided notoriety in connection with his miracles. First, he was exposed to constant danger from the prevalent misconception of the Messianic office, which led the people, whenever his miracles had created an unusual impression, to try to force on him the kingly office. Second, this interfered with his spiritual work. And third, it exposed him to the jealousy of the rulers. Fourth, in this case he purposely avoided him, that the right time might come for the disclosure. Jesus appears to have withdrawn at the moment the impotent man had stooped to take up his bed and the crowd had rushed to see the wonder which had been wrought. It was at a time, the passover, when every resort within and without the city was crowded. The same crowd that gave publicity to the miracle would permit Jesus easily to glide away unnoticed.
14. In the temple, where Jesus was wont to resort, and where the healed man probably went with pious spirit, according to the law, gratefully to make the appointed offering. Sin no more, etc. It is implied in what Jesus says to the man that his disease was the result of his sin; not only in the general way in which all human affliction is to be traced to sin, but as the direct result of a particular sin. Lest a worse thing come unto thee, *befall thee.* The worse thing against which Jesus warns him is probably final retribution. He would add to the cure of the body the permanent cure of the soul.
15. Told the Jews that it was Jesus. He thus justifies himself and makes known his benefactor. There has been much questioning about the motive which led the man to tell the Jews that it was Jesus who had made him whole. It is certainly unnecessary, and seems unnatural, to suppose that he was wicked enough to do it from ingratitude and malice to his benefactor. Neither does the charge of stupidity seem well grounded; but it simply completes his answer to their question in regard to his supposed violation of the law. And if we suppose that the man recognized Jesus as one who had performed many miracles, that would strengthen his reply given in ver. 11. In his grateful and honest simplicity he also probably hoped to influence the Jews in Jesus' favor by this demonstration of his power and goodness.
16–30. JESUS VINDICATES HIMSELF, IN REGARD TO THE CURE ON THE SABBATH.
16. The verbs used in this verse are in the imperfect tense, denoting continued and customary action. They not only persecuted him in this particular instance, but they *were persecuting* him. This was their continued attitude toward Jesus, and their reason for it was that he *was* in the habit of *doing* such things on the Sabbath. The plural, these things—not merely this one cure, but others like it—shows the same thing. The words, and sought to slay him, do not belong here, according to the most approved text. They have been interpolated, probably from ver. 18.
17. My Father worketh, etc., or, *My Father is working until now, and I*

18 hitherto, and I work. Therefore the Jews ᵏsought the more to kill him, ˡbecause he not only had ᵐbroken the sabbath, but said also that God was his Father, ⁿmaking himself equal with God.
19 Then answered Jesus and said unto them, Verily, verily, I say unto you, ᵒThe Son can do nothing of himself, but what he seeth the Father do; ᵖfor what things soever he doeth, these also doeth the Son like-

ᵏ ch. 7. 19, 20, 25; 10. 39.
ˡ Ps. 35. 11.
ᵐ ch. 7. 22, 23; Matt. 12. 5.
ⁿ ch. 8. 54; 10. 30, 33; 14. 9; Phil. 2. 6.
ᵒ ver. 30; ch. 8. 28; 9.4; 12. 49; 14.10.
ᵖ vers. 21, 25, 26;

comp. ch. 10. 18 with Acts 2. 24; Gen. 1. 1, 26 with ch. 1. 1-3; Ps. 50. 6 with 2 Cor. 5. 10; Prov. 2. 6 with Luke 21. 15; Isa. 44. 24 with Col. 1. 16; Jer. 17. 10 with Rev. 2. 23.

am working. Compare Matt. 12 : 3-8. In this reply to the Jews, Jesus takes the highest ground contained in any of his answers to the charge of Sabbath-breaking. He generally defends himself on the ground that such acts are no violation of the spirit of the law. But in this he asserts his superiority to the law, which he shares with the Father. The argument is as follows: *Whatsoever the Father does, I do.* God the Father is ceaselessly at work on Sabbaths as well as week-days, and has been from the first day until now. Though he rested on the seventh day from his work of creation, he never rests from his work of upholding, governing, and blessing the universe he has made. Jesus put himself side by side with God, and justified his healing on the Sabbath on the ground that his own activity, like that of the Father, was holy and unceasing.

18. **Therefore,** etc., *For this, therefore,* **the Jews sought the more to kill him ;** not only desired and formed the purpose to kill him, but began to form plans for legally apprehending and executing him. This became the settled habit of his enemies. The verse indicates an interval of time, longer or shorter, between Jesus' brief reply in ver. 17 and the longer defence in ver. 19. **Not only had broken the sabbath,** in their opinion, and according to their traditions. The charge that the Jews now brought against him was that he claimed equality with God in calling him *his Father.* The word translated *his* means *his own.* Compare Rom. 8 : 32. There is a sense, which the Jews themselves recognized, in which men may be the sons of God. Compare ch. 1 : 12, 13. But Christ here claims it in a sense peculiar to himself. And not only in a peculiar sense, but in a real sense, as denoting that identity of nature which is involved in sonship, so that he as the Son of God is himself God, just as the son of a man is a man. This necessarily implied equality with God—*i. e.,* equality of nature. The rulers understood him to claim this, which, to their minds, was adding to the crime of Sabbath-breaking the crime of blasphemy. If they had mistaken his meaning, Jesus would surely have corrected their misapprehensions. Instead of this, he publicly defends himself before the Sanhedrim or its representatives in the long address that fills the rest of this chapter, and in this plainly asserted his divine "authority, commission, dignity, and equality with God the Father."

19. **The Son can do nothing of himself.** Jesus declares in this verse the principle on which the statement of verse 17 is founded. The language is figurative. He represents himself as seeing what the Father does, and imitating it. What he wishes to convey in this figurative language is the community of action between them, based on their essential unity. Neither of them works independently, but the Father works through the Son, and the Son from the Father. The further thought expressed, besides that of community of action, is that the act originates with the Father. **What he seeth the Father do,** literally, *except he sees the Father doing something.* **For what things soever he doeth,** etc. The reason for what he had just asserted. "The words 'what things soever' are without limit; all that the Father does the Son does likewise. This is as high an assertion as possible of his being equal with God. If one does all that another does or can do, then there is proof of equality. If the Son does all that the Father

20 wise. For the Father loveth the Son, [q] and showeth
him all things that himself doeth; and he will show
him [r] greater works than these, that ye may marvel.
21 [s] For as the Father raiseth up the dead, and quickeneth *them;* [t] even so the Son quickeneth whom he will.
22 For the Father judgeth no man, but [u] hath committed
23 all judgment unto the Son; [x] that all *men* should
honor the Son, even as they honor the Father.
[y] He that honoreth not the Son honoreth not the
Father which hath sent him.

[q] ch. 10. 32; 15. 15; Prov. 8. 22-31; Luke 10. 22. [r] vers. 25, 28, 29. [s] Deut. 32. 39; 1 Kings 17. 21, 22. [t] ch. 11. 25, 43, 44; 17. 2; Luke 7. 14, 15; 8. 54, 55. [u] ver. 27; ch. 3. 35; 17. 2; Matt. 11. 27; 16. 27; 25. 31-46; 28. 18; Acts 10. 42; 17. 31; 2 Tim. 4. 1; 1 Pet. 4. 5. [x] ch. 10. 30; 14. 1; Heb. 1. 6. [y] ch. 15. 23, 24; 16. 14, 15; 17. 10; 1 John 2. 23; 2 John 9.

does, then like him he must be almighty, omniscient, all-present, and infinite in every perfection; or, in other words, he must be God."

20. **For the Father loveth the Son.** We have here the basis or reason for this community of action in the love which the Father bears the Son. Love is the principle which regulates the relations between them. And it contains further the reason for the second part of the preceding verse. It is not only true that the Son does nothing except what he sees the Father do, but also that he does whatever the Father does. His work not only corresponds to the Father's as far as it goes; it goes as far and embraces as much as the Father's. And this, the statement of the second part of ver. 19, is confirmed by the statement that the Father shows him all things that he himself does. And finally the verse asserts that the Father will cause him to perform greater works than these miracles of healing which have caused such excitement. **He will show him greater works than these.** *Greater* is emphatic: *Greater works than these will he show him.* What these greater works are, see next verse. **That ye,** probably the unbelieving hearers. The divine intention is expressed. **May marvel.** Though they might persevere in unbelief, it would be in face of such evidence as would excite their astonishment. "Faith they might withhold; astonishment he will compel."—LANGE.

21. **For as the Father raiseth up the dead, and quickeneth them,** etc. We have here a statement of one of the greater works to be done by the Son. The raising of the dead and quickening them is the spiritual, not the physical, act—the giving of life to those dead in trespasses and sins. This is proved, first, by the fact that it is an act based on the will and judgment of Christ, and involves, therefore, discrimination among men, while the resurrection is general and undiscriminating. See vers. 22 and 29. Second, by the grounding of the judgment, and the selection based upon it, on belief in the Father and the Son, which is the condition of eternal life. See ver. 24. And third, by the fact that the time of this resurrection is already present. See ver. 25; compare ver. 28. These points will be developed in the verses referred to. There are two divine prerogatives here ascribed to the Son—first, the giving of eternal life; and second, the selection of the persons to whom it is to be given.

22. This verse contains the confirmation of the second divine prerogative contained in the words *whom he will* of ver. 21. This, of course, involves the act of judgment, and this authority to execute judgment is here ascribed to the Son. **For the Father judgeth no man,** etc. This statement is harmonized with those passages which describe the Father as judging, by the general scriptural doctrine that whatever the Father does, he does through the Son, so that the direct agent in this, as in other spheres of divine action, is the Son. Compare Phil. 2:10, 11; Rom. 14:9, 12. This fact, that the quickening spoken of in the preceding verse is of those whom the Son wills, implying the selection of certain among men to receive it, and that it is, as this verse shows, an act of judgment, constitutes the first proof mentioned above that it is the spiritual quickening of dead souls, and not the resurrection of the body, for that is general.

23. **That all men should honor**

24 Verily, verily, I say unto you, ᵃ He that heareth my word, and believeth on him that sent me, hath everlasting life, and shall not come into condemna-
25 tion; ᵃ but is passed from death unto life. Verily, verily, I say unto you, The hour is coming, and now is, when ᵇ the dead shall hear the voice of the Son of
26 God; and they that hear shall live. For as the Father ᶜ hath life in himself, so hath he given to the
27 Son to have life in himself; and hath given him authority to execute judgment also, ᵈ because he is the

ᵃ ch. 3. 16, 18, 36; 8. 51; Gal. 3. 13.

ᵃ Col. 1. 13; 1 John 3. 14.

ᵇ Rom. 6. 4; Eph. 2. 1, 5; 5. 14; Col. 2. 13.

ᶜ Ex. 3. 14.

ᵈ Dan. 7. 13, 14; Phil. 2. 7-11.

the Son, even as they honor the Father. The object of this giving over of judgment to the Son is here stated, that men, seeing him invested with divine prerogatives, may give him divine honor as they do the Father. **He that honoreth not the Son,** etc. The result of withholding from the Son this honor, is to dishonor the Father who sent him, on the principle that a king is involved in the dishonor of his messenger or representative. "Our Lord is showing his *equality* with the Father. As the life-giving power which he had claimed proved his divine *omnipotence,* so does his ability to judge mankind prove his divine *omniscience.* And these are to be fully displayed, that he may be honored even as the Father, who, indeed, is not truly honored unless the Son is honored too."—*Annotated Parag. Bible.*

24. The **Verily, verily, I say unto you,** with which this statement opens, is intended to give solemn emphasis to it. Christ gives here the ground on which the judgment of vers. 21 and 22 is based—the test by which men are to be judged in selecting the recipients of the everlasting life—viz., listening to the Son and believing on him who sent him—that spiritual life which continues and increases for ever. Compare ch. 12 : 44; 17 : 3; 1 John 5 : 9-12. This constitutes the second proof mentioned above that it is the eternal life of which Christ is speaking in ver. 21—for it is this life which is conditioned by faith—and, furthermore, that is specified in this verse as the life meant. The *eternal life* is contrasted with **condemnation,** and is therefore to be connected with justification or pardon. Until the man believes he is condemned and dead; but with the act of faith he passes over from the state of condemnation and death, is pardoned, and receives eternal life. **Is passed,** *has passed* already, **from death,** of sin, unbelief, and guilt, **unto life—**a life of faith, righteousness, and bliss. Compare Rom. 8 : 1-6.

25. **The hour is coming, and now is,** etc. This verse reiterates with emphasis the statement of ver. 21, with the added particular that the Son is already exercising the power there ascribed to him. And in *this element of time* consists the third proof that it is not the physical resurrection there alluded to, since that is future. The spiritually **dead** shall hear his voice and live—have spiritual life, ch. 17 : 2, 3.

26, 27. These verses recapitulate summarily the arguments by which Christ sustains his claim of imparting eternal life. He has both the power and the authority necessary. The power, in that the Father has endowed him with the same life-giving power that he has himself—**life in himself.** Compare ch. 6 : 57; 11 : 25; 14 : 6, 19. The authority, in that the Father has authorized him to perform the act of judgment necessary in selecting men for the life eternal. **So hath he given to the Son; . . . hath given him authority.** In his divinity he needed not that this power and authority should be given him, but as man he needed that it should be conferred. Jesus speaks of it as an historical fact. *He gave*—that is, at his incarnation. The reason for investing the Son with this authority of judge is, that he is the Son of man. Christ is distinguished from the Father and the Spirit by his connection with man; and by virtue of this connection he is made the King and Judge of mankind. **Because he is the Son of man,** rather, *a son of man,* particularizing and thus emphasizing the fact. Judicial authority has been given him as the man Christ Jesus (1 Tim. 2 : 5),

28 Son of man. Marvel not at this: for the hour is coming, *in the which all that are in the graves shall 29 hear his voice, ʳand shall come forth; ᵍthey that have done good, unto the resurrection of life, and they that have done evil, unto the resurrection of damnation.
30 I can of mine own self do nothing: as I hear, ʰI judge, and my judgment is just; because ⁱI seek not mine own will, but the will of the Father which hath

* 1 Cor. 15. 42-54
Rev. 20. 11-13.
ᶠ Isa. 26. 19; 1 Cor. 15. 52; 1 Thess. 4. 16.
ᵍ Dan. 12. 2; Matt 25. 31-46; Rom 2. 6-10.
ʰ ch. 8. 15, 16.
ⁱ ch. 4. 34; 6. 38, Matt. 26. 39.

---

the Mediator. Compare Dan. 7 : 13, 14; Acts 17 : 31. See note on ch. 1 : 51.
28. Marvel not at this, for the hour is coming, etc., rather *an hour,* etc. Men are not to wonder at this claim of Christ to impart eternal life to men. For he has the power also to raise the physically dead, and the time is coming when he will exercise this power on all the dead. But this does not require the preliminary act of judgment, for this resurrection is general, and includes those who have done good and evil alike.
29. They that have done good, unto the resurrection of life, etc. Life in its highest form; a state of unending bliss. There is, however, a judgment connected with this resurrection. But it comes after it. And the terms and tests of this judgment are different from those which determine the gift of eternal life. In that case it was faith that was demanded; in the final judgment, of which this verse speaks, it is good works. But while the terms of judgment are different, the awards are the same. *Life* is connected with good works in this case, as it is with faith in the other, and evil works meet the same condemnation at the end as unbelief at the beginning. This is explained as follows: The faith of the Christian religion is a "faith that works by love," and "faith without works is dead." The uniform representation of the final judgment, therefore, is of a judgment based on the "works done in the body, whether they be good or evil." For this is the final test of Christian character, that the faith with which it starts has been fruitful of good works. But why have the two judgments to determine the same thing (see on vers. 21, 22, 26), the result of both being the gift of eternal life? The answer to this is also given us in the New Testament. The believer in this life receives only the assurance of eternal life in its highest and final form, and the Spirit as the first-fruits and pledge of his future inheritance. He is in the position of an heir to a large estate before he comes of age. The property is his, and he may have a certain income from it, but he is not yet in actual possession of it. He indeed has a spiritual life, but before he comes into the actual possession of his final inheritance tests are applied to determine the genuineness of his life, and of the faith by which the original gift was obtained. And so "he that believeth shall be saved," and "he that endures to the end shall be saved." **The resurrection of damnation,** rather, *of judgment*—a resurrection to death eternal—an unending state of misery. .
30. I can of mine own self, *of myself,* **do nothing: as I hear, I judge,** etc. This verse corrects any misapprehension that may have arisen from the preceding statement, by declaring that, though Christ is Judge, he does not act independently in this any more than in any other part of his works, but in connection with the Father and as his representative. The terms of judgment are those which he has received from the Father. He does not mean that his will is different from the Father's, but that he does not seek for that which shall determine his action in himself, but in the Father, or rather in himself, as his nature and will are determined by his connection with the Father. If we could conceive Christ acting independently of this, his judgment would not be just. **Because I seek not mine own will,** etc.; the reason why his judgment is just and right. Here, for **of the Father,** the

31 sent me. ᵏ If I bear witness of myself, my witness is
32 not true. ˡ There is another that beareth witness of
me, and I know that the witness which he witnesseth
of me is true.
33 ᵐ Ye sent unto John, and he bare witness unto the
34 truth. But I receive not testimony from man; but
35 these things I say, that ye might be saved. He was
a burning and ⁿ a shining light: and ᵒ ye were willing
for a season to rejoice in his light.
36 But ᵖ I have greater witness than *that* of John; for
the works which the Father hath given me to finish,
the same works that I do bear witness of me, that the

ᵏ Deut. 19. 15
Prov. 27. 2; Rev. 3. 14.
ˡ vers. 36,37; Matt. 3. 17; 17. 5; 1 John 5. 6, 7, 9.
ᵐ ch. 1. 19-34.
ⁿ Matt.11.11; Luke 1. 15-17; 2 Pet. 1. 19.
ᵒ Matt. 3. 5-7; 11. 7-9; 13. 20, 21; 21.26; Mark 6.20.
ᵖ 1 John 5. 9.

---

most approved text reads *of him which sent me.* Acting according to the oneness of nature and will with the Father, he therefore acts in perfect rectitude.

31-47. JESUS SHOWS THAT IT IS THE FATHER WHO BEARS WITNESS TO HIM IN HIS WORKS AND IN THE SCRIPTURES, AND ALSO POINTS TO THE UNBELIEF OF THE JEWS.

31. Christ comes in this verse to a consideration of the testimony by which these wonderful claims are confirmed. The emphatic word in the first clause is the subject, **If I,** *myself*, which is contrasted with the other witness spoken of in the following verse. The principle stated is, that if such claims were supported only by his word, without any accompanying testimony from God, they would **not** be **true,** or valid. They must have other confirmation than his witness.

32. This first clause, **There is another,** etc., is better translated, *It is another,* etc. Who this other is he proceeds to show, vers. 33-36. He is such, and his testimony is of such a sort, that he is assured of its truth. God had already testified of him by the descent of the Holy Spirit, by miracles, and by a voice from heaven.

33. Christ considers the testimony of John first: **Ye sent unto John.** They had shown their sense of the value of John's testimony by sending to him to make inquiries; and John had witnessed to **the truth** by pointing to One who was to follow him as the Messiah, and eventually by designating Jesus personally as the Christ, ch. 1: 19-36.

34. **But I receive not testimony from man;** *i. e., the* testimony—that of which he is speaking—is not human.

Christ does not deny in general that he receives such testimony, for that would not be true. John the Baptist was such a witness, and so were the apostles and Christians generally. He refers to this testimony of John for their benefit, that they **might be saved.** This purpose is not to be accomplished wholly nor principally by the citation of John, but it is one of the means used for it. Christ sets here the example followed by Paul, who "would by all means save some."

35. This verse, **He was a burning and a shining light: and ye were willing for a season to rejoice in his light,** is also improved by translation: *He was the burning and shining lamp; and you were willing to rejoice for a time in its light.* It is intended to correct any impression that he was depreciating John, by showing what John's real office was. He was the *lamp;* not an original and powerful source of *light* like the sun. See ch. 1: 8, 9. But notwithstanding this, the Jews were willing to exult temporarily in his light. "He was only as the light of the candle [lamp], for whose rays, indeed, men are grateful; but which is pale, flickering, transitory, compared with the glories of the Eternal Flame from which itself is kindled."—LIGHTFOOT, *On Revision,* p. 118. If they would, however, Jesus would have them believe on him through John's testimony.

36. **Greater witness.** This greater testimony is his works. Inasmuch, however, as these works are those which the Father has given him to do, they are really the witness of God himself. He is therefore the other witness of whom the Lord speaks. The thing to which they bear witness is that God sent him. They are God's endorsement

A. D. 28. JOHN V. 105

37 Father hath sent me. And the Father himself, which
hath sent me, ^q hath borne witness of me. Ye have
neither heard his voice at any time, ^r nor seen his
38 shape. And ^s ye have not his word ^t abiding in you;
39 ^u for whom he hath sent, ^x him ye believe not. ^y Search
the Scriptures; ^z for in them ye think ye have eternal
life; and ^a they are they which testify of me.
40 ^b And ye will not come to me, ^c that ye might have
41, 42 life. ^d I receive not honor from men. But I know

^q ch. 6. 27; 8. 18; Matt. 3. 17; 17. 5.
^r ch. 1. 18.
^s ch. 8. 37, 47.
^t Ps. 119. 11; Col. 3. 16; 1 John 2.
^u Mark 12. 24.
^x Isa. 53. 1–3.
^y Deut. 6. 6; Prov. 8. 33, 34; Isa. 8. 20; 34. 16.
^z See Luke 10. 25–29.

^s ch. 1. 45; 20. 31; Deut. 18. 15, 18; Luke 24. 27, 44; 1 Pet. 1. 11; Rev. 19. 10. ^b ch. 1. 1. 3. 19; 12. 37, 40; Matt. 22. 3; 23. 37; Rom. 10. 16–21; Rev. 22. 17. ^c ch. 14. 6. ^d ver. 31; ch. 6. 15; 1 Thess. 2. 6.

of him as a divine messenger. Instead of the same works, it should be rendered *the works themselves*. Christ often appealed to his miracles, ch. 10 : 25, 37 ; 14 : 10, 11; 15 : 24. The works may perhaps include the whole course of his teachings as well as his miracles. His teachings bore evidence of divine origin.

37. And the Father himself which hath sent me, etc. This should rather be translated, *And the Father who sent me, he has*, etc. The subject is repeated in the pronoun for emphasis, *He has borne witness of me*. There is not only this indirect testimony of the Father in the works of Christ; there is also direct personal testimony from him. This testimony has not been given, however, in personal intercourse with them, for they have never seen nor heard him.

38. Ye have not his word abiding in you. God has never spoken his word of truth within them. For they do not believe in his Son, *whom he sent*, which any inwardly enlightened man would do. They showed they did not receive the testimony of God by rejecting that of his Son.

39, 40. Search the Scriptures. Rather, *ye search the Scriptures*, the Old Testament Scriptures, to find out rites and observances in order to insure salvation. But they are a testimony of the Father to me, the Messiah and Saviour of men. He bases this appeal on their own recognition of the value and authority of these writings. In them ye think, he says, ye have eternal life. The *ye* is emphatic. And these very Scriptures in which you trust are the witness of which I have been speaking. They contain this personal testimony of the Father to me. And they

are they which testify of me. Moreover, the course of thought shows that they bear this special testimony to Christ as the source of the eternal life which the Jews believed that the Scriptures revealed. For the connection is, And ye will not come to me, that ye might, *may*, have life. "Although you look to the Scriptures for eternal life, and although they testify concerning me as the Source of that life, yet you will not come to me for it." And this claim, that he is the Author of eternal life, is the very one which Christ has made in the preceding part of the discourse (vers. 21–30), and which he has sought to substantiate by the testimony of these witnesses.

41. The connection of this verse is a little difficult. But it is probably a disclaimer of personal, self-glorifying ends in this discourse of self-defence. Although they rejected him, he was not dependent upon their esteem; neither did he seek or take to himself human applause. I receive not, *I appropriate not to myself*, honor from men. All of this has gathered about himself, and of course it seems to have his glory for its object. But this glory, if it was sought in this discourse, would be a glory coming from men, and that, Christ says, he does not receive.

42. But I know you, that ye have not the love of God in you, the reason why they rejected him. The real object that Christ is seeking is not that they should glorify him, but that they should love God. And the discourse has been to show them that they have not this really important love to God. For he is in such relation to the Father that their refusal to receive him reveals want of love to

5 *

43 you, that ᵉye have not the love of God in you. I am come in my Father's name, and ye receive me not; ᶠif another shall come in his own name, him ye will 44 receive. How can ye believe, ᵍwhich receive honor one of another, and seek not ʰthe honor that *cometh* 45 from God only? Do not think that I will accuse you to the Father; ⁱthere is *one* that accuseth you, *even* 46 Moses, ᵏin whom ye trust. For had ye believed Moses, ye would have believed me; ˡfor he wrote 47 of me. ᵐBut if ye believe not his writings, how shall ye believe my words?

ᵉ ch. 8. 42, 47; Rom. 8. 7; 1 John 2. 15.
ᶠ Acts 5. 36, 37.
ᵍ ch. 12. 43; Matt. 23. 5-7; Phil. 2. 3.
ʰ Rom. 2. 29; 2 Cor 10. 18.
ⁱ ch. 7. 19; Rom. 2. 12, 17-24.
ᵏ ch. 9. 28, 29; Gal. 3. 10.
ˡ ch. 1. 45; Luke 24. 27; Acts 26. 22.
ᵐ Luke 16. 29-31.

God. The following verse shows that by their conduct they did not love God.

43. **I am**, *or have*, **come . . . ye receive me not.** This verse combines the statement of the one which precedes, that the Jews do not really love God, for they reject him who comes in the name of God. Compare ch. 8 : 42. The argument is, that real love to God will show itself in the acceptance of One who comes in his name and is in perfect sympathy with him. But one coming **in his own name they will receive.** The sinful principle shown in this is twofold: First, there is the endorsement of one who sets aside God—comes in his own name instead of God's. And second, of one who seeks to exalt and glorify himself. They show thereby their sympathy with godlessness and selfishness. Their willingness to follow impostors would show their want of love to God. Thus false Christs afterward appeared, whom they followed to their own destruction.

44. **How can ye believe, which,** *who*, **receive honor one of another,** etc.? This seeking of human applause was, indeed, self-idolatry. This selfishness and desire for the praise of men is what stands in the way of their believing. Christ says that they cannot believe as long as they remain actuated by this principle. For faith seeks honor, not from men, but from God. The very essence of faith is humility and self-renunciation, while its supreme desire is the approval of God. In the last clause, instead of **from God only**, read, *from the only God*, pointing to the unity so clearly taught in the writings of Moses, of whom he proceeds to speak. God is the only source of true honor.

45. **Do not think that I will accuse you,** etc. That was not a part of his work, ch. 3 : 17. Nor was it needful, for Moses was their accuser. The emphatic word in the first clause is the **I**, which is contrasted with **Moses** in the following clause. They are to be accused, but not by him. They might have inferred easily from the tone of his discourse that he was to be their accuser. But they are to be accused notwithstanding, and that, too, by the very Moses in whom their hopes as a nation have been placed. Of course, this confidence in Moses had not been based on anything that he could do for them, but on his writings, and specially on the law which he had given them. **In whom ye trust**, or better, *have hoped*.

46. **For had ye believed Moses, ye would have believed me.** This verse confirms the statement that Moses would be their accuser. For their disbelief in Christ involves necessarily disbelief of Moses, who wrote concerning Christ. **For he wrote of me,** Deut. 18 : 15. An important testimony of Jesus to the writings of Moses, and the application of this and other passages to him as the Messiah.

47. **But if ye believe not his writings,** etc. We have here the reverse of the preceding. If they had believed Moses, they would have believed Christ. But if they do not believe what Moses wrote concerning Christ, how can they be expected to believe what Christ says concerning himself? The contrast is between Moses, whom they had been taught all their lives and by immemorial tradition to believe, and Christ, whose claims were new, and, moreover, utterly repugnant to their perverted views of the Messianic office.

PRACTICAL REMARKS.

1. The miracles of Christ are typical of his spiritual works of power. And this typical character is not only a general quality, but each miracle presents some special phase of the Lord's work and powers in the realm of spirit, vers. 1-9.

2. In this miracle the fact is emphasized that the disability removed was one of long standing, and the miracle represents, therefore, Christ's power to heal spiritual diseases and disabilities aggravated in the same way, vers. 1-5.

3. The immediateness of the cure is noticeable in the same connection, ver. 9.

4. The implicit faith of the man in his healer, accepting his word as that of one who had shown in the miracle his possession of divine authority, even in a matter about which current opinion was quite different, is also noticeable and commendable, vers. 6-9.

5. The acceptance of well-attested authority in matters of this kind is frequently quite reasonable, vers. 8, 9.

6. The connection between sin and suffering suggested here (ver. 14), and fully stated elsewhere, is that sin causes suffering, and that present sufferings are God's warnings against the greater evils with which sin is to be punished hereafter, vers. 5-14; 1 Cor. 11 : 30.

7. Jesus selects this worst case from the great multitude; so election frequently saves the most desperate, ver. 3; 1 Tim. 1 : 15, 16.

8. "Jesus would have our earnest will," ver. 6; Luke 13 : 24; Jer. 29 : 13.

9. Jesus will help when all human helpers fail us, ver. 7; Ps. 27 : 10.

10. "The word of Jesus has power; what he commands, he gives," vers. 8, 9.

11. To sin after special grace is to provoke the visitations of the worst judgments, ver. 14; Matt. 18 : 23-34.

12. There is a time to speak and a time to be silent. It is not best always to be babbling even of what grace Jesus has given us specially, ver. 15; Matt. 7 : 6.

13. Christ's answer to the charge of breaking the Sabbath contains some of his most instructive teachings in regard to his relations to the Father, vers. 10-18.

14. In the first place, he claimed the right to do what the Father did, ver. 17.

15. This claim rested on his Sonship, and the Sonship was of a peculiar nature that involved natural essential equality, ver. 18.

16. This relation was such that he could do nothing but what the Father did, and, on the other hand, did everything that the Father did, vers. 19, 20.

17. The relation was such, however, that the acts originate with the Father, rather than with the Son, vers. 19, 20.

18. Further, the authority for Christ's acts (vers. 22, 27), and the power, proceed from the Father, vers. 26-30.

19. To establish this claim he appeals to the witness of the Father—first, in his own works (ver. 36); second, in the inward witness given to the believer (ver. 38); and third, specially in the Scriptures, vers. 39, 40.

20. On the strength of this relation to the Father, Christ claims to impart eternal life (vers. 21 ff.); to select the persons to receive it (ver. 21); to perform the act of judgment necessary in such selection (vers. 22 ff.); to raise the dead at the last day (vers. 28, 29); and to judge them after they are raised, vers. 22, 29.

21. The significance of the *terms* of judgment—faith, in the act of justification, and works, in the last judgment—has been noticed in the critical notes. See on ver. 29.

22. To be the means of saving souls is a more glorious work than the miraculous healing of bodies, vers. 20, 21; John 14 : 12.

23. How simple the terms of salvation! Only implicit trust and loving obedience. Hear and live, vers. 24, 25. Just as we have, *look and live*, Isa. 45 : 22; John 3 : 14, compared with Num. 21 : 8, 9.

24. The personal experience of redemption taking effect in the spirit sufficiently encourages faith in the final redemption of the body, ver. 28; Rom. 8 : 23.

25. Aim to save an objector, even if you must press him with arguments from his own lower standpoint, vers. 33, 34; 1 Cor. 9 : 22.

26. "As a burning light while lighting others consumes itself, so Christian teachers should sacrifice themselves in the service of God and their fellowmen," ver. 35.

27. The testimony of Christ to the

Jesus miraculously feeds a multitude.   * Matt. 14. 13-21
VI. AFTER ᵃ these things Jesus went over the sea of   Mark 6. 32-44   Luke 9. 10-17.

divine authority of the Scriptures is very strong and positive. They contain the Father's personal witness to the Son—a witness more direct than Christ's own works, vers. 39, 45, 46, 47.

28. Scripture testimony is that by which men are to be judged, vers. 39-47.

29. The works of Jesus, perpetuating and multiplying themselves to this day in the progressive regeneration of the race, are more powerful as testimony than anything seen in his own lifetime on earth, ver. 36; John 12 : 24, 32.

30. The most powerful testimony to Jesus, the foundation and bulwark of his church, is the direct revelation to the spirit from the Eternal Father, ver. 37; Matt. 16 : 17.

31. The Scriptures, sufficiently searched, evince in themselves that they testify truly to the eternal life, and to Jesus Christ as the Prince of that life, ver. 39.

32. While the praise of every step of salvation must be ascribed to Christ, the guilt of refusal must always be referred to the sinner, ver. 40.

33. A devotion to the praise of men is one of the strongest snares to the soul, ver. 44; Prov. 29 : 25 ; John 12 : 43.

34. The wicked will be condemned even by their own standards, vers. 45-47; Luke 19 : 22.

CHAPTER VI.

We have in this chapter another of the principles on which John selects the few miracles recorded by him. The miracle of feeding precedes and prepares the way for the discourse on the bread of life. The discourses are the principal thing in this Gospel, and the miracles and other events serve mainly as the setting of these wonderful words. The symbolic character of the miracles is evident here too. Christ's power to supply the spiritual need of man is illustrated, and also his ability to multiply the few things of human instrumentality into the many of divine grace, vers. 1-14. During the night between the feeding of the multitude and the discourse on the bread of life occurs his walking upon the water, vers. 15-21;

and the next morning the multitude find Jesus at Capernaum, 22-27. The discourse that follows may be analyzed as follows: Men are to work for spiritual rather than bodily food, ver. 27. The work necessary to secure the latter is faith in Christ, vers. 29, 35, 40, 47, 51, 53, 54, 57, 58. If men seek a sign by which they may believe, Christ himself is that sign by virtue of his being the bread of life, vers. 30-35. Christ for ever satisfies the need of the soul that comes to him, so that it never hungers more—*i. e.*, for life. Other wants may be continually arising, and need constant replenishing, but this is satisfied once for all, vers. 35, 37, 39, 40, 47, 50, 51, 54, 58. Men exercise this faith in Christ, by which they secure eternal life, only as the Father draws them, vers. 36, 37, 39, 44, 45, 65. In accordance with what he has said about the permanent satisfaction of the believing soul, Christ keeps, and finally saves, those who have exercised faith, vers. 39, 40, 44. In the mutual relations between them, the Father draws men to the Son, and the Son reveals to men the Father, vers. 45, 46. The reason that Christ becomes thus the source of life to men is that he has life in himself, vers. 51, 57. That by which Christ becomes the bread of life is his sacrificial death, vers. 51, 53-56. Christ is not represented as the sustenance, but as the source, of life, vers. 33, 35, 53. Christ becomes the source of an eternal life to the soul, because there is an abiding of the soul in him and of him in the soul. The soul that once partakes of him has taken into itself an imperishable, life - giving substance ; that is, the result depends not on the continual partaking, but on the quality of that which the soul takes into itself once for all, ver. 56.

In the effect produced on his disciples by this discourse we see the beginning of a sad history. The cross becomes what it has always remained—the stumbling-block of the Christian religion. But Christ sees in this only the natural and, to the wise man, the expected result; the heart of man being what it is, such that only the grace of God can subdue it, vers 60-71.

2 Galilee, which is *the sea* of Tiberias. And a great

1-14. JESUS PASSES TO THE EASTERN SIDE OF THE LAKE, WHERE HE MIRACULOUSLY FEEDS THE FIVE THOUSAND, Matt. 14 : 13-21 ; Mark 6 : 31-44 ; Luke 9 : 10-17. The great importance of this account and miracle may be inferred from the fact that all the evangelists relate it. Mark and John are the fullest and enter most into details. Matthew and Luke are about equally concise. This is the third time in the life of Jesus that all four evangelists harmonize upon the same event. The two preceding are the departure of Jesus into Galilee, after his early Judæan ministry (John 4 : 1-4), and his arrival and teaching in Galilee, John 4 : 43-46. As this feeding the multitude was near the passover, A. D. 29, nearly a year had intervened between the last chapter and this. During that time Jesus labored actively in Galilee. John passes over this, as it was his purpose to record Christ's ministry in

SEA OF GALILEE.

Judæa rather than in Galilee. His Gospel also appears to be somewhat supplemental to those of the others. Compare *Author's Harmony*, ?? 31, 33, 76.

1. **After these things.** The events recorded in the preceding chapter were at the time of a passover. According to ver. 4, a passover was now near, and there is therefore an interval of a year between the two times. By reference to the parallel account in Matt. 14 : 13 we find that Jesus crossed the lake because he had just heard of the death of John the Baptist; and from Mark 6 : 31 we learn the additional reason, that the disciples had just returned from their missionary-tour in Galilee, and wished to be alone with the Lord for a time to talk over what had happened, but could not on account of the crowd. Being the passover season, there were crowds passing through Capernaum on their way to Jerusalem, who stopped on the way to see Jesus. **Jesus went over**, rather, *away, beyond* **the sea of Galilee, which is the sea of Tiberias,** an explanation for foreign and Gentile readers. The sea is twelve and a half miles long, and about six and a half broad.

"John is the only evangelist who mentions Tiberias; but he not only speaks of the city, but calls the lake by this name more than once. May we not find in this an incidental corroboration of the opinion that his Gospel was written last of all, and toward the close of the first century, and for those who by that time had come to know the lake most familiarly by the name of Tiberias? This supposition becomes the

multitude followed him, because they saw his miracles which he did on them that were diseased. 3 And Jesus went up into a mountain, and there he 4 sat with his disciples. (°And the passover, a feast 5 of the Jews, was nigh.) ᴾ When Jesus then lifted up *his* eyes, and saw a great company come unto him, he saith unto Philip, Whence shall ye buy

* ch. 2. 13; 5. 1; Lev. 23. 5, 7; Deut. 16. 1.
ᴾ Matt. 14. 14-21; Mark 6.35; Luke 9. 12.

---

more probable when we remember that it was quite a modern town when our Lord frequented this region, having been built and named by Herod about the time of his advent. Seventy years afterward Josephus found it an important city, and no other in Galilee is so often mentioned by him. Almost every other city was destroyed by Vespasian and Titus, but this was spared, and rewarded for its adherence to the Romans by being made the capital of the province. John, writing many years after these events, would naturally mention both the city and the lake, and call the latter by its most familiar name, Tiberias. But the other apostles wrote before these events had taken place, and therefore do not speak of Tiberias at all."—Thomson, *Land and Book*, vol. ii. p. 72. See on ver. 23.

2. **A great multitude followed him.** Doubtless made up in part of those going to the passover, ver. 4. Jesus crossed the lake for the very purpose of escaping this crowd. See Mark 6 : 31. But according to the same account (Mark 6 : 34), he gave up this purpose from compassion for them, and came out of his retirement to teach them. **Because they saw his miracles,** etc. This seems to refer to some recent miracles he had wrought. According to Luke, Jesus retired to an uninhabited region near the eastern Bethsaida, which stood on the northeastern side of the lake.

3. The first clause of this verse should read, *And Jesus went up into the mountain* — that is, the mountain in that place, the mountainous highlands near the lake. It seems, according to this account, that Jesus did get some little time with his disciples, and this therefore supplements the other accounts, which would otherwise leave the impression that his retreat was immedia'ely entirely cut off by the crowd, which ran round the head of the lake to intercept him. **There he sat with his disciples,** being the posture of teaching, Matt. 5 : 1. Though they came hither for retirement and rest (Mark 6 : 31), yet the time was not idly spent. The disciples had time for reporting more fully their missionary-journey (Mark 6 : 12, 13, 30, 31), for conversation and instruction.

4. **And the passover.** See on ch. 2 : 13. This verse is explanatory, but not parenthetical, as in our common version. **A feast,** rather, *the feast,* the great or principal feast, **of the Jews.** The explanatory clause about the passover is another proof that the Gospel was written for Gentile readers. This statement about the passover is intended to explain the presence of the *great multitude.* See on vers. 1, 2. This passover, A. D. 29, began April 17th.

5. **When Jesus then lifted up his eyes,** etc. It is better to retain the participial form of the original in the first part of this verse: *Jesus therefore having lifted up his eyes, and having seen, says.* In this part of the narrative the other accounts are fuller. We learn from them that previous to the feeding of the multitude Jesus went out and taught them many things (Mark 6 : 34), and healed their sick (Matt. 14 : 14), and also that the disciples brought the destitute condition of the people to his attention, probably before this question addressed to Philip. The course of the conversation is probably this: In answer to the suggestion of his disciples that they send the multitude away to purchase food for themselves (Luke 9 : 12), he tells his disciples to feed them. The disciples ask, Shall we buy two hundred denarii' (about thirty dollars', worth of bread (Mark 6 : 37)? knowing that that is a large sum for them to expend, but small for such a purpose, and suggesting, therefore, the impossibility of his requirement. Christ then turns to Philip, and the rest of the conversation is as given here. **Philip.** See on ch. 1 : 43. While Judas was treasurer

6 bread, that these may eat? (And this he said ⁹ to prove him: for he himself knew what he would do.)
7 Philip answered him, ʳ Two hundred pennyworth of bread is not sufficient for them, that every one of
8 them may take a little. One of his disciples, Andrew,
9 Simon Peter's brother, saith unto him, There is a lad here, which hath five barley loaves, and two small fishes: ˢ but what are they among so many?
10 And Jesus said, Make the men sit down. Now there was much grass in the place. So the men sat
11 down, in number about five thousand. And Jesus took the loaves; and ᵗ when he had given thanks, he distributed to the disciples, and the disciples to them that were set down; and likewise of the fishes as

ᵠ Gen. 22. 1.

ʳ Num. 11. 21-23.

ˢ 2 Kings 4. 12-44; Ps. 78. 19, 20, 41.

ᵗ 1 Thess. 5. 18.

Philip may have had charge of provisions. Perhaps, too, his faith needed strengthening. Compare ch. 14 : 8.
6. We are told here that Christ wished to prove Philip; that is, to test his faith. He had probably never performed such a miracle, and he wishes to see if Philip's faith is strong enough to go beyond the bounds of his actual experience of Christ's power and suggest a new miracle. For he knew himself what he would do, *was about to do*. Jesus did not ask for counsel. By this question it is shown that a miracle was not expected by Philip and the disciples.
7. Two hundred pennyworth, two hundred denarii' worth. The denarius was a Roman silver coin worth about fifteen cents. The whole amount mentioned is therefore thirty dollars. That every one of them may take a little. Even this would be a scant supply, just enough to stay hunger.
8. One of his disciples, etc. The particularity with which Andrew is described is an indication that this Gospel was not written for the Jewish church, which would be familiar with these facts. On Andrew, see ch. 1 : 40.
9. The bread was in the shape of what we call cakes rather than loaves—*i. e.*, flat and round. Philip shows the impracticability of purchasing what was necessary for such a multitude, and Andrew the entire insufficiency of anything that they had on hand. Barley loaves were an inferior kind of food, and the fishes were small.
10. The first time that the word men occurs here it is the general word denoting persons, including women and children. The second time it is the specific word for *men* alone. Matthew (14 : 21) says that the number, exclusive of women and children, was about five thousand. We cannot infer certainly from this how many there were in all, but probably at least seven thousand. The posture taken was not a *sitting*, but a *reclining*, posture. This is what the words used mean, *Make the men recline*, or *lie down*, and it was the ordinary posture at meals. Now there was much grass in the place, which then in the spring covered the ground. "The scene of this extraordinary miracle is the noble plain (Butaiha) at the mouth of the Jordan, which during most of the year is now, as then, covered with green grass."—DR. J. P. NEWMAN, *From Dan to Beersheba*, p. 395. "This Butaiha belonged to Bethsaida. At this extreme southeast corner of it the mountain shuts down upon the lake bleak and barren. . . . In this little cove the ships (boats) were anchored. On this beautiful sward at the base of the rocky hill the people were seated to receive from the hands of the Son of God the miraculous bread, emblematic of his body, which is the true bread from heaven."—DR. THOMSON, *The Land and the Book*, vol. ii. p. 29. This plain east of the Jordan forms a triangle, the shore of the lake making one side, the Jordan the second, and the eastern mountains the third.
11. The words, To the disciples, and the disciples, should be omitted, according to the best manuscripts. When he had given thanks, having praised God for it. Mark and Luke say he *blessed*, implored God's blessing

12 much as they would. When they were filled, he said unto his disciples, Gather up the fragments that remain, that nothing be lost. Therefore they gathered *them* together, and filled twelve baskets with the fragments of the five barley loaves, which remained over and above unto them that had eaten.

14 Then those men, when they had seen the miracle that Jesus did, said, This is of a truth ᵘthat prophet that should come into the world.

ᵘ ch. 1. 21; 4. 19, 25; 7. 40; Gen. 49. 10; Deut. 18 15–18; Mal. 3. 1; Matt. 11. 3.

on the bread, and praised God for it. The latter includes the former. The word translated *bless* is used in praising God for favors, Luke 1 : 64; also in invoking God's blessing, Luke 2 : 34; also in God's conferring favors, Heb. 6 : 14; Acts 3 : 26. These three senses really met in Jesus. For as a man he praised God and implored his blessing, while as God he granted it. So Matthew (15 : 36) has *gave thanks*, while Mark (8 : 7) has *blessed*. The same diversity is seen in the account of the Lord's Supper. Matthew (26 : 26) and Mark (14 : 22) have *blessed*. Luke (22 : 19) and Paul (1 Cor. 11 : 24) have *gave thanks*. **As much as they would,** or *desired*. They were satisfied.

12. **Gather up the fragments,** etc. John alone informs us that Jesus gave this command. This frugality in the presence of such power is one of the most striking things about this miracle. But Christ was not in the habit of supplying ordinary wants in this way. His own and his disciples' wants were provided for in the usual ways, and frugality was one of these.

13. **Twelve baskets,** the usual Jewish travelling-baskets. We do not know the size of these baskets, and cannot tell, therefore, how much remained. But the intention of the writer evidently is to give the impression of a great quantity, comparatively, of fragments even from the original five loaves. The Jews were proverbial for carrying a basket, probably to keep their food from being polluted by accidental contact with Gentiles. The number of baskets here was twelve; thus each apostle filled his basket. Thus there remained much more than the original provisions, showing an actual increase of food, and not a supernatural restraining and satisfying of the appetite. Some suppose that the provisions taken up were those broken by Jesus, but undistributed. The most natural supposition, however, is that they had been distributed, or mostly so, and that they were gathered up from the ground where the companies had eaten. And this is implied by the words, **which remained over and above unto them that had eaten.**

14. **Then** here is not temporal, but inferential, therefore, and instead of **those** it should be *the men*, the people. The word **Jesus,** too, is not found in the best text, and instead of **that prophet,** it should be *the prophet*. The whole verse reads as follows: *The men, therefore, having seen the miracle which Jesus did, said, This is truly the prophet that is coming into the world.* This nameless prophet, whom the Jews were expecting, is the one mentioned in Deut. 18 : 15 and 18, who was to be like Moses. Some of them explained this of the Messiah; others of a prophet attending his coming. In this case they evidently referred it to the Messiah, for they contemplated making him king, ver. 15. The multitude were blind to this deep spiritual import and design, but they felt the force of the miracle as an evidence of the Messiahship of Jesus. Possibly a tradition that the Messiah would rain manna from heaven may also have had its influence in leading them to this conclusion.

Various attempts have been made by neologists to explain away this miracle by endeavoring to trace it to natural causes, and even by supposing it originally a parable, related by mistake as an actual occurrence. But all such attempts are manifestly absurd and ridiculous. All of the four narratives clearly convey the idea of superhuman power. They do not tell how that power was exerted or how the food was increased, but they do clearly tell us that a few loaves and fishes, which a lad could carry in his basket, were

A. D. 29. JOHN VI. 113

The disciples return across the sea of Galilee: Jesus walks on the water.

15 When Jesus therefore ˣ perceived that they would come and take him by force, ʸ to make him a king, ᶻ he departed again into a mountain himself alone.
16 ᵃ And when even was *now* come, his disciples went
17 down unto the sea and entered into a ship, and went over the sea toward Capernaum. And it was now
18 dark, and Jesus was not come to them. And the sea
19 arose by reason of a great wind that blew. So when they had rowed about five and twenty or thirty furlongs, they see Jesus walking on the sea, and drawing

ˣ ch. 2. 24, 25; Heb. 4. 13.
ʸ ch. 12. 12, 13.
ᶻ ch. 5. 41.
ᵃ Matt. 14. 22-36; Mark 6. 45-51.

increased so that thousands satisfied their hunger, and there remained at least twelve times more of fragments than of the original provisions. It is not necessary to suppose creative power; for the laws and the elements of the natural world being under the direction of Jesus, he could bring together at his will all the elements constituting the bread and the fishes. The power in one case was as truly omnipotent as in the other. Similar exhibitions of divine power are recorded in the Old Testament, in giving the manna (Ex. 16 : 4) and in multiplying the widow's oil, 2 Kings 4 : 2-7. Compare the turning of water into wine, ch. 2 : 9.

15-21. JESUS WALKS UPON THE SEA, Mark 14 : 22-36; Mark 6 : 45-56. Mark as usual enters most into detail, but omits all reference to Peter's walking on the water, which is alone recorded by Matthew, who ever delights in giving the words and sayings of Jesus. John gives a brief but independent account, as of an eye-witness, with several additional particulars. Luke, who passes over very briefly the period of six months from the passover A. D. 29 to the feast of tabernacles (Luke 9 : 17-51), omits all reference to this voyage and miracle.

15. **When Jesus therefore perceived that they would come and take him by force, to make him a king, he departed again into a mountain himself alone.** This statement of the intentions of the multitude explains what we are told in the other Gospels of the urgency of Christ in sending away his disciples and dismissing the multitude. As to the former, he was probably afraid that they would second the endeavors of the multitude, and make it more difficult for him to restrain them. **Himself alone,** watching and praying. The other accounts tell us that he went into the mountain to pray. The mountain is that of ver. 3. They would take him with them to Jerusalem to the passover, and there make him king.

16. **And when even was now come,** beginning with sunset—from about six to nine o'clock — **his disciples went down unto the sea,** . . . **toward Capernaum.** Mark tells us (6 : 45) that Christ sent the disciples to Bethsaida. Probably one was the place for which they started, and the other the place to which they were driven by the stress of the storm. The other accounts leave no doubt that he sent the disciples away first. The order of events in these narratives is not necessarily the order of their actual occurrence, either as regards separate events or the different parts of the same event, unless temporal particles are introduced fixing the order.

17. **And it was now dark, and Jesus was not come to them.** This statement does not imply, of course, that they were expecting Jesus to come to them, but it anticipates the following statement that he did come to them, walking on the water.

18. **And the sea arose by reason of a great wind that blew.** These storms are frequent on this lake, which is subject to sudden gusts of wind that sweep down through the gorges of the mountains, and in a few moments produce a violent tempest. See HACKETT, *Illustrations of Scripture,* p. 329.

19. **So when,** *when therefore.* **About five and twenty or thirty furlongs.** A furlong was a little less than an eighth of a mile. As the lake is at this point

20 nigh unto the ship, and they were afraid. But he
21 saith unto them, ᵇIt is I, be not afraid. Then they ᵇ Ps. 93. 4.
willingly received him into the ship, and immediately
the ship was at the land whither they went.

Christ's discourse in the synagogue at Capernaum.

22 The day following, when the people which stood
on the other side of the sea saw that there was none
other boat there, save that one whereinto his disciples
were entered, and that Jesus went not with his dis-
ciples into the boat, ᶜbut *that* his disciples were gone ᶜ vers. 16, 17.
23 away alone; (howbeit there came other boats from

somewhere between four and five miles in width, they were at this time about two-thirds of the way across. It was about the fourth watch of the night, or between three and four o'clock in the morning, Mark 6 : 48. The reason of their fear when they saw Jesus was that they did not recognize him. The other accounts say that they thought it was a spirit.
20. Jesus no longer acts as if he would pass by them (Mark 6 : 48), nor does he any longer continue silent. They are sufficiently tried, and immediately upon their manifesting their terror by crying aloud, Jesus talked with them. The familiar and tender tones of his voice indicate who he is, and tend at once to allay their fears. His words, too, are adapted to dispel their superstitious alarm. **It is I, be not afraid.** *Fear not* any danger, since I, whom you know as your Lord and Teacher, am here. At this point Matthew relates the incident of Peter's vain desire and attempt to imitate his Master in walking on the water. Much has been written upon this miracle, and much to no purpose. The silly evasion of those who, to ex- plain away the miracle, would translate "walking on the shore of the sea," is opposed alike to the strict and natural meaning of the words, the evident de- sign and form of the narrative in relat- ing a miracle, and the surprise and ter- ror of the disciples at the sight. How Jesus could have walked on the water we are not informed—whether he sus- pended the law of gravity in his own case, or counteracted the force of gravity by divine power, or made the waters solid beneath his feet. The second sup- position seems to me the most plausible. But he was divine, and the laws of Na- ture were subject to him, of which he could easily make a use wholly un- known to us.
21. **Then they willingly received,** etc. Their willingness is contrasted with their previous fear. It would seem that in the immediate coming of the ship to the land there is another miracle. The ship **immediately** came, apparently with miraculous speed, to the land whither they *were going;* that is, to Capernaum, ver. 17. Yet in popular language we often use such expressions as *immediately, at once,* meaning *very soon.* Nor is it necessary to suppose that they landed at once. As it was very early in the morning, they may have rested a while in the boat.
22–59. JESUS DISCOURSES IN RE- GARD TO THE BREAD OF LIFE IN THE SYNAGOGUE AT CAPERNAUM. Re- corded only by John.
22. This paragraph, to verse 25, ac- cording to the most approved text, reads as follows : " On the morrow, the mul- titude that stood on the other side of the sea saw that there was not another boat there except one, and that Jesus did not go with his disciples into the boat, but his disciples went away alone. But other boats came out from Tiberias, near the place where they ate the bread, the Lord having given thanks. When therefore the multitude saw that Jesus was not there, nor his disciples, they embarked themselves in the boats, and came to Capernaum, seeking Jesus." The statement of ver. 22 is intended to explain the surprise of the multitude in finding Jesus on the other—that is, the western—side, expressed in ver. 25. There was only one boat there, and Jesus did not go in that. How, then, did he get there?
23. This verse explains how they came over themselves. **Howbeit,** *but,*

A. D. 29. JOHN VI. 115

Tiberias nigh unto the place where they did eat
24 bread, after that the Lord had given thanks:) when
the people therefore saw that Jesus was not there,
neither his disciples, they also took shipping, and
25 came to Capernaum, seeking for Jesus. And when
they had found him on the other side of the sea, they
said unto him, ^d Rabbi, when camest thou hither?   ^d ch. 1. 38.
26   Jesus answered them and said, Verily, verily, I say
unto you, ^e Ye seek me, not because ye saw the mira-   ^e Ezek. 33.31: Phil
cles, but because ye did eat of the loaves, and were   2. 21; 3. 19.

From Tiberias. See on ver. 1. This is the only mention of this city in the Bible. "Tiberias is situated on the lake, and is held by the Jews to be the place where the true Messiah (yet to come) will land as he rises from this sea and is about to establish his throne on Mount Safed. The great Jewish university was for three hundred years here, making the place the intellectual metropolis of the Jews. Here the *Mishna*, or oral law, was reduced to a written form, and the *Gemara*, or commentary on the *Mishna*, was compiled, forming what is now known as the Jerusalem Talmud. There are about 2000 inhabitants in Tiberias, half of whom are Jews—a poor, squalid, sickly-looking remnant of this ancient people."—DR. FISH, *Bible Lands Illustrated*, pp. 552, 553.

" Is it not somewhat strange that our Saviour never entered Tiberias? This is not quite certain, for he undoubtedly visited many places which are not mentioned by any of the evangelists. And if the tradition respecting the site of the present old church has any foundation in fact, he did actually enter it, and even after his resurrection. It is my opinion, however, that he never came to Tiberias; and for several reasons, which, by the aid of Josephus, we are able to discover. He tells us that Herod, in order to people his new city, brought many strangers and people called Galileans, and many not even freemen, but slaves. In short, Herod gathered up all classes and compelled them to settle in Tiberias. This was not a population with which our Lord and his disciples would choose to associate. Josephus further states that to make this place habitable was to transgress the ancient laws of the Jews, because ' many sepulchres were here to be taken away in order to make room for the city of Tiberias, whereas our law pronounces that such persons are unclean for seven days.' Jesus therefore could not enter this city without becoming ceremonially unclean, and we know that both he and his disciples scrupulously avoided any such violation of the law of Moses. He *never visited Tiberias*, and thus the silence of the evangelists in regard to it is explained."—DR. THOMSON, *Land and Book*, pp. 72, 75.

After that the Lord, etc., rather, *The Lord having given thanks.* A most noticeable and instructive reference to the exhibition of divine power in connection with giving thanks.

24. **They also took shipping.** The boats are those mentioned in the preceding verse as coming out from Tiberias. The multitude was convinced that Jesus had in some way gone to the other side, and so they came over to find him.

25. The multitude is curious to know not only how, but when, Jesus could have come over the lake; for they have been watching the coast all the time, and did not see him. **Rabbi.** See on ch. 1 : 38.

26. The **Verily, verily, I say unto you,** with which Christ begins, is his most impressive way of introducing a statement. He attributes to this multitude the lowest motives short of positive hostility for seeking him — **because ye did eat of the loaves, and were filled.** Next above these, and the most common class that Christ encountered, were those who were attracted by the miracles that he performed, and accorded to him a certain authority corresponding to these. Then there were those who admired his teachings, his character, and so on. But here were those who were influenced mainly by selfish interests of a low order. The

JOHN VI.   A. D. 29.

27 filled. Labor not for ᶠ the meat which perisheth, but ᵍ for that meat which endureth unto everlasting life, which the Son of man ʰ shall give unto you: ⁱ for him hath God the Father sealed.
28   Then said they unto him, What shall we do, that
29 we might work the works of God? Jesus answered and said unto them, ᵏ This is the work of God, that ye believe on him whom he hath sent.
30   They said therefore unto him, ˡ What sign showest thou then, that we may see, and believe thee? What
31 dost thou work? ᵐ Our fathers did eat manna in the desert; as it is written, ⁿ He gave them bread from heaven to eat.

ᶠ ch. 4. 13, 14; Isa. 55. 2, 3; Matt. 6. 19, 20; Luke 10. 41, 42.
ᵍ vers. 40, 51, 54, 68.
ʰ ch. 10. 28; 17. 2.
ⁱ ch. 1. 33, 34; 2. 2 5. 37; 8. 18; Ps. 2. 7; Isa. 42. 1; Matt. 3. 13, 16, 17; 17. 5; Mark 1. 11; 9. 7; Luke 3. 22; 9. 35; Acts 2. 22; 2 Pet. 1. 17.
ᵏ 1 John 3. 22, 23.
ˡ ch. 2. 18; Matt. 12. 38; 16. 1–4; Mark 8. 11; 1 Cor. 1. 22.
ᵐ Ex. 16. 4–15; Num. 11. 7; Neh. 9. 15; 1 Cor. 10. 3.
ⁿ Neh. 9. 15.

---

word translated **miracles** is significant. It means *signs*, and the idea is therefore *not because you saw signs* of divine authority. This is the word commonly used by John. On the words used in designating miracles see on ch. 2 : 11.
27. The connection between this verse and verse 28 is shown better by substituting *work* for **labor**. *Work not for the food*, make it not your chief business, as you are now doing by following me from place to place. They were following Christ for material food which *perishes*, and he warns them to seek instead *that meat*, the spiritual, eternal food, which he bestows. **Son of man**, see on ch. 1 : 51. The term is specially appropriate here, as it is only by virtue of his incarnation and Messianic office that Christ gives this enduring food. That he can give them this food is shown by the fact that he is **sealed** by the Father. To seal a thing is to attest it as a genuine product or possession of the person whose seal is attached to it. He had been attested by the Father in the wonders that attended his birth and his baptism, and in the works he had wrought, ch. 5 : 36–39. Compare ch. 3 : 33.
28. Their question is in answer to Christ's command in the preceding verse, "Work . . . for the food which endures." **What shall we do, that we might work the works of God?** They understood from Christ's words that he was to give them this food in the character of a messenger sent and sealed by God, and that the works necessary for obtaining it, therefore, were works appointed by God.
29. Christ in his answer points out the one **work**, in opposition to their many works (ver. 28), necessary to obtain this food—viz. to believe on him whom the Father sent. Here the human and the divine meet: God working in the heart, and man exercising a hearty freedom in saving faith. This work of God must be more than an intellectual belief; it is believing with the whole heart.
30. The Jews in reply ask the question by which they are accustomed to test any claims to divine commission and authority, **What sign showest thou then?** The question in general was pertinent, but it seems very strange that these men should have asked it just at this time, with the taste of the miraculous food scarcely out of their mouths. **See, and believe thee,** as one sent from God, not merely as a teacher, but one divinely commissioned as an object of faith.
31. **Our fathers did eat manna.** This verse gives an example justifying their demand. Moses claimed to be sent by God, and he gave our fathers proof of his claim in the manna which the Scriptures declare to be bread from heaven, Ps. 78 : 24. Can you show like proof of your claims? This adds to the strangeness of their demand. That they should have asked for any further sign is unaccountable. But that they should cite this precise counterpart of the miracle just performed before their eyes is only another and one of the strongest proofs of the power of the sinful nature to stultify the mind. Perhaps we may explain thus: They were ready to acknowledge him as a teacher whom the Father had sanctioned (vers. 27, 28), but to trust in him as one superior to Moses

32 Then Jesus said unto them, Verily, verily, I say unto you, ᵒMoses gave you not that bread from heaven; but my Father giveth you ᵖthe true bread
33 from heaven. For ᑫthe bread of God is he ʳwhich cometh down from heaven, and giveth life unto the
34 world. Then said they unto him, Lord, evermore give us this bread.
35 And Jesus said unto them, ˢI am the bread of life; ᵗhe that cometh to me shall never hunger; and he
36 that believeth on me ᵘshall never thirst. ˣBut I said unto you, That ye have seen me, and believe
37 not. ʸAll that the Father giveth me ᶻshall come to me; and him that cometh to me ᵃI will in no wise

ᵒ Ex. 16. 4, 8, 15.
ᵖ vers. 33, 35, 41, 50, 55, 58.
ᑫ vers. 38, 48, 51.
ʳ ch. 3. 13; 1 John 1. 1, 2.
ˢ vers. 48, 58.
ᵗ Matt. 5. 6; Rev. 7. 16.
ᵘ ch. 4. 13, 14; 7. 37.
ˣ vers. 26, 64; ch. 5. 38.
ʸ vers. 39, 45; ch. 17. 2, 6, 9, 11, 24.
ᶻ ch. 10. 28, 29; 2 Thess. 2. 13, 14; 2 Tim. 2. 19; 1 John 2. 19.

ᵃ Luke 23. 40-43; Heb. 7. 25; Rev. 22. 17.

---

they desired a sign greater than his recent miracle, one which should surpass the manna in the wilderness.

32. This verse should begin *Jesus therefore said*. **That,** more correctly *the,* **bread from heaven.** Jesus says that the bread which Moses gave them was not *the bread from heaven*, the true, the genuine heavenly bread. Moses indeed gave them manna, but not the heavenly bread. That the Father gives them.

33. This verse confirms the preceding statement by showing what the true bread of God is. **He which cometh,** etc., rather *that which comes down out of heaven and gives life to the world*. The pronoun in the predicate is not personal *he*, but *that*, referring to the bread. The personal reference to himself is not introduced till ver. 35.

34. **Evermore give us this bread.** These men were in the state common to men. As long as God's gifts were offered to them in a general way, they desired them, but as soon as they found out just what these gifts were, and the way to obtain them, their ardor died out. The word translated **Lord** has a wide range of meaning from merely *Sir* to *Master*, and then *Lord* as a divine title. In the mouths of these men it meant probably the second.

35. **I am the bread of life;** that is, the life-giving bread. To this explanation of the nature of the bread of life Christ adds in this verse a statement of its essential quality, that it for ever satisfies the cravings and needs of the person who partakes of it. In the first part of this he drops the figure. Instead of eating the bread, he substitutes the spiritual fact for which that stands—viz. *the coming* to him or *believing* on him. See on ver. 47. The coming and believing are simply different ways of expressing the same thing, the same as the *hungering* and *thirsting* are only different figurative expressions of the soul's need. A great deal of difficulty in connection with this statement may be avoided by keeping in mind that Christ is here speaking, not of the general wants of the soul, but of its one great want of eternal life. Other desires may be constantly recurring and constantly satisfied anew, but this want is satisfied once for all.

36. The connection has to be carefully studied in order to see the bearing of this verse. They have demanded of Christ a sign, that they may see and believe, and have mentioned among such signs that which Moses gave them of the manna. And here Christ tells them that he himself is the true heavenly bread, of which the manna was only a type. Here, then, was the sign that they demanded, only greater. He himself was that sign. Yet, he says, *You have also seen me, and do not believe*.

37. Christ, however, is not astonished in one sense at this unbelief. He several times tells the Jews that no man comes to him except the Father draws him. And so he says here, *All that the Father gives me will come to me*. I do not expect any others; and if you do not come, it is because you do not belong to that class. Compare Ps. 22 : 30; Isa. 53 : 10-12; Rom. 8 : 29. **Him that cometh to me,** etc. In the second clause he reiterates in another

38 cast out. For I came down from heaven, ᵇ not to do mine own will, but the will of him that sent me.
39 And ᶜ this is the Father's will which hath sent me, ᵈ that of all which he hath given me I should lose nothing, ᵉ but should raise it up again at the last day.
40 And this is the will of him that sent me, ᶠ that every one which seeth the Son, ᵍ and believeth on him, may have everlasting life; and I will raise him up at the last day.
41 The Jews then murmured at him, because he said,
42 I am the bread which came down from heaven. And they said, ʰ Is not this Jesus, the son of Joseph, whose father and mother we know? How is it then that he saith, ⁱ I came down from heaven?

ᵇ ch. 4. 34; 5. 30 Matt. 10. 28; 26 39; Rom. 15. 3 Heb. 5. 8.
ᶜ Luke12.32; Rom. 8. 28–31.
ᵈ ch. 10. 23; 17. 12; 18. 9; Col. 3. 3, 4; 1 Pet. 1. 5; Jude 1.
ᵉ ch. 11. 24–26; Rom. 8. 11; Phil. 3. 20, 21.
ᶠ ch. 3. 15, 16; 4. 14.
ᵍ vers. 35, 54; ch. 5. 24.
ʰ ch. 7. 27; Matt. 13. 55, 56; Mark 6. 3.
ⁱ 1 Cor. 15. 47.

form the statement that this coming to him is what decides the matter, and secures to the comer eternal life. Such a person, he says, he cannot reject, he will not cast out. If such casting out were possible, the person coming to him might not secure life for himself, or after securing it might lose it. But him who comes to him he **will in no wise cast out.** His salvation is fully assured.

38. **For I came down.** This last statement Christ confirms by the assurance that he came down **from heaven** to do the Father's will, which of course involves the keeping of what the Father has given him, instead of casting it out. Here is one of the comforts of the doctrine of free grace, that a work which has originated with the Father, as in this case the coming to Christ is represented as doing, Christ is under obligation to render permanent, and secure to it an eternal blessing. The doctrines of "election" and "perseverance or preservation" stand together. On the will of Christ and its relation to the Father's will, see on ch. 5 : 30.

39. **And this is the Father's will.** According to the best critical authorities, the word *Father* does not belong here, but in ver. 40. They make this verse read, *him which hath sent me,* and ver. 40, *the Father which hath sent me.* In either case the meaning is the same. Christ states here what the Father's will is, which, in connection with his purpose to do that will, makes it sure that he will not cast out any one who comes to him—viz. that he should **lose nothing** of all that the Father gives him. **The last day** is of course the day of Christ's second coming and of the judgment. Christ does not mean here the bodily resurrection only, for that is common to all, but both the spiritual resurrection referred to in ch. 5 : 21–27 and the resurrection to a glorified body, which is the culminating work of redemption. Compare note on ch. 5 : 29.

40. The verse should begin with *For* It confirms, therefore, the preceding statement about the Father's will. It is his will that Christ should lose nothing of all that he has given him, for it is his will that all such have eternal life. **Which seeth the Son,** gets or receives knowledge of him. Those whom the Father has given the Son and those who believe on the Son are the same. See ver. 37. The I in the last clause is emphatic, equivalent to *I, for my part.* Notice how this, *I will raise him up at the last day,* comes in as a refrain all through this passage (vers. 40, 44, 54), giving it a treble assurance.

41, 42. **The Jews,** the leaders, and perhaps their views spreading among the multitude, **then,** rather, *therefore,* **murmured at him.** According to Greek usage, the word translated *murmur* means "a murmuring of disdain." —THOLUCK. It was a fault-finding among themselves (ver. 43), with a contemptuous spirit. It was *at him,* denoting opposition, antagonism. They complained because Christ claimed a heavenly origin, whereas they knew, or supposed they knew, his earthly origin. In like manner, they disputed his Mes-

43 Jesus therefore answered and said unto them, Murmur not among yourselves. *k* No man can come to me, *l* except the Father which hath sent me *m* draw him; and I will raise him up at the last day. *n* It is written in the prophets, And they shall be all taught of God. Every man therefore that hath heard, and hath learned of the Father, cometh unto me. *o* Not that any man hath seen the Father, *p* save he which is of God, he hath seen the Father.

47 Verily, verily, I say unto you, *q* He that believeth

k ver. 65; ch. 3. 27
12. 37–40.
l Matt. 11. 25-27
16. 17.
m ch. 12. 32; Sol. Song 1. 4; Jer. 31. 3.
n Mic. 4. 2; Heb. 8. 10; 10. 16.
o ch. 1. 18; 5. 37.
p ch. 7. 29; 8. 19; Matt. 11. 27; Luke 10. 22.
q ch. 3. 15, 18, 36.

sianic claim by the statement that he came from Nazareth, instead of the Bethlehem of the Messianic prophecy; whereas a little inquiry would have shown that Christ had no earthly father, and that he came from Bethlehem.

43, 44. On **Murmur**, see ver. 41. Why ver. 44 should be given as a reason for the *Murmur not among yourselves* is difficult to see. It may be this: The claim which Christ set up to be the bread from heaven is the reason which he has given why men should come to him, ver. 35. They complained, on the other hand, that there was direct proof of his earthly origin. But he tells them not to complain about that, because it is not by weighing such arguments *pro* and *con.* that men are brought to him, but *by the Father's drawing*. It seems evident that the drawing here is something more than the use of motives and appeals which the man may yield to or resist; for the drawing, whatever it is, is that which decides the matter; and these Jews, whom Christ evidently does not regard as having this drawing, had all of mere external influences that man can have. In the last clause Christ states what he does in the matter: The Father draws men to him, and he on his part raises them up at the last day. They are graciously allured by divine love, ch. 12 : 32. On this resurrection see on ver. 39.

45. **Prophets.** So one division of the Old Testament Scriptures was called. This quotation is from the same passage (Isa. 54 : 13, quoted freely from the Septuagint version) which the apostle Paul quotes in Gal. 4 : 26, 27, where he refers it to the Jerusalem above. The children of this heavenly Jerusalem, "which is the mother of us all," are all to be taught of God. Compare Jer. 31 : 33; Joel 3 : 16; Mic. 4 : 2. This divine instruction is to characterize them rather than any human teaching, and therefore the Lord declares that it is such as have received this who come to him. **Every man therefore that hath heard.** The Father's instruction is effectual, but there must be not only the hearing, but also the *learning*. Compare Matt. 11 : 28-30.

46. The Lord guards his hearers, however, against the possible inference that any one has **seen the Father;** for this instruction is not outward and visible, the result of personal intercourse, but is imparted inwardly and secretly to the soul. **Save he which is of,** or *from,* **God,** etc. Only he himself, who comes from the immediate presence of God, has seen the Father. Christ does not speak here of his divine origin, as our version seems to imply, but of his coming *from* the presence of God. In that presence, from which he has come to earth, he has seen the Father. As far, therefore, as outward instruction by the ordinary processes is concerned, he reveals the Father and teaches men his nature and character, while the Father, on his part, by secret processes within the soul itself, draws men to Christ.

47. In this verse, after showing the way in which men are brought to him, Christ resumes again the main subject of his discourse by showing the result of coming to him or believing on him. The believer receives the gift of eternal life, for in believing he partakes of Christ, who is the bread of life. **He that believeth on me.** Here, as throughout the Scriptures, and especially the New Testament, faith is made the root of Christian life, the fundamental distinguishing characteristic of the Lord's disciples. Christians are "believers." This faith is not the mere

48 on me hath everlasting life. *I am that bread of life.
49 *Your fathers did eat manna in the wilderness, and
50 are dead. *This is the bread which cometh down from heaven, that a man may eat thereof, and not
51 die. I am the living bread *which came down from heaven; if any man eat of this bread, he shall live for ever. And *the bread that I will give is my flesh, which I will give *for the life of the world.

*vers. 33–35.
*ver. 31.
*vers. 51, 58; ch. 5. 24; 11. 26.
*ch. 3. 13.
vers. 52–57; Mat. 20. 28; Luke 22. 19; Eph. 5. 2, 25; Heb. 10. 5, 10.
*ch. 1. 29; 2 Cor. 9. 15; 1 John 2. 2; 4. 14.

---

conviction of judgment that Christ is what he claimed to be. It is also the taking of Christ to be for us what he offers to be; and thus it is the attachment of ourselves to him, to be for him what he requires. It is the acceptance of Christ as our Lord and Saviour, and the surrender to Christ in loyal, worshipful devotement. Thus it is the bond of union between Christ and Christ's, and the condition of all that fulness of manifold gracious life coming from the union. While at the first exercise of faith the believer is justified and everlasting life is secured, yet it is not to be regarded as something separate, merely done at the start and not continued—once for all wrought, and then left behind as history merely. It is perpetual, continuous, not to be interrupted; the constant present condition of a present life. Hence the words, "He that believeth," or, more exactly, "is believing"—*i. e.*, all the time—not "he that *did* believe." Sometimes God, and sometimes God's word, is spoken of as the object of faith; but it all comes to the same thing, because God's word exhibits God in his relation to us lost men, and to believe in it is to believe in him. But God meets us lost men in the person of Jesus Christ; and hence to believe in God as our God is to believe in Christ. See this taught in vers. 35–40.

48. It should read *the* instead of *that bread of life*. So also it is *the life* just referred to. Christ is the *life* as well as *bread*. It is the former which is at the root and makes him the living bread, ver. 51.

49. He states here again the contrast between himself and the manna eaten by their fathers. They ate that, and died. **Your fathers,** referring to their own words in ver. 31. **And are dead,** better, *and died*. Jesus shows what worthless desires and ambitions move them. They need more than a mere temporal Saviour.

50. This **bread,** on the contrary, comes down out of heaven in a sense of which the heavenly origin of the manna is only the type, and comes for this purpose—that he who eats of it may **not die.** That could only defer death, this prevents it. God had from the beginning been pointing men, and especially the Jews, to this infinite good, of which his self-righteous critics and foes seemed not to have the faintest suspicion. Having thus told them of *what kind* of bread man has need, he goes on again to tell them where only they can find it.

51. In the first part of this verse he merely reiterates the statement that he is this **living,** heavenly, **bread,** which imparts eternal life. **If any man eat of this bread.** If he would be saved, he must be active—receive, accept, and obey Christ. But in the last part he adds to this the further limiting statement that the bread is his **flesh,** which **he will give for the life of the world.** This in the original is introduced as something of special importance: *And indeed,* or *Yea, and this bread*. Several manuscripts omit the second **which I will give,** in which case it may be rendered, *Yea, and this bread, which I will give for the life of the world, is my flesh*. It was by his death he was to become bread, a Saviour. The cross is in his view. His flesh, given for the life of the world, is his sacrificial, his atoning death. Justification and salvation are secured on the part of the believer by faith in Christ's atoning work, Rom. 5 : 1, 12–21. This is the eternal life. Inseparably connected with justification is spiritual life in the soul, the union between Christ and the believer, presented in the fifteenth chapter, and the consequent fruit. Roman Catholics and

52 The Jews therefore *strove among themselves, saying, *How can this man give us *his* flesh to eat?
53 Then Jesus said unto them, Verily, verily, I say unto you, Except ᵇ ye eat the flesh of the Son of man,
54 and drink his blood, ye have no life in you. ᶜ Whoso eateth my flesh, and drinketh my blood, hath eternal
55 life; and I will raise him up at the last day. For my flesh is meat indeed, and my blood is drink indeed.
56 He that eateth my flesh, and drinketh my blood,

* ch. 7. 43; 9. 16; 10. 19.
* ch. 3. 9; 1 Cor. 2. 14.
ᵇ ch. 3. 36; Matt. 26. 26–28; 1 John 5. 12.
ᶜ vers. 27, 40, 63; ch. 4. 14.

---

others who believe in the saving power of the sacraments interpret the expressions used here literally, and find in them transubstantiation, or the changing of the bread and wine of the Lord's Supper into Christ's body and blood, and teach that there is salvation in the partaking of these. But Christ furnishes the corrective to such literalism by translating the *eating* and drinking into their spiritual equivalent—*coming* or *believing*. See vers. 35, 37, 40, 44. Eating here is only another name for faith. But, on the other hand, there can be little doubt that Christ is here speaking of the same spiritual facts as are represented in the Lord's Supper. The fact that the figure used is the same, and the explanation of the figure as referring to his atoning death in both cases, leave no room to doubt about that.

52. This idea of eating Christ's flesh seemed so strange and unaccountable to the Jews that they **strove**, fell to disputing, **among themselves**, what he could mean, how it could be possible for him to do such a thing.

53. The Lord, however, does not answer their question, but simply reiterates in the most impressive manner the statement that only by this eating can they secure eternal life. **Except ye eat the flesh, . . . and drink,** etc. Literal drinking of blood would be most abhorrent to a Jew, Gen. 9 : 4; Lev. 3 : 17; 7 : 26; 17 : 14; Deut. 12 : 23. The strangeness of the language would naturally suggest that his words should be taken in a deeper sense. Indeed, he makes the reference to his death still plainer by adding the drinking of his blood to the eating of his flesh. One naturally thinks of the Lord's Supper, but it is only as the Supper visibly exhibits the relation of Christians to Christ, and so speaks the same language which Jesus here uses. He is not speaking of the Supper, but both he and the Supper speak of our salvation through his death. Indeed, the phraseology in the original is definite and unmistakable. The eating and drinking are not, as we might expect, in order to sustain life, but *to give it*—to produce life where there is now death. You have no life, Christ says, unless you partake of these life-giving elements; and the tenses employed are such as to denote a single act. Indeed, this is the point of the argument, that *the one act secures eternal life*. And this corresponds with what we know of the spiritual facts represented. The one act of faith secures justification and eternal life. The same view is presented wherever Christ employs this figure.

54. This verse presents the positive side. It is not only true that without this act of faith one has no life, but also that *whoever* performs it has eternal life. It is indispensable and sure. **Hath eternal life.** The present is again used—has it *now*, as those Jews did *not* have it. **I will raise him up,** etc. The third time asserted within a few verses. See vers. 40, 44. Eternal life comes to its completeness at the resurrection.

55. **For my flesh is meat indeed, and my blood is drink indeed.** Christ means that they fulfil the expectations based on them. They do not deceive, as other articles of food and drink do, by leaving the person who partakes of them to die at last.

56. In this verse Christ explains how it is that the one eating, or the one act of faith, produces such permanent results. **Dwelleth in me, and I in him.** This is more than imitation: he who thus partakes of Christ *abides* in Christ, and Christ in him. There is a permanent union established between the soul and Christ, who thus becomes the source of eternal life. Compare ch. 15 : 5; 1 Cor. 6 : 17.

JOHN VI.   A. D. 29

57 ^ddwelleth in me, and I in him. As ^ethe living Father hath sent me, ^fand I live by the Father; so
58 he that eateth me, even he ^gshall live by me. ^hThis is that bread which came down from heaven; not as your fathers did eat manna, and are dead; he that eateth of this bread shall live for ever.
59 These things said he in the synagogue, as he taught in Capernaum.
60 Many therefore of his disciples, when they had heard *this*, said, This is an hard saying; who can

^d ch. 15. 4, 5; Eph 3. 17; 1 John 3. 21; 4. 12, 15, 16.
^e Ps. 18. 46; 84. 2; Jer. 10. 10; 1 Thess. 1. 9.
^f ch. 5. 26; 17. 21.
^g ch. 11. 25, 26; Gal. 2. 20; Col. 3. 3, 4.
^h vers. 49–51.

¹ ver.66; Matt.11.6

---

57. Here the Lord carries the source back further still, to the Father. The principle on which the statements of the verse are based is that life is the source of life. Compare ch. 17 : 21. Hence the three steps, **the living Father,** the Son living by the Father, and the man who partakes of the living Son living by him. The comparison is as follows: "Just as it was a *living* Father that sent me, and I *live* by him, even so he who eats of the *living* me shall *live* by me." The union of Christ and Christ's is here put in the strongest light, and the results of it again put in sublime contrast with mere earthly good. If we turn to the fifteenth chapter of John, we find the Saviour teaching this same doctrine of union with him by the similitude of the vine and its branches. There, as here, he shows that the union is to be both vital and voluntary. Because *vital*, its absence implies spiritual death; its presence life, and the same life that was in Jesus—a pure, lovely, and loving, and righteous life—a life all the fuller and stronger the closer and more perfect the union, as the life of the branch is at its best only in case its union with the trunk be complete, only as the strength of a man be full when he partakes to the full of proper food. It is a *voluntary* union, and therefore we have something to do—living not merely for Christ, but in him—first *in* him, and then *for* him.

58. **This is that,** or *the,* **bread,** etc. This verse sums up the entire statement. After giving the nature and various qualities of the heavenly bread, Christ recapitulates, saying, This which I have described is the bread from heaven, unlike that which your fathers ate in the wilderness in one important particular, since it gives eternal life, while those who **ate** of that died notwithstanding. It is well known that they **did eat manna, and are dead.**

59. **Synagogue** means *assembly, congregation,* and is applied both to a religious gathering having certain judicial powers (Luke 8 : 41; 12 : 11; 21 : 12; Acts 9 : 2) and to the place where the Jews met for their public worship on ordinary occasions, Luke 7 : 5. The synagogue appears to have been first introduced during the Babylonish captivity, when the people, deprived of their usual rites of worship, assembled on the Sabbath to hear the law read and expounded. Compare Neh. 8 : 1–8. The times of meeting were on the Sabbath and feast-days, and afterward on the second and fifth days of the week. Each synagogue had its president or ruler (Luke 8 : 49; 13 : 14; Acts 18 : 8, 17) and elders (Luke 7 : 3–5), who might chastise (Matt. 10 : 17; Acts 22 : 19; 26 : 11) or expel (ch. 9 : 34) an offender. In Mark 5 : 22 and Acts 13 : 15 the ruler and elders appear to be spoken of indiscriminately as *rulers.* It is, however, uncertain how perfect was the organization of the synagogue in the time of Christ. It was probably changed and developed after the destruction of Jerusalem by the Romans. **Taught.** For his manner of teaching in the synagogue see Luke 4 : 16–21. The heads of the synagogue were accustomed, after the reading of Scripture, to ask such grave and learned persons as might be present to address the people. Christ and the apostles constantly availed themselves of this privilege. **Capernaum.** John has not given before the place in which this discourse was delivered, except an intimation in ver. 24 that it was in Capernaum. See on ch. 2 : 12.

60–71. EFFECT OF OUR LORD'S DISCOURSE ON HIS DISCIPLES. Many dis

A D. 29.   JOHN VI.   123

61 hear it? When Jesus ^{j} knew in himself that his dis-   ch. 2. 24, 25.
ciples murmured at it, he said unto them, Doth this ^{k} ch. 3. 13; 16. 28;
62 offend you? ^{k} What and if ye shall see the Son of   Mark 16.19; Acts
                                                           1. 9; Eph. 4. 8, 10.
63 man ascend up where he was before? ^{l} It is the ^{l} Ps. 119.50; 2 Cor.
Spirit that quickeneth; the flesh profiteth nothing;   3. 6.
the words that I speak unto you, *they are* spirit, and ^{m} ver. 36; ch. 5. 42;
64 *they are* life. But ^{m} there are some of you that be- 10. 26.

ciples offended; Peter in behalf of the twelve confesses him. Related only by John.

60. This discourse not only caused murmuring among the Jews, but also disaffection among Christ's disciples. The word **disciples** appears to be used here in a general sense, meaning those who attended his teaching and adhered to him. The twelve seem not to be included (ver. 67), but perhaps Judas was among them, ver. 64. They said, **This is an hard saying;** that is, not difficult, hard to understand, but harsh, offensive, hard to listen to; **who can hear it?** or *listen to it?* Some perhaps stopped their ears, Acts 7 : 57. The thing which offended them was the evident allusion to his death, and salvation only through such a sacrifice.

61. **Jesus knew in himself,** by his divine knowledge, ch. 2 : 25. The word translated **offend** here means literally to *make one stumble* or *fall*, and is hence used of tempters or temptations, as things over which one falls. Does this prove a stumbling-block to you? or, Does this make you stumble? Compare Matt. 11 : 6. And as the noun from which the verb comes means a trap-stick, there is in it the idea of ensnaring, making one fall into a snare.

62. In this verse the emphasis comes on the word **see.** Now you have only *heard* of my returning to the Father; what, if you see it, will be the effect on you? Christ evidently refers here to his death, the mere mention of which had so affected his disciples. Others suppose that the disciples were offended at the eating of his flesh. Then the passage would be best explained as follows: These teachings of mine seem harsh and offensive. But if I ascend bodily to heaven, will not that prove to you that my teaching is true, and show that this eating of my flesh is not to be taken literally, but spiritually, and that my words and Spirit received into the heart give life? vers. 62, 63.

63. Out of the various interpretations of this difficult verse the following seems on the whole best: By the **Spirit,** Christ means the Holy Spirit; by **the flesh,** his bodily manifestation, his life on the earth. Now, the offence which his disciples had taken was because he had spoken of his death, of the removal of his bodily presence from them. And he removes this objection by declaring that the bodily presence would be no advantage to them, but that the Spirit, who would come after his death, is the quickener, the imparter of life. His meaning is substantially the same as in ch. 16 : 7 ff. Of course, Christ is speaking comparatively, and with reference strictly to the matter in hand—namely, the question of his remaining or departing. His flesh, his incarnate presence, had been of inestimable advantage, and it was to be through it that the work of redemption was to be wrought out on the cross. But it was not his permanent presence which his disciples desired, but the Spirit—that was to do the work and confer the blessing needed. There is also the question to be asked, in what sense the Spirit was to do this particular work of imparting life, which has just been ascribed to Christ, and him crucified. The answer seems to be that this life, dependent on union with Christ, is secured on the part of man by faith, and that the Spirit prepares the way for the exercise of this faith; that the Spirit, therefore, is the initiative and effective agent in the bestowal of this gift. In this sense, even while Christ had been on earth, the Spirit had been the quickener, and not he. **The words that I speak;** according to the most approved text, *The words that I have spoken*. They contain spiritual food and life, and by receiving them ye receive me. Thus they *are spirit, and are life*. See next verse.

64. The last clause of the last verse and the first clause of this are to be

lieve not. For ᵐJesus knew from the beginning who they were that believed not, and who should betray
65 him. And he said, Therefore ᵒsaid I unto you, that no man can come unto me, ᵖexcept it were given unto him of my Father.
66 ᵍFrom that *time* many of his disciples went back,
67 and walked no more with him. Then said Jesus
68 unto the twelve, ʳWill ye also go away? Then Simon Peter answered him, Lord, ˢto whom shall we
69 go? thou hast ᵗthe words of eternal life. ᵘAnd we believe and are sure that thou art that ˣChrist, the
70 Son of the living God. Jesus answered them, ʸHave not I chosen you twelve, ᶻand one of you is a devil?

ᵐ ch. 2. 24, 25; 13 11; Acts 15. 18.
ᵒ vers. 44, 45.
ᵖ 2 Tim. 2. 25, 26.
ᵍ ver. 60; Luke 9. 62; Heb. 10. 38, 39; 1 John 2. 19.
ʳ Luke 14. 25–33.
ˢ Ps. 73. 25; Acts 4. 12; 1 Cor. 3. 11.
ᵗ vers. 40, 63; Acts 5. 20; 1 John 5. 11–13.
ᵘ ch. 1. 49; 11. 27; 20. 31; Matt. 16. 16; Mark 8. 29; Luke 9. 20.
ˣ Ps. 2. 2–7.

ʸ ver. 64; ch. 15. 18; 17. 12; Luke 6. 13–16. ᶻ ch. 13. 2, 21, 27; 1 John 3. 8.

read together, with only a comma between. Christ does not mean to say that his words are this life-giving Spirit, in which case his remaining would be necessary, but that they contain these things as their message. His words were truth, and it is by the truth that the Holy Spirit works in the heart, James 1 : 18; John 17 : 17. Yet in spite of this character of his words, some do not believe. This statement of the unbelief of some John verifies by Christ's knowledge of them **from the beginning.** He did not have to wait for these signs of unbelief, but from the beginning, even when they were apparently genuine believers, he knew them in their real character. And this gives us the probable meaning of the phrase, *from the beginning.* Most naturally it refers to the beginning of their connection with him. **Who should betray him.** This first reference to Judas as the betrayer is significant. Very probably at this point began his first aversion to Christ and the doctrine he preached. See on ver. 71.

65. **Therefore,** because some do not believe, in spite of the fact that my words bring the message of the Spirit and of life, showing that not even the best words avail, but need to be reinforced by the gift of the Father. Compare vers. 39, 44.

66. **From that.** It is doubtful whether the words at the beginning of this verse mean *from that time* or *on that account.* In the latter case it would refer to the discourse just delivered and the offence that it had given. Its more natural reference is, however, to time. Both convey substantially the same idea, and Alford and Godet attempt to combine the two.

67. **Then,** or *therefore.* **Will** here is not the auxiliary, but means *Do you wish?* The form of the question is such as to expect a negative answer: *You do not wish to go away, do you?*

68. **The twelve,** the apostles. See at the end of ver. 70. **To whom shall we go?** implying that the time would never come when they would forsake him. In the second part of the verse it is not the subject **thou** which is to be emphasized, as might be supposed from our version, but the object— **words of eternal life.** These things which Christ has are the reason why they should not go to any one else; not because he, and no one else, has these words, but because no one else has anything better, nor as good: *Words of eternal life thou hast.*

69. **And we believe and are sure that thou art Christ.** The subject *we* is emphatic, contrasted with the unbelief of others. The correct text reads, *we have believed, and know, that thou art the Holy One of God.* They had believed, and now believe, all his claims, vers. 27, 39, 40, 47, 51, 58. They know him to be Christ the Messiah.

70. Christ emphasizes in this verse the fact that *he* has **chosen** them; which, of course, makes the defection of one of them the more strange and tragical. The article belongs before twelve—**you** *the* **twelve**—which adds to the impressiveness of the statement. He himself has chosen them as his twelve most intimate friends and per-

A. D. 29.　　　　　　　　JOHN VI.　　　　　　　　125

71 He spake of Judas Iscariot *the son* of Simon; ᵃ for he
it was that should betray him, ᵇ being one of the
twelve.

ᵃ Ps. 109. 6-8; Acts 1. 16-20; 2. 23.
ᵇ Ps. 41. 9; Matt. 26. 14-16.

sonal followers, yet one of them is a **devil.** The word *devil* means a traducer, a false accuser, and was probably here applied to Judas as a traducer and traitor, whose treason was inspired by the evil one, ch. 13 : 27. "As Christ in Matt. 16 : 23 gives the name Satan itself to Peter as the organ of Satan, he can surely the more readily here give to Judas, who has abandoned himself to satanic influence, the name of *a* devil—that is, a man resting under diabolic influences."—THOLUCK. Some high authorities put the interrogation-point after *the twelve,* making what follows an exclamation of holy sadness, "And one of you a devil!" It is also worthy of notice that here and in ver. 68 is the first reference to *the twelve* as a body in this Gospel, showing that their appointment was well known, Luke 6 : 13. This is in sad contrast with the confession by Peter of the faith of the twelve as a body.

71. **Judas Iscariot.** Some manuscripts make the word Iscariot here belong to Simon; others refer it to *Judas.* The question is not an important one. The name means man or inhabitant of Kerioth, a town south of Jerusalem, Josh. 15 : 25. Judas Iscariot was probably the only one of the apostles who was not by birth a Galilean. He carried the bag, and appropriated part of the common stock to his own use, ch. 12 : 6. The climax of his sins was the betrayal of Jesus, which was speedily followed by suicide. His infamous character doubtless accounts for the position of his name as last in each of the catalogues in the Gospels. **That should,** or *was about to,* **betray him, being one of the twelve.** An apostle and traitor, a terrible union, incurring fearful guilt. It was part of infinite wisdom that Christ should have chosen his betrayer among the twelve. God works even through wicked men, as in the case of Balaam. The churches of Christ have never yet found absolute purity on earth; some of the chaff ordinarily remains among the wheat. The defection of those who have been regarded great in the church has never yet caused its ruin, and never will.

PRACTICAL REMARKS.

1. Curiosity always draws together a crowd, but the preaching of strong doctrine, however true, is apt to repel, vers. 2, 66.
2. We should never under any circumstances withhold our pity from the spiritually destitute and ignorant, vers. 1-3; Zech. 7 : 9; Rom. 15 : 3.
3. The broad benevolence of the Christ-like spirit concerns itself with all human needs, those of the body as well as those of the soul, ver. 5. See also nearly all of Christ's miracles.
4. Often God's providence seems most perplexing just before proving most bountiful, vers. 6, 7.
5. Jesus is far more compassionate than it is possible for his people to be, vers. 5-10; Luke 18 : 39-42; Ps. 103 : 11, 13.
6. Fear not to proffer to Christ even a very little, if it be really all that circumstances permit, ver. 9; Luke 21 : 1-4; 2 Cor. 8 : 2.
7. In straitened circumstances, and even in poverty, we should practise Christian benevolence, trusting in Christ, who can make the desert teem with plenty. ver. 7; 1 Cor. 16 : 1, 2; Ps. 78 : 19-22; 107 : 33-37; Isa. 32 : 8.
8. Whatever Jesus directs we should do, confiding in his wisdom and power, ver. 10; Mark 3 : 5; Matt. 6 : 33.
9. Christ by example commends to us a due regard to order and system, ver. 10; 1 Cor. 14 : 33, 40; Tit. 1 : 5; Acts 6 : 1-4.
10. If our faith and obedience were more largely exercised in making ready for a blessing, we should more often receive to the full, ver. 10; 2 Kings 3 : 16 ff.
11. We have the example of Jesus as a sanction for the custom of giving thanks at our meals, ver. 11; Mark 8 : 6; Eph. 5 : 20; 1 Tim. 4 : 4, 5.
12. Not even a bounty great enough to be miraculous will excuse the waste of a fragment, ver. 12; Matt. 7 : 6; Mark 8 : 8.

13. The "bread-and-butter argument" is sometimes irresistible to men who are impervious to all other appeals, ver. 14.

14. Christ's way is the right and best way, but often contrary to the inclinations of his people, ver. 15; Mark 10 : 29; Matt. 16 : 24.

15. Men who would crucify the "King of the truth" are eager to crown the "king of the commissary," vers. 14, 15.

16. Solitary devotion (Luke 6 : 12) is the best refuge from the urgings of unholy ambition, ver. 15; Luke 6 : 12; 9 : 28; 22 : 40; Gal. 4 : 12; James 4 : 2.

17. Jesus never loses sight of his people in this sea of strife; in due time he will come to their relief, ver. 19; 1 Cor. 10 : 13; Ps. 78 : 19–22; Heb. 13 : 5, 6.

18. Jesus tries our faith. That which at first seems threatening with destruction often turns out to be full of mercy, ver. 19; Rev. 1 : 17, 18; Isa. 43 : 1, 2; Ps. 119 : 67.

19. "Man's extremity is God's opportunity" (ROBERT HALL), vers. 18, 19.

20. Nothing brings Jesus to us like trouble, ver. 20; Ps. 46 : 1.

21. When Christ comes among his people and takes possession of the soul, human passions are stilled and opposition is banished, ver. 21; Eph. 2 : 4–6.

22. The presence of Jesus helps us quickly to finish the hardest toil, ver. 21.

23. "Those that would find Christ must diligently observe all his motions and learn to understand the tokens of his presence or absence, that they may steer accordingly" (MATTHEW HENRY), vers. 22–25.

24. "These seekers are a type of all false friends of religion, who seek not the kingdom of heaven in earthly advantages, but only earthly advantages in the kingdom of heaven" (LANGE), ver. 26.

25. The temporal benefits accruing from Christianity are in some degree a sign and a seal of its eternal blessings, ver. 27.

26. A carnal mind has no other thought than that everlasting life is the wages of one's own good works, ver. 28; Rom. 10 : 3.

27. The thing vital to salvation is not at all what we shall do, but simply and solely our trust in Christ, vers. 29, 40, 47; ch. 3 : 15, 36; ch. 11 : 26.

28. How stubborn is wilful skepticism. One who wills not to believe would demand signs even in Capernaum, where the most miracles were wrought. He would even appear with the miraculous bread in his teeth, face to face with Jesus himself, demanding a sign, ver. 30; Luke 16 : 30, 31.

29. Most men, like these Jews, are secretly sighing for a millennium of indolence and luxury, with its manna, as it were, rained from heaven, instead of bread earned by the sweat of the brow, ver. 31.

30. In drawing men's thoughts toward heavenly things, let us imitate the wonderful tact of the Great Teacher, vers. 32–34.

31. Jesus Christ satisfies the deepest yearnings of the human heart, ver. 35.

32. Faith springs not so much from external evidence, however clear, as from an internal divine drawing, vers. 36, 37, 44.

33. What encouragement Jesus here gives to take the great decisive step, simply taking him at his word! ver. 37. Scores have been saved merely by seizing the promise in this one passage, ver. 37.

34. God's elect are sure to come to Christ, sure to be accepted, and sure to be kept in the perseverance, or preservation, of the saints unto final salvation, vers. 37–39.

35. Look, trust, live! ver. 40; ch. 3 : 14, 15; Num. 21 : 8, 9; Isa. 45 : 22.

36. Murmuring spoils prayer and plunges the mind into deeper darkness, vers. 34, 41, 52, 66.

37. Whoever will, may come; yet that very will is the inward drawing of God, ver. 44.

38. Observe the fourfold assurance given of the exaltation of the believer at the last day, vers. 39, 40, 44, 54.

39. Everlasting life for the believer is a present possession, ver. 47.

40. There is no true life without a personal appropriation of the "flesh and blood," or Christ in his atoning sacrifice, ver. 51, 53–58.

41. In Christ is found the only satisfying good for the soul. Without him is want and woe, vers. 51–53; Heb. 10 : 20–25, 35–39.

42. Murmuring against Jesus, if indulged, becomes striving, and finally a forsaking him altogether, vers. 41, 52, 66.

JOHN VII.

Jesus still continues in Galilee.

VII. AFTER these things Jesus walked in Galilee: for he would not walk in Jewry, c because the Jews sought to kill him.   a ch. 5. 16, 18.

43. A preacher may lose his hearers through no fault of his own (STARKE, quoted by LANGE), ver. 66.

44. In a time of general declension the appeal of Jesus to the faithful comes with peculiar tenderness and power, ver. 67.

45. At such a time hearty testimony for Christ is peculiarly fitting and acceptable, vers. 68, 69.

46. There is light enough in the present age to show us that we must either have the religion of Jesus or be left utterly irreligious, ver. 68.

47. However thoroughly the followers of Jesus are winnowed, all the chaff will not be excluded until the final burning, vers. 70, 71 ; Matt. 13 : 29.

CHAPTER VII.

Having given an account of the feeding of the five thousand and the events immediately following, the evangelist informs us in a single verse where Jesus was during the next six months, from April to October, A. D. 29, and why his labors were at that time confined to Galilee. The passover that year, the third in our Lord's public ministry, began April 17th, and was evidently not attended by him for the reason given in ver. 1, *because the Jews were seeking to kill him.* The feast of tabernacles, which followed, began on the 19th of October. A few days previous to this, his brothers urged him to go up to Jerusalem. He replies, *My time has not yet come,* vers. 2-9. Afterward he goes up, unattended by a multitude, and in the midst of the feast he appears in the temple and teaches, ver. 10. The Jewish rulers soon manifest a desire to seize him, and send forth officers for that purpose, 11-32. The officers are restrained from laying hands on him, and bring back the report, *Never man spake like this man,* 33-46. This occasions a colloquy between the leading Pharisees and chief priests and Nicodemus, 47-52.

1-9. JESUS CONTINUES IN GALILEE. HIS BROTHERS ASK HIM TO GO UP TO THE FEAST OF TABERNACLES. This account is not contained in the other Gospels. Between the defection of many of his disciples (ch. 6 : 66) and the ensuing feast of tabernacles (7 : 2), as we learn from the other Gospels, occurred the discourse of Jesus to the Pharisees and scribes concerning unwashed hands and the tradition of the elders, the healing of the Canaanitish woman's daughter, the healing of a deaf and dumb man and many others, the feeding of the four thousand, his cautioning the disciples against the leaven of the Pharisees, healing a blind man, visiting the vicinity of Cæsarea Philippi and declaring the necessity of self-denial, his transfiguration, curing a demoniac whom the disciples could not cure, providing tribute-money, and discoursing on humility, on dealing with an offending brother, and on forgiveness. See Matt. 15 : 1-18 : 35; Mark 7 : 1-9 : 50; Luke 9 : 18-50. Compare *Author's Harmony,* §§ 80-96.

1. **After these things,** after his feeding the five thousand, declaring himself the Bread of Life, being forsaken by many professed disciples, and nobly acknowledged by Peter, ch. 6 : 1-71, **Jesus walked,** *went about,* attending to his public ministry of teaching and healing the people. See Acts 10 : 38. It is worthy of notice that John mentions no single act or word of Jesus during all these months. They did not bear on the design of his Gospel. **In Galilee,** the northern division of Palestine, where many Jews resided and the field was still open for his labors. **In Jewry,** *Judæa,* as in ver. 3; 11 : 7; and elsewhere in the New Testament, except Luke 23 : 5; the southern division of Palestine. **He would not walk in Jewry,** *Judæa,* because the time had not come for him to expose his life by doing this, and he had also a work in Galilee to accomplish. Compare vers. 6-8. Hence he did not that year attend the feast of the passover. **Because the Jews,** not the common people, but the rulers and other leading men. See Mark 12 : 37 Though Galilee was also

2 ᵈNow the Jews' feast of tabernacles was at hand. ᵈ Lev. 23. 34–43.
3 ᵉHis brethren therefore said unto him, ᶠDepart hence, ᵉ Matt.12.46; Mark 3. 31; Acts 1. 14.
and go into Judæa, that thy disciples also may see the ᶠ Jer. 12. 6.
4 works that thou doest. For *there is* no man *that* doeth
any thing in secret, and he himself seeketh to be
known openly. If thou do these things, ᵍshow thy- ᵍ ch. 18. 20.

---

inhabited by Jews, the leading men of the nation lived in Judæa, and the seat of the Jewish ecclesiastical power was at Jerusalem. **Sought to kill him.** It was a settled purpose with them, which they cherished in their hearts (vers. 19, 25) and were ready to manifest whenever an occasion was presented. See vers. 30, 32.

2. **The Jews' feast of tabernacles,** more exactly, *the feast of the Jews; the feast of tabernacles.* It is styled *feast of the Jews,* because it had been enjoined on *the Jews* and was observed by them. It was also soon to be laid aside, along with the other merely Jewish institutions. **Was at hand,** probably within four or five days, as the festival caravan would need three or four days to go from the vicinity of the Sea of Galilee, about seventy-five miles, to Jerusalem. (See HACKETT, *Illustrations of Scripture,* p. 16.) **Feast of tabernacles,** or *booths,* so called because the Israelites were to dwell, during its continuance, in booths or tents made of branches of trees (Lev. 23 : 40–42; Neh. 8 : 14–16), to remind them of their forefathers' dwelling in tents or booths, instead of permanent habitations, while God was leading them through the wilderness, Lev. 23 : 43. It was also called the *feast of ingathering,* because it occurred after they had gathered in the various fruits of the earth for the year; and they were to rejoice before the Lord their God in grateful acknowledgment of his abundant provision for their need, Ex. 23 : 16; Deut. 16 : 13–15. It was a season of so great joy that the rabbins were wont to say, "The man who has not seen these festivities does not know what jubilee is." It commenced on the fifteenth day of their *seventh* month, corresponding nearly to our *October,* and was observed eight days, on the first and eighth of which was to be a holy convocation, and solemn assembly, and no servile work was to be done, Lev. 23 : 34–36, 39. They were also to make the prescribed offerings to the Lord on each of the eight days, Lev. 23 : 36–38. This feast is mentioned only here in the New Testament. It was the third and last of the great feasts which God commanded all the male Israelites to attend every year, Deut. 16 : 16. The feast of the dedication (ch. 10 : 22) was instituted by Judas Maccabeus, 165 years before Christ, to commemorate the cleansing of the temple after its defilement by Antiochus Epiphanes.

3. **His brethren,** *his brothers,* probably younger sons of Joseph and Mary, and not his cousins, nor his step-brothers, sons of Joseph by a former marriage. See on ch. 2 : 12 and the Author's *Notes on Matthew,* 13 : 55, and *Notes on Mark,* 6 : 3. From these passages we learn that the brothers' names were James, Joses, Simon, and Judas. **Go into Judæa,** which contains the national capital, and where the men of power and influence reside, and secure the reception of your claims there. As Jesus had not been in Judæa since the second passover in his ministry, eighteen months previous (vers. 21, 23; comp. 5 : 1–16), these brothers thought it strange that he should waste his time in the obscure region of Galilee and the borders of Phœnicia and Peræa, instead of proclaiming himself to the chief men of the nation at the capital, and especially during the great feasts. **Thy disciples,** all thy adherents assembled at the feast, but especially those living in Judæa and Jerusalem. **That thy disciples also may see the works,** rather *thy works,* his miracles which he wrought. With these the brothers were favorably impressed, and they concluded others must be similarly influenced.

4. **There is no man that doeth,** or, *no one does anything,* that is remarkable, and adapted to secure the favorable attention of men, **in secret,** in a hidden or obscure place, such as they regarded Galilee in contrast with Judæa for Messianic purposes. **Seeketh to be known openly,** or *seeks to be in*

5 self to the world. For ʰ neither did ˡ his brethren believe in him.
6 Then Jesus said unto them, ʲ My time is not yet
7 come: but your time is always ready. ᵏ The world cannot hate you; ˡ but me it hateth, ᵐ because I tes-
8 tify of it, that the works thereof are evil. Go ye up unto this feast: I go not up yet unto this feast; ⁿ for my time is not yet full come.

ⁿ ver. 6; ch. 8. 20.

ʰ ch. 1. 11; Mark 3. 21.
ˡ Acts 1. 14.
ʲ vers. 8, 30; ch. 2 4; 8. 20; 13. 1.
ᵏ Luke 6. 26; James 4. 4; 1 John 4. 5.
ˡ ch. 15. 18, 19; 17. 14; Rom. 8. 7; 1 John 3. 13.
ᵐ ch. 3. 19.

public, so as to gain the general attention, acquaintance, and good-will of the people. **If thou do**, not indicating doubt, but expressing an acknowledged fact, and putting it in this form to give their argument the greater force. **Show,** or *manifest*, **thyself to the world,** as thou wouldst do in Jerusalem at the feast, in contrast with thy labors in this obscure region.
5. **For neither,** *not even,* **did his brethren believe in him.** While many of his disciples had withdrawn and walked with him no more (ch. 6 : 66), and the rulers and chief men were seeking to take his life (ver. 1), not even his brothers were exercising a settled faith in him as the promised Messiah, nor did they have any just conception of his Messianic mission and work. From this point of view we perceive that their remarks to him may have exhibited something of impatience and of a taunting tone. We have also here an insight into the domestic trials of our Saviour, in accordance with the saying, "A prophet hath no honor in his own country," ch. 4 : 44; or "A prophet is not without honor, but in his own country and among his own kin, and in his own house," Mark 6 : 4.
6. **Jesus said,** or *says*, in the present tense, bringing the scene vividly before the reader. **Then Jesus;** better, *Jesus therefore says,* in order to reply to his brothers' request, and show them why he cannot go up to the feast. **My time,** in contrast with *your time* in the succeeding member of the sentence, **is not yet come.** He evidently does not mean the time for going up to this feast, but the time had not fully come for him to go up to Jerusalem and make a public manifestation of himself there, such as his brothers desired, and such as he would make at the next great feast, the passover, by going up to Bethany six days before the feast

(ch. 12 : 1), and into Jerusalem the next day and on days following. Such a manifestation would provoke the active hostility of the world (ver. 7), and bring on the *time* of his sufferings. **But your time is always ready.** Any convenient time is suitable for you, because you have no public work to perform adapted to call forth the enmity of the world. You may always, and in any manner, show yourselves to the world without its taking hostile notice of you.
7. **The world,** the people who have a worldly spirit and an unrenewed state of heart, **cannot hate you,** because you are not so different from them as to be exposed to their ill-will, nor do you sustain a public relation to them requiring you to reprove their sins. **But me it hateth,** for the reason that, as long as men are unwilling to part with any sin, they hate and are angry with the one who faithfully reproves them for it, see Mark 6 : 18, 19. **Because I testify;** the I is emphatic, and should be prominent, keeping up the contrast with the preceding *you : Because I am testifying of it;* his work also being *continuous.* The period had now arrived in his public ministry when he must bear a decided and continued testimony respecting the **evil works of** men, ver. 19; 8 : 21, 24, 37-45. He must cry aloud and spare not; he must lift up his voice like a trumpet, and show his people their transgressions and the house of Jacob their sins (Isa. 58 : 1), that thus the way might be prepared for them to repent, believe, and be saved.
8. **Go ye up ;** *do you go up,* the **you** being emphatic, in contrast with the **I** in the clause following. **Unto this feast,** rather, with the critical editors, *to the feast,* serving to give significance to *this feast* in the next clause. **I go not up yet unto,** making the **I** prom-

6*

9 When he had said these words unto them, he abode *still* in Galilee.

Jesus goes up to the feast of tabernacles privately; teaches in the temple; the rulers attempt to seize him.

10 But when his brethren were gone up, then went he also up unto the feast, not openly, ᵒ but as it were in secret.   ᵒ Isa. 42. 2.
11 Then ᵖ the Jews sought him at the feast, and said,   ᵖ ch. 11. 56.
ᑫ ch. 9. 16; 10. 19.
12 Where is he? And ᑫ there was much murmuring among the people concerning him: for ʳ some said, He is a good man: others said, Nay; ˢ but he deceiv-   ʳ ver. 40; Luke 7. 16.
ˢ ver. 47; Matt. 27. 63.

inent because emphatic; **this feast,** the word **this** being emphatic and significant, because he would not go up now, with the festal train, to *this* feast, although to the next great feast he would go up early. See on ver. 6. Some of the oldest and best manuscripts omit **yet.** In this case his answer is enigmatical; he could not explain himself to them. Something is implied, as if he had said, "I go not up *now* to this feast," **For my time is not** *fully come,* so as to render it proper for me to go. While others would consult only their own pleasure, convenience, and interest, Jesus would consult in all things *the Father's will.*

9. **When he had said these words unto them.** Instead of *unto them,* the most able critical authorities, by a slight change in a Greek word, read *he himself.* **Abode still in Galilee.** While his brothers went up, most likely with the festal caravan, as they had urged him to do, *he himself* did not go with them, but *remained in Galilee,* awaiting the proper time for him to go more privately with his disciples.

10-53. JESUS GOES UP TO THE FEAST, AND TEACHES IN THE TEMPLE. THE PEOPLE EXPRESS VARIOUS OPINIONS CONCERNING HIM. THE RULERS ATTEMPT TO SEIZE HIM, BUT ARE THWARTED. Found only in John.

10. **When his brethren,** see on ver. 3, **were gone up, then went he also up unto the feast,** or, with the oldest manuscripts and the best critics, *had gone up to the feast, then he also went up,* **not openly,** in a large festal caravan and as a festal pilgrim, but having only his disciples with him, and going probably, not on the most public roads, **but as it were in secret,** *in a private manner,* as he would ordinarily travel. Compare Luke 9 : 51-62, which is believed to give some particulars of this journey, and harmonizes well with this verse and its context. Compare *Author's Harmony,* § 97, and *Notes on Luke,* 9 : 51-56. On this occasion he did not wish to appear as an ordinary pilgrim attending the feast, but as the Prophet, the Messenger of Jehovah, coming forth from his concealment suddenly into his temple (Mal. 3 : 1) in the midst of the feast (ver. 14), and teaching the people the insufficiency of the festal symbols, in contrast with their fulfilment in his person and work.

11. **Then the Jews,** better, *the Jews therefore,* because he had not come (ver. 9), but they were looking for him, and could not see him there. **The Jews,** especially the people of Judæa, but primarily those hostile to Christ (see ver. 13), who had evidently been expecting him, and expecting with all the more anxiety from the fact that he had not attended the last passover. **Sought him;** the original implies that they sought him from day to day, **at the feast,** more exactly, *in the feast,* during its first three days, when he had not yet arrived there (see ver. 14), **and said, Where is he?** more exactly, *Where is that man?* The hostile Jews (ver. 13) in making this inquiry showed that they wished to continue even to death the persecution which they had commenced against Jesus at the feast of the passover eighteen months previous. See ver. 25; ch. 5 : 16, 18.

12. In this and the next verse we

A. D. 29.   JOHN VII.   131

13 eth the people. Howbeit no man spake openly of
him, *for fear of the Jews.
14 Now about the midst of the feast "Jesus went up
15 into the temple, and taught. 'And the Jews marvelled, saying, How knoweth this man letters, having never learned?

*ch. 9. 22; 12. 42;
19. 38.
"See refs. Matt.
21. 12.
'Luke 4. 22; Acts
2. 7.

have various opinions concerning Jesus. There was much murmuring, suppressed talk, not complaining, but conversing or disputing, with a low voice and in a private manner, so that what they said would not be easily understood by the rulers (see ver. 13), among the people, rather, *the multitudes*, attending the feast, for some said. The word *for* should be omitted, as there is nothing representing it in the Greek text, and the sense is clear without it. He is a good man—*i. e.* he is honest and kind, a righteous man. Compare the reply which follows. Others said, Nay, *No*, a simple denial that he was good. But, introduces a positive charge of evil, he deceiveth the people ; *he leads the multitude astray,* giving them erroneous views, and raising in them false hopes. How utterly unjust, and how completely opposed to the truth, was this hostile assertion! David might well pray, "Let me fall now into the hand of the Lord, but let me not fall into the hand of man," 1 Chron. 21 : 13.

13. Howbeit no man spake openly of him, *spoke freely* and publicly *concerning him,* especially as to what they thought in regard to his being the Messiah, for fear, *because of his fear,* distinctly assigning the reason why no one of the people spoke freely and openly, of the Jews, the rulers, the chief men of the Jews. Those of the multitude who favored Jesus' claims to the Messiahship did not dare to let it be known, and those who rejected his claims were careful not to utter all that they felt. "The bondage of conscience was such that no one ventured to utter fully the thoughts of his heart before the hierarchy had spoken."— LANGE.

14. Jesus comes into the temple and teaches publicly; the Jews in wonder question his capability, vers. 14, 15. Now about the midst of the feast, the first three days of the feast having passed, Jesus went up, the temple being situated on the top of the hill Mount Moriah (2 Chron. 3 :1 ; Ezra 3 : 10–12; 5 : 11), into the temple. He emerged from his obscurity, came suddenly and unexpectedly into the temple (see on ver. 10), and appeared openly among the multitude there assembled. The presence of this vast multitude, many of whom cherished the belief that he was the Christ, served as a shield for him, because the hostile rulers did not dare provoke the displeasure of the people by proceeding abruptly and publicly against him. Thus, while the people had a timid fear of the rulers, on the other hand the rulers had a salutary fear of the people. And taught, especially of matters pertaining to the feast of tabernacles, applying to those matters passages from the Old Testament Scriptures, and explaining them. See on ver. 15.

15. And the Jews, rather, with the best critical authorities, *The Jews therefore, because of* the nature and extent of knowledge which he exhibited in his teaching, and the unusual character of his explanations of Scripture. The *Jews,* some of the leading and learned men, most likely chief priests or scribes. Marvelled, or *wondered,* saying, How knoweth this man, how can he possess reliable knowledge on such elevated and difficult subjects? Their surprise would seem to indicate that Jesus had not before this taught publicly at Jerusalem, or perhaps that these Jews had never before heard him. Letters, *i. e., writings, scriptures, learning;* here doubtless referring to the Jewish *Scriptures* of the Old Testament, the kind of *learning* which they cultivated almost exclusively, and some portion of which, especially as applying to the feast of tabernacles, he had just very clearly and forcibly presented. See ver. 14, and compare Luke 4:16–22. Having never learned, more exactly, not having been taught by their doctors of law, nor gone through their usual course

16 Jesus answered them, and said, *My doctrine is not
17 mine, but his that sent me. ʸIf any man will do his
will, he shall know of the doctrine, whether it be of
18 God, or *whether* I speak of myself. ᶻHe that speaketh of himself seeketh his own glory; but he that
seeketh his glory that sent him, the same is true, and
19 no unrighteousness is in him. ᵃDid not Moses give

ˣ ch. 3. 11; 8. 28;
12. 49; 14. 10, 24.
ʸ ch. 8. 31, 32, 43;
Ps. 25. 12; 119.
10, 101, 102; Hos.
6. 3; Mic. 4. 2;
Mal. 4. 2.
ᶻ ch. 5. 41; 8. 50;
Phil. 2. 3–8.
ᵃ ch. 1. 17.

of training; not having "been schooled as a rabbi."—DR. P. SCHAFF. They seem to have asked the question, not to express admiration of his teaching, but to excite doubt in the minds of the common people and hinder them from receiving his instructions. See his answer in vers. 16–19, and the people's response in ver. 20 to his question.

16. In reply, Jesus asserts the divine authority of his teaching and its self-commending power, vers. 16-18. **Jesus answered.** The best critical authorities add *therefore*, or *then*, in a similar sense: *Jesus then answered them, and said*, letting them know that he had understood both their question and the motives which prompted it. **My doctrine,** the instruction which I give, **is not mine.** It is not to be considered mine so much as *his who sent me*, and by whose authority I act; and it is not a mere system of doctrine or teaching, but is pre-eminently *his message* of life to you. It was also not devised by me as a man, or by me irrespective of the Father; and it is what he himself sanctions and has enjoined on me to communicate to the people.

17. **If any man will do,** rather, *desire to do*, implying that kind of desire which is carried out in corresponding earnest action, **his will,** the will of God as made known in Nature and by inward conviction, by the Old Testament, and by the explanations and teachings of the Lord Jesus, **he shall know of the doctrine,** *know concerning the teaching;* he shall feel in his own soul the glow and divine power of that teaching, which, to his consciousness, will prove it to be from God, and not from any mere man. **Whether it be of God,** not spoken hypothetically, but positively, **or whether I speak,** giving prominence to the emphatic **I,** and expressing Christ's *continuous* work of publicly teaching the people; **of myself,** better, *from myself,* self-prompted, self-directed, instead of being commissioned and sent by God. The phrase *of myself* might mean *concerning* myself, a sense not appropriate in this passage.

18. **He that speaketh of himself,** *from himself* (see on ver. 17), **seeketh his own glory,** is ambitious to promote his own interests and his own honor, instead of the interests and honor of him who sent him; he is an unfaithful, untrusty messenger; **but he that seeketh his glory that,** or, *the glory of him who,* **sent him,** by faithfully delivering his message, and seeking only his honor, **the same is true;** he is upright, faithful, and worthy of confidence; he is no impostor, **and no unrighteousness is in him,** no abuse of his trust, and no transgression of the law; see ver. 21. His message should therefore be received in full confidence.

In vers. 17, 18 Jesus presents two facts in confirmation of his teaching only what is agreeable to God's will: 1. His teaching is such as commends itself to a heart piously inclined, and every such heart will *feel* that the teaching is true. See Matt. 7 : 28, 29. 2. He seeks not honor for himself, but for the Father who sent him, and thus proves his own sincerity and fidelity in the work assigned him.

19. In this and the next verse Jesus reproves the Jews for their hostility, and in vers. 21–24 he shows that healing a man is not so great a violation of the Sabbath as the practice of circumcising a man on that day. **Did not Moses give you the law?** *Moses,* their highest legal authority, making prominent the fact of *their* having received the law, and under such circumstances as rendered them inexcusable for not keeping it. Most of the critical editors close the question with *the law,* making what follows a direct assertion or charge: *Yet none of you keepeth the law!* This harmonizes with the succeeding con-

you the law, ^b and *yet* none of you keepeth the law? Why go ye about to kill me?
20 The people answered and said, ^d Thou hast a devil: who goeth about to kill thee?
21 Jesus answered and said unto them, ^e I have done
22 one work, and ye all marvel. ^f Moses therefore gave unto you circumcision; (not because it is of Moses, ^g but of the fathers;) and ye on the sabbath day cir-

^b Rom. 2. 17-29.
^c See ch. 5. 16, 18; 10. 31, 39; 11. 53; Matt. 12. 14; Mark 3. 6.
^d ch. 8. 48, 52; 10. 20.
^e ch. 5. 9-11.
^f Lev. 12. 3.
^g Gen. 17. 10-14; Acts 7. 8.

text and with ver. 7. The law says, "Thou shalt not kill," "Thou shalt love thy neighbor as thyself," "Thou shalt love the Lord thy God with all thine heart" (Lev. 19 : 18; Deut. 5 : 17; 6 : 5), yet the rulers were seeking to *kill* Jesus, and the thoughtless people were as evidently failing to perform the law. And with such a state of heart they were utterly disqualified to judge of him and his teaching, as he proceeds to show in vers. 21-24. **None of you keepeth the law,** or, *no one of you performs the law.* **Why go ye about,** why are you watching for an opportunity, **to kill me?** This specific charge of murderous intent was adapted to lead the people as well as the rulers to reflection and self-examination, from the fact that while the rulers were seeking to kill Jesus, they were encouraged in their high-handed course by the mental indolence and timidity of the people, especially of those in Judæa, who must have known that the rulers were hating and persecuting him "without a cause," ch. 15 : 25. Having spoken of his *teaching* in vers. 16-18, Jesus by this question prepares the way to defend his *works* in vers. 21-24.
20. **The people answered;** not those of Jerusalem and its vicinity (ver. 25), but the festal pilgrims who had come in from a distance and were unacquainted with the designs of the rulers. **And said;** some spoke, and others acquiesced. The rulers remain silent under Christ's charge of murderous intent, because, though they may safely plot against him and watch their opportunity in private, they consider it dangerous to have their design so soon canvassed in public before the vast festal throng. See Matt. 26 : 4, 5. **Thou hast a devil,** rather *a demon.* The original Scriptures recognize only one devil, but many demons, an inferior order of evil spirits subject to the devil, or Satan their prince, Matt. 12 : 24; 25 : 41; Rev. 12 : 9. See the Author's *Notes on Matthew,* 4 : 24; *Notes on Mark,* 1 : 23. As those possessed by demons were in most cases deranged persons or melancholy, the prominent idea intended to be conveyed here may have been that Jesus was melancholy and beside himself to suppose they were seeking to take his life. See ch. 10 : 20. Still the expression was disrespectful, and adapted to try the patience of Jesus. **Who goeth about to kill thee?** See on ver. 19.
21. **Jesus answered,** spoke in his turn, **and said unto them;** those whom he was especially addressing in vers. 16-19, the Jewish rulers and leaders—not the multitude, who interposed their disrespectful, even if well-meant, language. **I have done one work,** referring to a work which had been especially displeasing to them—his curing the infirm man at the pool of Bethesda when he was last in Jerusalem at the feast of the passover, eighteen months previous, ch. 5 : 8, 9. **And ye all marvel,** or *wonder* at it, but in such a way as to complain of it as a violation of the Sabbath, ch. 5 : 16, 18. Notice that out of the hundreds of beneficent acts which Jesus had done they selected this *one* to complain of and use against him. They wonder, not at the grandeur of the miracle performed, but that he should presume to do a *work* on the Sabbath. To their charge that he had violated the Sabbath by doing this *one work* he proceeds to reply.
22. **Moses therefore,** or *for this reason Moses,* has given you circumcision, not because it originated with him, or first appears in the enactments under him, but because it came from the fathers of the nation, and primarily from Abraham, on whom, together with his posterity, it was specially and positively enjoined by God. **Gave unto you; he**

23 cumcise a man. If a man on the sabbath day receive circumcision, that the law of Moses should not be broken; are ye angry at me, because ʰ I have made a man every whit whole on the sabbath day? ¹ Judge not according to the appearance, but judge righteous judgment.

ʰ ch. 5. 8, 9, 16; Luke 13. 15, 16; 14. 1-6.
¹ ch. 8. 15; Deut. 1. 16, 17; Ps. 58. 1; Prov. 24. 23; 2 Cor. 10. 7; James 2. 1-4.

has recorded the injunction, and it stands in his writings as obligatory on the descendants of Abraham, Gen. 17 : 10-14. **Circumcision (not because it is of Moses, but of the fathers); and ye on the sabbath day,** or *on the Sabbath you,* in obedience to the requirement of Moses, perform this ritual service, *you* **circumcise a man,** a human being, a male child. See ch. 16 : 21.

23. **If a man on the sabbath day receive circumcision.** This was a well-known and constantly-recurring fact. **That the law of Moses,** the law particularly respecting circumcision, which requires every male child to be circumcised when eight days old, Gen. 17 : 12. To this superior and positive unconditional law the inferior law respecting the doing of work on the Sabbath must yield if they appear to conflict. But do they really conflict? I think not when rightly understood; for the kind of "work" in the prohibition—"In it thou shalt not do *any work*"—must be ascertained and defined by the context. In Deut. 5 : 12-15 we find the command concerning the Sabbath clearly stated and enforced : "Keep the sabbath day to sanctify it," to consecrate it, to set it apart from ordinary or common uses to the service of God, "as the Lord thy God hath commanded thee." This implies that his covenant people were individually to be wholly subject to the commands and appointments of their God. "Six days thou shalt labor, and do all thy work." The Hebrew word here for "work" is properly service or work which one person is *sent* to do for another. Notice the command, "*Thou* shalt labor, and do all *thy* work," personally, and by the help of others, and do it "all" within the "six days." "But the seventh day is the sabbath of the Lord ;" literally, "is a rest to Jehovah thy God"—a *rest from* "all thy work," to be devoted "*to* Jehovah thy God," to perform his will. Conse-quently, the repetition of the command in a negative form, "In it thou shalt not do any work," must necessarily be explained and limited by what precedes, and must mean, "Thou shalt not do any of *thy* work" on that day—*i. e.* "any work" to accomplish thine own ends or promote thy worldly interests. This view is confirmed by the clauses which follow: "thou, nor thy son," etc., "that thy man-servant and thy maid-servant may rest as well as thou"—*rest* from *thy* service and "*thy* work" which thou *sentest* them to do. But circumcision is *commanded* by God, and therefore it cannot be classed under the Sabbath law as "thy work." Hence there is no inconsistency between the two laws. Also, Jesus does not intimate any such inconsistency, but seems to imply the contrary. In Matt. 12 : 5, where he introduces the matter in another aspect, the explanation is: "The priests in the temple profane [or *render common*] the Sabbath" by doing what seems like the common week-day work which men do for their own purposes. They slay and cut up sheep and goats and bullocks, and then burn them on the altar (Lev. 16 : 3, 5, 31 : Num. 28 : 9, 10, 18-25), "and are blameless," because they do it not to serve their own ends, but to obey the commands of God. **Should not,** *may not,* **be broken,** the *may not* corresponding with the preceding *receive,* **because I have made a man every whit whole,** or *altogether well;* literally, *made an entire man, sound,* or *well,* intimating that the infirm man's whole body had been diseased, but was entirely restored to health. And whereas circumcision affected only a small part of the body, which must subsequently be cared for and healed, Jesus had by a word healed *the whole body* of a man, and restored him at once from an eight-and-thirty years' sickness to perfect health. Surely this was an act unselfish and divine!

24. **Judge not according to the**

A. D. 29.   JOHN VII.   185

25 Then said some of them of Jerusalem, Is not this
26 he, whom they seek to kill? But, lo, ʲ he speaketh ʲ Matt. 22. 16.
boldly, and they say nothing unto him. ᵏ Do the ᵏ ver. 48.
rulers know indeed that this is the very Christ?
27 ˡ Howbeit we know this man whence he is: but ˡ ch. 6. 42; Matt.
when Christ cometh, ᵐ no man knoweth whence he   13. 55; Mark 6.
is.   3; Luke. 4. 22.
                                                   ᵐ vers. 41, 42.
28   Then cried Jesus in the temple as he taught, saying,

appearance. Judge not superficially, not as the matter first *appears* to be; but **judge righteous judgment**—judgment which is in accordance with the weight of evidence and the nature of things, with the principles of truth and right and with the word of God. The law commands, "Thou shalt not kill," implying our duty to use every proper means for *preserving* life, and "Thou shalt love thy neighbor as thyself," Ex. 20 : 13 ; Lev. 19 : 18. It is therefore our duty to seek to preserve the lives of ourselves and others, on the Sabbath and on all other days. And while it was right for Jesus to heal on the Jewish Sabbath, it is also right for us on the Lord's Day to administer appropriate remedies and care to the sick, to partake of food and drink, and do whatever else is necessary to preserve life and health, and cannot be done before that day nor neglected till after. Such a course is unselfish and in harmony with the revealed will of God.

25. Further opinions and doubts concerning his Messiahship, vers. 25-27. **Some of them of**, or *from*, **Jerusalem**, showing that the murderous designs of the rulers were known to more or less of the inhabitants of Jerusalem; **whom they, "the rulers"** (see ver. 26), **seek to kill**. See on ver. 19.

26. **But, lo, he speaketh boldly**, uttering all that he wishes to say, **and they**, those in authority, "the rulers" (see below), **say nothing unto him**, nothing to restrain or intimidate him. **The rulers**, the members of the Sanhedrim especially, which was the highest civil and ecclesiastical court of the Jews, and consisted of seventy-one persons, from the three classes of chief priests, elders, and scribes. **Do the rulers know indeed?** Have they come to this knowledge lately, forsooth, so that they have given up the idea of seizing and putting him to death? These Jerusalemites presume to call in question the zeal and watchfulness of their rulers, and treat them with irony. **That this is the very Christ?** rather, with the oldest manuscripts and the critical editors, *the Christ?*

27. **Howbeit**, or *but*, **we know this man**, the word this is emphatic, **whence he is**. From the mean and despised town of Nazareth in Galilee, and from the low family of Joseph the carpenter. **But when Christ cometh**, the *when* indicating an indefinite time somewhere in the unknown future. *The Christ*, with the article as in verse 26, referring to him in his official character as the promised Messiah of the Old Testament. **No man knoweth whence he is.** This opinion seems to have been at that time common among the Jews, and may have originated in their ideas of Mal. 3 : 1 : "The Lord, whom ye seek, shall suddenly come to his temple, even the messenger of the covenant, in whom ye delight," compared with such passages as Isa. 53 : 8 ; Dan. 7 : 13, 14. It seems to have raised in some minds the expectation that the Christ would suddenly appear, and no one be able to give an account of his parentage ; and in other minds the expectation that he would retire for a time from the notice of men, and then make a sudden appearance, without any one knowing whence he came. See Matt. 24 : 23, 26. But when these arrogant complainers declared *no man knoweth whence he is*, how entirely they ignored such plain passages as Deut. 18 : 15 ; Ps. 132 : 11, which point out from whom the Christ as Prophet and King was to come : " From the midst of thee, *of thy brethren*," of the *offspring of David*, and Mic. 5 : 2, pointing out the place from which—Bethlehem Ephratah, in Judah, see ver. 42; Acts 2 : 30; Matt. 2 : 4-6 !

28. In this and the next verse Jesus asserts again and more distinctly his divine origin. **Then cried Jesus,**

ᵃ Ye both know me, and ye know whence I am. And
ᵒ I am not come of myself, but he that sent me ᵖ is
29 true, ᵠ whom ye know not: but ʳ I know him: ˢ for
I am from him, and ᵗ he hath sent me.
30 Then ᵘ they sought to take him: but ᵛ no man laid
hands on him, because ʷ his hour was not yet come.
31 And ˣ many of the people believed on him, and said,
When Christ cometh, will he do more miracles than
32 these which this *man* hath done? The Pharisees
heard that the people murmured such things concerning him; and the Pharisees and the chief priests
ʸ sent officers to take him.

ᵃ ch. 8. 14.
ᵇ ch. 5. 43; 8. 16, 42.
ᵖ ch. 5. 32; 8. 26; Rom. 3. 4.
ᵠ ch. 1. 18; 8. 54, 55; 16. 3.
ʳ ch. 10. 15; 17. 25; Matt. 11. 27.
ˢ ch. 3. 16, 17.
ᵗ 1 John 4. 14.
ᵘ ver. 19; ch. 8. 37; Mark 11. 18; Luke 19. 47; 20. 19.
ᵛ vers. 6, 8, 44; ch. 8. 20; Ps. 31. 15.

ʷ ch. 13 1   ˣ ch. 3. 2; 8. 30; Matt. 12. 23.   ʸ vers. 45, 46.

speaking boldly and loudly, with direct reference to what those from Jerusalem had said, **in the temple as he taught,** more exactly, *teaching in the temple, and saying,* **Ye both know me, and ye know whence I am.** You know my person, my parentage (ch. 6 : 42), and the place of my early residence, vers. 41, 52. **And I am not,** or *I have not,* **come of myself.** Though you may know my human origin and residence, yet I have come forth by divine authority, and not from my own will or purpose. **But he that sent me is true.** He has a real existence, and has truly sent me; therefore his sanction of my claims should be acknowledged. Compare ch. 5 : 32-39. **Whom ye know not,** the ye being emphatic and requiring prominence; with whose true character and his design in sending me you are not acquainted.
29. **But I know him.** I is emphatic, in contrast with **ye** of the preceding clause. *I know him,* have an intimate acquaintance with him and with his purposes and plans; **for I am from him, and he hath sent me.** He has sent me forth, from himself and by his own authority, to do his work in his appointed way.
30. Some seek to seize Jesus; others believe on him. Therefore the rulers send officers to take him, vers. 30-32. **Then they,** "the rulers," ver. 26, **sought to take him,** being urged on to it by their anger at what he had just said. **But no man laid hands on him,** to seize him as a prisoner. Though the desire to do it was in the *heart,* they were not suffered to lay on him the hand. **Because his hour was not yet come,** the time when he should actually be delivered into the hands of his enemies.
31. **And many of the people,** or *multitude,* **believed on him.** While the rulers rejected him, and were watching their opportunity to seize and kill him, the great mass of the people had a very different feeling. Many of them believed he might be the Messiah, and cautiously expressed that belief. Their conviction, however, needed confirming, and was doubtless in many cases destitute of the love to him which would admit his claim to their personal obedience. **When Christ cometh,** see on ver. 27, **will he do more miracles,** or *work more signs,* which were of a miraculous character, and adapted to excite wonder, **than these which this man hath done?** or, according to some, *than those which this man is working?* This was an important proof of his Messianic character; see ch. 3 : 2; Isa. 35 : 5, 6; 42 : 6, 7.
32. **Heard that the people murmured,** or *heard the multitude murmuring.* They not only heard that the thing was done, but themselves heard the murmuring, and readily learned what it was which the multitude said. Compare ch. 1 : 37. *Murmuring,* see on ver. 12. **Such things,** rather *these things,* **concerning him; and the Pharisees and the chief priests;** the best critical authorities reverse the order and read, *the chief priests and the Pharisees.* Thus the Pharisees watch the multitude, hear their suppressed talk in implied acknowledgment of Jesus as "the Christ," and report these facts to the chief priests. The latter are then

33 Then said Jesus unto them, ᵉYet a little while am
34 I with you, and *then* I go unto him that sent me. Ye
ᵃshall seek me, and shall not find *me*: and where I
am, *thither* ye cannot come.
35 Then said the Jews among themselves, Whither
will he go, that we shall not find him? will he go
unto the ᵇdispersed among the Gentiles, and teach
36 the Gentiles? What *manner of* saying is this that
he said, Ye shall seek me, and shall not find *me:*
and where I am, *thither* ye cannot come?
37 ᶜIn the last day, that great *day* of the feast, Jesus
stood and cried, saying, ᵈIf any man thirst, ᵉlet him

ᵉ ch. 12. 35, 36; 13.
1, 33; 16. 16–22.
ᵃ ch. 8. 21–24; 13.
33; Prov. 1. 24–
31; Hos. 5. 6;
Luke 13. 24, 25,
34, 35.
ᵇ Isa. 11. 12; Zeph.
3. 10; Acts 21.
21; James 1. 1;
1 Pet. 1. 1.
ᶜ Lev. 23. 36.
ᵈ ch. 6. 35; Isa. 41.
17, 18; 55. 1;
Rev. 21. 6; 22. 17.
ᵉ Matt. 11. 28.

ready to take the lead in the actual persecution of Jesus. See also ver. 45. **Sent officers to take him,** that they might watch for the opportunity when they could seize him without exciting the multitude.

33. In language which the people do not understand Jesus intimates his speedy removal, vers. 33-36. **Then said Jesus unto them,** rather *Jesus therefore said,* omitting *unto them,* and making his remarks which follow as general as those in vers. 28 and 29, **Yet a little while,** it being now six months before his actual departure, **am I with you,** implying to the officers, You must let me freely speak a little longer here; and to the multitude, My work among you is drawing toward its close; improve, therefore, while you can, the opportunity now afforded you. **And then I go unto him that sent me.** This expression is made somewhat enigmatical by that which follows, and therefore these Jews either ignore it or pretend not to understand it.

34. **Ye shall seek me, and shall not.** The time is coming when you will long for the Messiah, but in vain. Rejecting me, you will find in no other the Messiah whom you desire. **And where I am, thither ye cannot come. I am,** "the present of vivid representation" (THOLUCK); or spoken by anticipation, and meaning, where in a few months he would be, in the heavens at the right hand of God, Acts 7 : 56. **Ye cannot come,** the *you* being emphatic. See ch. 8 : 21, 24.

35. **Then said the Jews,** their inquiry being occasioned by the statement Jesus had just made, **will he go unto the dispersed among the Gentiles?** or *among the Greeks,* meaning those Jews who were scattered among surrounding nations, where the Greek language was more or less spoken and understood. Such were regarded by the Palestine Jews as less orthodox and less respectable and intelligent than themselves. **And teach the Gentiles,** rather *the Greeks;* will he even go so far as to teach the Greeks, toward whom, by his treatment of the law (ch. 5 : 8-16) and his liberal utterances (ch. 5 : 24-28; 7 : 17), he seems inclined? Those Jews who did not live in Palestine were called *the dispersion* or *the dispersed ones,* because they were scattered abroad outside the Promised Land. See James 1 : 1; 1 Pet. 1 : 1. Of such Jews there were many in Asia Minor, Syria, Egypt, Greece, and Rome, where the Greek language was in general use; and the nations living in those countries were classed by Palestine Jews under the general term, "the Greeks." See Acts 14 : 1; 18 : 4; 21 : 28; Rom. 1 : 16; 10 : 12.

36. **What manner of saying is this that he said?** What are we to understand by it? They cannot but give some attention to the saying, and seem to feel the dark, fearful mystery it contains. But, like Pilate on another occasion, having asked the question, they let the matter drop.

37. JESUS INVITES THE PEOPLE TO THE FOUNTAIN OF LIFE, vers. 37-39. **In the last day, that great day,** or *Now in the last, the great day of the feast,* which brought this great festival to a solemn close. This was the eighth day of the festival, on which there was to be a holy convocation, a solemn assembly, and no servile work was to be done (Lev. 23 : 36), and the day on which, at least in every seventh year, the year

38 come unto me, ʳand drink. ᵍHe that believeth on me, as the Scripture hath said, ʰout of his belly shall

ʳch. 6. 55; 1 Cor 10. 4; 11. 25.
ʰDeut. 18. 15.

ᵇch. 4. 14; Job 32. 18, 19; Prov. 18. 4; Isa. 12. 3; 44. 3; 58. 11; Zech. 14. 8; Gal. 5. 21, 22.

of release, they finished the reading of the law, which they commenced at the beginning of the feast, Deut. 31 : 10-13. According to the Jewish rabbinical writings, during the first seven days of this feast—and Rabbi Juda says on this day also—with still greater expressions of joy, occurred the ceremony of drawing water from the pool of Siloam and carrying it in solemn procession to the altar. A priest filled a golden pitcher, of about two and a half pints, with water from the fount of Siloam (ch. 9 : 7), which was borne with great solemnity, attended with the clangor of trumpets, through the gate of the temple; and, being mixed with wine, it was poured upon the altar of burnt-offering, while meantime the Hallel, of Ps. 113 : 1-118 : 29, was sung. As the booths commemorated the tent-life of the Israelites in the wilderness, so this pouring of water might serve to commemorate the miraculous springs which God opened to supply the thirst of his people. Others connect this ceremony with their prayer for rain on the seed sown during the coming year, and others connect it with Isa. 12 : 3: "With joy shall ye draw water out of the wells of salvation," and with the effusion of the Holy Spirit in the days of the Messiah. This ceremony, so indefinite in its teaching, seems to have been a mere human invention, yet the opportunity which it afforded Jesus improved in calling the attention of the people to the water of life, which he will bestow, and which alone can satisfy the cravings of the soul. Compare ch. 4 : 10-14. But others hold that the ceremony of bringing water was omitted on the last day of the feast. If so, then Jesus could very naturally, in the absence of this ceremony, call attention to himself as the source and fountain of living water. **Jesus stood** (he usually sat when teaching, Matt. 5 : 1; 13 : 1; 24 : 3), in the temple, amidst the thousands of the people then present, **and cried** out in a loud voice, so that the vast multitude might hear. Like a herald he cries out aloud, announcing an important truth. **If any man**

thirst, if any one feel that he is destitute of true happiness, yet earnestly desires it, as one who has the natural bodily thirst, and longs for water to satisfy it; yea, if any one feel that he is a guilty, perishing sinner, and longs to be saved from his sins and restored to the favor and enjoyment of God (see ch. 4 : 14; Matt. 5 : 6; Rev. 22 : 17), **let him come;** the invitation is full and free to all the thirsting; *if any one thirst*, no matter who or of what age he is, or to what class he belongs, the invitation is to him; if *any one* thirst, let him come **unto me, and drink.** Tischendorf omits **unto me**, but most critical authorities retain the words. The sense, however, is sufficiently clear in either case, because the next clause distinctly points out, in plain language, what is to be done.

38. **He that believeth on me,** he that acknowledges me as the Christ (ver. 31), and with a penitent and obedient heart trusts in me for salvation from sin, **as the Scripture hath said,** in a general way, in such passages as Prov. 18 : 4: "The words of a man's mouth are deep waters; the well-spring of wisdom as a gushing stream."—*Conant's Proverbs.* Isa. 58 : 11: "Thou shalt be like a watered garden, and like a spring of water, whose waters fail not." Or, considering the believer's body as a living temple of the Holy Spirit, such passages as Ezek. 47 : 1-12, Joel 3 : 18; Zech 14 : 8. **Out of his belly;** better, *his heart.* The Greek word thus translated properly signifies a *hollow place*, a cavity, and hence is appropriately used to represent the *stomach* and the *bowels*, as in Matt. 2 : 40; 15 : 17; the inward parts, the inner man, the *heart*, as here. Compare Jer. 31 : 33; Heb. 8 : 10. **Shall flow.** He shall have within him, not only a well-spring of happiness, but a fountain, from which *shall flow forth* perennial streams for the refreshment of others. **Rivers,** implying abundance—a full supply. Compare ch. 4 : 14. **Of living water,** pure, running water, ever-flowing streams; the opposite of stagnant,

39 flow rivers of living water. ¹But this spake he of the Spirit, which they that believe on him should receive: ʲfor the Holy Ghost was not yet *given:* because that Jesus was not yet ᵏglorified.
40 Many of the people therefore, when they heard this
41 saying, said, Of a truth this is ˡthe Prophet. Others said, ᵐThis is the Christ. But some said, Shall Christ
42 come ⁿout of Galilee? °Hath not the Scripture said, That Christ cometh of the seed of David, and out of
43 the town of Bethlehem, ᵖwhere David was? So ᑫthere

ch. 14. 16, 17, 26; Isa. 44. 3; Joel 2. 28; Acts 2. 17, 33, 38; Eph. 1. 13, 14.
ʲ ch. 16. 7.
ᵏ ch. 12. 16; Acts 3. 13.
ˡ ch. 1. 21; 6. 14; Deut. 18. 15, 18.
ᵐ ch. 4. 42; 6. 69.
ⁿ ver. 52; ch. 1. 46.
° ver. 27; Ps. 132.

11; Isa. 11. 1; Jer. 23. 5; Mic. 5. 2; Matt. 2. 5; Luke 2. 4. ᵖ 1 Sam. 16. 1, 4. ᑫ ver. 12; ch. 9. 16; 10. 19; Acts 14. 4.

malarious, poisonous water; also life-giving water. See on ch. 4 . 10. The gospel of Christ, which is the truth of God received into the heart by the Spirit, brings life, health, and joy; the errors of sin and Satan bring disease, misery, and death.

39. **But this spake he of the Spirit,** the Holy Spirit, in his more copious and abundant influences on the hearts of men, in connection with the preaching of Christ as the atoning Saviour, **which they that believe on him should receive,** after his resurrection from the dead, both on the day of Pentecost and subsequently. **The Holy Ghost,** or, according to the best text, *the Spirit.* Compare note on ch. 1 : 33. **Was not yet given,** in this copious measure, so as to become, by his enlightening, renewing, sanctifying, and comforting influences, as "rivers of living water" in the disciples of Jesus. **Because that,** is not now used. In such a connection *that* has become superfluous. **Jesus was not yet glorified.** He had not yet risen from the dead and ascended to heaven to the glory there awaiting him, where he would act as the High Priest and Intercessor for his people, and whence, as Head over all things to his church, he would send forth upon them the abundant influences of his Spirit, procured by his sufferings and death as their atoning Lord and Redeemer. See Ps. 110; John 14 : 16, 17; 16 : 7-15; Acts 1 : 5; 2 : 4; Rom. 5 : 5-10; Eph. 1 : 19-23; 4 : 7, 8.

40. A new dispute arises concerning Jesus, but no one molests him, vers. 40-44. **Many,** or, according to the best reading, *some,* **of the people therefore, when they heard this saying.** There were those of the common people who heard these words of Jesus, received an impression from them, and proceeded to state that impression. **Of a truth this is the Prophet.** With some, the Prophet foretold by Moses in Deut. 18 : 15-19—*i. e. the Christ;* but with others, the one whom they expected to precede the coming of the Messiah, and to prepare the way for and assist him; especially Elijah or Jeremiah. See ch. 1 : 21; Matt. 16 : 14; Mal. 4 : 5, 6.

41. **But some said.** Tischendorf, Alford, and Schaff, on good manuscript authority, read, *Others said.* **Shall Christ come out of Galilee?** not distinguishing between his birthplace, Bethlehem in Judæa, and the place where he was brought up, Nazareth in Galilee. Had they been anxious to learn the real character of Jesus, this erroneous impression could easily have been corrected.

42. **That Christ cometh of the seed,** or *offspring,* **of David.** See Ps. 89 : 19-29; 132 : 11; Isa. 9 : 6, 7, 11 : 1-5; Jer. 23 : 5, 6. **And out of the town of Bethlehem, where David was?** Where he was born and lived for about sixteen years, till he was called into the service of King Saul. See Mic. 5 : 2; Luke 2 : 4; 1 Sam. 16 : 1, 5, 18; 17 : 12-15, 58.

43. **So there was a division among the people,** in consequence of their having different opinions about him. There was (1) a division into friends and enemies of Christ, as we see from ver. 44; (2) a division of those who were friendly, because of the differing views they entertained concerning him. These all might allow that he was "the Prophet" (ver. 40), but when they proceeded to define what they understood by this expression,

44 was a division among the people because of him. And ʳsome of them would have taken him; but no man laid hands on him.

45 Then came ˢthe officers to the chief priests and Pharisees; and they said unto them, Why have ye not brought him? The officers answered, ᵗNever man spake like this man. Then answered them the Pharisees, ᵘ Are ye also deceived? ᵛ Have any of the rulers or of the Pharisees believed on him? But ʷ this people who knoweth not the law are cursed.

ʳ ver. 30.
ˢ ver. 32.
ᵗ Matt. 7. 29; Luke 4. 22.
ᵘ ver. 12.
ᵛ ver. 26; ch. 12. 42; Acts 6. 7; 1 Cor. 1. 20, 22–28; 2. 8.
ʷ ch. 9. 34; Isa. 5. 21; 65. 5; 1 Cor. 1. 20, 21; 3. 18–20; James 3. 13–18.

they differed. For while some readily assented to his being the prophet foretold by Moses—*i. e.* "the Christ" (ver. 41)—others were perplexed by their erroneous views of his pedigree and birthplace, and thought he might be the prophet spoken of by Malachi, who should precede the Christ. See on ver. 40.

44. And some of them would have taken him, desired to seize him and deliver him up to his enemies. These hostile persons, mingled among the multitude, were either urged on by the chief priests and Pharisees, or were ready to act the part of zealots and proceed on their own responsibility against Jesus. Yet they were fettered on the one hand by fear of the adherents of Jesus, and on the other by the secret power of God, impressing them with an involuntary awe, so that they dared not proceed. **But no man laid hands on him,** not even those who had been commanded to do it. See vers. 32, 45.

45. Deeply impressed, the officers did not seize Jesus. They are reproved by the Pharisees, vers. 45–49. **Then came the officers,** those who had been sent to watch for the opportunity and seize Jesus, ver. 32. These men were so impressed and awed by the appearance and surroundings of Jesus, and by the words which he uttered, that they dared not take him. They consequently came back and made their report to those who had sent them. **And they said unto them,** the chief priests and Pharisees said to the officers, **Why have ye not brought him?** having expected that they would find occasion to seize him.

46. The officers answered, Never man spake like this man. Tischendorf, with two of the ancient manuscripts, and with ancient Latin and Syriac versions, gives the officers' language a little more fully, and in a style which seems in harmony with the occasion and the character of the men: *Never did a man so speak as this man speaks;* words expressing wonder and astonishment. Some of the oldest documents read, *Never man spoke thus!* This testimony came, too, from men who had been watching every word and every look. With what convincing power had his teaching come home to their consciences and hearts! Compare Matt. 7 : 28, 29. Augustine remarks: "Of him whose life is lightning, his words are thunders."

47. Then answered them the Pharisees, being quite ready to take the lead in speaking on this subject, prompted by their own feelings, **Are ye also deceived?** With their views of the character and work of the Messiah, they take it as a matter of course that Jesus is an impostor, and they speak and act accordingly, without searching into his claims, and bringing them to the test of Scripture and evidence, to learn whether they are well founded.

48. Have any of the rulers or of the Pharisees believed on him? For them the authority and example of the rulers must be everything. And we should notice that the testimony of the officers makes not the least wholesome impression on the rulers, but rather disturbs and excites them. **Or of the Pharisees;** this great, learned, aristocratic, and influential body,—has any of them believed on him? How mistaken these questioners were in regard to both the classes they referred to is shown directly afterward by the example of Nicodemus, vers. 50, 51.

49. But this people, this *multitude,* or rabble, as distinguished from men of letters, of intelligence, and influence,

50 Nicodemus saith unto them (ˣhe that came to Jesus by night, being one of them), ʸDoth our law judge any man, before it hear him, and know what he doeth? 52 They answered and said unto him, Art thou also of Galilee? Search, and look: for ᶻout of Galilee

ˣ ch. 3 1, 2.
ʸ Deut. 1. 17; 17. 8 etc.; 19. 15-19.
ᶻ ver. 41; ch. 1. 46 Isa. 9. 1, 2; Matt. 4. 15, 16.

who knoweth not the law, have not been instructed in the schools of the Pharisees, and taught how to read and interpret the Old Testament. Hence, they are not qualified to judge for themselves in these matters, and must not presume to set up their opinion in opposition to that of their rabbins and leaders. Hence, too, they are easily led astray (ver. 47), and induced to credit and receive an impostor who pretends to be the Christ. **Are cursed,** or, *accursed are they!* execrable, doomed to error and deception, and worthy of contempt and perdition. This was evidently an outburst of Pharisaic madness, indicating their disappointment, and designed to intimidate and control the officers. It is also in harmony with the rabbinical writings, which show great contempt for the common people.

50–53. NICODEMUS HAS THE COURAGE TO SUGGEST THAT JESUS SHOULD NOT BE CONDEMNED UNHEARD, BUT IS TAUNTED TOO; WHEN EACH GOES TO HIS HOME.

50. **Nicodemus,** see 3 : 1, **saith unto them,** to those Pharisees who had been raging against the officers and Jesus, and against the people for believing in him. Tischendorf omits **he that came to Jesus by night,** but Alford and Meyer retain the clause with the exception of *by night;* better still, *he who formerly came to him,* ch. 3 : 1, 2. See ch. 19 : 39, where this clause certainly belongs, as it is found there in all the manuscripts. **Being one of them,** one of the rulers and of the Pharisees (ver. 48; 3 : 1), a member of the Sanhedrim, or great national council. Thus God placed this good man in the national council to vindicate his honor and law, and to keep the wicked and unprincipled in check.

51. **Doth our law judge,** pass sentence upon, *condemn.* The law is here put for the authority which is to hear and decide the case according to law. **Any man,** rather *the man,* the one who is accused of some crime. The Pharisees, by their manner of speaking, had already denounced Jesus as a deceiver who was leading the people astray, vers. 47–49. See ver. 12; Matt. 27 : 63. **Before it hear him, and know what he doeth?** give him opportunity to defend himself against unjust accusation, and make known what he has really done. See Deut. 1 : 16, 17; 19 : 15-19. To the legality and justness of this principle the accusers must assent. But the officers had spoken in favor of Jesus; now Nicodemus does so, though in an indirect way, by an admonition from a judicial point of view. Yet under the circumstances this admonition has an edge which the accusers cannot but feel, so as inwardly to acknowledge themselves foiled in their attempts against Jesus. "Pleasingly, and at the same time in a mode psychologically correct, are presented the tokens of the growing faith of Nicodemus. Still fettered in part by that same fear of man which had allowed him only with caution and by night to come to Jesus, he confines himself to requesting a procedure in accordance with the principle of legal rectitude. . . . To their blinded passion this love of rectitude on the part of Nicodemus is at once a suspicious matter; they express in their scornful question the idea that none but a man from the despised province would be among the followers of Jesus."—THOLUCK.

52. **Art thou also of Galilee?** *thou* being emphatic, and rallying Nicodemus, or implying their readiness to class him too among the adherents of the despised Galilean. As they hate Jesus, they use to his injury the fact of his having resided so much in Galilee and chosen his disciples from that region. Also, being destitute of evidence and scriptural argument in the case, they resort to ridicule to accomplish their purpose. **Search and look: for,** rather, *and see that.* Here they direct impliedly to the right source for information, but at the same time show they have not themselves thoroughly *searched.* **Out of Galilee ariseth**

53 ariseth no prophet. *And every man went unto his * Job 5. 12, 13.
own house.

no prophet. But it was definitely predicted in Isa. 9 : 1, 2 that "a great light" should shine in the region north and west of the Sea of Galilee on the people walking in darkness and dwelling in the land of the shadow of death; and this clearly indicated not only a *prophet*, but *the great prophet*—the Messiah himself. See Matt. 4 : 15, 16. And they entirely ignore the fact that while Jesus performed the very works predicted of the Messiah (Isa. 35 : 4-6), he was also born in Bethlehem of Judæa and of the offspring of David. See on ver. 42. Besides, several prophets had *risen out of Galilee*, instead of Judæa, such as Elijah (1 Kings 17 : 1), Elisha (1 Kings 19 : 16), Jonah (2 Kings 14 : 25), Nahum (Nah. 1 : 2), and Hosea, Hos. 7 : 1; 8 : 5, 6. These petulant Pharisees assumed that Nicodemus viewed Jesus as a *prophet*, though he had said no such thing. He had simply stated in the interrogative form what was the dictate of their law and of plain justice, and the principle thus advanced would apply to all persons accused of crime, to the worst of criminals as well as to the innocent Saviour. See Acts 25 : 16.

53. **And every man went unto his own house,** spoken of the members of the Sanhedrim, and intimating that, instead of coming to a unanimous decision against Jesus, they were discordant in their views, and were so confused and frustrated in their counsels that they willingly adjourned and withdrew each to his home, leaving the victim of their hatred unmolested for some months longer. Thus God overruled the plans and controlled the passions of these selfish, wicked men for the accomplishment of his own purposes. See Ps. 76 : 10; Job 5 : 12-15.—*Conant's Revision.*

The verses from ch. 7 : 53 to 8 : 11 inclusive are omitted by all the ancient manuscripts except one, the Cambridge, and by the most ancient versions, such as the Syriac, Sahidic or Upper Egypt, Coptic or Lower Egypt, Gothic and Armenian, and five copies of the Itala or old Latin. In four of the cursive manuscripts written after the tenth century they are placed at the end of Luke 21, where they fit well and harmonize with the narrative. They should be bracketed or placed in the margin, as is done by the critical editors Lachmann, Tischendorf, Tregelles, and Alford. Tischendorf says: "It is very certain the passage concerning the adulteress was not written by John. But from the third century onward it began to be read in Greek and Latin manuscripts. . . . It seems to have been received by use among the Latins sooner and more than among the Greeks." "Grotius conjectures that some who heard the story from the apostle's mouth recorded it, with the approbation of Papias and other eminent persons in the church."— DODDRIDGE. Augustine defended it as genuine, and suggests that it was thrown out of the text by enemies or weak believers from fear it might encourage their wives to infidelity.—*Tract* xxxiii. *De Conj. Adult.* II., 7. That it was so early received into the text to be read in the churches proves it was believed to be a truthful account. It appears also in harmony with other wise and compassionate teachings and acts of Jesus. Hort thinks it was brought into the text from "an extraneous independent source."

PRACTICAL REMARKS.

1. "Gospel light is justly taken away from those who endeavor to blow it out" (M. HENRY), ver. 1; Matt. 21 : 43.
2. "When we cannot do *what* and *where* we *would*, we must do *what* and *where* we *can*" (HENRY), Mark 6 : 5, 6.
3. "Hasten not after suffering; it will come soon enough." — STARKE. "Then, and not till *then*, we are called to expose our lives, when we cannot save them without sinning" (HENRY), Matt. 10 : 23, 28, 32, 39.
4. "Christians still celebrate their feast of tabernacles when they heartily praise God for his shelter and defence" (CRAMER), ver. 2.
5. "Follow not the voice which urges thee to seek a great name and become renowned in the world" (CANSTEIN), ver. 3; Jer. 45 : 5.
6. The true Christian heart desires not to display itself; the more secret, the happier, ver. 4; Matt. 6 : 1-4.

7. "Grace runs in no blood in the world if not in that of Christ's family" (HENRY), ver. 5; Ps. 51 : 5; Rom. 3 : 9; Eph. 2 : 1, 3.
8. "God does everything exactly at the right time, but men do much out of season" (EBRARD), ver. 6; Matt. 25 : 10–12; Luke 14 : 18–20, 24.
9. "One hawk does not pick out another's eyes. He who accommodates himself to the world will be loved by it" (EBRARD), ver. 7; John 15 : 19.
10. "It is better to incur the world's hatred by testifying against its wickedness than gain its good-will by going down the stream with it" (HENRY), ver. 7; James 4 : 4.
11. "He who loves God lets all his moments depend on the will and indication of God" (GOSSNER), ver. 8; Acts 16 : 6–10.
12. "It bespeaks humility and prudence for a man to wait God's time, keeping himself quiet till it come" (CANSTEIN), ver. 9; Luke 24 : 49, 53.
13. "God knows the true and better time to appear and help" (STARKE), ver. 10; Acts 7 : 25, 30, 34.
14. If we would *see* Christ at the feast, we must *seek* him there, ver. 11; 1 Chron. 28 : 9; 2 Chron. 15 : 2.
15. "Christ and his religion have been, and will be, the subject of much controversy, Luke 12 : 51, 52. When some receive light and others resolve against it, there will be murmuring" (HENRY), ver. 12.
16. Because nothing can justly be said *against* Christ, some will have nothing said *of* him, ver. 13; Acts 5 : 28, 40.
17. Since the Jewish priests did not teach the people as they ought, Jesus went into the temple and taught them. "When the shepherds of Israel made a prey of the flock, it was time for the chief Shepherd to appear (Ezek. 34 : 22, 23; Mal. 3 : 1)," (HENRY), ver. 14.
18. "That neither Christ nor his apostles were instructed by men shows the heavenly origin of his doctrine" (STARKE), ver. 15.
19. If we follow Christ's teaching, we enjoy the comfort that it is divine— *of God and not of men*, ver. 16; Hos. 6 : 3.
20. "He who uses not the word of God with the true purpose of learning and doing it, will not be sure of its divinity." — MAJUS. Many are ever learning, yet come not to the knowledge of the truth, because they hear much, but *do it not*, ver. 17; Ezek. 33 : 31, 32; 2 Tim. 3 : 7, 8.
21. Those who do God's will, and are thus brought to *resemble* him, are most likely to *understand* him, ver. 17; 1 Cor. 2 : 9–13; 2 Cor. 3 : 18–4 : 2.
22. "A preacher must seek not his own glory, but only God's."—QUESNEL. "They who speak *from* God will speak *for* God" (HENRY), ver. 18; 2 Cor. 4 : 5.
23. "Those that support themselves and their interest by persecution and violence, whatever they pretend, are not keepers of the law of God" (HENRY), ver. 19; John 16 : 2, 3; 1 Cor. 15 : 9.
24. "Those who would be like Christ must put up with affront and pass by indignities done them. When he was *reviled*, he *reviled not again*" (HENRY), ver. 20; 1 Pet. 2 : 23.
25. We should be quite as ready to praise what is commendable as we are to censure what seems questionable, ver. 21; 5 : 16; Luke 13 : 14; 6 : 7–12.
26. We should receive the ordinances of God as his *gifts*, and use them *according to his will*, ver. 22; Mark 14 : 22–24; 1 Cor. 11 : 23–26.
27. The Sabbath was violated, not by obeying a command of God, but by *doing one's own work and finding one's own pleasure*, ver. 23; Isa. 58 : 13.
28. We cannot consistently censure in others, and condemn them for, what we practise ourselves, ver. 23; Rom. 2 : 1–3, 21–23.
29. "Those that have the means of knowledge and grace, if not *made better* by them, are commonly *made worse*" (HENRY), ver. 25; Matt. 12 : 20, 45.
30. "The worst persecutions have been carried on under color of the support of authority and government" (HENRY), ver. 26; 18 : 30; 19 : 7; Acts 8 : 1–3; 9 : 1, 2.
31. We should be anxious, above all things, to *know Christ as ours*, and should at once acknowledge and obey him, ver. 27; Phil. 3 : 8–10.
32. "God has wicked men in a chain, and whatever mischief they *would do*, they *can do* no more than he suffers. . . . When Satan *fills their hearts*, God *ties their hands*" (HENRY), ver. 30;

VIII. JESUS went unto the mount of Olives.

Acts 4 : 1-3, 21 ; 5 : 17, 18, 33, 40 ; 12 : 4, 19.

33. We must not measure the prosperity of the gospel by its success among the great, nor say we labor in vain even if none but the poor receive it, ver. 31; 1 Cor. 1 : 26-29 ; Mark 12 : 37; Luke 4 : 18 ; 7 : 22.

34. "Even weak faith may be true faith, and so *accepted* by the Lord Jesus, who *despises not the day of small things*" (HENRY), Mark 9 : 24 ; Zech. 4 : 9, 10.

35. Persecutors act on the principle, "The most effectual way to disperse the flock is to *smite the shepherd*" (HENRY), ver. 32; Matt. 26 : 4, 31.

36. We should "seek the Lord while he may be found, and call upon him while he is near" (Isa. 55 : 6), for "the time is short," 1 Cor. 7 : 29 ; ver. 33.

37. If we now seek Christ, we shall find him ; but the day is coming when those who now *refuse* him will *seek and not find him*, ver. 34 ; Prov. 1 : 28.

38. We should thirst after the waters of life, and come to Christ and drink. "The wells of salvation are open to all men who are like dry ground" (MAJUS), ver. 37; Isa. 55 : 1 ; 44 : 3.

39. "Where there are *springs* of grace and comfort in the soul, they will *send forth streams*."—HENRY. "True faith is like a copious fountain : it cannot restrain itself from gushing forth in holy love" (MAJUS), ver. 38; Cant. 4 : 12-15.

40. We should expect and pray for the measure of the Spirit which God has promised to give, ver. 39 ; 16 : 7-14.

41. "He who loves and seeks the truth, finds it; but he who contemptuously asks, What is truth ? falls into error" (CRAMER), ver. 41 ; Prov. 2 : 3-6 ; 23 : 9 ; John 18 . 38.

42. "The preaching of the gospel sometimes restrains the violence of *the hand* when it works no change in *the heart*" (BURKITT), ver. 44; Acts 24 : 25 ; 26 : 28-32.

43. "Mischievous men fret that they cannot do the mischief they would (Ps. 112 : 10 ; Neh. 6 : 16)," (HENRY), ver. 45; Matt. 2 : 16 ; Acts 12 : 19.

44. "Those who are sent *to take* Jesus are themselves *taken*."— HEUBNER. "Unlettered, honest simplicity is much better fitted to know the truth of God than the swelling, conceited wisdom of the schools" (ZEISIUS), ver. 46; Matt. 11 : 25.

45. "Christianity has from its rise been represented as a great cheat, and they that embrace it as men *deceived* when they began to be *undeceived*" (HENRY), vers. 47, 12; 2 Chron. 6 : 8.

46. "The cause of Christ has seldom had rulers and Pharisees on its side. . . . *Self-denial* and the *cross* are hard lessons to" them (HENRY), ver. 48; 18 : 36 ; 1 Cor. 2 : 8.

47. The Pharisees' saying that the people who inclined to believe in Jesus were *accursed*, did not make them so, for "*the curse causeless shall not come*," Prov. 26 : 2; ver. 49.

48. "Many believers, who at first were ready to *flee at the shaking of a leaf*, have at length, by divine grace, grown courageous and able to *laugh at the shaking of a spear*" (HENRY), ver. 50 ; Lev. 26 : 36; Prov. 28 : 1.

49. "God still always has his own, even among apostate masses" (ZEISIUS), who, when he calls for it, bear witness to the truth, ver. 50 ; Rom. 11 : 1-5 ; 1 Pet. 2 : 9-10 ; 2 Pet. 2 : 5-8.

50. Persons are to be judged, not by what *is said* of them, but by what they themselves *do*, ver. 51 ; Matt. 5 : 11, 16.

51. "It is a sign of a bad cause when men cannot bear to *hear reason*, and take it as an affront to be reminded of its maxims" (HENRY), ver. 52 ; 9 : 34.

52. "One man with God on his side is stronger than any majority" (P. SCHAFF), ver. 53 ; Deut. 32 : 30; Rom. 8 : 31.

CHAPTER VIII.

Jesus returns, goes unto the Mount of Olives, in the morning into the temple; and a large number of the people coming to him, he sits down and teaches them, vers. 1, 2. While he is thus employed the scribes and Pharisees bring before him an adulteress, and seek to induce him to pronounce a judgment on her case. This artful attempt to ensnare him he foils by writing on the ground with his finger, and replying to their persistent questions, "He that is without sin among you, let him first cast the stone at her." The accusers, hearing this, go out one by one till they have all left. Jesus, raising himself up, and hearing from the woman that no one has condemned her, says, "Neither do I condemn thee; go, and sin no more," vers. 3-11.

He then resumes his teaching of the people, but is soon interrupted by the Pharisees, who question the sufficiency of his testimony respecting himself, ver. 12. He replies that his testimony is true, because he knows of what he testifies; and his testimony is also confirmed by that of the Father, vers. 13-19. He continues teaching with great frankness and answering inquiries, until the Jews become angry and call him a Samaritan, possessed by a demon, vers. 20-48. He meekly and most nobly replies, and then continues a discussion with them, until

MOUNT OF OLIVES.

he is led to declare, "Before Abraham was, I am," vers. 49-58. They then take up stones to cast at him, but he hides himself from them, and passes out of the temple, ver. 59.

1-11. JESUS' OPINION IS ASKED CONCERNING AN ADULTERESS. Found only here. On the genuineness of these verses see the last paragraph of ch. 7. The ancient documents containing this passage vary much from one another. The scribes and Pharisees try to ensnare Jesus and bring him into trouble. Should he judge the case and condemn the woman to death, they could accuse him of usurping power which belonged only to the civil authorities existing in the nation. He might thus come in collision with the Roman government. On the other hand, should he speak differently from the law of Moses, or from *their view* of that law, they might raise a popular tumult against him as an opposer of Moses and a violator of their sacred law, and thus be able to procure his death. Compare Matt. 22 : 15-23.

1. **Jesus went**, a contrast to what the members of the Sanhedrim did; for while they went each to his home, Jesus had no earthly home of his own to go to. Besides, when the people withdrew for the night from the temple, Jesus also withdrew even from Jerusalem, on account of the hostility of his enemies. This verse should not have been sundered from the preceding chapter. **Mount of Olives**, lying east of Jerusalem, beyond the brook Kidron. To this mount Jesus now began to retire for the night; and when attending his last passover in Jerusalem he retired thus every evening. See Mark 11 : 1, 11; Luke 21 : 37; 22 : 39. The garden

The opinion of Jesus asked concerning an adulteress.

2 And early in the morning ᵇhe came again into the temple, and all the people came unto him; and he sat down and taught them.
3 And the scribes and Pharisees brought unto him a
4 woman taken in adultery. And when they had set her in the midst, they say unto him, Master, this
5 woman was taken in adultery, in the very act. ᶜNow Moses in the law commanded us, that such should
6 be stoned; but what sayest thou? This they said, ᵈtempting him, that they might have to accuse him. But Jesus stooped down, and with *his* finger wrote on

ᵇ ch. 4. 34; 7. 14.

ᶜ Lev. 20. 10; Deut 22. 21-24.

ᵈ Matt. 19. 3; Luke 20. 20-23.

---

of Gethsemane, to which he frequently resorted with his disciples (John 18 : 2), was on the western side of the mount; and Bethany, the abode of Martha and Mary and their brother Lazarus, on its eastern side, ch. 11 : 1.

2. And early in the morning he came again into the temple. As soon as the people had assembled there in considerable numbers the next morning, Jesus also returned and resumed his work among them. The people of the East are accustomed to early rising. **And all the people came,** those who had come up to Jerusalem to attend the feast and remained the day after the feast had closed. Having resorted to the temple early in the morning, they spontaneously *came to* the place where Jesus was. While the chief priests and scribes and Pharisees were plotting against his life and were deaf to his instructions, the common people, the great multitude, heard him gladly (Mark 12 : 37) and with an attentive ear. **And he sat down,** as the Jewish teachers did when giving instruction to their pupils. See Matt. 5 : 1, 2; Luke 4 : 20. Having sat down, he *was teaching* the people when the adulteress was brought in.

3. The scribes, a class of learned men, who preserved, copied, and expounded the Old Testament Scriptures and the Jewish traditions. They were interested and supposed to be skilled in all questions relating to the Mosaic law, and could readily unite with the **Pharisees** in the attempt to entrap Jesus on a question of law. **A woman taken in adultery,** having been betrayed into it, perhaps, as Doddridge suggests, among those intemperances which too often attended public feasts. **Had set her in the midst,** *placed her in the midst* of the people, before Jesus.

4. Master, or, *teacher,* **this woman was taken.** This, with the attending circumstances, seems to imply that the crime had been committed quite recently. The man who had participated in the crime, and was also liable to the penalty of death (Lev. 20 : 10; Deut. 22 : 22, 24), appears either to have escaped or to have been overlooked. **In adultery, in the very act;** a case, according to their showing, not at all doubtful, but perfectly clear and conclusive.

5. Now Moses in the law commanded us. With all their pretence, it is evident they were not anxious for the honor of the law nor for the virtue of the people, but wished to bring Jesus into difficulty; **that such should be stoned.** The unfaithful betrothed virgin, certainly, was to be stoned to death (Deut. 22 : 23, 24), but this passage may be only a more particular description of the death-penalty uniformly appointed for the adulterer and the adulteress. See Lev. 20 : 10; Deut. 22 : 22-24. **But what sayest thou?** the thou being emphatic, in contrast with **Moses** in the first part of the verse. This question was artfully contrived and put to induce Jesus to say something, either positive or negative, which they might construe against him. Compare Luke 20 : 20-26.

6. This they said, tempting him, or, *trying him,* putting him to the test, to see if they could not take him suddenly, when off his guard, and lead him to say something hasty and imprudent. **That they might have to accuse him,** or *have something to accuse him of,* so that they could get him

7 the ground, *as though he heard them not.* So when they continued asking him, he lifted up himself, and said unto them, 'He that is without sin among you, 8 let him first cast a stone at her. And again he 9 stooped down, and wrote on the ground. And they which heard it, g being convicted by *their own* conscience, h went out one by one, beginning at the oldest, even unto the last; and Jesus was left alone, and the

* Ps. 38. 12-14; 30. 1; Eccles. 8. 7.
f Deut. 17. 7; Matt. 7. 1-5; Rom. 2. 1-3.
g Eccles.7.22;Rom. 2. 15, 22; 1 John 3. 20.
h Job 5. 12, 13; Ps. 9. 16.

condemned to death. See ch. 7 : 1, 19. **With his finger wrote,** *was writing,* a continuous act. **On the ground;** just as the ancient writer, with his iron stylus, *wrote* or marked *on the wax* of his tablet or writing-board, or as some persons now write in the smooth, compact sand of the ocean beach. Since Jesus was at this time in one of the courts of the temple, he could easily write on the earth or in the dust lying on the pavement. In doing this he appeared not to heed his questioners, and showed that he was not to be drawn into useless disputes or dangerous decisions. He also drew the attention of the people from the woman to himself, and prepared them to notice the very appropriate and important directions which he was about to give. The phrase **as though he heard them not,** printed in italics by the authority of King James's revisers, should be dropped, since the Greek text authorizes no such addition.

7. **So when they continued asking him;** they will not give it up, but, thinking they have him at a disadvantage, they persist in pressing the question; and their persistence causes him to raise himself up and give them, in one brief sentence, a most searching and pointed moral principle and practical test, to be applied first to themselves and then to the accused woman. **He that is without sin among you,** more exactly, *He of you that is without sin,* this particular sin of adultery (comp. ver. 11), at that time very prevalent among the Jews (see Matt. 16 : 4; 19 : 9; Mark 8 : 38), the sin of unchastity in general, and perhaps any other sin heinous as adultery in the sight of God. This test was adapted to soften any harsh judgment against the accused woman, and especially if they let her male accomplice go unpunished. **Let him first cast a stone at her.** On the testimony of two or three witnesses the accused person could be put to death. And when the criminal had been thus proved deserving death, the hands of the witnesses were to be first upon him in casting the stone, and then the hands of all the people till he should die, Deut. 13 : 9, 10; 17 : 5-7. This imposed a fearful responsibility on the witnesses, and in any ordinary case they would not be likely to assume such responsibility without just cause. This responsibility Jesus threw upon the accusers of the woman, and at the same time charged them first to inquire into their own character and conduct, and when they could prove, in the court of conscience their own innocence, they might then execute sentence upon her. This searching appeal, and the consequent double pressure on their individual conscience and heart, was more than they could endure; and being thus completely baffled, they gave up the unequal contest, and one by one quietly withdrew.

8. **And again he stooped down, and wrote on the ground,** still intimating thereby that he was not to be drawn into useless discussions or into dangerous and illegal decisions; nor would he assert any Messianic authority, so as to change the law of civil procedure.

9. **And they which heard it, being convicted by their own conscience,** or, with some critical authorities, *But they, having heard it,* went out one by one; a simple statement of the fact. The accusers, having heard his response to their demands, saw that they were baffled, and, pressed with a sense of his majesty and their own personal guilt, they availed themselves of the opportunity to withdraw before he should still further reprove and expose them. "It is

10 woman standing in the midst. When Jesus had lifted up himself, and saw none but the woman, he said unto her, Woman, where are those thine accusers?
11 Hath no man condemned thee? She said, No man, Lord. And Jesus said unto her, ¹ Neither do I condemn thee; ᵏ go, and sin no more.

Jesus continues to teach in the temple: the Jews in anger attempt to stone him.

12 Then spake Jesus again unto them, saying, ¹ I am the

¹ ver. 15; ch. 3. 17; Luke 9. 56; 12, 13, 14.
ᵏ ch. 5. 14; Prov. 28. 13.
¹ ch. 1. 4, 5, 9; 3. 19; 9. 5; 12. 35, 36, 46.

historically attested that at that time many prominent rabbins were living in adultery."—THOLUCK. "And some of them must have feared that when he should lift up himself again they might hear something further, which would be still less pleasant."—MUSCULUS, *in Lange's Commentary.* **Beginning at the eldest,** rather, *with the elders,* those of official dignity, as well as maturity of age and of high standing in society. See Matt. 15 : 2; 27 : 1, 3, 12, 20. **Even unto the last;** from the most honorable in official station down to those of inferior rank, the accusers all retired. **And the woman standing in the midst**—*i. e.* in the midst of the multitude, where she had been placed by her accusers, ver. 3.

10. **When Jesus had lifted up himself, and saw none but the woman, he said unto her, Woman, where are those thine accusers?** Those crafty, insolent, blood-thirsting tempters had disappeared from the scene, and left the case for Jesus to dispose of. **Hath no man condemned thee?**—in a legal manner, according to the customary judicial forms of proceeding?

11. **She said, No man, Lord. And Jesus said unto her, Neither do I condemn thee,** in a legal and judicial manner. To me belong not the functions of the civil magistrate, whose office requires him to try cases and decide on them by the law of the land, and condemn to the prescribed punishment. Compare Luke 12 : 13, 14. **Go, and sin no more,** or, with high critical authority, *and henceforth sin no more.* Yet Jesus recognizes the fact that she is a sinner. What a grand moral decision is this! How full of encouragement and hope on the one hand, and of solemn and fearful warning on the other, not only to the accused sinning woman, but also to the whole listening multitude as transgressors of the law of God! How adapted to arouse their conscience, induce reflection and searching of heart, and stimulate to the confession of "sin" to God, and to earnest prayer for pardon and for grace and strength to obey the command!

12–59. JESUS CONTINUES TEACHING IN THE TEMPLE. THE JEWS IN ANGER ATTEMPT TO STONE HIM. Some suppose that Jesus uttered this discourse on the last day of the feast of tabernacles, being a continuation of the discourses of the preceding chapter. But if the incident just related (vers. 1–11) has its true place at the beginning of this chapter, then this discourse was more probably delivered on the day after the feast, ver. 1. He represents himself as the Light of the world, and declares, "He that followeth me shall not walk in darkness, but shall have the light of life." The Pharisees question the validity of his testimony, vers. 12, 13. He insists that it is valid, because he knows of what he affirms, and the Father also sanctions it, 14–20. As he continues speaking many Jews appear to believe on him, 21–31. He assures such, "If ye continue in my word, ye shall know the truth, and the truth shall make you free." They reply, "We be Abraham's seed, and were never in bondage to any man." He shows that in committing sin they are in bondage to sin, but the Son of God can set them free, 31–38. He then proves from their works whose children they are (39–47), and they reply, "Say we not well that thou art a Samaritan, and hast a devil?" With great dignity and composure he answers, "I have not a devil, but I honor my Father, and ye do dishonor me." Resuming his teaching, he declares,

light of the world; ᵐ he that followeth me ⁿ shall not walk in darkness, ᵒ but shall have the light of life.
13 The Pharisees therefore said unto him, ᵖ Thou bear-
14 est record of thyself; thy record is not true. Jesus answered and said unto them, Though I bear record of myself, *yet* my record is true; ᵠ for I know whence I came, and whither I go; but ʳ ye cannot tell whence

ᵐ Hos. 6. 4.
ⁿ ch. 12. 46; Isa. 50. 10.
ᵒ ch. 7. 17; 14. 6; Job 22. 21–23, 26–28; Ps. 36. 9; 97. 11.
ᵖ ch. 5. 31.
ᵠ ver. 42; ch. 7. 29.
ʳ ch. 7, 28; 9. 29.

"If a man keep my saying, he shall never see death." They reply, "Now we know that thou hast a devil. Abraham is dead, and the prophets.... Whom makest thou thyself?" 48–53. He proceeds to show that they know not God, but declares, "Your father Abraham rejoiced to see my day, and he saw it, and was glad," 53–58. They question his assertion, and he replies, "Before Abraham was, I am." Then they take up stones to throw at him, but he withdraws from among them, 57–59. The whole narrative illustrates how Jesus "endured such contradiction of sinners against himself," Heb. 12 : 3.

12. **Then spake Jesus again,** the *again* referring back to ch. 7 : 37, and *then*, in the sense of *therefore*, to 7 : 52, 53, and perhaps to 8 : 11. See the beginning of the preceding paragraph. **Unto them,** the people who were about him in the temple, ver. 2. **I am the light of the world.** As Jesus, in ch. 7 : 37, has alluded to the *water* poured upon the altar on the successive days of the feast, so here he may allude to the *lights* used for the purpose of illumination. "In the court of the women stood great golden candelabras, which were lit on the evening of the first day of the feast, and spread their light over all Jerusalem, while by the men a torch-light dance with music and singing (expressing their joy, Deut. 16 : 14) was performed before these candelabras (see Winer).... According to Maimonides, this illumination took place also on the other evenings of the festival."—LANGE. This illumination seems to have been intended to serve as an emblem of the pillar of fire which accompanied the Israelites in their pilgrimage through the wilderness, and their sojourn there in tents, Ex. 13 : 21, 22. Or perhaps the rising sun, just coming up over the Mount of Olives, gave occasion for this language. See ver. 2, "early in the morning." **Of the world,** not of the Jews alone, but of *the world* of mankind that are in the night of sin and death. *Light* is in all languages used to represent *knowledge*, that which enables us to discern our duty, and which saves us from the evils of ignorance and error. "Whatsoever doth make manifest is light," Eph. 5 : 13. Light is also emblematical of *happiness* and *joy*. "Light is sown for the righteous, and *gladness* for the upright in heart," Ps. 97 : 11. **He that followeth me,** as the Israelites *followed* the pillar of cloud and fire in the wilderness; he that submits to my guidance, or becomes my disciple, obeys my instructions, and imitates my example; **shall not walk in darkness;** he shall no longer live in the ignorance and misery of sin, **but shall have the light of life;** have the knowledge which relates and leads to eternal life, and the happiness that flows from the pardon of sin and the favor of God, and endures for ever.

13. THE PHARISEES QUESTION HIS EVIDENCE. **Thou bearest record,** or *witness,* **of thyself;** thou art a witness in thine own case. See ch. 5 : 31. Since the law required two or three witnesses in a criminal case (Deut. 17 : 6), they allege, as the only evidence Jesus furnishes is his own assertion, therefore it cannot be entitled to belief. **Thy record,** or *testimony,* **is not true;** is not to be received as true and sufficient to establish the thing asserted. But in this instance, where Jesus presents himself as the sure Guide through the darkness of this world to the true life, his credential must be *the certainty of his own conviction*—*i. e.* his positive knowledge of his own origin, his character and work, and the goal toward which he is moving, as he himself proceeds to show.

14. In this and the four verses following Jesus shows that his own testimony is credible, and to it is added that of his Father. **Though I bear record of myself,** in a case of this kind, **yet my record,** or *testimony,* **is true,** and can

JOHN VIII. A. D. 29

15 I come, and whither I go. ᵇYe judge after the flesh;
16 ᶜI judge no man. ᵈAnd yet if I judge, my judgment is true; for ˣI am not alone, but I and the Father
17 that sent me. ʸIt is also written in your law, that
18 the testimony of two men is true. ᶻI am one that bear witness of myself, and ᵃthe Father that sent me beareth witness of me.

ᵇ ch. 5. 31-34, 37.

ᶜ ch. 7. 24; 1 Sam. 16. 7.
ᵈ ver. 11; ch. 3. 17; 12. 47; 18. 36.
ᵘ ch. 5. 22-30.
ˣ ver. 29; ch. 16. 32.
ʸ Deut. 17. 6; Matt. 18. 16; 2 Cor. 13. 1; Heb. 10. 28.
ᵃ vers. 12, 25, 58.

---

be depended on. Jesus had a perfect knowledge respecting himself and the work assigned him, and no one else on earth either had such knowledge or was qualified to bear a different or contradictory testimony. His perfect knowledge was also accompanied with perfect integrity. Therefore his testimony that he was the Light of the world, and a sure Guide to those in darkness, should have been accepted and heartily believed. **For I know whence I came, and whither I go;** I know my heavenly origin and my destination; know by whom I am sent, what commands he gave me, and what I am to accomplish; but you cannot know these except as I myself declare them to you. **But ye cannot tell whence I come, and whither I go;** therefore you are not qualified to judge of these things. An ambassador from a foreign court knows the will and purposes of the sovereign who sent him, and is competent to testify concerning them. The court to which he is sent has no way to judge of these except by his testimony, which is received as sufficient. All that can be demanded to prove his claim and his right to be heard is that he present his credentials of appointment duly signed and sealed. Jesus had done this by his miracles (ch. 3 : 2) and by the matter and manner of his teaching.

15. **Ye judge after the flesh**—*i. e.* by wrong standards, according to the outward, finite appearance, or with earthly, selfish views and carnal and prejudiced feelings. Hence you judge and condemn the internal character of the Son of man from his humble outward appearance, and you are unfitted to judge of the spiritual and heavenly nature of his Messianic reign. **I judge no man,** either as a civil ruler, or by such wrong standards as yours. Jesus did not come to judge and condemn the world (ch. 3 : 17), nor to judge in their hasty, prejudiced, censorious, and harsh manner,

vers. 48, 52, 59. Judgment was not the object of his mission on earth, ch. 3 : 17; 12 : 47.

16. **And yet if I judge;** I emphatic, along with **judge**, and still keeping up the contrast contained in the preceding verse—if even I express my judgment of men or of things. He was not limited, nor forbidden to judge, nor restrained by fear of judging erroneously. **My judgment,** more emphatically, *this judgment of mine,* whenever I do express it, **is true,** is in accordance with truth, or with the character of men and the nature of things as they really are. **For I am not alone,** in forming this judgment, **but I and the Father that sent me.** All Christ's judging is the estimation of men and things as they truly are, the discrimination of sinner and sin, and the separation of believer and unbeliever. "The *ground* of this judgment, of his being thus true, is that the Father by the actual course of things executes these same decisions, separations, and judgments, which the Spirit of Christ passes."—LANGE.

17. **It is also written in your law,** or, following the order of the Greek, *And in your own law also it is written,* **that the testimony of two men is true,** is sufficient to establish a matter, provided the witnesses are both intelligent and honest. See Deut. 17 : 6; 19 : 15; compare Matt. 18 : 16. *Your own law,* in which you boast, the very letter of which also binds you.

18. **I am one that bear witness of,** or *concerning,* **myself,** from my own conviction and positive knowledge. See on vers. 13 and 14. **And the Father that sent me beareth witness of me,** in the numerous prophecies of the Old Testament which relate to the Messiah, and by the direct exercise of his power in the miracles which I work in connection with my teaching. Hence this testimony of the Father, thus combined and harmonizing with the testi-

19 Then said they unto him, Where is thy Father? Jesus answered, ᵇ Ye neither know me, nor my Father; ᶜ if ye had known me, ye should have known my Father also.
20 These words spake Jesus in ᵈ the treasury, as he taught in the temple. And ᵉ no man laid hands on him; for ᶠ his hour was not yet come.
21 Then said Jesus again unto them, I go my way, and ᵍ ye shall seek me, and ʰ shall die in your sins; ⁱ whither I go, ye cannot come.

ᵇ vers. 54, 55; ch 7. 28; 16. 3.
ᶜ ch. 10. 30; 14. 6-9; Col. 1. 15; Heb. 1. 3; 2 John 9.
ᵈ 1 Chron. 9. 26; Mark 12. 41.
ᵉ ch. 7. 6, 30, 44; Luke 13. 13-33.
ᶠ ch. 7. 8.
ᵍ ch. 7. 33, 34; 12. 35; 13. 33.
ʰ ver. 24.
ⁱ ch. 13. 33.

mony of him whom he has sent, ought to be acknowledged and received as sufficient. See ch. 3 : 2; 5 : 36; 10 : 37, 38; 14 : 10, 11.

19. WHERE IS HIS FATHER? **Then said they unto him,** in consequence of what he had just stated, **Where is thy Father?** They ask this question in derision. They have been repeatedly informed by Jesus that when speaking of his Father he means God (ch. 5 : 17-24, 26, 36, 37, 43, 45), yet now they ignore this, and affect contempt at his mentioning his Father as a witness in the case, as though they understand him to mean an interested earthly father. **Jesus answered,** meekly and patiently, **Ye neither know me, nor my Father.** Their words and actions showed that they had no just conceptions of the real character, either of Jesus or his Father. **If ye had known me, ye should have known my Father also;** if you received me as the Christ, and became acquainted with my true character as such, you would at the same time become acquainted with the Father, for in character and purpose we are one, ch. 10 : 30; 14 : 9. These Jews needed more knowledge, higher views, and a spiritual frame of mind to judge correctly either of Jesus as the Christ or of the design of the Father in sending him.

20. WHERE JESUS SPOKE THESE WORDS. **These words spake Jesus in the treasury, as he taught in the temple.** This was an apartment of the temple, in what was called the Court of the Women (*i. e.* the court beyond which the women did not venture; the men, however, either stopped there or passed on, Mark 12 : 41-43), where thirteen chests were kept, in which were deposited and *treasured* up the offerings of the Jewish people, both the annual and all the other offerings, for the support of the temple-service. The evangelist mentions this locality, because it was a very public place; here every one deposited his gifts. It was also in the immediate vicinity of the chamber where the Sanhedrim met. **And no man laid hands on him; for his hour was not yet come.** See ch. 7 : 30, 44. This comes in here as the refrain of the history, with an air of trust and triumph in God.

21. In this and the three verses that follow, Jesus warns the Jews. It was apparently the last time he spoke in the temple before the assembled crowds scattered to their distant homes, many never to see or hear him again. Hence the solemnity of the address. **Then said Jesus again unto them** (see on ver. 12; 7 : 33-35), **I go my way,** rather, *I am going away,* the **I** being emphatic, and the expression intimating, to those who wished to enjoy his instructions, the importance of heeding them now, because soon the opportunity would be over. The ridicule prompted by unbelief (ver. 19) is here to our Saviour a new signal of his approaching death, as persecution was at ch. 7 : 34. In both instances he declares his freedom in his death. In the former he also foretells their disappointment: *Ye shall not find me;* here, their condemnation: *Ye shall die in your sins.* **And ye shall seek me,** being impelled to it by your trials and your desires (see on ch. 7 : 34), **and shall die in your sins;** more exactly, *in your sin,* under the weight of its fearful guilt and condemnation. The Messiah that you will seek and long for will not come, and as you reject me, and there is no other Saviour provided, you must die in your

152 JOHN VIII. A. D. 29

22 Then said the Jews, Will he kill himself? because
23 he saith, Whither I go, ye cannot come. And he said unto them, ᵏ Ye are from beneath, I am from above; ˡ ye are of this world, I am not of this world.
24 ᵐ I said therefore unto you, that ye shall die in your sins; ⁿ for if ye believe not ᵒ that I am *he*, ye shall die in your sins.

ᵏ ch. 3. 31; 1 Cor. 15.47,48; 1 John 2. 15, 16.
ˡ ch. 15. 18, 19; 17. 14, 16; 1 John 4. 5.
ᵐ ver. 21.
ⁿ ch.3. 18,36; Prov. 8.36; Mark 16.16; Heb. 2. 3.
ᵒ ch. 13. 19; Matt. 11. 3.

---

sin. **Whither I go, ye cannot come**—that is, to heaven—because you continue under the guilt and power of sin, and will not accept God's way of deliverance from sin. Compare ch. 13 : 33.

22. **Then said the Jews**, in consequence of Jesus' statement in verse 21, **Will he kill himself?** A little particle in the Greek, equivalent to *then*, adds to the meaning of this question: *Will he kill himself, then?* Is that what we are to expect of him? This was a wicked and spiteful insinuation, doubtless called forth by his declaration, "Ye shall die in your sins," ver. 21. They evidently regarded Jesus as a deceiver (Matt. 27 : 63), who had broken the law of Moses (John 5 : 18), and might be suffered to go on and commit the great crime of self-murder and be consigned to the pit of woe. They thus speak with hatred and contempt, as of a wicked impostor going onward to his deserved place, to which they have no expectation or fear of going. See on ver. 21. In ch. 7 : 35 the Jews used the irony, "Whither will he go that we shall not find him? Will he go unto the dispersed among the Gentiles, and teach the Gentiles?" Here they rise to the impudent sarcasm, *Will he kill himself, then?* **because he saith, Whither I go, ye cannot come.** "They think he has set himself far above them in saying they cannot reach him. They revenge themselves by suggesting that he will sink far below them. 'An orthodox Jew,' they would say, 'utterly abhors suicide.' According to Josephus (*De Bello Jud.*, iii. 8, 5), the self-murderer goes to the darker under-world. Thus, . . . the suicide falls to the lowest hell [part] of Hades, and is separated by a great gulf from Abraham's bosom (Luke 16 : 26), into which they hope to go."—LANGE.

23. **And he said unto them**, giving instruction that naturally followed their spiteful insinuation, as well as what he had said in ver. 21, **Ye are from beneath**—*i. e.* they were low and earthly in their views, and even hellish in their disposition and feelings, as their foolish and wicked insinuation against him clearly showed. To be *from beneath* and to be *from above* are the direct opposites of each other. Compare Col. 3:2. **I am from above**—*i. e.* from heaven, having a disposition and character, with views and aims, corresponding with my heavenly origin. Therefore my words should be thus received and interpreted. He then repeats the same thought in other words, after the manner of a Hebrew parallelism: **Ye are of this world, I am not of this world**—not of this world as it is now deranged, defaced, and corrupted by the sin and depravity of fallen men. *This world, kosmos,* "according to the Jewish Christology, denoted pre-eminently the ancient heathen world, which was to come into condemnation."—LANGE. Jesus does not stop to speak of their contemptuous language in virtually imputing to him the design of self-murder, with all its horrid consequences, but proceeds to warn them of their sinful condition, and of the doom which awaits them if they persist in their impenitent course and their rejection of him. See next verse.

24. **I said therefore unto you, that ye shall die in your sins.** Their being "from beneath," and "of this world" as their principle of life, is the reason why they *will die in their sins.* **For if ye believe not that I am he**, that I am what I profess to be, the One sent by the Father, the Son of God, the Life-giver (ch. 5 : 21, 23, 25), the Light of the world, the One from above, 8 : 12, 23. He could not say to these Jews, *I am the Messiah*, because they had wrong views of the person and work of the Messiah, and consequently would misunderstand him. Hence he says to them, *I am he*, and leaves them

25 Then said they unto him, Who art thou? And Jesus saith unto them, ᵖEven *the same* that I said
26 unto you from the beginning. I have many things to say and to judge of you; but ᑫhe that sent me is true; and ʳI speak to the world those things which I
27 have heard of him. *They understood not that he spake to them of the Father.

ᵖ ver. 12; ch. 3. 14-17; Heb. 13. 8.
ᑫ ch. 7. 28.
ʳ ch. 3. 32; 15. 15.
* ver. 43.

to interpret the *he* by what he had said of himself. **Ye shall die in your sins,** and be in effect self-murderers of your own souls, because, rejecting the only way of deliverance, they wilfully and necessarily remain as they are, under the power and guilt of their sins, and must receive the wages of sin, which is death, Rom. 6 : 23. Thus their indirect charge of *self-murder* he throws back on them with a fearful significance and weight.

25. In vers. 25-27 Jesus discourses on his dignity, intimating who he is. **Then said they unto him,** in consequence of the declarations he had just made, **Who art thou?** This was probably a sly question to decoy and force Jesus to an explicit avowal (see ch. 10 : 24), that they might get an accusation against him. But Luther, Meyer, Doddridge, Henry, Trollope, Bloomfield, Barnes, and others understand it as asked in contempt, as if they would say, *Who art thou* that art assuming such authority and making such fearful threats? When we bear in mind that they regarded him as a mere pretender from Galilee, that he was poor and without friends among them, and that he was persecuted by those in power, we cannot but admire the meekness and patience with which he endured their insolent language, and the cool and calm manner in which he replied to them. See Matt. 11 : 29. **And Jesus saith unto them, Even the same that I said unto you from the beginning.** I am of that kind of character which I have been speaking out to you and showing forth in my varied instructions from their beginning at the middle of the feast, ch. 7 : 14. He had declared to them that he was sent by God, his teaching was from God, and he was unselfish in his work; that he would abundantly satisfy the thirst, the inward longing, of the believer on him; that he was the Light of the world, and those who followed him should have the light of life; and that he was attested in his character and work by the Father, who had sent him. He had also declared, in his visit at Jerusalem eighteen months previous, that he was the Son of God and the Life-giver, to whom all judgment was committed by the Father, ch. 5 : 21, 22. The careful study of these points would answer their question and acquaint them with his true character.

26. **I have many things to say and to judge of,** or *concerning,* **you.** They had erroneous, worldly views of the Messiah, and consequently were not prepared to understand and appreciate him in his true character. They needed first to know themselves, to become acquainted with their own condition and wants as sinners, to feel the guilt of their pride, selfishness, deception, and unbelief, and then they could understand the important points in his character which adapted him as a Saviour to their own souls' need. Hence he *had many things to speak and to judge concerning them,* by way of instruction and of condemnation and reproof, before he could plainly declare to them that he was the Christ. See Matt. 16 : 20. This duty he must faithfully perform, painful though it was in some of its aspects. **But he that sent me is true.** He judges and *acts* toward men in accordance with what they are, and with the principles of *truth* and right; and I, as sent by him, judge and *speak* in the same way. **And I speak to the world those things which I have heard of him.** The order of the Greek is, *And what things I have heard from him, these I speak to the world,* as his ambassador to men.

27. **They understood not,** because of their wilful unbelief and their persistently expecting and longing for a temporal, worldly Messiah, **that he spake to them,** or *was telling them* (a different verb from those in the two verses preceding), **of the Father,**

JOHN VIII. A. D. 29

28 Then said Jesus unto them, When ye have ᵗlifted up the Son of man, ᵘthen shall ye know that I am he: and ˣthat I do nothing of myself; but ʸas my Father hath taught me, I speak these things. And
29 ᶻhe that sent me is with me; ᵃthe Father hath not left me alone; ᵇfor I do always those things that please him.
30 As he spake these words, ᶜmany believed on him.

ᵗ ch.3.14; 12.32-34
ᵘ Matt. 27. 50-54; Acts 2. 36-41; Rom. 1. 4.
ˣ ch. 5. 19, 30.
ʸ ch. 3. 11.
ᶻ ch. 14. 10, 11.
ᵃ ver. 16.
ᵇ ch. 4. 34; 5. 30; 6. 38; 14. 31.
ᶜ ch. 2. 23.

when he used the words, "*He that sent me.*"

28. In this and the two following verses Jesus refers to his crucifixion, and intimates that the saving truths connected with his death will ultimately convince his followers. **Then said Jesus unto them,** because he knew the vagueness of their ideas, and the perverse cause of it, **When ye have lifted up,** alluding to his anticipated crucifixion (see ch. 12 : 32, 33, and 3 : 14), and showing, as he clearly foresaw, that their murderous hatred would be satisfied with nothing less than his death. He purposely employs this ambiguous Hebraistic expression, which may mean either to *lift up* to honor and official dignity or to *lift up* to shame and death. See Gen. 40 : 19, 20. These Jews probably understand him as meaning, Whenever you have acknowledged the Son of man as the Messiah, and proclaimed him in political form. **The Son of man;** as such he could be *lifted up* on the cross, and there pour out his soul unto death, be made an offering for sin, and bear the iniquities of his believing people, Isa. 53 : 10-12. **Then shall ye know that I am he;** they would know that he was what he professed to be—was *the Son of man,* and the Messiah foretold by the prophet Daniel, Dan. 7 : 13, 14; 9 : 25, 26. Some of them would *know* this after his crucifixion and ascension by the outpouring of the Holy Spirit and their own conversion; others by the severe judgments which would come on them to their dismay and ruin; and all might know by the wonderful phenomena accompanying his crucifixion—the supernatural darkness, the torn veil of the temple, the quaking of the earth, the rending of the rocks, the opening of the graves, the descent of the angel and his rolling away the heavy stone from the door of the sepulchre, and especially by his resurrection from the dead (Matt. 27 : 45, 51, 52; 28 : 2, 7, 9); and subsequently by his ascension to heaven, and the pouring out of the Holy Spirit and his mighty work on the consciences and hearts of men, together with the miracles wrought by the apostles in the name of Jesus, Acts 1 : 9-11; 2 : 4, 17, 33, 37, 41, 47; 3 : 6-8; 5 : 12. **And that I do nothing of myself,** *nothing* independently and of my own will (see on ch. 7 : 16, 18, and compare 5 : 19, 30); **but as my Father hath taught me,** referring to his having received instructions as an ambassador before being sent by the Father upon his embassy. See next verse. It was his constant aim, undeviatingly, to speak and act *according to* his instructions.

29. **And he that sent me is with me,** *with* him in working miracles and in all that he performed as God's ambassador—*with* him to support and vindicate him in declaring the truth as to men's guilt and need and his own Messiahship. **The Father hath not left me alone.** How different from earthly sovereigns, who cannot be present with their ambassadors! And this fact of the abiding presence made each thoughtful mind understand of whom Jesus was speaking. See ver. 30. **For I do always,** the I being emphatic; though others disobey him, I am always doing his will. Also, *because* I obey him, he does not leave me nor hide his face from me. See Isa. 59 : 2. **Those things that please him,** the kind of things, both as to motive and act, which he has declared are pleasing in his sight. See 1 John 3 : 22. Christ's *undertaking* the work of redemption was pleasing to the Father, and his whole progress in *the execution* of it was equally pleasing. See Isa. 53 : 10; Luke 3 : 22; 2 Pet. 1 : 17, 18.

30. THE EFFECT OF HIS WORDS ON MANY OF HIS HEARERS. **As he spake these words,** the words contained especially in the preceding para-

A. D. 29. JOHN VIII. 155

31 Then said Jesus to those Jews which believed on him, ¹If ye continue in my word, *then* are ye my dis-
32 ciples indeed; ᵏand ye shall know the truth, and ¹the truth shall make you free.
33 They answered him, ᵐWe be Abraham's seed, and were never in bondage to any man; how sayest thou, Ye shall be made free?

12; 1 Pet. 2. 16. ᵐ ver. 39; Lev. 25. 42; Matt. 3. 9.

¹ ch. 15. 4-9; Acts 14. 22; 2 Tim. 3. 14; Heb. 3. 14; 10. 38, 39; James 1. 25.
ᵏ ch. 7. 17.
¹ Ps. 119. 45; Rom. 6. 14-18, 22; 8. 2, 15; Gal. 5. 1, 13; James 1. 25; 2.

graph, vers. 28-30; but they may extend farther back, into paragraph vers. 21-27; **many believed on him;** believed he was the Christ, and received his instructions so far as to become his disciples in an historical sense—that is, they had the belief of the *head*, but not the established faith of the *heart*, Rom. 10 : 10. "A faith, however, which was but superficial, for it did not find in the words of Jesus *words of life*, ch. 6 : 63, 68. They stand upon the footing of the disciples mentioned in ch. 6 : 66; hence, *to abide* (ver. 31) is required of them."—THOLUCK. There was doubtless something in the manner and expression of Jesus which brought conviction in the minds of many. But their faith needed to be tested, and, if genuine, to be confirmed. Hence he proceeds now to address them.
31. In this and the next verse Jesus promises true freedom to them that believe. **Then said Jesus.** The fact that they believed on him and that he knew the character of their belief *caused* him to address them in particular. **To those Jews which believed on him,** had believed his testimony respecting himself, and in their minds hastily accepted him as the Christ. **If ye continue in my word,** if you heartily receive and habitually obey it, and thus *rest* in it as a person *dwells* in his habitation from day to day and from month to month. *My word*, in contrast with the teaching of the Jewish scribes and rabbis. **Then are ye my disciples indeed;** you will thus prove yourselves such, and really be such, chap. 14 : 21; 15 : 14. While in this way instructing them, he also *warns* them against trusting to their present feelings, giving them to understand that their faith will be tested by time, and if it does not lead to holy living, in obedience to his word, it will by this failure be proved spurious and of no value. See James 2 : 17, 26.
32. **And ye shall know the truth;** you shall discern what is true in regard to human nature and its wants and God's provision for the soul's need, and shall know more and more of the power of this truth on your own hearts; **and the truth shall make you free**—free from the bondage of ignorance, error, and sin; free from the slavery of evil passions, grovelling views, and corrupt propensities. God's word elsewhere teaches that the sinner, obeying the promptings of an evil heart and of a corrupt nature, is a slave, or *bond-servant*, of sin, ver. 34. " Ye were the servants of sin. . . . Ye have yielded your members servants to uncleanness and to iniquity," Rom. 6 : 17, 19, 20. "Thou art in the gall of bitterness, and in the bond of iniquity," Acts 8 : 23. *The truth* of Christ, received into the understanding and heart and practised in the life, sunders the chain, breaks off the heavy yoke of bondage, and sets the sinner free. And it is indeed a blessed freedom, "the glorious liberty of the children of God" (Rom 8 : 21)! a freedom from the galling yoke of sin and Satan; a liberty to approach God as our Friend and reconciled Father, and to enter even "into the holiest by the blood of Jesus," Heb. 10 : 19. The setting free which is here ascribed to *the truth* is in verse 36 ascribed to Christ, "the Son," showing it is the truth in Jesus (Eph. 4 : 21), and not some other department of truth, which accomplishes this great work.
33. In vers. 33-38 Jesus shows that the Jews, though Abraham's seed, needed freedom from sin. **They answered him.** Some of the most forward among them make this reply, and perhaps the others assent. **We be Abraham's seed,** his natural posterity or descendants, **and were never in**

34 Jesus answered them, Verily, verily, I say unto you, ⁿWhosoever committeth sin is the servant of 35 sin. And °the servant abideth not in the house for

• Rom. 6. 16, 19, 20
2 Pet. 2. 19; 1
John 3. 8-10.
• Gal. 4. 30.

bondage to any man. Overlooking or rejecting the fact of their bondage to error and sin, and their need to be set free from these by "the truth," they become excited, and spurn the idea that they, descendants of the freeman Abraham, to whom such divine promises of national superiority and leadership were made, should be represented as needing to be "set free." The nation had, because of its idolatries and other sins, been in subjection to the Chaldæans, and temporarily to others, and it was then under the authority of the hated Romans. But they either ignore this subjection or, in their lofty and independent spirit, cannot bear to have it called being *in bondage*, and be charged on them as such. Also, as Jesus was then speaking to a few individuals, and those near or associated with them, they probably thought of *personal servitude*, or being the slaves of some man as a master; and in such bondage they had never been. Nay, like their father Abraham, they were freemen! The same independent spirit has been felt by other descendants of Abraham who have not walked in the steps of his faith (Rom. 4 : 12), the Ishmaelites, down to the wild Bedouin Arabs of the present day, Gen. 16 : 12. **How sayest thou.** The word **thou** is emphatic. Respecting such as we, *How dost thou say*, **Ye shall be made free?** or, more exactly, *Ye will become freemen?* How utterly inadequate are their views, and how entirely they misapprehend the words of Jesus!

34. **Jesus answered them, Verily, verily**—*i. e. Truly, truly*—affirming the certainty and truth of what follows, and calling attention to it as something of importance. **Whosoever committeth sin,** better, *every one who commits sin*, no matter who he is, whether high or low in society, whether rich or poor, young or aged—every human being, of whatever age, sex, or condition—**is the servant,** more exactly, *is a bond-servant*, **of sin,** being under its authority and subject to its control as really as the slave is subject to the authority and control of his master. See on ver. 32. Therefore these Jews, with all their pride and boasting, being *bond servants* of sin, had no right to the privileges which belong only to the *free children* in God's family. Jesus here "utterly expels the political question from his scope. He states first the principle, then the application. The *committing* of sin is to be taken with emphasis. He whose tendency and habit is to commit sin, . . . he is the servant, the slave, of sin; fallen into the worst conceivable bondage. . . . The application was obvious. Jesus implied that they, not only for being born of the flesh, but for being carnally-minded and practically hostile to the truth, committed sin. . . . They were therefore in the hardest slavery, and in the utmost need of liberation by the truth."—LANGE.

35. **And the servant abideth not;** he is not the heir, but merely a bond-servant; he has no right or legal claim to remain. If he is disobedient and wicked, he is sold or turned away by his master. **In the house for ever**—*i. e.* permanently, during the whole of his natural life. "The bond-servant is not an organic member of the household, has no inheritance, and can be expelled or sold, Gen. 21 : 10; Gal. 4 : 30."—LANGE. Consequently, these Jews, while continuing the slaves, or bond-servants, of sin, had not the rights of children in the family of God, and were liable to be cut off from both the household and its general privileges at any hour when the Master should please. The words of Sarah, sanctioned by God, were: "Cast out the bond-woman and her son ; for the son of the bond-woman shall not be heir with the son of the free-woman," Gal. 4 : 30; Gen. 21 : 10. Thus, Abraham had two kinds of seed. That only by the free-woman was heir of the promise, Gal. 4 : 22-31. **But the Son abideth ever.** The last word is the same as that translated *for ever* in the former part of the verse. The son, being heir, as long as he lives has a legal right to abide in the house and to inherit and dispose of the property. In accordance with the father's will, he has also legal authority to act in the management of the affairs of the household.

36 ever: *but* ᵖ the Son abideth ever. ᑫ If the Son there- 37 fore shall make you free, ye shall be free indeed. I know that ye are Abraham's seed; but ʳ ye seek to 38 kill me, because my word hath no place in you. ˢ I speak that which I have seen with my Father; and ye do that which ye have seen with your father. 39 They answered and said unto him, ᵗ Abraham is our father.
Jesus saith unto them, ᵘ If ye were Abraham's chil- 40 dren, ye would do the works of Abraham. But now ye seek to kill me, a man that hath told you the

ᵖ Gal. 4. 4–7; Heb. 7. 24, 25.
ᑫ vers. 31,32; Rom. 8. 1, 2; Gal. 5. 1.
ʳ ver. 40; ch.7. 1, 19.
ˢ ch. 3. 32; 5. 19, 30; 14. 10, 24.

ᵗ ver.33; Matt. 3. 9.

ᵘ Rom. 2. 28, 29; 9. 7; Gal. 3. 7, 29; James 2. 22–24.

36. If the Son therefore. The term *Son* is manifestly applied here to the Son of God, who is the "heir of all things" (Heb. 1 : 2), the Son in his Father's house, who has a right and possesses authority there. **Shall make you free.** He employs his "truth" in setting men free, and "the truth" (ver. 32) presents **the Son** as the great Liberator. **Ye shall be free indeed.** Drawing his illustration from a usage with which they were familiar, Jesus applies it with great force to his own work in saving his people from the bondage of sin: *If, etc., ye will be freemen indeed,* you will possess a freedom that is worthy of its name.
37. I know that ye are Abraham's seed, or *offspring.* "The acknowledgment of their claim to natural descent from Abraham serves only to strengthen the reproof that follows."— LANGE. What a contrast! Abraham's offspring, yet seeking to murder Christ! **But ye seek,** you persist in the wicked design, **to kill me, because my word,** the truth which I declare, **hath no place in you;** no room is found for it there, because the space is preoccupied by your pride, selfishness, prejudices, and false notions respecting the Messiah; or, *makes no progress in you* (MEYER, LANGE, T. S. GREEN), does not thrive there and bear its appropriate fruit.
38. Jesus proceeds to correct their mistake in claiming distinguished privileges on the simple ground of being Abraham's natural descendants. He shows that they are morally and in the sight of God his children whose spirit they possess and whose conduct they imitate. **I speak,** habitually in my discourses to the world. The great work of his life was to bear testimony to the truth of God. The **I** is emphatic in contrast with the first *you* in the latter member of the verse. **That,** or *the things,* **which I have seen with my Father**—that is, with God—which things consequently I am well acquainted with, and communicate intelligently and truthfully. Compare ch. 3 : 11–13. But the perfect **have seen** also extends down beyond his assumption of his human nature. Compare ch. 3 : 34; 16 : 13. **And ye do,** you practise now and habitually, **that which ye have seen with,** or, with some critical editors, *what things you heard from,* **your father.** He does not yet inform them whom he means by their father, whose lessons they are practising; but he is gradually leading them to see that he regards them as exceedingly sinful, opposed to God, and in heart and works like the evil one.
39. In this and the two verses that follow Jesus shows that the Jews were not in the highest sense children of Abraham. **Abraham is our father,** rather, *Our father is Abraham, father* being the subject, and *Abraham* the predicate, in the sentence. This order of the words gives an emphasis to their claim. However it may be with others, our father is Abraham. **If ye were Abraham's children,** if you had his spirit and possessed a faith like his, ye **would do the works of Abraham,** would be faithful and obedient as he was.
40. But now, as your spirit and character really are, **ye seek to kill me.** How this plain and direct statement of Jesus, made in ver. 37, and here reaffirmed, was adapted to show them that he could look into their hearts and read the thoughts, feelings, and motives which they were cherish-

JOHN VIII.   A. D. 29

41 truth, which I have heard of God; this did not Abraham. Ye do the deeds of your father.
Then said they to him, We be not born of fornication; ˣ we have one Father, *even* God.
42 Jesus saith unto them, ʸ If God were your Father, ye would love me; ᶻ for I proceeded forth and came from God; ᵃ neither came I of myself, but he sent me.
43 ᵇ Why do ye not understand my speech? *even* because

ˣ Ex. 4. 22; Isa. 63 16; 64. 8; Mal 1. 6.
ʸ 1 John 5. 1.
ᶻ ch. 1. 14; 16. 27, 28; 17. 8, 25.
ᵃ ch. 5. 43; 7. 23, 29; 1 John 4.9, 10, 14.
ᵇ ch. 7. 17; Prov. 28. 5.

ing, or that he was taught these by the immediate agency of God's Spirit, and in either case, that in thus discrediting and opposing him they were opposing God himself! **A man.** Jesus here brings out distinctly the fact of his complete humanity. He applies the term to himself nowhere else, but he often uses the expression, "the Son of man." He does not yet charge them with seeking to murder *the Christ.* But notice the gradation of the charge: 1. You are seeking to kill me, *a man;* 2. A man that has *spoken* to you *the truth;* 3. The truth which I heard *from God.* **This did not Abraham.** Abraham neither cherished a murderous purpose against any one, nor rejected a truth which God revealed to him. On the contrary, he was distinguished for his love to both God and men. He nobly liberated captives (Gen. 14 : 14–16) and welcomed and generously entertained strangers, Gen. 18 : 1–8. He also received without faltering the revelations of God to him, however mysterious they were or however trying the duties they imposed, Gen. 12 : 1–4; 15 : 4–6; 22 : 1–16. On these accounts we find him highly commended in the New Testament, Rom. 4 : 9, 13; 9 : 9; Heb. 11 : 8, 17; 13 : 2.

41. Ye do the deeds of your father, the *you* being emphatic. Whatever others may do, your course is decisive; *you* exhibit the spirit and perform acts like those of your father. See on ver. 38. These Jews now see to what conclusion Jesus is leading them, and resolutely maintain that they are genuine children of Abraham and of Abraham's God. **Then said they to him, We be not born of fornication;** that is, We are not bastards or of a spurious stock, but are genuine descendants of Abraham. Bastards were excluded from the Jewish congregation, Deut. 23 : 2. **We have one Father, *One*** above all others, one and the same that Abraham had, **even God.** The terms *adultery* and *fornication* are often used in the Bible to signify apostasy from God and the adoption of *idolatry*, Isa. 1 : 21; 57 : 3–5; Hos. 1 : 2; 2 : 4. These Jews therefore now go at one bound from the literal to the spiritual, and maintain that they have not apostatized from God, and are neither idolaters nor descendants from idolaters, but, like Abraham, they are genuine worshippers and children of God.

42. THE JEWS HAVING CLAIMED GOD AS THEIR FATHER, JESUS SHOWS THEM WHO IS THEIR FATHER, vers. 42–45. **If God were your Father.** Facts exhibited in their disposition and conduct proved that they were not the spiritual children of God. Their treatment of Christ, though he came from God and by his authority, and faithfully delivered his message and performed his work, showed conclusively that their spirit, choice, and bent of mind were wholly at variance with God. Therefore Jesus said to them, **If God were your Father, ye would love me.** They would love him because he was the brightness of the Father's glory and the express image of his person (Heb. 1 : 3), "and every one that loveth him that begat, loveth him also that is begotten of him" (1 John 5 : 1) and bears his image. **For I proceeded forth and came from God.** Of course, *came hither*, thus marking the source and the termination of his act of coming. **Neither came I of myself,** self-prompted, self-authorized, and self-sent. **But he sent me,** he called me, gave me my commission, and sent me forth on his embassy to perform the work he assigned me. See on ver. 14.

43. Why do ye not understand my speech? or *this speech of mine?* as to its form, tone, and manner of delivery, so as to recognize the loving voice of the Good Shepherd. See ch 10 : 3, 4. **Even because ye,** or, sim

44 °ye cannot hear my word. ᵈ Ye are of *your* father the devil, and the lusts of your father ye will do. ᵉ He was a murderer from the beginning, and ᶠ abode not in the truth, because there is no truth in him. ᵍ When he speaketh a lie, he speaketh of his own; ʰ for he is

ᶜ ch. 6. 60; Jer. 6. 10; Rom. 8. 7, 8.
ᵈ vers.38, 41; Matt. 13. 38; Acts 13. 10; 1 John 3. 8–10.
ᵉ Gen. 3. 3–6; Rom. 5. 12; 1 Pet 5. 8; Rev. 12. 9.   ᶠ 2 Pet. 2. 4; Jude 6.   ᵍ 2 Chron. 18. 20–22; Job 1. 11; 2 Thess. 2. 9–11; Rev. 13. 14.   ʰ Acts 5. 3.

ply, *because you*, **cannot hear my word**, as to its matter or substance. This feature of the word they did not approve and love, because it was opposed to their pride, vanity, prejudices, and preconceived opinions, and therefore they gave little attention to the word itself, did not wish to understand it, and could not bear to hear it.

44. Having gradually prepared the way, Jesus now comes out plainly, and calls by name him whom he has previously hinted at as their father. **Ye are of your father the devil;** more exactly, *You are of the father the devil*. The *you*, being emphatic, implies, Whatever others may be, your character is decisive; your whole spirit and conduct, especially toward me as God's ambassador, proves you to be from the fatherhood of the devil. Compare Acts 13 : 10; 1 John 3 : 8–10. **And the lusts,** or *longings*, **of your father ye will do,** you choose and wish to do, and take delight in doing. Jesus proceeds to mention two traits of the devil in which these Jews resemble him and prove themselves his children rather than children of God. These are, the spirit of murder and a dislike of the truth. Their desire to put Jesus to death and their dislike of his truthful teaching proclaim unmistakably their moral resemblance to Satan. **He** (emphatic) **was a murderer**, or *mankiller*, **from the beginning**, from the beginning of the history of our race. He tempted our first mother, Eve, and thus caused death to come on Adam and Eve and all their descendants, Gen. 2 : 17; 3 : 4–6; Rom. 5 : 12. He instigated Cain to kill his brother Abel, and has instigated others to murder in every age since; "Cain, who was of that wicked one, and slew his brother. 1 John 3 : 12. **And abode not,** rather, *he stands not*, **in the truth, because there is no truth in him,** or, simply, *because truth is not in him*. If he speaks the truth in part, it is with the purpose of deceiving by the admixture of error, and thus seeking to gain his point. He does not *stand in the truth* as in a position from which he is not to be moved, or in a congenial element ont of which he cannot be drawn. He is false and deceitful, because it is his habit and his delight to be so, and *because truth is not in him* as a regulating and controlling power, to guide his judgment and his will. **When he speaketh a lie,** or *the lie*, which he purposes to utter in his persuasive way, **he speaketh of his own,** *out of his own feelings*, from the promptings of his own deceitful heart. **For he is a liar,** in his feelings, habits, and choice, **and the father of it;** some interpret, he is *the father of lying*, so far as our race is concerned, for he *first introduced it* among mankind; by speaking base insinuations and falsehoods he deceived Eve and drew her away from the truth, and is ever instigating falsehood to her descendants to lead them also astray. Some eminent scholars, however, hold it more consistent with the original to interpret, *father of the liar*, the *liar* being used in an indefinite sense, implying that every liar is the devil's son.

In this verse *the existence of the devil as a real, living being* who deceives and ruins our race is distinctly and positively taught. Because—1. So to understand the verse is to take it in *its natural and obvious sense,* and make it easy of comprehension and practical application; whereas to understand it otherwise is to deprive it of intelligible meaning and turn it into nonsense. 2. The devil is here called a *father*, and these Jews are called *his children*. But they were *living beings;* consequently, he must be *a living being,* or the comparison is inappropriate. 3. *Personal acts and attributes* are ascribed to him. He is represented as having *lusts* or *longings;* as being *a murderer;* as *wandering from the truth;* as *speaking falsehood;* as being *a liar*, and the father of lying or liars. 4. The power

JOHN VIII.   A. D. 29.

45 a liar, and the father of it. And ¹ because I tell you
46 the truth, ye believe me not. ᵏ Which of you convinceth me of sin? And if I say the truth, why do
47 ye not believe me? ¹ He that is of God heareth God's words; ye therefore hear *them* not, because ᵐ ye are not of God.
48 Then answered the Jews, and said unto him, Say we not well ⁿ that thou art a Samaritan, and ᵒ hast a devil?

ⁱ ch. 3. 19; 7. 7
Gal. 4. 16.
ᵏ ver. 7; Isa. 53. 9.
¹ ch. 1. 12, 13; 6. 45; 10. 26, 27; 1 John 4. 6.
ᵐ 1 John 3. 10.

ⁿ ch. 4. 9.
ᵒ ver. 52; ch. 7. 20; 10. 20.

of free *choice* is ascribed to him. He is a murderer, and wanders from the truth and speaks falsehood because *he chooses* to do these things. But the power and act of choice implies an intelligent *chooser*, capable of understanding and of accepting or refusing. 5. *Design* is ascribed to him. He is a murderer, because *he designs* and plans to be so; and he wanders from the truth and speaks falsehood, because he designs to do this and accomplish his object thereby. But design always implies *a personal, intelligent designer*, who lays his plans to bring about the object he has in view. And this can never be affirmed of dead matter or of a mere attribute.

45. **And because I,** in contrast with *your* desire to perform the longing of your father and to act out murder and falsehood like him, **tell you the truth,** especially in regard to my own origin, character, and mission, **ye believe me not,** implying, should I utter *false* religious teachings, and profess to be the Messiah in accordance with *your mistaken notions* of his character and work, you would believe me. Compare ch. 5 : 43.

46. The unbelief of the Jews a proof that God is not their Father, vers. 46, 47. **Which of you convinceth,** rather, *convicts,* **me.** To *convince* is to satisfy *a man's own mind* of some particular truth; to *convict* a man is to prove him guilty of unfaithfulness, deception, or some other crime against men or against God. **Convicts me of sin?** of error, deception, imposture, of any departure from what is true and right and in accordance with the word f God? And the sinlessness of his life was a pledge of the truthfulness of his teaching. **And if I say the truth,** truth free from error and imposture, truth in harmony with God's word, **why do ye not believe me?** He

here implies: If you cannot convict me of imposture and deception, nor prove me guilty of teaching error and departure from the Scriptures, then you are morally bound to receive me as God's ambassador and to accept my words.

47. **He that is of God**—that is, a child of God by the new birth and moral resemblance to God—**heareth God's words,** the words delivered by the authority and with the approbation of God; hears them with the reverence and affection of a child, with a sincere desire to understand what they teach and to practise what they enjoin. These Jews did not exhibit a childlike, teachable, affectionate, obedient spirit toward God and toward his beloved Son, whom the Father had sent forth to instruct and save them. With good reason, then, did Jesus add, **Ye therefore hear them not, because ye are not of God.**

48. The Jews further revile Jesus. **Then answered the Jews.** The most approved text omits *Then,* and reads, *The Jews answered,* making the narrative concise and forcible. **Say we not well that thou art a Samaritan,** an expression of reproach and contempt. In Jewish estimation it had the force of charging Jesus with being a *heretic* or *schismatic,* because they so regarded the Samaritans, and of affiliating with *a spurious race* that descended from a mongrel people made up of idolaters and Jews. See ch. 4 : 9, 20, 40; 2 Kings 17 : 24, 41. **And hast a devil?** or, *a demon?* See on ch. 7 : 20. As Jesus had shown that they were not genuine children of Abraham in a moral and spiritual sense which they did not comprehend, perhaps they intended to retort by calling him *a Samaritan.* And as he had proved that in spirit and works they were not the children of God, but were chil-

A. D. 29. JOHN VIII. 161

49 Jesus answered, ᵖI have not a devil; but I honor
50 my Father, and ye do dishonor me. And ᑫI seek not
mine own glory; ʳthere is one that seeketh and judg-
51 eth. Verily, verily, I say unto you, ˢIf a man keep
my saying, he shall never see death.

ᵖ 1 Pet. 2. 23.
ᑫ ch. 5. 41; 7. 18.
ʳ ch. 5. 20–23.
ˢ ch. 3. 15, 16; 5
24; 11. 26.

---

dren of the devil, they may have sought to match this by suggesting that he was *possessed by a demon.* Their language on both points was bitter and insulting, and was used by them in a self-justifying as well as a revengeful spirit: Do we not *well* say thou art a Samaritan, and hast a demon?
49. In this and the two verses that follow, Jesus reasserts his intimate relation to the Father, and the life-giving power of his doctrine. With what meekness and magnanimity Jesus responds! As to the first part of the charge, that he was a Samaritan, he makes no reply, except incidentally. To the second part he does reply by the direct denial, **I have not a devil,** or, *a demon.* He adds, **but I honor my Father,** thereby showing inferentially that he neither was a Samaritan, in their sense of the term or in any sense, nor had a demon. He did honor his Father by teaching the doctrines of the Holy Scriptures (2 Tim. 3: 15), which tend to exalt God; by teaching explicitly that God is holy, just, and true, yet compassionate and gracious; by himself doing the Father's will; and by seeking to bring men to love and obey God. An evil spirit or demon, from its very nature, neither would nor could do this, so that here was conclusive proof that Jesus was controlled by no such spirit. **And ye do dishonor me.** In their whole course, from verse 33 onward, they had spoken and acted toward him in a disrespectful and insulting manner, as if he were an impostor or a man beside himself; and this, with the blindness of their corrupt hearts, kept them from discovering his real character and merits.
50. **And,** or *yet,* **I seek not,** the *yet* expressing the contrast of his aim to that of ambitious men, **mine own glory,** as if Jesus would say: I am not seeking my glory apart from that of the Father; nor do I seek to exalt or to vindicate myself. I am willing to be reproached and despised, and I leave to another the vindication of my honor.

There is one that seeketh and judgeth—One who seeks my honor and welfare, and who will vindicate my character; One who always judges on principles of justice and truth, so that while he acquits and justifies the righteous, he condemns and overwhelms the wicked, Rom. 2: 6–9. To him I commit my cause, and patiently await his time. See 1 Pet. 2: 21–23; Ps. 37: 5, 6.
51. **Verily, verily,** indicating the certainty and importance of what follows. See on ver. 34. **If a man keep my saying,** or, *my word,* as in vers. 31, 37, 43, **he shall never see death,** more accurately, *shall by no means,* there being two negatives in the Greek, which emphasize or give increased force to the assertion, as in ver. 12, *see death for ever,* or, in the order of the Greek, *Death he shall by no means see for ever.* Since, in *judging* (ver. 50) the wicked and impenitent, God assigns them to *death,* according to the nature and desert of their sins (Rom. 6: 21, 23; Ezek. 18: 4, 31, 32), Jesus here points out how men may with certainty avoid that fearful result in its final issue, specifically called in Rev. 2: 11; 20: 6, 14, *the second death.* The penalty attached to the original law was: "In the day that thou eatest thereof, thou shalt surely *die,*" Gen. 2: 17. In the very day when Adam and Eve disobeyed God and partook of the forbidden fruit they became mortal—they were under sentence of death, were tending toward death, and were liable to be cut off at any hour. They were also forthwith spiritually dead—dead in sin (Eph. 2: 1, 5), deprived of the image and life of God in the soul; and having themselves become morally corrupt and under sentence of death, they could beget no other than a corrupt and mortal posterity. "Adam lived a hundred and thirty years, and begat a son *in his own likeness, after his image,* and called his name Seth," Gen. 5: 3. "By one man sin entered into the world, and death by sin; and *so death passed upon all men,* for that all have sinned," or on

52 Then said the Jews unto him, Now we know that thou hast a devil. *Abraham is dead, and the prophets; and thou sayest, If a man keep my saying, 53 he shall never taste of death. Art thou greater than our father Abraham, which is dead? and the prophets are dead; whom makest thou thyself?
54 Jesus answered, "If I honor myself, my honor is

*Zech. 1. 5; Heb 11. 13.

"ver. 50; ch. 5. 31; 7. 18.

---

the ground that all sinned, Rom. 5: 12. But the soul that lays hold of and keeps Christ's word of salvation will safely pass through both stages of God's judgment, in the death of the body and in the full and final execution of sentence at the judgment-day: *he shall by no means see death for ever.*

52. In this and the next verse the Jews still further revile Jesus and his teaching. We have here "the answer of blind enmity to his enticing call of mercy."—LANGE. **Then said the Jews, . . . Now we know that thou hast a devil, or a demon,** and our former suggestion (ver. 48) is proved true, because thou affirmest what is contrary to all human experience, and is in the nature of things impossible; and surely no sane man would venture such an assertion. **Abraham is dead,** rather, *Abraham died,* the historic past, simply stating the matter of fact which their argument also requires. Jesus has unqualifiedly declared how any man can be preserved from death. Understanding death in the physical sense, these Jews join issue with him, and attempt to rebut his assertion by presenting what they suppose an unanswerable argument, founded on universally conceded facts in the history of their nation. *Now we know that thou hast a demon,* because *Abraham,* the father and founder of our nation, *died,* good and obedient to God as he was, **and the prophets,** faithful as they were in proclaiming his word and conforming to his will. **And thou sayest,** or, *yet thou sayest,* notwithstanding these acknowledged and indisputable facts, **If a man keep my saying,** or *word,* **he shall never taste of death.** See on ver. 51. Notice that they change the expression *see death* into *taste of death.* Among the Jewish rabbins, according to Schoettgen and Wetstein, to *taste* of death is the figure of *drinking the cup* of death.

To *see* death and to *taste* of death are therefore in one respect equivalent expressions, both of them signifying to *die.* These Jews seem to have mentally reasoned: He who promises bodily immortality to others ought himself to possess it in a still higher degree. But since even Abraham and the prophets died, it is senseless and demon-like for you to claim exemption from death, either for yourself or your followers. They thus, in their blindness and hatred, entirely overlook the real meaning and the preciousness of Jesus' declaration, and deprive themselves of its practical benefits.

53. **Art thou greater,** art thou more exalted in thy nature, or possessed of a higher and self-sustaining power, **than our father Abraham, which is dead?** *one who died,* the historic past, as in ver. 52. The pronoun in this passage is not the simple relative **which,** or *who,* but a compound relative, meaning *whoever, some one who, one who* (see LIDDELL, and ROBINSON'S *Lex.*); thus taking one person as a specimen in general to represent the whole class to which he belongs. They add, **and the prophets are dead,** or *died,* as above, stating a literal fact of history; **whom makest thou thyself?** whom dost thou pretend to be? Although so great and good a man as Abraham died, and the faithful and devoted prophets could not escape death, yet thou, a despised Nazarene, a Samaritan, a demoniac, pretendest that thou canst keep thy followers from dying! Forsooth, *whom makest thou thyself?* What contempt and scorn are expressed in this question as they put it! And what a grandeur of patience Jesus exhibits in bearing with them as he does under their repeated provocations and insults!

54–56. JESUS ASSERTS THAT HIS FATHER HONORS HIM, AND DECLARES ABRAHAM'S KNOWLEDGE AND JOY CONCERNING HIM. 54.

A. D. 29.   JOHN VIII.   163

nothing; ˣ It is my Father that honoreth me; of
55 whom ʸ ye say, that he is your God: yet ᶻ ye have
not known him, ᵃ but I know him; and if I should
say, I know him not, ᵇ I shall be a liar like unto you;
56 but I know him, ᶜ and keep his saying. Your father
Abraham ᵈ rejoiced to see my day; ᵉ and he saw it,
and was glad.

ˣ ch. 5. 22-29, 41; 16. 14; 17. 1; Ps. 2. 6-12; 110. 1-4; Acts 3. 13.
ʸ ver. 41.
ᶻ ver. 19; ch. 7. 28, 29; Jer. 4. 22; 9. ?.
ᵃ ch. 1. 18; 6. 46; Matt. 11. 27.

ᵇ 1 John 2. 4, 22; 5. 10.   ᶜ ch. 15. 10; Heb. 5. 8, 9.   ᵈ Luke 10. 24.   ᵉ Gen. 22. 13, 14, 18; Rom. 4. 18-22; Gal. 3. 7-9, 14-18; Heb. 11. 13.

These Jews have just reproached him as claiming unreasonable glory for himself in pretending to be greater than even Abraham and the prophets. He tacitly assents to the implied claim of being greater than those ancient worthies, but so speaks as to let them know he is not anxious to vindicate himself from their reproaches. **If I honor myself,** shall proceed to praise and exalt myself, impelled by a spirit of self-glorying, **my honor,** or *glory,* **is nothing,** is of no value. **It is my Father that honoreth me.** The glory which I have and the vindication I seek come from him. See on ver. 50. **Of whom ye say, that he is your God.** When they said, "We be Abraham's seed," "Abraham is our father" (vers. 33, 39), they virtually claimed also Abraham's God, as they did in a direct manner when they affirmed, "We have one Father, even God," ver. 41. They therefore not only said once, but persisted in saying or claiming, *He is our God.*
55. **Yet ye have not known him,** you have not been even acquainted with him as a person may be with his neighbor or townsman, **but I know him,** I *have seen him,* been intimate with him, and have a direct and thorough knowledge of him. **And if I should say,** rather, *if I say,* to harmonize with its corresponding verb *shall be* that follows in the sentence, **I know him not, I shall be a liar like unto you.** Such was his intimate knowledge of the Father, and his consciousness of the Father's presence with him (Matt. 11 : 27), that to deny it would be to utter a falsehood and make himself a liar like them, who pretended to know God and be his children, yet at the same time desired and eagerly practised the works of the devil (ver. 44), and hence were hypocrites and liars. **But I know him,** **and keep his saying,** by laying up his word in my heart (Ps. 119 : 11) and constantly practising it in my life. How striking is the contrast between their ignorance of God and Christ's knowledge of the Father!
56. **Your father Abraham,** thus conceding their claim in its literal sense, **rejoiced,** rather, *exulted,* as one does who leaps on account of the exuberance of his joy, **to see my day,** that he was allowed the privilege of seeing, by faith, *this day of mine,* this time of peculiar favor—the day of the Messiah. This day of Jesus as the Christ, however, is not to be limited to the time of his life on earth from his birth to his crucifixion, but is to be extended to his whole Messianic reign, in the present world and the world to come. Such a view, though dim and imperfect, might well cause Abraham to *exult.* **And he saw it,** in anticipation, by faith in the promises which he received, Gen. 15 : 4-6; 22 : 1-18. Or, as some think, he saw it as those redeemed ones who have passed away see what is transpiring in this world which they have left. **And was glad,** or *rejoiced,* as the word is translated in John 3 : 29; 4 : 36; 14 : 28, and many other passages. As seeing is twice mentioned in this brief allusion to Abraham, so is also his accompanying joy. He *exulted to see,* he *saw* and *rejoiced.* The implied testimony of Abraham is here brought forward by Jesus, because the Jews considered it a great honor to be his descendants, ver. 39. And as they regarded the words and deeds of Abraham as peculiarly illustrious and worthy of their imitation, consistency would require that they cheerfully and patiently listen to what he, by his inward faith and outward acts, had expressed concerning the Messiah. Compare Gal. 3 : 16.

JOHN VIII. A. D. 29.

57 Then said the Jews unto him, Thou art not yet fifty years old, and hast thou seen Abraham?
58 Jesus said unto them, Verily, verily, I say unto you, ᶠBefore Abraham was, ᵍI am.
59 Then ʰtook they up stones to cast at him; but Jesus hid himself, and went out of the temple, ⁱgoing through the midst of them, and so passed by.

ᶠ ch. 1. 1, 2; 17. 5, 24; Mic. 5. 2.
ᵍ Ex. 3. 14; Isa. 43. 13; Col. 1. 17.
ʰ ch. 10. 30–33; 11. 8; Lev. 24. 16.
ⁱ ver. 20; ch. 10. 39, 40; Luke 4. 30.

---

57. THE INSULTING RETORT OF THE JEWS. **Then said the Jews unto him,** in consequence of his remark about Abraham, **Thou art not yet fifty years old.** Why should they say *fifty* years, when Jesus is supposed to have been only *thirty-three* years old? They may have said *not yet fifty,* to prevent the possibility of a denial on that point. Had they said *forty* years, they might have apprehended such a denial, and the consequent depriving their argument of its intended force. Hence they would be sure to have the number *sufficiently large.* Or, as "the fiftieth year was the full age of a man, Num. 4 : 3" (THOLUCK), possibly they mentioned this age "as though they magnanimously granted more than could be demanded, in order to give an appearance of absurdity to his language." — BRAUNE. **And hast thou seen Abraham?** They here pervert the language of Jesus, and raise a false issue. He did not say *he* had seen Abraham, but *Abraham saw his day,* and rejoiced. By this seeing and rejoicing, Abraham, great as he was, acknowledged his own inferiority to the Messiah. This point they either failed to perceive or wilfully overlooked, and thus cut themselves off from the benefit they might otherwise have received.

58. This leads Jesus to assert his pre-existence. **Verily, Verily,** a strong affirmation, denoting the truth and importance of what is about to be said. See on ver. 34. **Before Abraham was,** more accurately, *was born,* as also in Rom. 1 : 3; Gal. 4 : 4, twice. This is a different verb from that at the end of the sentence: this refers to the *origin* of a creature or created being—his coming into existence; that denotes simply *existence* or *being,* without reference to origin, and is used to express the perpetual existence or being of the ever-living God. **I am**—both words emphatic—as applied here to Christ in his divine nature, implies his past and future eternal existence. Compare Ex. 3 : 14: "*I am* that *I am,*" or "He who I am;" the Greek version of the Old Testament, called the Septuagint, has it, "I am he who is." Also, "*I am* hath sent me to you;" the Septuagint and the Latin Vulgate render, "He who is hath sent me." It is manifest that by "I am" in these passages is indicated the eternity of God, or his perpetual existence independent of all time. This idea is beautifully expressed in Ps. 90 : 2: "From everlasting to everlasting *thou art* God." Jesus, therefore, in these words to the Jews, claims this attribute of the Godhead, and they so understand him. See ver. 59. So that while they, in ver. 57, disregard the instruction and pervert the meaning of his words just uttered, he, in the verse before us, follows up their words, and claims for himself a still more exalted character than he then claimed. Then he intimated that as the Messiah he was more exalted than Abraham; here he claims to be divine.

59. In rage the Jews attempt to stone Jesus, but he escapes. **Then took they up stones,** in consequence of what Jesus had just said, and because they regarded it as blasphemy (see ch. 10 : 33), **to cast at him,** as a blasphemer. Because the law required that the blasphemer of the name of Jehovah should be stoned to death (Lev. 24 : 16), through the impulse of religious frenzy and personal hatred these Jews were about to execute the penalty on Jesus at once, without waiting to go through any forms of law to prove whether he was guilty of the blasphemy which the law condemned. Compare John 10 : 36. The leaders in this movement probably belonged to the class called Zealots, who considered themselves authorized to proceed in this summary manner. See ch. 10 : 31–33. Small stones or fragments of stone might easily be lying about the

courts of the temple, which they could readily obtain and use for the purpose. "The stones were probably the building-stones in the vestibule (see Lightfoot, p. 1048)."—MEYER, in *Lange*. But Jesus hid himself, most likely by mingling with the multitude, and thus concealing himself from his opposers (comp. Luke 4 : 30), **and went out**, more exactly, *went forth out of the temple*. In this we see a special providence, rather than a miracle. Of the latter there is no intimation here. The words, **going through the midst of them, and so passed by,** are omitted by the best critical authorities.

PRACTICAL REMARKS.

1. "It is prudent to go out of the way of danger whenever we can without going out of the way of duty" (M. HENRY), ver. 1; Matt. 10 : 23; Acts 8 : 1.
2. "He went *early* to his work; the people came *early* to hear him. *Early* let our souls be given to him, for he comes *early* into his temple, the heart" (GOSSNER), ver. 2 ; Ps. 5 : 3 ; Prov. 8 : 17.
3. "Though no magistracy can be without sin, it should nevertheless not be chargeable with the sins which it must visit with bodily punishments upon others" (HEDINGER), ver. 3; 2 Sam. 23 : 3, 4; Job 29 : 11–17.
4. "Men may be zealous for the divine law with evil hearts" (HEUBNER), Matt. 26 : 65; John 19 : 7.
5. "It is common for those that are indulgent to their own sin to be very severe against the sins of others."—HENRY. "Thou hypocrite! look into thine own bosom" (HEDINGER), ver. 4; 2 Sam. 12 : 5; Matt. 7 : 3–5; Rom. 2 : 1.
6. "Those that promise themselves secrecy in sin, deceive themselves." "Better our sin should *shame* than *damn* us, and be set in order for our conviction, than for our condemnation" (HENRY), Gen. 4 : 10; Num. 32 : 23; Josh. 7 : 18–21; 2 Sam. 12 : 12, 13.
7. "The heartless cruelty of modern society turns the seduced adulteress over to perpetual infamy, while it winks at the greater crime of the seducing adulterer" (P. SCHAFF), ver. 5; Lev. 20 : 1); Deut. 22 : 18-24.
8. "Worldlings and hypocrites have a passion for bringing good people into perplexity with entangling questions" (HEUBNER), Luke 10 : 25; 11 : 53, 54; 20 : 22, 23.
9. "The pulpit should not meddle in secular affairs, and much less should the secular order meddle with spiritual matters" (HEDINGER), ver. 6; Luke 12 : 13, 14; Acts 4 : 19; 5 : 29.
10. " *The heart of the righteous studieth to answer.*" See Prov. 15 : 28. "It is safe, in many cases, to be deaf to that which it is not safe to answer, Ps. 38 : 13" (HENRY), Prov. 18 : 7.
11. "When we cannot make our point by steering a *direct course*, it is good to *fetch a compass*" (HENRY), ver. 7 ; 2 Sam. 12 : 1–7.
12. "The answer of Jesus puts their cunning to shame, without infringing the law, justice, or love" (GERLACH), Isa. 11 : 2–5.
13. "Prudence and love require that we should give persons an opportunity to withdraw, without ado and disgrace, from a bad cause into which their passion has seduced them" (QUESNEL), ver. 8; Gen. 12 : 18–20; 1 Sam. 24 : 10, 18, 19.
14. "Happy they who have no reason to be afraid of Christ's writing" (HENRY), Jer. 17 : 13; Dan. 5 : 24–30; Rev. 20 : 12.
15. "*In the net which they hid is their own foot taken.* See Ps. 9 : 15. They came with a design to accuse him, but were forced to accuse themselves."—HENRY. "They themselves must come to shame who seek to put others, especially faithful teachers, to shame; treachery comes home to him that forges it" (ZEISIUS), ver. 9; Esth. 7 : 10; Dan. 6 : 24.
16. "Wonderful is the power of conscience, even in hypocrites."—HEUBNER. "To drive these hypocrites away needs only a word of the Lord, which strikes the heart like a hammer that grinds the rock" (GERLACH), Matt. 27 : 3–5.
17. "Our care should be more to save our souls than to save our credit. . . . Those that are *convicted* by their consciences will be *condemned* by their Judge, if they are not *justified* by their Redeemer" (HENRY), Matt. 16 : 24–26.

18. "Preachers must be, no doubt, earnest and zealous with great sinners, but not with gross harshness, for this does not improve and edify" (ZEISIUS), ver. 10; 2 Tim. 2 : 24-26.

19. "*No man, Lord:* it sounds like a sigh of anguish, shame, and faith."—HEUBNER. "True penitents find it enough to give account of themselves to God, and will not undertake to give account of other people" (HENRY), ver. 11; Luke 18 : 13, 14.

20. "Those whose cause is brought before our Lord Jesus will never have occasion to remove it into any other court, for he is the refuge of penitents. . . . Let his gospel *rule us*, and it will infallibly *save us*" (HENRY), Acts 4 : 12; 13 : 38, 39.

21. "Christ's favor in the remission of the sins that are past should prevail with us to *go and sin no more*, Rom. 6 : 1, 2."—HENRY.

22. "Despair not of improving those who have fallen very low."—HEUBNER. "Those who help to save the *life* of a criminal should, as Christ here, help to save the *soul*" (HENRY), Luke 7 : 44-48; 8 : 2, 35, 39.

23. Christ "reverses the judgment of the world, which casts the stone of infamy at the ruined, and leaves the author of the ruin unharmed" (MUHLENBERG, in *Schaff*), Col. 3 : 25.

24. "One sun enlightens the whole world; so does one Christ."—HENRY. Therefore no other can give us the light we need, ver. 12; Mal. 4 : 2; Luke 2 : 32; Acts 4 : 12.

25. "It is not enough to *look at* and *gaze* upon this light; we must follow it, believe in it, and walk in it; for it is a light to our *feet*, not to our *eyes* only" (HENRY), Ps. 119 : 105; John 12 : 35, 36.

26. "He who follows Christ never misses the right way, Isa. 11 : 3, 4."—HEDINGER. "The following of Jesus casts out all uncertain, restless groping" (HEUBNER), vers. 12, 31, 32.

27. Christ "is the Light of the world, and it is the property of light to be *self-evidencing*."—HENRY. "Does not the sun bear witness even to its own existence? Set it aside, if you can" (BRAUNE), ver. 13; Eph. 5 : 13.

28. "The believer always knows the source and the goal of his life" (HEUBNER), ver. 14; John 1 : 4; 17 : 3.

29. "The first coming of Christ was for the purpose of administering, not *justice*, but *medicine*" (HENRY), ver. 15; John 3 : 17; 12 : 47; 1 Tim. 1 : 15.

30. "If Christ had a *commission* from the Father, and the Father's *presence* with him in all his administrations, no doubt his *judgment* was *true* and valid; no exception lay *against* it, no appeal lay *from* it" (HENRY), ver. 16; Isa. 11 . 2-5.

31. "If the Father and the Son testify the very same thing, how strong, how invincible is the testimony" (HEDINGER)! ver. 18; Matt. 17 : 5, John 5 : 37.

32. "These witnesses *to* the world now, will be witnesses *against* those that perish in unbelief; and *their* word will judge men" (HENRY), John 3 : 32-34; 12 : 48, 49; Rom. 2 : 8, 9.

33. "None are so incurably *blind* as those that *will not see*."—HENRY. "Stiffnecked enemies of the truth deride what they do not and will not understand; and when they can go no further they start something ridiculous" (HEDINGER), ver. 19; John 9 : 32-34.

34. "The knowing of the Father and the knowing of the Son are inseparable."—HEUBNER. "The reason why men are ignorant of God is, they are unacquainted with Christ" (HENRY), John 17 : 3.

35. "Those become vain in their imaginations concerning God that will not learn of Christ" (HENRY), John 3 : 19, 20; 5 : 40; Rom. 1 : 21-25.

36. What a contradiction! "The *treasury of God* surrounded by a God-forsaken people, whose offerings were as heartless as the coin clinking in the chest" (BESSER)! ver. 20; Luke 21 : 1-4.

37. "God wonderfully protects faithful teachers and confessors of his word."—HEDINGER. He makes them impregnable till their work is done, Acts 4 : 21; 5 : 40; 12 : 11; 23 : 15, 30.

38. "Those are for ever undone who die in unbelief."—HENRY. "Heaven is inaccessible to the assaults of the wicked" (HEUBNER), v. 21; John 3 : 36; Rev. 21 : 27; 22 : 14, 15.

39. "Christ, and Christians with him, go above to heaven, because they are from above; but the servants of sin and the devil go down, because they are from beneath" (BESSER), ver. 23; Matt. 6 : 20, 21, 24; Col. 3 : 1-6.

40. "Unbelief is the damning sin; it is a sin *against the remedy*" (HENRY), ver. 24; John 3 : 18, 19 ; 5 : 40.

41. "Christ is *one with himself;* what he has said from the beginning he says still. He is an *everlasting gospel*" (HENRY), ver. 25; John 18 : 19-21 ; Rev. 14 : 6, 7.

42. "Whatever discoveries of sin are made to us, he that searches the heart has still *more to judge* of us, 1 John 3 : 20" (HENRY), ver. 26.

43. "Jesus says nothing but what the Father bids him say; therefore should his ministers also preach nothing but what they have learned of him, Rom. 15 : 18" (QUESNEL), Acts 20 : 24.

44. "The plainest things are riddles to those who are resolved to hold fast their prejudices; day and night are alike to the blind" (HENRY), ver. 27; Ezek. 20 : 49.

45. "The cross is the knot in which humiliation and exaltation are entwined. In the cross the deepest humiliation ended; in the cross exaltation began" (BRAUNE), ver. 28; Phil. 2 : 8-11.

46. "Who, except Jesus, ever did or could truly say, 'I always do the things that please him'?"—T. SCOTT. Every day we need our atoning Saviour, ver. 29; 1 John 1 : 8; Gal. 2 : 20.

47. "I wish that when I speak many may believe, not on me, but with me on him" (AUSTIN, in *Henry*), ver. 30; 1 Cor. 9 : 19-22.

48. "At their entrance into his school he lays down this rule, that he will own none for *his disciples* but those that *continue in his word*" (HENRY), ver. 31; John 15 : 7-10; Col. 1 : 23.

49 "Did we not need to *be taught*, we should not need to *be disciples.*" "Christ's scholars are sure to be well taught" (HENRY), John 14 : 26 ; 16 : 12-14.

50. "It is a very great privilege *to know the truth;* ... to know what is truth, and what proves it to be so" (HENRY), ver. 32; John 16 : 13, 14.

51. "Gospel truth makes us free *from* our spiritual enemies, free *in* the service of God, free *to* the privileges of sons, and the free *of* the Jerusalem above" (HENRY), Gal. 4 : 2-7, 26 ; 5 : 1.

52. "Of what avail is it to have pious parents and ancestors, and not to be pious ourselves? to be of noble blood, but ignoble in soul" (ZEISIUS)? ver. 33 ; Rom. 4 : 12.

53. "A state of sin is a state of bondage."—HENRY. Yet hardened sinners prate of *freedom* while glorying in their self-chosen tasks and their willing bonds! vers. 33, 34; Prov. 14 : 9.

54. "Jesus Christ in the gospel offers us *our freedom;* he has authority and power to *make free*" (HENRY), ver. 36 ; Matt. 11 : 28; Rom. 8 : 2.

55. "As it is common for families that are sinking to boast of their pedigree, so churches that are corrupt and depraved value themselves upon their antiquity and the eminence of their first planters" (HENRY), ver. 39; Luke 3 : 8.

56. All who have God for their Father have a true and abiding love to Christ. "He who loves not Jesus is not born of God, but of the devil" (in LANGE), vers. 41, 42 ; 1 John 3 : 8-10 ; 5 : 1.

57. *Ye cannot hear:* "A wicked, unruly *will* lay at the bottom of this." "As long as a man cannot endure truth he is incapable of faith" (LANGE), ver. 43; Isa. 6 : 9, 10; John 12 : 37-40.

58. *Abode not,* or *stands not.* "Hence the earliest Fathers of the church called the devil an apostate (*apostatēs*). Apostasy from truth leads to the entire loss of truth" (HEUBNER), ver. 44; 2 Thess. 2 : 3, 4, 8-10.

59. "It is the old way of the world to love and hearken to the devil's lies, hypocrisy, and flattery rather than truth" (ZEISIUS), ver. 45; Matt. 24 : 4, 5, 11; John 5 : 43.

60. "A Christian is bound to appeal to his good conscience when his enemies revile and slander him without cause" (LANGE), ver. 46 ; Acts 23 : 1; 24 : 16.

61. "When wicked men are convinced of their wickedness and have nothing to answer, they resort to abuse, invective, and calumny, Acts 6 : 10, 11" (LANGE), ver. 48.

62. "Jesus is the sublimest pattern of meekness."—RAMBACH. Though Moses' example, Num. 12 : 3-13, was excellent, that of Christ surpasses his, ver. 49; Heb. 3 : 5, 6; 7 : 26.

63. "Those who can truly say they make it their constant care to honor God are sufficiently armed against the censures and reproaches of men" (HENRY), 1 Sam. 2 : 30; Ps. 91 : 14.

Jesus on the sabbath heals a blind man; questions by the rulers respecting the miracle and its Author; he is excommunicated for his bold confession.

IX. AND as *Jesus* passed by, he saw a man which was 2 blind from *his* birth. And his disciples asked him,

64. "Perverse world! It honors what is despicable, and despises what is honorable" (LANGE), Mal. 3 : 15; Luke 16 : 15.

65. "The wicked trample the most precious promises under foot, and draw only poison from the fairest flowers of the divine word" (LANGE), ver. 52; Prov. 9 : 7, 8; 23 : 9; Matt. 7 : 6.

66. "Self-honor is no honor, and the affectation of glory is the forfeiture of it" (HENRY), ver. 54; Prov. 25 : 27; 27 : 2; John 5 : 30, 31, 41.

67. "Many *claim kindred* to God who yet have no acquaintance with him." "The best proof of our acquaintance with God is our obedience to him" (HENRY), ver. 55; 1 John 2 : 3, 4.

68. "The longings of gracious souls after Jesus Christ will be fully satisfied when they come to heaven" (HENRY), ver. 56; Ps. 17 : 15; Matt. 13 : 17; Phil. 3 : 20, 21.

69. "God never forsakes any till they have first provoked him to withdraw and will have none of him" (HENRY), ver. 59; Prov. 1 : 23–31; Isa. 65 : 11, 12; Matt. 21 : 41, 43.

CHAPTER IX.

Whether the miracle recorded in this chapter was wrought on the same Sabbath on which Jesus escaped from the angry Jews, as related in the preceding chapter, or took place on a subsequent Sabbath, is a debated question. The opening words, "And as Jesus passed by," seem to connect closely with the close of the preceding verse, "going through the midst of them, and so passed by;" but the genuineness of these last-quoted words is seriously questioned. The calm demeanor of the disciples, and their interest in the problem concerning the connection between sin and suffering when they observe that Jesus is looking at the blind man, do not accord with the excitement into which they must have been thrown by the violence with which their Master had been threatened. Nor would the enraged mob, whose persecuting fury had just driven him into concealment, have suffered him quietly and openly to perform this act of healing in the vicinity of the temple. It seems more probable that this miracle was wrought on a Sabbath near the time of the feast of dedication, about two months later than the feast of tabernacles, at which the Jews attempted to stone Jesus. Compare *Author's Harmony,* ¿ 111. The place where the miracle was wrought was near Jerusalem. The incidents of this chapter are related only by John.

1. **And as Jesus passed by.** The language does not necessarily connect with what precedes. It may mean, On a certain occasion, as he was passing along, etc. **A man which was blind from his birth.** Blindness was then, and is still, a malady of common occurrence in the East. But this was a peculiar case, for the man was "blind from birth;" hence his case was beyond the power of medical skill. Perhaps he was accustomed to proclaim this fact to excite more sympathy and charity from the passers-by. When the disciples noticed that Jesus was regarding him with attention, they thought it a favorable opportunity to ask a question.

2–5. CONVERSATION BETWEEN JESUS AND HIS DISCIPLES CONCERNING THIS BLIND MAN. The disciples take occasion to ask the opinion of their Master upon the perplexing and oft-discussed question concerning the connection between sin and suffering. Christ first corrects their mistaken assumption that all suffering is a punishment for some particular sin, and then teaches them what his mission requires him to do when such cases are presented to him.

2. **Master, who did sin?** This question assumes that special sin is the cause of special suffering. Just as the three friends of Job insisted that his sore afflictions were a sure proof that he had been a great sinner, so the disciples take for granted that this case of blindness is the penalty for some particular

saying, Master, [k] who did sin, this man, or his parents, that he was born blind? Jesus answered, Neither hath this man sinned, nor his parents; [l] but that the works of God should be made manifest in him. [m] I must work the works of him that sent me, while it is

[k] ver. 34; Luke 13. 1-4.
[l] ch. 11. 4.
[m] ch. 4. 34; 5. 19, 36; 11. 9, 10; 12. 35; 17. 4; Eccles. 9. 10; Eph. 5. 16.

transgression. Had blindness come upon him after he reached youth or manhood, there would have been no problem to solve, in their view. But he **was born blind.** Firmly believing that this blindness was the punishment of some particular sin, they were in doubt who was the sinner. They could suggest only two parties—the man himself and his parents. Evidently, it was not satisfactory to ascribe the sin to the man himself, and they hesitated to ascribe it to his parents. Having disagreed among themselves, they propose the question to Christ. This view of the origin of this question, and of the reason why they proposed it to Christ in this form, renders it unnecessary to assume that the disciples were inclined to the heathen doctrine of the transmigration of souls, as some have conjectured, or that they believed in antenatal sin, or that they were wavering between the doctrine of the Greek philosophers, who taught that souls may sin in a pre-existent state, and the teachings of the Jewish rabbis, that the child may bear the punishment of a parent's sin. These disciples can hardly be supposed to have been familiar with these speculations of the schools. Nor does the view of Tholuck seem probable, that they supposed the man to be punished by anticipation for predestined sin. Nothing in the answer of Christ in what follows seems to hint at any such speculative tendencies on the part of the disciples.

3. Neither hath this man sinned, nor his parents. We must supply the words, "that he was born blind," to complete the thought. Manifestly, Jesus does not intend to deny that the blind man was a sinner, nor that his parents had committed sin; but he does deny that this special form of suffering was visited upon him by reason of any special sin on his part or on the part of his parents. This answer of Christ directly contradicts the assumption upon which the question of the disciples was based, that a particular sin is the cause of a particular evil. When this was done, the perplexity was removed. It was unnecessary to pursue the search for a person who had specially sinned in this instance. We are not, however, to make our inference from these words too broad. Children may *suffer* in consequence of the iniquities of their parents, and thus the iniquities of the fathers may be visited upon the children. But this is quite different from saying that one person is *punished* for the sin of another. Compare Jer. 32:18 and Ezek 18:20. But while we may not say the a man is a great sinner because he is a great sufferer, the general doctrine is true that suffering comes in consequence of sin. **That the works of God should be made manifest.** "The *works of God* here meant are primarily his saving, redeeming works."—STIER. Christ turns the attention of his disciples to a new aspect of the case. In stead of groping back into the hidden mysteries of the divine purposes, and striving to trace the connection between sin and suffering, they were to look forward and see what the mercy and grace of God would accomplish. This man's blindness was the divinely-ordained means of bringing him in contact with Christ. He was to receive eyesight, and with it the blessing of salvation. His bodily infirmity was one of the prearranged conditions of obtaining spiritual eyesight. More than this—it would furnish an opportunity for Christ to give a new proof that he is the Light of the world.

4. I must work. The true text reads, *We must work.* Thus Christ associates his disciples with himself in the obligation to perform duty whenever opportunity offered. Since the enmity of the Jews was daily becoming more bitter, the healing of this man on the Sabbath would furnish fresh occasion for malignant accusations, and so the disciples may have wished that Jesus should hasten from the scene of peril. He tells them that he *must* execute his commission, and even in face of danger

5 day; the night cometh, when no man can work. As long as I am in the world, ⁿI am the light of the world. • ch. 1. 5, 9; 3. 19; 8. 12; 12. 35, 46 Isa. 49. 6; 60. 1.
6 When he had thus spoken, ᵒhe spat on the ground, and made clay of the spittle, and he anointed the eyes of the blind man with the clay, and said unto • Mark 7. 33; 8. 23; Rev. 3. 18.
7 him, Go, wash ᵖin the pool of Siloam (which is by interpretation, Sent). ᵠHe went his way therefore, and washed, and came seeing. ᵖ Neh. 3. 15, *Siloah*. ᵠ 2 Kings 5. 10–14.

do what has been assigned to him. **While it is day; the night cometh.** *Day* is the period of work, *night* the time for cessation from labor. Every man has his *day* of opportunity, but when *night* comes these opportunities cease. Christ was under the same law. He had an allotted time for his personal ministry, and was under obligation to work while it continued. Already night was drawing near. Some have found a difficulty in the application of these words to Christ, because his work of salvation did not cease with his death. They attempt to give this proverbial expression too broad an application. It simply states that every man has a day for labor. If he neglects it, he cannot accomplish his task after his night comes. Christ himself had his work as a man, which he must do before he laid down his life. For *this* work his opportunity would cease when death came.

5. I am the light of the world. Truth is aptly compared to light. Benevolence and mercy with equal propriety may be called light. Christ, while personally among men, was the great source of this heavenly light, and hence himself made it *day* for the world. As he was about to open the eyes of a blind man, it was fitting that he should make this declaration. Since he was the Sun, appointed to give light to those who sit in darkness, he would rescue this beggar from the gloom of the night in which he had thus far lived. It was a work of mercy, and it forms a fitting illustration of giving sight to those who are spiritually blind. Compare Isa. 35: 5.

6, 7. SIGHT GIVEN TO THE BLIND MAN. Having spoken these words, Jesus now performs the miracle. The blind man, despised on account of his infirmity, called a sinner by the Pharisees, who passed by him, must have listened with eager interest to the words, "Neither hath this man sinned, nor his parents." They had doubtless won his heart and prepared him for prompt obedience.

6. Spat on the ground, and made clay. In ancient times a medicinal value was attributed to the saliva. Christ employed it in other instances, Mark 8: 23 and 7: 33. But we are not to imagine that our Lord used the saliva or the clay as *remedies*. There was no inherent virtue in them to give sight to this man. The man had been attracted to Jesus by his kind words, and may have had awakened in his heart a faint hope that God's purpose, of which Jesus had spoken, was now to be accomplished in him. But he must in some way be made sensible of a personal contact with Jesus, who came to work the works of God—who is the Light of the world. Jesus chose this method to bring the man into a direct contact with his power. He used the anointing with clay as the channel through which to communicate the blessing. Thus he aided and strengthened the new-born faith and hope of the man.

7. Go, wash in the pool of Siloam. This pool is mentioned under the name Siloah in Neh. 3: 15 and Shiloah, Isa. 8: 6. It was south-east of Jerusalem, and its site is undisputed. Its length is fifty-three feet and its breadth eighteen, according to Robinson. Its full depth was nineteen feet, but it usually contained only three or four feet. Compare DR. FISH's *Bible Lands Illustrated*, pp. 227–229. To this pool the blind man was told to go and wash his eyes, not because there was any medicinal virtue in the waters, but as a test of his faith. No reason was given; he was to do it simply because Jesus commanded it. Yet John seems to suggest that there was a reason,

8 The neighbors therefore, and they which before had seen him that he was blind, said, Is not this he
9 that sat and begged? Some said, This is he; others
10 said, He is like him; but he said, I am he. Therefore said they unto him, How were thine eyes opened?
11 He answered and said, ʳ A man that is called Jesus   ʳ vers. 6, 7.

or at least a fitness in sending the man to this pool, for he adds, **which is by interpretation, Sent.** This is the meaning of the name Siloam. Its Hebrew form, which appears in Isaiah *Shiloah*, is derived from *shalach*, "to send." Why this name was given to it we need not inquire. In Isaiah "the waters of Shiloah that go softly" are used to image forth the divine blessings that came upon Israel like the gentle flow of an unfailing stream. It was peculiarly appropriate that the waters thus employed in the prophet's discourse should bear the name **Sent,** a designation of Christ—the One sent to bless and save. Compare Heb. 3 : 1, where the word *apostle*, another form of the word here translated *sent*, is applied to Christ. It was fitting that this man should receive sight by washing in those waters so intimately associated in the mind of the devout Jew with God's gracious blessings. "The healing virtue imparted to the water is to be denoted as symbolical of him *who was sent*, and whose mission it was to give the healing water of life."—ALFORD. The prompt obedience of the man, as well as his immediate cure, showed his faith. He raised no objections and exhibited no reluctance, and hence the happy result: **He went his way therefore, and washed, and came seeing.**

8–12. DISCUSSION OF NEIGHBORS WITH EACH OTHER AND WITH THE MAN HIMSELF. The account of the conversations of this man's neighbors and acquaintances concerning this event is so true to life, so minute and distinct, that we feel at liberty to conjecture that the evangelist must have heard it from the man who was healed; his testimony was direct, positive, and frank.

8. The neighbors. From this verse it appears that the man did not return to our Lord, but went from the pool to his own home. So marvellous a change in his appearance excited much discussion among his acquaintances. Instead of reading **that he was blind,** the best critical authorities read, *that he was a beggar.* He now abandoned that occupation, and this circumstance first attracted notice. The reason of it was readily learned: he had received sight. Hence their first question, **Is not this he that sat and begged?** implying what he was accustomed to do. It is the change in his conduct that is first observed. And this is what the world usually notices first in those to whom spiritual eyesight is given. And such a change occasions debate, as in this case.

9. **Some said, This is he; others said, He is like him;** opinions differed. These people were under the influence of the Pharisees, and had the fear of censure if they should too enthusiastically confess that Jesus had wrought a miracle on the Sabbath. The more frank and candid portion of them asserted the identity of this man with the beggar whom they had known. The more timid and sceptical admitted that he bore a strong resemblance to the beggar, but doubted his identity. How has human ingenuity taxed its powers of invention to discover some plausible explanation of what Christ does, without admitting his divine power! In this instance the man's own explicit statement, **I am he,** ended the debate among the common people.

10, 11. **How were thine eyes opened?** When the question of identity . is settled, they begin to inquire how the cure was effected. He replies by narrating the facts. In the clause, **he answered and said,** the best authorities omit **and said. A man that is called Jesus.** He cautiously refrains from expressing any opinion concerning the character and mission of his benefactor at this time, and contents himself with a simple and artless statement of the facts. Whether this caution in reference to the Messiahship of Jesus arose from a prudent desire to avoid controversy, or from a

made clay, and anointed mine eyes, and said unto me, Go to the pool of Siloam, and wash; and I went
12 and washed, and I received sight. Then said they unto him, Where is he? He said, I know not.
13 They brought to the Pharisees him that aforetime
14 was blind. And *it was the sabbath day when Jesus   * ch 5. 9.

want of settled conviction in his own mind, is not clearly apparent. We are not informed what his previous opportunities for a knowledge of Christ had been. He does not appear desirous to put himself forward. He was an intelligent, thoughtful observer, not hasty in forming opinions, but positive in his convictions when once formed. We should infer that he had not yet become fully settled in the belief of the Messiahship of Jesus, but was in a teachable and inquiring frame of mind.

12. **Where is he?** This is the next question on the part of the people. They do not seem to have been ill-disposed toward the man or toward Jesus. They do not suggest any cavils concerning the reality of the miracle, nor does it appear that they had any hostile purpose against Jesus in making this inquiry. But they were under the influence of the Pharisees; they knew that this miracle had been done on the Sabbath, and that the Pharisees regarded such works as a violation of the law of the Sabbath. Respect for their religious teachers, combined with interested curiosity, moved them to refer this examination to the Pharisees. The man's answer to the inquiry where Jesus is was, **I know not.** From the pool of Siloam he had gone directly to his home. At the time when Jesus sent him to this pool, Jesus himself was going to some place with his disciples. He was "passing by," and only stopped to perform this act of mercy. Hence the man had no means of knowing where Jesus was at this time.

13 17. THE FIRST EXAMINATION BEFORE THE JEWISH AUTHORITIES. We are not to assume that all which is related in this chapter occurred in a single day. This examination may not have taken place on the same day on which the man received sight. It had already been decided that any one who acknowledged Christ should be excommunicated (ver. 22). This fact made the people timid in assuming any responsibility. Hence they deemed it prudent to bring this case before the rulers. It is generally supposed that it was not the great council, composed of seventy members, but a minor council, said to have twenty-three members, before whom this man was brought. This lesser Sanhedrim is mentioned by the Talmud, but not by Josephus, and held its meetings on Mondays and Thursdays. Hostility to Christ was predominant among all the leading men, though there were a few individuals, like Nicodemus and Joseph of Arimathea, who in heart were favorably disposed toward him. An unprejudiced investigation was not to be expected from the members of this council.

13. **Brought to the Pharisees;** literally, *They bring,* etc. The word *Pharisees* here means the leading men of that sect, just as the term "Jews" in verse 18 and elsewhere in John means the chief men of the nation, and not the whole people. The Sanhedrim was not composed entirely of Pharisees, but they were the most numerous and influential party in this body, and the bitterest enemies of our Lord. **Him that aforetime was blind.** These words show that the people were convinced of the reality of the miracle—that the question presented to the rulers was not concerning the identity of this man, though something like that question was subsequently raised by the council, but concerning the time and manner of performing the cure.

14. **It was the sabbath day when Jesus made the clay.** Because this miracle was wrought on the Sabbath, it seemed questionable to the people. They knew of the complaints of the Pharisees on former occasions because Jesus had performed cures on the Sabbath. Compare ch. 5: 16; Mark 3: 4; Luke 13: 14. In this instance the Saviour *made clay,* he did *work,* on the Sabbath. This certainly was a small criticism, but these Pharisees were noted for fine-spun distinctions and pretentious quibbles. It

15 made the clay, and opened his eyes. Then again the Pharisees also asked him how he had received his sight. He said unto them, He put clay upon mine 16 eyes, and I washed, and do see. Therefore said some of the Pharisees, ᵗ This man is not of God, because he keepeth not the sabbath day. Others said, ᵘ How can a man that is a sinner do such miracles? And ˣ there 17 was a division among them. They say unto the blind man again, What sayest thou of him, that he hath opened thine eyes? He said, ʸ He is a prophet.

ᵗ ver. 24.
ᵘ vers. 30–33; ch. 3. 2.
ˣ ch. 7. 42, 43; 10. 19.
ʸ ch. 4. 19; 6. 14.

furnished the enemies of Christ with a pretext for their accusation. The more unreasonable it was, the more confidently they asserted their charge.

15. **Then again.** The question that had been asked by his neighbors is repeated by the Pharisees. Doubtless those who brought the man hither reported the conversation that had been held with him. But the rulers chose to hear the story from the man's own lips, hoping to detect something that would give them an opportunity to accuse Christ. In asking him **how he had received his sight**, they by implication admit the miracle. He answers them by a simple statement of the facts: **He put clay upon mine eyes**, etc. Meyer calls attention to the fact that the man omits all mention of the saliva, and testifies only to what he *felt*. At the time he could not see what Jesus did. He is careful not to state anything except what he actually knew.

16. The answer leads to a discussion among the Pharisees themselves. The incontrovertible fact which the man stated, **I . . . do see**, admitted of no dispute. The party, bitterly hostile to Christ, at once exclaim, **This man is not of**, or *from*, **God**. It would seem as if they were replying to their own inward convictions, for no one had then suggested anything concerning the divine mission of Jesus. They appear to introduce the name of God with reverence, but speak contemptuously of Jesus as *this man*. It was no satisfaction to them that a sufferer had been relieved, but it stirred their malignant hate that Jesus had given another illustration of his divine authority. On the reason which they give see note on verse 14. There were some more conscientious judges present, who asked, **How can a man that is a sinner do**

such miracles? These men were in the minority. They seem to speak with timidity, simply suggesting that such miracles as this show at least that the man is not a sinner. If there were any Sadducees present, they may have sided with the more candid minority for the purpose of making a division in the ranks of their theological opponents, the Pharisees. Evidently, the debate waxed somewhat warm, as the **division**, or *schism*, **among them** shows. This circumstance certainly gave the man who had been healed more courage to speak his honest convictions at a later stage of the investigation, for he saw that his examiners were not of one mind. Yet so small a minority, composed of timid men, would soon be silenced by the arrogant and determined majority. Logic, however forcible, never convinces prejudiced and unscrupulous adversaries. Bitter partisans never weigh evidence or argument honestly and candidly.

17. **They say,** etc.; according to the oldest manuscripts, *They say, therefore.* The discussion of conflicting opinions by members of the council was unseemly and embarrassing. If it appeared that Jesus had advocates and defenders in that body, what would these spectators think who had brought this man there? Evidently, they had been intimidated by the Pharisaic teachers, so that they feared to put faith in Jesus; but the potent spell of this influence would be dissolved if the Sanhedrim was divided in opinion. *Therefore* they turn to the blind man with the question, **What sayest thou of him, that he hath opened thine eyes?** Conant translates the last clause, *seeing that he opened thine eyes?* The word **thou** is specially emphatic in the Greek. It is not two questions, but a single one, ad-

18 But the Jews *did not believe concerning him, that *Isa. 26. 11.
he had been blind, and received his sight, until they
called the parents of him that had received his sight.
19 And they asked them, saying, Is this your son, who
ye say was born blind? How then doth he now see?

dressed to the man as if they thought his opinion of importance. It was designed to throw him off his guard, so that he would be betrayed into some imprudent or rash expression. Thus they would check the debate among themselves by provoking a controversy with him. He was too clear-headed and self-possessed to be caught in their artifice. He was ready with an answer: **He is a prophet,** one who is endued with power and sent with a message from God. He seems not yet to have reached the full conviction that Jesus is the Son of God, the Messiah, but he is persuaded that he is one sent by divine authority. He boldly and manfully stated his belief. His answer brought upon him the hostility of those who had just asserted "This man is not of God;" but they could not then condemn the man for believing Jesus to be a prophet.

18-23. THE EXAMINATION OF THE PARENTS OF THE BLIND MAN. Baffled in their efforts to weaken the evidence of a miracle by questioning the subject of the cure, the enemies of Christ now turn to the parents of the man, hoping to prove that he was not really born blind, and that a deception had been practised upon the people. The parents are too honest to deny that their son was born blind, but too timid to say anything in favor of his benefactor. Thus this device avails nothing.

18. **The Jews,** rather, *The Jews therefore.* See note on verse 13. The same party which above is called the Pharisees is here designated *the Jews.* Perhaps more persons were at this time taken into the consultation. The leading men of the nation are here referred to, but by the term "Jews" John seems to mean also that they were opposers of Christ. Incidentally, we may notice that this peculiar use of the word *Jew* shows that this Gospel was written when the word had come to mean an enemy of Christ as well as a descendant of Jacob. At least in the latter part of the apostolic age this was the use of the term among Christians. **Did not believe concerning him, that he had been blind.** The attempt to cast odium on Jesus by the accusation of Sabbath-breaking had not been successful. His enemies now endeavor to discredit the miracle. Had they proceeded systematically, this would naturally have been the first point investigated. Evidently, they did not think at first of questioning the reality of the miracle; but when they saw that if the miracle was admitted the charge of violating the Sabbath could not be sustained, they must either show that a fraud had been committed or give up their accusation. Few persons could be induced to believe that an open violator of God's law would be empowered to show such signs of divine authority. **Until they called the parents.** The inquiry has been made whether these words imply that the Jews were convinced of the miracle after they had taken the testimony of the parents. It is sufficient to reply that they failed to find any testimony to countenance their theory of fraud. As a matter of fact they had no reason to suspect any deception, but having needlessly invented such a theory, they signally failed to establish it. Unintentionally they have done Christianity a service. They have shown that the most searching scrutiny of bitter foes was unable to find any flaw in the evidence which attested the reality and truthfulness of the miracle.

19. Three questions are really addressed to the parents, though no opportunity was given to make answer until all the inquiries had been propounded. Putting them in legal form, the questions would be: 1. Is this your son? 2. Was he born blind? 3. How did he recover his sight? The careful reader will notice that the first and second inquiries are blended together, and language is used which seems designed to intimidate the parents. **Is this your son, who ye say was born blind?** The manner of putting the question, the insertion of the words

20 His parents answered them and said, We know that
21 this is our son, and that he was born blind: but by what means he now seeth, we know not; or who hath opened his eyes, we know not. He is of age; ask him; he shall speak for himself.
22 These *words* spake his parents, because ᵃ they feared the Jews; for the Jews had agreed already, that if any man did confess that he was Christ, he ᵇ should
23 be put out of the synagogue. Therefore said his parents, He is of age; ask him.

ᵃ ch. 7. 13; 19. 38;
Prov. 29. 25;
Matt. 10. 26, 28;
Acts 5. 13.
ᵇ ver. 34; ch. 12 42; 16. 2.

who ye say, shows that the interrogators would have been glad to awe them into a denial of the blindness of their son at birth, or at least into an admission that his case was not as bad as had been represented. The answer to the last question would depend upon the answer to this. It was intended to make them feel that the last and main question would be embarrassing to answer if they continued to assert the blindness of their son from the first.

20. The crafty plans of wicked men do not always succeed. The parents decline to be accomplices in fraud or falsehood. They give explicit answers to the two points involved in the first inquiry. **We know that this is our son.** This is a positive and indisputable evidence. They were just as explicit on the next point, that he was born blind. These parents were honest. It has been suggested that they were beggars also, but there is no proof of this. Doubtless they were in humble circumstances, or their blind son would not have been compelled to resort to begging.

21. **By what means he now seeth, we know not.** The shrewd Pharisaic lawyers were matched by shrewd witnesses. These persons were not present when the eyes of their son were opened, but they had heard him tell the story. In the common acceptation of the term they *did know* by what means his eyes were opened. But the tribunal before which they were examined could not demand of them any hearsay evidence, any statement beyond what they knew from direct personal observation. Evidently, these inquisitors perceived that these witnesses understood their privileges, and therefore the questions were not pressed. But why do they add the words, **or who hath opened his eyes, we know not?** If their reticence was only due to a scrupulous regard for their duty as witnesses, why were they so forward to disclaim all knowledge of the benefactor of their son? It is in this statement especially that their timidity appears. "They lack strength to prove their gratitude for the healing of their son by uniting their testimony to his."—LANGE. It is not for any want of respect to the Jewish tribunal that they are censured, but for their lack of moral courage, their selfish caution, their great anxiety to disavow all knowledge of Jesus, who had blessed them in the person of their child. **He is of age; ask him.** It is stated by some authorities that the Jews allowed a person to testify at the age of thirteen. This person had evidently reached full manhood. This is implied in the expression *of age*, and is apparent from what he said and did. His parents admired his courage, though they did not imitate it. They had confidence in his ability to state his own case, but they do not wish to become involved with him in the controversy.

22, 23. **Because they feared the Jews.** The evangelist gives this explanation of the conduct of these parents. What power of intimidation these enemies of Christ had may be inferred from ch. 12 : 42, from which it appears that even men of rank and influence were awed into a suppression of their honest convictions. **Had agreed already.** This does not seem to mean that a public formal decree had been passed by the Sanhedrim, yet it was more than an agreement among private individuals. Lange suggests that it refers to "a regulation made by the Jews in Jerusalem concerning excommunication from the synagogue." Confess

24 Then again called they the man that was blind, and said unto him, ᵉGive God the praise; ᵈwe know 25 that this man is a sinner. He answered and said, Whether he be a sinner *or no,* I know not; ᵉone thing I know, that, whereas I was blind, now I see.

ᶜJosh.7.19; 1 Sam 6. 5.
ᵈ ver. 16.
ᵉ Eph. 2. 1-10; 5 8; 1 John 3. 14 5. 10.

that he was Christ—that is, openly *acknowledge* him as the Messiah, the Anointed One promised in ancient prophecy. This was equivalent to becoming an avowed disciple of his. **Should be put out of the synagogue.** A majority of commentators hold that there were three degrees of excommunication: (1) *Seclusion* from the congregation for thirty days, in which the person was required to keep at a distance of four cubits at least from his friends and acquaintances. He might approach the door of the temple or synagogue, but was not allowed to participate in the worship. If at the expiration of this period the person continued obstinate, it could be extended. (2) The *curse,* to which severer penalties were attached. The offender was prohibited from teaching or being taught in company with others. He could not hire or be hired; he could neither sell nor buy, except to purchase the necessaries of life. In addition, a solemn malediction was pronounced upon him. (3) A final and total *separation* from the congregation, in which curses from earth and Heaven were invoked upon the offender. Some have maintained that the second and third degrees cannot well be distinguished from each other. It will be seen that one who had incurred the first form of excommunication, if he continued obstinate, would come under the second form. Thus, those who were put out of the synagogue became social outcasts; their friends were alienated from them, and their lives made dreary and bitter. The parents of the man who had been blind shrank from the danger of incurring any of these hardships, and therefore they avoided any expression that could be construed as a confession of Jesus as Christ.

24-27. THE SECOND EXAMINATION OF THE MAN WHO HAD BEEN BLIND. He was probably required to be absent while his parents were examined; but since nothing had been gained by questioning them, another attempt was made with him. His inquisitors endeavor to influence his statements by a decided expression of their own opinion, but the result is to make him firmer and bolder in declaring his own convictions.

24. **Give God the praise,** or *glory.* Some make this phrase to mean *Praise God for thy cure,* and refer to 1 Sam. 6: 5; Jer. 13 : 16; Luke 17 : 18. Others regard it as a solemn form of appeal to a witness to tell the truth. Compare the words addressed to Achan, Josh. 7 : 19. It was reminding him that he stood in the presence of God, and that reverence for his sacred Majesty should move him to speak the truth and attempt no further concealment. Such were these words in the mouth of Joshua, but in the mouths of these Pharisees they would have been hypocritical mockery, a blasphemous farce. **We know.** As much as to say, "We have probed this matter and ascertained the real facts." It was a bold attempt to browbeat the man and draw from him something unfavorable to Christ. **That this man is a sinner.** This is their opinion, and by so confidently stating it they hope to influence the man to speak ill of his benefactor. The impression they would convey is that they had gained important evidence from his parents. The man himself had not been allowed to know what his parents said. The dishonesty and malignity of these Jewish rulers, and their perversion of the forms of justice, cannot be characterized in too strong terms.

25. **Whether he be a sinner, . . . I know not.** Observe the caution and discretion of the man. The rulers had said, "*We know* that this man is a sinner." He is too sagacious to contradict them flatly. Hence he declines squarely to join issue with them on the question whether Jesus is a sinner, or to dispute the opinion of these learned teachers. We are not at liberty to press his language so far as to make him admit that Jesus might be a sinner. He evidently intended to make no such admission. He only designed to avoid a debate

26 Then said they to him again, What did he to thee? 27 how opened he thine eyes? He answered them, ʳI have told you already, and ye did not hear; wherefore would ye hear *it* again? Will ye also be his disciples? 28 Then ᵍ they reviled him, and said, Thou art his disciple; but we are Moses' disciples. ʰ We know that

ʳ vers. 10-15; Luke 22. 67.

ᵍ Matt. 5. 11; 1 Pet. 4. 14.
ʰ Num. 12. 2-8; Deut. 34. 10.

upon the intricate and confusing subtleties of the scribes, and to remain steadfastly upon the firm ground of common sense and known facts. Waiving all debate on their opinion, he tells them, **one thing I know, that, whereas I was blind, now I see.** This was a fact quite independent of their authority. His bold, unequivocal statement of it thwarted their plan of drawing from him any declaration that would make Christ appear to be a deceiver. This utterance "is rightly taken as a model for all who have been enlightened through Jesus."—STIER. " He will speak the thing that he does know, and let them draw their own conclusions." —TRENCH.

26. Then said they to him. His inquisitors, foiled in their effort to prove any deception on the part of Jesus, now require him to repeat the story of his cure, hoping to detect some contradiction to his former statement, or to find something which they can use as an accusation against Christ; or they may have done this with no definite purpose except to gain time in which to devise some new plan of procedure.

27. I have told you already, and ye did not hear. Their evident malignity and want of candor roused the indignation of the man. He had come before them simply to state the truth, and they wished him to dishonor his manhood, violate his sense of justice, and deny all sentiments of gratitude. His soul revolted against their vile plot. He could no longer patiently submit to their inquisitorial scrutiny. His manhood asserts itself, and he gives them to understand that further questioning is useless. Ye were not willing to accept my statement before; **wherefore would ye hear it again?** The man uses few words, but they are keen and incisive. He pushes them with a question that cut to the quick: **Will ye also be his disciples?** In the use of the word *also* Chrysostom de-

tected a virtual admission that he himself was already a disciple at heart. With mingled humor and irony he inquires of these men if they wish him to repeat his story again because they are inclined to become disciples with him. Nothing could have stung them more sorely than the suggestion of such a suspicion. It ended their examination and brought the matter to an immediate issue. "God gave to this poor man grace and strength to make a bold confession of the truth and completely to confound his subtle examiners."— BARNES.

28, 29. THE ANGRY REPROACHES OF THE RULERS. These examiners can no longer restrain their wrath. They were mortified that this humble man, by his sharp-witted replies, had overmatched them in every instance. They were specially embittered because he had presumed to speak as if he suspected them of a favorable disposition toward Christ. They lost control of their passions and burst forth in reproaches.

28. They reviled him; a common procedure on the part of men in a bad cause when argument fails them. John has not recorded the harsh epithets which they used, nor would it be of interest to us to know them. **Thou art his disciple; but we are Moses' disciples.** As on previous occasions, they set Moses over against Christ, as if the teaching of the one were contrary to the other. Probably they intend to intimate that being healed on the Sabbath rendered this man a participant in the Sabbath-breaking of which they accused Christ, while they were zealous observers of the law of Moses concerning the Sabbath. They did not realize that they were incurring the curse which Moses denounced upon all who should refuse to listen to Jesus, the Prophet whom Moses foretold, Deut. 18 : 18, 19.

29. We know that God spake

God spake unto Moses; as for this *fellow*, ¹we know 30 not from whence he is. The man answered and said unto them, ᵏ Why herein is a marvellous thing, that ye know not from whence he is, and *yet* he hath 31 opened mine eyes. Now we know that ¹God heareth not sinners; but if any man be a worshipper of God,

¹ ch. 7. 27; 8. 14.
ᵏ ch. 3. 10; 12. 37.
¹ Job 27. 8, 9; 35. 12; Ps. 34. 15; Prov. 15. 29; Zech. 7. 13.

unto Moses. In this they were correct. God did speak to Moses; and had they been honest and true disciples of Moses, they would have acknowledged Christ. Compare ch. 5 : 43–47; 6 : 30–32, where they boast of Moses and his miracles. They do not venture to say, as the Pharisees had before said, that Jesus was in league with the prince of demons. Compare Matt. 9 : 34. **As for this fellow.** It is not certain that they intended to express so much contempt as our translation implies. There is no word in the original corresponding to "fellow." It is more accurate to render *this man.* The rulers evidently were becoming a little cautious in their expressions. Their sharp encounters with this man constrained them to be a little guarded, Just before they confidently *knew this man* to be a sinner; now they *know not* whence he is. They *feel* just as much contempt, but are more careful in avowing it. They *insinuate* that Jesus may have derived his extraordinary powers of healing from demons, but they only *say* that there is no evidence that he came from above. We shall see how much they gain in the debate by this modification of their tactics.

30–34. THE FINAL REPLY OF THE MAN TO THE JEWS, AND HIS EXCOMMUNICATION. In giving way to anger the rulers exposed themselves to the crushing blow which their keen-sighted and self possessed adversary aimed at them. He was neither slow nor hesitating in using his advantage. Beaten in debate, they resort to the weapon of tyrants, and excommunicate him.

30. **Herein is a marvellous thing.** Some translate *in respect to this man*, instead of "herein." The Greek admits of either translation; but on the whole the common version seems the more appropriate in the connection, as the majority of critics think. It was wonderful that these men, the teachers of the people, should have so much perplexity in this case. **And yet he hath opened mine eyes.** This was the undoubted fact which all of their investigations had failed to set aside. From this uncontradicted evidence of his divine mission these men could come to no conclusion with all their skill in reasoning and their knowledge of divine truth. Here is certainly a thrust at their pretensions which they must have felt.

31. **Now we know that God heareth not sinners.** Since the rulers confessed themselves unable to come to a decision, this man proposed to give them his mode of reasoning in this instance. The term *sinners* is here used in the same sense as in verse 24, when these Pharisees said, "We know that this man is a *sinner*"—that is, an open and known transgressor. It is only in this specific and emphatic sense of the term that this proposition would be admitted. The word *hear* must be understood in the sense of *favorably regard* or *answer.* Jesus in some instances prayed in connection with working miracles. Elijah prayed that the rain might be withheld, James 5 : 17, 18. To the well-known truth that the miracles of former times were evidences of answered prayer, reference is here made. God will not answer, and thus honor open offenders of his law. Compare Ps. 66 : 18; Prov. 28 : 9; Isa. 1 : 15. With the express declarations of Scripture before them that God will not hear the prayers of the openly wicked or those wicked in heart, the rulers could not assert that an impostor would be able to do such a miracle as this. On the other hand, **if any man be a worshipper of God, and doeth his will, him he heareth.** Such passages as "the eyes of the Lord are upon the righteous, and his ears are open unto their cry" (Ps. 34 : 15) clearly establish this proposition. These general principles concerning the manner in which God deals with the prayers of men cannot be questioned.

A. D. 29.   JOHN IX.   179

32 ᵐand doeth his will, ⁿhim he heareth. Since the
world began was it not heard that any man opened
33 the eyes of one that was born blind. ᵒIf this man
34 were not of God, he could do nothing. They answered
and said unto him, ᵖThou wast altogether born in sins,
and dost thou teach us? ᵠAnd they cast him out.
35 Jesus heard that they had cast him out; ʳand when
he had found him, he said unto him, Dost thou be-

ᵐ ch. 7. 17.
ⁿ 1 Kings 17. 20-22; 18. 36-38; 2 Chron. 30. 20, 21; Ps. 99. 6; Heb. 11. 6.
ᵒ ver. 16; ch. 3. 2.
ᵖ ver. 2; Isa. 65. 5.
ᵠ ver. 22.
ʳ ch. 5. 14; Ps. 27. 10.

32. **Since the world began was it not heard**—that is, *it was never heard*—that any man opened the eyes of one that was born blind. If these rulers had been able to cite an instance, they would have done it. Here, then, was the fact that Christ had accomplished what had never before been done in the history of the race. It was a miracle, and more— such a miracle as neither Moses nor any of the prophets had wrought. Did bringing water from the rock prove that Moses was a prophet? Did the raising of the widow's son prove Elijah to be a man of God? What, then, is the conclusion to be drawn in view of this wonderful work? Could Jesus be an impostor? Had these rulers, who pretended to be able to distinguish between a false and a true prophet, any reason for saying that they were unable to determine whence Jesus was?

33. **If this man were not of God, he could do nothing**; that is, was not a *prophet*, as he had before stated in ver. 17. It needs an encounter with opposition to bring some men out decidedly. A lover of truth, of a cautious, modest nature, will have his soul stirred and roused by such injustice, equivocation, and hypocrisy as these Jews showed. He will be impelled and constrained to speak out decidedly.

34. His adversaries have no arguments to offer in reply. They were indignant that the man whom they had attempted to inveigle into giving false testimony or to entrap in contradictions should give them such a lesson in honesty and truth. And so they reproach him for his misfortunes. **Thou wast altogether born in sins.** His imperfection of body was, in their view, a mark of a deformed soul. Thus he was *altogether*, in body and in soul, born in sins. For such a man to teach them was the height of presumption and arrogance. If these men could not maintain themselves in the debate, they certainly knew how to abuse and revile one who opposed them. Trench well remarks: "It is characteristic enough that they forget that the two charges—one that he had never been blind, and so was an impostor, the other that he bore the mark of God's anger in a blindness which reached back to his birth—will not agree together." **And they cast him out.** See note on vers. 22, 23. It is believed by some that they inflicted on him the first degree of excommunication, since it appears from what follows that he was not wholly cut off from social intercourse. Others think that he was violently thrust out of the audience-hall at this time, and that afterward, at a regular meeting of the Sanhedrim, they proceeded to pass sentence upon him. Thus by the arbitrary exercise of authority the rulers sought to hinder men from confessing Christ. Compare Pharisaic violence in ch. 11 : 43, 47.

35-38. THE PERSECUTED MAN'S INTERVIEW WITH JESUS. The report that the rulers had cast out this healed man spread rapidly. Jesus found him and drew from him a full confession of faith, and accepted his homage.

35. **Jesus heard.** Evidently the action of the rulers caused no little excitement in the community, and through some of his disciples Jesus heard of it. So when John the Baptist was beheaded the report was carried to Jesus (Matt. 14 : 12). Thus the trials of all his disciples are brought to the Master. **When he had found him.** Now that the man is persecuted, the Saviour finds him, searches him out, just as he does all his followers. **Dost thou believe on the Son of God?** It was more

JOHN IX.   A. D. 29.

36 lieve on ᵃthe Son of God? He answered and said, ᵃ ch. 10. 36; Matt. 14. 33; 16. 16; Mark 1. 1; 1 John 5. 13.
37 Who is he, Lord, that I might believe on him? And Jesus said unto him, Thou hast both seen him, and
38 ᵇit is he that talketh with thee. And he said, Lord, ᵇ ch. 4. 26; Ps. 25. 8, 9, 14.
 I believe. And he worshipped him.
39 And Jesus said, ⁿFor judgment I am come into this ⁿ ch. 3. 17; 5. 22, 27; 12. 47; Luke 2. 34; 2 Cor. 2. 16.

common for Christ to style himself "the Son of man," and such is the reading of some ancient documents; but the most approved reading is, *the Son of God*, which he also claimed to be. It needed only such a confession from this man to show that he had received *spiritual* eyesight and was in heart a disciple. Hence the question in this form. The Messiah of ancient prophecy is a divine being. Comp. Ps. 45 : 6 and Heb. 1 : 8. But the great body of the Jews did not look for such a Messiah. See Smith's *Dict. of Bible*, art. "Son of God;" see also on ch. 1 : 34. The healed man recognized in Jesus a prophet from God; would he also confess him to be the real Messiah of ancient prophecy, the Immanuel, the Son of God?

36. **Who is he, Lord, that I might believe?** This was the first time that this man had actually *seen* Jesus. He had heard his voice and had heard of him. He knew that he was sent from God, and he was ready to listen to any instruction from his lips. But the same calm, self-possessed intelligence which he exhibited in his examination before the Pharisees is apparent here. He must understand to whom this designation, "the Son of God," applies. He may have felt in his heart that it belongs to Jesus, but he knows his own ignorance, and he desires to be instructed, that he may have an intelligent faith. Hence he asks this question before he makes answer to the question of Jesus.

37. **It is he that talketh with thee.** As in the case of the Samaritan woman Jesus plainly declared himself to be the Messiah (ch. 4 : 26), so to this man he declares himself to be the Son of God. Thus the man whom the Jews cast out of the synagogue was permitted both to see and listen to the Son of God—an honor that vastly counterbalanced the reproach which had been heaped upon him.

38. His reply is prompt. **Lord, I believe.** The simple word of Jesus was enough for him. He acted as well as professed. **He worshipped him.** It was not a simple expression of reverence for a great man that he offered, but adoring worship for Jesus as the Son of God. So the connection plainly shows. And Jesus accepted that worship; for, beyond a doubt, he taught this man to believe in his divinity. Here, then, is an instance where Jesus accepted the homage that belongs to God only. It cannot be said that this man misconstrued the words of Christ, for he evidently was an honest inquirer for the truth, and Jesus would not have allowed a mistake on such a vital point to pass uncorrected. The last record of the man born blind is his full confession of faith and his act of worship.

39-41. CHRIST'S WORDS OF REBUKE TO THE PHARISEES. The discourse of which these words form the introduction ends at verse 18 of the next chapter. The interview of Christ with the man who had been healed may have been private, but the conversation of Christ with him would attract attention and draw others around them. Stier suggests that we must assume an interval of time and a change of place between verses 39 and 40; but the question in the latter verse seems to spring from the remark in the former, so that we cannot disconnect them.

39. **For judgment I am come into this world.** It is not for passing the final sentence of condemnation, but for drawing the line of separation between the righteous and the wicked, that Christ came. This was the foreseen result, since some would disbelieve and reject him. The opening of the eyes of this blind man suggested the terms by which believers and unbelievers are here designated. More than this: the man had received spiritual eyesight, and was an illustration of

world, ˣ that they which see not might see; ʸ and that they which see might be made blind.

40 And *some* of the Pharisees which were with him heard these words, ᶻ and said unto him, Are we blind
41 also? Jesus said unto them, ᵃ If ye were blind, ye should have no sin: but now ye say, We see; ᵇ therefore your sin remaineth.

ˣ Matt. 13. 13.
ʸ Isa. 6. 9, 10.
ᶻ Luke11.45; Rom. 2. 19.
ᵃ ch. 15. 22-24; Luke 12. 47; Heb. 10. 26, 27.
ᵇ 1 John 1. 8.

what Christ by his grace will do for those born in the blindness of sin, while the Pharisees were a sad example of those who remained in unbelief, growing more blind under the light of truth and grace. **They which see not** are those who *are conscious* of their blindness. These will come to Christ to obtain sight. **They which see** are those who claim to themselves a knowledge of God's truth, and glory in their own righteousness. Like those night-birds whose eyes are dazzled and blinded by the sunlight, these men were made more blind by the light of gospel truth. The one party was separated from the other. The unbelieving Pharisees will not have the believing man in their synagogue, for light and darkness cannot affiliate.

40. **Some of the Pharisees.** Who they were is not clearly determined. Tholuck thinks they were spies from the hostile party. Lange supposes them to be a remnant of the pharisaically-minded followers of Christ. It matters little whether they were once his professed followers or not: they were at this time imbued with the pharisaical spirit. They well understood the meaning of Christ's words, and ask, **Are we blind also?** There is a tone of scorn in the question. They would indignantly deny their blindness.

41. **If ye were blind, ye should have no sin.** These words are brief and pointed. *To have sin* is to incur the guilt of sin, to acquire and hold possession of the fruits of sin. If these Pharisees had truly become conscious of their blindness, they would not continue to cling to their sin of unbelief, the great sin under the gospel. They would not have been possessors of the guilt that is involved in rejecting Christ. **Now ye say, We see.** This word **say** furnishes the key to the interpretation of the passage. These men *assert* that they are not blind, but really do see, and hence persist in their self-righteousness, in their hypocritical pretensions to piety, and in their opposition to Christ. Therefore should be omitted, according to the highest critical authorities. The expression is concise. Thus, their sin and all the guilt connected with it abide with them. In their infatuation they called Christ a sinner and themselves the disciples of Moses—reviled a man for believing Jesus to be a prophet, and claimed for themselves the authority to declare the will of God. Had they really known their own blindness and ignorance, they would have come to Christ, that the eyes of their understanding might be enlightened. Men's sins will always remain unpardoned while they continue self-confident and trust in their own wisdom.

PRACTICAL REMARKS.

1. Suffering and sorrow attract the attention and move the compassion of Jesus, as in the case of this blind man, ver. 1; Mark 1 : 41.
2. A curiosity to pry into the secret history of the lives of others may lead to uncharitable conjectures and false surmises, as the question of the disciples concerning this man's blindness illustrates, ver. 2; Job 4 : 7.
3. The greatest sufferers are not to be regarded as the greatest sinners. While there is a connection between sin and suffering, while there are instances in which it is impossible to mistake the relations between sin and punishment in the life of an individual, yet this by no means explains all the allotments of suffering and sorrow to individuals. Upon some large measures of affliction fall, in order that God's grace and glory may be manifested to them, ver. 3; Luke 13 : 1-4.
4. It is characteristic of a servant of God to improve opportunities for doing good when they present themselves, ver. 4; ch. 4 : 34; 2 Pet. 3 : 9; Rev. 3 : 19.

The Good Shepherd.

X. VERILY, verily, I say unto you, ^c He that entereth not by the door into the sheepfold, but climbeth up

^a Jer. 14. 15; 28. 15; Ezek.13.2-6; Matt.7.15; Heb. 5.4; 1 John 4.1.

5. Jesus opens the eyes of the spiritually blind, so that they may behold him, the true Light, ver. 5; ch. 1:9, 12.
6. Faith in Christ is shown by cheerful and prompt obedience to his precepts; and this secures the blessing, ver. 7.
7. The inclination of many to question the reality of Christ's beneficent works finds an illustration in some of the neighbors and acquaintances of this healed man, vers. 8, 9.
8. There is convincing power in the simple statement of personal experience of what Christ has done, as is often seen in our times by the testimony of young converts, vers. 10-12.
9. The enemies of Christ are ready to seize upon any circumstance which they can use to disparage his works of benevolence and grace, vers. 14, 16.
10. The more fully true miracles are investigated, the more does their reality appear; but in false miracles the more does their deceit become manifest, vers. 15, 30-32.
11. It is good to tell what the Lord has done for us—a duty also to acknowledge Christ before his enemies, vers. 17, 25, 30, 35-38; Ps. 103:1; Acts 4: 9, 10.
12. There is no greater blindness than moral, spiritual blindness, vers. 18, 34, 39, 40.
13. Avowed unbelief will not yield to evidence in favor of Christ so long as there is any hope of finding a pretext for rejecting it, ver. 18.
14. Bigots and tyrants, who do not believe in the self-protecting power of truth, would by force compel the opinions of others, vers. 22, 34.
15. A lack of moral courage often indicates that the truth has not a deep root in the heart, vers. 19-23.
16. If a believer cannot answer the objections that the enemies of Christ make, he may appeal to his own experience of what Christ has done for himself, and thus confound opposers, ver. 25.
17. How many, through fear or shame, keep silent, instead of testifying to the truth for Christ's sake! vers. 20-23.

18. Men who bitterly reproach the disciples of Christ may make loud professions of piety and of regard for the divine law; they may be tenacious of forms and traditions, adhering to the letter that killeth, and rejecting the Spirit that giveth life, vers. 28, 29.
19. The worldly wise have often been baffled by the arguments of some humble seeker after truth, vers. 30-33.
20. The reasoning of plain common sense often confounds the sophistries and perversions of the enemies of truth, vers. 30-33.
21. Jesus finds and comforts his disciples when trials overtake them. Then he makes to them fuller revelations of himself, vers. 35, 37.
22. Faith prompts to worship, ver. 38.
23. "Conscious humble ignorance dwells nearer the porch of wisdom than arrogant genius and science."—SCOTT. Those who know and confess their blindness can come to him who will "anoint their eyes with eye-salve;" while those who claim for themselves knowledge and righteousness will grope on in spiritual blindness, and come to final ruin, vers. 39-41.
24. All to whom a knowledge of Christ comes are either subdued or hardened—won to the faith or roused into more decided hostility. Thus, the line of separation is drawn between those who fear God and those who fear him not, that the thoughts of many hearts are revealed, ver. 39; Luke 2: 35.
25. None is so ignorant of his condition as the hardened sinner. None think they can see so well as the spiritually blind, ver. 40.
26. The self-confidence of sinners is their ruin, ver. 41.

CHAPTER X.

This chapter, to the 21st verse, is a continuation of the preceding one. The Pharisees had denied that Jesus was of God (ch. 9:16), because he had healed the blind man on the Sabbath day, or even that God spoke through him. They finally ask him in derision if they

A. D. 29. JOHN X. 183

some other way, the same is ᵈa thief and a robber. 2 But he that entereth in ᵉby the door is ᶠthe shepherd 3 of the sheep. ᵍTo him the porter openeth; ʰand the sheep hear his voice: ⁱand he calleth his own sheep 4 by name, ᵏand leadeth them out. And when he putteth forth his own sheep, he goeth before them,

ᵈ vers. 8, 10.
ᵉ vers. 7, 9.
ᶠ Isa. 40. 14.
ᵍ 1 Cor. 16. 9; Col. 4. 3; Rev. 3. 7, 8.
ʰ 1 Thess. 5. 12, 13; Heb. 13. 7, 17.
ⁱ Tit. 2. 1-6.

ᵏ Ps. 23. 2, 3; Jer. 31. 9; Phil. 3. 17; 1 Tim. 4. 12; 1 Pet. 5. 2-4.

are the blind whose eyes he came to open. In the parable of the Good Shepherd, and the interpretation of it, he replies to them—rebukes them as robbers and hirelings over God's heritage, and shows that he is the true divine Saviour, Guide, and Protector of God's people, vers. 1-21. At the feast of the dedication, the Jews—probably some of the same that had heard his parable of the Good Shepherd (ver. 20)—came and asked him to tell them in unequivocal words if he really was the Messiah, 21-24. He refuses to answer their request directly, because they have not credited what he had already said, nor believed the testimony of his works, which was sufficient to convince those who were willing to hear and know the truth. When he does tell them "plainly" of his oneness with the Father, they accuse him of blasphemy and take up stones to stone him, 25-31. Jesus escapes from them when they attempt a second time to take him, 31-39. Again, as before, after the discourse on the Good Shepherd, there is a division of opinion in regard to him, and many believed on him. Jesus goes into Peræa, 40-42. Compare *Author's Harmony*, ¿¿ 112-114.

1-6. THE THIEF AND THE SHEPHERD DESCRIBED AND CONTRASTED.

1. **He that entereth not by the door.** The shepherd, or, if he had an assistant, the porter, guarded the door by night, and therefore enemies must climb up some other way if they would gain access to the sheep. Of all domestic animals, our Lord could not have chosen a better than *the sheep* to illustrate and enforce what he desired. Defenceless by nature, weak, and even foolish in character, it is utterly dependent on human protection; but at the same time it is noted for its docility, learning the human voice and implicitly following its human guide; and in doing this is its safety against not only the changes and severity of weather and climate, but especially against the depredations of thieves and ferocious animals. Similar use of *sheep* for illustrating the people of God is found in the Old Testament, Ps. 79: 13: Ezek. 34:6; Zech. 13:7. **Sheepfold,** enclosure for the sheep. See quotations below. The *sheepfold* represents God's kingdom. We must not, however, press the comparisons of a parable too far. **A thief and a robber;** a false teacher, who steals and robs the sheep by drawing them away after himself. The true teacher engages in his work for Christ, whom he honors and obeys, and to him the flock readily responds. Thus he resembles the Good Shepherd, 1 Pet. 5: 1-4.

2. **The shepherd of the sheep,** the guide, leader, and teacher of the true children of God, wherever they may be found, ver. 16.

3. **To him the porter openeth,** etc. See on ver. 1. The *porter* represents the Father rather than the Holy Spirit, as some suppose, Acts 14: 27; 2 Cor. 2: 12; Col. 4: 3. (See DR. VAN LENNEP, quotation, ver. 4.)

4. **And when he putteth forth his own sheep,** rather, according to the most approved text, *When he putteth forth all his own,* **he goeth before them,** etc. "Those low flat buildings out on the sheltered side of the valley are sheepfolds.... When the nights are cold the flocks are shut up in them, but in ordinary weather they are merely kept within the yard. This is defended by a wide stone wall, crowned all around with sharp thorns, which the prowling wolf will rarely attempt to scale.... The sheep are so tame and so trained that they follow their keeper with the utmost docility. He leads them forth from the fold or from their houses in the villages just where he pleases.... The shepherd calls sharply from time to time to remind them of his presence. They know his voice, and follow on;

and the sheep follow him: for they know his voice.
5 And ¹a stranger will they not follow, but will flee from him: for they know not the voice of strangers.
6 This parable spake Jesus unto them: but they understood not what things they were which he spake unto them.
7 Then said Jesus unto them again, Verily, verily, I say unto you, ᵐI am the door of ⁿthe sheep. °All that ever came before me are thieves and robbers:
9 ᵖbut the sheep did not hear them. ᑫI am the door:

¹ Prov.19.27; Luke 8. 18; 2 Tim. 4 3, 4; 1 John 4. L

ᵐ ch. 14. 6; 15. 5 Eph. 2, 18; 3. 12
ⁿ Ps. 74. 1.
° Jer. 6. 13, 14; 23. 2, 11, 15.
ᵖ Matt. 7. 15.
ᑫ vers. 1, 7.

but if a stranger calls they stop short, lift up their heads in alarm, and, if it is repeated, they turn and flee, because they know not the voice of a stranger. This is not the fancy costume of a parable; it is a simple fact. I have made the experiment repeatedly." — THOMSON'S *Land and Book*, vol. i. pp. 299-301. Also, in regard to several of these points, Dr. H. J. Van Lennep says (*Bible Lands*, p. 185): "The sheepfold, however, often consists of a mere enclosure surrounded by a palisade of thorn-bushes, or a wall of loose stones with thorn-bushes upon the top, and is usually an effectual barrier against the wolves. The door consists of a few sticks laid across the entrance, and here the shepherd and his dog watch all night. Thieves sometimes climb up the wall and push aside the bushes, and sheep-stealing is as much a profession in Turkey as horse-thieving is in some other countries. By the mention of a porter in our Lord's parable we are not to understand that there is a special porter to the sheepfold, but simply that a shepherd acts as porter, opening or shutting the door. Our Lord's object in mentioning it was to allude to the great Porter in God's kingdom, who is Jehovah himself, and who has opened the door of the church to the great Shepherd to enter in and govern his people."

5. **A stranger**, a false and irreligious teacher, **will they not follow**, etc. The true believer may for a time be imposed upon by plausible men, but in due time he will discover their true characters and turn from them.

6. **This parable**, or, more nearly, *allegory*. The word is different from that translated "parable" in Matt. 13, etc. This familiar incident, illustrating a great moral truth, **they understood not**. They understood what he said, but not how the illustration was to be applied—that the parable was aimed at them. So, generally, the Jewish leaders understood not our Lord's parables, Matt. 13 : 13-15.

7-9. JESUS THE DOOR.

7. **I am the door of the sheep**; the Way by which the sheep enter the fold (ch. 14 : 6; Eph. 2 : 18); the only Entrance to the fold and family of God; the only Mediator between God and man; the only One by whom we must attain to salvation.

8. **All that ever came before me**, claiming the same high dignity for themselves and the same authority for their teachings as I have done, **are thieves and robbers**, not having in view the good of the sheep, but their own selfish ends. Our Lord doubtless has reference to the scribes and Pharisees, and others like them, who demanded of the people implicit submission to themselves, as being superior in wisdom and alone competent to teach the way to God. Compare ch. 9 : 24, 34. This has been regarded as a difficult passage, but the above interpretation is simple and natural, and is doubtless the true one. All founders of false religions, and many professed teachers of the gospel, have claimed to be the "door of the sheep," the way to happiness and heaven. To such this verse applies. This could not apply to Moses and the prophets, who wrote of Christ and by faith looked for him, nor to John the Baptist, who pointed the people to Jesus. **But the sheep did not hear them**—that is, did not heed and follow them. **The sheep** are true believers, who were never led astray by false prophets and teachers, but were as Simeon and Anna at our Lord's appearing—like sheep without a shepherd.

9. **I am the door**; emphasized by

r by me if any man enter in, he shall be saved and
10 shall go in and out, *and find pasture. t The thief
cometh not, but for u to steal, and to kill, and to destroy: x I am come that they might have life, and
11 that they might have it y more abundantly. z I am
the good shepherd. The good shepherd a giveth his
12 life for the sheep. But b he that is an hireling, and
not the shepherd, whose own the sheep are not, seeth
c the wolf coming, and leaveth the sheep, and fleeth:
and the wolf catcheth them, and scattereth the sheep.

r Rom. 5. 1, 2; Heb. 10. 19-22.
s Ps. 23. 1, 2; 100. 3, 4; Isa. 40. 11.
t Ezek. 34. 2-4.
u Col. 2. 8.
x ch. 3. 17; 6. 33, 51; Matt. 18. 11; 20. 28; 1 Tim. 1. 15; 2 Tim. 1. 10.
y Rom. 5. 15-21; Heb. 7. 25.
z Ps. 23. 1; Ezek. 37. 24.

a ver. 15; Eph. 5. 2; Tit. 2. 14; 1 Pet. 2. 24.   b Ezek. 34. 3-8.
c Acts 20. 29.

its repetition. **By me if any man enter in, he shall be saved.** Access to God is to be gained *immediately through Christ;* there is no other door, either to shut out or to admit, between the soul and salvation. **Shall go in and out,** etc. He shall "go in," as to a place of safety and repose; and he shall "go out," as to green pastures and still waters (Ps. 23 : 2) for nourishment and refreshing. Compare Num. 27 : 16, 17; 1 Tim. 4 : 16. " By these words, therefore, our Lord meant to express this idea: Every one who enters by the door into the sheepfold shall find with me all that is necessary for the illumination, the sanctification, the confirmation, the joy, the tranquillity, and the felicity of the soul."—TITTMANN.

10-15. JESUS THE GOOD SHEPHERD CONTRASTED WITH THE HIRELING.

10. Our Lord now drops the figure of the door, and presents himself as the "Shepherd." He contrasts the objects of the false teachers with his own. They are represented by the **thief.** They come to kill; he to make alive. Their design is to lead to destruction; his purpose is to bring his followers into the enjoyment of a perfect and full salvation. **I am come that they might have life,** life from the dead, spiritual life, **and that they might have it more abundantly,** or simply *abundantly.* "Our Lord promises those who shall seek salvation through him not life merely, but felicity, and that supreme and perfect— a life in which we shall not only have all things that are necessary to our felicity, but shall have them in rich and overflowing abundance."—TITTMANN.

11. **I am the good shepherd,** not simply " a," but " the Good Shepherd " foretold in the Scriptures. See Ps. 23; Isa. 40 : 11; Ezek. 34 : 11-23; 37 : 24; Zech. 13 : 7. Compare also Heb. 13 : 20; 1 Pet. 2 : 25; 5 : 4. The Greek word translated "shepherd" and the corresponding Hebrew term denote in their figurative sense one who rules over a body of people, defends them from violence and injury, and generally watches over and provides for their comfort and safety. See Jer. 23 : 1; Ezek. 34 : 1, 23, 24. Christ therefore claims to be the Guide, Guardian, Defender, and Prince of his people. Our Lord now gives the distinguishing marks of a good shepherd: he is not only watchful and loving, but self-sacrificing. **Giveth his life,** *layeth down his life,* as the same words are translated in vers. 15, 17, **for the sheep.** In their behalf he perils his own, that they may not suffer violence from robbers and beasts of prey. See 1 Sam. 17 : 34-37.

12, 13. The marks of false shepherds, or **hirelings,** those who set themselves up as guides and defenders of the people, having their own gain in view, are very different. Our Lord, doubtless, has in mind some of those whom he was addressing, and also the false prophets of old. They failed the people at the critical moment, in the time of danger, and left the flock scattered and shepherdless. This was the condition of the Jewish people in Christ's day. The words, **the sheep, the hireling fleeth,** at the end of ver. 12 and the beginning of ver. 13 should be omitted, according to the best text. It will read: *Leaveth the sheep and fleeth; and the wolf catcheth and scattereth them, because he is an hireling,* etc.

JOHN X.

13 The hireling fleeth, because he is an hireling, [d] and careth not for the sheep. I am the good shepherd, 15 and [e] know my *sheep*, and [f] am known of mine; as the Father knoweth me, even so know I the Father: 16 and I lay down my life for the sheep. And [g] other sheep I have, which are not of this fold: [h] them also I must bring, [i] and they shall hear my voice; [j] and

[d] Phil. 2. 20, 21.
[e] ver. 27; Ps. 1. 6; 1 Cor. 8. 3; 2 Tim. 2. 19; Rev. 2. 2.
[f] ch. 17. 8; Eph. 1. 17; 2 Tim. 1. 12; 1 John 5. 20.
[g] Gen. 49. 10; Ps. 72. 10, 11, 17; Isa. 56. 8; Ezek. 34. 11, 12; Rom. 15. 9–12.
[h] Mark 16. 15; Luke 14. 22; Acts 15. 14; Rom. 10. 12–15.
[i] ch. 6. 37; Rev. 3. 20.
[j] Ezek. 37. 22; Eph. 2. 14; 1 Pet. 2. 25.

---

13. Because he is an hireling. The *hireling* is one who serves merely for gain; he is a worldly pastor, and has no personal interest in the sheep. They are not safe in his hands, for he will risk and suffer nothing for them. "The life of a shepherd is arduous. His duties are too severe to be faithfully performed by hirelings. It is rare, therefore, to find any one engaged in this calling simply for hire. Owners of flocks engage shepherds generally by bargaining for the delivery of a certain amount of curdled milk and cheese, and a fixed number of lambs and sheep, yearly, besides maintaining the flock undiminished, while the shepherds are paid for their trouble by whatever they can obtain beyond this."—Dr. H. J. Van Lennep, *Bible Lands*, p. 184.

14, 15. I am the good shepherd. This is made more emphatic by its repetition and by the contrast just made between the false and the true shepherd. **And know my sheep, and am known of mine**, etc. Our common version wrongly makes ver. 15 an independent sentence, and thus the true and full sense is obscured. The two verses should be connected and read as follows: *And know mine, and mine know me, just as the Father knows me and I know the Father.* The term "to know" is used here in the peculiar and endearing sense of 2 Tim. 2: 19, and is synonymous with "to love." The mutual knowledge of Christ and his people is as deep, intimate, and loving as the mutual knowledge of the Father and the Son. Our Lord means to show by these words that he has the characteristic marks of a true shepherd in that he has an intimate acquaintance with his flock, and is about to lay down his life for their salvation. **And I lay down my life for the sheep.** Christ plainly implies that it is his fixed purpose to lay down his life; that he does it of his own free choice; and that there is a necessity for his doing so in the condition and danger of those who are called his sheep. He gives his life **for the sheep**—that is, in their behalf, for their benefit. As the sheep are in danger, and would die were not the life of the shepherd interposed, the doctrine of substitution, or the vicariousness of Christ's death, is implied, though not directly stated, in this passage. It should be noted that the Good Shepherd lays down his life for the *sheep*, and not to confirm the truth of his doctrines. The sense in which the words are to be taken will be explained by such passages as Matt. 20: 28 and Rom. 5: 6.

16–18. The Extent of His Flock for which He Willingly Lays down His Life.

16. By this fold Jesus no doubt means believers on him from among the Jews. **Other sheep** are those who should believe on him from among the Gentiles. Though unconverted, he *has them;* they are already his in the purpose of his grace. Compare Acts 18: 10: "I have much people in this city." "They were yet without, among the Gentiles, predestinated, not yet gathered in. These he knew who had predestinated them : he knew who had come to redeem them with the shedding of his own blood. He saw those who did not yet see him. He knew them who yet believed not in him."—Augustine, as quoted by Ryle. **Them also I must bring**, in the fulfilment of prophecy and to carry out the great purpose of his coming. In carrying out this purpose Christ uses his people as instruments. Yet he is chief in the matter, for the saints are "the called of Jesus Christ," Rom. 1: 6. **They shall hear my voice, so as**

17 there shall be one fold, ᵏ *and* one shepherd. Therefore doth my Father love me, because I lay down my
18 life, that I might take it again. ¹No man taketh it from me, but I lay it down of myself. I have power to lay it down, and I ᵐ have power to take it again. ⁿ This commandment have I received of my Father.
19 ᵒ There was a division therefore again among the
20 Jews for these sayings. And many of them said, ᵖ He hath a devil, and is mad; why hear ye him?
21 Others said, These are not the words of him that hath a devil. Can a devil open the eyes of the blind?

ᵏ Ezek. 34. 23; Heb. 13. 20.
ˡ ch. 19. 11; Matt 26. 53–56.
ᵐ ch. 2. 19–21.
ⁿ ch. 6. 38; 14. 31 15. 10; Acts 2 24, 32; Heb. 5. 6–9.
ᵒ ch. 7. 40–43; 9. 16.
ᵖ ch. 7. 20; 8. 48, 52.

Jesus at Jerusalem at the Feast of Dedication: Jews charge him with blasphemy, and again attempt to seize him.

22 And it was at Jerusalem the feast of the dedication.

---

to believe and obey. There is implied here a purpose to draw them to himself by an inward efficacious call. There was a cheering promise in these words for the disciples, for the sheep among the heathen to whom they were to preach would listen and be converted. **There shall be one fold**, or *one flock*, as the same word is translated in Matt. 26 : 31; Luke 2 : 8; 1 Cor. 9 : 7. This will be completely fulfilled only when "the fulness of the Gentiles be come in," and "all Israel shall be saved," Rom. 11 : 25, 26. "The disciples of Jesus, whether Jews or Gentiles, shall be essentially 'one flock,' united in their relations to the 'one Shepherd.' Our Lord does not say 'one fold,' for this unity is not that of any mere external organization."—*An. Par. Bible.* This is a most important distinction, since there may be many *folds*, but only one *flock*. All true followers of Christ make up the one body. Compare Eph. 2 : 13–18. One kingdom, but many local churches.

17. **Therefore** (compare Isa. 53 : 12 and Phil. 2 : 6–11) **doth my Father love me,** etc. As the Son showed his love to the Father by his voluntary humiliation and self-sacrifice in behalf of the flock, so the Father's love to him finds its justification in the same act. **That I might take it again;** his rising from the dead was as necessary as his dying, for by his resurrection he secured the fruits of his death. Compare Rom. 4 : 25.

18. **No man taketh it from me,** etc. His sacrifice was purely voluntary. Neither in his death nor in his resurrection was Christ passive; he rose by his own divine power. Compare Acts 2 : 24, 32; 1 Pet. 3 : 18; John 2 : 19. From which we infer that in every part of Christ's mediatorial work the three persons of the Trinity concurred and co-operated. **This commandment,** etc. "My death is my own voluntary act (see ch. 18 : 5–8), for I have the right of my own life; yet it is also an act of obedience to the commandment which 'I have received from my Father.' It is the combination of this right or power with obedience that gives value to the sacrifice of Christ."—*An. Par. Bible.*

19–21. FRESH DISCUSSION AND DIVISION AROUSED BY THE WORDS OF JESUS.

19. **There was a division,** as twice before, because of Christ's words. See ch. 7 : 43 and 9 : 16. That he should be the cause of division was foretold. See Isa. 8 : 14; Luke 2 : 34.

20, 21. Different impressions are made by the same words of Christ on different hearers. In his claim to be the Good Shepherd, and to have power to lay down his life and to take it again, the one saw only the senseless talk of a madman, the other compared his words with his work, and concluded that **These are not the words of him that hath a devil,** or *demon*. The fact that Jesus had opened the eyes of the blind (ch. 9) seemed too great to have been wrought by the agency of demons. Such could only be produced by the power of God.

22–39. JESUS AT THE FEAST OF DEDICATION.

23 And it was winter, and Jesus walked in the temple ^q in Solomon's porch.
24 Then came the Jews round about him, and said unto him, How long dost thou make us to doubt? ^r If thou be the Christ, tell us plainly.
25 Jesus answered them, *I told you, and ye believed not. The works that I do in my Father's name, they
26 bear witness of me. But ^t ye believe not because ye

^q Acts 3. 11 · 5. 12.

^r ch. 8. 25, 53; Luke 22. 67-70.
^s ch. 5. 17-43.
^t vers. 14, 27; ch. 6. 37, 44, 45, 65; 8 47; 1 John 4. 6.

22, 23. **The feast of the dedication**, rather, *And the feast of the dedication came* (or *occurred*) *at Jerusalem*. Some time probably intervened between the last verse and this. This was instituted by Judas Maccabeus, B. C. 164, to commemorate the purging of the temple and the rebuilding of the altar after the profanation by Antiochus Epiphanes. It commenced on the 25th of Chisleu (that is, December 20th, A. D. 29), and lasted eight days, but did not require attendance at Jerusalem, being celebrated by the Jews at their homes by festivity and the illumination of their dwellings, 1 Macc. 4 : 52-59; Jos., *Antiq.*, xii. 7, 6, 7. From John's narrative it appears that Jesus remained in Judæa after the feast of tabernacles, which I believe to be confirmed by a proper view of Luke's narrative, and hence was at Jerusalem at this festival. The fact that the Jews did not go up to Jerusalem to observe this feast is a confirmatory argument for our Lord's stay at Jerusalem and its vicinity during the seven weeks between the feast of tabernacles and that of dedication. **It was winter**, suggests the weather of that season, and the reason why he **walked** in the covered porch of Solomon instead of the open courts of the temple. It was a protection, not only from the cold, but perhaps from the wintry storm. **Solomon's porch,** the eastern colonnade of the temple, probably where that of Solomon formerly stood. (For the connection of events and the probable position of this section see *Author's Harmony,* pp. 276, 277.)

24. **Then came the Jews**, the rulers, not the common people, **round about him.** The words seem to come from an eye-witness. Quite likely John was with him. **How long dost thou make us to doubt ? . . . tell us plainly.** " Do not keep us in doubt by the use of ambiguous words and figurative terms." Our Lord had frequently spoken to the Jews regarding himself in such a way as to leave them in no doubt as to who he was; but for wise reasons he had not said plainly, " I am the Messiah." Their request at this time was no doubt intended to draw from him a declaration for which they might stone him on the spot as a blasphemer. It seems very probable that these who encircled Jesus were some of the persons spoken of in verses 19-21, and that their presence calls to mind the illustration of the shepherd and the sheep, vers. 26-29.

25. **I told you**, in such discourses as are recorded in ch. 5 : 17-47; 8 : 12-59. The immediate reference here is no doubt to the proclamation of himself as the Good Shepherd. **Ye believed not,** " You did not credit my words when I declared myself to be the Messiah; but," he says in substance, " further declarations are not necessary to show who I am." **The works that I do in my Father's name, they bear witness of me**—" they confirm all I have said, and furnish the clearest evidence that I am from God, for no man can do the miracles that I do except God be with him." See ch. 3 : 2 ; 5 : 36 ; 7 : 31 ; 9 : 33, 34; Acts 2 : 22. " Our Lord's ministry was accredited by the miracles which, like flashes of the indwelling Deity breaking through the veil of the flesh, proved him to be more than man." — *God's Word Written*, GARBETT, p. 96.

26. **Because ye are not of my sheep.** " Faith is one of their marks. Not being Christ's sheep was not the cause of the unbelief of the Jews, but their unbelief was the evidence that they were not Christ's sheep."—RYLE. **As I said unto you.** See ch. 8 : 47 and ver. 3, 4 of this chapter. The clause is omitted by the oldest and best critical authorities, but retained by others. If genuine, it would seem best to connect it with the following verse,

27 are not of my sheep, as I said unto you. My sheep hear my voice, and I know them, and they follow
28 me: ᵘand I give unto them eternal life; and ᵛthey shall never perish, neither shall any *man* pluck them
29 out of ʷmy hand. My Father, which gave *them* me, is greater than all; and no *man* is able to pluck *them*
30 out of my Father's hand. ˣI and *my* Father are one.
31 Then ʸthe Jews took up stones again to stone him.
32 Jesus answered them, ᶻMany good works have I

ᵘ ch. 6. 27; 17. 2
Rom. 6.23; 1 Cor. 2. 12; 1 John 2. 25; 5. 11.
ᵛ ch. 3. 15; 6. 39, 40; 17.11,12; 18. 9; 1 Sam. 2. 9;
Rom. 8. 1, 33–39; Col. 3. 3, 4.
ʷ Deut. 33. 3; Isa. 49. 16; 2 Tim. 1. 12.

ˣ ver. 38; ch. 14. 9–11; 17. 11, 21, 22. ʸ ch. 8. 59. ᶻ 1 Pet. 1. 21–23.

and read, *As I said unto you, my sheep hear my voice*, etc.

27. My sheep hear my voice is in contrast with, *But ye believe not*, in the preceding verse; "*to believe on him*" and "*to hear his voice*" are terms expressing the same idea.

28. And I give unto them, etc. We have seen the character of the "sheep," and now our attention is directed to their blessed privileges—eternal life and eternal security from all foes. **I give**, in the present, not "*I will give*," in the future. Eternal life is the present possession of believers. **They shall never perish.** They shall in no wise be lost, ch. 6 : 35, 39, 40; Rom. 8 : 30–39. **Neither shall any man**, *any one*, man, angel, or devil. The Good Shepherd is superior in wisdom and might to all the enemies of his people. Neither life nor death, nor angels nor principalities nor powers, nor things present nor things to come, nor height nor depth, nor any other created thing, shall ever be able to separate them from his loving care. The perpetuity of grace in believers, and the certainty that they shall never be cast away, could scarcely be asserted in more plain and positive language. To interpret these words to mean, " They shall never perish so long as they remain my sheep," or, " They shall never perish through any defect on my part," is only to say that Christ attempts to secure eternal life for his people, but in some cases makes a humiliating failure. The gift of eternal life is, it may reverently be said, of little worth to us unless it includes a guarantee against our own weakness.

29. My Father, which gave them me, is greater than all; he is almighty, no adverse power can contend with him, Isa. 27 : 2–4. **And no man,** *no one,* **is able to pluck them.** "*Them*" is not in the Greek, but is implied. Our Lord by these words seems to say, " No one, however powerful, can snatch my sheep from my care, any more than from the care of my Father, who is almighty." The reason is given in the next verse.

30. I and my Father are one. From the connection in which these words stand, we must interpret the union here expressed to be a harmony of power and operation. The main thought intended to be conveyed in this and the two verses preceding appears to be that Christ's people are perfectly safe in his keeping, because he, like his Father, is infinite in power. Unity of interest, design, and essence are all implied in the context, but not directly stated here. "One in power, or of the same power. But if one in power, one in Godhead, essence, and nature; therefore when he said, ' I and the Father,' he signified a duality of persons, a distinction of substances; but when he added, ' we are one,' he signified a oneness of Godhead, an identity of nature, essence, and power."—EUTHYMIUS ZIGADENUS, as quoted by Tittmann. The Saviour has now answered indirectly the request made by the Jews in the twenty-fourth verse.

31–38. THE JEWS REGARD THE HIGH CLAIMS OF JESUS AS BLASPHEMY, AND ARE ABOUT TO STONE HIM.

31. Took up stones again to stone him. They had perhaps come prepared to do so if in his answer he should again assert his equality with God, as in ch. 8 : 58, 59. There were probably stones lying about which had been brought there for the temple, which was not yet completed. The Jews appear to have caught up the stones in a tumultuous manner.

32. While the stones are in their hands Jesus proceeds with calmness

showed you from my Father; *for which of those works do ye stone me? 33 The Jews answered him, saying, For a good work we stone thee not; ᵇbut for blasphemy; and because that thou, being a man, ᶜmakest thyself God. 34 Jesus answered them, ᵈIs it not written in your law, I said, Ye are gods? 35 If he called them gods, ᵉunto whom the word of God came (ᶠand the Scripture cannot be broken), 36 say ye of him, ᵍwhom the Father hath sanctified, and ʰsent into the world, Thou blasphemest; ⁱbecause I said, I am ʲthe Son of

* Ps. 35. 12; 109. 4, 5.
ᵇ Lev. 24. 16.
ᶜ ch. 5. 18.
ᵈ Ex. 22. 28.
ᵉ Rom. 13. 1.
ᶠ Matt. 5. 18; Luke 16. 17.
ᵍ ch. 3. 34; 6. 27.
ʰ ch. 3. 17; 5. 36, 37; 6. 38, 39, 57; 8. 42.
ⁱ ver. 30; ch. 5. 17, 18.
ʲ ch. 9. 35-37; Luke 1. 35.

and dignity to answer them. We never see him showing signs of fear or terror in the presence of human passion. His bearing throughout the gospel history is like that of the Son of God. **Many good works.** He had fed the hungry, he had restored the maimed, he had cleansed the lepers, he had cured the sick, he had cast out demons, he had recovered the paralytic, he had raised the dead, he had employed his energies solely in doing good, Acts 10 : 38. **Have I showed you.** All these things were not only *done*, but *showed*—exhibited before their eyes as a proof of what he was, ch. 2 : 11; 17 : 6; 1 Tim. 3 : 16; 1 John 1 : 2; 3 : 8. **From my Father.** These good works he was commissioned by the Father to do; they were done by his will and authority. By these words Jesus would repel their charge that he was assuming prerogatives to which he had no right. **For which of those works do ye stone me?** He appeals to their sense of justice, and says in effect, "It cannot be that you are about to stone me for any of those good works."

33. **For a good work we stone thee not.** They could not deny that his works were *good*, for even the healing of the blind man on the Sabbath day (ch. 9) was a good work, and, as they knew, not against the spirit of the Sabbath law. They therefore charge him with **blasphemy**, which according to their law was punishable with death by stoning (see Lev. 24 : 14-16). But being under Roman dominion, they had no *right* to execute such a law. The exact nature of the blasphemy was that **thou, being a man—** only a man they mean—**makest thyself God**, that is, equal to God. It seems plain from these words that the Jews understood Christ to claim for himself a divine nature, equality with God. Ryle observes with great force: "This 'contemporaneous exposition,' to use a legal phrase, of our Lord's words deserves great respect and carries with it great weight and authority." If Jesus in calling God his Father, and in saying that he and the Father were one, did not mean to claim equality with him, he might easily have corrected the erroneous interpretation which the Jews put upon his words. He does not do so here or on any other occasion. Compare ch. 5 : 18.

34. **Is it not written in your law.** Law here includes the whole Old Testament. Jesus shows by their own Scriptures that he does not blaspheme in claiming to be the Son of God. **Ye are gods.** "I have said, Ye are gods; and all of you are children of the Most High." Ps. 82 : 6. Jesus quoted part of the verse, leaving his hearers to recollect the rest. Magistrates and judges, being earthly rulers under Jehovah, the supreme Ruler, had applied to them the title of *gods* and *sons of God*.

35. **If he called them gods**, etc. The reference is to princes and judges who were commissioned to rule and judge in God's name. **And the Scripture cannot be broken;** this they acknowledge—this Scripture cannot be explained away. It is therefore true that magistrates may be called gods without injury to the majesty of the one living and true God. Since our Saviour's argument here turns upon the one word, *gods*, the bearing of this passage on the verbal inspiration of the Scriptures is evident.

36. **Whom the Father hath sanctified,** set apart, appointed for an of-

A. D. 30.   JOHN X.   191

37 God? *If I do not the works of my Father, believe   k ch. 15. 24.
38 me not: but if I do, though ye believe not me, ¹be-   l ch. 5. 36; 14. 10, 11.
lieve the works: that ye may know, and believe,
39 ᵐthat the Father *is* in me, and I in him. ⁿTherefore   m ver. 30; ch. 14.
they sought again to take him: °but he escaped out   10, 11; 17. 21.
of their hand,   n ch. 7. 30, 44; 8. 59.
    o Luke 4. 29, 30.

Jesus retires beyond Jordan.

40 And went away again beyond Jordan into the   p ch. 1. 28; Judg.
place ᵖwhere John at first baptized; and there he   7. 24.

fice, **and sent into the world;** this was never said of any of the princes or judges. He was appointed and sent into the world; he was an ambassador from above. They were of the earth, and the word of God came to them, giving them a very limited authority to speak or rule; his position was infinitely superior to theirs. Our Lord's argument was meant merely *to free himself from the charge of blasphemy.* If these magistrates of old could be called gods—and God had called them so—he who came from heaven with a great work to do for humanity can without blasphemy claim equality with God. Jesus does not lower his claim in the least in this argument, but if he seems to do so, he at once takes up the same ground as at first in the following verses.

37. **If I do not the works of my Father,**—the works which he doeth, works showing the same wisdom, power, and goodness,—**believe me not.** That is, If you do not witness miraculous works done by me, I do not ask you to credit my words. If you do not see me do the works appropriate to one "whom the Father hath sanctified and sent into the world," do not believe my assertion that "I and my Father are one." Compare ver. 25; ch. 5 : 17, 19–23.

38. **But if I do, though ye believe not me,** though you have not that spiritual perception which my sheep have, and which would lead you to give credence to my words when I claim equality with God, **believe the works,** that is, "believe what the works teach concerning me," or, as in ch. 14 : 11, "believe me for the works' sake." The works, then, were not the objects of *faith*, but the objects of *sight*, leading on to *faith in the worker.* Miracles are themselves evidences of power; their extent and character show the extent and character of the worker's commission and give authority to his claims. Christ appeals not simply to his works as manifestations of power, but to their nature as "good works," "works of the Father." **That ye may know, and believe,** etc. Verses 38 and 39 have a close connection with what precedes. Christ says here, in effect: Though you have not that spiritual insight that fixes its faith on me at once, let the works that I do show you that I am not merely a man; let them remove your prejudices, so that you may afterward come to the fuller belief in my oneness with the Father. Compare ver. 30; 5 : 19.

39. **Therefore they sought again,** etc. Carried away by their passion, they refused to regard any appeal to their reason, but they clearly saw one thing that many who read his words now fail to see—that he did not relinquish his high claim of equality with God. **But he escaped** (see ch. 8 : 59; Luke 4 : 30) literally, *he went forth out of their hand,* out of their power. Christ's enemies were probably awed and restrained, so that they were powerless to carry out their designs. (For similar instances of his divine influence over men witness the cleansing of the temple (ch. 2 : 13–16) and the overpowering of the soldiers who came to take him, ch. 18 : 6.)

40. **Beyond Jordan,** etc. This was Bethany (according to the correct reading of ch. 1 : 28, note on which see), on the east side of the Jordan. We do not read that Jesus ever before revisited the scene of his own baptism and the place where he began his public ministry. **And there he abode;** probably not, as some suppose, in quiet retirement, but in teaching and healing His stay beyond Jordan probably occupied about six weeks, and the time

41 abode. And many resorted unto him, and said, John
42 did no miracle: ⁿbut all things that John spake of this man were true. ʳAnd many believed on him there.

ᵠ ch. 1. 15–27; 29–36.
ʳ ch. 2. 23.

---

was in part filled up by the events recorded in Luke's Gospel from ch. 13 : 10 to 17 : 10. See *Author's Harmony*, notes on §§ 114, 125.

41. **And many resorted unto him,** doubtless from Jerusalem, as they did to John's preaching. **John did no miracle,** "yet we believed him," and now we see indeed that he had a divine commission, *for* **all things that John spake of this man were true.** "A very important testimony against those who explain the miracles of Jesus as fables springing from the morbid love of marvels is found in this observation that the Baptist, though it might certainly be looked for from him as a prophet, performed no miracle." — THOLUCK. The *place* would recall the testimony of John. In comparing what John had said with what Christ had done, they were forced to acknowledge that all that John had said was true— that Jesus was indeed "the Lamb of God, that taketh away the sin of the world," ch. 1 : 29. Probably only a small part of what John had said concerning Jesus is recorded. Specimens are to be found in ch. 1 : 27, 29 ; 3 : 27–36. He proved himself a *prophet*, though he wrought no miracle.

42. Convinced by the testimony of Christ, fulfilling the testimony of John the Baptist, **many believed on him there.** Thus John, being dead, yet spoke, and proved indeed a harbinger of the Messiah to many there.

PRACTICAL REMARKS.

1. Christ is our chief Shepherd, and he will recognize none as shepherds who are not in personal and spiritual union with him, ver. 1; Heb. 13 : 20; 1 Pet. 2 : 25 ; 5 : 4.
2. The shepherd and sheep all enter the same way; the rightful owner, however, enters as one having authority, ver. 2.
3. Only those are true disciples or ministers of Christ who believe in him and keep his commands, ver. 3.
4. True Christians have discernment and love for the truths of the gospel, ver. 4; 1 Cor. 2 : 14, 15.
5. Those who are under the guidance of Christ, his word, and his Spirit, are quick to detect error and false teachers, and have no relish for either them or their teaching, ver. 5 ; 1 John 4 : 1.
6. How many read our Saviour's words, but, like the Pharisees, understand not! ver. 6 ; Acts 28 : 26, 27.
7. Christ is the Door, open to his friends, shut against his enemies, vers. 7–9.
8. The Scriptures may also be styled the door, in the same sense that they manifest Christ and he is the manifestation of the truth, vers. 7–9; ch. 5 : 39.
9. How tender the care that Christ the Shepherd exercises over his people! vers. 9–11; Ps. 23.
10. How hearty should be our submission to Christ! how safe in his hands! vers. 9–14, 27–30.
11. Christ put his love for his people to an actual test in dying for them, ver. 11; ch. 15 : 13; Rom. 5 : 8.
12. Times of trial determine whether one is a shepherd or a hireling, vers. 12, 13 ; 2 Tim. 4 : 10, 14.
13. False shepherds make the world their object, and cause the flock of God to minister to their own selfishness, vers. 12, 13.
14. The relations of Christ to his people are most intimate, and will be eternal, vers. 14, 15 ; Ps. 112 : 6 ; Isa. 31 : 5.
15. Christ's death was necessary in procuring the salvation of his people, vers. 15, 17 ; 1 Pet. 2 : 24 ; 3 : 18.
16. Christ knows every one of his flock. Not one, however humble, poor, or weak, will be forgotten, neglected, or forsaken, vers. 14–16, 27–30.
17. How extensive Christ's love! All his people, of every time and place, will in due time be gathered into one flock under one Shepherd, ver. 16.
18. The voluntariness of Christ's death shows how great his love and how great its necessity, vers. 17, 18.
19. Christ's words have in every age produced division among men, ver. 19; Matt. 10 : 34–38.

Jesus receives news of Lazarus' sickness.
XI. NOW a certain *man* was sick, *named* Lazarus, of

20. How greatly does prejudice blind the mind against the truth! What need of the Holy Spirit to enlighten us to discern the teachings of Christ! vers. 19, 20; 1 Cor. 2 : 14; 3 : 1.
21. The life, character, and works of Christ are such as to convince a candid mind of the truth of his doctrine, vers. 20, 21.
22. Days of dedication, thanksgiving, and prayer are proper and productive of good if kept in accordance with the teaching of Christ, ver. 22.
23. "The Jews pretended that they only *doubted;* Christ declared that they did *not believe.* Scepticism in religion is no better than *infidelity*" (M. HENRY), vers. 24, 25.
24. Infidelity and unbelief have their root in a depraved heart, ver. 26.
25. Christ's sheep are Christ-like: they learn his doctrine, obey his words, and imitate his example, ver. 27.
26. The true disciple is not driven, but drawn, by Christ's love. He follows him, ver. 27.
27. The believer is secure, because he is kept by an almighty hand, vers. 28, 29.
28. The saint's perseverance is made certain by the power of God vouchsafed in his behalf, vers. 28, 29.
29. The divinity of Christ is a source of comfort and hope to God's people, and was so presented by Christ, ver. 30.
30. The more Christ is presented, the more are his enemies aroused in their opposition, vers. 31-33.
31. The enemies of Jesus can find no just ground for their opposition, vers. 32, 33.
32. Professed Christians who deny the divinity of Christ are condemned by the Scriptures, as were the Jews of old, vers. 33-36.
33. Jesus proved his Messiahship and divinity by his divine works, vers. 37, 38.
34. Christ attached high importance to the Scriptures, and put high honor upon his miracles, vers. 35-37.
35. Jesus does not require a blind faith without proof, but a faith grounded on his divine words and works, vers. 35-38.

36. It does no good to reason with men who are blinded by prejudice and human tradition, ver. 39.
37. The simple-minded and candid find evidence where the prejudiced find none, vers. 41, 42.
38. The preacher's success is not confined to his lifetime, vers. 41, 42.
39. Preaching repentance prepares the way for preaching the fulness of gospel grace, vers. 41, 42.

CHAPTER XI.

We find recorded in this chapter one of the most remarkable miracles of our Lord. In the working of the miracle, and in the events attending it, we see manifested in a wonderful manner both the divine power and glory of Christ and also his keen and tender human sympathy. The events of this chapter are narrated by John alone. It has seemed strange to some that such an important circumstance in our Lord's history—one that appears to have decided the course of the Jewish rulers with regard to him—should have been passed over in silence by the other evangelists. Older writers have explained this by saying that the other evangelists wrote while Lazarus was still living, and omitted it from delicacy or for the sake of saving him from notoriety or danger from hostile Jews. But no one of the Gospel historians, nor the four combined, record all the words and works of Jesus. Indeed, it would have been impossible, as the words of John imply ch. 21 : 25. Each writer, guided by the Spirit, seizes upon those events in his Master's career which will best serve his purpose in writing. Now this miracle is purposely recorded by John alone in accordance with his design to set forth Christ as the light and *life* of men—to give unto us the "gospel of the Son of God." The motive of our Lord in working this miracle just when and where he did may have been to supply the Jewish rulers one more incontrovertible proof that he was the Son of God, the promised Messiah. It may also have been intended to prepare the

Bethany, the town of *Mary and her sister Martha. • Luke 10. 38-42.

minds of the people for his own resurrection. After the raising of Lazarus they could not say that the resurrection of Jesus was *incredible*. Of all the miracles of Jesus, this is supported by the strongest evidence and is the most thoroughly credible. When we regard all the circumstances—the time, the place, its great publicity—it requires more credulity to deny it than it does to believe it.

It was while Jesus was in Peræa, whither he had retired for a while from the fury of his enemies, that news came to him that Lazarus his friend was sick, vers. 1-4. After waiting two days where he was, he informs his disciples that Lazarus was really dead, vers. 5-14.

BETHANY.

Braving now all danger from his enemies, he departs for Bethany for the purpose of raising Lazarus from the dead, vers. 15-18. On his arrival, he finds him already buried, and many Jews present with Mary and Martha, comforting them, ver. 20. Martha, hearing that the Master has come, goes out to meet him, and a precious dialogue concerning the resurrection is carried on between them, until Martha confesses her implicit faith in him as the Messiah, vers. 20-27. Mary, being sent for, comes to Jesus weeping, followed by the Jews, also weeping, vers. 28-32. Jesus is deeply moved by the sight, and he, weeping too, arrives at the grave, vers. 33-38. He directs them to open the tomb, prays to the Father, bids Lazarus come forth before all, and commands them to loose him and let him go, vers. 39-44. Many of the Jews who witnessed the miracle believed, and others were hardened in their unbelief, vers. 45, 46. The rulers, having been informed of what was done at Bethany, formally resolve to put Jesus to death, vers. 47-53. He again departs from the vicinity of Jerusalem until his time should come to be delivered into the hands of his enemies, ver. 54. The rulers, seeking opportunity to take him, speculate as to the probability of his coming to the approaching passover, vers. 55-57.

1. **Lazarus**, the Greek form of the

2 (¹ It was *that* Mary which anointed the Lord with ointment, and wiped his feet with her hair, whose 3 brother Lazarus was sick.) Therefore his sisters sent unto him, saying, Lord, behold, ᵘ he whom thou lovest is sick.
4 When Jesus heard *that*, he said, ᵛ This sickness is not unto death, ʷ but for the glory of God, ˣ that the Son of God might be glorified thereby.
5 Now Jesus loved Martha, and her sister, and Laza-

ᵗ ch. 12. 3; Matt. 26
7; Mark 14. 3.

ᵘ Heb. 12. 6, 7.

ᵛ ver. 40; ch. 9. 3.
ʷ ch. 13. 31, 32.
ˣ ch. 5. 23; 8 54.

Hebrew name Eleazar, meaning *God is his help*. We know nothing of his history aside from this narrative. It is worthy of notice that John assumes that his readers had heard of Mary and Martha, but probably not of Lazarus. **Of, from, Bethany the town,** *the village*, **of Mary and her sister Martha,** so named to distinguish it from the Bethany beyond Jordan, twenty-five miles distant, ch. 1 : 28; 10 : 40. " Bethany is now a poor village of some thirty or forty families, without thrift or industry. The present name of the place is *El-Azariyeh*, a corruption of Lazarus—a lasting memorial of the miracle connected with the spot. Even now the little village clinging to the gray hillside of Olivet, and sprinkled with fig, almond, olive, and pomegranate trees, has a peaceful and quiet aspect,

'Not wholly in the busy world, nor quite Beyond it.'

One can readily imagine the charming seclusion which made it to Jesus a second Nazareth."—*Bible Lands Illustrated*, by H. C. FISH, D. D., p. 248.
2. **It was that Mary,** etc. There were three other persons by this name mentioned in the Gospels: (1) The mother of our Lord; (2) the wife of Cleophas; and (3) Mary Magdalene. Hence this explanation. The deed of Mary is mentioned here by anticipation, since it did not happen until later. See ch. 12 : 3-7. The event was well known among Christians in John's time, and therefore this allusion would readily serve to distinguish Mary, the sister of Martha, from others of the same name. We see here, incidentally, the striking fulfilment of Christ's prophecy in regard to the anointing, Matt. 26 : 13. This verse is explanatory, but not parenthetical, as in our common version.
3. **Sent unto him;** it was about a day's journey from their home to the Bethany beyond Jordan. **Lord, behold, he whom thou lovest is sick.** " Very beautiful is it to observe their confidence in him; they take it for granted that this announcement will be sufficient, and say no more; they do not urge him to come; they only tell their need, as being sure that this will be enough; he does not love, and forsake them whom he loves."—TRENCH.
4. **This sickness is not unto death;** this was the reply to the messenger. This must have greatly perplexed the sisters and tried their faith, for by the time the messenger arrived home again Lazarus must have been dead and buried. "Could it be possible," they would think, "that the Master would so deceive us, or is he himself deceived?" The words must, of course, be taken with some qualification, for *Lazarus did die;* he ceased to breathe, and became unconscious. The meaning probably is that death was not to be the final issue of the sickness. **But for the glory of God,** etc.; for the manifested honor of the Father and of the Son. " The Father is glorified when the Son is glorified; and the Son was glorified by the miracle to which this event gave occasion; by his own *death*, which was hastened by the miracle (see ch. 12 : 23; 13 : 31; 17 : 1); and doubtless also by the *spiritual benefit* which resulted to Lazarus and to many others."—*Annotated Paragraph Bible*.
5. **Now Jesus loved,** etc. This is mentioned, probably, to show that it was not without a beneficent purpose that sickness and death were permitted to enter this household. It also explains why the sisters sent the message which they did to Jesus. The verse has also, no doubt, connection with the two following. He loves them, yet he tarries (ver. 6); this love even leads him to tarry, that he may prove and perfect their faith. He loves them,

6 rus. When he had heard therefore that he was sick, ʸhe abode two days still in the same place where he was.　　ʸ ch. 10. 40; Isa. 30. 18; 55. 8, 9; Matt. 15. 22-28.

Jesus goes into Judæa, and raises Lazarus from the dead.

7 Then after that saith he to *his* disciples, Let us go
8 into Judæa again. *His* disciples say unto him, Master, ᶻthe Jews of late sought to stone thee; ᵃand goest　　ᶻ ch. 10. 31, 39.
9 thou thither again? Jesus answered, Are there not　　ᵃ Matt. 16. 21-23; Acts 21. 12, 13.
twelve hours in the day? ᵇIf any man walk in the　　ᵇ ch. 9. 4.
day, he stumbleth not, because he seeth the light of
10 this world. But ᶜif a man walk in the night, he　　ᶜ ch. 12. 35.
stumbleth, because there is no light in him.

and therefore he says, "Let us go into Judæa again," ver. 7. It is worthy of notice that the word in the original translated *love* in ver. 3 is that of affection, while the one in this verse is that of esteem and friendship.

6. When he had heard therefore that he was sick. Jesus purposely delayed his journey, and by this delay permitted Martha and Mary to suffer intense mental pain, and Lazarus to endure the agony of death and the sorrow of parting. We should rather expect to read: "When, therefore, he heard that he was sick, he immediately departed," etc. But Jesus loved all his people as well as the family of Bethany. Therefore he tarries and permits a few to suffer, and the wonderful miracle is wrought. As a result, the faith of the sisters was perfected, the minds of the weak disciples were raised to hope and confidence, his whole church is benefited, and his own glory and the glory of the Father are most signally displayed. **Abode two days;** thus he gave time for the death and burial of Lazarus. These two days may coincide with the *to-day and to-morrow* of Luke 13 : 32, 33. So Wieseler and Ellicott. If so, then the interesting narrative of Luke 14 : 1 to 17 : 10 records incidents which took place after the reception of the message from Bethany and before his arrival there. See *Author's Harmony*, §§ 116-124, and notes on them.

7. After that, *after this*, the two days. When the time of waiting had expired and of duty in Judæa had come. Christ's hour always came at the right moment. "Our Lord moves by the clock of his Father's timekeeping."—WHEDON.

8. The Jews of late sought to stone thee, *were but now seeking* (at the feast of dedication, ch. 10 : 31; also at the feast of tabernacles, ch. 8 : 59), **and goest thou thither again?**—to the place of the greatest peril, to almost certain death? Words of warm but mistaken affection.

9, 10. If any man walk in the day, etc. He says in effect to his disciples: There are certain hours when the natural sun will shine and cannot be obscured, and he who travels then can depend upon enjoying the light. In like manner, my day lasts while the work that the Father gave me to do remains undone. This is my day, and the Jews cannot harm me. But "I must work while it is day," for the night is coming when, if I shall attempt to work, I shall surely perish, ch. 9 : 4. The time is coming when I must say to my enemies, "This is your hour and the power of darkness." The words of Jesus, however, are in such a form as to be of universal application. Those who are in the path of duty walk ever in the light and cannot fall, while those who seek to escape it walk in the dark and are sure to stumble. A man is immortal till his work is done. **Because there is no light in him.** Some would render, *because the light*—that is, of the world, of day—*is not in it;* is not in the night. While this seems the most natural view, yet the more common translation, *in him*, is to be explained by regarding the eye as the light of the body (Matt. 6 : 22, 23), and if there is no light in the

11 These things said he: and after that he saith unto them, Our friend Lazarus ^d sleepeth; but I go, ^e that
12 I may awake him out of sleep. Then said his dis-
13 ciples, Lord, if he sleep, he shall do well. Howbeit Jesus spake of his death: but they thought that he
14 had spoken of taking of rest in sleep. Then said Je-
15 sus unto them plainly, Lazarus is dead. And I am glad ^f for your sakes that I was not there, ^g to the intent ye may believe; nevertheless let us go unto him.
16 Then said ^h Thomas, which is called Didymus, unto

^d So Deut. 31. 16; Dan. 12. 2; Matt. 9. 24; Acts 7. 60; 1 Cor. 15. 18, 51; 1 Thess. 4. 13, 14.
^e vers. 43, 44.
^f ch. 12. 30; 17. 19.
^g ver. 4; ch. 2. 11.
^h ch. 20. 24-29.

eye, then are we in darkness and we stumble.

11. Our friend Lazarus. An illustrious title from such lips! It was given to Abraham alone of all the Old Testament saints. It should be noted how Christ takes his disciples into his friendship. **Sleepeth,** or *has fallen asleep.* Thus in words of great beauty and tenderness he breaks the news of Lazarus' death. He represents in this pleasing and tender image that which the Scriptures call the king of terrors, Job 18 : 14. The figure of *sleep* is often used in the Bible with reference to the death of Christians (see references); it is used also by heathen writers. "The nearest motive to this image may probably have been the likeness of a dead body to one sleeping. Yet there may well lie in it a deeper thought, of the state of the dead being that of sleep—not indeed a dreamless sleep, but the separation of the soul from the body, as the appointed, and indeed necessary, organ of its activity, may and must bring about, not a suspension, but a depression of the consciousness. Wherefore, the state of the soul apart from the body is never considered in the Scriptures as itself desirable, nor as other than a state of transition, the Scriptures acknowledging no true immortality apart from the resurrection of the body."—TRENCH.

12. Lord, if he sleep, he shall do well—that is, *shall recover.* The disciples, supposing Jesus to refer to natural sleep, thought that this indicated a favorable change in the condition of Lazarus. They would also intimate to Jesus that, such being the condition of Lazarus, there was no longer any need for him to expose himself to peril. For a similar mistake see Matt. 16 : 11. As the disciples were so slow to comprehend the words of Jesus while he was with them, it does not seem probable that they could have invented the remarkable sayings and sublime discourses which they record.

13. Howbeit Jesus spake, rather, *But Jesus had spoken.* **They thought that he had spoken,** that *he was speaking,* of the repose of sleep.

14. Then said Jesus unto them plainly, without using any figure of speech. This is spoken also positively, without any qualification and without hesitancy. There is no room in the narrative to suppose that Jesus regarded Lazarus as in a deep swoon, or that a second messenger had informed him of Lazarus' death.

15. And I am glad, not for the sake of Martha and Mary and Lazarus, but **for your sakes that I was not there**—not that Lazarus was dead—**to the intent ye may believe.** Not that they might believe for the first time, but that their faith might be confirmed. In the presence of him who was the Prince of life death could not have entered the home at Bethany. The glory of God and the good of the disciples and of all Christians could not have been so well served by the preservation of Lazarus from death as by his resurrection from the dead. The sympathies of Jesus were still with his three friends, but they took in also the wider circle of his disciples, and through them and along with them the whole of our suffering humanity.

16. Thomas in Aramæan, and **Didymus** in Greek, both signify a *twin.* He was probably from Galilee. He was impulsive, as shown in this verse, of an inquiring mind (ch. 14 : 5, 6), and slow to be convinced, ch. 20 : 24-29. Tradi-

his fellow disciples, Let us also go, that we may die ⁱwith him.

17 Then when Jesus came, he found that he had *lain* in the grave four days already.

18 Now Bethany was nigh unto Jerusalem, about fif-
19 teen furlongs off: and many of the Jews came to Martha and Mary, ʲto comfort them concerning
20 their brother. Then Martha, as soon as she heard that Jesus was coming, went and met him: but Mary sat *still* in the house.

ⁱ ver. 8; ch. 13. 37; Matt. 26. 35.

ʲ Gen. 37. 35; Job 2.11; Rom. 12. 15.

---

tion affirms that he preached the gospel in India and suffered martyrdom. **Let us also go, that we may die with him.** The news of the death of their friend touched the sympathetic and impulsive heart of Thomas, and he was willing to share with Lazarus that which, to the friends of Christ, was but a momentary sleep, ver. 11. It is worthy of notice that the disciples made no objection now to their Master's return to Judæa. By his answer (vers. 9, 10) he had quieted their solicitude for his safety. The intimation also in ver. 15 that some great work was to be performed in connection with the visit to Bethany probably made the disciples all the more willing to return. Commentators, for the most part, see in the question of the disciples (ver. 8), taken in connection with this verse, a fear for their own personal safety. Thomas, according to this interpretation, says in effect: If our Master goes, he goes to certain death. Let us not desert him, but stand by him, and, if needs be, suffer death with him. We do not find, however, that the Jews, in their attempts to stone and kill Jesus, had ever molested the disciples. It does not appear from the narrative that the disciples, when at Bethany, were in fear for their personal safety. The first word of the verse, **Then,** seems to point to the verses preceding, beginning with ver. 8. He had said nothing in these about their personal danger; he had even quieted their apprehension concerning his own peril.

17–27. JESUS ARRIVES AT BETHANY. HIS CONVERSATION WITH MARTHA.

17. **Then when Jesus came,** *Having come, therefore, Jesus.* **Four days already.** If Lazarus died the same day that the messenger announcing his illness arrived, he would most likely have been buried the same day, according to Eastern custom. This would be reckoned as one day; two days our Lord remained in Peræa, and one day would be consumed in the journey to Bethany. This would make four days; but we do not know exactly where Jesus was, nor how long a time would be occupied by the journey. Enough time had intervened to place the death of Lazarus beyond all doubt and to extinguish in the sisters all hope of his restoration.

18. **Now Bethany was nigh.** This explanation indicates that John was writing for readers not well acquainted with Palestine. It accounts also for the fact mentioned in the following verse, that so many had come from Jerusalem. The use of the past tense here harmonizes with the general view that John wrote after the destruction of Jerusalem and the laying waste of the neighborhood. **About fifteen furlongs off;** nearly, or about, two miles.

19. **And many of the Jews came,** *had come.* Thus we see that in a natural way many witnesses of the miracle were secured. The presence of so many Jews from Jerusalem indicates that the family of Lazarus was well known. These visitors evidently supposed that Lazarus was dead. **To Martha and Mary.** This is the most approved reading. Tischendorf, however, reads, *To those who were about Martha and Mary* — to them, their relatives, and the mourning and wailing women.

20. **Then** (*therefore*) **Martha, as soon as she heard,** etc. Jesus probably tarried outside of the village near where Lazarus was buried, and from here he suffered tidings to go before him that he was near at hand. He would, if possible, have his first interview with the bereaved sisters alone.

21 Then said Martha unto Jesus, Lord, ^k if thou hadst
22 been here, my brother had not died. But I know,
that even now, ^l whatsoever thou wilt ask of God,
23 God will give *it* thee. Jesus saith unto her, Thy
24 brother shall rise again. Martha saith unto him, ^m I
know that he shall rise again in the resurrection at
25 the last day. Jesus said unto her, I am ⁿ the resurrection, and the ^o life: ^p he that believeth in me,

^k ver. 32.
^l ch. 3. 35; 9. 31; Ps. 2. 8.
^m ch. 5. 28, 29; Job 19. 25-27; Ps. 49. 15; Isa. 26. 19; Dan. 12. 2; Luke 14. 14.
ⁿ ch. 5. 21; 6. 39, 40, 44; 1 Cor. 15. 20-26; 2 Cor. 4. 14; Phil. 3. 20, 21; Col. 3. 3, 4.
^o ch. 1. 4; 5. 26; 6. 35; 14. 6; 1 John 1. 1, 2; 5. 11; Rev. 1. 18.
^p ch. 3. 36; Rom. 8. 10, 11, 38, 39.

Martha first hears of his arrival and goes out to meet him. But **Mary sat still in the house**, rather, *sat in the house*, not having heard, probably, that Jesus had come; for when she did hear (vers. 28, 29) " she arose quickly, and came unto him." "For when Mary on that former occasion (Luke 10 : 39) chose to sit still, it was because it was at the feet of Jesus she was sitting. This nearness to him, and not the sitting still, was then the attraction. The same motive that kept her on that other occasion in stillness there would now have brought her with the swift impulse of love to the place where Jesus was."—TRENCH.

21. **Lord, if thou hadst been here.** As both sisters say the same thing (ver. 32), it would seem that they had made similar remarks to each other while waiting for his coming. It showed also what had been their hope in sending for him, ver. 3. It was probably in their heart to ask, Why wast thou not here in time to spare us this bereavement? Yet the words show faith in Christ, since they believe that he could have restored their brother. They manifest a certain lack of faith, in that they supposed that Jesus could not heal without being present.

22. Martha, however, encouraged by his coming and presence, is not without hope that Jesus will in some way come to their relief. **But I know, that even now.** She has great confidence in the powers of the Master. She has witnessed his miracles, and knows that great possibilities reside in him. Yet she hardly ventures to name or hope for the boon she so much desires—the restoration of her dead brother. Martha's faith appears weak in this respect, that while she believes him to have favor with God, she does not regard him as having in himself the fulness of divine power.

23. Jesus assures her that the ungessed desire of her heart shall indeed be granted. He had come as the Lord of life and death, Rev. 1 : 18. **Thy brother shall rise again.** He purposely speaks in general terms, to try her faith still further. He will not work a miracle to gratify the simple impulse of natural affection. He would show now, as he did once before (ch. 2 : 3, 4), that his miraculous power was not at the bidding of private friendship, but for a higher end. He will first broaden Martha's view of himself and lift her up into a higher plane of life, so that when the desire of her heart is granted it may not be an empty gift. To realize that we have a present Saviour, who is the resurrection and the life, is more than the mere temporary restoration of our departed friends.

24. **I know that he shall rise . . . at the last day.** As a pious Israelite she believed in the resurrection of the dead, but finds little comfort in the doctrine. She does not yet venture to believe that Jesus is about to grant her desire. She knows that her brother will rise at the last day. She would rather be able to say, I know that he shall rise *now*.

25. **I am**—not *shall be*—**the resurrection, and the life.** Jesus says in effect to Martha: My triumph over death does not await that final hour for its manifestation. *Even now* the whole power to impart, maintain, and restore life resides in me. **He that believeth in me, though he were dead, yet shall he live ;** *even though he die, he shall live*. Those who, like Lazarus, are believers in him, still live spiritually, though their bodies perish. Thus he presents himself as the Author not only of the resurrection, but of that spiritual life which death cannot touch and which is eternal.

JOHN XI.   A. D. 30.

26 though he were dead, yet shall he live: and �q whoso- q ch.3.15-18; Luke
ever liveth and believeth in me shall never die. Be- 20.36; Rev. 21. 4.
27 lievest thou this? She saith unto him, Yea, Lord:
I believe that thou art the Christ, the Son of God, r ch. 4. 42; 6. 14, 69;
ˢ which should come into the world. Matt. 16. 16.
28 And when she had so said, she went her way, and ˢ ch. 6. 14; Matt.
called Mary her sister secretly, saying, ᵗ The Master 11. 3.
29 is come, and calleth for thee. ᵘ As soon as she heard ᵗ ch. 13. 13; 20. 16.
30 *that*, she arose quickly, and came unto him. (Now ᵘ Ps. 27. 8.
Jesus was not yet come into the town, but was in
31 that place where Martha met him.) ᵛ The Jews then ᵛ ver. 19.
which were with her in the house, and comforted her,
when they saw Mary, that she rose up hastily and
went out, followed her, saying, She goeth unto the
grave to weep there.

26. **And whosoever,** etc. Over such death shall have no power; their continued life and happiness are assured in him, and their resurrection also. Hanna (in his *Life of our Lord,* vol. iii. p. 261) expresses well the thought of this passage: "Would that I could get you and all to look to me in another and far higher character than the assuager of human sorrow, the bringer of a present relief—that I could fix your faith on me as the Prince of life, the Author, the Bestower, the Originator, the Supporter, the Maturer of that eternal life within the soul over which death hath so little dominion that whosoever hath this life begun, in dying still lives, and in living can never die." How striking the appeal and the application to Martha!—**Believest thou this?**

27. **Yea, Lord: I believe**—according to the most approved reading, *I have believed* (and now believe)—**that thou art the Christ, the Son of God.** Though Martha may not have comprehended, yet she evidently means to assert her belief in the truth of all that Jesus had said. She believed him to be the Anointed One, the Son of God, the subject of the prophecy, and she was willing to believe all glorious things concerning him. Trench observes that her faith was "as that of most persons at all times must be—implicit rather than explicit." "And this faith prepared her to regard her brother's restoration, not as a social blessing from the hand of friendship (ver. 21), but as a living 'sign' of the Messiahship of Jesus and a living symbol of 'the resurrection and the life.'" —*Annotated Par. Bib.* "Martha declares her faith in Christ with a steadfast assurance which places her testimony by that of Peter's (Matt. 16 : 16), whom in so many features she resembles."—DE PRESSENSÉ, *Life of Christ,* p. 400.

28-38. MARY, BEING CALLED, GOES TO MEET JESUS. THE WEEPING COMPANY ARRIVE AT THE TOMB.

28. **And called Mary her sister,** at the bidding of Jesus, as we infer, **secretly;** wishing the interview to be confidential, and doubtless also fearing lest some of the Jews who were present from Jerusalem might be unfriendly to Jesus and take occasion to inform the rulers of his presence. The fear was well founded. See ver. 46. **The Master** (the *Teacher*) **is come, and calleth for thee.** The first intimation we have that Jesus had made mention of the absent sister. All the conversation that passed between Jesus and Martha is not recorded. Jesus never forgot the courtesies of social intercourse.

29. See notes on ver. 20. Some of the oldest manuscripts have the present tense : *She rises quickly, and comes to him.*

30. This verse is not parenthetical, but explanatory. Jesus remains in the same place where **Martha met him.** See on vers. 20, 28.

31. **The Jews . . . followed her.** Thus it was ordered that the miracle should be witnessed by many even of the enemies of Christ. **She goeth unto the grave,** etc. The custom is still re-

32 Then when Mary was come where Jesus was, and saw him, she fell down at his feet, saying unto him, *Lord, if thou hadst been here, my brother had not 33 died. When Jesus therefore saw her weeping, and the Jews also weeping which came with her, ˣhe 34 groaned in the spirit, and was troubled, and said, Where have ye laid him? They said unto him, Lord, 35, 36 come and see. ʸ Jesus wept. Then said the Jews,

* ver. 21.
ˣ ver. 38; Heb. 4 15; Mark 7. 34 8. 12.
ʸ Luke 19. 41.

---

tained in the East. "I noticed every morning, since coming to Sidon, that women come forth very early to visit the graves. They move about under the trees and among the tombs in the gray dawn, wrapped up from head to feet in their white sheets, and looking for all the world like veritable ghosts. Sometimes I hear the voice of prayer, some weep and sob, while others sing or chant in a low monotonous tone."—THOMSON'S *Land and Book*, vol. i. p. 144.

32. **Fell down at his feet.** To show peculiar respect to friends on meeting or receiving them, it was common in the East to bow the body downward almost to the ground or to fall entirely prostrate. The prostration of Mary at the feet of Jesus was more than the observance of a formal custom; it was most likely both the natural expression of feelings, overcome as she was with grief, and of earnest pleading, Mark 7 : 25. **Lord, if thou hadst been here.** See ver. 21. She utters the same words of sorrow as Martha; but while she makes no expression of hope (ver. 22), she shows no lack of faith. She leaves it all with the Lord. Hers was the silent pleading of an agonizing soul, to which words could give no adequate expression.

33. **When Jesus therefore saw her weeping.** The reality of our Lord's humanity is beautifully brought out here. We are so constituted that the sight of grief moves us to tears; so Jesus wept when he saw others weeping. **He groaned in the spirit, and was troubled.** Considerable difference of opinion exists as to the meaning of this clause. Literally translated, it means, *He was indignant in spirit, and troubled himself.* The word rendered *groaned* is used four times in the New Testament. Compare its use in Matt. 9 : 30; Mark 1 : 43 and 14 : 5. It probably means here to *be deeply moved,* perhaps with a suppressed sound. And *troubled himself* may be regarded as a Hebrew mode of expression, equivalent to *was troubled*. It seems best, therefore, to consider the phrase as "expressing the highest and deepest kind of agitation of mind—an agitation in which grief, compassion, and holy detestation of sin's work in the world were all mingled and combined." But this agitation is for the moment concealed from view; it is inward, in the spirit, in his human spirit, in himself, ver. 38. The word *spirit* here is aptly used in speaking of holy, spiritual emotion.

34. **Where have ye laid him?** A question asked not for information, but as a friendly inquiry; and also, perhaps, to show that there was no collusion between Christ and the sisters, and no suspicion of imposture about the raising of Lazarus.

35. **Jesus wept;** *shed tears* is the exact meaning of the word. It is different from the word used to express the weeping of Mary and the Jews in ver. 33. That denotes a loud wail; this, silent tears. The tears of Jesus were tears of sympathy: he wept when he saw the sisters and their friends weeping, ver. 33. His human tenderness stands out all the more strongly here in contrast with his divine power, displayed so soon afterward, ver. 43. The tears of Jesus were also, doubtless, tears of pity for human misery. These scenes of sorrow could not have been witnessed *by him* without their *cause* being suggested. The words of Pressensé may also have much force: " With his great pity for fallen humanity mingled a tender and intimate sympathy with the bitter suffering of separation. Standing by the grave of Lazarus, he bears on his heart the burden of all mourners. He knows what it is to see a beloved form brought down to the silence and stillness of the tomb."—*Life of Christ*, p. 401.

36. **Then said the Jews.** Even

37 Behold how he loved him! And some of them said, Could not this man, *which opened the eyes of the blind, have caused that even this man should not 38 have died? Jesus therefore again groaning in himself cometh to the grave. It was a cave, and a stone 39 lay upon it. Jesus said, Take ye away the stone. Martha, the sister of him that was dead, saith unto him, Lord, by this time he stinketh: for he hath

* ch. 9. 6, 7; Luke 7. 21.

his enemies, disarmed for the moment by his tears, are moved to admiration and sympathy for him. The greatness of Christ's love is acknowledged by his enemies.

37. **And some.** Some, however, of those present who had witnessed the miracle wrought upon the blind man are disposed to find fault with Jesus for not interposing his great power to keep his friend from dying. Perhaps they were among those who asked, "How can a man that is a sinner do such miracles?" ch. 9 : 16. It indicates that our Lord's miracles were admitted as true.

38. **Groaning** (see ver. 33) **in himself**, equivalent to *in spirit* in ver. 33. Jesus was again deeply moved at the sight of the grave. It suggested to him the cause of all this sorrow and misery. **It was a cave, and a stone lay upon it.** "The tomb, as the whole course of the narrative shows, was without the town (ver. 30); and this is according to the universal custom of the East (Luke 7 : 12), which was not to place the dead among the living. It was a cave. Such was commonly the family vault of the Jews—sometimes natural (Gen. 23 : 9), sometimes artificial and hollowed out by man's labor from the rock (Isa. 22 : 16; Matt. 27 : 60), in a garden (John 19 : 41), or in some field, the possession of the family (Gen. 23 : 9, 17–20; 25 : 9; 2 Kings. 21 : 18), with recesses in the sides, wherein the bodies were laid—occasionally with chambers, one beyond another. Sometimes the entrance to these tombs was on a level, sometimes there was a descent to them by steps." —TRENCH. Dr. H. C. Fish, who felt assured that he saw the very locality where this tomb was, thus says (*Bible Lands Illustrated*, p. 246): "Not far beyond, toward Bethany [a little west of Bethany], we find a rocky knoll with several ancient caves, where, probably, was the *grave of Lazarus*. It could not have been *in* the village of Bethany (where the monks would show it), and everything in the inspired record points to this locality. 'It was a cave, and a stone lay upon it' (John 11 : 38), *i. e.* over its mouth. One of these cavities (no doubt used of old for burying the dead) I entered, finding no difficulty in standing erect after creeping through the mouth. Was it to this very grave that the Saviour pointed as he said, 'Take ye away the stone' (John 11 : 39)? Was it where I stood that he, in the hushed silence, first raised his eyes to heaven, and then in tones of sonorous authority cried, 'Lazarus, come forth'?"

39–44. JESUS CAUSES THE GRAVE TO BE OPENED; PRAYS TO THE FATHER; RAISES LAZARUS FROM THE DEAD.

39. **Take ye away**, etc., spoken to the attendants of Mary and Martha. They would be all the more impressed with the greatness and reality of the miracle by being called upon to assist in this way. **Martha, the sister,** etc. The relationship is mentioned probably to account for her remonstrance. She was the proper guardian of the remains. This is another incidental touch in the narrative that shows the reality of Lazarus' death. Martha, his sister, who ministered to him in his sickness and saw him die, publicly declares that he has been dead four days. **Lord, by this time**, etc. In the East it is said that all the marks of corruption appear within four days. We must, however, remember that this took place in the *winter*. It seems best to take these words as the conclusion which Martha draws from the time he has been buried, rather than as expressing an experience which she now makes. She shrank from the exposure which she naturally supposed would be made. The faith, and hope too, which the

A. D. 30.   JOHN XI.   203

40 been *dead* four days. Jesus saith unto her, ªSaid I
not unto thee, that, ᵇif thou wouldest believe, thou
41 shouldest see ᶜthe glory of God? Then they took
away the stone *from the place* where the dead was laid.
And Jesus lifted up *his* eyes, and said, Father, I
42 thank thee that thou hast heard me. And ᵈI knew
that thou hearest me always: but ᵉbecause of the
people which stand by I said *it*, ᶠthat they may be-
43 lieve that thou hast sent me. And when he thus had
spoken, he cried with a loud voice, Lazarus, come
44 forth. ᵍAnd he that was dead came forth, bound
hand and foot with grave-clothes: and ʰhis face was
bound about with a napkin. Jesus saith unto them,
Loose him, and let him go.

ª vers. 23–26.
ᵇ 2 Chron. 20. 20.
ᶜ ver. 4.
ᵈ ch. 8. 29; Matt. 26. 53; Heb. 5. 7; 7. 25.
ᵉ ch. 12. 30.
ᶠ ch. 5. 34–36.
ᵍ ch. 5. 21, 25; 1 Sam. 2. 6; Ps. 33. 9; Luke 7. 11–15.
ʰ ch. 20. 7.

---

words of Jesus (ver. 23) had awakened in her had become clouded. She hesitated to believe such great things of Christ—that he could raise her brother after being so long time dead.

40. Therefore, to confirm Martha's faith, Jesus reminds her of the conversation they held upon his first arrival (vers. 22–27): **If thou wouldest believe**, etc. This may be taken as the general import of this conversation, or it may have been a part of it that was not recorded before. Jesus thus demands a certain degree of faith corresponding to the miracle. **See the glory of God**, as manifested in the exercise of divine power.

41. Martha now no longer objects. **Then they took away the stone.** The words, **from the place where the dead was laid**, according to the best authorities, should be omitted. **Hast heard me**, in his communion with the Father which he had ever enjoyed in his work among men. He publicly acknowledges this; and now the miracle was to be a sign not only of this intimate communion, but also of his Messiahship.

42. **And I knew.** The communion of the Father and the Son and their unity of mind and purpose were always perfect. This Jesus knew, yet he prayed. He knew this, but the Jews did not know it, for they accused him of working his miracles by the power of Beelzebub. Hence, **because of the people which stand by, I said**, etc. "At other times our Lord prayed in silence. On this occasion he prayed aloud, for the sake of the people which stood by, that if they should perceive that he was heard, and that he wrought a great miracle by the power of God, they might thence conclude that whatever he did was in accordance with the will of God, and might no longer doubt that he was really sent by God into the world."—TITTMANN.

43. **Cried with a loud voice**, not that Lazarus might be made to hear, but that the bystanders might all observe what was about to take place—that they might see that it was by no magical mutterings or words of enchantment (Isa. 8:19, 20), but by his own word of power, that the deed is done. This same voice shall be the cause of a greater awakening, John 5: 28, 29; 1 Thess. 4:16; 1 Cor. 15:52. **Lazarus, come forth;** speaking to the dead as to the living, knowing the state of both alike. Sublime words! words of power! Truly this is the "voice of the Son of God." It has been happily remarked that Jesus said "*Lazarus*, come forth," lest all the dead should rise. It is worthy of note that even this greatest of all his miracles is wrought by Christ without any apparent effort; he speaks and it is done.

44. **And he that was dead came forth, bound,** etc. Some would make it a new miracle that he was able to come forth bound in this way. But this seems needless. Locomotion was most likely hindered by the grave-clothes, but not rendered impossible. His face was probably encircled with a napkin, bound around the chin. There is force in the remark of Ryle: "My own private feeling is that the slow, gradual, tottering movements of a figure encumbered by grave-clothes

JOHN XI. A. D. 30.

45 Then many of the Jews which came to Mary, ¹ and had seen the things which Jesus did, believed on him. 46 But some of them went their ways to the Pharisees, and told them what things Jesus had done.

A council to put Jesus to death: he retires to Ephraim.

47 ʲ Then gathered the chief priests and the Pharisees a council, and said, ᵏ What do we? for this man doeth

¹ ch. 2. 23; 10. 42; 12. 11, 18.

ʲ Ps. 2. 2; Matt. 26. 3; Mark 14. 1; Luke 22. 2; Acts 4. 25-28.
ᵏ ch. 12. 19; Acts 4. 16.

would impress a crowd far more than the rapid, ghost-like gliding out in air of a body of which the feet did not move." **Loose him, and let him go.** Lazarus came forth before the eyes of all; he came forth with all his grave-clothes upon him. Some of the spectators handled the clothes, and even Lazarus himself. The reality of the miracle could scarcely be denied, at least by these persons. Even the enemies of Jesus could not deny its reality, as they acknowledge, ver. 47. "Of Lazarus himself we have but one further notice (12 : 2), but that, like the command to give meat to the revived maiden (Mark 5 : 43), like the Lord's own participation of food after the resurrection (Luke 24 : 42; John 21 : 13), is a witness against anything merely *phantastic* in his rising again. He is generally assumed to have been much younger than his sisters. One tradition, mentioned by Epiphanius, makes him thirty years old at this time, and to have survived thirty years more. The tradition of his later life, as that he became bishop of Marseilles, rests upon no good authority."—TRENCH. The evangelist passes over in silence the effect of the miracle upon the two sisters of Lazarus. He leaves us to imagine their joy—a joy which, as Trench observes, "was well nigh theirs alone among all the mourners of all times,

'Who to the verge have followed those they love,
And on the insuperable threshold stand;
With cherished names its speechless calm reprove,
And stretch in the abyss their ungrasp'd hand.'"

A veil is thrown over all this, and we are shown the effect of the miracle upon the witnesses of it and upon the Jewish rulers, and the part it played in bringing about, according to the determinate decree and counsel of God, the death of Jesus upon the cross.

45-54. EFFECT OF THE MIRACLE UPON THE WITNESSES AND THE SANHEDRIM.

45. **Then many of the Jews . . . believed on him.** A majority of them, as we may infer. They regarded such a mighty miracle as possible only to divine power. Whether this faith of theirs was unto salvation or not, we do not know, but it is very likely that these mourners of Bethany helped to swell the ranks of the converts on the day of Pentecost. They realized the truth of the Preacher's words: "It is better to go to the house of mourning than to go to the house of feasting," Eccles. 7 : 2.

46. **But some of them**, not convinced, but rather hardened in heart, by this evidence of Jesus' Messiahship, **went their ways to the Pharisees,** his bitter and open enemies, **and told them what things Jesus had done,** evidently in order that they might put him to death. Some suppose that the purpose of these persons was to present this miracle as a conclusive argument against the views of the Pharisees, and that they were really the friends of Jesus and intended to do him a favor. But it is evident from the first part of the verse that there is a great difference in the disposition toward Jesus of the persons mentioned here and of those who believed on him. "The Jews were aware of the deadly enmity of the Pharisees toward Jesus; if these informants had been friends, they must have witnessed for Jesus with heroic martyr-courage, and they would have secured a firm and conspicuous station in the evangelistic history."—LANGE.

47. **Then,** *therefore*, because they were informed of the resurrection of Lazarus, **gathered the chief priests and the Pharisees a council,** This was the Sanhedrim, the great ecclesiastical council of the Jews. **What do we?** "Why are we so inactive?" This man, whom they hated and attempted

48 many miracles. If we let him thus alone, all *men* will believe on him: and the Romans shall come and
49 take away both our place and nation. And one of them, *named* ¹Caiaphas, being the high priest that same year, said unto them, ᵐ Ye know nothing at all,
50 ª nor consider that it is expedient for us, that one man should die for the people, and that the whole nation

¹ ch 18. 14; Luke 3. 2; Acts 4. 6.
ᵐ ch. 7. 48, 49; 1 Cor. 1. 20; 3. 18, 19.
ª ch. 18. 14.

but recently to kill, and whom they had, as they supposed, driven from Judæa for ever, is again at Bethany, near by, and again drawing the multitude after him. They see that something must be done to stem the tide of his popularity. There is great need that they should bestir themselves, **for this man doeth many miracles,** or *signs.* They certainly would have denied, if they could, that Christ wrought any miracles, but the miracles were too many and too public for them to do so. The most that the bitterest enemies of Christ could do *in his day* was to attribute these miracles to an evil source. It was left for his enemies of a later date to deny their *occurrence* or that they were even *possible.*

48. **All men will believe,** etc. They probably refer to the multitude, the common people, whom they despised, but who were generally favorably disposed toward Jesus. **The Romans shall (*will*) come and take away both our place and nation.** They profess to fear that the people will acknowledge Jesus as the Messiah and set him up as their king—that as a result the Romans will come and abolish their nationality and destroy their temple. There was some pretext for such fear in the fact that the Romans were exceedingly jealous of their authority, and were not slow to use the vast power they swayed to crush the first appearance of rebellion. The first question which the Roman governor Pilate asked Jesus was, "Art thou the king of the Jews?" The council does not seem once to consider whether the miracles of Jesus are wrought by the power of God or whether he may not indeed be the Messiah. The truth or falsehood of his claims is not discussed at all. The only purpose of their consultation appears to have been to gratify their hatred by putting Jesus to death under color of a regard for the public safety; for Jesus had never aspired to an earthly kingdom, but, on the contrary, he proclaimed that his kingdom was not of this world, and taught the people to "render to Cæsar the things that were Cæsar's." The insincerity of their fear and their concern for their nation is evident also from the fact that they themselves looked for one who should deliver their nation from the Roman yoke; and if Christ had claimed such a mission and wrought the miracles which he did, they would most probably have gladly received him.

49. **Caiaphas,** more bold and unscrupulous than the rest. Joseph Caiaphas was high priest about nine years, during the whole procuratorship of Pontius Pilate, but was deposed by the proconsul Vitellius soon after the removal of Pilate. He was son-in-law to Annas, who had been formerly the high priest, and who still exerted great influence as the father-in-law of Caiaphas, and is thought by some to have shared the office with him—the latter as actual high priest, the former as president of the Sanhedrim — or else that Annas acted as the vicar or deputy of Caiaphas. It would seem from Acts 5 : 17 that Caiaphas was a Sadducee. Compare Matt. 26 : 3; Luke 3 : 2; John 18 : 13, 19, 24; Acts 4 : 6. **Being the high priest that same year.** The fact is mentioned to explain why his words have such weight and significance. The historical fact that the office of high priest is now no longer a life office, but subject to the caprice of the Roman governors, is also implied. **Ye,** emphatic, **know nothing at all.** He had a great contempt for the tardy movements of the rest, who were chiefly Pharisees.

50. **Expedient for us,** or, according to some high authorities, *for you.* The whole deliberation of the council was based on *expediency,* and *not principle.* The argument of Caiaphas was that it was better that Jesus should suf-

51 perish not. And this spake he not of himself: but being high priest that year he prophesied °that Jesus
52 should die for that nation; and ᵖnot for that nation only, ᵠbut that also he should gather together in one ʳthe children of God that were scattered abroad.
53 Then from that day forth they took counsel together
54 for to put him to death. Jesus ˢtherefore walked no

° ch. 10. 15; Isa. 53. 5–8; Dan. 9. 26.
ᵖ ch. 1. 29; Isa. 49. 6; 1 John 2. 2; Rev. 5. 9; 7. 9, 10.
ᵠ ch. 10. 16; Isa. 55. 5; 56. 8, Eph. 2. 14–22.
ʳ Acts 18. 10; Rom. 9. 25, 26; 2 Thess. 2. 13, 14.
ˢ ch. 4. 1, 3; 7. 1; 10. 40.

fer death, whether innocent or not, than that the whole nation should be imperilled. He did not know, of course, the full import of the words he uttered.

51. And this spake he not of himself, or *from himself*—that is, in giving utterance to his views he was unconsciously the mouthpiece of the Spirit to utter a prophecy concerning Christ's atoning death. **But being high priest**, etc. The prophetic gift was not always connected with the office, but God in ancient times often used the high priests as interpreters of his will. "God, who sometimes uses the wicked to accomplish his purposes, caused the Aaronic priesthood, just when it was about to be abolished, to speak prophetically, though unconsciously, by its representatives, of the great Sin-offering then about to be presented for the sins of the world. Caiaphas thus occupies in relation to the Mosaic and the Christian dispensations the same place as Balaam fills in respect to the patriarchal and the Mosaic economies."—*Annotated Par. Bib.* **For that nation**—that is, the Jewish nation.

52. And not for that nation only. The benefits of his death were to be enjoyed by the Gentiles as well as by the Jews. "All believers, of all nations and every region of the earth, shall partake of his salvation," ch. 10:16. "The best parallel of this verse is 1 John 2:2: 'He is a propitiation for our sins; and not for ours only, but also for the sins of the whole world.' Not the law, as the Jews supposed, but the atoning death of Christ, was that which should bind together all men into one fellowship. 'I, if I be lifted up from the earth, will draw all men unto me.' The law was only a wall of separation; it was only that death which could knit together. We may compare Eph. 2:13–22 as the great commentary of St. Paul on the words of St. John."—TRENCH. **In one**—that is, into one people or spiritual nation, having one Lord, and enjoying access to him by one Spirit.

53. Then, being easily persuaded that it was most expedient to follow the advice of Caiaphas, all they did now was to consider *how* they could best bring about his death. The wonderful miracle just wrought at Bethany would greatly increase the number of our Lord's adherents, so that an open attempt to stone him would probably have created a tumult among the people for which the rulers would have been held accountable. As they could not *legally* carry out their design of putting Christ to death, and could not do it unlawfully with safety to themselves, they were compelled to work through the Roman governor, who alone held the power of capital punishment. **From that day**, the day of the decisive and final rejection of Jesus by the Jewish rulers. An organized movement against him had been going on (Mark 3:6; John 5: 16–18; 7:25, 32; 9:22), but not till now does it appear that the Sanhedrim, in formal session, determined that he should die.

54. Walked no more openly—that is, for the present, not until the passover season. His time had not yet come, and therefore he does not needlessly expose himself to the daily assaults of these wicked men. He probably desired also to give further instruction and training to his disciples, and therefore retires with them from the excitement in and about Jerusalem. He probably remained at or near Bethany but a day or two, and does not appear to have visited Jerusalem. **Near to the wilderness** of Judæa, that uninhabited and uncultivated district between the hill-country of Judæa and Jerusalem and the Jordan. **Ephraim.** Nothing is certainly known of this place. It is conjectured to be identical

more openly among the Jews; but went thence unto a country near to the wilderness, into a city called ᵗEphraim, and there continued with his disciples.   ᵗ 2 Sam. 13. 23; 2 Chron. 13. 19.

Jesus sought at Jerusalem.

55 ᵘ And the Jews' passover was nigh at hand: and many went out of the country up to Jerusalem before 56 the passover, ˣ to purify themselves. ʸ Then sought they for Jesus, and spake among themselves, as they stood in the temple, What think ye? That he will 57 not come to the feast? Now both the chief priests and the Pharisees had given a commandment, that, if any man knew where he were, he should show *it*, that they might take him.   ᵘ ch. 2. 13; 5. 1; 6. 4. ˣ Ex. 19. 10, 14; Num. 9. 6; 2 Chron. 30. 17-19; Acts 24. 18; 1 Cor. 11. 28. ʸ ch. 7. 11.

---

with Ophrah (Josh. 18:23) and Ephraim (2 Chron. 13:19) and the modern village Taiyibeh, situated on a hill about five miles east of Bethel and sixteen from Jerusalem. (See *Author's Harmony*, p. 266.) This was a fitting place for retirement on the borders of Samaria, and for commencing the journey a little later "through the midst of Samaria and Galilee," Luke 17:11. It was probably about the middle of February, and Jesus remained here about three weeks.

55-57. JESUS SOUGHT AT JERUSALEM. For the incidents in our Lord's life occurring between this and the events mentioned in the former section, see *Author's Harmony*, pp. 141-161. This embraces our Lord's last journey through Samaria and the lower part of Galilee, and through Peræa, occupying about two or three weeks, Luke 17:11 to 19:27, 28.

55. John states here what was the common custom, explaining for the sake of readers who were not Jews. **To purify themselves** (2 Chron. 30:17-19) from ceremonial uncleanness before eating the passover. These services consisted in bathing, visiting the temple, offering prayers and sacrifices, abstaining from certain kinds of food, and similar ceremonies. From one to six days were thus occupied according to circumstances.

56. The common theme of conversation among these multitudes was Jesus and his works, and the probability of his appearing at the feast. His fame had spread throughout the country, and now, if not before, they had learned of his last great miracle. **What think ye? That he will not**, etc. Both of these should be united in one question, separated only by a comma. They thought that perhaps he had come, and *therefore sought for Jesus.* But finding him not, some may have concluded that he would not come on account of the order of the Sanhedrim, whilst others thought differently. *What think ye, that he will not come to the feast?* Yes, he will come. The rulers especially hoped Jesus would come, so that they might seize him. Their wish was, in their case, father of the thought.

57. **Now both the chief priests and the Pharisees,** etc. This is mentioned to account for the doubt expressed as to his coming. It is probable that the people sought him chiefly out of a curiosity to see and hear him, and not in order to inform the rulers about him. The rulers sought him from a different motive. **Had given a commandment.** "They did not lay a price upon his head, but they enjoin all good citizens to be informers against him. Where he is they know not; but he was lately heard of at Bethany, and must still be lurking somewhere near the capital. Alas for them! This hunted refugee will yet enter the capital in triumph, will face them down in the temple, and, even in yielding to be their *victim*, will give them abundant evidence of being their *Lord.*"—DR. D. D WHEDON.

PRACTICAL REMARKS.

1. Christians are not exempt from sickness and suffering, nor are these evidences of God's displeasure, ver. 1; Job 1 : 7-12; James 5 : 11.
2. All our labors of love, however small, are treasured in God's book of remembrance, ver. 2; Mal. 3 : 16-18.
3. While we use every means for the restoration of our suffering friends, the heavenly Physician alone can make them effectual. Effectual prayers need not be long ones. We can safely leave our case with the Lord, ver. 3; 2 Kings 19 : 14.
4. The sickness of believers may be unto death; yet God may be glorified thereby, ver. 4; Rom. 14 : 7, 8.
5. The Lord loves all his own, though of very different dispositions. They are all his dear children, and bear his image, ver. 5.
6. The Lord will answer our prayers, though not at the time or in the way we may expect, ver. 6; 2 Cor. 12 : 9.
7. "He would let the need come to the highest before he interposed. He comes in with his mighty help, but not till every other help has failed " (TRENCH), ver. 7.
8. Christ never leads his people into danger without going with them, vers. 7, 8; Isa. 41 : 17; 42 : 16.
9. The life which God gives us on earth is sufficient for all he has given us to do, ver. 9.
10. He who seeks to learn and do the will of God will find his way made plain before him; but he who seeks his own ends will sooner or later fail and perish, vers. 9, 10.
11. With singular beauty and tenderness the death of the Christian is described as a sleep. Sleeping life is not the highest type of life, but always gives promise of it. So the death of the Christian is not to be desired except as the prelude of a glorified life, ver. 11; Isa. 26 : 19; 57 : 2.
12. Like the disciples, we are apt to put the wrong meaning upon our Lord's words. Hence the need of the Spirit to help us to understand spiritual things, vers. 12, 13; ch. 16 : 13; 1 Cor. 2 : 13, 14.
13. Christ takes cognizance of the death of every saint, ver. 14; Ps. 116 : 15.
14. Death separates us from our friends, but brings us near to Christ, ver. 15; Phil. 1 : 23.
15. Different dispositions and temperaments are tested and brought out in the Christian life, ver. 16.
16. Human sympathy is sweet, but the Lord alone can fully sympathize with us, ver. 16; Heb. 4 : 15, 16.
17. Jesus comes to his people at the right time and the best time, ver. 17; Matt. 14 : 27.
18. "Grace will keep sorrow from the *heart*, not from the *house* " (M. HENRY), ver. 19; ch. 14 : 1.
19. We may have much love for Christ, yet fail to see the fulness of his love and power, vers. 21, 22.
20. We often increase our troubles by pondering over what might have been, ver. 21.
21. All our hopes of future life centre in Jesus, vers. 23-26.
22. "To die in the fulness of light, in the calm glory of the life which is in Jesus, is no longer that which human language calls by the name of death " (GODET), vers. 25, 26.
23. To know that Christ is the Son of God, the promised Saviour, is the alphabet of Christian knowledge, ver. 27.
24. We should be ever ready to go at the call of Jesus, vers. 28, 29.
25. In all our trials it is best to refer our case to Jesus, and leave all to his disposal, ver. 32.
26. Jesus still has his human nature, and can be touched with the feeling of our infirmities and understand our tears, vers. 33-35; Heb. 4 : 15.
27. How much suffering attended the work which Christ accomplished for us! vers. 36-38; Matt. 8 : 17.
28. How does love arrest the attention of the world! ver. 36; ch. 3 : 13-16.
29. Our weak faith often needs to be strengthened by the words of Christ, vers. 39, 40.
30. Christ, by example, has shown us the importance of public prayer, vers. 41, 42.
31. God requires us to do our part, but does that which we cannot do, vers. 39, 41, 43.
32. The raising of Lazarus was a foreshadowing of the general resurrection, vers. 43, 44.
33. We see how differently different

Jesus, journeying toward Jerusalem, arrives at Bethany.

XII. Then Jesus, six days before the passover, came to Bethany, *where Lazarus was which had been dead, *ch. 11. 1, 43.

persons are affected by the same event, vers. 45, 46.

34. It needs more than a miracle to lead men to repentance and faith, ver. 46; Luke 16 : 31.

35. Many who neglect spiritual things through fear of losing things temporal, finally lose both, vers. 47, 48; Matt. 6 : 33.

36. Even the enemies of Christ are compelled to acknowledge and witness to his works, ver. 47 ; Phil. 2 : 10, 11.

37. How strong and blinding are prejudice and ill-will! vers. 49, 50.

38. God uses even wicked men in carrying out his purposes, vers. 51, 52 ; Ps. 76 : 10; Isa. 10 : 5–7.

39. "The unworthiness of the individual does not affect the sanctity of his office," ver. 51.

40. "The conclusions of great ecclesiastical councils are sometimes wicked," ver. 53.

41. Wicked men confirm one another in their sins by taking counsel together, ver. 53.

42. Jesus did not expose himself to danger when duty did not require it, ver. 54.

43. Ecclesiastical leaders are often foremost in their opposition to the gospel, vers. 55–57.

44. Unbelief does not result from a want of evidence, but from a depraved heart and a perverted will, vers. 46–57.

45. Persons may seek Jesus from wrong motives or with bad intent, ver. 56.

46. "Rulers increase their own sins by making their subjects the instruments of their unrighteousness," ver. 57.

CHAPTER XII.

In this chapter we have two events depending closely upon the raising of Laza us from the dead. The first is Mary's anointing at the supper in Bethany. Jesus received the anointing of the Holy Spirit when he entered upon his prophetic office, Acts 10 : 38. He deigns to accept the anointing of human affection as he enters upon his priestly office. The second event consequent upon the raising of Lazarus is the public greeting of our Saviour as king, vers. 12–19. But the whole chapter is solemn with the shadow of the cross, to which Christ has now nearly approached. The account of the Greeks seeking an interview introduces the thought of his propitiation for the sins of the whole world, vers. 20–34. This is followed by the remarks of our Saviour, warning the Jews on account of their unbelieving cavil concerning this matter (vers. 35, 36); also by the reflections of the apostle on their unbelief (vers. 37–43); and the chapter concludes with a summary of the teachings of Jesus concerning his acceptance or rejection.

1–8. THE SUPPER AND THE ANOINTING AT BETHANY, Matt. 26 : 6–13; Mark 14 : 3–9. The three evangelists evidently relate the same event, with merely the variations of independent narrators. The anointing related in Luke 7 : 36–50 is altogether different from this in time, place, and circumstances. That took place much earlier, in Galilee, probably in the vicinity of Nain; this at Bethany, just before the crucifixion—the one at the house of Simon the Pharisee, the other at the house of Simon the leper. That both were named Simon is not strange in a country where that name was very common. There were even two Simons among the apostles. Wednesday evening, April 5, A. D. 30.

1. **Six days before the passover.** Jesus was journeying toward Jerusalem, probably from Jericho. According to the more usual force of the language in the original, these "six days before" would mean that he arrived *on* the sixth day before the passover commenced. Now, the passover began on Thursday evening at sunset. The sixth day before would begin on Friday evening at sunset. The time of his arrival, then, falls within the Jewish Sabbath. But so long a journey as the distance from Jericho would not have been undertaken by our Saviour on the Sabbath; but it would not have been inconsistent even with strict Jewish custom for him to have completed the journey a few

2 whom he raised from the dead. *There they made him a supper; and Martha served: but Lazarus was one of them that sat at the table with him.
3 Then took ᵇMary a pound of ointment of spikenard, very costly, ᶜand anointed the feet of Jesus, and wiped his feet with her hair: and the house was filled with the odor of the ointment.
4 Then saith one of his disciples, ᵈ Judas Iscariot,
5 Simon's *son*, which should betray him, Why was not this ointment sold for three hundred ᵉpence, and
6 given to the poor? This he said, ᶠnot that he cared for the poor; but because he was a thief, and ᵍ had

* Matt. 26. 6–11
  Mark 14. 3–7.

ᵇ ch. 11. 2; Luke 10. 38, 39.
ᶜ Luke 7. 37, 38.

ᵈ ch. 6. 70, 71.

* Matt. 18. 28.

ᶠ Prov. 29. 7.

ᵍ ch. 13. 29.

---

minutes after the Sabbath commenced, or a little after sunset on Friday evening. There he quietly "rested the Sabbath day, according to the commandment." The words, **which had been dead**, are omitted in the best text. **Bethany, . . . Lazarus.** See on ch. 11 : 1.

2. There they made him a supper. It was in the house of Simon the leper, Matt. 26 : 6. The time of this supper is not certainly known. It was quite customary with the Jews to close the Sabbath with a joyful meal, and the language in Matt. 26 : 16 would seem to indicate that Judas must have commenced his dark plottings at least several days before the betrayal. But, on the other hand, two days before the passover we find evidence indicating that Judas had not yet given the rulers the opportunity they were seeking (Matt. 26 : 2–5) and the language of our Saviour in verse 7—literally, "For the day of my preparation for burial hath she kept this"—would be inappropriate unless the time was very near the crucifixion, making the supper most probably at the close of Wednesday. (See *Author's Harmony*, § 158.) **Martha served.** This is one indication that she was, as has been supposed, a relative of Simon. She as well as Mary took her own characteristic way of showing devoted gratitude for the raising of a brother from the dead, Luke 10 : 38–42.

3. Then took Mary, sister of Lazarus (ch. 11 : 1, 2), **a pound.** It was probably about three-fourths of a pound avoirdupois. **Ointment of spikenard.** An aromatic oil, produced probably from the jatamansi plant of India. **Anointed the feet of Jesus.** His *head*, according to Matthew and Mark;

but here is no contradiction, for there was nard enough to lavishly anoint both. Matthew and Mark notice only the first act, anointing the head; John dwells upon the final and longest, and, on her part, the most humble and devoted, act—the anointing the feet and wiping them with her hair. Washing the feet before an entertainment was usual with the sandalled Orientals, and the accompanying anointing was not infrequent. According to Lightfoot, children performed this office for their parents, and sometimes a disciple for his teacher. **Wiped his feet with her hair.** A mark of the profoundest reverence. It was the glory of a woman (1 Cor. 11 : 15) laid in humblest tribute at Jesus' feet. **The house was filled with the odor of the ointment.** Mentioned only by John, but according to the other evangelists it was destined that the whole household of God should ever be fragrant with the memorial proclamation of this costliest and most beautiful tribute ever tendered to Christ, Matt. 26 : 13; Mark 14 : 9.

4. Judas Iscariot, see on ch. 6 : 71. Only John gives the name of the speaker, though he probably spoke the disapproval of the others, Matt. 26 : 8; Mark 14 : 4. **Which should betray him;** rather, he who was *about to deliver him up*. Matthew says "the disciples;" but John, pointing out the leader and instigator, says, "one of his disciples, Judas Iscariot." We have here a beautiful illustration of the independent and truthful statements of the three evangelists. The three accounts taken together are lifelike. The suggestion of Judas is caught up and inconsiderately repeated by the rest.

5, 6. Three hundred pence, about

7 the bag, and bare what was put therein. Then said Jesus, Let her alone: against the day of my burying
8 hath she kept this. For ʰ the poor always ye have with you; ⁱ but me ye have not always.
9 Much people of the Jews therefore knew that he was there: and they came not for Jesus' sake only, but that they might see Lazarus also, ᵏ whom he had
10 raised from the dead. ˡ But the chief priests consulted
11 that they might put Lazarus also to death; ᵐ because that by reason of him many of the Jews went away, and believed on Jesus.

ʰ Deut. 15. 11; Matt. 26. 11; Mark 14. 7.
ⁱ ver. 35; ch. 8. 21.
ᵏ ch. 11. 43, 44.
ˡ Luke 16. 31.
ᵐ ver. 18; ch. 11.45.

---

forty-five dollars, but it would purchase manifold what that amount would now. It was about a laborer's wages for a whole year. See Matt. 20 : 2. **Given to the poor.** A good reason under ordinary circumstances, and doubtless uttered honestly by all except Judas, who **was a thief,** and desired the money for his own use rather than for the poor. **And bare,** better, *and was wont to take away what was put therein* (ch. 20 : 15). But this selfish instigator soon after sold the life of his Master for thirty shekels, about a third of this amount, the price of a slave, Ex. 21 : 32. **Bag,** *box, pouch,* or *purse.*

7. **Then said Jesus, Let her alone.** The harsh rebuke of Judas was probably spoken to Mary. Jesus hastens to relieve and vindicate her. Matthew (26 : 10) says, "When Jesus understood it," which implies that the murmuring and the reproof of the disciples were intended for the woman, and not for the ear of Jesus, who was the recipient of such honor. Their disapprobation would naturally confuse her. But Jesus takes up her defence. **Against the day of my burying hath she kept this;** the best text reads, *Let her keep it against the day of my burial,* instead of selling it. She was still in the act of anointing. Bodies were anointed and usually embalmed previous to entombing, John 19 : 39. The language of our Saviour implies a prophetic consciousness on the part of Mary that the event of his death was very near, Matt. 26 : 2. As there would be no time for this after his death, this anointing and embalming, as it were, for the sepulchre took place, in the divine arrangement, while he was yet alive. This anointing was not only a symbol of what was about to take place, but was an act performed with definite reference to his death. The language seems to imply a *motive* on the part of Mary; she seems to have had a presentiment, a knowledge beyond his disciples, of his approaching death. It also gave Jesus another opportunity of referring to his death. Her act of love and faith stands out in striking contrast to the avarice of Judas and the murmurings of the others.

8. **The poor always . . . me . . . not always.** Jesus puts himself not above the poor, but with them, Matt. 25 : 40. But he means that they would ever have opportunities of doing good to the poor, but their opportunity to honor him would be short and soon gone.

9. **Much people of the Jews,** see Acts 6 : 7. According to Alford "the Jews" in the Gospel of John always mean, not the great mass of the common people, but the ruling "persons of repute." The time here goes back to that of verse 1.

10. **The chief priests.** Alford and Tholuck both suggest that these priests were of the sect of the Sadducees, believing in no resurrection, but desirous to get Lazarus out of the way because he drew attention to Jesus.

11. **Many of the Jews went away,** *many were withdrawing* from the Jews—not openly and formally, but gradually transferring their confidence from their leaders to Jesus.

12-19. THE TRIUMPHAL ENTRY OF JESUS INTO JERUSALEM, Matt. 21 : 1-11; Mark 11 : 1-11; Luke 19 : 29-44.

Luke is the fullest, John the briefest. While Mark occupies about the same space as Matthew, he is specially minute and vivid by the use of the pres-

212 JOHN XII. A. D. 30.

The first day of the week Jesus enters Jerusalem publicly.

12 ⁿ On the next day much people that were come to the feast, when they heard that Jesus was coming to Jerusalem, took branches of palm trees, and went forth to meet him, and cried, ° Hosanna! Blessed *is* ᴘ the King of Israel that cometh in the name of the Lord!
14 ᑫ And Jesus, when he had found a young ass, sat 15 thereon; as it is written, ʳ Fear not, daughter of Sion! Behold, thy King cometh, sitting on an ass's colt.
16 These things ˢ understood not his disciples at the first; ᵗ but when Jesus was glorified, ᵘ then remembered they that these things were written of him, and *that* they had done these things unto him.

n Matt. 21. 1-9;
Mark 11. 1-10;
Luke 19. 29-38
o Matt. 21. 2-9.
p ch. 1. 49; 19. 15.
q Matt. 21. 7.
r Isa. 35. 4; 40. 9, 10.
s Luke 18. 34.
t ch. 7. 39; 13. 31,32.
u ch. 14. 26.

ent tense, and surpasses the others, throughout the chapter, in his careful specifications of time.
12. **On the next day.** The Sunday after the Sabbath rest of verse 1. **Much people**, already eager to know whether Jesus would be at the feast, ch. 11 : 56.
13. **Took branches of palm trees.** There were then very many palms growing on that road. The palm was the emblem of triumph, Lev. 23 : 40; Rev. 7 : 9. The people met Jesus with these royal honors boldly and enthusiastically, because of the miracles they had seen, and especially because of the raising of Lazarus. Luke also adds that certain Pharisees wished Jesus to rebuke the applause, and also that when he came near and beheld the city, he wept over it. While the multitude continue to shout his honors he weeps over the wicked, the unbelieving, and devoted city. **Hosanna!** an abbreviated compound of two Hebrew words meaning "Save now!" It was equivalent to the exclamation, "Salvation!" The brevity of John's account of this triumph seems to imply that his readers were already acquainted with the fuller descriptions of the other three evangelists. **Blessed is the King of Israel that cometh in the name of the Lord!** This was a distinct Messianic recognition. See Ps. 118 : 25, 26.
14. **A young ass.** The ass was used by persons of the highest rank, Judg. 5 : 10; 10 : 4. But this was not the king's mule (1 Kings 1 : 33, 38, 44), one kept for the use of royalty; nor the horse, which the Scriptures invariably associate with the idea of war (Ex. 15 : 21;

Ps. 76 : 6; Prov. 21 : 31; Jer. 8 : 6), and which the kings of Israel were forbidden to multiply unto themselves (Deut. 17 : 16), but the colt of a beast of burden—one used in hard labor, Matt. 21 : 5. The time had come for Jesus to claim and receive Messianic honors, and this he could not well do on foot in a procession. He therefore rides in triumph into Jerusalem, but in a way which was significant, appropriate, and suited to the nature of his kingdom. The horse was an animal of pride and war, the ass of humility and peace. Thus Jesus publicly claimed and received honors as the Messiah, yet not as a proud, worldly monarch, but as the Prince of Peace. His meekness and lowliness in thus entering Jerusalem were in harmony with the nature of his kingdom, and inconsistent with the views of some rationalistic interpreters, that Jesus really designed to head a military movement, deliver the Jews from the Roman yoke, and become a temporal monarch. How unfounded the last supposition is appears from the facts that the multitude were without arms, and that the Roman authorities failed to take any notice of the triumphal procession as in any degree wrong or disloyal. Jesus probably took the southern road, the direct one from Jericho over the Mount of Olives.
15. **As it is written, Fear not**, quoted not literally, but in an abbreviated form, agreeing with Zech. 9 : 9 in sense.
16. **Understood not at the first;** the evident unconsciousness of the disciples in so many things, not only in what they did, but in what they wrote,

A. D. 30. JOHN XII. 213

17 The people therefore that was with him when he called Lazarus out of his grave, and raised him from
18 the dead, ˣ bare record. ʸ For this cause the people also met him, for that they heard that he had done
19 this miracle. The Pharisees therefore said among themselves, ᶻ Perceive ye how ye prevail nothing? behold, ᵃ the world is gone after him.

Greeks desire to see Jesus: his return to Bethany at night.

20 And there ᵇ were certain Greeks among them ᶜ that

ˣ ch. 11. 43.
ʸ vers. 9-11.

ᶻ ch. 11. 47, 48.
ᵃ ch. 3. 26; Acts 17. 6.
ᵇ Acts 17. 4.
ᶜ 1 Kings 8. 41, 42; Acts 8. 27.

is excellent evidence of their entire simplicity and truthfulness in recording things in realms higher than they knew. **But when Jesus was glorified, then remembered they.** After the ascension and the descent of the Holy Spirit, then was fulfilled the promise of Jesus, ch. 14 : 26 and 16 : 13, 14.

17. **The people ... with him when he called Lazarus out of his grave,** ch. 11 : 42, 43. The raising of Lazarus was the immediate occasion of this ovation. **Bare record,** or *testimony,* that Jesus raised Lazarus. By the change of a single letter many manuscripts read: "The multitude which was with him bare witness that he called Lazarus out of the tomb." Their hosannas were a public testimony to the miracle, ver. 13 ; Luke 19 : 37, 38.

18. **The people also met him.** Two different multitudes are mentioned: one from Bethany accompanying him (ver. 9), and one from Jerusalem meeting him. Each chanted his praises in responsive chorus, Mark 11 : 9, 10. **For this cause.** It was the raising of Lazarus that caused both companies now to attend Jesus in his triumphal march.

19. **The Pharisees therefore said.** What follows is the language of enemies in their rage and despair, seeking to stir each other up to acts of violence. This discussion or expression of reproach was perhaps aimed at the Sadducean policy of Caiaphas, ch. 11 : 48-50. **The world.** A strong popular expression—everybody.

20-36. CERTAIN GREEKS DESIRE TO SEE JESUS. HE RETURNS TO BETHANY AT NIGHT. On the last point, Matt. 21 : 17 ; Mark 11 : 11. Sunday, April 2d. "In the application of these Gentiles our Lord sees a token of his glory as the Redeemer of the world, and therefore of that 'hour' of mortal suffering through which he must pass in order to 'reconcile both [Jew and Gentile] unto God in one body by the cross.' See ch. 10 : 16 ; 11 : 51, 52 ; Eph. 2 : 13-22. Hence the conflicting emotions by which his 'soul is troubled,' ver. 27 ; hence also his allusion to the lesson so clearly taught by his death, that self-sacrifice is necessary to usefulness (ver. 24), and indispensable to the eternal well-being and acceptance of the servant of Jesus, vers. 25, 26. Such a lesson was fitted to dissipate any hopes which his triumphant entry into Jerusalem might have excited of a kingdom of earthly glory."—*Annotated Paragraph Bible.*

20. The time of this approach of these Greeks to Jesus was probably on the same day as the triumphal entry. It would seem natural to suppose that their attention was attracted to Christ by the procession. The language of Jesus (vers. 23-33) and the voice from heaven (ver. 28) were also in harmony with the day, the *tenth* of Nisan, when he, the great Paschal Lamb, was selected, as it were, in the temple for our passover. The 36th verse, which leads Robinson, Ellicott, and others to suppose that this occurred just before his final departure from the temple, may be explained as referring to his departure for the night to Bethany. It is certainly more natural to suppose a break of three or four days after verse 36 than between verses 19, 20, especially as John does not, with the other evangelists, relate the incidents of those days. It is preferable, therefore, with Lightfoot, Newcome, Greswell, and others to place the interview with the Greeks here. See *Author's Harmony,* §§ 139, 140. Neander also inclines to this view. The place of this colloquy is within the area of the temple (Matt. 26 : 55), probably in

21 came up to worship at the feast: the same came therefore to Philip, ^d which was of Bethsaida of Galilee, and desired him, saying, Sir, we would see Jesus.
22 Philip cometh and telleth Andrew: and again Andrew and Philip tell Jesus.
23 And Jesus answered them, saying, ^e The hour is
24 come, that the Son of man should be glorified. Verily, verily, I say unto you, ^f Except a corn of wheat fall into the ground and die, it abideth alone: but
25 ^g if it die, it bringeth forth much fruit. ^h He that loveth his life shall lose it; and he that hateth his

^d ch. 1. 44.

^e ch. 7. 8; 13. 31, 32; 17. 1-5.
^f 1 Cor. 15. 36-38.
^g vers. 32, 33; Isa. 53. 10-12; Heb. 2. 9; 12. 2.
^h Matt. 10. 39; 16. 25; Mark 8. 35; Luke 9. 24; 17. 33.

the porch and in the Court of the Gentiles. **Certain Greeks.** They were proselytes of the gate, uncircumcised, but observers of the moral code of the Old Testament, and also regular attendants upon the great feasts, probably journeying thither from some foreign country, for they were of **them that came up to worship at the feast.**
21. **The same came therefore to Philip.** Philip and Andrew are Greek names. Perhaps these strangers spoke to them first, because they may have been more intimately associated with the Greeks than were the other apostles. There is a tradition that the labors of these two were afterward largely among the Greeks. **Sir, we would see Jesus.** They showed the Messianic expectations of the Jews, and their profound respect for the Saviour is shown in their modesty in refusing to press upon him without permission, and also by the reverence with which they salute even one of his disciples. "Chaldæans from the East had sought his cradle; these Greeks from the West came to his cross." **Bethsaida.** See on ch. 1 : 44.
22. **Philip cometh and telleth Andrew.** Jesus had just been hailed with acclamations as King of Israel. Philip evidently hesitates to compromise him by pressing upon him an immediate interview with Gentiles. It was natural that he should first consult his friend and fellow-townsman Andrew, who was also of Bethsaida, ch. 1 : 44. Perhaps we may see too in this evident deliberation and their coming together the awe in which they held our Saviour's person. So suggests Farrar in his *Life of Christ.*
23. **Jesus answered them.** Whom? Tholuck says his disciples, after the Greeks had been admitted to audience and dismissed. This supposition seems altogether too circuitous for the natural sense of the passage. Alford maintains that our Saviour did not grant the Greeks audience at all. Lange thinks that this discourse was uttered in the presence of the Greeks, but addressed directly to his disciples. This last view accords best with our Saviour's breadth of charity and with the sentiments of his discourse. **The hour is come.** The death-hour must have been an abiding shadow in the life of Jesus, Luke 12 : 50. The universality of his mission and his death are in his mind inseparably connected, ch. 10 : 15, 16; 17 : 1, 2. **That the Son of man should be glorified.** Humanity (Son of man), irrespective of nationality, was to be glorified in and with him.
24. **Except a corn,** *the grain,* **of wheat fall into the ground and die.** This emphatic utterance is the great truth fundamental to Christianity. It is a beautiful expression of the great law of sacrifice, through death to life. "The seed-corn must undergo a process analogous to dissolution in order to yield a harvest; so must I die in order to achieve this great result. And my disciples (ver. 25) must 'follow me' herein (ch. 13 : 16); for life, if unduly loved, will be *fruitless.*" **But if it die, it bringeth forth much fruit.** The "much" here is emphatic. Through the death of Christ and the persecution of the church by the Jews the fulness of the Gentiles was to be gathered in.
25. **He that loveth his life shall lose it.** Nursing one's selfishness is a process of moral death. **He that hateth his life in this world shall keep it unto life eternal.** What glorifies the Son of man is likewise the

26 life in this world shall keep it unto life eternal. If any man serve me, let him follow me; and where I am, there shall also my servant be: if any man serve 27 me, ʰ him will *my* Father honor. ᵏ Now is my soul troubled; and what shall I say? ˡ Father, save me from this hour. But for this cause came I unto this 28 hour. Father, glorify thy name.

ʰ ch. 14. 21-23.
ᵏ ch. 13. 21; see refs. Matt. 26. 38, 39.
ˡ Mark 14. 36.

---

true glory of each redeemed soul—that is, not the mortification of the life as a mere penance, but sacrifice for others—the seed dying for the sake of the harvest. "The central principle of Christian life stated in the form of a double paradox. Though, as we have seen, Christ had his own death in view, he yet speaks of the principle in its universal application. The spirit which took him to death, and through death to glory, and in all this made him abound in fruit, is the spirit that must live and reign in every disciple. We all come to glory by his path, dying with him, and so living with him—his fellows in crucifixion and in glory. To love one's life or soul, according to Christ's meaning, is so to make self first and chief that self-gratification becomes the law or principle of all action. To do this is to lose the life or soul; for, *first*, this is a wrong or wicked principle, and hence is itself the soul's ruin; and, *second*, this principle works out ruin, because it is at war with the nature of God, with the nature of the human soul, and so with the constitution of all society, human and angelic, earthly and heavenly. It has come to be understood, as never before, that all true national and international law, and all prosperous commerce and intercourse between men generally, rest ultimately upon the law of impartial love to man and of supreme love to God. To hate the life in this world is the opposite of loving it, and is to make first and chief God's will, and to find in it the law of action. This keeps the life or soul unto life eternal; *first*, because such a spirit is in its own nature the very spirit or life of God himself, or eternal life; and, *second*, being this, it works out results and will come out into manifestations in keeping with itself, into the eternal glory which alone is and constitutes heaven."
—DR. G. D. B. PEPPER.

26. **If any man serve me, let him follow me.** A practical answer to these Greek inquirers. They might enter his service by following him in sacrifice. "This shows that he had his own impending death in mind in choosing his illustration. To follow him is to enter, in self-sacrifice, into his suffering. Not that we must go through the same or similar experience externally, but we must have and live out his spirit at whatever risk. The promise that the servant shall be where he is looks to his declaration that he was now to be glorified, to enter into glory. The promise is partially fulfilled in the Christian as he passes along in life, for Christ the glorified is with him always. But its full realization is future, when we go to be 'with the Lord,' especially 'when he shall appear' and 'we shall appear with him.' This is said by him to be honor from his Father, because it will be shown to be of God as the absolute and supreme Sovereign."—DR. G. D. B. PEPPER. **Where I am, there ... my servant ... him will my Father honor.** Eternal life, ver. 25; companionship with Christ here and hereafter; honor from the Father,—these, last of all, are held out as the rewards of this service.

27. **Now is my soul troubled.** The message to the Greeks being finished, he unbosoms the feelings that their application had occasioned. Well might he be troubled, for never mortal had so much to apprehend. **What shall I say?** Contending emotions struggle for utterance. **Father, save me from this hour.** This is not an interrogation, as some interpret, but a veritable ejaculatory prayer, occasioned by an overwhelming consciousness of the horrors so near him. See Matt. 26 : 39 and Ps. 22. **But for this cause.** This expression is emphatic: I came to this hour for this very purpose. Here he controls his natural shrinking from the sacrificial death by reflecting that for this cause, the redemption of humanity, to be honored of the Father (ver. 26), he had come to the bitter hour.

28. **Father, glorify thy name.**

JOHN XII.   A. D. 30

ᵐThen came there a voice from heaven, *saying*, I
29 have both glorified *it*, ⁿand will glorify *it* again. The
people therefore, that stood by, and heard *it*, said that
it thundered: others said, ᵒAn angel spake to him.
30 Jesus answered and said, ᵖThis voice came not be-
31 cause of me, but for your sakes. Now is ᑫthe judgment of this world: now shall ʳthe prince of this
32 world be cast out. And I, ˢif I be lifted up from the

2 Cor. 4. 4; Eph. 2. 2; 6. 12; Col. 2. 15.   ˢ ch. 3. 14; 1 Pet. 2. 24.

ᵐ See refs. Matt
3. 17; Acts 9. 7
22. 9.
ⁿ ch. 13. 31, 32.
ᵒ Acts 23, 8, 9.
ᵖ ch. 11. 42.
ᑫ ch. 16. 11.
ʳ ch. 14. 30; Gen.
3. 15; Matt. 12.
28, 29; Luke 10
18; Acts 26. 18;

Love and hope for the perishing (Heb. 12 : 2) and the highest possible motive, zeal for the glory of God, combine to lift the Saviour high above all apprehensions into the blissful consciousness of perfect harmony with the will of the Father. Self was lost. The emphasis of the prayer is, "Father, glorify *thy* name." **Then came there a voice from heaven.** Here there has been much vain rationalizing. Some say this was only a peal of thunder, which was interpreted as an endorsement of the prayer; others, that with the thunder there was mingled a voice; but we have no right to understand the record in any other way than it reads, "a voice from heaven," though it was not understood by all. This is the third time that Jesus had this kind of a sanction; the first being at his baptism, and the second at his transfiguration. **I have both glorified it,** as Creator and Preserver, and in all the history, types, and prophecies of the Old Testament. **And will glorify it again.** Again is emphatic, showing that the glorification about to be effected was no mere repetition, but a glory in a much higher degree. Through the sufferings of Christ there was to be manifested a glory of God surpassing all before.

29. **The people said . . . it thundered.** Voices in heaven are more than once compared with thunder, Rev. 6 : 1; 14 : 2; 16 : 17, 18; Job 40 : 9. A casual consciousness perceived nothing more than thunder, according to a recognized principle, Matt. 13 : 12. See also Acts 9 : 7, compared with 22 : 9, and it will be seen that the attendants of Saul at his conversion heard the sound of the voice, but could not distinguish the words spoken. Others said, **An angel spake to him.** **To** him is emphatic. Others with a higher faith recognized the thundering sound **as speech,** but, not understanding the words, they affirmed that it was a message intended expressly for him.

30. **Jesus answered, . . . This voice came . . . for your sakes.** The Spirit always witnessed to the inner consciousness of our Saviour, John 11 : 42. The Saviour here addressed all who were within hearing. The voice came for the sake of all. To John, and probably to the other apostles, it was intelligible speech—to the others it was a token more or less clear according to their spiritual development.

31. **Now is the judgment of this world.** *This world* means all who do not belong to the kingdom of Christ. The word *judgment* here has the same essential meaning as in the expression "day of judgment," Matt. 10 : 15 and 12 : 36. The crucifixion was truly a pre-judgment of the world. Nothing so convicts the world as the Lamb slain, Rev. 5 : 6 and 6 : 16. The god of this world hath blinded the minds of them that believe not (2 Cor. 4 : 4), but the cross reveals the carnal mind as enmity against God and murderous in its hate, Acts 2 : 23. So, too, on the other hand, the cross is a declaration of God's love (John 3 : 16) and holiness, and of sin's deserved penalty, Gal. 3 : 13. **Now shall the prince of this world—** that is, Satan—**be cast out.** The nations shall be undeceived by this revelation, and Satan shall lose his power over them. My sacrifice shall procure the Spirit (Gal. 3 : 14), convicting the world (John 16 : 8), following and leading into all truth.

32. **And I, if I be lifted up from the earth,** *crucified,* as explained in ver. 33. Jesus does not here express a doubt, but a certain event which he knew was soon to take place. Compare ch. 3 : 14; 8 : 28. **Will draw all men unto me;** not the totality of the human race, but, as plainly seen in the

33 earth, will draw ᵗall *men* unto me. ᵘThis he said, signifying what death he should die.
34 The people answered him, We have heard out of the ˣlaw that Christ abideth for ever: and how sayest thou, The Son of man must be lifted up? Who is this Son of man? Then Jesus said unto them, ʸYet a little while ᶻis the light with you. ᵃWalk while ye have the light, lest darkness come upon you: for ᵇhe that walketh in darkness knoweth not whither he goeth. While ye have light, believe in the light, that ye may be ᶜthe children of light.
36 These things spake Jesus, and departed, and ᵈdid hide himself from them.

Reflections on the unbelief of the Jews.

37 But though he had done so many miracles before

ᵗ ch. 1. 7, 29; Isa. 49. 6; Rom. 5. 18; 1 Tim. 2. 6; Heb. 2. 9; Rev. 5. 9.
ᵘ ch. 18. 32.
ˣ comp. 2 Sam. 7. 13; Ps. 72. 17; 89. 4, 29, 36, 37; 110. 4; Isa. 9. 7; 53. 8; Ezek. 37. 25; Dan. 2. 44; 7. 14, 27; Mic. 4. 7.
ʸ ch. 7. 33; Heb. 3. 7, 8.
ᶻ ch. 1. 9; 8. 12; 9. 4, 5.
ᵃ vers. 36, 46; Jer. 13. 16; Rom. 13. 12-14; Eph. 5. 8; 1 Thess. 5. 5-8.
ᵇ ch. 11. 10; 1 John 2. 10, 11.
ᶜ Luke 16. 8; Eph. 5. 8; Col. 1. 9-13; 1 Thess. 5. 5; 1 John 2. 9-11.
ᵈ ch. 8. 59; 11. 54.

context, "all," irrespective of nationality—a highest encouragement to the hope of these Greeks.
33. **What death, *what kind of death;*** that is, death by being lifted up on the cross.
34. **We have heard out of the law,** the Old Testament, ch. 10 : 34. **Christ abideth for ever.** See references. **Son of man.** See on ch. 1 : 51. Dan. 7 : 13, 14 speaks of this Son of man as possessing everlasting dominion, but "the Son of man lifted up" meant, as these people understood our Saviour, removed from the earth into glory, vers. 23, 32. They had no thought that our Saviour was predicting his crucifixion. **Who is this Son of man?** This here is emphatic, showing the signification of the cavil to be as follows: The law says that Christ, the *true* Son of man, abideth for ever, but who is *this* Son of man that tells of his removal from earth?
35. **Then Jesus said unto them.** He deigns not to answer the cavil, but utters a solemn warning: "Cavil if you will, *yet* a little while *I* (ver. 46) am among you. Walk as ye have the light, lest darkness come upon you, Rom. 1 : 21." Moreover, the true answer of their question could be received only by spiritual hearts, prepared for such truth. Jesus is therefore silent in respect to it, and only exhorts them to improve the light which they have. **Knoweth not whither;** you know not the unparalleled horror of that fate into which you are slowly passing—that is, siege, slaughter, dispersion, the fate of the Jew in time (Matt. 24 : 21), and worse beyond, Matt. 10 : 28.
36. **While ye have light, believe in the light,** put faith in the degree of light that ye have, **that ye may be** (or *become*) **the children of light.** Walking according to the light we have is the only way to enter into full light, John 7 : 17. **Did hide,** retired to Bethany, Matt. 21 : 17; Mark 11 : 11.
37-50. REFLECTIONS ON THE UNBELIEF OF THE JEWS. Recorded only by John.
37. These reflections (vers. 37-43) properly come after Jesus had given his last public discourse to the Jews, Matt. 23 : 1-39, and was about to leave the temple. This was on the afternoon of Tuesday, the third day of the week—an interval of about two days after the words spoken concluding with v. 36. See *Author's Harmony,* ₰ 153. "The evangelist closes his account of our Lord's public ministry among the Jews by some reflections upon their obstinate unbelief, which, however, had been long ago foreseen and predicted (vers. 37-43); and he shows how unreasonable and inexcusable it was by adducing some of our Lord's own clear and explicit declarations respecting his divine mission and the danger of rejecting him (44-50)." **So many miracles, . . . yet they believed not on him.** Though a few did believe, yet as a people they rejected him.

38 them, yet they believed not on him: that the saying of Esaias the prophet might be fulfilled, which he spake, ᵉ Lord, who hath believed our report? and to whom hath the arm of the Lord been revealed? 39 Therefore ᶠ they could not believe, because that Esaias 40 said again, ᵍ He hath blinded their eyes, and hardened their heart; that they should not see with *their* eyes, nor understand with *their* heart, and be converted, 41 and I should heal them. ʰ These things said Esaias, 42 when he saw his glory, and spake of him. Nevertheless among the chief rulers also many believed on him; but ⁱ because of the Pharisees they did not confess *him*, lest they should be put out of the synagogue:

ᵉ Rom. 10. 16.
ᶠ ch. 6. 44, 65; Isa. 44. 18, 19.
ᵍ Matt. 13. 13–15.
ʰ Isa. 6. 1–5.
ⁱ ch. 7. 13; 9. 22. Prov. 29. 25.

---

38. That the saying of Esaias, Isa. 53 : 1, one of the most noted Messianic prophecies. Even this rejection was only a prophetic evidence in his favor. **That . . . might be fulfilled.** *In order that,* etc. is the uniform meaning of this phrase in the New Testament, referring to the direct fulfilment of some prediction, type, or typical prophecy. We catch here a glimpse of a twofold reason for the fulfilment of prophecy: First, that the power, truth, and faithfulness of God should not be compromised; second, that his purposes as revealed should be carried out. Hence it is said, "Now all this was done that," etc., Matt. 1 : 22. Types and prophecies are not the cause of events, but simply the revelation of God's will concerning them. **Report,** testimony, instruction. **Arm of the Lord;** the strength of Jehovah manifested in miracles, in the work of redemption, and the preaching of the gospel.

39. Therefore they could not believe. *Therefore* introduces the reason for the unbelief.

40. This was a typical prophecy, applying first to the Jewish people of Isaiah's time, but more fully to the Jews in our Saviour's time and under the gospel dispensation. That hardness of heart exhibited under the preaching of Isaiah was but a type of that greater hardness of heart which would be shown by the unbelieving Jewish people in the rejection of Christ and his gospel. Reference to the fulfilment of this prophecy, which was, and indeed is still, so complete under the gospel, is also made in Matt. 13 : 14, 15; Acts 28 : 26, 27; Rom. 11 : 8. The quotation is not literal, but free and according to the sense. In Isa. 6 : 9 the insensibility of the people under the preaching of the prophet is predicted under the form of a command or exhortation to themselves. Here the imperative, by a sort of "solemn irony," according to Alexander, is a future in meaning. In the Septuagint it is translated as a future, and is so quoted in Matt. 13 : 14, 15; Acts 28 : 26. In Isa. 6 : 10 the prophet is commanded to make the heart of the people fat, etc.—another form of prediction that this would be the direct effect of his faithful warnings. The underlying thought is, that the grossness, blindness, and hardness resulting from these neglected warnings are judicial; hence the pertinency of the quotation here. **Should . . . be converted, and I should heal them,** rather, *and turn, and I should heal them.* In all this God did not take away their freedom. He was ready to heal them if they did but turn; which, however, they would not, and indeed could not, do; for they were morally unable, because they were unwilling. Their moral inability was the result of their moral unwillingness, John 5 : 40. *Healed* of their spiritual malady, or, according to Mark (4 : 12), their sins *forgiven.*

41. These things—*i. e.* the unbelief declared in ver. 38, and the reason for it in ver. 40. **When he saw his glory,** Isa. 6 : 1. It was really the glory of Christ which the prophet saw, and this vision was the occasion of his predictions.

42. Nevertheless among the chief rulers; rather, *Nevertheless*

43 ᵏ for they loved the praise of men more than the praise of God.
44 Jesus cried and said, ˡ He that believeth on me, believeth not on me, but on him that sent me. And
46 ᵐ he that seeth me seeth him that sent me. ⁿ I am come a light into the world, that whosoever believeth
47 on me should not abide in darkness. And if any man hear my words, and believe not, ᵒ I judge him not: for ᵖ I came not to judge the world, but to save the
48 world. ᵠ He that rejecteth me, and receiveth not my words, hath one that judgeth him: ʳ the word that I have spoken, the same shall judge him in the last

ᵏ ch. 5. 44; Matt. 6. 2; 23. 5-7; 1 Thess. 4. 6.
ˡ ch. 13. 20; Matt. 10. 40; Mark 9. 37; 1 Pet. 1. 21.
ᵐ ch. 14. 9, 10; 2 Cor. 4. 6.
ⁿ vers. 35, 36; ch. 3. 19; 8. 12; 9. 5, 39.
ᵒ ver. 48; ch. 5. 45; 8. 15, 26.
ᵖ ch. 3. 17.
ᵠ Luke 9. 26; 10. 16.
ʳ ch. 3. 17-20;

Deut. 18. 19; Mark 16. 16; Luke 12. 47, 48.

---

even among the rulers. Though generally rejected, yet even these gave an assent of the intellect to the truth of Christ's claims; but . . . **they did not confess him,** so it was not saving faith, Rom. 10 : 9, 10. Some, however, like Nicodemus and Joseph of Arimathea, did afterward openly *acknowledge* him, ch. 19 : 38, 39; Mark 15 : 43.

43. **They loved the praise of men,** such as fellowship in the synagogue, ch. 9 : 22. The apostle here assigns Christ's own reason for their unbelief. See ch. 5 : 44.

44, 45. The passage from these verses to the end of the chapter was formerly thought by all the older commentators to be a part of some other discourse of our Saviour, or a direct address made in a loud voice after Christ had withdrawn from the temple to some little distance. But because no occasion is specified here it is now generally conceded that the words following are a sort of a summary of the teaching of Jesus on the question the apostle has just been discussing—that is, the unbelief of the Jews. This view is supported still further by the consideration that these words are taken mostly from various discourses already given in this Gospel. **Jesus cried and said.** "This does not necessarily mean a shout from a distance or a vehement outcry." —LANGE. The word is employed by John in the sense of loud public declarations, ch. 1 : 15 and 7 : 28, 37. The meaning, then, is that what follows is the substance of our Saviour's *preaching* to those that rejected him. **Believeth on me . . . on him that sent me. . . . seeth me seeth him that sent me.** He who by faith becomes experimentally acquainted with me believes on and becomes acquainted with the Father, who is revealed by me, the Word, ch. 1 : 1, 18. These expressions are to be taken as in close connection with ver. 41, sustaining the position of the evangelist that the glory of Christ and that of Jehovah were the same. Compare ch. 5 : 24; 8 : 19, 42; 10 : 30, 38; 14 : 10.

46. **I am come a light into the world**—a Saviour, one who bestows truth, knowledge, and bliss (see references)—**that whosoever believeth on me should not abide in darkness.** *Abide* expresses the idea that all are originally in darkness. It means a state of alienation from God. Its finality will be fearful, Matt. 8 : 12; 2 Pet. 2 : 17; Jude 13.

47. **Hear my words, and believe not, I judge him not**—that is, not at present. This does not contradict the assurance that Jesus will at the day of judgment perform that office, John 5 · 22, 27; Rom. 2 : 16. His present mission is to save, ch. 3 : 17. Christ does not bring misery and condemnation, but mercy and salvation.

48. **Hath one that judgeth him: the word . . . shall judge him.** The word of Christ will convict. To sin against it is to sin against light, offered mercy, and emphatic warnings. It will judge, too, in the sense of pronouncing penalty, as, "he that believeth not shall be damned," Mark 16 : 16 and ch. 3 : 18. Notice that Christ here makes a distinction between himself and the word or instruction which he imparts. The sinner's final destruction can be traced to neither Christ nor his word, but to his own unbelief and perverseness.

49 day. For *I have not spoken of myself; but the Father which sent me, he gave me a commandment, 50 ʰ what I should say, and what I should speak. And I know that ⁿ his commandment is life everlasting. Whatsoever I speak therefore, even as the Father said unto me, so I speak.

* ch. 7. 16-18; 8. 26 38; 14. 10; 15. 15; 17. 8.
ʰ Deut. 18. 18.
ⁿ 1 John 3. 23, 24; 5. 11-13, 20.

The word of God, however, is the sword of the Spirit, living and powerful, Eph. 6 : 17; Heb. 4 : 12.

49. For I have not spoken of myself; but the Father. This word must inevitably judge men, for every syllable of it—**what I should say, and what I should speak**—is uttered by direct commission from the eternal Father. The eternal word, like its eternal Source, must abide to judge us when the heavens and the earth pass away.

50. I know that his commandment is life everlasting. This is the testimony of the Son to the Father, John 8 : 55. The Son claims full consciousness of the Father; accordingly, he gives clear testimony that on the words spoken by the Father's commandment hangs not only condemnation, but eternal life. For this gravest of reasons our Saviour adds the emphatic clause, **even as the Father said unto me, so I speak.**

PRACTICAL REMARKS.

1. Let us each do what we can do best to show gratitude to the Saviour, vers. 2, 3; Mark 14 : 8.
2. Give to the Redeemer not merely what can easily be afforded—give rather what is " very costly ;" give, too, not with closely-calculated economy; give lavishly, even in ministering in the humblest service as it were at the Master's feet, ver. 3; Matt. 10 : 8; 2 Cor. 9 : 7.
3. Love counts nothing too precious for Jesus, ver. 3; 2 Cor. 5 : 14.
4. A covetous and selfish spirit begrudges the gifts and sacrifices of love to Christ, ver. 4; 1 Tim. 6 : 10.
5. Many hypocritically plead the wants of the poor as an excuse for withholding their offerings to Christ and his cause, ver. 5.
6. Beware of harsh interference with the service of any one who is devoted to Jesus. The intuitions of a warm heart may, after all, suggest what is most beautifully appropriate, vers. 7, 8.
7. A malignant spirit not only strikes at the object of its hatred; it scruples not to make way with one having no part in its quarrel if he helps even indirectly to sustain an adversary. Such is the sinfulness of the human heart, vers. 10, 11; Jer. 17 : 9; Rom. 3 : 13-16.
8. It is God's plan that the poor should always be with his people to receive their sympathy and aid, ver. 8; Deut. 15 : 11; Prov. 22 : 2; Luke 18 : 22; Rom. 15 : 26, 27.
9. Whatever honors our Saviour's death is pleasing to him. For example, baptism and the Lord's Supper, ver. 7.
10. Christians share in the honors of the gospel. Their deeds of love are held in everlasting remembrance, ver. 7; Ps. 112 : 6; Mal. 3 : 16; Acts 10 : 31.
11. To what lengths a person may go in a false profession of religion! How many a false professor has turned against Jesus for the sake of worldly gain! vers. 4, 5; 1 Tim. 6 : 9, 10; 2 Tim. 4 : 10; 2 Pet. 2 : 14, 15.
12. Most of those who saw Lazarus had no saving faith. How stubborn, then, is unbelief! vers. 1, 9. See Luke 16 : 31.
13. How vain to be elated by popular favor! The voice of the multitude on the first day of the week was " Hosanna! Blessed is the King of Israel!" But on the sixth day it was, " Crucify him!" vers. 13-18; Mark 15 : 13, 14.
14. Persons, animals, and things are received, employed, and required in Christ's service, ver. 14; Num. 22 : 28-33 ; 1 Cor. 1 : 26-29.
15. We should do our part in honoring Jesus, our Prophet and King, thankful to engage in any service, however humble, vers. 12, 13; Isa. 52 : 7; Zeph. 5 : 14-17; Hos. 4 : 6.
16. Jesus had often sought retirement (Matt. 12 : 15-21), but now for wise purposes he makes his coming to Jerusalem most public. It was meet that his

A. D. 30.   JOHN XIII.   221

Our Lord's last passover; Jesus washes his disciples' feet.
XIII. NOW ˣ before the feast of the passover, when Jesus   ˣ Matt. 26. 2.

sufferings and death should be before angels and men, vers. 12-16; John 3: 14; Acts 23: 22-24; 10: 39.

17. Jesus was meek and lowly, even in his triumphal entrance into Jerusalem. How unbecoming, then, are pride, avarice, and ambition in his followers under any circumstances! ver. 14; Phil. 2: 3-5; Eph. 4: 1, 2; James 3: 13-18.

18. The faithful testimony of Christ's people to what they have seen and experienced of his saving power is ever attended with marked results, vers. 16, 17.

19. It is well to be regular in attendance on the appointed worship of God. Sometimes surprising blessings await us there, ver. 20, following.

20. When we stand in doubt, it is best to take counsel with some friend, and then together ask Jesus, ver. 22; Prov. 11: 14; 24: 6; Matt. 18: 19.

21. There is no great spiritual harvest, either for this world or the next, without deep humiliation and willing self-sacrifice, vers. 23, 24.

22. "Truth is a seed that is never lost. Even when it seems overcome and buried, it is often planted where it will the more surely germinate, and in due time bring forth the more abundant crop," vers. 24-27.

23. In prayer we should pour out the real feelings of our hearts. Prayer to be saved from trouble is not inconsistent with patience and submission, ver. 27; Ps. 62: 8.

24. The supreme moment in prayer is reached when every other thought and feeling is lost and absorbed in this one petition: Father, glorify thy name! ver. 28; Dan. 9: 19.

25. "The shrinking of Christ's sensibilities from the appalling horrors of the cross does not detract anything from his divinity; it rather adds to it a sacred tenderness, and brings him near to us as having a nature like our own—our God, and yet our brother," vers. 27, 28.

26. Preachers and teachers best attract and win souls by the use of those themes that most exalt Christ, and him crucified, ver. 32; 1 Cor. 1: 18, 23, 24.

27. "The attractions of the cross are God's power unto salvation. They appeal with equal force to men of every race and condition. How great is that number who from age to age yield to those attractions, and are won to receive Christ as their Saviour and Lord!" vers. 32, 33.

28. Answer a caviller not according to his folly, but rather in the language of solemn warning, vers. 34-36; Prov. 26: 4.

29. "Preconceived opinions, however imbibed, are often a fatal hinderance to spiritual illumination. It is no less the dictate of wisdom to hold ourselves accessible to a new truth than to hold firmly that which we have tested and settled," vers. 34-38.

30. "It is not for want of evidence that men ever reject the gospel. The source of unbelief is a hardened heart," vers. 37-40.

31. An undue love for the praise of men has ever proved a fatal snare, vers. 42, 43; John 5: 44; Prov. 29: 25.

32. Jesus in person, Jesus even in his word, tests men's hearts. To reject either is to reject God and all good, and hopelessly to condemn one's self, vers. 44-48; Luke 2: 34, 35; Mal. 3: 2, 3.

33. Preachers and teachers should not proclaim their own notions. The eternal life of their hearers depends upon the faithful delivery of the messages of God, vers. 49, 50; Acts 20: 26, 27.

CHAPTER XIII.

In this chapter we begin to enter the fragrant atmosphere of sacrificial love. The very first verse speaks of a love to the end, and the incident that follows shows us not, indeed, love in its agony, but love in its lowliness—a Master ministering, tender as a mother, at his disciples' feet, vers. 1-17. But there is a dark background to this benignant scene. One of these disciples, favored with this wealth of affection, is accused on the spot as a traitor, and goes out into the night, vers. 18-30. Relieved of his presence, the Saviour manifests a fondness never recorded before. For the first time he calls his

knew that his hour was come ʸ that he should depart out of this world unto the Father, ᶻ having loved his own which were in the world, ᵃ he loved them unto the

ᵃ Ps. 37. 28; Isa. 49. 14-17; Jer. 31. 3; Rom. 8. 37-39; Heb. 12. 8.

ʸ ch. 14. 28; 16. 5 28; 17. 11.
ᶻ ch. 15. 9, 10; Eph. 5. 25-27; Rev.1.5.

disciples little children, and then gives them, as with his dying breath, his new commandment of love, vers. 31-35. At the end of the chapter Peter breaks in with his boasting of fidelity, but is at once rebuked by the prediction that he will very soon deny his Lord thrice, vers. 36-38.

1-20. WASHING THE DISCIPLES' FEET. Having reclined at table, Jesus discourses thereon, and intimates the presence of a traitor. Recorded only by John.

1. **Before the feast of the passover.** See on ch. 2 : 13. This was early Thursday evening. "The expressions used here and in other passages in this Gospel (vers. 27-30; 1 : 28; 19 : 14, 31) seem to imply that the Jewish passover night had not yet arrived. Whence it would follow that the meal of which our Saviour partook with his disciples (see Matt. 26 : 17-20 and parallel passages) was eaten on the day before the regular passover-day. Some think that Christ, the true Paschal Lamb, was to be offered up at the exact time of the eating of the passover, and either regard the Last Supper as an ordinary meal, solemn only on account of our Lord's peculiar circumstances, or believe that he celebrated the passover with his disciples a day before the usual time. But this appears to be directly opposed to the statements in the other Gospels, that on the day 'when the passover must be' (*i. e.* ought legally to be) 'killed,' 'in the evening,' 'when the hour was come,' 'he sat down with the twelve,' and said that he had earnestly 'desired to eat this passover' before he suffered. It has been suggested that there may have been a difference among the Jews themselves, and that our Lord and his disciples ate the passover at the legal time (Luke 22 : 7), whilst the greater part of the people and their rulers partook of it at a day later. But of this there is no adequate proof."—*Annotated Paragraph Bible.*

The festival of the passover began at six o'clock, and his language may be variously explained: (*a*) It may mean *just before the passover,* just as the sun was setting. So Lange and Bäumlein. (*b*) Or it may be equivalent to *festival-eve,* the evening immediately before the festival proper, the commencement of the 15th of Nisan, as the opening day of the festival of unleavened bread, distinct from the mere paschal supper, Num. 28 : 16, 17. So Robinson and others. (*c*) Or John may merely state the fact that Jesus, knowing before the passover that his time of suffering had come, loved his disciples unto the end, in which case the language could decide nothing in regard to the time of this Last Supper. So Meyer. There appears, therefore, no necessity for supposing that John meant twenty-four hours before the passover, or of inferring that the paschal supper, which is doubtless mentioned immediately after, took place a whole day before its regular time, contrary to the plain testimony of the other evangelists.

It may also be added that it is most natural, with Campbell, Robinson, Tholuck, Meyer, and many others, to regard ver. 1 *as an independent sentence,* forming an introduction to what follows.

It should also be remembered that John was writing for Greeks and others unacquainted with the Jewish mode of reckoning time, and that the word *before* should not be pressed too closely. See the whole question of the time discussed in *Author's Harmony,* p. 297, following. **When Jesus knew that his hour was come.** Rather, *Jesus knowing that his hour has come,* or, *was coming*—the awful hour which forced from him such prayers as John 12 : 27; Luke 22 : 42-44; Mark 15 : 34. **Having loved his own,** etc. "*His own* were not simply the faithful eleven, and others who heard and followed him during his ministry, but all disciples of all time, ch. 10 : 16; 17 : 20, 21. Hence it is neither mere general benevolence nor simply compassion for the

2 end. And supper being ended (ᵇ the devil having now put into the heart of Judas Iscariot, Simon's *son*, to be-
3 tray him), Jesus knowing that the Father had given all things into his hands, and that he was come from God,
4 and went to God; ᶜ he riseth from supper, and ᵈ laid aside his garments; and took a towel, and girded him-

ᵇ ver. 27; Luke 22. 3; Acts 5. 3.

ᶜ Luke 22. 27; Phil. 2. 7, 8.
ᵈ 1 Kings 18. 46; Luke 12. 37; 17. 8.

---

lost. It is the Shepherd's love for the sheep of his flock, because they are his flock—a very special love, a love at once for the saved, and which saves. As the Greek word shows, and the connection requires, it was not the love of mere sentiment, feeling, affection, but the higher love of moral regard, involving choice. Christ so loved as to take to himself, keep, care for, and give himself instead of, his own. They are designated as 'his own which were in the world,' because their 'in-the-world' condition was the condition of peril, exposure to wolves and robbers and destruction, which required the Shepherd to defend them with his life. See ch. 10."—DR. G. D. B. PEPPER. **He loved them unto the end.** Fully conscious of the horrors at hand, and in their very presence as it were, his love is so self-forgetful that to the very end he ministers to his beloved (ver. 4 and following), and comforts them with words that are the richest legacy of love. See ch. 14 : 1-3, 12-14, 16-18, 23, 27; ch. 15 : 11; 16 : 22-24. "What a Saviour! Weeping for his enemies in the midst of the highest triumph of his life (Luke 19 : 41), and dealing out deeds and words of comfort for his friends on the very verge of the most awful death! The Greek phrase here translated *unto the end* is in Luke 18 : 5 translated 'continual' (continually). It implies that no obstacle or hinderance in the way turned Christ out of the way. The horrors of death and hell—nay, death, hell, and all the powers of hell—rose in his path of love to drive him from that path. Drive him from it they could not. He went straight on to meet all, bear all, suffer all, and in suffering to conquer—conquer for his own—deliver them, save them, bring them to glory. What a truth! The grand theme, burden, inspiration of holy writ from end to end of the heavenly book, the burden of the song of Moses and the Lamb, filling heaven and eternity with inexpressible sweetness. God's self-sacrificing, sin-atoning, rebel-saving love."—DR. G. D. B. PEPPER.

2. And supper being ended. Rather, *supper being served.* They had already reclined. **The devil having now put into the heart of Judas . . . to betray him.** Mentioned here still more to magnify the love of Jesus. Reading that traitor's heart, the Saviour could yet wash his feet. The presence of the traitor was, indeed, an important reason for what he was doing, vers. 10, 11, 18.

3. Jesus knowing. His condescending love is magnified by this third consideration, his consciousness of being divine in sovereignty, origin, and destiny. An obvious reason for this statement of Christ's kingly, lordly consciousness is the emphasis given by it to his act of lowest, most menial service to each disciple, including even Judas, known by Christ to have already covenanted his betrayal, ver. 11. **The Father had given all things into his hands,** etc. All power had been given him (ch. 5 : 22; 13 : 3; Ps. 2; Acts 13 : 33, 34; Matt. 11 : 27; 25 : 34), and won and openly declared by his death and resurrection. As the Christ, the Mediator between God and men, *the God-man,* he, in his resurrection and ascension, took full possession of that glory which he had before the foundation of the world, and of that inheritance and kingdom which was the special purchase of his blood, ch. 17 : 5; Luke 24 : 26; Rom. 14 : 9; Phil. 2 : 9-11; Eph. 1 : 20-23; 1 Pet. 3 : 22; Rev. 5 : 5-14. Compare Acts 13 : 33, 34; Rom. 1 : 4; Matt. 28 : 18.

4. He riseth from supper, where he had been reclining with the twelve, **and laid aside his garments,** those on the upper part of his person. **Took a towel,** or a linen cloth that might be used as an apron. **Girded himself,** assuming thus the badge of a servant. "The attendant carries a napkin over his shoulders, which is used to

5 self. After that he poureth water into a basin, and
began * to wash the disciples' feet, and to wipe *them* *1 Sam. 25. 41; 1
with the towel wherewith he was girded.   Tim. 5. 10.
6   Then cometh he to Simon Peter: and Peter saith

---

wiping the hands and mouth. This napkin is white and often embroidered, as anciently; another of dark blue striped with red is often worn about the loins like an apron or tucked into the girdle by any person performing menial duties, especially washing the feet."— Dr. Van Lennep, *Bible Lands*, p. 476.

5. After that he poureth water, etc. How vivid and detailed the de-

EASTERN TABLE WITH COUCHES.

scription! An eye-witness writes—one whose memory remained indelibly fixed every incident of that evening, every word and motion, especially of his Lord. How often, how sadly and fondly, must the beloved disciple have recalled that evening and lived it over again! We notice that he puts some of the verbs in the present tense, as though he saw and heard as he wrote. **Began to wash the disciples' feet.** How this must have rebuked them! At the Bethany supper they had indignation (Matt. 26 : 8) because their *Lord's* feet were anointed. Now *he* washes *theirs*. Lange says: "Since the foot-washing was ordinarily done by slaves previous to the commencement of a meal, in the absence of a slave the duty naturally devolved upon the humblest of the circle. In this lay the fuze that kindled the last strife for pre-eminence," Luke 22 : 24. If this be true, how effectually this final strife was silenced by our Saviour's expressive action! "As sandals were ineffectual against the dust and heat of an Eastern climate, washing the feet on entering a house was an act both of respect to the company and of refreshment to the traveller." The sandals of one coming in were always taken from the feet at the door. "Immediately that a guest presented himself at the tent-door it was usual to offer the necessary materials for washing the feet, Gen. 18 : 4; 19 : 2, etc."

6. Then cometh he to Simon Peter. Alford says he came to Peter first. Lange, on the other hand, agrees with Meyer that Peter was not washed the first. The latter supposition seems best sustained by the natural sense of the narrative and the force of the emphasis in the original. **Dost thou wash my feet?** *My* here is strongly

7 unto him, Lord, ᶠdost thou wash my feet? Jesus answered and said unto him, What I do thou knowest
8 not now; ᵍ but thou shalt know hereafter. Peter saith unto him, Thou shalt never wash my feet. Jesus answered him, ʰ If I wash thee not, thou hast no part
9 with me. Simon Peter saith unto him, Lord, not my
10 feet only, but also *my* hands and *my* head. Jesus saith to him, He that is washed needeth not save to wash his feet, ⁱ but is clean every whit: and ᵏ ye are clean,

ᶠ Matt. 3. 14; Luke 5. 8.
ᵍ vers. 12, 14, 15; Ezek. 14. 23; Hab. 2. 1–3; James 5. 7–11.
ʰ ch. 3. 5; Zech. 13. 1; 1 Cor. 6. 11; Eph. 5. 26; Tit. 3. 5, 6; Heb. 10. 22; Rev. 1. 5; 7. 14.

ⁱ Song Sol. 4. 7; Jer. 50. 20; 2 Cor. 5. 17.   ᵏ ch. 15. 3.

---

emphatic. Peter's rebuke sprang doubtless from his reverence for his Master (Matt. 16 : 22), but the true degree of reverence would have kept him humbly silent.

7. The Saviour answers Peter's emphatic "thou" and "my" with emphasis of still stronger significance, thus: **What I** (thy Lord) **do thou** (who shouldst be a submissive disciple) **knowest not now; but thou shalt know hereafter.** When was Peter to know? Sufficient for his scruples was our Saviour's immediate explanation. Peter was to know in a deeper significance after the Spirit was given, but not in its full depth of meaning until he should be in the eternal world, where we know as we are known.

8. **Thou shalt never wash my feet.** In disputing with his Lord what is due to his Master's dignity Peter becomes warmer. It is as if he had said, "Hereafter, dost thou say? So far am I from consenting that thou shouldst so degrade thyself, *my* feet thou shalt never wash." "A praiseworthy *modesty*, were it not that with God *obedience* is better than service."— CALVIN. Such a rejoinder demands from the Master a sternness that will bring the impulsive Peter into due subjection. Jesus answers decisively: **If I wash thee not, thou hast no part with me.** It is literally true that direct and persistent disobedience must exclude any disciple from his part in Christ. Symbolically, in the sense explained by the Saviour in verse 10, it is also true that the disciple who would continue to walk with his Lord must be subjected to partial but frequent and thorough cleansings.

9. **But also my hands and my head.** Love cannot give up its Lord. A devoted loyalty, eager to maintain its allegiance for ever, together with a sense of the sin of resisting the Lord's will, and perhaps a deep consciousness of his sinful state in general, all unite to prompt this impassioned utterance; but in the rebound the impetuous disciple has gone too far. His reply was perfectly characteristic of the impulsive apostle.

10. **He that is washed,** rather, *He that hath bathed himself.* The verb in the original is not the one translated *wash* in the preceding verses and also at the end of this verse. It means *bathe*—an ablution of the whole body. Many ancient and modern expositors have considered this a reference to baptism, as the "bath of regeneration," Tit. 3 : 5; Eph. 5 : 26. But it cannot well refer to literal baptism, which is an ordinance performed by another, and not by a person upon himself. There is nothing, however, in this fact to prevent a symbolic reference, as given below. It is better to suppose the figure taken from the customary ablutions or bathings among the Jews. He who has thus bathed himself needs not, as he goes forth to a meal, to wash, save his feet. The full bath is the symbol of regeneration. **Needeth not save to wash his feet.** Regeneration never needs to be repeated. The footwashing is the symbol of the daily or occasional cleansings of the partly defiled but still regenerate man. One who has experienced this washing of regeneration, by contact with things of earth will still continue more or less to contract defilement, as do sandalled feet in the dust of the way; but to give up to an excessive feeling of guilt, to cry with Peter, "Not my feet only, but also my hands and my head," is to impugn the work of God in regeneration, as if it needed to be repeated. **Ye are**

11 but not all. For ¹he knew who should betray him; therefore said he, Ye are not all clean.
12 So after he had washed their feet, and had taken his garments, and was set down again, he said unto them, Know ye what I have done to you? ᵐ Ye call me Master, and Lord: and ye say well; for so I am. ⁿ If I then, *your* Lord and Master, have washed your feet; ᵒ ye also ought to wash one another's feet.

¹ ch. 2. 25; 6. 64, 65; 17. 12.
ᵐ Matt. 23. 8, 10; Luke 6. 46; 1 Cor. 8. 6; 12. 3; Phil. 2. 11.
ⁿ Luke 22. 26, 27; Phil. 2. 5-8.
ᵒ Rom. 12. 10, 16; Gal. 5. 13; 6. 1, 2; 1 Pet. 5. 5.

clean, but not all. All were regenerate but Judas. "'Sometimes a bath was taken before a meal, and on leaving the bath the feet again became soiled. Now, if Jesus and his disciples had bathed that evening, these words may be regarded as simply furnishing the reason why the feet only needed to be washed at that time. . . . It is, to be sure, merely problematical that Jesus and his disciples had bathed, but there is no difficulty in supposing a reference to what usually occurs; as when a person comes from the bath it is common for him to have need afterward to wash his feet, yet is otherwise clean. Thus, the *heart* of the inner man is pure in you.'" —NEANDER. "If even the action had not been intended to have the symbolical meaning, yet this very exclamation of Peter which preceded it—in which was so beautifully revealed the pure depths of his soul, and at the same time was brought out the contrast between this genuine disciple and the betrayer,—this very exclamation must have given occasion to this turn of it. His declaration had shown anew how thorough was the internal hold which Christ had upon him, ch. 6 : 68, 69. Now he who had received Christ's word so deeply into his inner nature was pure (ch. 15 : 3); only the extremities were yet to be purified. It was only needful that the internal principle should unfold itself further and penetrate the whole man, while in the case of a Judas this principle was wholly wanting. In these words, as in the whole scene of love in which he too was allowed to be a partaker, there was for Judas a final persuasion and warning."—DR. A. THOLUCK, *Com. on John.*

11. He knew who should betray him, or *his betrayer.* Judas had already engaged to betray him, and was watching his opportunity, Mark 14 : 1, 10, 11. This whole chapter is a beautiful illustration of the faithful use of the means of grace to bring into allegiance a false disciple. "Ye are clean, but not all," was an arrow for the conscience of Judas. Had *he* answered, "Lord, it is I. Wash not my feet only, but also my hands, my head, my heart," our Saviour never would have said those saddest words, "It were good for that man had he never been born."

12. Was set down again; that is, *reclining again at table.* **Know ye what I have done to you?** He does not pause for an answer. The question is merely introductory to his own immediate application of the lesson.

13. Ye call me Master, and Lord, that is, *Teacher, and Master.* These were titles frequently given to a rabbi by his scholars. One to whose instruction they should listen, and whose word they should obey. In this they said well, for so he was. And, correspondingly, they were disciples and servants.

14. Ye also ought to wash one another's feet. This does not mean, as held by the sect of Tunkers, a literal ceremonial feet-washing. This is to stop short with the hard and bitter husk of the command. Such a practice savors more of a grovelling humiliation than of gentle humility. According to Alford, it is not found in the church in any form before the fourth century. The pope of Rome and Roman Catholic monarchs on Maundy Thursday, with great pomp, wash the feet of twelve poor old men, already made scrupulously clean for the occasion; but this is as foreign as possible from the spirit of the command. Nor is this duty, enjoined by the Lord, to be interpreted merely in the light of Oriental hospitality. True, feet-washing was customary and essential to comfort with those who wore merely the open sandal (1 Tim. 5 : 10), but our Saviour means more than "Refuse not hospitality,

15 For ᵖI have given you an example, that ye should do
16 as I have done to you. ᵠVerily, verily, I say unto you, The servant is not greater than his lord; neither
17 he that is sent greater than he that sent him. ʳIf ye
18 know these things, happy are ye if ye do them. I speak not of you all: I know whom I have chosen: but that the Scripture may be fulfilled, ˢHe that eateth bread with me hath lifted up his heel against me.
19 ᵗNow I tell you before it come, that when it is come

ᵖ Matt.11.29; Rom. 15.5; Eph. 5.2; Phil. 2.5; 1 Pet. 2.21; 1 John 2.6.
ᵠ ch. 15.20; Matt. 10.24, 25; Luke 6.40.
ʳ Ps. 19.11; Matt. 7.24, 25; James 1.22-25; 3.13; 4.17.
ˢ ver. 21; Matt. 26.23.
ᵗ ch. 14.29; 16.4; Isa. 41.23; 48.5.

render even the humblest form of service if necessary to your guest." What, then, is the true meaning? As we have seen on ver. 10, the washing of the feet is a symbol of the constant cleansings that are needful on account of our daily defilement. "Ye ought also to wash one another's feet" means that there should be mutual helpfulness in these purifications. The restoring of defiled wanderers demands a humility that is well symbolized by the expression "washing his feet." "Restore such a one," says the apostle, "in the spirit of meekness," Gal. 6: 1.

15. **For I have given you an example.** No more striking example could have been given than the washing of the feet of his betrayer just before he went after the blood-money. The humility of no disciple ever will reach so low.

16. **Verily, verily.** The importance of this duty is still more strongly enforced by this emphatic "verily," and by the repetition in substance of the plea of ver. 14. **The servant is not greater,** etc. A proverbial expression, Matt. 10: 24.

17. **Happy are ye if ye do them.** Duties involving humiliations, though seemingly repulsive, are found in the doing to be attended with the highest blessedness, Matt. 7: 24; Luke 11: 28. A knowledge, too, is essential to a proper performance and to the attainment of the blessing that attends: **If ye know these things.**

18. **I speak not of you all.** This is the third time there is an allusion to Judas in connection with this washing. Is not this significant? The intimate connection between the ministering at the feet of the Lord (Matt. 26), and the Lord's ministering at the feet of his disciples, has been too much neglected. When Mary ministered so bountifully at the feet of our Lord, in Judas the indignant rancor rose so high that we read, "From that time he sought opportunity to betray him." Now see how our Lord aimed to overcome evil with good. To the indignant protest of some of them, and to the bloody purpose of Judas occasioned because one ministered at *his* feet, he responds by ministering himself at *their* feet. It would seem that our Saviour meant to melt them all down, that he might prepare them for that matchless discourse that followed immediately, so fragrant with the very breath of heaven, so unparalleled in its divine love and peace. We gain new light on this whole scene if we reflect that it was a last attempt made to save Judas. If anything would break that traitor heart, it would seem that it must have been the spirit of full forgiveness speaking out in silent eloquence in the tender touch of overcoming love on those defiled feet. **I know whom I have chosen.** This treachery, our Saviour affirms, is no surprise to him. It is a part of the determinate counsel and foreknowledge of God. Jesus, too, knew what kind of persons he had chosen as apostles. He was not ignorant of the character of any of his professed disciples. **He that eateth bread,** etc. Quoted freely from the Septuagint, Ps. 41: 9. Treachery on the part of a most intimate friend. *Lifting up the heel* is a figure taken from the kicking of a horse, here applied to one who rose from a supper of love and from the washing of his feet by his Master to consummate an act of betrayal.

19. **Now I tell you before it come, . . . when it is come**—that is, this betrayal—. . . **ye may believe that I am he**—that is, "the very person to

20 to pass, ye may believe that I am he. "Verily, verily, I say unto you, He that receiveth whomsoever I send receiveth me; and he that receiveth me receiveth him that sent me.

*ch. 12. 44–48; Matt. 10. 40; 25. 40; Luke 10. 16.

The passover meal continued; Jesus foretells the treachery of Judas.

21 ˣ When Jesus had thus said, ʸ he was troubled in spirit, and testified, and said, Verily, verily, I say unto you, that ᶻ one of you shall betray me. ᵃ Then the disciples looked one on another, doubting of whom
23 he spake. Now there was leaning on Jesus' bosom
24 one of his disciples, ᵇ whom Jesus loved. Simon Peter therefore beckoned to him, that he should ask who it

ˣ Matt. 26. 21–25; Mark 14. 18–21; Luke 22. 21–23.
ʸ ch. 12. 27.
ᶻ vers. 2, 18; Acts 1. 17; 1 John 2. 19.
ᵃ Matt. 26. 22.
ᵇ ch. 19. 26; 20. 2; 21. 7, 20–24.

whom the psalm typically refers." So Lange. See Ps. 49.

20. He that receiveth whomsoever I send. What is the connection here? The thought would seem to be as follows: Though one of you proves a traitor, do not let your faith fail. Remember that I predicted it, and remember, too, that notwithstanding the awful fall of one of you, ye, my chosen ones, are yet God's ambassadors. Go forth, then, with all confidence, for he that receives you receives, as it were, God himself.

21–30. JESUS FORETELLS HIS BETRAYAL, AND POINTS OUT THE TRAITOR (Matt. 26:20–24; Mark 14:17–21; Luke 22:14–18, 21–30) AT THE PASSOVER MEAL. The accounts of Matthew and Mark are quite similar, with occasional differences, such as we would expect in independent narratives. Luke and John exhibit greater divergences. The latter is most detailed in his account of the traitor. The time was Thursday evening, or, according to the Jewish mode of beginning the day with sunset, Friday, April 6th.

21. He was troubled in spirit. Jesus plainly saw that all his kindness and his appeals to the conscience of Judas failed to soften him. He was troubled to see a trusted apostle, an ambassador of God, so hardened in sin and so hopelessly sinking into perdition. He now evidently seeks by his plainness to move the traitor to withdraw; hence the first unmistakable testimony, **one of you shall betray me.**

22. Looked one on another; this shows that they had not till then distinctly apprehended the intimations of Jesus.

23. On Jesus' bosom one of his disciples, whom Jesus loved. It was John (see the references). It was the custom to eat reclining on the left side, while the food was conveyed to the mouth by the right hand. John must then have been immediately on the right of Jesus. "The tables were usually square or oblong, and the couch either semicircular, as seen among the remains of Herculaneum at the Naples museum, or there were three couches set against the three sides of the table, leaving one side open for the servants to set on the food and attend to the wants of the guests. Three persons usually took their seats upon each couch, but there were sometimes as many as four, or even five. They reclined upon their left elbows, supported by cushions, the feet being extended outwardly, and the back of each guest turned toward his next neighbor. The faces and hands thus verged toward a common centre, where was set the dish from which they all partook with their fingers, according to the Oriental mode. Thus we can understand how John, the beloved disciple, leaned upon Jesus' bosom, and how it was practicable for Jesus to hand the sop to either of the disciples." — DR. VAN LENNEP, *Bible Lands*, p. 600.

24. Simon Peter therefore beckoned to him, or bent toward the same (John). Peter, on account of what our Lord had said in verse 8, was still nervously apprehensive at such an utterance as that recorded in verse 21.

25 should be of whom he spake. He then lying on Jesus'
26 breast saith unto him, Lord, who is it? Jesus answered, He it is to whom I shall give a sop, when I have dipped it. And when he had dipped the sop,
27 he gave it to Judas Iscariot, *the son* of Simon. ^cAnd after the sop Satan entered into him. Then said Jesus
28 unto him, That thou doest, do quickly. Now no man at the table knew for what intent he spake this unto
29 him. For some *of them* thought, because ^d Judas had the bag, that Jesus had said unto him, Buy *those things* that we have need of against the feast; or, ^ethat he

^c ver. 2; ch. 6. 70; Luke 22. 3.

^d ch. 12. 6.

^e ch. 12. 5.

That he should ask who it should be of whom he spake. He wished him to be definitely pointed out.

25. He then lying on Jesus' breast; rather, *falling back on Jesus' breast,* in affectionate trustfulness. The circumstances seem to indicate that Peter reclined a little to the right of John. **Saith unto him, Lord, who is it?** Probably speaking in a low tone or a whisper, he merely echoes, with childlike simplicity and confidence, the words that Peter had put into his mouth.

26. To whom I shall give a sop, when I have dipped it; rather, *for whom I shall dip the morsel and give it him;* the reply especially for John, and probably was heard only by him. The sop was a piece of the flexible, unleavened bread, dipped, partially folded, into the broth of bitter herbs, so as to take up a small portion like a spoon. Given to another, it was an expression of the most confiding affection. Thus the Saviour continued to heap coals of the fire of love on the head of Judas, but, as was inevitable, unless he was subdued by them, they only served to kindle to a flame the Satanic malignity that smouldered in his heart. **He gave it to Judas.** Judas must have reclined very near Jesus, probably next to him on the left. The answers of Jesus regarding the traitor may be harmonized as follows: The answer given by Mark (14 : 20) may be regarded as the first; then the sign to John while several disciples continue to ask, *Is it I?* Then, having dipped his hand into the dish with Judas, and given him the sop, he makes the reply recorded in Matthew (26 : 23); literally, *He that dipped his hand with me,* etc. These replies of our Saviour seem to have been better understood by Judas than by the others, for when Judas went out no one appears to have understood the intent of our Lord's language to him, John 13 : 28, 29. The object of Jesus was not to expose the traitor, but to give him all necessary warning against committing so terrible a crime.

27. After the sop Satan entered into him, took full possession of him, so that he was now bent on the betrayal, without the least wavering. Perhaps up to this point Judas was vacillating, not knowing whether to do the dreadful deed; but now his determination is fully fixed. He is given over to death. Jesus can do no more to save him. **Do quickly;** the last merciful barrier to the downward plunge is now removed. Longing to be alone with his beloved ones, the Saviour himself hurries the doomed soul away. A fearful moment in the history of a soul! Given up to mortal sin!

28. No man at the table knew for what intent he spake this. This shows that Judas acted entirely alone in his treachery. Though some of the disciples shared in his first resentful feelings, yet it speaks well for them that Judas apparently had not even ventured to approach them with proposals to betray their Master.

29. Buy . . . that we have need of against the feast. The whole feast lasted eight days. For such a length of time the provision before them was not sufficient; hence the understood direction to buy. It also implies that it was not yet very late in the evening. **Or, that he should give something to the poor.** The poor were specially aided at this time, as is customary with us on Thanksgiving.

20

30 should give something to the poor. He then, having received the sop, went immediately out; and it was night.

Jesus speaks of his departure, and foretells the denial of Peter.

31 Therefore when he was gone out, Jesus said, ᶠNow is the Son of man glorified, and ᵍGod is glorified in 32 him. ʰIf God be glorified in him, God shall also glorify him in himself, and ⁱshall straightway glorify him.
33 Little children, yet a little while I am with you. Ye shall seek me: ᵐand as I said unto the Jews, Whither 34 I go, ye cannot come; so now I say to you. ⁿA new commandment I give unto you, That ye love one

ⁿ ch. 15. 12; Lev. 19. 18; Rom. 12. 10; Gal. 6. 2; Eph. 5. 2; Phil. 2. 1-8; Col. 3. 12-14; James 2. 8; 1 Pet. 1. 22; 2 Pet. 1. 7; 1 John 3. 16, 23; 4. 21; 2 John 5.

ᶠ ch. 12. 23; 16. 14; Heb. 5. 25.
ᵍ ch. 12. 28; 14. 13; 17. 1; Isa. 49. 3; Rom. 15. 6-9; Eph. 1. 12; Phil. 2. 11; 1 Pet. 4. 11.
ʰ ch. 17. 4-6; Isa. 53. 10-12.
ⁱ ch. 12. 23.
ᵐ ch. 7. 33, 34; 8. 21.

---

30. He then, having received the sop, went immediately out. Judas understood the significance of the sop. Conscious that his sinister aim is read, the situation becomes intolerable to him. He hastens out into the darkness like a beast of prey that skulks from the light. **And it was night.** One dark stroke here paints a picture; but the effect is appalling. The sun had gone down; the last gleam of twilight was lost in the gloom. So too it was night in the soul of Judas. The last ray of his day of probation was quenched. He was in the outer darkness. How great is that darkness! Thus he leaves before the institution of the Lord's Supper.

31-38. JESUS FORETELLS THE FALL OF PETER, Luke 22 : 31-38. Compare Matt. 26 : 30-35; Mark 14 : 26-31, where Jesus foretells the second time the fall of Peter and the dispersion of the disciples. This occurred before the institution of the Supper; that related by Matthew and Mark after Jesus and the disciples had left the upper room on their way to the Mount of Olives. Compare *Author's Harmony,* §§ 163, 169, with notes.

31. Now is the Son of man glorified. The first act in the glorious tragedy of redemption now really begins, as Judas goes to arrange for the arrest. **God is glorified in him.** By his perfect obedience realizing the ideal humanity.

32. The best text omits the first clause, and reads, *And God will* **glorify him** in himself, by his resurrection, ascension, and enthronement on high, **and shall straightway glorify him.** These events, commencing with the trial that issued in the crucifixion, were to begin that very night. Hence he is led to say further—

33. Little children, yet a little 1 am with you. This is the only time our Saviour is recorded to have used this appellation of endearment. He feels as a father about to leave his children, but he pronounces the whole comforting discourse that follows, to show that he does not leave them uncared for—orphans, literally—ch. 14 : 18. **As I said unto the Jews, Whither I go, ye cannot come; so now I say to you.** Why quote this saying to the Jews? It was a considerate way of breaking to the disciples the assurance that his immediate glorification was by his immediate death, ch. 16 : 6; also 8 : 21, 22.

34. A new commandment I give unto you, That ye love one another. Why new? Is not the commandment, Thou shalt love thy neighbor as thyself, as old as the Pentateuch. ? Lev. 19 : 18. The answers to this question have been very diverse. Lange cites a dozen different views, but objects with considerable force to every one of them, and then proposes one of his own, which Schaff accepts and commends for its ingenuity. Lange says : "The new commandment is indicative of the institution of the Lord's Supper." "That ye love one another," Lange

35 another; as I have loved you, that ye also love one another. ° By this shall all *men* know that ye are my disciples, if ye have love one to another. 36 ᴾSimon Peter said unto him, Lord, whither goest thou? Jesus answered him, ᑫ Whither I go, thou canst not follow me now; but ʳthou shalt follow me afterwards. 37 Peter said unto him, Lord, why cannot I follow thee now? I will lay down my life for thy sake. 38 Jesus answered him, ˢWilt thou lay down thy life for my sake? Verily, verily, I say unto thee, The cock shall not crow, till thou hast denied me thrice.

ⁿActs 4.32; 1 John 2.5.
ᵖ Matt. 26. 31-35; Mark 14. 27-31; Luke 22. 31-38.
ᑫ ver. 33.
ʳ ch. 21. 18, 19, 22; 2 Pet. 1. 14.
ˢ Prov. 16. 18; 28. 26.

translates, "In order that ye may love one another." The Lord's Supper, he maintains, is to be the channel for the conveyance of light, impulse, and strength for such brotherly love. Meyer's objections to this singular interpretation cannot be overlooked. He observes that it is contrary to the parallel passage, 1 John 2 : 8; and though it was doubtless very near to this time that the Lord's Supper was instituted, yet John does not indicate this at all in this connection. Besides these objections of Meyer, it ought to be insisted that the Lord's Supper is not a channel of sacramental grace, but designed to be a memorial ordinance: "This do in remembrance of me;" "For as often as ye eat this bread and drink this cup ye do show the Lord's death till he come." It is better to suppose that Jesus instituted the Supper just after foretelling the denial of Peter, between this and the following chapter. See last paragraph on ver. 38.

A simpler, more direct interpretation, and more nearly in accord with received evangelical views, would be this: The commandment is new, not in letter, but in spirit. Christ gave this commandment new vitality. The mere mandate, *Love one another*, never could give life and nourishment to love. Love is something spontaneous. It cannot be forced imperatively; as well attempt to force the growth of flowers without sunshine. But when Jesus says, Love one another, he lets the sunshine stream freely where he plants this word. All the commands of Jesus, like his words to the palsied, the prostrate, and the dead, become enabling in the very act of obeying. This commandment of Jesus is a virtual promise of the grace of obedience, while at the same time it gives to the law of love new life by adding to *Love one another* the words following—**as I have loved you.** He puts back of the law the force of his own life and death, when lo! the world's winter is over; the frost melts, the seed of truth bursts its husk, it grows mightily, and now no tree is so spreading and beautiful.

35. **By this shall all men know,** or *take notice.* The keeping of the characteristic commandment of the new covenant is the best mark of a true disciple, 1 John 3 : 10. It was preëminently so in primitive Christianity. The heathen said with admiration, See how these Christians love one another! There will yet be a glorious revival of this spirit, ch. 17 : 21.

36. **Simon Peter said unto him, Lord, whither goest thou?** Peter, still flushed and warm, is eager for an occasion to express a devotion stronger than the dread of death. Jesus answers to his thought, **Thou canst not follow me now,** it is not thy time to follow me now, neither hast thou the spiritual power and grace to do it yet; **but thou shalt follow me afterwards.** An obscure intimation of Peter's final martyrdom. See ch. 21 : 18, 19.

37. **I will lay down my life for thy sake.** An impulse generous but proud. It needed chastening before it became the true spirit of the martyr strong in Christ alone. He was unable to do it now, but he did it afterward, ch. 21 : 19.

38. **The cock shall not crow, till thou hast denied me thrice.** *A cock,* etc. So in the other Gospels the indefinite article is used, which is in harmony with the supposed scarcity of this fowl. Fowls are very abundant in

the East at the present day. Later Jewish writers affirm, though not always consistent with themselves, that the inhabitants of Jerusalem and the priests everywhere were forbidden to keep fowls, because they scratched up unclean worms. But even if this were so, the Roman residents, over whom the Jews could exercise no power, might keep them. Mark says, "Before the cock crow twice." The first about midnight, the second about three o'clock. The latter more generally marked the time, and was the one meant when only one cock-crowing, as here, was mentioned. The expression, therefore, means the same in both Gospels. **Hast denied me**—denied that I am your Lord and Teacher, and that you are or ever have been my disciple; disowned me. At this point Jesus probably instituted the Lord's Supper. There is a sufficient break between this and the following chapter. Besides, after announcing the fall of Peter and the institution of the Supper, fraught to them with a sad significance, it was especially fitting to address them—"Let not your heart be troubled," ch. 14 : 1. See *Author's Harmony,* §§ 164, 165, and notes.

PRACTICAL REMARKS.

1. The love wherewith Christ unites himself to his own is indissoluble; it outlasted his death; it will outlast theirs, ver. 1: Rom. 8 : 38, 39; John 10 : 28.

2. Jesus, in keeping the passover, has taught us to attend faithfully to those ordinances which are now in force, ver. 2; 1 Cor. 11 : 2.

3. The King of kings ennobled the humblest drudgery by girding himself with the badge of a servant; so any mere servant, girding himself in his toil with the spirit of Christ, will yet become a king and a priest unto God, ver. 4 ; Rev. 1 : 6.

4. The most fitting rebuke to an exhibition of a wrong spirit is frequently not so much in words as in acting out its opposite, ver. 5 ; 1 Sam. 24 : 1–16.

5. "It is no dishonor to true greatness to perform any needful service, however humble," vers. 4, 5.

6. Many things, most fitting in themselves, seem incongruous in the dim light of the present. In eternity they will shine out in their true glory, vers. 6, 7 ; 1 Cor. 13 : 12.

7. "The mysteries of divine providence will one day be revealed to us; and we shall read in them lessons of wisdom, of benevolence, and of holiness that will dispel every doubt and fill us with everlasting joy," vers. 6, 7.

8. Our Saviour sternly rebukes those who put their own notions of taste and propriety above his plainly-intimated will. This inference has an important bearing on the objections urged by some against baptism, ver. 8; Matt. 7 : 21; Luke 6 : 46, following.

9. "The Christian has daily need to 'bathe his feet' from the defilements which constantly gather upon him in his pilgrimage. They are not like the sins of the unrenewed, for they do not get into his heart, but they are unsightly and grievous to him who has called him to his service. Blessed be his grace that the fountain in which he may be cleansed is ever open!" vers. 9, 10.

10. Hearest thou the Saviour's voice in thy conscience saying to thee, "Unclean!"? Harden not thyself, lest presently thou art doomed, vers. 11 and 30; Rom. 14 : 22.

11. Jesus is the Searcher of hearts, and knows all of the plans and purposes of his professed followers, ver. 11; Rev. 2 : 23.

12. There is no work more Christlike and blessed than the restoring of backsliders, vers. 14–17.

13. In this work we should faithfully apply all gracious instrumentalities, however hopeless the case of the one we seek to save. Thus did our Saviour with Judas, vers. 12–21.

14. As one of the highest evidences that Jesus is the Messiah, prophecy should by no means be neglected, ver. 19; John 5 : 39; Luke 16 : 29 and 24 : 25.

15. Whatever the defections of others, ministers should be unmoved, in the assured consciousness that they themselves are nevertheless ambassadors of God, ver. 20 ; 2 Cor. 5 : 20.

16. The sins of God's people are the more aggravated on account of their relation to him, ver. 21; Zech. 13 : 6; Heb. 6 : 6.

17. The thought of dishonoring Jesus or sinning against him is sad to the re-

Christ's valedictory discourse; reasons for his departure; promise of the Comforter. ᵗ ver. 27; ch. 16. 22, 23; Matt. 14. 27.

XIV. Let ᵗnot your heart be troubled: ᵘye believe in ᵘch. 5. 23.

newed heart, 'ver. 22; Mark 14 : 72; 2 Cor. 7 : 8, 9.
18. Sin in a minister is an especial grief to the Master, vers. 21, 22.
19. The truly humble and pious heart is ever ready to suspect itself, rather than condemn others, ver. 22; 1 Sam. 24 : 17; 2 Sam. 24 : 17; Isa. 6 : 5.
20. Our Saviour feels an especial affection for those who are pre-eminent for resting on him in complete trustfulness, ver. 23.
21. The wicked act freely in sinning, even though in the divine arrangement they fulfil the divine purposes, ver. 27; Acts 4 : 25-28.
22. Self-examination should precede the reception of the Lord's Supper, vers. 20-31; 1 Cor. 5 : 8; 11 : 28.
23. To sin against special grace is not only to shut off every communication from above; it is also to open up every avenue to the soul from beneath, ver. 27; Matt. 12 : 43-45.
24. See in this wonderful discourse how our Saviour, in a sort of unconscious flash or two of his glory, photographs, as it were, his own character: " Love one another, as *I* have loved you." Let it be remembered that Jesus was speaking to those who had been his inseparable attendants for three years in closest intimacy, and we see the force of our Saviour's appeal to his own love —a love that never once became bitter or ceased to flow out toward its object. Doubtless, love at that moment, just on the verge of the midnight agony, shone in his face with beams that kindled the same feeling in the disciples' hearts.
25. " Nowhere in the universe is the glory of God so revealed to his creatures as in the cross of Christ. It is to be the song of the redeemed and of admiring angels for ever," ver. 31; Rev. 5 : 9, 12.
26. " Christ's love to his people is not only a new motive to holiness, but a new standard and measure of it. It is well to esteem the virtuous; it is a duty to return gratitude to a benefactor; it is noble to bestow charity on the poor; but the highest summit of goodness is reached only by him who, like Jesus, loves his enemies and does good to his persecutors," vers. 34, 35.
27. The highest evidence of Christianity is the life of love, ver. 35.
28. Learn the weakness of human resolution and the folly of trusting thereon, vers. 36-38; Prov. 28 : 26.
29. Beware of boasting of an extraordinary consecration or a higher life, ver. 37; Matt. 26 : 33; John 21 : 15; Prov. 27 : 2; Job 9 : 20, 21.

CHAPTER XIV.

This chapter introduces us into what Olshausen fitly calls " The holy of holies of evangelical history." It is perfectly in harmony with John's own character and with the aim of his narrative that he alone, of all the evangelists, should open for us a door into this sanctuary. Judas having gone out, Jesus is now alone with his faithful disciples, and hence he speaks more freely concerning his future and theirs. He first addresses to them words of comfort. Though he goes away, it is to his Father and theirs—to his home and theirs—to prepare a place for them. He will return again. He is the way to the Father and the perfect manifestation of him, as his words and works declare. He promises them extraordinary powers and answers to their prayers. If they keep his commandments, he will give them another Comforter, to abide with them for ever. They live through and in him ; both he and they have eternal life. By keeping his commandments their love to him will be made manifest, and they shall be blessed with the peculiar love of the Father and the manifestation of the Son. He tells them how to enjoy his continued presence, and that the Comforter, the Holy Spirit, will give them fuller instruction. His peace he leaves with them, and assures them that his going away should be to them a cause of rejoicing. All these things he has spoken to them to prepare them for what is about to come to pass.

1-4. ENCOURAGEMENT IN DESPONDENCY.

1. Let not your heart be troubled.

2 God, believe also in me. In my Father's house are ᵃ Luke 14. 22; 2 Cor. 5. 1; Heb. 11. 10, 14-16.
many ˣ mansions; if *it were* not *so*, I would have told
3 you. ʸ I go to prepare a place for you. And if I go ʸ ch. 13. 36; 17. 24; Heb. 4. 14; 6. 20; 11. 16.
and prepare a place for you, ᶻ I will come again, and
receive you unto myself; that ᵃ where I am, *there* ye ᵃ vers. 18, 28; Acts 1. 11; Heb. 9. 28. ᶻ ch. 12. 26; 17. 24; Rom. 8. 17; 1 Thess. 4. 17; Rev. 3. 21.

The disciples with their limited knowledge might well be perplexed and anxious from a variety of causes. They perhaps observed (13 : 21) that their Master was "troubled in spirit" while he declared that one of them should betray him. The sudden departure of Judas (13 : 27-30) was to them also a mystery. The Lord has just announced to them, too, that he will be with them only a short time (13 : 33), and that whither he goes they cannot come; that they shall all be scattered like the sheep of a smitten shepherd (Matt. 26 : 31); and, finally, that the foremost among them in professions of attachment shall thrice deny him. **Heart.** The heart represents that which is deepest and innermost. In Scripture language it is the organ of faith, Rom. 10 : 9, 10. Jesus knowing, as the disciples did not, the end from the beginning, knew that there was nothing in the events about to transpire that should shake their confidence in him, for all shall at last redound to the glory of God and to their good. Therefore he continues: **Ye believe in God, believe also in me.** Some would read, *Believe in God, believe also in me.* Others, however, dissent from this reading. They say no indication had been given of a want of faith in God, and there was no apparent danger that their faith in him would fail. But there was special need that in this important crisis they should not lose their confidence in Jesus as the Christ, the Son of the living God. Hence they think the words of the Lord mean, " Your confidence in God is firm, let not your faith in me be shaken." Jesus had just said to them (13 : 13), " Ye call me Master, and Lord; and ye say well; for so I am." This confidence he would have them maintain when they should see him arrested, condemned, and crucified.

2. Christ's rejection by the Jews, his crucifixion and departure, were all in accordance with his plans for the salvation of his people. Therefore his disciples should be comforted by all he was about to say to them. **Father's house.** Heaven is meant, whence he came and whither he is going (13 : 3), where the divine glory dwells—his own *home,* from which he has been temporarily absent. **Many mansions.** " Mansions " is derived from a word signifying "to remain," and therefore denotes a permanent dwelling-place. *The Father's house* is set in strong contrast with the *earthly house.* Here Christ's disciples are pilgrims and strangers, having no continuing city (1 Pet. 2 : 11; Heb. 13 : 14), but there they have a home which is abiding. These mansions are **many.** They might find no refuge or resting-place on earth, but in the Father's house there would be room enough for all. **If it were not so, I would have told you.** In him is no guile; he speaks the simple truth. If they had been entertaining false hopes, it would have been inconsistent with his character to permit them to remain until now ignorant of the fact. **I go,** rather, *For I go,* **to prepare,** etc. This is meant to confirm the assurance just given that there were many mansions in his Father's house. His going to prepare a place for them all implies that there were "many mansions." **For you,** the reason for his departure. It was not for himself, but for them. Love brought him down to earth, love leads him back. He came to save; he departs to complete the work of redemption and open heaven to believers. The preparation he makes is evidently by his atoning death. He enters heaven as a High Priest, and presents the merits of his sacrifice for his people's sins, and claims for them the right of entrance into his Father's house.

3. **If I go and prepare,** etc., as he was about to do, for there was no uncertainty about his going, **I will come again, and receive you.** The fact that he departs for such a purpose is a pledge that he will take care to bring them into the enjoyment of **the place**

A. D. 30. JOHN XIV. 235

4 may be also. And ᵇwhither I go ye know, and ᶜthe
way ye know.
5 Thomas saith unto him, Lord, we know not whither
6 thou goest; and how can we know the way? Jesus
saith unto him, I am ᵈthe way, ᵉthe truth, and ᶠthe
life: ᵍno man cometh unto the Father, but by me.
7 ʰIf ye had known me, ye should have known my
Father also: and from henceforth ye know him, and
have seen him.
8 Philip saith unto him, Lord, show us the Father,
9 and it sufficeth us. Jesus saith unto him, Have I

ᵇ See Matt. 16. 21;
  Luke 18. 31-33.
ᶜ ch. 3. 16; 6. 68, 69.
ᵈ ch. 10. 7, 9; Acts
  4. 12; Rom. 5. 2;
  Eph. 2. 18; Heb.
  7. 25; 10. 19, 20.
ᵉ ch. 1. 14, 17; 8.
  32; 18. 37.
ᶠ ch. 11. 25; 3. 15;
  Rom. 5. 21.
ᵍ ch. 10. 9; 1 Pet.
  3. 18.
ʰ ch. 8. 19.

he has prepared. The promise of his coming again will only be realized in its fulness at his second advent at the end of the world, for not until then do Christ's people enjoy all the fruits of his completed redemption, 1 Thess. 4 : 16, 17.

4. And whither I go, etc. According to the best text, *And ye know the way whither I go*. They should recall their Master's words, both in public and private. The goal was his Father's house; the way was through faith in him.

5-7. THE QUESTION OF THOMAS ANSWERED.

5. Thomas, the doubting, slow-minded believer. Peter was silent, humbled perhaps by the sad and solemn words of his Lord, ch. 13 : 38. We know not whither. And this after all that Jesus had said! The disciples may have felt that their knowledge on this subject was not as definite and clear as they could wish. On account of their present fears they could appreciate but faintly the loftiness of their Lord's discourse, and comprehend but little of its meaning.

6. The somewhat complaining question of Thomas draws from the Saviour one of the most precious texts of Scripture: **Jesus saith unto him, I am the way.** Christ is not only Leader and Forerunner of his people, showing the way to heaven, but the Way "in and on which we must go, having an inner union with and in him." He is not only to be followed as an example, but to be trusted in as the propitiation for sin, and as the only One able "to bring us to glory," Heb. 10 : 20. **The truth.** Christ is more than the great expounder of truth, more than a truth-speaking man; he is the complete revelation of God, and hence the sum and substance of all truth, "in whom are hid all the treasures of wisdom and knowledge," Col. 2 : 3. **The life.** Christ is the mediatorial source of all spiritual grace and salvation, Acts 4 : 12. He is also the creative Word of God, by whom all existence has been spoken into being and is sustained, ch. 1 : 3; Col. 1 : 16, 17. **No man cometh unto the Father, but by me.** Christ is not only the all-sufficient, but the only, Mediator between God and man.

7. **If ye had known me**—as perfectly as they might have known him; he is grieved at their tardy apprehension of the great truths he had taught them concerning himself—**ye should have known my Father also.** A just and full view of the Lord Jesus Christ is equivalent to an actual beholding of him who is invisible. **Henceforth ye know him,** etc. From this time forward, especially after his death, they would have clearer views of Jesus, and hence of the Father.

8-11. THE REQUEST OF PHILIP.

8. **Show us the Father,** etc. This petition utters the longing of man in every age — to have a view of God through the bodily senses, like Moses: "Show me thy glory," Ex. 33 : 18. Philip was right in believing that the manifestation of the Father's special presence would suffice to dissipate their doubts and fears, but wrong in failing to learn from both the words and works of Jesus that he who had been "so long time with them" was the "image of the invisible God." This calls forth the gentle but decided rebuke in verse 9 : **Have I been so long time with you,** etc. Philip was among the first disciples chosen (ch. 1 : 43), and had

JOHN XIV. A. D. 30.

been so long time with you, and yet hast thou not known me, Philip? ¹he that hath seen me hath seen the Father; and how sayest thou *then*, Show us the
10 Father? Believest thou not that ᵏ I am in the Father, and the Father in me? the words that I speak unto you ¹I speak not of myself: but the Father ᵐ that
11 dwelleth in me, ⁿ he doeth the works. Believe me that I *am* in the Father, and the Father in me: or
12 else believe me for the very works' sake. ᵒ Verily, verily, I say unto you, He that believeth on me, the works that I do shall he do also; ᵖ and greater *works* than these shall he do; because I go unto my Father.

ᶦ ver. 20; ch. 12.45; Col. 1. 15; Heb 1. 3.
ᵏ ch. 10. 30; 17. 21, 23.
ᶦ ch. 3. 32-34. See refs. 5. 19.
ᵐ 2 Cor. 5. 19.
ⁿ ch. 5. 17; Acts 10. 38.
ᵒ Matt.21.21; Luke 10. 17; Acts 3. 6-8; 8. 7; 9. 34.
ᵖ Acts 2. 4-11, 41, 44.

been with Jesus about three years. During this time he had looked with his bodily eyes upon the incarnate God, in whom dwelt the fulness of the Godhead, and yet asked for a vision of the Father! He had yet to learn that the Father and the Son could not have a separate manifestation. **He that hath seen me hath seen the Father,** so perfect is the manifestation of God in the Son. **How sayest thou**—an old disciple, who should have known my true character—**Show us the Father?** Another mild rebuke.

10. **Believest thou not,** after so much instruction upon this mysterious subject (ch. 5 : 19; 10 : 30, 38), **that I am in the Father, and the Father in me?** The relation existing between the Father and the Son was of so close and vital a nature that the Father could not be revealed apart from the Son. The relation was one of mutual indwelling so intimate and continuous that the words and works of the Son must be considered as proceeding also from the Father. **Words** and **works** include all thought, speech, and action. The entire person, life, and work of Jesus reveals the Father.

11. **Believe me,** etc. The Lord now addresses all the disciples, for Philip was not alone in needing instruction. **Or else believe me,** etc. Believe my words, or, if you will not do this, believe me because of my works. The simple declaration of Jesus should have been sufficient for the disciples; but if they cannot yet trust him personally, they can go back to the lower plane with the Jews (ch. 10 : 38), and begin with his works, and see that only one who was in union with the Father could do them.

12-14. PROMISE OF EXTRAORDINARY POWERS, AND ANSWERS TO THEIR PRAYERS.

12. **He that believeth on me.** Faith in Jesus as the Son of God is to be a wonder-working power. **The works that I do,** etc. This promise has reference—in part, at least—to the physical miracles which many of the first generation of Christians had power to perform, but also to the influence on the world of their teaching and lives. We must not reason from our Lord's words that miracles would still be wrought if the faith of Christians was sufficiently strong. The necessity for miracles which existed at the beginning, the critical period, of the church's history, no longer exists. **And greater works than these shall he do.** The physical miracles of the apostles and early Christians were more numerous than those of Christ, but in no other respect were they *greater*. Reference is doubtless made in this promise to the marvellous results of their preaching, thousands being converted in a single day, Acts 2 : 41. The conversion of a soul is a greater miracle than the opening of blind eyes or the raising of a dead body; but this occurs more frequently even now, under the labors of many preachers, than it did under the ministry of Christ himself. Believers are said to do these works, yet they are only instruments in the hands of Christ. **Because I go unto my Father.** As afterward appears, it was only on condition of his going away that the Comforter would come, ch. 16 : 7. It was after the Lord's ascension that the Holy Spirit was poured out and so many miracles of conversion were wrought, Eph. 4 : 8.

13 ᑫAnd whatsoever ye shall ask ʳin my name, ˢthat will I do, ᵗthat the Father may be glorified in the Son. 14 If ye shall ask any thing in my name, I will do it. 15, 16 ᵘIf ye love me, keep my commandments. And ˣI will pray the Father, and ʸhe shall give you another Comforter, that he may ᶻabide with you for 17 ever; even ᵃthe Spirit of truth; ᵇwhom the world cannot receive, because it seeth him not, neither knoweth

ᑫ Matt. 21. 22.
ʳ Eph. 2. 18; 3. 12; Heb. 7. 25; 13. 15.
ˢ ch. 4. 10.
ᵗ Phil. 2. 9–11.
ᵘ vers. 21, 23, 24; ch. 15. 10, 14;
Gal. 5. 6.
ᶻ Rom. 8. 34; Heb. 7. 25.
ʸ Acts 9. 31.
ᵃ ch. 4. 14.

ᵃ ch. 16. 13.   ᵇ Prov. 14. 10; 1 Cor. 2. 14; Rev. 2. 17.

13. Whatsoever ye shall ask. Whatever strength, comfort, wisdom you need in doing these works of faith. No restriction is put upon the asking, for the same faith that looks to the power of Christ looks also to his wisdom to be guided in asking. **That the Father may be glorified in the Son,** through the power of his grace and the triumphs of his Spirit.

14. The promise is emphasized by its repetition, **I will do it.** After all, it is Christ, and not the disciples, who does the works. The disciples are omnipotent only through the omnipotence of their Master.

15–18. PROMISE OF THE COMFORTER AS A FURTHER SOURCE OF CONSOLATION.

15. **If ye love me,** as they surely will do, seeing that he has so loved them, and is ever ready at their request to show fresh proofs of it, **keep my commandments.** This is the only practical way to express this love. The injunction very appropriately stands between two most gracious promises. Jesus says, **my commandments.** It is the language of one who has authority to lay down laws for his people. The path of loving obedience is one in which greater blessings are to be obtained. Hence the following promise:

16. **And I will pray the Father,** rather, *ask* or *request* as one equal with the Father, **and he shall give,** *he will give.* The Father willingly responds to the request of the Son. It is worthy of note that the three Persons of the Trinity are mentioned in this verse: the Son asks, the Father gives, the Spirit comforts. The language here is accommodated to our comprehension, for it cannot literally be said that the gift of the Spirit depends on Christ's asking, as though the Father and the Spirit had no part in the matter. In chs. 15 : 26 and 16 : 7 Christ says he will send the Spirit. Though the Spirit is now for the first time said to be given or sent, it must not be supposed that he was not in the world and in the hearts of believers before this time. He comes now with greater fulness, influence, grace, and manifestation than in the old economy. **Another Comforter.** The word translated "Comforter" occurs only in this place and in ver. 26; 15 : 26; 16 : 7; 1 John 2 : 1. In the last passage cited it is applied to Christ and translated "advocate." It means "one called or sent for to assist another, an advocate who pleads the cause of another; hence generally, one present to render various beneficial services." Christ calls the Spirit "another Advocate" or *Helper*—that is, one who should be to them what he had been, or, who should be to them on earth during his absence what he still is in heaven. For Christ's relation to his disciples did not terminate at his departure, though the sphere and manner of his official actions were changed. "Now we have an advocate, a *Paraclete,* with the Father, 'Jesus Christ the righteous.' And we have another Paraclete, even the Spirit of truth, to abide *with us* for ever. This Comforter is not a substitute for Christ, nor a successor to Christ, as though he took the place and office which Jesus vacated."—JAMES INGLIS, in *Waymarks,* vol. x. pp. 110, 111. Christ is our advocate with the Father; the Spirit is Christ's advocate with us. **Abide . . . for ever,** and not like Christ, who was with them only a little while. The Spirit will be with Christians till Christ comes again.

17. The Spirit of truth, so called

him: but ye know him; ^cfor he dwelleth with you, 18 ^dand shall be in you. ^eI will not leave you comfort- 19 less; ^fI will come to you. Yet a little while, and the world seeth me no more; but ^gye see me: ^hbecause I 20 live, ye shall live also. At that day ye shall know that ⁱI am in my Father, ^kand ye in me, and I in

^a Isa. 57. 15; Rom. 8. 9, 11; 1 Cor. 3. 16; 6. 19; 2 Tim. 1. 14; 1 John 3. 24; 4. 12, 13.
^d Gal. 4. 6; 1 John 2. 27.
^e Isa. 51. 12; Matt.

28. 20.   ^f ch. 16. 22; Matt. 18. 20.   ^g ch. 12. 35; 16. 16.   ^h ch. 11. 25.
ⁱ ver. 10.   ^k ch. 6. 56; 15. 1; Gal. 2. 20; Eph. 3. 17.

---

because he possesses and communicates the truth of God. He is the Spirit of revelation, Eph. 1 : 17. He alone knows the mind of God, 1 Cor. 2 : 10. He takes of the things of Christ, who is "the truth," and shows them unto believers, and guides into all the truth, 14 : 6; 16 : 14. The truth thus revealed he makes effective in the life. "The Spirit is truth," 1 John 5 : 6. **Whom the world,** in its natural state, carnal and sinful, **cannot receive,** 1 Cor. 2 : 14. It neither believes that he is nor is cognizant of his operations. The inward feelings of conviction, repentance, faith, hope, fear, love, which he produces the world cannot understand. **But ye,** in contrast with the world, being spiritually-minded, **know him,** as comforter, monitor, helper, advocate; **for he dwelleth with you, and shall be in you**—*is in you.* "It is the Spirit alone who, by dwelling within us, gives us the knowledge of himself, being otherwise unknown and incomprehensible."—CALVIN.

18. **I will not leave you comfortless;** rather, *orphans* or *bereaved.* The word is peculiarly appropriate, since Christ had so recently called the disciples "little children," 13 : 33. "Orphans are children left alone in their incapacity to face trials to which only mature men are equal." **I will come to you;** rather, *I come*, for the verb is present. That is, he will come soon, without delay, in the person of the "Spirit of truth." The presence and grace of Christ are essential to the disciples, and they shall not be deprived of them. The presence of the Comforter, though he be "another," Christ regards as virtually the same as his own presence. Thus he asserts the essential and vital unity of himself and the Comforter.

19-24. SPIRITUAL LIGHT AND LIFE THROUGH THE INDWELLING OF THE COMFORTER.

19. **A little while,** less than twenty-four hours. **The world** saw him no more after his crucifixion and burial, **but ye see me.** Even after the world shall cease to behold him, the disciples shall see him—not only during the forty days when he showed himself alive unto them, but always as a real, living, present Saviour. Though separated from them in body, they will recognize him as present in the spirit. **Because I live, ye shall live also,** or, *for I live, and you will live.* This last is perhaps the preferable rendering of this clause. It does not therefore necessarily teach the dependence of the Christian's life upon that of Christ—a precious truth taught elsewhere—but gives the reason why the disciples shall always see Jesus. The meaning of the whole verse seems rather to be this: "The world will see me no more; in a little while I shall be to the world as one who has ceased to exist. But though I depart I do not perish; and since you too have eternal life and a spiritual insight not possessed by the world, you may take comfort in the thought that you shall evermore behold me." The translation, *Because I live, ye shall live also*, has, however, eminent defenders, and should not be hastily set aside, but seriously considered.

20. **At that day,** when the Comforter shall have come, **ye shall know,** etc. "What they were slow to learn in the days of his flesh they will learn rapidly in the days of the Spirit."—BOWEN, *Love Revealed.* The Holy Spirit will produce in them a clear perception of Christ's peculiar relation to the Father and to them. Thus the believing, loving soul is brought not only to see Christ and to share in his victory, but into most intimate and perpetual fellowship with God

21 you. ¹He that hath my commandments, and keepeth them, he it is that loveth me: and he that loveth me shall be loved of my Father, and I will love him, and will manifest myself to him.   ¹ 1 John 2. 5; 5. a
22 ᵐ Judas saith unto him (not Iscariot), Lord, how is it that thou wilt manifest thyself unto us, and not unto the world?   ᵐ Luke 6.16; Matt 10. 3, *Lebbeus*.
23 Jesus answered and said unto him, If a man love me, he will keep my words: and my Father will love him, ⁿ and we will come unto him, and make our abode with him. ᵒ He that loveth me not, keepeth not my sayings: and ᵖ the word which ye hear is not mine, but the Father's which sent me.   ⁿ ver.17; Rev. 3. 20. ᵒ Matt. 19. 21, 22; 2 Cor. 8. 8, 9; 1 John 3. 16-20. ᵖ ver. 10.
25 These things have I spoken unto you, being *yet*

---

21. He that hath my commandments, has them in memory, **and keepeth them**, observes them in his life, showing that he has them also in his heart, **he it is that loveth me.** As in verse 15, so here obedience is set down as the test of love. The commandments of Christ are responses to the believer's loving inquiry, "Lord, what wilt thou have me to do?" When he said to Peter, "Lovest thou me?" the prompt answer was, "Yea, Lord," and the ready response, "Feed my sheep." **He that loveth me shall be loved of my Father,** who loves those who love his Son with a love that is peculiar—that differs widely from the general love of pity and compassion with which he regards the rest of mankind. **And I will love him.** Even Christ himself makes special revelations of his love and special manifestations of his glory to those who give special evidence of love to him.

22. The disciples failed to understand the nature of the manifestation just spoken of, and hence the question of Judas. **Not Iscariot,** for the traitor had already gone out, 13 : 30. John distinguishes the two men as having wholly different characters. This Judas is also called Lebbeus, or Thaddeus, Matt. 10 : 3; Mark 3 : 18; Luke 6 ; 16. **Lord, how is it,** etc. Rather, *What has come to pass*, etc. The disciples were looking for the immediate establishment by their Master of an earthly kingdom. What has occurred that Jesus should no more present himself to the people. They could not see how he should confine himself to them.

23. Their Lord, instead of answering them directly, throws them back upon the explanation in ver. 21, which they had not duly considered; and by repeating it emphasizes the fact that the manifestation he asks of is spiritual and is given to those who love and obey him. **And my Father will love him.** "In ver. 15 we find Jesus saying, 'If ye love me, keep my commandments,' and this injunction introduces the promise of the Spirit. In verse 21 we have the same injunction introductory to the promise of the manifestation of Christ. In verse 23 we read again, 'If a man love me, he will keep my words;' and in connection with it the promise of the manifestation of the Father, and of the permanent abode of both the Father and the Son with the believer. It would be difficult to conceive of any addition to this promise."
—BOWEN.

24. The same great principle that he has already laid down, that love and obedience are inseparably united, Jesus here states in the negative form, **And the word which ye hear,** etc. The importance of keeping Christ's commandments is seen in the fact that they are of such dignity and authority; they are not his alone; they proceed equally from the Father.

25, 26. FULLER INSTRUCTIONS TO BE GIVEN BY THE COMFORTER.

25. **These things,** the things spoken to them in this valedictory discourse. It was not all he might say to them, but all they were prepared to receive, and all that was necessary to arm them for the events so soon to follow.

26 present with you. But ᑫ the Comforter, *which is* the Holy Ghost, whom the Father will send in my name, ʳ he shall teach you all things, ˢ and bring all things to your remembrance, whatsoever I have said unto you.
27 ᵗ Peace I leave with you, my peace I give unto you: ᵘ not as the world giveth, give I unto you. Let not your heart be troubled, neither let it be afraid. Ye have heard how I said unto you, I go away, and come *again* unto you. If ye loved me ye would rejoice, because I said, ˣ I go unto the Father: for ʸ my Father

ᑫ ch. 7. 39; Luke 24. 49.
ʳ ch. 16. 13; 1 John 2. 20, 27.
ˢ ch. 2. 22; 12. 16; Acts 11. 16.
ᵗ ch. 16. 33; Rom. 1. 7; 5. 1; Eph. 2. 14–17; Phil. 4. 7; Col. 1. 20; 3. 15.
ᵘ P's. 28. 3.
ˣ ch. 16. 16; 20. 17.
ʸ ch. 13. 16; Isa. 42. 1; 1 Cor. 11. 3; 15. 28; Heb. 2. 9–16.

26. But the Comforter, when he *shall come,* will impart fuller knowledge to you. **In my name,** at his prevailing request, in his behalf, for the accomplishment of his work. **He shall teach you all things,** that concern Christ and his words, his person, and his teaching: not all knowledge, but all knowledge needful for the spiritual well-being of the soul. **And bring all things to your remembrance,** etc.; a very consoling promise to the disciples. Often they had heard the words of Christ without understanding them, and even without remembering what they did understand. The writings of the apostles give ample evidence that the promise was literally fulfilled. Since this promise was given in the first place for the apostles, we find in it our impregnable authority for the trustworthiness and completeness of the Scriptures of the New Testament. They contain Christ's words and the inspired comments on them. "It is on the fulfilment of this promise to the apostles that their sufficiency as witnesses of all that the Lord did and taught, and consequently the authority of the gospel narrative, are grounded."— ALFORD. The Spirit, through whom we possess a complete and authoritative record, enlightens our minds in its reading and seals its truths upon our hearts.

27–31. FURTHER COMFORTING ASSURANCES.

27. Peace I leave with you. Jesus saw that his disciples were disturbed by the intimation that he was to depart out of the world. They could not appreciate without actual experience the marvellous compensations of the Spirit and the spiritual presence of Christ and the Father. It seemed impossible to them that anything but trouble could come to them when the bodily Christ whom they knew should be taken away, and only a shadowy Christ whom they knew not should remain. Yet they have their Master's own word for it that it shall not be so. **My peace I give unto you.** Christ's own peace, the peace which he enjoys, he gives unto them. This peace, which "passeth all understanding" (Phil. 4 : 7), arose from the consciousness that he possessed almighty power, infinite wisdom, and perfect holiness. Through their faith in him the disciples should possess this peace. **Not as the world giveth,** etc. It is the custom in Eastern countries for persons to separate with wishes of peace. These wishes from their frequency become mere formal expressions, and even at best are ineffectual in securing peace. But Christ gives from a sincere and loving heart, and uses means to make his offer effectual. He gives himself, the just for the unjust; he sends the Holy Spirit, that the things which concern salvation may be known more clearly. Hence arises in us a peace that flows from a sense of pardoned sin, the hope of heaven, and the constant presence of a living Saviour. **Let not your heart be troubled;** a repetition of the words which begin the long list of consoling thoughts in this chapter.

28. Ye have heard how I said unto you. See vers. 2, 3, 12 and ch. 13 : 33–36. They heard that his absence would be temporary; that during this time the Holy Spirit would be to them "another Comforter;" that, so far from their losing by his departure, they would gain unspeakably in wisdom, in power with God and with man, and in

A. D. 30.   JOHN XIV.   241

29 is greater than I. And *now I have told you before
it come to pass, that, when it is come to pass, ye
30 might believe. Hereafter *I will not talk much with
you: *for the prince of this world *cometh, *and hath
31 nothing in me. But that the world may know that I
love the Father; and *as the Father gave me commandment, even so I do. *Arise, let us go hence.

*ch. 13. 19; 16. 4.
*ch. 16. 12.
*ch. 12. 31; 16. 11.
*See Luke 22. 53;
   Eph. 6. 12.
*Isa. 53. 9.
*ch. 4. 34; 10. 18;
   15. 10; Ps. 40. 8;
   Phil. 2. 8; Heb.
   5. 7, 8.   *ch. 18. 1-4.

all perfections. **If ye loved me,** with such a love as they ought to cherish toward him. They did love him, but their love was too carnal; it was not sufficiently spiritual and intelligent; they failed to recognize his true nature and the character of his work. **Ye would rejoice, because I said, I go unto the Father;** the best authorities omit "*I said*" from this passage; **for my (*the*) Father is greater than I.** This gives the reason why his going to the Father ought to be to them a cause of rejoicing. "When Christ speaks of the Father as greater than himself, he refers not to his own nature, but to his office, condition, and work as Mediator, and it implies no inferiority in his original dignity, wisdom, power, and glory." — *New, Test. with Notes*, Amer. Tract Soc. He says in effect to his disciples: "My Father is greater than I. In ascending to him I ascend to a far higher greatness than you have yet seen investing me. I am in some sense despoiled of my proper greatness by my life in the flesh. I have made myself lower than the angels for the suffering of death. I have been encompassed about with the infirmities incident to humanity. I go to the Father that I may be clothed with the glory of the Father. I go not into darkness, but into light unapproachable, to glory inconceivable."—BOWEN. If, therefore, you love me, rejoice, not for your own sakes alone, but for my sake also. See ch. 17:5 and Phil. 2:7.

29. **And now I have told you before it come to pass.** His suffering, ascension, and the coming of the Comforter are referred to here. **That, when it is come to pass, ye might believe.** Their faith, instead of being shaken by the events about to happen, will be confirmed when these events are seen to be but the fulfilment of his prophetic words.

30. **Hereafter I will not talk much with you:** the time intervening before his crucifixion was brief, and but a small portion of this was to be spent in communing with them; **for the prince of this world.** Satan is meant. He rules in the hearts of the majority of mankind. "The whole world lieth in the Wicked One." Judas, the Roman soldiers, the Pharisees, and rulers were coming to apprehend him, but all these were only the agents of Satan. **Cometh,** as he had done all through our Lord's earthly ministry, but now with special violence and wrath, to make his last attack on him in Gethsemane and on Calvary, **and hath nothing in me**—nothing in common with himself; no sin or weakness of which he can take advantage.

31. **But that the world may know,** etc. Christ bears all that is about to befall him—the conflict with the prince of this world and the sufferings of the cross—by the Father's appointment, that he may show to the world his love for the Father and his desire to glorify him in the salvation of sinners. **Arise, let us go hence.** These words were not, according to some interpreters, followed by an immediate departure. They think that the first verse of chapter 18 indicates that Jesus went forth from the upper room only at the close of his intercessory prayer. The consoling words of this chapter were spoken, as they think, at the table immediately after the institution of the Supper. Then, in obedience to the Saviour's command, all arose from their couches and gathered about him, but their immediate departure was delayed by Christ's addressing them afresh. Standing and grouped around their Master, they listened to his last words and heard his last prayer. Godet takes a different view of the whole verse. The idea, in his view, is, "In order that the world may know, . . . arise, let us go hence." By going out to Gethsem-

ane Jesus was moving toward Calvary. Luke tells us: "When the time was come that he should be received up, he steadfastly set his face to go to Jerusalem," Luke 9 : 51. So now he says to his disciples, "Arise, let us go hence," in order to meet the treachery of Judas, the deadly hatred of the Jews, and the death on the cross. Thus, the cup that the Father gave him he would willingly drink, and by his obedience in this to the Father's will show the fulness of his love for him. Godet thinks the subsequent addresses were made as they went out on their way to Gethsemane.

Practical Remarks.

1. In the world Christians will have trouble on account of apostasies, the many mysteries of Providence; on account of their own conscious weakness and unworthiness; but an abiding faith in the person and work of their Lord is an antidote for it all, ver. 1; ch. 16 : 33.

2. Christ leads his followers to a place where troubles never come. He gives us many positive and comforting assurances concerning heaven. It is our Father's house, and therefore home. In it is room for all; the poorest and weakest believers shall have a place there. It is an abiding place, where we shall dwell eternally. It will be the abode of Christ our Saviour, vers. 2, 3; Phil. 1 : 23; 1 Thess. 4 : 7; Rev. 21 and 22.

3. Though Christians mourn the absence of their Lord and long for and love his appearing, they have the consolation that it was for them he went away. "Look upon the person of Christ as a vase filled with celestial gifts; the breaking of the vase is the diffusion of the gifts" (BOWEN), ver. 3; ch. 16 : 7; Rom. 8 : 34; Heb. 7 : 25; 9 : 28.

4. The Lord is often more charitable to his people than they are to themselves. To know Christ as our Saviour is to know the way of life, however ignorant we may be of many things that concern salvation. Failing to take heed to the words of the Lord is the too frequent cause of our limited knowledge, vers. 4, 5; Heb. 2 : 1; 5 : 12; 6 : 1.

5. The only way of access to God, either to his "house" or to a state of reconciliation with him, is through faith in the Lord Jesus Christ. Christ as the "way" begins just where man by nature is in his sins—shows him the truth and gives him life. 'To use Christ daily as the way—to believe Christ daily as the truth—to live on Christ daily as the life,—this is to be a well-informed, a thoroughly furnished, and an established Christian" (RYLE), ver. 6; Acts 4 : 12; 1 Tim. 2 : 5.

6. If we would know more of the invisible God, we must know more of his image. The glory of God must be veiled in flesh that man may behold it. The rebellious world knows not the nature of its request when it asks for a more direct revelation of God. Those who refuse to see him in Jesus Christ shall never see him, save as the God of judgment, vers. 7-9; ch. 12 : 44, 45; 2 Cor. 4 : 4; Col. 2 : 9; Heb. 1 : 3.

7. It should humble us when we consider how many opportunities we have for gaining the most important of all knowledge, and how little we improve them. The knowledge of temporal and earthly things, how easily acquired and retained! How slow we are to learn, and how soon we forget the words of Jesus! vers. 8, 9; Luke 24 : 25; Heb. 5 : 12.

8. If Jesus was not what he claimed to be, he was either deceived himself, and so deserves our pity, or he was a deceiver, and merits the reprobation of all men. The evidence for the justness of his claim is many-sided. To those who have entered into personal relation with him and know him, what he asserts is the truth. To those who are ignorant of him, his works testify of his character, and show it to be such that he will always speak the truth. There is evidence suited to all the different classes and states of mind, vers. 10, 11; chs. 5 : 36; 10 : 25, 38.

9. Faith in Christ not only gives rest to the troubled heart, but also prepares its possessor for eminent usefulness in the world. Conscious of being saved ourselves, we are free to labor for the good of others. All duty is possible to the believer, ver. 12; Matt. 21 : 21; Mark 16 : 17; Phil. 4 : 13; Col. 1 : 11.

10. "Let us admire the condescension of our Master in allowing more success to the ministry of his weak servants than to his own." "Ou

Lord is working with us and for us, though we cannot see him. It was not so much the sword of Joshua that defeated Amalek as the intercession of Moses on the hill, Ex. 17 : 11."—RYLE. "Christ ascended up on high that he might the more widely diffuse his grace and glory in the earth; that he might in his disciples visit every nation and flash forth upon mankind the evidences of his power to bless unto the uttermost" (BOWEN), ver. 12.

11. Christ ascended unto the Father, and all his followers ascend with him and enter into the very treasury of God's power; these treasures they may have for the asking. The name of Christ is their only plea at this storehouse of blessing. "They stand in Christ before the throne, and receive in Christ the expression of the Father's love to Christ," vers. 12-14; ch. 15 : 7, 16; 16 : 23, 24; Matt. 7 : 7; 21 : 22.

12. To ask in the name of Christ is to pray resting on the merits of his atonement and intercession, trusting wholly in the righteousness of his will, and confiding in the risen Saviour, to whom is given all power in heaven and earth, vers. 13, 14; Heb. 4 : 14-16.

13. We best show our love to Christ not by lamenting the degeneracy of the times and the wickedness of the world, but in seeking to right the world's wrongs by practising and teaching the words of Christ. Active and contemplative piety ought ever to be conjoined. There are times to sit at Jesus' feet, and times to put in practice the lessons we have learned there, vers. 15, 21, 23; Luke 10 : 38-42; 1 Cor. 15 : 58; James 2 : 20, 24; 1 John 5 : 3; 2 John 6.

14. Christians have the most precious promises for the times of the greatest need. Christ's work *for us* is all-sufficient, but provision is made that it shall be made effectual *in us* through the ministry of the Spirit. "Christ could not come sufficiently near his people while imprisoned in a body of clay upon the earth, and the body was broken like an alabaster box of ointment, that he might come nearer to his own and communicate himself to their very souls" (BOWEN), vers. 16-18; Rom. 8 : 13-16, 26-28; 2 Cor. 12 : 9, 10.

15. "The Holy Spirit is meant to supply all the needs of believers and to fill up all that is wanting while Christ's visible presence is removed." "Next to the whole truth about Christ, it concerns our safety and peace to see the whole truth about the Holy Spirit." "Any doctrine about the church, the ministry, or the sacraments which obscures the Spirit's inward work or turns it into mere form is to be avoided as deadly error" (RYLE), vers. 16-18; 1 John 2 : 27.

16. Those who leave all for Christ will never be forsaken by him, ver. 18; Matt. 28 : 20; Mark 10 : 28-30.

17. The world regards Christ as dead, but the Holy Spirit reveals him as a living Saviour to living souls. Through the illumination of the Spirit, Christians enjoy now exalted views of Christ and his salvation, but brighter and clearer visions await them in the day of his coming, vers. 19, 20; 1 Pet. 1 : 3; Acts 25 : 19; 1 John 3 : 1, 2.

18. Those who have most real practical love to Christ will have the clearest and deepest spiritual vision—will know most of the heart of Christ. Though we are saved "by grace," yet special honors are awarded to special faithfulness. "Those who follow Christ most closely and obediently will always follow him most comfortably and feel most of his inward presence" (RYLE), ver. 21; 1 John 2 : 5; 4 : 12.

19. Christ would have us set a high value upon his words, for they, as well as his work, show that he is one with the Father—reveal the Father's character and will. No matter what a person may profess, if he does not observe Christ's words, he does not love Christ, vers. 21-24; Ps. 119; Matt. 7 : 21-23; 1 John 2 : 24.

20. The revelation we have is sufficient for our needs, but the Holy Spirit must aid us to understand, interpret, and apply it. As the Spirit could not have recalled the words of Christ to those who had never heard them, so his people now cannot expect the Spirit to recall to their minds words of Scripture which they have never heard and never read, ver. 26.

21. If the world has peace, it is because it is ignorant of its danger. If Christians are troubled, it is because they are ignorant of the true grounds of their peace, vers. 27, 28; Isa. 48 : 22; 59 : 8; Rom. 3 : 17; 5 : 1; 8 : 1.

22. Christians ought to rejoice be-

JOHN XV.   A. D. 30

The abiding union between Christ and his disciples.

XV. I AM the true vine, and my Father is ᵍ the husband- 2 man. ʰ Every branch in me that beareth not fruit he taketh away: and ⁱ every *branch* that beareth fruit, he purgeth it, that it may bring forth more fruit.

ᵍ Isa. 27. 2, 3; 1 Cor. 3. 9.
ʰ Matt. 3. 10; 7. 19; 15. 13; Luke 13. 7-9; Heb. 6. 7, 8.
ⁱ Matt. 13. 12; Heb. 12. 11.

---

cause Christ went to the Father, since through his resurrection and ascension we have hope of acceptance with the Father, ver. 28; 1 Cor. 15 : 17; Rom. 4 : 25; 1 Pet. 1 : 3.

23. "Our Lord intended that his people should have continually new arguments for faith." "One of the reasons for which prophecy was given is that the fulfilling providence of God may be made to bear testimony to the Scriptures of truth" (BOWEN), ver. 29.

24. It is a sad commentary on the state of this world when the prince of darkness, the father of lies, is its god—that all men by nature are in subjection to him. "Christ alone could say, 'He hath nothing in me;' God had everything in him."—BOWEN. "Let us thank God that we have such a perfect, sinless Saviour—that his righteousness is a perfect righteousness, and his life a blameless life" (RYLE), ver. 30; ch. 12 : 31; 16 : 11; 2 Cor. 4 : 4; Eph. 2 : 2; 1 John 5 : 19; Rev. 12 : 9.

CHAPTER XV.

Our Lord in this chapter treats of the abiding and vital union between himself and his disciples, implying that this is in no wise impaired by his going away. " By the allegory of a vine and its branches he illustrates the nature of this union and many of its beneficial results. As one consequence and chief fruit of this union he commands them to show their participation in his Spirit by their mutual love, resembling his self-sacrificing love to them. As another he warns them of the hatred of the world toward himself and all united with him, but he cheers them by reminding them that they suffer it with him; that it is not their fault, but the effect of the ignorance and perverseness of their enemies; that they are not left to bear it alone, for the Holy Spirit will help them to work through it."—*Annotated Paragraph Bible.*

In the previous chapter the words of Jesus were chiefly intended to calm and comfort the timid and troubled dis- ciples. Now he proceeds to give instruction rather than consolation, and to press on their attention certain great truths which he would have them especially remember when he is gone.

1-8. THE VITAL AND ABIDING UNION BETWEEN CHRIST AND HIS PEOPLE.

1. Many ingenious but needless attempts have been made to explain why Jesus selected the vine and its branches to illustrate his discourse on this occasion. The figure of the vine, like that of the shepherd which he uses in chapter 10, was familiar to the Jews. Old Testament language (see Jer. 2 : 21; Ezek. 15 : 2-8; Hosea 10 : 1; Ps. 80 : 8), together with the sight of the wine-cup that had been so recently consecrated and divided, may have easily suggested it. The vine is the noblest of plants, and its fruit the most abundant and generous. The figure is therefore the most beautiful and suggestive that could have been used. **I am the true vine.** True, not as opposed to false, but true in the sense of original and essential. He says in effect, "I am the true, original vine, of which all other vines are but types and shadows." Compare ch. 6 : 32—" the true bread." Christ is the vine of which his people are the branches, for he is to them the source of all spiritual life and vigor, and they are as dependent on him as are the branches on the parent stem. **My Father is the husbandman.** Not the hired laborer, the vine-dresser, but the Owner of the vineyard, the original Planter, Possessor, and Cultivator of the vine. The Saviour speaks of himself as the subject of his Father's care and cultivation. The pruning-knife was not withheld even from him; he was perfected through suffering, Heb. 2 : 10. His coronation was the fruit of his triumphant endurance. In the Father's care for the vine is implied also his care for the branches. What he does to the *branches* is expressly stated in the next verse.

2. It appears to be the Saviour's pur-

A. D 30.	JOHN XV.	245

3 ᵏ Now ye are clean through the word which I have   ᵏ ch. 13. 10; 17. 17; Eph. 5. 26, 27.

pose in this passage (vers. 1–8) to teach how intimate the relationship is between himself and his people, and to show further that the natural and necessary result of such union is that they will bring forth the fruits of the Spirit. We are taught also that the heavenly Husbandman takes measures to promote this bearing of fruit. As the owner or keeper of a vineyard sees to it that dead and superfluous branches are removed and that the bearing branches are carefully pruned, so our heavenly Father in his infinite wisdom cares for his own, and through the ministry of his Spirit in the sacred word and in providence prepares them for fruit-bearing. If, then, it be the Saviour's aim to teach these truths, we must interpret the several parts of the passage in harmony with this general purpose. It is well to observe that there is not, and cannot be, a perfect analogy between the Father and a husbandman, between Christ and a vine, between Christians and the branches of a vine. A vine with its branches may wither and decay, but Christ is "the life." Branches may die, be cut off and burned, but we are assured that those who are in Christ Jesus are new creatures and have everlasting life. We must not, therefore, by laying undue stress upon certain forms of expression in this figurative language, draw from the passage doctrines opposed to the plain teaching of the rest of God's word. **Every branch in me**—his disciples are the branches (ver. 5)—**that beareth not fruit.** Jesus is speaking only of such as are *in him*, and hence are real branches. As a matter of fact there are no Christians who do not manifest *some* graces of the Spirit. **He taketh away.** We are not to understand, as some do, that the Father takes away graceless and worldly Christians by death, for this is contrary to fact; or that he permits those who have been born again to come under the condemnation of eternal death, for this is contrary to Christ's own words on other occasions. This clause represents a part or one aspect of the process of training to which our heavenly Father subjects us. (See below.) The other part or aspect is represented in the next clause—**every branch that beareth fruit, he purgeth it;** more exactly, *cleanses it*. This is effected by the word (ver. 3; ch. 17 : 17; Eph. 5 : 26; Ps. 119 : 9; 2 Cor. 7 : 1; Col. 1 : 6), also by afflictions and trials, Heb. 12 : 6–11; 1 Pet. 1 : 6, 7; James 1 : 2–4. Concerning pruning the vine in the East, Dr. Van Lennep (*Bible Lands*, p. 115) says: "Besides the general pruning, however, as soon as the fresh branches have come out upon the stems and show their young blossoms, the vine-dresser goes from one stem to another, cutting off the branches which bear leaves only, in order to afford more nourishment for those which give promise of fruit, and not sparing altogether even these last." **That it may bring forth more fruit.** By these means "our fellowship with Christ is consciously enlarged, and he sends forth through us his own rich fruit."—CHARLES CAMPBELL, in *Grace and Truth*, vol. ii. p. 373. The meaning of the whole verse is in substance this: The object of the husbandman in keeping a vineyard is to obtain fruit; therefore, if there are branches that are useless or that hinder the vine from producing its full burden of fruit, he removes them entirely. Those that remain he trains and prunes in such a manner that the full force of the sap which comes from the parent stock may be used for the production of fruit. Just so the Father treats each branch of the true Vine, for he too is glorified when we bear much fruit. Whatever there is in us or about us—sin or its unnatural fruits—that would hinder us in glorifying him he removes; whatever graces or powers for good we possess he takes measures to improve. The purpose of all this care is that we may bring forth more fruit.

3. **Now ye are clean,** etc. The meaning will be clearer if we read with Alford, *Ye are clean already, by reason of the word which I have spoken unto you*. They are clean, yet (ver. 2) needing to be cleansed. They need daily purging in order to fruit-bearing, because daily exposed to defilement; yet they are born, through the uncorruptible Word, with a birth to which no uncleanness attaches (1 Pet. 1 : 23; James 1 : 18), and therefore, in regard

4 spoken unto you. ¹Abide in me, ᵐand I in you. ⁿAs the branch cannot bear fruit of itself, except it abide in the vine; no more can ye, except ye abide 5 in me. I am the vine, ᵒye *are* the branches. He that abideth in me, and I in him, the same bringeth forth much ᵖfruit: for without ᵍme ye can do nothing. 6 If a man abide not in me, he is cast forth as a branch, and is withered; and men ʳgather them, and cast

ʳ See Matt. 13. 40–42.

¹ ch. 8. 31; Gal. 2. 20; 1 John 2. 6; 2 John 9.
ᵐ ch. 17. 23; Eph. 3. 17.
ⁿ 2 Cor. 12. 8–10; Phil. 4. 13.
ᵒ 1 Cor. 10.17; 12.12.
ᵖ Hos. 14. 8; Phil. 1. 11.
ᵍ Acts 4. 12.

---

to their standing before God, they are absolutely clean. Similar apparent contradictions may be seen by comparing 1 Cor. 6 : 11 and 1 Thess. 5 : 23; Heb. 10 : 14 and Phil. 3 : 12; 1 Pet. 1 : 22 and 1 John 3 : 3.
4. The thought most prominent in this and the four succeeding verses is that as Christ is the source of all the fruit brought forth by the branches, it is essential that they should abide in him and he in them. **Abide in me—**continue, dwell, remain in me. This exhortation implies that the disciples were already in Christ, and also that their fellowship with him was liable to be interrupted for a time, though it might never end, 1 John 2 : 27. To abide in Christ is to have sustained conscious communion with him and a satisfying view of our completeness in him —to continue in the joyful recognition of the value of his perfect sacrifice and the efficacy of his precious blood. **And I in you.** This is an exhortation, and not a promise: "See to it that I abide in you." "He seems to make us responsible not only for our abiding in him, but for his abiding in us. Again, a distinction must be made between his being *in us* and his *abiding in us.* He is ever in us by his Spirit, and is the source of all our comfort and power. As by *our abiding in him* is meant the happy conscious fellowship of our union with him in the discernment of what he is for us, so by his *abiding in us* is meant the happy conscious recognition of his presence in us, in the discernment of his power and grace and goodness, as himself the resource of our souls in everything."—CHARLES CAMPBELL. **As the branch,** etc. A strong statement of the necessity of maintaining our fellowship with Christ.
5. **I am the vine, ye are the branches.** This truth was implied in the preceding verses, but is now for the first time distinctly stated. What follows is a repetition and enlargement of what has already been said, showing that the truth so repeated claims our special consideration. **Bringeth forth much fruit.** The fruit of the Spirit is love, joy, peace, etc., Gal. 5 : 22, 23. **For without me,** *outside of* or *severed from me,* not maintaining communion with me, **ye can do nothing.** Christ claims, and justly, all the fruit which the Christian bears as his own. "We have a warning here to the regenerate man that he never seek to do aught of himself, not a declaration that the unregenerate is unable to do aught. Christ does not mean, 'Out of and apart from me ye are powerless for good;' but 'Being in me, only through putting forth of my power, suffering me effectually to work in and through you, can you accomplish anything.'"— TRENCH.
6. **If a man abide not,** etc. Abiding in Christ is not only essential to our fruit-bearing, but also to show that we are in him—that we have that union with Christ which is essential to our personal salvation. The very fact that believers are in the true and living Vine, and share his life, makes it certain that they will continue to abide in him. See ch. 6 : 39; 10 : 28, 29; 17 : 12; Rom. 8 : 34–39. For a similar mode of teaching a similar truth see Heb. 6 : 4-6. **And men gather them;** more correctly, *they gather them.* "The reapers are the angels," Matt. 13 : 39. **And cast them into the fire,** etc., the dreadful doom of all who have no vital connection with the true Vine. "All that is here expressed or implied of the fire (Matt. 3 : 10), the flame (Luke 16 : 24), the flaming fire (2 Thess. 1 : 8), the furnace of fire (Matt. 13 : 42), the gehenna of fire (Mark 9 :

7 *them* into the fire, and they are burned. If ye abide in me, and *my words abide in you, 'ye shall ask
8 what ye will, and it shall be done unto you. " Herein is my Father glorified, that ye bear much fruit; so shall ye be my disciples.
9 ˣ As the Father hath loved me, so have I loved you:
10 continue ye in my love. ʸ If ye keep my commandments, ye shall abide in my love; even as I have kept my Father's commandments, and abide in his love.
11 These things have I spoken unto you, that my joy might remain in you, and ᶻ *that* your joy might be full.

* Col. 3. 16.
ᵗ ch.14. 13,14; 16.23.
ᵘ Matt. 5. 16; Phil. 1. 11; 1 Pet. 2. 12.
ˣ ch. 17. 23, 24, 26.
ʸ ch. 14. 15, 21-23; Heb. 10. 38; 1 John 2. 5.
ᶻ ch. 16. 24, 33; 17. 13; Acts 13. 52; Rom. 5. 11; 1 Pet. 1. 8; 1 John 1. 4.

---

13), the lake of fire (Rev. 21 : 8), the everlasting fire (Matt. 25 : 4; Jude 7), with all the secrets of anguish which words like these, if there be any truth in words, *must* involve, demands rather to be trembled at than to be expounded."—TRENCH.
7. If ye abide in me, and my words abide in you. "To abide in Christ means to keep up a habit of constant and close communion with him—to be always leaning on him, resting on him, pouring out our hearts to him, and using him as our fountain of life and strength. To have his word abiding in us is to keep his sayings and precepts continually before our minds and memories, and to make them guide our actions and rule our daily conduct and behavior."—RYLE. The former is dependent on the latter, according to 1 John 2 : 24. **Ye shall ask,** etc. The promise is without conditions to those abiding in him; for, being in him, their minds are in harmony with the divine mind, and their wills submissive to the divine will; therefore their requests will be such as the Lord will hear and answer, for they will include only the things that are according to his mind and for his glory.
8. Herein is my Father glorified, etc. Here is another inducement, in addition to the promise above, for our abiding in Christ. The good character and works of those who abide in him will testify to the power and blessedness of the truth concerning him—will lead sinners to receive him, and so bring glory to the God of salvation. The glory of God is the great end and aim of our being. **So shall ye be my disciples;** according to some good authorities, *and become my disciples,* making no pause between this and the clause preceding. The meaning, then, is that by abiding in Christ we bear much fruit and become disciples of Christ worthy of the name, such as he can acknowledge as his own (8 : 31, 32); and in all this the Father is honored. Thus, while we aim at the higher object, the glory of God, we secure the lower, the blessings of true discipleship.
9-11. THE LOVING RELATIONSHIP BETWEEN THE VINE AND THE BRANCHES.
9. As the Father hath loved me, etc. The love of one person of the Trinity to another is something of which we can have no adequate conception, but we know it must be perfect and infinite. Such is the measure of Christ's love to his own. **Continue ye in my love.** The word translated here "continue" is the same that is in previous verses rendered "abide." **My love** is Christ's love for us, not ours to him. To abide in this love is to rest our souls continually on it, being assured that it is exercised toward us—to live and labor under a constant sense of it, being fully persuaded that nothing shall separate us from the love of Christ. See Rom. 8 : 35-39. The warrant for our assurance is that he "gave himself" for us.
10. If ye keep my commandments, etc. The meaning is, that we cannot have an abiding sense of Christ's love except in the path of obedience. It was because of Christ's perfect obedience to the Father that he possessed without interruption a sense of his love. The measure of our conscious fellowship with Christ will ever be according to the measure of our conformity to his words.
11. These things, concerning their

248 JOHN XV. A. D. 30.

12 *This is my commandment, That ye love one another, as I have loved you. ᵇGreater love hath no
13 man than this, that a man lay down his life for his
14 friends. ᶜYe are my friends, if ye do whatsoever I
15 command you. ᵈHenceforth I call you not servants; for the servant knoweth not what his lord doeth: but I have called you friends; ᵉfor all things that I have heard of my Father I have made known unto you.
16 ᶠYe have not chosen me, but I have chosen you, and ᵍordained you, that ye should go and bring forth fruit, and *that* your fruit should remain: that ʰwhatsoever ye shall ask of the Father in my name, he may

* See refs. ch. 13. 34; see also 1 Thess. 4. 9; 1 Pet. 4. 8; 1 John 3. 11.
ᵇ ch. 10. 11, 15; Rom. 5. 6-8; Eph. 5. 2; 1 John 3. 16.
ᶜ ch. 14. 21; Matt. 12. 50.
ᵈ ch. 12. 26; Rom. 8. 15; Gal. 4. 1-7.
ᵉ ch. 17. 26; Gen 18. 17; Matt. 13. 11; Luke 10. 23,

24.   ᶠ ch. 6. 70; 13. 18; Luke 6. 13; Rom. 9. 16; 1 John 4. 10, 19.
ᵍ Matt. 10. 1-5; 28. 19; Mark 16. 15; Col. 1. 6.   ʰ ch. 14. 13.

---

mutual fellowship and love. **That my joy.** See 2 Cor. 2 : 3. This is the joy which Christ has in the consciousness of his Father's love and their abiding unity. It may also refer to the joy our Lord feels in the redemption of his people, Heb. 12 : 2. Christ desires that his disciples should not only be free from trouble, but that they may also be full of joy. Abiding in him, they will rejoice in whatever affords joy to their Lord, and thus the joy which they feel from a sense of his love and presence will be increased to the limit of their capacity and satisfaction.

12-16. THE LOVE OF HIS DISCIPLES TOWARD ONE ANOTHER.

12. **This is my commandment.** Jesus recurs to 13 : 34. By repeating this truth he emphasizes its importance. He calls it " his commandment" because he exalted it into the ruling principle in the new dispensation—because he first gave to us an illustration of its meaning, and it is only by his aid that it can be kept. **That ye love one another.** They were branches of the same Vine, equally dependent on him, loved and nourished by him; on a footing of spiritual equality, they were to love one another **as I have loved you;** this is the measure of their love. Our love cannot, humanly speaking, be the same in quantity as the perfect, infinite love of Christ, but it may and ought to be the same in quality. If it is pure, unselfish, enduring, patient, and hopeful, it is Christlike and divine.

13. **Greater love hath no man than this.** Christ shows his disciples the measure and degree of the love they should cherish toward one another by showing them the greatness of his love. No love could be greater, since he laid down his life for them who are now his friends.

14. **Ye are my friends,** etc. Jesus says in effect, Let no one suppose he is a friend of mine if he is not keeping my commandments. He only returns once more to the great principle laid down in ver. 14 and ch. 14 : 15, 21, 23.

15. Christ's exaltation of his disciples to be his friends is a further evidence of his love to them. **Henceforth I call you not servants,** *no longer I call,* etc. A servant does not know all his master's will, his purposes and plans; he is expected simply to execute his commands without knowing the reason why they are given or all that is to be accomplished. Up to this time the disciples had held a similar relation to their Master, in that they were practically ignorant of his design and work. But now they were to be taken into his confidence as friends. **All things that I have heard.** All things which they were able to bear (16 : 12); all things concerning their salvation, needful for their spiritual good; all things which, as his friends and ambassadors, they were to teach the world.

16. The greatness of Christ's love is seen further by the fact stated in this verse. **Ye have not chosen me.** Pupils among the Jews generally selected their own rabbi or teacher; Jesus reverses the order and calls his disciples, Matt. 4 : 18-22; Mark 2 : 14. He selected twelve from among all his followers to be his chosen and constant companions, endowing them with power to work miracles and to fulfil a special

17 give it you. ¹These things I command you, that ye love one another.
18 ᵏIf the world hate you, ye know that it hated me
19 before *it hated* you. ˡIf ye were of the world, the world would love his own: but ᵐbecause ye are not of the world, but I have chosen you out of the world,
20 therefore the world hateth you. Remember the word that I said unto you, ⁿThe servant is not greater than his lord. If they have persecuted me, they will also persecute you: °if they have kept my saying, they

¹ See refs. ver. 12.
ᵏ ch. 7. 7; Matt 10. 22; James 4 4; 1 John 3. 1, 13.
ˡ 1 John 4. 4, 5.
ᵐ ch. 17. 14–16; Tit. 3. 3–7.
ⁿ ch. 13. 16; Matt. 10. 24, 25; Luke 6. 40.
° Ezek. 3. 7.

---

mission, Matt. 10 : 1; Mark 3 : 13–15; Luke 6 : 13–16. Their appointment to this high office was purely of grace. They were not his champions, noble of birth, powerful in influence, or of great wealth, but chosen vessels to whom he was pleased to commit the great treasures of the gospel, 2 Cor. 4:7. **Ordained** *(appointed)*, . . . **that ye should go and bring forth fruit.** This expresses the object of their appointment to the apostolic office. They were to go into all the world and bring forth fruit, by their godly lives and earnest teaching winning souls to Christ, founding churches, instructing and confirming believers in the faith. The fruit they thus gathered in their personal ministry was "unto eternal life," but the fruit of their labors as apostles remains for us in the Scriptures of the New Testament. **That whatsoever ye shall ask.** It was a part of his purpose and plan that while thus pursuing the labors to which he had appointed them they should obtain by prayer everything they needed for their work.

17–21. THE WORLD'S HATRED OF THE BRANCHES OF THE TRUE VINE. Having spoken of the close and loving relationship between himself and his disciples, and among the disciples themselves, Jesus now speaks of the disciples' relation to the world and the world's attitude toward them.

17. **These things I command you.** For the third time this command falls from the lips of the Master in this evening discourse. He knows the absolute necessity, as well as propriety, of their loving one another. They must stand together and work together, for the world is combined to hate and oppose them. **These things.** We might expect several commands to follow this plural form, but there is only one. It is as though the Lord had said, The sum of all I have to say to you on this subject is, Love one another. This is my first commandment, and the second and third are like unto it.

18. **If the world hate you,** as it does most intensely, **ye know,** *know ye,* **that it hated me before it hated you.** This knowledge brings comfort, 1 Pet. 4 : 12, 13. In this and the following verse the word "world" is used six times. Its deep-seated and protracted hatred is set over against the profound and inexhaustible love of Christ. The disciples were assured that they would be hated as fiercely as they were loved strongly and tenderly, and that finally this hatred would flame into persecution.

19. **If ye were of the world.** This saying gives a reason for the world's hatred, and at the same time affords comfort to the disciples. The world's hatred of them is proof that they have a different Master, a different life and aims and hopes, from the world. The world loves only its own Prince, its own spirit, tone, character, faith, and life.

20. **Remember the word** (13 : 16; Matt. 10 : 24; Luke 6 : 40), for the proverb will prove true in your case. **If they have persecuted me,** which they have done, **they will also persecute you: if they have kept my saying,** which they have not done, **they will keep yours also.** "The Lord was accompanied with credentials from Heaven. He did the work of him who sent him: he was manifestly the Son of God." "Though in human form, he was attended with majesty and power. The winds and waves obeyed him; devils trembled at his

21 will keep yours also. But ^p all these things will they do unto you for my name's sake, ^q because they know
22 not him that sent me. ^r If I had not come and spoken unto them, they had not had sin : ^s but now they have
23 no cloak for their sin. ^t He that hateth me hateth my
24 Father also. If I had not done among them ^u the works which none other man did, they had not had sin : but now ^x have they both seen and hated both
25 me and my Father. But *this cometh to pass,* that the word might be fulfilled that is written in their law, ^y They hated me without a cause.

^p ch. 16. 3; Matt 10. 22 ; 24. 9.
^q ch. 8. 19, 54, 55.
^r ch. 3. 18–21 ; 9. 41 ; 12. 48 ; Luke 12. 46, 47.
^s Rom.1.20; James 4. 17.
^t ch. 10. 30; 14. 9; 1 John 2. 23; 2 John 9.
^u ch. 3. 2 ; 5. 36; 7. 31 ; 9. 32 ; Matt. 9.33 ;11.5;Mark 2. 12.

^x ch. 6. 36.   ^y Ps. 35. 19 ; 69. 4.

presence and fled at his command; angels waited upon him. All his words and works gave evidence that his was a mission of benevolence and love to man. And yet the world hated and persecuted him. It would therefore be vain to expect for his followers a serene path through life."—In substance from BOWEN.

21. **But all these things will they do unto you,** persecute, hate, reject both you and your teachings. The martyrology of the Christian church, written and unwritten—more unwritten than written—is comprehended under the words, "all these things." **For my name's sake.** They were persecuted not only because they bore the name of Christ, but because they exemplified his life and doctrines. See Tacitus, xv. 44; Suetonius, *Nero,* xvi. Yet this suffering was a source of joy and comfort to them, Acts 5 : 41; 2 Cor. 12 : 10; Gal. 6 : 17. **Because they know not him that sent me.** "Ignorance of God is the great cause of hostility to Christ and his servants."—ALFORD. Jesus was sent that he might remove this ignorance, for he was the image of God and came to reveal him. Had the world at once received Christ, it would have been a proof that it already knew God and that the Saviour's mission was useless.

22–25. THE SINFULNESS OF THE WORLD'S HATRED.

22. **If I had not come and spoken unto them,** with such words as never were spoken before, teaching truths that no one ever taught before, showing plainly that he came from heaven, **they had not had sin.** This sin is that of hating Christ and his people. It is not meant that they would not have been sinners at all, but that the light which shone in Christ and his words only revealed the virulence of their hatred and caused their guilt to be more clearly seen. **No cloak for their sin,** no pretext or excuse by which to cover up their conduct, 9 : 41.

23. This verse gives a reason why the guilt of the world in hating Christ was so great. He was one with the Father; to hate him was to hate the Father, and to show that they did not love holiness, and hence were full of sin, 14 : 9. This truth was especially pertinent to the Jews, who professed to reject Christ because they loved God.

24. **If I had not done among them the works,** etc. They had not only the evidence of Christ's words, but the added testimony of his works; and therefore their guilt and condemnation were greatly increased. The works of Christ did not so much surpass in wonderfulness and extent the miracles of Moses, Elijah, Elisha, and the apostles. They were greater in this respect, that he wrought them in his own strength by a mere word, without effort. Their works revealed the power of God in them; his works revealed his own power, and showed that all creation was obedient to his will.

25. **But this cometh to pass,** the world's treatment of Christ and his disciples, **that the word might be fulfilled.** Compare Matt. 1 : 22. The purpose expressed here is the purpose of God, and not that of the world. The world in hating Christ had no intention of fulfilling prophecy, but their sinful hatred did lead them unconsciously to fulfil it. **That is written in their law.** See Ps. 35 : 19; 69 : 4. **Law** is here a gen-

26 ᵃ But when the Comforter is come, whom I will send unto you from the Father, *even* the Spirit of truth, which proceedeth from the Father, ᵃ he shall 27 testify of me: and ᵇ ye also shall bear witness, because ᶜ ye have been with me from the beginning.

ᵃ cf. 14. 16, 17, 26; 16. 7, 13; Luke 24. 49; Acts 2. 33. ᵃ ch. 16. 14, 15; 1 John 5. 6. ᵇ Luke 24. 48; Acts 1. 8, 21, 22; 2. 32; 3. 15; 4. 20, 33; 5. 32; 10. 39; 13. 31; 1 Pet. 5. 1; 2 Pet. 1. 16–18. ᶜ Luke 1. 2, 3; Acts 1. 21, 22; 1 John 1. 1, 2.

eral term denoting the Old Testament. **They hated me without a cause.** These words David uses concerning his enemies' conduct toward himself. But David was a typical person, chosen of God to be a type of Christ, and hence the treatment he received from his enemies was typical also. The circumstance of his being hated without a cause was typical, and for this reason prophetic of the world's causeless hatred of Christ. In this way there was an indirect though proper fulfilment of prophecy. It is thus a typical prophecy.

26, 27. THE PROMISE OF HELP TO ENDURE AND TO OVERCOME THE WORLD'S OPPOSITION.

26. **But when the Comforter is come**—*i. e.* the Holy Spirit—**whom I will send unto you from the Father.** Christ here contemplates himself as already seated at the right hand of the Father. Therefore he says, **I will send.** It is a style of language suitable to him in his state of exaltation, being on an equality with the Father. In the preceding chapter (ver. 16) he says: "I will pray the Father," which is another style of speech, according with his state of humiliation. **Which proceedeth from the Father,** indicating a close and vital relation with the Father, for the word translated "proceedeth" is a strong term, signifying literally "to go out of." It does not appear, however, that we are to derive from this clause the doctrine of the eternal procession of the Holy Spirit. But we are plainly taught that the Spirit is a person distinct from the Father, and yet is one with him in his essential nature—that although a distinct person from the Son, and having a different part in the work of redemption, it can be said of him as of the Son, that he was "in the beginning" and "was God" (ch. 1 : 1), was one with the Father (10 : 30), came down from heaven (3 : 13), from God (13 : 3), from the Father, 16 : 27, 28, 30. He, emphatic, "he" in opposition to the world, **shall testify of me,** in such a manner that the testimony of the Spirit and of the disciples cannot be resisted. The events in Acts 2 were the beginnings of the fulfilment of this promise. We see also in that chapter the manner in which the Spirit's testimony is given. "The Spirit testifies of Jesus to the believer, and teaches the believer to testify of Jesus." For it was by reason of the truth which the Spirit inspired the apostles to utter on the day of Pentecost that about three thousand enemies of Christ were subdued.

27. **And ye also shall bear witness,** or, *and ye also are bearing witness.* Christ looks upon his disciples as already engaged in the work which they should enter upon more fully "when the Comforter is come." "With great power gave the apostles witness of the resurrection of the Lord Jesus," Acts 4 : 33. Some take the verb in the imperative, *and bear ye also witness.* I prefer the other as the more natural. Here is a double testimony; yet each not independent of the other. "The Spirit will witness in and by them. Of the human side of this testimony of the Spirit we have a summary in the inspired Gospels —the divine side in his own indwelling testimony in the heart and life of every believer in all time."—ALFORD. **Because ye have been with me from the beginning,** of his ministry; an important qualification of the apostles as witnesses, Acts 1 : 21, 22; 10 : 40, 41; 13 : 31. Paul's lack of this was made up by a direct call and revelation of the risen Jesus. This promise of the presence and aid of the Spirit was intended to so encourage the disciples that they should not be depressed in view of the hatred and opposition of the world.

PRACTICAL REMARKS.

1. It is only by union with Christ, the "True Vine," the only Mediator, that our lost souls can be restored to their

true relationship with God, ver. 1; Rom. 6 : 8, 11; Eph. 5 : 30-32.

2. The fruit we are to bear as branches of the True Vine is not first and chiefly religious activity, but the graces which pertain to personal character. There may be much activity where there is little fruitfulness. The external rites of religion may be observed by those who are destitute of the inward spirit, ver. 2; Rom. 14 : 17; Gal. 5 : 22, 23.

3. The process of pruning and culture is in our Father's hands. If any part of it for the present seems to be grievous, we know that in the end it must result in good to us and in glory to him, ver. 2; Rom. 8 : 28; 2 Cor. 4 : 17; Heb. 12 : 11; Job 42 : 12-17; 1 Sam. 3 : 18; Ps. 119 : 67, 71; Prov. 3 : 11, 12.

4. Every one who is in Christ by faith is spiritually cleansed, is sanctified, and therefore prepared at once to bear the fruits of righteousness. It is a false notion that it is necessary for us to have persecutions or chastisements before we are ready to glorify God in our lives. It is not to our honor, but to our shame, that we need daily cleansing, ver. 3; ch. 13 : 10; 1 Cor. 6 : 20; 1 John 1 : 7.

5. Occasional, fitful fellowship with Christ produces only barrenness of soul. Constant, close, and habitual communion with him forms a strong spiritual character, which naturally bears rich and abundant fruit. "By their fruits ye shall know them" may be fitly applied in marking the differences between true Christians, ver. 4; Col. 1 : 23; 2 : 5-7; 1 Cor. 15 : 58.

6. Our glory is that we are branches of the True Vine. All our power for good is from Christ, and can only be obtained by continual communion with him. Christ does not merely supplement our wisdom and strength, but he gives all, ver. 5; 2 Cor. 12 : 9; Phil. 1 : 11; 4 : 13.

7. The Lord would keep his disciples close to him by motives of fear as well as by motives of love. Yet the ultimate motive is always love, for while he says, "Beware of the doom of the wicked!" he says, in effect, "It is from this I have saved you, *therefore* abide in me," ver. 6; 2 Cor. 10 : 12; Heb. 3 : 12; 6 : 4-6.

8. Let us observe the importance of Christ's words. They are an expression of Christ himself, so that he abides in us by means of his words. Compare ver. 4. When his words abide in us our wills become one with his will. Hence we obtain what we ask when we ask what we thus will. This is asking in Christ's name. "We must keep up intimate friendship with the great Advocate in heaven if we wish our petitions to prosper" (RYLE), ver. 7.

9. All things are made and the creation is ruled for God's glory, and this also is the end of our salvation. By fulfilling our duty to bring forth much fruit we glorify him. But let us be content to bear fruit in God's own order, love, joy, peace, long-suffering, etc., and then not seek to glorify ourselves by any fruit that may be given us to bear, ver. 8; Matt. 5 : 16; Rom. 11 : 36.

10. Christ's love to us, though so great, is unchanging; our consciousness of a participation in that love should be equally abiding. The Saviour is no more willing to give us a sense of his love at first than he is to grant a continuance of it. If we are full of fervor and zeal a part of the year, and dead and cold the other part, it is because we have not sought by earnest watchfulness and prayer to continue in Christ's love, ver. 9; Jude 20, 21; ch. 13 : 1; Rom. 8 : 35, 39; Eph. 6 : 17, 18; 1 John 4 : 16.

11. "Holy living and assurance of an interest in Christ are closely connected. Our happiness and enjoyment of religion are inseparably bound up with our daily practical living. 'Joy and peace in believing' will never accompany an inconsistent life. 'Hereby we do know that we know him, if we keep his commandments,' 1 John 2 : 3" (RYLE), vers. 10, 11.

12. The importance of the new commandment is set forth in 1 Cor. 13 : 4-7. This love must break down all social barriers, even as Christ's love is without respect of persons. He only truly loves men who earnestly and constantly plans and seeks their highest good, ver. 12; 2 Cor. 5 : 13-21; Gal. 3 : 28; Col. 3 : 11; James 2 : 1-9.

13. "'All that a man hath will he give for his life,' and the gift of his life includes all possible gifts. When we receive such a gift we receive the highest expression of love that can be given among men."—BOWEN. What, then, must we think of Christ's love to us,

Persecution foretold: his return: acceptable prayer.
XVI. THESE things have I spoken unto you, that ye

who, though he was holy, harmless, undefiled, and separate from sinners, gave his life for us while we were yet sinners? vers. 13, 14; Rom. 5 : 6-8; Eph. 5 : 2; 1 John 3 : 16; 4 : 9, 10.

14. The history of the disciples is, or should be, the experience of every Christian. We first know Christ as our Lord and Master, but by doing his will and by growth in the knowledge of him we enter more and more into his confidence as friends. The dignity of the believer is an ever-growing dignity, ver. 15; ch. 20 : 17; 1 Cor. 2 : 9, 10; Col. 2: 2, 3; Phil. 3 : 8-10.

15. That is a counterfeit faith which imagines that it creates love in Christ by coming to him. Faith simply recognizes a love that already exists and is freely proffered, 1 John 4 : 16. The election of the Scriptures is an election to fruitfulness as well as to eternal life, ver. 16; 2 Thess 2 : 13; Eph. 1 : 4-6; 2 : 10; Rom. 8 : 29; 1 John 4 : 10.

16. The Christian is not to seek the cause of the world's hatred solely in himself. If he were perfect in every grace, the world would hate him all the more. It hated the Saviour, and the closer our likeness to him the more opposition we may expect, vers. 18-21; 2 Tim. 3 : 12; 1 Pet. 2 : 19-21; 3 : 14-17; 4 : 13, 14.

17. "The same character and the same principles that were embodied in Christ will, wherever embodied, and according to the degree in which they are so, meet with repulsion from men as long as men are what they are." "Some men glory in the mere fact that they are hated, but this is no sure indication of their piety. The opposition they encounter may be not on account of the truth they declare, but because of the austere and truculent way in which they declare it" (BOWEN), ver. 20; Matt. 10 : 16; 2 Pet. 2 : 2; ch. 13 : 16; Phil. 2 : 14, 15.

18. "With malevolence man combines the wisdom of the serpent, and the glorious intellect which, if consecrated to God, would make him the companion of God, spends itself on the invention of ways and means for the gratification of its hostility to all that reflects the image of God" (BOWEN), vers. 20, 21; Ps. 2 : 2, 3; ch. 11 : 47; Acts 4 : 16, 17.

19. Man invents many theories and entertains many fair fancies of human nature with a view to cover up or to excuse sin, but the gospel is a light that reveals the fallacy of them all. As in the days of his flesh the more the scribes and Pharisees knew of Christ the more they hated him, so now, when the gospel of his grace is best known, man's enmity to him assumes its worst forms, vers. 22-24; Luke 12 : 47, 48; Mark 23 : 13, 37; 11 : 20-22; Rom. 1 : 20, 21.

20. "The gospel declares Jesus to be ineffably kind, condescending, conciliatory, gentle, refined, wise, a physician, a shepherd, a teacher, a brother, an advocate, an ally, a light, a sun, a shield, one that washeth the feet of his disciples and sheddeth his blood as a propitiation for their sins. Ten thousand arguments for love there were, but not one for hate" (BOWEN), ver. 25.

21. Numbers may be on the side of the world, but right and might are on the side of the followers of Jesus. Though weak in themselves, they are strong in the strength of their Helper. Those who have the most intimate acquaintance with Christ can but testify of him, vers. 26, 27; Ps. 56 : 11; 118 : 6, 7; Luke 12 : 32; Rom. 8 : 31; 2 Cor. 12 : 10.

CHAPTER XVI.

Our Lord in this chapter continues his discourse without any interruption in the thought. He has told his disciples of the persecutions they will have to suffer after he leaves them, so that when the trial comes they may not lose confidence in him. Though persecution will follow his going away, too great sorrow ought not to fill their hearts, since it is all for their good; for only at his departure will the "Comforter" come to perform his work of conviction in the world and to instruct them in all the truth, thus preparing them for their work as witnesses. But before persecutions shall come he warns them that their faith

254 JOHN XVI. A. D. 30.

2 ᵈshould not be offended. •They shall put you out
of the synagogues: yea, the time cometh, ᶠthat whosoever killeth you will think that he doeth God ser-
3 vice. And ᵍthese things will they do unto you, be-
4 cause they have not known the Father, nor me. But
ᵇthese things have I told you, that when the time
shall come, ye may remember that I told you of them.
And ⁱthese things I said not unto you at the beginning, because I was with you.

ᵈ Matt. 11. 6; 24
10; 26. 31.
• ch. 9. 22, 34; 12
42; Luke 6. 22.
ᶠ Matt. 24. 9; Acts
8.1;9.1;26.9-11.
ᵍ ch. 8. 19; 15. 21;
Rom. 10. 2; 1
Cor.2.8;1 Thess.
2. 14, 15; 1 Tim.
1. 13.
ᵇ ch. 13. 19; 14. 2⁹.
ⁱ See Matt. 9. 15.

Renewed promise of the Comforter, and of his own return.

5   But now ᵏI go my way to him that sent me, and

ᵏ vers. 10, 16; ch.
7. 33;13.3;14. 28.

will be put to a very severe test. Only
a little while and his body will be laid
in the grave, and with it, apparently,
all his promises and all their hopes.
They will mourn, while the world re-
joices at their seeming defeat and disappointment. But soon they shall see
him in his resurrection life, and their
sorrow will be turned into joy. Then
they shall offer acceptable prayer in
his name and greatly increase their
knowledge; their joy shall be full on
account of the blissful visions they
shall obtain. The disciples are encouraged by his words to declare anew
their faith in him. But he warns
them that an emergency is already at
hand that will prove the weakness
and insufficiency of their present faith.
Yet they shall have peace in him, and
obtain through him the victory.

1–4. PERSECUTION FORETOLD.
1. **These things have I spoken,**
concerning the hatred and persecution
of the world and the promise of the
witnessing Spirit, **that ye should not
be offended,** be so surprised and dis-
concerted as to lose your confidence in
me. "Offended" is the translation of
a Greek word which means to cause to
stumble or fall into sin. See Matt. 5:
29; 13 : 21; 18 : 7.
2. **They shall put you out of the
synagogues.** They shall be cut off
from the worship and from all the privileges, religious and social, that pertain
to the synagogue—a very severe punishment for a Jew. An element of
special bitterness in this suffering was
that it was inflicted by their own brethren and by those professing to be the
religious guides of the people. **Yea,
the time cometh** when they shall
have to encounter the bloody fanaticism
of both Jew and Gentile, for **whosoever killeth you will think that
he doeth God service.** The world
will become so blinded by hate that it
will deem it a religious duty to cut
them off from the earth. **That he
doeth God service;** literally, "That
he brings an offering to God"—a most
solemn religious act. See Acts 26 :
9-11.
3. **Because they have not known.**
As in ch. 15 : 21, he points to blind ignorance as the cause of this hatred and
persecution. See 1 Tim. 1 : 13.
4. **But these things,** etc. See 14 :
29 and notes. **Said not unto you at
the beginning.** He revealed truth
to them gradually, as they needed and
were able to bear it. He had spoken
of these things before in an incidental
way (Matt. 5 : 10; 10 : 16), but had never
dwelt upon them so particularly as at
this time. It was very important that
they should first of all know him and
believe on him. This saving knowledge would prepare them to encounter
earthly loss and opposition. **Because
I was with you.** While Jesus was
with them the malice of the world was
directed chiefly against him, but his
removal would leave them to bear it,
apparently, alone. It was not necessary
to disturb their minds on this subject at
an earlier date.

5-11. THE EXPEDIENCY OF CHRIST'S
DEPARTURE, AND THE HOLY SPIRIT'S
MISSION TO THE WORLD.
5. **But now I go my way.** This
is the reason why he is so careful to
notify them of the coming days of trial.
**And none of you asketh me,
Whither goest thou?** A reproof of
their slowness to apprehend the true
state of affairs. They had asked this

6 none of you asketh me, Whither goest thou? But because I have said these things unto you, ¹sorrow hath filled your heart.
7 Nevertheless I tell you the truth; ᵐ It is expedient for you that I go away: for if I go not away, ⁿ the Comforter will not come unto you; but ᵒ if I depart, I will send him unto you. And when he is come,
8 ᵖ he will reprove ᵠ the world of sin, and of righteousness, and of judgment: ʳ of sin, because they believe

ˡ ver. 22; ch. 14. 1.
ᵐ ch. 14. 28.
ⁿ ch. 7. 39; 14. 16, 26; 15. 26.
ᵒ I's. 68. 18; Luke 24. 49; Acts 1. 4, 5; 2. 33; Eph. 4. 8.
ᵖ Zech. 12. 10; Acts 2. 37.
ᵠ ch. 8. 9, 46.
ʳ ch. 8. 24; 15. 22-25; Rom. 3. 19,20.

---

question before (13 : 36; 14 : 5), but apparently with more thought of his going away than of the place, purpose, and benefits of his departure.

6. **Sorrow hath filled your heart,** " filled it to the exclusion of all regard to the object of my leaving you." A true answer to the question as to where he was going would dissipate their grief and strengthen them for the scenes to follow. In place of giving way to sorrow, they should have improved the brief time that remained to learn from their Saviour's lips concerning his place and work in heaven.

7. **Nevertheless,** although they have not asked him, he will tell them the real state of affairs. The reference is to the fifth verse. **It is expedient for you that I go away.** This is the real truth, though it differs widely from the thoughts of the disciples. **For if I go not away,** etc., the reason why his going away is expedient for them. According to the divine counsels, there is an order that must be observed in the work of redemption. The Son must suffer death, be raised again and exalted, before the dispensation of the Spirit in its fulness can begin, 7 : 39. The reason for this order we cannot give; its reasonableness we may not question. **But if I depart, I will send him unto you.** The Saviour clearly implies that his work for his disciples could not be completed unless he went to the Father, and that the ministry of the Comforter was more desirable for them than his bodily presence. "The dispensation of the Spirit is a more blessed manifestation of God than was even the bodily presence of the risen Saviour."—ALFORD.

8. **Will reprove,** *convince, convict.* The word means to convince by conclusive argument. See 8 : 9, 46; James 2 : 9. **The world,** the same hating, persecuting world already spoken of. **Of sin, and of righteousness,** *concerning sin, concerning righteousness.*

9. **Of sin.** He will convince the world *concerning sin.* The word here translated "sin" denotes sin generically as a principle or quality of action; sin in the nature, in distinction from outward acts of transgression. The world's idea of sin is, that it consists solely in the violation of certain laws. The world's idea of its own sin is, that it is chargeable only with wrong deeds, and that when a wrong course of action is forsaken there is no more sin. The Holy Spirit will set sin in its true light before the world—will exhibit it in its deep-seated nature, and show the great guilt of the world on account of it. The one conclusive argument which he will use to convince the world of sin is that the world rejects Christ. **Because they believe not on me;** no other proof is needed. The rejection of Christ is an act which lays open man's heart and shows it to be full of sin. Christ was holy, the manifestation and embodiment of all moral excellence and beauty. If men were holy, they would be drawn at once toward him on the principle which he himself laid down in ch. 8 : 42. Christ's atoning sacrifice was a gift of God's love and grace to man; man's rejection of it shows that in his heart there is no true love to God, but rather a settled state of enmity. Hence the world is seen to be wholly corrupt, the very fountain of man's life is poisoned. The very common interpretation of this passage, that the Holy Spirit is to convict or convince the world that unbelief is a great sin, does not appear to do justice to the words themselves or to the context. Want of faith in Christ is regarded not simply as a great sin in itself, but as a fact that forcibly tes-

10 not on me; ᵗof righteousness, ᵘbecause I go to my
11 Father, and ye see me no more; ᵛof judgment, because ˣthe prince of this world is judged.
12 I have yet many things to say unto you, ʸ but ye

ᵗ ch. 3. 14; 5. 32.   ᵘ Acts 17. 31; 26. 18.   ˣ ch. 12. 31; Luke 10. 18;
Eph. 2. 2; Col. 2. 15; Heb. 2. 14.   ʸ Mark 4. 33; 1 Cor. 3.1,2; Heb. 5. 12.

ᶻ Isa. 45. 24, 25;
Dan. 9. 24; Acts
2. 32; Rom. 1. 17;
3. 21-26; 10. 4;
2 Cor. 5. 21.

tifies of man's inherent sinfulness, since only a sinful being would reject the sinless Saviour.

10. Of righteousness. He will convince the world *concerning righteousness*. The word translated righteousness means "righteousness in general, including the whole range of that conception, without reference to any particular form of its embodiment."— CREMER'S *Lexicon*. The world believes that righteousness consists solely in right deeds, and that a man by his own efforts may attain to a life so perfect as to find favor with God. The Holy Spirit will set the subject in its true light, and show the world that it is destitute of the righteousness that God requires. **Because I go to my Father, and ye see me no more.** This will furnish him the argument. At Christ's baptism (Matt. 3 : 17), and again at his transfiguration (Matt. 17 : 5), the Father bore witness that with his Son he was well pleased. This complacency was in the *person* of Christ, in whom was no sin; he was the brightness of the Father's glory and the express image of his person, and therefore perfect in holiness. Christ's departure to the Father and acceptance by him, as shown by his resurrection and exaltation, prove that the Father was well pleased also with the *works* of the Son. The righteousness, then, which God requires is seen to consist in a perfectly holy nature, out of which comes a holy life. Thus, while the Spirit convinces men of the nature of righteousness, he will also convince them of their need of it as found alone in Christ.

11. Of judgment. He will convince the world *concerning judgment*. The word translated "judgment," means first "separation, and then judicial procedure instituted against the guilty and leading to their condemnation." The world rests secure in its own fancied goodness, but the Spirit will bring home to it the reality and danger of God's judgment. **Because the prince of this world is judged,** *has been judged.* Jesus looks upon future events as already passed. The argument of the Spirit will be that Christ has meted out judgment to, has destroyed the works of, Satan, the prince of this world, the author and embodiment of all evil, and that therefore he has condemned and will punish all evil-doers. Christ judged Satan when he resisted his temptations and frustrated all his designs to hinder the accomplishment of his mission of mercy; when he cast out demons and healed the sick; and, most of all, when he arose from the dead and ascended in triumph to the Father's right hand. This demonstration of the Spirit will result in the salvation of some and in the condemnation of others, according as the truth is accepted and appropriated or rejected, 2 Cor. 2 : 16. This work of the Spirit upon the world is accomplished in part, at least, through the disciples of Christ, for it results from his coming to comfort and enlighten them. Accordingly, the apostles afterward speak of themselves as having preached the gospel *with the "Holy Ghost sent down from heaven."*

12-15. THE PROMISE OF INSPIRATION TO THE APOSTLES.

12. I have yet many things to say, etc. The things referred to were doubtless higher, fuller, and deeper views of himself and his kingdom. Some of these he taught them after his resurrection, when "he opened to them the Scriptures" (Luke 24 : 32) and spoke of the "things pertaining to the kingdom," Acts 1 : 3. Many additional instructions and revelations were left to the teaching of the Spirit, who was to guide them "into all truth." They were not now prepared, by reason of their sorrow and apprehension for the future, to receive and digest all these things. They had scarcely realized or apprehended what he had already told them; as their capacity to receive in-

13 cannot bear them now. Howbeit when he, ᵉ the
Spirit of truth, is come, ᵃ he will guide you into all
truth: for ᵇ he shall not speak of himself; but whatsoever he shall hear, that shall he speak: and ᶜ he
14 will show you things to come. ᵈ He shall glorify me:
for ᵉ he shall receive of mine, and shall show it unto
15 you. ᶠ All things that the Father hath are mine:
therefore said I, that he shall take of mine, and shall
show it unto you.

ᵃ ch. 14. 17; 15. 26.
ᵃ ch. 14. 26; 1 Cor. 2. 12; 1 John 2. 20, 27.
ᵇ ch. 3. 32; 7. 16-18.
ᶜ Joel 2. 28; Acts 11. 28; 21. 9-11; 2 Thess. 2. 3; 2 Tim. 3. 1-5; 2 Pet. 1. 14; Rev. 1. 1, 19.
ᵈ 1 Cor. 12. 3; 1 Pet. 1. 10-12; 1 John 5. 6.   ᵉ ch. 15. 26; 1 John 4. 13.   ᶠ ch. 3. 35; 13. 3; 17. 10.

creased further revelations would be made.
13. **Howbeit when** (*but when*) **he, emphatic as in ver. 8, the Spirit of truth, is come.** Christ endeavors to impress upon the disciples a high conception of the dispensation of the Spirit. Much precious truth remained to be communicated, yet he, their Master, was about to depart out of the world. But neither they nor the future church shall suffer any loss, for **he,** the Spirit, **will guide you into all truth,** *all the truth.* The Spirit will guide them into the truth— that is, will impart to them gradually, as they are able to receive and as it is necessary, the things which Jesus began to teach them, until the whole circle of truth is completed. What Christ taught the disciples we now have in the four Gospels; what he left unsaid, the additional teaching of the Spirit, we have in the books that follow. The Gospels, as well as the Acts and Epistles, come to us through the agency of the Spirit, for he it is who called to the remembrance of the disciples what Jesus had said, 14: 26. Whatever, therefore, came from the apostles personally or was sanctioned by them is Christian truth and of binding authority upon us. Since they were to be guided into all the truth or the whole truth, what we have from them is complete and all-sufficient, and not to be added unto either by tradition or in any other way. **For he shall not speak of himself.** It is not meant that he will not speak *concerning* himself (all the revelation we have concerning the Spirit comes to us through the Spirit), but that he will not speak "*from himself,*" literally—that is, independently of Christ the Son. Jesus uses similar language about himself in his relation to the Father, 12: 49. **But whatsoever he shall hear, that shall he speak.** As Jesus revealed the mind of the Father and of the Spirit, so the Spirit shall reveal the mind of the Father and of the Son. The essential unity of being and entire oneness of purpose in the Trinity are here clearly implied. **And he will show you things to come,** or, rather, *tell you the things to come,* These were a part of the whole truth which they were to be taught. "Scattered traces of the fulfilment of this part of the promise are found in the Acts and the Epistles; its complete fulfilment was in the giving of the Apocalypse, in which the 'things to come' are distinctly the subject of the Spirit's revelation, and with which his direct revelation closes. See Rev. 1 : 1, 10; 22 : 16, 17."—ALFORD.

14. **He shall glorify me.** As the Son glorifies the Father in appearing to ransom the lost, so the Spirit glorifies the Son in making this redemptive work effectual in saving the lost. A mysterious rivalry of divine love! **For he shall,** etc., *Because he will,* etc. The reason given, *why* and *how* the Spirit will glorify Christ. **Shall show:** better, *will tell it to you.* "The Holy Spirit glorifies Christ by revealing his glory to his disciples upon the earth. *Glory* in the realms of glory Christ hath never wanted. . . . The Father glorified Christ by raising him from the dead and from the earth, exalting him above principalities and powers and placing him at his own right hand. The Holy Spirit glorifies Christ by making him known as glorious to the believer."—BOWEN.

15. **All things that the Father hath are mine;** therefore when the Spirit shows them the truth concerning Christ he declares the things of the Father also, and glorifies both alike. **Therefore said I;** this is the ground or justification of the assertion made in the previous verse. There is here an

16 ᵍA little while, and ye shall not see me: ʰand again, a little while, and ye shall see me, ⁱbecause I go to the Father.
17 Then said *some* of his disciples among themselves, What is this that he saith unto us, A little while, and ye shall not see me: and again, a little while, and ye shall see me: and, Because I go to the Father?
18 They said therefore, What is this that he saith, A little while? We cannot tell what he saith.
19 Now ᵏJesus knew that they were desirous to ask him, and said unto them, Do ye inquire among yourselves of that I said, A little while, and ye shall not see me: and again, a little while, and ˡye shall see
20 me? Verily, verily, I say unto you, ᵐThat ye shall weep and lament, ⁿbut the world shall rejoice: and ye shall be sorrowful, but ᵒyour sorrow shall be turned

ᵍ vers. 5, 10; ch. 7 33; 13. 33; 14. 19.
ʰ ch.20. 19, 20; 21. 1.
ⁱ ver. 28; ch. 13. 3.

ᵏ ch.2. 24, 25; Matt. 6. 8.
ˡ Matt.16. 10; Luke 24. 17.
ᵐ Matt.9. 15; Luke 6. 21.
ⁿ Matt. 27. 39–43.
ᵒ Ps. 30. 5; Acts 2. 46, 47.

---

incidental though convincing argument for the doctrine of the Trinity.

16-24. CHRIST'S WITHDRAWAL; ITS EFFECT UPON THE WORLD AND UPON THE DISCIPLES.

16. A little while, and ye shall not see me, because in a very short time death would remove him from their sight. Even this "little while" was shortened by their own lack of courage and devotion, Mark 14 : 50. **And again, a little while,** the period between his burial and resurrection, **and ye shall see me;** after his resurrection he manifested himself to them during forty days, and they saw him with their bodily eyes. See 14 : 19 and notes. According to the best authorities we should omit entirely the words **because I go to the Father.**

17. **What is this that he saith unto us, A little while, etc.?** They could not understand what he meant by his *speedy* departure and *speedy* return, for they looked upon his going to "him that sent him" as a long and hopeless withdrawal.

19. **Now Jesus knew,** etc. Here, as often elsewhere, he displays his perfect knowledge of their thoughts.

20. Jesus does not answer their question directly, but by the words, **Verily, verily, I say unto you,** he indicates that what he is about to utter is of more importance than the mere matter of time. **That ye shall weep and lament.** This, it would seem, was literally fulfilled. See Luke 23 : 27;

John 20 : 11. They were already sorrowful at the thought of his departure, but this sorrow would be greatly increased when they saw their Lord and Master taken by his enemies, subjected to all manner of indignities, crucified between two thieves, and finally buried. Their faith received an almost fatal shock when Christ suffered himself to be taken and put to death; all their hopes were buried for a time in his tomb, Luke 24 : 21. **But the world,** with its different hopes and different feelings in regard to Christ, **shall rejoice,** because of its supposed triumph over the despised Nazarene, Matt. 27 : 39-44. **But your sorrow,** profound as it is, **shall be turned into joy.** The time of the Saviour's sojourn in the tomb was a period the like of which has never been seen on any other occasion. For the disciples were not only without their Master, but without the Spirit, for he had not yet come as the Comforter. "The Son of God, in taking unto him the sin of the world, had also taken unto him all its most sacred interests: all these went down with him into the night of the grave, and we may conceive of the guardian angels of humanity standing on the edge of this gulf trembling, wondering if from such a profound abyss there should be a resurrection of these precious interests, a return of the self-sacrificing One."—BOWEN. This suspense was brief, that "dark and critical hour" was of short duration. When Christ left the grave and "was raised

21 into joy. ᵖ A woman when she is in travail hath sorrow, because her hour is come: but as soon as she is delivered of the child, she remembereth no more the anguish, for joy that a man is born into the world. 22 ᑫ And ye now therefore have sorrow: but I will see you again, and ʳ your heart shall rejoice, and ˢ your 23 joy no man taketh from you. And in that day ye shall ask me nothing. ᵗ Verily, verily, I say unto you, Whatsoever ye shall ask the Father ᵘ in my

ᵖ Isa 26. 17.
ᑫ ver. 6.
ʳ ch. 14. 1, 27; 20. 19, 20; Luke 24. 40, 41, 52; Acts 2. 46; 13. 52; 1 Pet. 1. 8.
ˢ Job 34. 29; Prov. 14. 10; Rom. 8, 35–39.
ᵗ ch. 14. 13; 15. 16; Matt. 7. 7.
ᵘ Eph. 2. 18.

again for our justification" (Rom. 4 : 25), the sorrow of the disciples was *changed into joy*, the very matter of grief becoming a matter of joy, as Christ's cross of shame has become the glory of the Christian, Gal. 6:14. Peter describes their joy (1 Pet. 1 : 3): "Blessed be the God and Father of our Lord Jesus Christ, who, according to his abundant mercy, begot us again unto a living hope through the resurrection of Jesus Christ from the dead."—*Bible Union Version.* Though not stated, it is clearly implied that the rejoicing of the world shall be turned into ceaseless sorrow.

21. **A woman,** etc. Not an uncommon symbol in Scripture, Isa. 21 : 3; 37 : 3; 66 : 7; Hos. 13 : 13. "The pains of childbirth are acute, but there is alleviation in the thought that they are introductory to the existence of an immortal creature, in whom the image and glory of God may be revealed throughout eternity. How unutterably more sublime the considerations—had the disciples been in a position to entertain them —connected with the return from the dead of the Saviour of the world, made perfect through suffering, leading captivity captive, and having the keys of death and hell!"—BOWEN.

22. **Your heart shall rejoice.** See ch. 20 : 20; Luke 24 : 52. **Your joy no man taketh from you.** The joy they had hitherto possessed as followers of Jesus the Nazarene was soon to be taken away. Not until his resurrection did they fully understand who their Master was or what was the nature of his mission. This event attested all his teaching, confirmed all his promises, and "with their risen Saviour their buried hopes rose and mounted on high, no more to fade." Amid all the world's hate and persecution they had a peace and joy which the world could not understand and which never forsook them.

23. **In that day;** a day dawning with his resurrection and fully ushered in at Pentecost, when the Spirit descended. It was a day of much clearer light than the preceding one—a day of exceeding brightness compared with the awful darkness of that night in which the Sun of Righteousness was eclipsed by the world's sin. **Ye shall ask me nothing.** The English word "ask" is used in this verse to translate two Greek words of somewhat different meaning. The one in this clause means "to question," "to ask for information," and is the same that is used in verses 19, 30. The one in the following clause means "to entreat," "petition," and is used in verses 24 and 26. By keeping this distinction in mind the apparent difficulty of this passage will be removed. The meaning of the Saviour's words, about which they had desired to ask him (ver. 19), would soon be made apparent by his death, resurrection, and by his teaching (Luke 24 : 25-49), so that they would not need to question him concerning them. They did, however, think it necessary to ask him a question on a subject that was perhaps in their minds on this occasion, but the answer of the Lord could not have been very satisfactory. See Acts 1 : 6, 7. The coming day was also to be the dispensation of the Spirit, and he would give them light upon their difficulties. **Verily, verily, I say unto you.** As much as to say, Not only will there be clearer light and fuller knowledge in the coming time, but the doors of heaven's treasury may be opened in my name. **In my name, he will give it you—***He will give you in my name.* Whatever is given to Christians is as though it were given to Christ, since he and they are one. The promise is to

24 name, he will give it you. Hitherto have ye asked nothing in my name: ask, and ye shall receive, *that your joy may be full.
25 These things have I spoken unto you in proverbs: but the time cometh ʸ when I shall no more speak unto you in proverbs, but I shall show you plainly
26 of the Father. ᶻ At that day ye shall ask in my name: and I say not unto you, that I will pray the
27 Father for you: ᵃ for the Father himself loveth you, because ye have loved me, and ᵇ have believed that I
28 came out from God. ᶜ I came forth from the Father, ᵈ and am come into the world: again, ᵉ I leave the world, and go to the Father.

ˣ ch. 15. 11; Phil 4. 4.
ʸ Luke 24.27; Acts 1. 3.
ᶻ ver. 23.
ᵃ ch. 14. 21; 17. 23.
ᵇ ch. 17. 8.
ᶜ ch. 1. 1; 3. 13; 13. 3; 17.5; 1 John 1. 2.
ᵈ ch. 3. 19.
ᵉ ch. 14. 28.

---

the disciples as believers, and is therefore without limitation. To give such a promise to a lover of the world would only be to hurry him down to ruin, just as, according to the story, that one who asked for the power of converting everything he touched into gold, when his desire was granted died of famine. See chs. 14 : 13 and 15 : 16 and notes.

24. **Hitherto have ye asked nothing in my name,** Matt. 6:9-13. They had not yet fully realized that the Master whom they followed and looked to as a Teacher and Friend, and even as the promised Messiah, was the only Mediator between God and man. For this reason they were not yet prepared to pray in his name. Besides this, it was not possible to pray in his name until his resurrection should attest the efficacy of his atonement. This access of all believers to the Father through the Lord Jesus Christ was one of the special privileges of the new dispensation, Eph. 2 : 18. **That your joy may be full.** As vast as the capacity of the human heart is for enjoying the love and goodness of God, so broad and full is the promise.

25-33. CONCLUDING WORDS OF PROMISE, WARNING, AND COMFORT.

25. **Spoken unto you in proverbs** —*parables* or *dark sayings.* The reference is to this whole discourse. His words on the subjects treated of seemed very dark and mysterious to the disciples. **The time cometh ;** the hour mentioned in vers. 16, 23. **I shall show you plainly of the Father,** no longer using parables and figures to express his meaning. The Son is the only one who can reveal the Father, ch. 1 : 18; Matt. 11 : 27. Through the clearer revelation that should be made of himself by his resurrection, by his own teachings (Luke 24 : 25-49), the teaching of the Holy Spirit, the Father also would be revealed in the fulness of his character. He would henceforth be known not only as the Almighty, Wise, and Eternal One, but as the Just One, yet the Justifier of the ungodly—as the God of love who sent his Son to suffer and die for sinners—as God in Christ reconciling the world unto himself.

26. "The Lord is now describing the fulness of their state of communion with himself and the Father by the Spirit. He is setting in the strongest light their reconciliation and access to the Father."—ALFORD. Hence he says, **At that day ye shall ask in my name.** When they shall have reached that more advanced state of knowledge they will not hesitate, but it will be their custom to ask whatever they need in the name of Christ. **I say not unto you, that I will pray the Father for you,** etc. "I say not this simply, but something more. The Saviour does not mean to deny that he will intercede with the Father for his disciples, but rather to lead their minds beyond this truth, which he had frequently stated, to another — that the Father is one with him in loving them (ver. 27), so that his intercession for them must prevail."—*N. T.* Am. Tr. Soc. **From God,** better, *from the Father.*

28. This verse seems to be a general summary of our Lord's office and mission. Its connection with what has preceded appears to be this: The disciples have believed, and rightly too, that he came from God. But **in order**

29 His disciples said unto him, Lo, *f* now speakest thou
30 plainly, and speakest no proverb. Now are we sure
that *g* thou knowest all things, and needest not that
any man should ask thee: by this *h* we believe that
thou camest forth from God.
31, 32 Jesus answered them, Do ye now believe? *i* Behold, the hour cometh, yea, is now come, that ye shall
be scattered, *k* every man to his own, and shall leave
me alone: and *l* yet I am not alone, because the Fa-
33 ther is with me. These things I have spoken unto
you, that *m* in me ye might have peace. *n* In the world

f vers. 16-19.
g ch. 21. 17. See Matt. 9. 4.
h ver. 27; ch. 17. 8.
i Zech. 13. 7.
k ch. 20. 10.
ch. 8. 16, 29; 14. 10, 11.
m ch. 14. 27; Isa. 9. 6; Rom. 5. 1; Eph. 2. 14; Col. 1. 20.
n ch. 15. 19-21; Acts 14. 22; 1 Thess. 3. 4; 2 Tim. 3. 12; Heb. 11. 25; Rev. 7. 14.

to accomplish his work as man's Redeemer he must endure the cross, pass through the grave, and ascend to the Father again. Their faith, therefore, should embrace the latter truth as well as the former. That view of Christ, however exalted it may be, which includes only his holy and beneficent life, and leaves out of account his atoning death, is but partial and incomplete.

29. **His disciples said unto him, Lo, now speakest thou plainly.** Even now, as they catch a glimpse of his meaning, though he appears to speak with no greater plainness, he seems to them to anticipate the coming time, ver. 25.

30. **Now are we sure** (*now we know*) **that thou knowest all things.** He knew the difficulty they hesitated to express (ver. 19), and answered it to their satisfaction. If he could thus read their thoughts and feelings, they were persuaded that he knew the secrets of all hearts, that he knew all things. **And needest not**, etc. No open inquiry is necessary, for, as in their case, even the secret desire is known to him. **By this**—that is, by the revelation of his wonderful knowledge which he had just made. They seem now for the first time to be particularly impressed with this, yet he had on several previous occasions given utterance to their thoughts and the thoughts of his enemies, showing his superhuman knowledge. **We believe that thou camest forth from God.** They are very confident that they have understood his meaning, but it is evident that they had not risen to the full conception of his words in verse 28. Through his humiliation they perceive his high origin, but are blind to the fact of his sufferings and the glory to follow. Yet, as Olshausen remarks, "the words of Christ were not spoken in vain. The disciples divined the richness of their meaning, and preserved them in their hearts till subsequently the Spirit caused these seeds to germinate and bring forth their abundant fruits" according to promise, 14 : 26.

31, 32. **Do ye now believe?** Jesus makes no further attempt to correct their misapprehension, but leaves this for the coming day of the Spirit. He, however, would dissuade them from too much self-confidence, for he plainly intimates that their faith, though loving and sincere, is weak and imperfect. Very similar was his treatment of Peter, 13 : 37, 38. **Behold, the hour cometh,** the hour of his arrest, trial, and persecution; **yea, is now come;** "immediately following the hours of sweet and serene companionship with Christ, in which he had washed their feet and in which he had cleansed their hearts by his gracious words."—BOWEN. **That ye shall be scattered** as sheep (Zach. 18:7), **every man to his own** home or business (20 : 10), **and shall leave me alone,** showing that their faith was not so strong and so deeply grounded in the knowledge of him and his works as they now supposed, **And yet I am not alone, because the Father is with me.** Said for his own comfort. The unfaithfulness of the disciples would not deprive him of all comfort and companionship. He was, indeed, in that hour of darkness deprived of the sensible manifestation of the Father's presence, but only of this. Christ, as a man, felt keenly the need of human sympathy, and the temporary desertion of his disciples in the hour of need must have deeply pained him.

33. The words just spoken contained

ye shall have tribulation: but be of good cheer; ᵒ I have overcome the world. ᵒ ch. 12, 31; Rom. 8 37; 1 John 4. 4 5. 4.

a mild rebuke, which the disciples must have felt. It was not intended, however, to discourage them, but all **these things** which he had spoken to them in this discourse, beginning with ch. 13:31, were said in order that in him they **might have peace**—his own peace, 14:27. This "peace embraces all that constitutes rest, contentment, and true happiness of heart on the basis of the Christian's salvation and vital union with Christ."—SCHAFF in *Lange*. **In the world ye shall have tribulation,** *ye have tribulation*. It is their normal state in the world; what they might always expect here below. This fact itself was a comforting sign that they were not of the world. Their love to Jesus and their faith in him, though but feeble, transferred their citizenship to a higher world. This "tribulation is both persecution from without and distress from within. The happiness of Christians in this life is subject to frequent interruptions and disturbances from their remaining infirmities and sins, as well as from an ungodly world. Yet deep down at the bottom peace continues to reign, however much the surface of the ocean of life may be agitated by wind and storm." —SCHAFF in *Lange*. **But be of good cheer; I have overcome the world.** The world might gain a temporary advantage over them, as foretold, ver. 32. But Christ has overcome the world by resisting the temptations of its prince, and enduring the severest sufferings it could inflict, and has triumphed at last over death itself. Christ has done this for his people, and hence their final victory over the world is assured in him. The discourse closes, as it begins, with exhortations to trust in Christ and to take comfort in him, 14:1.

PRACTICAL REMARKS.

1. The teachings of the Bible and the aid of the Holy Spirit are helps and means, provided beforehand, to keep Christians from falling. Christ's words are to us, as they were to the disciples, signal-lights to show us where danger lies, vers. 1, 4; Ps. 37:31; 119:11, 98; 2 Tim. 1:13, 14; 3:16, 17.

2. When God renews the soul he does not change its surroundings nor remove it from the world. But he clothes the Christian with the power of patience, meekness, humility, and self-denial, and thus fits him to endure all the trials of life, vers. 2, 33; I's. 34:19; 2 Cor. 4:17, 18; 2 Tim. 3:11-14; Matt. 5:5; Gal. 5:22, 23; Luke 21:19; ch. 17:15.

3. That a man is sincere is no evidence that he is right. His conviction may be the result of his inexcusable ignorance of God. Conscience is a safe guide only when enlightened by the word of God, vers. 2, 3; Acts 26:9; Rom. 9:31-33; 10:2, 3.

4. We often suffer from doubts and fears and sorrow of heart when there are in the Bible truths and promises, most clear and precious, that would remove them all. Like the disciples, we fail to appropriate and apply what we have heard, and neglect the opportunities we have for gaining more knowledge, such as will be adapted to our case, vers. 5, 6.

5. What seems to us best is often not expedient. Especially is this true of man's views with respect to the work of redemption. What is necessary to atone for sin and secure man's salvation and the blessing of the Spirit's ministry only the Author of salvation knows. Not what we think, but what God says, is the truth concerning this matter, ver. 7; Matt. 17:5; Acts 3:22, 23; Luke 24:26, 46; Acts 17:3; 1 Pet. 1:11.

6. The Holy Spirit is not only a Comforter dwelling in God's people, but he is also their Helper against the world, for he makes their testimony for the truth and against sin effective. He causes men to see more clearly the nature of sin, the need of righteousness, and the certainty of judgment; revealing the truth concerning Christ to Christ's disciples, he also prepares the way for the entrance of that truth into the minds and hearts of others, ver. 8; Acts 2:37; 4:4; 16:30; 7:54; 24:25.

7. The preaching of Christ; his divine character; the glory he renounced; the state of humiliation he assumed; his labors for the good of man; the things he suffered and the reason of his suffer-

ing; his present exaltation; his coming kingdom and glory; and his long suffering toward sinners,—are the means the Holy Spirit uses to reveal the world's guilt, helplessness, and condemnation, vers. 8-11.

8. "We must teach people as they are able to bear, and be patient. A man may be a good man, and yet not able to bear the whole truth."—RYLE. Still, in proportion to our diligence in learning the first principles of the doctrine of Christ shall we be able to receive and profit by the new treasures of wisdom and knowledge which God is ever ready to bestow. If, therefore, we cannot bear certain doctrines of Scripture, it is because we have neglected those that naturally come before them and prepare the way for them, vers. 12, 13; Heb. 5 : 11-14; 6 : 1.

9. We should ever seek to exalt Christ—in our lives to reveal his mind and will. All the faculties of our being should be so yielded to his control that he shall be glorified in us in all things. Thus it will be seen that we have been taught by the Spirit and that our religion is the religion of the Spirit. "All true teaching agrees with the testimony of the Spirit in glorifying Christ," vers. 14, 15; 1 Cor. 6 : 20; Gal. 2 : 20; 5 : 24; 1 Cor. 2 : 2.

10. There are many truths in the Bible so plain that all can understand them, yet there are depths in it which none can fathom. We need to search with painstaking care even those portions most familiar to us, and ask as we read, "What is this that he saith?" If we do not obtain what we expect, we shall find something better, vers. 16-24; ch. 5 : 39; Acts 17 : 11; 1 Pet. 1 : 10; 1 Kings 3 : 9, 11, 12; Prov. 2 : 3-5; James 1 : 5.

11. "The cross of our Lord was the source of his glory, Phil. 2 : 8, 9; Rev. 5 : 9, 13. And so it is still with the Christian, whose sharpest sufferings are the birth-pangs of his highest joys (2 Cor. 4 : 17), and with the whole church collectively" (*Annotated Paragraph Bible*), ver. 20.

12. Sorrow the Christian will have so long as he is in a world where sin is, but the privilege of rejoicing even in the midst of this sorrow is a gift that accompanies salvation. Men may take away his property, health, liberty, and all his social privileges, but they cannot take away his Saviour nor undo the work that he has done; and therefore they cannot rob him of his joy, ver. 22; Acts 5 : 41; Rom. 5 : 8; 12 : 12; 2 Cor. 7 : 4; Phil. 3 : 8; 1 Tim. 4 : 10; 2 Tim. 1 : 12.

13. The Christian's joy may be voluntarily surrendered for a time by his ceasing to abide in Christ's love, by neglect of duties, especially the duty of prayer, for there must be fulness of faith and prayer if we would have fulness of joy, vers. 23, 24.

14. A correct knowledge of God is a matter of great importance in the Christian faith, and it always includes a just apprehension of the person and mission of Christ, vers. 25-28.

15. "Alas for those who love not Christ! The Father loves them not. Ten thousand mighty merits will go for naught if they have no love to Christ to show. The very mention of such merits will prove that they have not the love of Christ in them" (BOWEN), ver. 27.

16. "When Christ came forth from the Father, he so came into the world as never to leave the Father; and he so left the world and went unto the Father as never to leave the world" (AUGUSTINE, as quoted by Burgon), ver. 28.

17. The same truth heard at different times makes a different impression on the mind. This shows the need of the guidance of the Spirit, that we may receive the correct impression when we hear or read the word of God. When the truth is not relished or understood the hearer, and not the teacher, may be at fault. Hence the frequent need of the Saviour's exhortation, Matt. 11 : 15; vers. 29, 30.

18. It is well to occasionally present the truths of Christianity in their strongest light as evidences, in order to confirm weak believers in the faith, if for no other reason, vers. 29, 30.

19. In hours of prosperity we have great confidence in ourselves; only in times of trial do we learn our weakness, vers. 31, 32; Matt. 26 : 35, 69-74; Mark 14 : 50.

20. If the Christian wanders from Christ, he forsakes One whom the Father would not forsake—One with whom are life and light and hope and heaven

Our Lord's intercessory prayer.

XVII. THESE words spake Jesus, and lifted up his eyes to heaven, and said, Father, ᵖ the hour is come; glorify thy Son, that thy Son also may glorify thee: ᵖ ch. 7. 30; 12. 23; 13. 31, 39

and all angelic hosts—to find only his own miserable heart of fear, his own helplessness and sinfulness. But though we wander from him, he forsakes not us; for his love to us, not ours to him, like an unseen cord binds us to him, and suffers us to go so far away and no farther, vers. 31, 32.

21. There is no true abiding peace for the wicked. Peace is only for the righteous, and righteousness is found alone in Christ. Sin is in the world, and therefore only sorrow and tribulations abound, ver. 33.

22. The way to heaven is not all sunshine and flowers; in the Christian warfare there are always the cross and the battle before the crown and the eternal rest. But why should we fear when our Captain is the world's Conqueror? This is the victory that overcometh the world, even our faith in him, ver. 33; 1 John 5 : 4, 5.

CHAPTER XVII.

In the temple of revelation this chapter is the inner sanctuary. It consists of Christ's sacerdotal or high-priestly prayer, in which he anticipates the completion of his sacrifice for sin, and on the ground of that finished work intercedes for his people. Thus absorbed in his communion with the Father, his thoughts are withdrawn from the immediate present; the glorious future is before him, and he views his earthly work as completed and in the past. (See especially ver. 12.) It thus enables us better to understand the assertion that "he ever liveth to make intercession for them," Heb. 7 : 25. We are made to see and feel what Jesus is now doing for us. The prayer divides itself into three main sections. The first (vers. 1-5) respects primarily himself; the second (vers. 6-19), the apostles; the third (vers. 20-26), believers generally.

1-5. PRAYER ESPECIALLY FOR HIMSELF. Those things which he seeks for himself were preparatory to the conferring of blessings on his apostles and disciples.

1. **These words**; those just spoken to the eleven, chs. 14-16. He begins to speak of his disciples to the Father as soon as he ceases to speak of the Father to his disciples, passing at once from his teaching on earth as Prophet t is intercession in heaven as Priest. **Lifted up his eyes to heaven.** Presenting him vividly as John saw and vividly remembered him. Perhaps he was in the open court around which the house was built, and thus under the open sky (ch. 14 : 31; 18 : 1), which is the symbol of God's home because of its exaltation, purity, beauty, unchangeableness, and infinity. The upward look befits his triumphant state. In his prayer of agony he was prostrate on the ground, Matt. 26 : 39. **Father.** The fact of his Sonship is the foundation of his plea; the sense of his Sonship is its spirit; hence the word *Father* often recurs in the prayer, as it here begins it. Not here "*my* Father," because he takes with him his disciples; not here or ever "*our* Father," because God is not their Father as he is Christ's. They have their sonship in the Son, and hence do not go to the Father with him, but are taken to the Father by him. When under a sense of his humiliation he said "My Father" (Matt. 26 : 39, 42), but now, as representing the intercessions of a glorified Mediator, "Father" was the most fitting. **The hour is come;** that hour which was ever clear and full in his view and often mentioned in his later ministry—the completion of his work in his self-sacrifice on the cross. Hence, naturally, he simply says *the hour.* To his thought, as he enters upon this holy communion with the Father, the end is already reached, the sacrifice accomplished. **Glorify thy Son,** since by divine purpose, covenant, and right this glory was at once to succeed that sacrifice. The glory intended is his exaltation to be "Head over all things to the church," Eph. 1 : 22. He says not *me,* but *thy*

2 ⁴ as thou hast given him power over ʳ all flesh, ˢ that
he should give eternal life to as many as thou hast
3 given him. And ᵗ this is life eternal, that they might
know thee ᵘ the only true God, and Jesus Christ,

q ch. 5. 21-27; Dan. 7. 14; Heb. 2. 8.
r Luke 3. 6
s ch. 4. 14; 10. 28.
t Isa. 53. 11; Jer. 9. 24; 1 John 5. 20.
u Jer. 10. 10; 1 Cor. 8. 4; 1 Thess. 1. 9.

Son, to express most strongly the reason why this prayer could be answered, and must be answered. (See above.) Both the Sonship and the glory are those not simply of the divine Lord, but of the divine-human Jesus Christ. **That thy Son also may glorify thee.** Christ's exaltation was in order that he might save men (Acts 5 : 31), but in saving men he glorifies the Father, because the purpose of salvation was of the Father's love (ch. 3 : 16), and hence the accomplishment of salvation is the revelation of that purpose and the manifestation of that love. Compare Eph. 1 : 17-23. Thus the one love of Christ has here three movements—toward himself, toward his people, and toward his Father.

2. **As**—more exactly, *according as,* introducing both a measure and a reason for the preceding request—**thou hast given him power,** from eternity, by purpose and promise. The *power* or *authority* was redemptive, and thus founded on his sacrifice, Matt. 28 : 18. Hence for its exercise and ends he must be glorified. (See Phil. 2 : 9.) **All flesh;** all mankind viewed as sinful and guilty. Only through atonement for sin did Christ gain such authority or right over sinful men that he could impart to them eternal life. None the less was the authority "given" by the Father, for the Son himself was by the Father " given " to make atonement, **that** (*in order that*) **he should** (*may*) **give eternal life.** The "power" to save was the Father's gift to the Son for men ; the exercise of that power would be the Son's gift to men for the Father. The salvation given is " eternal life " **to as many as thou hast given him;** only to those given in the election of love (Rom. 8 : 28-30; compare ch. 6 : 44)—to each and every one of these without failure. The Greek emphasizes the last of these points as a translation cannot: *That all which thou hast given him, to them he should give eternal life.*

3. **And this is life eternal** (*and the eternal life is this*)*,* **that they might know** (rather, *that they know,* or, simply, *to know*) **thee,** etc., the expression being about equivalent to the infinitive mood. Compare a very similar construction in ch. 13 : 34. The knowledge of God and Christ is eternal life ; and this knowledge is not a mere conception of the mind or an excitement of the feelings, but a *personal* and *experimental knowing,* which is commenced on earth and consummated in heaven, and is connected with, and rests upon, the partaking by believers of the divine nature, 2 Pet. 1 : 4. This knowledge of God also is only manifested through Jesus Christ, Matt. 11 : 27; John 1 : 18; 14 : 9; 1 John 4 : 12; 2 Cor. 3 : 18; 4 : 6. " Knowing is, in John's style of thought, invariably to be regarded as simultaneous with believing (see on ch. 6 : 69); but in believing the object of belief becomes the possession of man—passes over into his subjectivity. See on Heb. 11 : 1; 4 : 2. In faith and knowledge, consequently, eternal life is embraced."—THOLUCK. The following pertinent remarks of Dr. A. Carson on this passage (*Knowledge of Jesus,* p. 195) accord with the above view : " This passage not only identifies the character of the Son with that of the Father, but by ascribing eternal life to the knowledge of this character identifies both with the gospel. It could not be life eternal to know the Son if he were not the same God with the Father. It could not be eternal life to know both the Father and the Son unless this knowledge is substantially the same with the knowledge of the gospel ; for he that believeth the gospel shall be saved ; he that believeth not the gospel shall be damned. . . . The very knowledge of God is eternal life. Now, without faith in the gospel it is impossible for any one who hears it to be saved. If to know God is eternal life, the knowledge of God implies the belief of the gospel. Knowledge and faith are very different things in themselves, and may often exist in opposition with respect to the

4 ˣ whom thou hast sent. ʸ I have glorified thee on the earth: ᵃ I have finished the work ᵃ which thou gavest me to do. And now, O Father, glorify thou me with thine own self, with the glory ᵇ which I had with thee before the world was.

ᵃ ch. 3. 17, 34; 5. 36; 6. 29; 7. 29; 10. 36; 11. 42; Isa. 61. 1.
ʸ ch. 13. 31, 32; 14. 13.
ᵇ ch. 4. 34; 19. 30.

ᵃ ch. 14. 31; 15. 10.   ᵇ ch. 1. 1, 2; 10. 30; Phil. 2. 6; Col. 1. 15, 17; Heb. 1. 3, 10.

---

same object; but with respect to the gospel in the divine character, knowledge cannot exist without faith, and faith cannot exist without knowledge; for eternal life is promised to each of them, and denied to the want of either of them. In this case, then, the one cannot exist without the other in unison. . . . The existence of the one secures the existence of the other." **The only true God;** the only Being who is truly God, in contrast with all else that is called or treated as such. Man, made in God's image, finds his life, his supreme and eternal good, only in loving communion with him. **And Jesus Christ, whom thou hast sent.** By the knowledge of the Son we attain a knowledge of the Father, ch. 14: 9. (For this order see 1 John 1: 3; 5: 20.) He was sent in order to reveal the Father and be "the way" to the Father. Christ both was sent and came, acting equally of his Father's and of his own will. It was the design of God that eternal life should be limited to those who recognize and glorify the true God as opposed to all false gods, and Jesus Christ as opposed to all false Christs, 1 Cor. 8: 5, 6; 1 John 5: 20. It is worthy of note that this is the first and only time that the Lord couples his own name and the title of Christ or Messiah together. The apostles after this seem to have been ordinarily accustomed to speak of him thus, as Jesus Christ or Christ Jesus. (See the multitude of cases in the Acts and the Epistles.)

4. **I have glorified thee**—*I* and *thee* both emphatic, as also in the next verse. In this verse it is, *I* have glorified *thee;* in the next it is reversed: Do *thou* glorify *me*. Notice that he now for the first time in his prayer says "I," as though the mention of his earthly mission and of his own name had made him conscious of himself. The glorification of the Father here is other than that in verse 1, since that was future, but this past. Yet the work of Christ in heaven is a continuation of his work on earth. The two constitute one complete work, which throughout reveals the redemptive love of the Father or glorifies him, ch. 1: 14. **On the earth,** conceiving his earthly sacrifice as already ended and of the past. **I have finished**—the approved reading gives *having finished; i. e. by finishing*—**the work which thou gavest me to do,** stating why the Father may and must do what is asked in ver. 5. Yet it is not a hireling's demand for his pay, but filial love meeting paternal love, and urging that which "the law of love" in both demanded, and which "love as a law" could not fail to bestow.

5. **And now**—at this time, pleading the completion of the work just stated—**O Father, glorify thou me with thine own self.** The order in the Greek is, *Glorify me thou, Father, with thyself,* by which the words referring to the Father are together, as though the thought on touching the Father clung to him. "With thyself," or *by the side of thyself,* shows a painful sense of present removal and the longing of love to be wholly with its object. The consciousness of Christ's single personality was determined not less by his human nature and experiences than by his divine nature and relations. While in the flesh, bearing sin, he was absent from the Father. The completion of sin-bearing would be a return to the Father. After that he would be by the side of his Father. Herein the Christian's experience conforms to that of Christ, 2 Cor. 5: 1-8. **With the glory which I had with thee before the world was.** Here appears the purely divine consciousness, as in the preceding clause the purely human. *Before the world was*—that is, from eternity. There was the purely divine glory of the eternal Son with the eternal Father. Christ asks to be glorified with this, yet not to have simply a return of that very state, save in respect of being with, or by the side of, the Father. This is shown by repeating and emphasizing

6 *I have manifested thy name unto the men ᵈwhich thou gavest me out of the world: ᵉthine they were, and thou gavest them me; and they have kept thy 7 word. Now they have known that all things what- 8 soever thou hast given me are of thee. For I have given unto them the words ᶠwhich thou gavest me;

* ch. 1. 18; Ps. 22. 22.
ᵈ ch. 6. 37, 39; 10. 29.
ᵉ Rom. 8. 28–30; Eph. 1. 4–11; 2 Thess. 2. 13, 14.
ᶠ ch. 8. 28; 12. 49.

the words *by the side of thyself.* The states in that respect are identical, but differ in the fact that the original state was that of a simply divine being, the final state that of the divine human being. Compare ch. 1 : 1. That Christ refers to a past glory from eternity enjoyed by him with the Father, and not the future glory from eternity decreed to him by the Father, is too plain for rational doubt.

6–19. PRAYER FOR THE APOSTLES. Here begins the second section of the prayer. That he prayed for himself first was not because he made first his own interests, but because his power to serve the interests of his people depended upon his attainment of that which he asked for himself. Thus, the first section is as truly *intercession* as are the second and the third.

6. I have manifested thy name. The "name" of God is here, as often in Scripture, the real nature and character of God. Hence we see the importance of making his name fully known. To *know not* God is to be in a lost condition—a state of death; to *know* God in his real nature and character is life and blessedness. . This manifestation is "the work" referred to in ver. 4, and is spoken of as though quite ended and of the past. It consisted of Christ's words and works during his whole life, not excluding the final sacrifice of himself, which, for the moment, he conceives of as completed. This view of Christ, as the Revealer of God to man, is made prominent in many passages and is embodied in his title of "the Word." The corruption of human nature had destroyed the moral image of God in which man was made. But even a sinless man, if he were not also a divine person, could not adequately reveal the divine nature. **Unto the men which thou gavest me out of the world.** Christ's work was public, but through the blindness of the many it became a manifestation of God only to a few. Them the Father "gave" in eternal covenant to Christ. See on ver. 2. But even these in their original state differed not from the rest of mankind, being *of the world,* which here means unbelieving, ungodly mankind. They were made to differ by the Father's "drawing," which completed his "giving." **Thine they were, and thou gavest them me.** This must mean that the men given to Christ were the Father's in some special sense before they were given, and were given because they were already his, and not that they became the Father's by coming to Christ. They were his in the election of grace. The election was of the Father, and the mission of Christ to earth was to give effect to that election, and was also of the Father. **And they have kept thy word.** This was the evidence that the apostles were the Father's chosen ones and had been given to Christ. The Spirit of God in them responded to the word of God to them. This word was a part of Christ's manifestation of the Father's name.

7. Now they have known that all things whatsoever thou hast given me are of (or *from*) **thee.** He perhaps refers to the confession in ch. 16 : 29, 30. The word *now* indicates that the apostles had been coming to this knowledge up to that time. The most approved reading is, *Now they know,* etc. The knowledge was a fruit of the obedience mentioned in the preceding clause. To know God as one whom we should obey is one thing; to obey God is another thing; and to know God differs from both and follows both. It is the most precious of all knowledge, ver. 3. God's Spirit created a bond of union between the apostles and Christ, and this union drew them to an obedient reception of his doctrine, and this reception gave an experimental knowledge of the character of that doctrine. This is ever the method of grace, ch. 7 : 17.

8. For I have given unto them

and they have received *them*, ᵍ and have known surely that I came out from thee, and they have believed 9 that thou didst send me. ʰ I pray for them: ⁱ I pray not for the world, but for them which thou hast given 10 me; for they are thine. And all mine are thine, and

ᵍ ch. 16. 27, 30.
ʰ Luke 22. 32; Heb. 7. 25; 1 John 2. 1.
ⁱ 1 John 5. 19.

the words which thou gavest me. Christ here asserts, what in the preceding words he implied, that he had been a perfectly faultless revelation of God, not in intention only, but also in actual execution. And his argument is that because of this, to those who have the Spirit of God, the revelation approves itself by experience to be of God, as otherwise it could not. We ought to mark both the great strictness of this claim and the great value placed upon it, and not make light of any part of Christ's teachings unless we are prepared to reject him wholly. The word *gavest*, instead of *hast given*, presents Christ's revelations of the Father, not as continuously communicated to him, but as made over to him once for all. Either conception may be used to suit the connection. **Have received, ... have known surely**, or rather, *really knew*; that is, they received and came thus to a knowledge which was and is genuine—to an experimental knowledge or *acquaintance*. **That I came out from thee.** This fact as to the *person* of Christ underlies the fact just before stated as to his revelations. This *coming forth* is that of ch. 1: 5, 14. Compare ver. 5. **And they have believed that thou didst send me.** As faith results in experimental knowledge (ver. 7), so does this knowledge in turn result in a further and firmer faith. There is a law of gracious progress. The act of the Father in sending is mentioned last, because the Saviour wants to present God as the end of faith and knowledge.

9. **I pray for them.** The word here translated *pray* means *to ask in view of considerations*, and not from a mere sense of destitution. It is thus nearly like our word *plead*, and does not necessarily imply inferiority in the one who asks. Christ has given in vers. 7, 8 some of the considerations which constitute his plea, and others follow. **I pray not for the world.** This affirms what the preceding statement implied, that in *this* pleading, and in this kind of pleading, he advocates the cause, not of God's enemies, but only of his friends. Christ is and can be the Head only of those who are members in him, and therefore cannot desire or ask that the blessings of salvation be communicated to men while separate from him, and as separate. Such request would imply another method of salvation than that of faith in him. But though he can advocate the cause of those only who are in him, it may yet be his heart's desire that those out of him might be in him, and such desire he might pour out to God in prayer; and so also may we, Luke 13: 34; 23: 34; Matt. 5: 44; 1 Tim. 2: 1. Indeed, such a prayer was his whole life. **For they are thine.** *Thine*, though "given to *me*," because given to Christ only to be prepared for the Father and brought to the Father, but not to be alienated by the Father. Thus they were kept when given—nay, taken anew by giving—and hence they are his not less, but more, while and because Christ's; and in such way and sense are they his that to deny them would be to deny himself. Thus is this plea as strong as the very nature of God.

10. **And all mine are thine, and thine are mine;** or, *And all things that are mine*, etc. Not simply all persons, but all possessions and interests. So the original. This is grounded in the oneness of nature taught in ch. 1: 1, and in the oneness of will and life consequent upon that prior oneness. Now, since all the interests of the Father and Son are the same, the Son's interest in the apostles is a plea as strong as was that of the Father's direct ownership of them, since to deny the Son would also be to deny himself. The Father must disown the Son before he can neglect the Son's own. **And I am** (rather, *have been*) **glorified in them.** This "glorification" was the possession and manifestation of the very life of Jesus Christ. Such a glorification was at once the fruit and the evidence of the

A. D. 30. JOHN XVII. 269

11 ᵏthine are mine; ˡand I am glorified in them. ᵐAnd
now I am no more in the world, ⁿbut these are in
the world, and I come to thee. Holy Father, ᵒkeep
through thine own name those whom thou hast given
12 me, ᵖthat they may be one, as we *are*. While I was
with them in the world, ᵠI kept them in thy name:
those that thou gavest me I have kept, and ʳnone of

ᵏ ch. 10. 30; 16. 15.
ˡ Phil. 1. 20; 2 Thess. 1. 10; Rev. 5. 11-14.
ᵐ ch. 13. 1, 3; 16. 28.
ⁿ Matt. 10. 16.
ᵒ Ps. 17. 8; 1 Pet. 1. 5.
ᵖ Rom. 15. 5; 1 Cor. 1. 10; 12. 12; Eph. 4. 4. ᵠ ch. 6. 39; Heb. 2. 13. ʳ ch. 18. 9; 1 John 2. 19.

closest and highest possible union between them and him, and therefore of the most precious and supreme ownership of them by him. Thus does he specialize and intensify the argument which in its general form was contained in the preceding statement. If every interest of the Son, even the least, is also the Father's, and hence must be cared for by him, how much more *this* interest, which is that of his very NATURE!

11. And now I am no more in the world, but these are in the world, and I come to thee. Here he thinks and speaks of his final separation from the disciples as though it were already a present fact. This separation brings a new relation between them and him; and consequently new needs to them, and so to him new interest in them. Thus is this fact at once another special argument in the plea, and an introduction to the following statement of a special item of the plea. The contrast between their future condition in the world and his with the Father was like, though less than, that between his earthly and his heavenly state, ver. 5. His contrast moves his sympathies for them, and his earthly experience taught him what would be both their needs and their support. **Holy Father,** *holy* in contrast to the character of "the world" in which the disciples were to be left, **keep through thine own name those whom thou hast given me.** It is generally conceded that the reading of the oldest and most numerous manuscripts is, *keep them in that name of thine which thou hast given me.* Alford says: "The name of God was that which was to be in the Angel of the Covenant, Ex. 23 : 21. See also Isa. 9 : 6; Jer. 23 : 6. This name—not the essential Godhead, but the covenant name, Jehovah our Righteousness— the Father hath given to Christ, and it is the being kept in this, the truth and confession of this, for which he prays." **That they may be one, as we are,** or, *even as we.* "The world" is one in unholy discord, but the disciples are one in holy love. The one nature or *name* of God becomes a life to those who are in it and in whom it is; and so far, though not in every respect, the union of believers with one another and with God is the same as that of Christ and his Father. It is a union *grounded* in the divine nature, and hence as imperishable as though it were a union constituted by *identity* of their nature and his.

12. While I was with them in the world. Many of the oldest manuscripts omit *in the world.* Jesus in his communion with his Father contemplates his earthly work as completed. **I kept them in thy name.** This describes that personal ministry for the disciples which was now to end, and the word *kept* describes *what* was done. **I have kept,** or *guarded;* in the Greek a different word from that translated *kept* in the first part of the verse. The disciples could be kept within the name of God only by guarding them, since, though in that name, they were also in a hostile world. Its hostile influence against them must be counteracted by a friendly influence for them. It is due as much to divine power that we remain Christians as that we become Christians. **And none of them is lost, but the son of perdition.** The thought is not that *only* one, but rather *not* one, perished. One, Judas, not of them, but officially associated with them, perished. He was thus shown to have been not of the given, that holy family whose Father is God, but of that other family whose character in its very root is sin. Sin, because it surely *brings* perdition, may be said to *be* perdition. Hence perdition is per-

them is lost, *but the son of perdition; ᵗthat the
13 Scripture might be fulfilled. And now come I to
thee; and these things I speak in the world, ᵘthat
they might have my joy fulfilled in themselves.
14 I have given them thy word; ˣand the world hath
hated them, because they are not of the world, ʸeven
15 as I am not of the world. I pray not that thou
shouldest *take them out of the world, but *that
16 thou shouldest keep them from the evil. They are
not of the world, even as I am not of the world.

*ch. 6. 70; 13. 18.
ᵗPs.109.6-20; Acts 1. 20-25.
ᵘch. 15. 11; 1 John 1. 4.
ˣch. 15. 18, 19.
ʸch. 8. 23.
*Luke 8. 38, 39; Phil. 1. 20-26.
*Luke 11. 4; 2 Thess. 3. 3; 2 Tim. 4. 18; 1 John 5. 18.

---

sonified as being the mother of all such as Judas. Judas perished not by fault of Jesus, but by his own. **That the Scripture might be fulfilled.** The prediction did not affect the nature of the event, but showed its importance and its relation to the counsel and work of God. Hence this reference.

13. And these things I speak in the world, that they might (rather, *may*) **have my joy fulfilled in themselves**, or, *made full in them*. This joy is that which Christ experienced on earth, and not simply that which he gives. It resulted from his conscious fellowship with the Father, and was never greater than when, as now, in the midst of his extremest perils. This fellowship and this result of it he asks the Father to secure to the eleven by "keeping them." But even the keeping, and much more the joy, must come to them in the way of their own faith, and this faith must have the fit revelation on which to fasten; and such a revelation is that which this prayer constitutes. Hence Christ did not keep it in his own heart, but spoke it and so by words carried it into their hearts, to be the ground of preserving and rejoicing faith. Christ's consciousness of both the Father on the one hand and of the disciples on the other was needful to intercession, and determined not less fitly the form than the substance of the intercession.

14. I have given them thy word. See on vers. 6, 8. This statement is made to explain what follows. The need of the disciples is occasioned by the agency of the Father's Son and by the instrumentality of the Father's word; and hence must be met by the Father's help, unless he will disown both his own word and his own Son. **And the world hath hated them.** It did hate them while Jesus was with them, and hence would yet more when he was gone. Hence their need of God's help. **Because they are not of the world, even as** (or, *according as*) **I am not of the world.** The world was in antagonism to Christ—not through a misunderstanding, but because of an antagonistic spirit. But the disciples were of Christ's Spirit, as shown by the fact that they received his words. Living by those words and teaching those words as he had done, they must encounter the same kind of hostility and need the same kind of succor. And all the reasons which had held the Father to help his Son would hold him to help them.

15. I pray (or, *plead*) **not that thou shouldest take them out of the world.** Christ was about to go to the Father, and it might seem that the highest love would ask that his disciples might go with him. But as the Son did not go till his work was finished, so the sons had a work which must be finished before they should go. Jesus thus does not ask to have them taken before their time, and so he does virtually ask to have them remain till their service is completed. The world needs Christians not less truly than it needed Christ. The apostolic work is doubtless in mind. **But that thou shouldest keep them from the evil.** Possibly here, as certainly in 1 John 5 : 18, we should translate, *from the evil one—i. e.* from Satan. The difference, however, is rather of form than of substance. The kingdom of God and the kingdom of Satan are in collision, and Jesus asks God to care for those who are fighting God's battles. How reasonable! How certain to be done! Compare 2 Tim. 4 : 18. But compare note on Matt. 6 : 13.

16. They are not of the world, even as (or, *according as*) **I am not**

17 ᵇSanctify them through thy truth: ᶜthy word is truth. ᵈAs thou hast sent me into the world, even so have I also sent them into the world. And ᵉfor their sakes I sanctify myself, ᶠthat they also might be sanctified through the truth.

ᵇ ch. 15. 3; Ps. 19. 7-9; 119. 9; Acts 15. 9; Eph. 5. 26; 2 Thess. 2. 13; 1 Pet. 1. 23.
ᶜ ch. 8. 40; Ps. 12. 6; 119. 142, 151.
ᵈ ch. 20. 21; 2 Cor. 5. 20. 10. 10.
ᵉ 1 Cor. 1. 2, 30; 1 Thess. 4. 7; Heb. 2. 11;
ᶠ Acts 4. 32; Col. 3. 11, 12.

of the world. See ver. 14. Emphatic repetition. It sums up negatively the plea as thus far made. It affirms by implication that they are of the Father, according as Christ is, and hence must have like care with him.

17. Sanctify them. The verb in the original means—(1) *to separate, set apart* for a religious purpose, *devote, consecrate;* (2) *to make holy.* When it is used of inanimate things or of the brute creation, it necessarily takes the first signification, for holiness cannot be possessed by them, Lev. 16 : 19; Matt. 23 : 17; 1 Tim. 4 : 5. It is also used in the same signification of holy beings, for they are already holy, and cannot be made so, 1 Pet. 3 : 15. But of men, who need both consecration and holiness, it may be used in either sense, and also in the two senses combined. Yet he who is consecrated to God needs the inward holiness to carry out that consecration; and so he in whom the work of sanctification is going on will, as a natural result, consecrate himself to God and his work. In actual human experience, therefore, the two senses of the verb must be more or less united. In this passage the verb specially takes the second meaning—*to make holy.* The apostles were already called and set apart to their work. What they needed was increased holiness. The same is true of all believers. Besides, Jesus had prayed that they might be kept while they were in the world, and kept from the evil, vers. 11, 15. This was the negative side. Now he prays positively, *Sanctify them*—separate them more and more from the world, from sin and sinners, by making them more and more holy in body, soul, and spirit—more like thyself and myself, 1 Thess. 5 : 23. **Through thy truth;** rather, *in thy truth.* The word of God is the element in which the process of sanctification goes on. "They who are true disciples of Christ live and move in the word of truth as their element. They breathe it. This element, like all means of grace, has a sanctifying tendency."—DR. SCHAUFFER. It may therefore be styled a medium or means of sanctification. The truth also has an assimilating power upon those who receive it, 2 Cor. 4 : 2-6; 3 : 18; 1 John 3 : 2. **Thy word**—thy revealed word—**is truth.** Christ is himself the embodiment of truth, ch. 14 : 6. It may be added, as confirmatory of the above, that the word translated *sanctify* is kindred to, and derived from, that translated *holy* in ver. 11—"holy Father"—where the moral perfection of God in contrast to the world's pollution is meant. Thus, in the sanctification of believers there is a separation from the world and a holiness of heart and life, according to God's revealed will, by which this holiness and separation are effected, and even constituted. Compare James 1 : 18.

18. As thou hast sent (rather, *didst send*) **me into the world, even so have** (omit *have*) **I also sent them into the world.** In his holy and intimate communion with the Father he still views his earthly work as already accomplished. He says *I sent*, as though he had already given the final commission. A further reason why they should be kept in God's truth, and thus sanctified, is this fact that they are to represent and serve God and his cause on earth even as Christ had done. Only in so far as identified with the truth could they do this. See ch. 18 : 37. God is bound thus to sanctify them, unless he will be misrepresented and unserved.

19. And for their sakes I sanctify myself. In his high spiritual state Jesus had viewed his completed work (ver. 4), but now his mind once more turns to his earthly work as still in progress. He had already devoted and consecrated himself in coming into the world, Heb. 10 : 7. His whole life

20 Neither pray I for these alone, but for them also
21 which shall believe on me through their word; ᵍthat
they all may be one; as thou, Father, *art* in me, and
I in thee, that they also may be one in us: that the

ᵍ ch. 10. 16; Rom. 12. 5.

was one of consecration to his mission. He is about to devote himself to his sacrificial death; and this sacrifice and obedience were perfectly voluntary, ch. 10 : 17, 18. Jesus thus asserts that he is doing to himself what he had asked the Father to do for them, ver. 17. He does not, however, intend to assert that the Father bears to their sanctification a relation different from that which he bears to his. Not less truly did the Father sanctify him than them. His human nature was made holy through the Holy Spirit and the power of the Highest, Luke 1 : 35. He was "sanctified and sent into the world," ch. 10 : 36. There was also a similarity between their mission and his (ver. 18), and no less truly did they sanctify themselves than did he himself, ch. 5 : 19; Phil. 2 : 12. Both in them and him sanctification is made complete by holding fast unto God, and accomplishing each the work assigned to each by the divine will. In the words *for their sakes* Christ, however, distinguishes his sanctification from theirs as being primarily vicarious, and especially as about to end in a vicarious sacrifice. It is also implied that they can be sanctified only in him and on the ground of his earthly work. His sanctification was an example, but not that merely. He sanctified himself *for their sakes*, **that they also might** (better, *may*) **be sanctified through the truth**. This should be *in the truth*, or literally *in truth*—absolutely, as the element. See note on ver. 17. Compare 2 John 3; 3 John 3, 4.

For their sakes I sanctify myself. The word here translated *sanctify* is not synonymous with *purify*. "The *holy* is not opposed to the *impure*, but to the *natural*. To *sanctify* is to consecrate to a religious use anything pertaining to common life."—GODET. The Lord means that he consecrates himself heartily, entirely, without reserve, to the great work which the Father had given him to do; and the result of his entire consecration will be seen in working also in them a corre- sponding consecration to the great work for which he was sending them into the world. When a believer in Christ dedicates his whole heart, strength, and life to promote the glory of God in the salvation of men, he realizes the highest idea of Christian holiness. This Jesus did, and in so doing he presented the bright example which his apostles and his people in every age have striven in their own measure to imitate. Thus, his *sanctifying himself, his consecration*, have always ministered to theirs.

20-26. PRAYER FOR BELIEVERS GENERALLY. This third section of the prayer fitly ends the Lord's requests. It presupposes answers such as he desired to the two former sections of his prayer, for they were both necessary to such an enlargement of the number of believers as this section of the prayer implies.

20. **Neither pray** (*plead*) **I for these alone, but for them also which shall believe,** etc. According to some editors, the original should be read as in the present tense, and translated *those believing*. The petition in either case would include all believers to the end of time. **Through their word.** The Lord implies that those who come to believe are led to the exercise of faith through the words of the apostles, and also that their word was not to be fruitless, but attended with large success.

21. **That they all may be one.** Here is asked for all what in verse 11 was asked for the eleven. In the whole family of God there is one nature, and that a nature of loving oneness. Christ makes the grand division to be between his people and the world, not between a higher and a lower class of his people. **As** (*according as*) **thou, Father, art in me, and I in thee, that they also may be one in us.** See above, on verse 11, where there is the same thought, but less fully expressed. Christ guards here, where it needed guarding, the precious doctrine and fact that the least Christian of any and every time has the same immediate personal union with God that the apostles

22 world may believe that thou hast sent me. And ᵇthe glory which thou gavest me I have given them;
23 ˡthat they may be one, even as we are one: ᵏI in them, and thou in me, ˡthat they may be made perfect in one; and that the world may know that thou hast sent me, and hast loved them, as thou hast loved me.

ᵇ ch. 1. 16; Rom. 8. 17; 2 Cor. 3. 18; Phil. 3. 21; Col. 3. 4; 2 Tim. 2. 12; 1 John 3. 2.
ˡ 1 John 1. 3; 3. 24.
ᵏ ch. 6. 56; 14. 23; Rom. 8. 10, 11; 2 Cor. 5. 21; Gal. 3. 28.

ˡ Eph. 4. 12; Col. 2. 2.

enjoyed, and could never be separated from him by ordinances, organizations, persons, or aught else. Only this union secures oneness of holy life. If Christ here refers to conviction and action, he does not ask that Christians may unite in action at the sacrifice of their convictions, but that they may come to have and act upon convictions that are according to "the truth" of God, and therefore identical. **That the world may believe that thou hast sent** (*didst send*) **me.** This may mean either, That the world may come to believe in me, and so cease to be a godless world, or, That the world, remaining ungodly, may yet, to their condemnation, be convicted of my divine mission. The former meaning best fits the use of words 'n this prayer (ver. 8), as well as its general tone.

22. **And the glory which thou gavest** (*hast given*) **me I have given them.** It is desirable that believers ascertain if possible what is meant by this petition. This glory, which Jesus says that he had given to his own, whatever it may be, is of course what was first given by the Father to himself. Various writers have given their views on this subject, and some of them make the glory to be something which was never given by the Father to the Son. It is very certain that the work which Jesus was sent to perform was a glorious work. He came to enter on a divine life and service on earth in fulfilment of the work given him to do. There was a glory in this life and work, and a great glory as the reward. Jesus, "for the joy that was set before him, endured the cross, despising the shame, and is set down at the right hand of the throne of God," Heb. 12 : 2. He himself, after his resurrection, said to his disciples, "Ought not Christ to have suffered these things, and to enter into his glory?" Luke 24 : 26. Again, the apostle says he took on himself the form of a servant, and became obedient even unto the death of the cross; "Wherefore, God also hath highly exalted him, and given him a name which is above every name," Phil. 2 : 9. To this divine life and service Jesus called his disciples, to imitate his trust in the Father, his zeal in his service, his readiness to suffer in carrying out his Father's will. See Phil. 1 : 29. This life and service, as in the case of the Lord, are the earnest and the precursor of the heavenly glory. With emphatic repetition he again mentions the unity of believers in the divine life and love as the aim of his ministry, and consequently of the Father's will in giving him that ministry.

23. **I in them, and thou in me, that they may be made perfect in one,** or, *may be perfected into one*. This oneness is here spoken of as the final goal, the realization of the perfect ideal. The union between Jesus and his Father was perfect. There was no defect either in degree or in extent. Hence to see the Son was to see the Father. The life of the Son was the Father's life. Believers in becoming believers have such *kind* of oneness, but not such *degree*. The Holy Spirit both reveals and imparts to them in regeneration the mind of Christ, and therefore the mind of the Father; but the revelation is not completed by one stroke, but, as Jesus here indicates, is carried forward progressively toward that perfection which he himself in his life exhibited as a standard. This is primarily a prayer for believers on earth as a collective and progressive body, but with an application also to the individual believer. **That the world may know,** etc. (see on ver. 21), **and hast loved** (*didst love*) **them, as thou hast loved** (*didst love*) **me.** This presents the time of sending the Son as the time of the Father's love of the Son

274 JOHN XVII. A.D. 30.

24 ᵐFather, I will that they also, whom thou hast given me, be with me where I am; that they ⁿmay behold my glory, which thou hast given me: for thou
25 lovedst me before the foundation of the world. °O righteous Father, ᵖthe world hath not known thee: but ᵍI have known thee, and these have known that
26 thou hast sent me. ʳAnd I have declared unto them thy name, ˢand will declare it: that the love ᵗwherewith thou hast loved me may be in them, ᵘand I in them.

ᵐ ch. 12. 26.
ⁿ 1 Cor. 13. 12; 2 Cor. 4. 6; 1 John 3. 2.
° 1 Pet. 2. 23.
ᵖ 1 Cor. 1. 21; 2. 8.
ᵍ ch. 7. 29; 8. 55; 10. 15.
ʳ ver. 6; ch. 15. 15.
ˢ Luke 24. 45.
ᵗ ch. 14. 23; 15. 9.
ᵘ ver. 23; Gal. 2. 20; Eph. 3. 17; Col. 2. 10.

and of believers, and thus the act of sending the Son as an act of love to both him and them. This love, however, can be known experimentally only in the method just mentioned, and perfectly only in the full fruitage of that method. God's love to us is shed abroad in our hearts in a measure whenever we receive Christ; fully when we fully receive him.

24. **Father, I will that they also, whom thou hast given me, be with me where I am.** In the words *I will* kingly authority blends with intercession. As believers were given him, so was "all power" or authority given; and this he here asserts. In saying *where I am* he again conceives of himself as already returned to the Father, and done with his fleshly life on earth. Thus his prayer here advances to a claim for the eternal companionship of his disciples, and so supplements the words of ver. 15. As he passed from his earthly service to the Father's side (ver. 5), so shall they from their earthly service to his side. **That they may behold my glory, which thou hast given me.** This is the glory prayed for in ver. 5, and also doubtless that spoken of in ver. 22, which see. This fulness of glory is here conceived of as already received —*hast given.* He would have them *behold* it, because this vision of his glory was at once the evidence and the method of their participation in it. They would be like him because they would see him, and would see him because they would be like him. **For thou lovedst me before the foundation of the world.** From eternity—not as one who was to *become*, but as one who from the beginning *was.* The fellowship of the Father and the Son in the eternal oneness of their divine nature underlay and determined the perpetual fellowship of the Father with the Son in his divine human nature. The human nature was made a sharer of the divine glory in the respects of both quality and perpetuity, and the human disciples shared the same destiny with the human Son. Thus this clause refers to the whole preceding request, and not merely to its last clause.

25. **O righteous Father, the world hath not known** (rather, *did not know*) **thee.** It might seem that with ver. 24 the prayer should end, but Jesus remembers that his eleven and the whole body of saints represented by them were to serve on earth before they could reign in heaven, and so he comes back to make the last words of his great plea a helping hand reached down to lift them up into his heaven. He here calls the Father *righteous* or just by contrast with the world, and with the treatment which the world had accorded, and would accord, to him and his. The original inserts *and* before *the world*, in the sense either of *and yet* or of *and therefore.* **But I have known** (rather, *knew*) **thee.** Because unlike the world, Jesus had the spirit of righteousness in harmony with God; **and these have known,** rather *knew*, etc. In them, too, was a spirit of righteousness to receive and know Jesus and the Father. Thus the world's hatred and persecution should encourage, and not discourage, them. It was the evidence that God was for them and in them.

26. **And I have declared** (rather, *made known*) **unto them thy name, and will declare it;** rather, *make it known.* The past and the future are here his earthly and his heavenly work respectively. In the sending of the Spirit and of ministers of the gospel, etc. he continues to make known God's

name. **That the love wherewith thou hast loved** (*didst love*) **me may be in them, and I in them.** See the last clause of ver. 23, and comments on it. How fitly does this prayer of perfected love close with the avowed purpose to perfect the love of God in man, and so perfect man in the love of God, and thus make man's perfection to be also God's perfection! For this Jesus died and lives—*I in them.*

PRACTICAL REMARKS.

1. Prayer fittingly follows religious instruction, and fittingly precedes and prepares for approaching trial. It is an avenue of blessing to the suppliant, and often of consolation and encouragement to those who hear, ver. 1; ch. 11 : 42.
2. The mutual glorification of the Father and the Son is the ultimate design of mediatorial authority, vers. 1, 2.
3. Since eternal life is the gracious gift of Christ, it should be received with penitence and thankfulness as an undeserved favor to the guilty, ver. 3.
4. Without an experimental acquaintance of God in Christ there can be no eternal life, ver. 3; Ps. 34 : 8.
5. We should strive so to live as to say at last, "I have finished the work which thou hast given me to do," ver. 4; 2 Tim. 4 : 7, 8.
6. Jesus prays for what had been designed and promised—exaltation after humiliation; so the designs and promises of God should encourage our prayers, ver. 5; Phil. 2 : 5-7.
7. Christ manifests God to men; but only Christians, who are a gift of the Father to Christ, spiritually discern this manifestation, and as a result obey God, ver. 6; ch. 1 : 18; 2 Tim. 2 : 19.
8. Christians learn experimentally that their salvation is all of grace, a gift of God through Jesus Christ, ver. 7.
9. Faith and obedience are the evidences that we are given to Christ by the Father. Thus let us "make our calling and election sure," ver. 8; 2 Pet. 1 : 10.
10. How cheering the thought, if we are Christ's, that he, in the most sacred and elevated moment of his life, prayed for us, and that he ever liveth as an intercessor! vers. 9, 20; Heb. 7 : 25.
11. Christ is glorified in the salvation of men, in the apostles and all true believers, ver. 10; Isa. 53 : 10, 11.
12. It is unity in the Father's name, which Christ has revealed, for which he prays, ver. 11.
13. Christ's care for his disciples was not in vain; so his prayers in their behalf will be availing. Whoever of his professed followers is lost will be, like Judas, a son of perdition, ver. 12; Ps. 109 : 8; Acts 1 : 20.
14. Through the words of Christ the joy of believers is made perfect and lasting, ver. 13.
15. At the word of God, and the exemplification of this word in Christians, the hatred of the world is developed, ver. 14.
16. Work for Christ, even amid trials and afflictions, is better than to depart before our work is done. Our times we should commit to Christ, ver. 15; Ps. 31 : 15.
17. We should so live as to show that we are not of the world, ver. 16.
18. As God's word is the great means of sanctification, the better it is understood and the more closely it is obeyed the more holy will men be, the happier and the more useful, ver. 17.
19. Like Christ from the Father, so the apostles from Christ had a special mission in the world, ver. 18; Acts 1 : 21, 22.
20. Christ's vicarious sacrifice and work are the foundation of the apostolic mission and of the church, ver. 19 ; 1 Cor. 3 : 11; Eph. 2 : 20.
21. The weakest and humblest of Christ's followers were included in Christ's intercessory prayer, ver. 20.
22. The union for which Christ prayed was spiritual—a union of true believers in a loving and obedient knowledge of God's character and will, by being in the Father and the Son, and by having Christ in them, vers. 6, 11, 21, 23.
23. As this union is spiritual, so must the means for realizing it be spiritual, vers. 21-24; 2 Cor. 10 : 4.
24. The union for which Christ prayed is modelled after the perfect union of the Father and the Son, vers. 11, 21-23.
25. The union of individual believers with Christ lays the foundation for their union one with another, ver. 23; Eph. 4 : 12, 13.

Jesus is apprehended; taken before Annas and Caiaphas; denied by Peter.

XVIII. WHEN Jesus had spoken these words, ᵛ he went forth with his disciples over * the brook Cedron, where was a garden, into the which he entered, and his disciples.

ᵛ Matt. 26. 30, 36–46; Mark 14. 32; Luke 22. 39.
* 2 Sam. 15. 23.

26. The union of believers, which is begun on earth, will find its fullest and most perfect consummation with Christ in heaven, ver. 24; 1 John 3 : 1, 2.

27. "The death of believers is in answer to the prayer of Christ, and for the purpose of removing them to the perfect and everlasting enjoyment o' his presence in heaven," ver. 24.

28. Christ is the original fountain of all the saving knowledge that believers have of God, ver. 25.

29. Love is the bond in which the union of believers finds its perfection, ver. 26; Col. 3 : 14; Jude 21.

30. We should use all diligence to keep ourselves in the knowledge and love of God, meditating upon God's truth, praying over it, and putting it into practice, and in love striving to keep the unity of the Spirit in the bonds of peace, ver. 26; ch. 15 : 5; 1 Thess. 4 : 9, 10; 1 Pet. 1 : 22.

CHAPTER XVIII.

With the last chapter John closes his account of the *prophetic* ministry of Jesus. In this he proceeds to his *sacrificial* work, unless, indeed, we prefer to make the division at the beginning of ch. 13. Evidently the two overlap. John's narrative omits many things related by Matthew, Mark, and Luke, and contains others of great importance not named by them. This is as might be expected, both from the fact that John was more fully and continuously an eye-witness than any of the other evangelists, and also from the evident purpose of the writer, which was to supplement the other Gospels, to bring out more fully the divinity and the deep teaching of our Lord, and so to counteract rising heresies in regard to his person and work.

The topics of chs. 18 and 19 (which form one continuous division of this Gospel) are: The arrest of Jesus (vers. 1-11); his examination before Annas and Caiaphas successively (vers. 12-27); the denial of his Lord by Peter (vers. 15-27); the examination of Jesus by Pilate, who pronounces him innocent and proposes to release him (vers. 28-38); the clamor of the Jews against this, who prefer Barabbas (vers. 39, 40); the scourging and mocking of Jesus (ch. 19 : 1-5); Pilate's renewed effort to release him (vers. 6-12); his final yielding and order for the crucifixion (vers. 13-16); the crucifixion, with various incidents related only by John (vers. 17-37); the Lord's burial, vers. 38-42.

1-11. ARREST OF JESUS; TREACHERY OF JUDAS; RASHNESS OF PETER. Matt. 26 : 47-57; Mark 14 : 43-52; Luke 22 : 47-53. With the former part of each of these passages John (chs. 13-17) harmonizes in point of time. When John wrote, the three other Gospels were well known and the church and her ordinances were established things. Hence he omits particulars concerning the Jewish conspiracy against Christ, the contention among the Twelve, the institution of the Lord's Supper, and the agony at Gethsemane. But John alone preserves for us the unspeakably precious legacy of the Saviour's valedictory address, and his "intercessory prayer," which was also the Saviour's report of his work on earth to his Father.

1. **When Jesus had spoken these words**—namely, of his parting conversation and prayer (chs. 14-17), which followed the eating of the passover and the institution of the Lord's Supper—he **went forth**, accompanied by the eleven, from the house, as it would seem, as well as from the city, passing down the deep gorge on the eastern side, crossing **over the brook** (or *torrent*) **Cedron** — properly, *Kedron*, a winter torrent, but dry in summer—about where a small bridge now spans the dry channel, and soon came to a **garden**, owned, no doubt, by a friend, and situated at or near the foot of the Mount of Olives. It may have been a few steps up the slope of the hill. This

2 And ᵃJudas also, which betrayed him, knew the place: ʸfor Jesus ofttimes resorted thither with his disciples.
3 ᶻJudas then, having received a band of men and officers from the chief priests and Pharisees, cometh thither with lanterns and torches and weapons.
4 Jesus therefore, ᵃknowing all things that should come upon him, went forth, and said unto them,
5 ᵇWhom seek ye? They answered him, Jesus of Nazareth. Jesus saith unto them, I am *he*. (And Judas also, which betrayed him, stood with them.)
6 As soon then as he had said unto them, I am *he*, ᶜthey went backward, and fell to the ground.

ᵃ ch. 13. 2, 27-30.
ʸ Luke 21. 37; 22. 39.
Matt. 26. 47-52; Mark 14. 43-47; Luke 22. 47-53; also Acts 1. 16.
ᵃ ch. 13. 1; Matt. 16. 21.
ᵇ Prov. 28. 1.
ᶜ 2 Kings 1. 9-12; Ps. 27. 2; 40. 14.

is the *garden of Gethsemane*, where he was wont to resort with his disciples. The traditional site of this garden is probably the exact spot. Here, as related by the other evangelists, it being now late in the evening, Jesus remained for some time, underwent fearful agony, *and his sweat became as it were great drops of blood*, Luke 22 : 44. Here he prayed three times, and was strengthened by an angel. "This notice of the garden would suggest the scene to all familiar with the other Gospels. John's intention is to exhibit its issue—the repose of Jesus."—LANGE.

2. Here Jesus was arrested late at night. The treachery of Judas, who well **knew the place** and his Master's habits, enabled the Sanhedrim to arrest him without a public disturbance. Hence they changed their plan (Matt. 26 : 5), and sent Judas and a force of men sufficient, with full commission and authority, to apprehend Jesus and bring him before them.

3. **A band** (true text omits the words *of men*), properly, *the band—i. e.* the Roman cohort, which consisted of from three hundred to six hundred men, was quartered in the tower of Antonia, and guarded the peace of the city. The Sanhedrim could procure its services to effect an arrest. Probably only part of the band was now present. Then there were the officers—*i. e. the captains of the temple* (Luke 22 : 52) with their men, who guarded the temple and kept order. Some of the chief priests and elders (Luke 22 : 52) came also, to make sure of their prey, accompanied by some servants, as Malchus. This force was armed with **weapons** (swords and staves) to overcome any resistance, and was provided with **lanterns and torches** (better, *torches and lamps*), which they might need, although it was moonlight, if it should be necessary to search the shady recesses of the garden or the rock-caverns and tombs of the valley of the Kedron.

4. Jesus well knew and understood *all the things that were coming upon him*, as the phrase should read. His acquaintance with the Old Testament prophecies (Luke 24 : 27) was perfect; his knowledge of the nature of his work and of the counsel of God was complete. He had full foreknowledge (indeed, long beforehand) of all his appointed sufferings. Hence he was not, like his disciples, surprised. Besides, he had emerged from the conflict of Gethsemane calm and firm. Instead, therefore, of hiding, he **went forth** boldly to meet his enemies, and asked them, **Whom seek ye?**

5. They answered, **Jesus of Nazareth,** rather, *Jesus the Nazarene*, not probably recognizing him. At this point many place the kiss of Judas. He **stood** (rather, *was standing*) **with them,** and came forward to identify Jesus by the concerted signal—a treacherous kiss—and received a mild but terrible reproof, Matt. 26 : 48-50; Mark 14 : 44-46; Luke 22 : 47, 48. The calm courage of Jesus rendered this signal quite unnecessary, for he avowed himself the man they sought, without awaiting arrest or question. He said, **I am he.** The Judas kiss became "a meaningless farce through Jesus' self-declaration."—LANGE. But others place this after verse 9. See *Author's Harmony,* §§ 170, 171.

6. As the Son of God confronted them with calm majesty they were seized

7 Then asked he them again, Whom seek ye? And
8 they said, Jesus of Nazareth. Jesus answered, I have
told you that I am *he:* if therefore ye seek me, ᵈ let
9 these go their way: that the saying might be fulfilled,
which he spake, ᵉ Of them which thou gavest me have
I lost none.
10 ᶠ Then Simon Peter having a sword drew it, and
smote the high priest's servant, and cut off his right

ᵈ ch. 13. 1; Isa. 53. 6; 1 Cor. 10. 13; Eph. 5. 25.
ᵉ ch. 6. 39; 17. 12.
ᶠ Matt. 26. 51; Mark 14. 47; Luke 22. 49, 50.

with a sudden panic, started back in dismay, and **fell to the ground.** Some of these very men, in all probability, were of the number sent on a former occasion by the Sanhedrim to arrest him, and, being overawed by his teaching, dared not fulfil their commission, ch. 7 : 45, 46. Now, amidst the darkness of night and the sombre shades of the deep valley and the garden, they remembered too that Jesus was the great miracle-worker, and his majestic composure affrighted them. This accounts for the panic. LANGE: The channel of the miracle was " terror of conscience." " Tholuck cites kindred instances. When before Mark Antony, Marius, and Coligny, the murderers recoiled, panic-struck." But also the divine power deprived them for the moment of strength—even of power to stand. Thus it was shown to the Saviour's enemies, as he had previously taught his disciples (ch. 10 : 17, 18), that if he was taken and crucified, it was not for want of power to resist, but because he voluntarily yielded himself into their hands. Compare ch. 19 : 11. He also compelled every person present to be a witness of his arrest, legally effected.

7. When they had recovered themselves and returned, he **asked them again, Whom seek ye?** This reassured them. He evidently intended no resistance or harm to them, and they replied as before. This scene rendered any treacherous violence to Christ impossible.

8. **I have told you,** etc.; I have already told you; you know it from my own lips. **If therefore,** etc.—*i. e.,* if I am the person you are sent to arrest, **let these go their way.** Let these my friends, with whom you have no concern, go in peace. The Saviour's object was to give his disciples an opportunity to escape.

9. John here refers to the saying of Christ, ch. 17 : 12. It is not meant that this instance of thoughtful, unselfish care was the full or principal fulfilment, but that this was a partial fulfilment, one special instance, of that preserving of soul and body. As before, and as afterward he cared for them, even unto eternal life. In this case it was not bodily safety alone which the Saviour provided for, but the apostles' spiritual safety and the future of the church; for they were not strong enough for martyrdom, and they had a great work to do, for which they must be spared.

It may be that here Judas came forward, nerving himself to go through his part. (See on verse 5.) At any rate, the officers now laid violent hands on Jesus. The arrest was effected. The disciples, seeing what would follow if something were not done, inquired, "Lord, shall we smite with the sword?" Luke 22 : 49. They would not flee till they knew that Jesus would not deliver himself. If he encouraged, they were ready to fight, in full confidence that he could give them the victory against any odds.

10. **Simon Peter** did not wait for an answer. In accordance with his impetuous nature, and doubtless emboldened by the supernatural awe which Jesus had just previously caused to fall upon the multitude, also anxious to show that the Saviour's estimate of his strength was mistaken (Luke 22 : 31-34), Peter drew his sword and commenced the conflict, not doubting the power of Jesus to give the victory. His first onset was upon **Malchus,** the servant of the high priest, who perhaps had laid hands upon Jesus. This sword was one of the two mentioned in Luke 22 : 38. **And cut off his right ear,** aiming doubtless at his head. This rash act, contrary to the will of God, and threatening great harm to the cause and danger to the disciples, would not

11 ear. The servant's name was Malchus. Then said Jesus unto Peter, Put up thy sword into the sheath: *the cup which my Father hath given me, shall I not drink it?

*Matt. 20. 22; 26 39, 42.

12 Then the band and the captain and officers of the

have been performed if Peter had properly watched and prayed, Luke 22 : 37, 38. The earlier evangelists do not mention Peter's name, perhaps for prudential considerations.

11. In one expression the Saviour restrains Peter and answers the question of the disciples (Luke 22 : 49)—**Put up thy sword into the sheath.** This was a kind but firm reproof. **The cup**—thus he designates his sufferings and death (compare Mark 10 : 38 ; Luke 22 : 42, etc.)—**which my Father hath given me.** It was of divine appointment, a part of the Saviour's predestined work, and necessary for human redemption. This did not in any way lessen the freedom or excuse the guilt of the Jews or of Judas. A thing may be righteously and wisely predestined of God, and yet be freely and most wickedly done by men. There is no difficulty in this except the general difficulty, or rather impossibility, of fully harmonizing the idea of God's sovereign rule with the responsible free agency of man. Both are patent facts, the reality of which is in no way affected by our inability fully to comprehend their mutual relations. Compare Acts 2 : 23 ; John 19 : 11 ; Matt. 26 : 24. **Shall I not drink it?** Shall I not meekly accept the divine appointment? Thus the Saviour said in his agony, *not as I will, but as thou wilt,* Matt. 26 : 39, etc. To resist by force would be, in the circumstances, rebellion against the known will of God.

We learn from Matthew (ch. 26 : 52-54) that Jesus gave three other reasons for not resisting : (1) The unsuitableness of doing so: "For all they that take the sword shall perish by the sword." The Saviour does not here assert that all who resort to arms, under any circumstances, " perish." This is obviously untrue; indeed, this course very often preserves life, friends, and country. Much less does he utter the meaningless platitude that fighting is dangerous. The great principle is announced that religions founded or preserved by the sword will perish by the same means. Islam was so established, and will doubtless perish amidst civil convulsions. But Christianity is immortal. It cannot be propagated by the sword nor destroyed by the sword. Christians must not use carnal weapons in its defence, but spiritual. The reference is to religions and principles rather than to the fate of individuals. This passage has no reference to ordinary self-defence from robbers, murderers, etc., nor to military operations by human governments, and does not forbid governments from protecting the civil rights of Christians as of others—even their religious liberty—by force. (2) Peter's puny sword was superfluous. If force was needed, prayer would bring more than twelve legions of mighty angels. (3) "How, then, shall the Scriptures be fulfilled?" which is nearly equivalent to the question here. The Scriptures must be fulfilled, because they reveal the counsel of God.

We learn from Luke that Jesus immediately touched Malchus's ear and healed it. This prevented any harm to Peter or the others from his rash act, conciliated the officers so as to facilitate the apostle's escape from arrest, and strongly disavowed resistance to civil authority on the part of Jesus. The Saviour also addressed a temperate and dignified remonstrance to the members of the Sanhedrim present, and to the temple-captains, for the time and manner of his arrest. He protests, though he does not resist or flee. Then he quietly suffered himself to be arrested, pinioned, and led away. At this point all his disciples, perceiving that he did not mean to deliver himself, lost heart, forsook him, and fled for their lives. One only, not one of the Twelve, ventured to follow, and he was seized by the temple-guards, but escaped from their grasp and fled. (See for all in this and preceding paragraph Matt. 26 : 51-56 ; Mark 14 : 47-52 ; Luke 22 : 50-53.)

12-27. PRELIMINARY EXAMINATION OF JESUS BEFORE ANNAS. PETER'S

13 Jews took Jesus, and bound him, and ᵇ led him away to ⁱ Annas first; for he was father-in-law to Caiaphas, 14 which was the high priest that same year. ʲ Now Caiaphas was he which gave counsel to the Jews, that it was expedient that one man should die for the people.
15 ᵏ And Simon Peter followed Jesus, and *so did* another disciple. That disciple was known unto the

ᵇ Matt. 26. 57, 58, 69–74; Mark 14. 53, 54, 66–72; Luke 22. 54–60.
ⁱ Luke 3. 2.
ʲ ch. 11. 49–52.

ᵏ Matt. 26. 58; Mark 14. 54; Luke 22. 54.

DENIAL OF HIS MASTER, Matt. 26: 57, 58, 69–75; Mark 14: 54, 66–72; Luke 22: 54–62. Before Jesus was brought before Caiaphas, as related by the other evangelists, he was conducted, for a preliminary examination, before Annas. This old man had formerly been high priest, and, though deposed by the foreign power that ruled Judæa, was still the legitimate high priest according to the law of Moses (the office being for life, Num. 20 : 28; 35 : 25), and may have been so regarded by the Jews. Annas appears to have possessed vast influence, and as father-in-law to Caiaphas doubtless exerted a very controlling influence over him. It is probable that they occupied jointly the official residence, so that Annas, after examining Jesus, sent him across the court to the apartment occupied by Caiaphas. Peter's denial took place in this court, and thus all difficulties are removed.

12. **Then the band;** rather, *So the band.* See ver. 3. **Bound,** pinioned his arms. "To apprehend and bind *One* all gave their help, the cohort, the chiliarch, the Jewish officers.... Only by the help of all did they feel themselves secure. And thus it was ordered, that the disciples might escape with the more safety."—LUTHARDT. (The "chiliarch" was commander of the Roman cohort.) The time of the arrest was probably past midnight.

13. **And led him away to Annas first.** On account of Annas's high position and influence Jesus is led for a preliminary examination to him first. He was **father-in-law to Caiaphas,** the incumbent of the high priest's office at this time. The two men acted in harmony. It is said that Caiaphas was **high priest that same year.** (Omit *same.*) This expression occurs before in ch. 11 : 49. Probably a popular form of speech. God made the high priesthood a life-office, but under the desecrating Roman supremacy it had become a mere annual office.

14. Refers to facts stated in ch. 11 : 49. The high priest was the head of the priesthood and of all religious affairs. Aaron was the first high priest (Ex. 28 : 1–38), and the office continued in his family about fifteen centuries; but Herod, and the Roman governors after him, changed the incumbents at pleasure, so much so that the office became almost annual. **Caiaphas.** Joseph Caiaphas was high priest about nine years, during the whole procuratorship of Pontius Pilate. He was son-in-law to the deposed and rightful high priest. See on ch. 11 : 49. But why is Caiaphas mentioned just here? To intimate that both old Annas and his son-in-law were of one mind in bitter and murderous hostility to the Lord Jesus. The legal proceedings were merely a form and a mockery. The death of Jesus had been fully determined upon. His trial and condemnation and final death constituted a base and predetermined judicial murder. Here John gives us fair warning of the character of the proceedings which he is about to relate. The conclusion was decided upon before even the preliminary examination of the accused began. Annas appears, more than any other single man, to be the central figure in this conspiracy. He and his friends were Sadducees. They hated Christ with a deadly hate, partly as a reprover of their wickedness, partly as being a rival in influence with the people, and partly, perhaps, because in "cleansing the temple" he had interfered with corrupt practices by which they probably received large profits. The Pharisees also hated him because he threatened the reign of formalism and tradition.

15–18. FIRST DENIAL BY PETER. Jesus being before Annas, Matt. 26 : 58, 69, 70; Mark 14 : 54, 66–68; Luke

A. D. 30.   JOHN XVIII.   281

high priest, and went in with Jesus into the palace
16 of the high priest. ¹But Peter stood at the door ¹ Matt. 26. 69;
without. Then went out that other disciple, which   Mark 14. 66;
was known unto the high priest, and spake unto her   Luke 22. 54.
17 that kept the door, and brought in Peter. Then saith
the damsel that kept the door unto Peter, Art not
thou also *one* of this man's disciples? ᵐ He saith, I ᵐ Luke 22. 31.

22 : 54, 56, 57. See the *Author's Harmony*, ? 173, also table of the four accounts in his *Notes on Mark*, p. 285. There is not the slightest difficulty in harmonizing the three other accounts with each other and with John's. They, for convenience, group together the three denials; John, who alone relates the examination before Annas, mentions them, as related to that and other events, in the order of time.

15. And Simon Peter followed Jesus, and so did another disciple ; literally, *And there followed Jesus Simon Peter and another disciple.* All forsook him and fled when he was arrested, but Peter and John recovered some courage, and soon followed to see what would become of their beloved Master. It is evident from John's statement that the two started in company. The other nine had not courage to follow at all, but had hidden themselves. John **was known to the high priest,** was an acquaintance of Annas, and therefore, being recognized as a friend by the servants, was allowed to enter. From his statement that he **went in with Jesus**—*i. e.* at the same time he did—he must have been close to the Saviour. From Mark 14 : 54 we learn that Peter "followed him afar off." John only adds that Peter was standing at the door without; his modesty prevents his comparing himself with Peter to the disadvantage of the latter; but from all the facts given it seems that Peter hung back, as they entered the city, while John kept near, and that Peter soon after ventured to come up and stand outside. Farrar thinks that the two came to the gate together, John being admitted as an acquaintance, while the portress refused admission to Peter as a stranger. **Palace of the high priest;** rather, *court of the high priest.* The court was an enclosed square, open to the sky, around which the house was built. It was entered by a street-door and through a passage or outer court. Through these and across the court Jesus was led into the apartment of Annas, doubtless on the first floor, and raised one step or more above the court. Compare Mark 14 : 66. The doors being open, John, and afterward Peter, standing in the court, would look in and observe what passed.

16. But Peter stood (rather, *was standing*) **at the door without.** He had come up to the street-door. **Then went out,** etc. John, knowing that Peter would soon come to the gate (or possibly having left him there), went out and found him there, and by speaking to the maid-servant **that kept the door,** and who knew John, he was enabled to bring in Peter. Peter put a bold face on it, and sat down by the fire (Luke 22 : 56) among the servants of the high priest and the officers. John made less show of bravery, and had more.

17. Then saith the damsel (rather, *maid-servant*) **that kept the door unto Peter.** She probably observed Peter carefully when she let him in, and afterward as he sat by the fire. Something about his appearance excited her suspicions. Then she thought she remembered having previously seen him with Jesus. She approaches him, looks sharply at him (Luke 22 : 56), and remarks to those around, "This man was also with him." She tells Peter so (Matt., Mark) and then asks him directly, **Art not thou also one of this man's disciples?** Some think that the word "also" refers to John, who was known to be a disciple of Jesus. The maid-servant speaks rather contemptuously of Jesus—only *this man!* She may have feared being blamed for admitting Peter. He seems to have been in no great danger, except as he might be recognized as the assailant of Malchus. But he has passed from the extreme of natural bravery and rashness to the other extreme of pusillanimous cowardice. His careless, confident manner is a mere **expedient of fear.**

JOHN XVIII. A. D. 30

18 am not. And the servants and officers stood there, who had made a fire of coals; for it was cold: and they warmed themselves: and Peter ⁿ stood with them, and warmed himself.   ᵃ Ps. 1. 1; Matt. 26. 41; 1 Cor. 15. 33.
19 The high priest then º asked Jesus of his disciples,   • Luke 11. 53, 54.

Taken by surprise, he answers the maid, **I am not.** From the other evangelists we learn that he not only denied, but assumed ignorance, and tried to pass himself off as a stranger and mere casual observer. Alas for poor fallen Peter!

18. **Servants and officers stood.** The servants of the high priest, and officers (temple-captains and their men,

EASTERN FIRE-PAN, WITH COALS.

or some of them). These were standing in the court. Some of them were of the party who had arrested Jesus, ver. 26. Having **made a fire of coals;** a charcoal fire, mineral coal being unknown. Perhaps the fire was in a pan used for the purpose. "The wealthy, however, use a brazier, or stand of brass or copper two feet in height, in the centre of whose upper surface is set a chafing-dish of like material, which contains the fire. This was, doubtless, the pan containing a 'fire of coals' at which Peter stood and warmed himself in the court of the high priest's house." —DR. VAN LENNEP, *Bible Lands,* p. 464. **It was cold,** as it well might be in April, at midnight or probably later, even in that climate. Fire was needed for comfort. "The nights at Jerusalem at that season of the year are cool, though the day may be warm. The air after sundown becomes chilly. . . . Coal (charcoal) is one of the articles of fuel which the inhabitants of Jerusalem burn at the present day."— DR. HACKETT, in *Smith's Dictionary,* art. "Coal." **Peter stood.** Uneasy at being questioned, he had arisen, yet was not prepared to abandon the assumed boldness with which he had mingled with the officers and servants, imagining that he could pass off for a stranger. LANGE: "An assumed boldness is a characteristic of fear." John seems to have adopted the more sensible plan of keeping himself more retired and quiet. Besides, he was protected by his acquaintance with the high priest.

19–23. EXAMINATION OF JESUS BY ANNAS. This important circumstance John only mentions. Characteristically, not only as writing a supplementary Gospel, but also because, if the eternal Son of God is to be condemned by his own people, it should be known that the legitimate high priest took a con

20 and of his doctrine. Jesus answered him, P I spake openly to the world; I ever taught in the synagogue, and in the temple, whither the Jews always resort; 21 and q in secret have I said nothing. Why askest thou me? Ask them which heard me, what I have said unto them: behold, they know what I said. 22 And when he had thus spoken, one of the officers which stood by r struck Jesus with the palm of his hand, saying, Answerest thou the high priest so?

p ch. 7. 14, 26, 28; 8. 2; 10. 23, etc.; Matt. 26. 55; Luke 4. 15.
q Matt. 10. 27.
r Isa. 50. 5, 6; Jer. 20. 2; Acts 23. 2.

---

trolling part in the proceedings, and because all that followed resulted from this.

19. **The high priest** (Annas, who was the legitimate high priest, exercised great authority and was greatly reverenced, though deposed) **asked Jesus of** (*concerning*) **his disciples, and of** (*concerning*) **his doctrine,** or *teaching,* evidently assuming in advance that Jesus was a dangerous and seditious man. Annas inquired as to the number and standing of his disciples, and as to the nature of the teaching by which he had attached them to himself. The crafty old inquisitor hoped by these general questions to draw out of the prisoner a statement which could be used against him, perhaps also against his disciples.

20. **I spake**—such has been my habit—**openly**—without secrecy or disguise—**to the world,** to the public. Jesus had delivered his instructions publicly to all who would listen. **In the synagogue**—*i. e.* wherever I found one. Jesus preached in the synagogues of many towns. **In the temple**—there was but the one temple, and it was the most public place in the nation—**whither the Jews always resort,** for worship and religious ceremonies, especially at the time of the great annual festivals, when all the men were required by the law to appear before Jehovah. Jesus took such opportunities for preaching, John 5: 1 ff.; 7: 14, 37, etc. His out-door teaching on the lake or mountain or in the fields was of the same public, open character. Hence he adds, **in secret have I said nothing;** nothing as a teacher or rabbi. Jesus was no conspirator, holding secret meetings and giving secret instructions. Even the things which he from time to time (and necessarily) said confidentially to the Twelve were not secret plottings, and, as Lange remarks, were destined for ultimate publicity, Matt. 10 : 27.

21. **Why askest thou me?** It was unjust and evinced a malicious purpose. An accused person has a right to be confronted with the charges against him and with witnesses from whom testimony should be taken. He should not himself be called on to answer questions in order to find ground or pretext of conviction. This is now a recognized principle observed in our courts. **Ask them which heard me, what I have said unto them.** More exactly, Bring forward as witnesses those who from time to time have heard my instructions as a public teacher. **Behold, they know what I said** when teaching. They are earwitnesses. It is implied that an impartial trial would triumphantly vindicate the character of Jesus, and that he recognized the *animus* of his enemies. Thus the cunning of the aged priest was foiled and his injustice exposed by a few words of simple truth and the manly demand for just proceedings. The language of Jesus was calm and respectful. Compare with Paul's heated manner, Acts 23 : 3, for which, however, he made a noble apology as far as he had spoken hastily, Acts 23 : 5. Jesus, the all-perfect, always speaking the right and wise word, had no occasion for apology.

22. **One of the officers,** doubtless the temple-officers who had aided in the arrest of Jesus. Some of these were warming themselves in the courtyard, ver. 18; others were in attendance on Annas and were guarding the prisoner. One of these **struck Jesus with the palm of his hand;** literally, *gave Jesus a blow,* or slap, *on the face,* smiting him in the mouth to indicate that he had spoken disrespect-

23 Jesus answered him, *If I have spoken evil, bear witness of the evil: but if well, why smitest thou me?
24 ᵇNow Annas had sent him bound unto Caiaphas the high priest.

*2 Cor. 10. 1; 1 Pet. 2. 20-23.
ᵇ Matt. 26. 57.

---

fully and to silence him. This seems to be the natural meaning. See Acts 23 : 2. Yet the expression may mean, *struck Jesus with a rod.* **Answerest thou the high priest so?** This taunting question accompanied and explained the blow. "The prohibition, Ex. 22 : 28, had been by the Jews extended into an ordinance instilling a bigoted veneration for superiors, and for the high priest especially."—LANGE. Probably the officer was enraged at the discomfiture of the high priest. The whole transaction confirms the view that the Jews regarded Annas, though deposed, as the real or lawful high priest.

23. The answer of Jesus shows his perfect presence of mind, serene dignity, and absence of passion, as also his clear sense of the indignity he had received, and readiness to assert his right. **Jesus answered him**, the officer who struck him, **If I have spoken evil,** in what I just said, **bear witness.** "Come forward as a witness against it. Accusing and testifying are here thy business; not so [is] judging, much less punishing before sentence is passed."—LANGE. **But if well, why smitest thou me?** A reprimand sharp and clear, but in perfect temper, of his unjust conduct, and indirectly of Annas for allowing such an outrage in a court of justice. "It has been often and well observed that our Lord here gives us the best interpretation of Matt. 5:39—that it does not exclude the remonstrance against unjust oppression, provided it be done calmly and patiently."—ALFORD.

24-27. PETER'S SECOND AND THIRD DENIALS, Jesus being before Caiaphas. The examination before Annas developed nothing which our Lord's enemies could use against him—rather the contrary; hence perhaps it is omitted by the other evangelists.

24. **Now Annas had sent him.** This unfortunate mistranslation originated probably in the desire to avoid a supposed discrepancy. Confounding the examination before Annas with that before Caiaphas, as related by Matthew, Mark, and Luke, this forced rendering was adopted to avoid contradiction. But so John's account is obscured, and a real difficulty is made where none existed. John alone narrates the examination before Annas, and then says, as it should be rendered, *Annas sent him*, probably across the courtyard, to the apartment of the actual high priest. An impressive warning against tampering with the true text or with a true translation to avoid apparent difficulties. **Bound.** Jesus had been unbound for examination. The attempt to treat him as a secret conspirator had signally failed. His enemies found that they would be obliged to make distinct charges and suborn false witnesses. He is therefore bound again by order of Annas, just as if the examination had confirmed the idea that he was a dangerous character, and is thus sent to Caiaphas. Note the flagrant injustice. John does not record the particulars of the preliminary examination before Caiaphas found in Matt. 26 : 57-66; Mark 14 : 53-65; Luke 22 : 54-65.

It was now past midnight. A formal trial before the Sanhedrim in the night was unlawful, nor could one be sentenced to death before daylight by Roman law. Caiaphas, however, assisted by leading members of the Sanhedrim, proceeded to examine Jesus on a charge of blasphemy. Perjured witnesses testified, but their statements were so discordant as to be worthless. (Did Joseph or Nicodemus cross-examine? They may not have been invited to this sitting.) Jesus maintained perfect silence even when questioned. The evidence being worthless, no defence was called for. Caiaphas by his conduct and words showed that it was utterly insufficient (Mark 14 : 60, 61); then as a last resort he called upon Jesus to answer under oath whether he was "the Christ, the Son of the Blessed," Ps. 2 : 7; Mark 14 : 61. The Saviour did not think it proper to refuse, when solemnly adjured, to affirm his divine Messiahship before the rulers of the chosen

A. D. 30. JOHN XVIII. 265

25 And Simon Peter ᵘ stood and warmed himself. ᵘ ver. 18.
ᵛ They said therefore unto him, Art not thou also *one* ᵛ Matt. 26. 69, 71;
of his disciples? ʷ He denied *it*, and said, I am not. Mark 14. 69.
Luke 22. 58.
ʷ Prov. 29. 25.

people to whom he had come. A truthful answer would furnish no just charge against him. He therefore not only declared himself the Christ, the Son of God, but added the startling words, "Ye shall see the Son of man sitting on the right hand of power and coming in the clouds of heaven." The high priest and his associates were goaded to madness by this bold and unexpected answer. They decided at once, without considering whether in this confession Jesus had spoken the truth, that no further testimony was needed, since, by claiming to be sharer in the power and glory of God and final Judge of all mankind, he had "spoken blasphemy." Thus Jesus declares *who he is*, and is blasphemously charged with blasphemy, and declared worthy of death for speaking the truth under oath.

The Jews expected a Messiah, and called him "the Son of God" or "Son of the Blessed." Why, then, could they consider the Saviour's claim as blasphemy? (1) Because they assumed that the claim was false. (2) They do not appear to have understood the full meaning of "Son of God." Hence, when the Saviour used it so as obviously to claim divinity for himself they considered him a blasphemer. See ch. 10: 33. Compare the questions and answers in Luke 22: 67-71, which refers, however, to the next stage of the trial— namely, before the Sanhedrim in formal session. The Jews neither understood the spiritual nature of Messiah's kingdom nor the full divine grandeur of his person; hence they accounted the claims of Jesus as blasphemous, and condemned him accordingly, 1 Cor. 2: 8. But their blindness was wilful and guilty beyond measure.

He was not as yet legally condemned. Meanwhile he was mocked, spit upon, and buffeted (smitten with the fist) by, it would seem, even his examiners; and the "servants" (officers) abused him. "The officers, with blows, took him in charge" (Mark 14: 65, *Bible Union version*, after best authorities) till he could be formally tried by the Sanhedrim. The "blows" were with their open hands, or perhaps with staves or rods. Thus insult was added to insult, Isa. 52: 14. They make his Messiahship the object of scorn and mockery, and treat him as a base pretender and outlaw, mingling their revilings with violence. The "patient Son of God" endured in silence.

25. PETER'S SECOND DENIAL, early during the examination before Caiaphas. **And Simon Peter stood and warmed himself.** We learn from Mark that, disturbed by the first questioning (by the maid who kept the door), Peter "went out into the porch," through which he had entered the court from the street, and that "a cock crew." It was then probably between twelve and one o'clock. Peter was not recalled to fidelity by the sign predicted by the Saviour. Perhaps in his anxiety and fear he did not at the moment heed its significance. He is now standing probably in the door from the court into the porch, with the blaze of the fire shining upon him. It is between one and two o'clock. **They said therefore unto him,** those about him noticing him narrowly, thus exposed to observation. The recent transfer of the prisoner from the apartment of Annas to that of Caiaphas would have excited attention. This may explain why Peter dared remain where he was. His policy was to act boldly the part of a curious stranger; besides, he was anxious to see what became of Jesus. **Art (omit not) thou also one of his disciples?** Several questions were asked by different persons at this time, all to the same effect —by a second maid (Matt. 26: 71), by the maid who kept the door (Mark 14: 69), by one of the men standing by (Luke 22: 58), and possibly by others. The different records of the four evangelists show how independent yet perfectly harmonious are their narratives. **He denied** (omit it), **and said, I am not.** He denied his discipleship. Matthew tells us that he also denied knowing Jesus, and that too with an oath, calling God to witness, and with

26 One of the servants of the high priest, being *his* kinsman whose ear Peter cut off, saith, Did not I see thee
27 in the garden with him? Peter then denied again: and ᶻ immediately the cock crew.

ˣ ch. 13. 38; Matt. 26. 74; Mark 14. 72; Luke 22. 60.
ʸ Matt. 27. 1, 2, 11–14; Mark 15. 1–5; Luke 23. 1–5; Acts 3. 13.

Jesus before Pilate, who pronounces him innocent and seeks to release him.

28 ʸ Then led they Jesus from Caiaphas unto ᵃ the hall

ᵃ Matt. 27. 27.

the somewhat contemptuous form, "I know not the man;" as if he had come from curiosity to learn the cause of this gathering without any interest in it, without possibly even knowing the name of the person on trial. This denial is thus a step in advance of the first. He was then taken by surprise, perhaps confused; now he has had time to reflect. This, therefore, is more deliberate. The number now questioning him doubtless excited him to falsehood, irritated him, and led to a cowardly denial and a rash, wicked, false oath. Profanity is no sign of bravery, yet his real danger seems to have been small.

26, 27. PETER'S THIRD DENIAL. Jesus still before Caiaphas. Mark tells us it was "a little after" the second—about one hour after, Luke 22 : 59. Peter was now probably again in the court, anxious about the examination, which was not yet over. It was between two and three o'clock. It appears from Mark that "they that stood by," having doubtless discussed the matter among themselves, and having noted his Galilean provincialisms and accent, conclude that the maid-servant is right. They therefore say to him, "Surely thou art one of them, for thou art a Galilean." Matthew says they add, "For thy speech bewrayeth (betrays) thee."

26. **One of the servants,** etc., a relative of Malchus. **Did not I see thee in the garden with him?** Doubtless this man was one of the arresting party. Thus is Peter hemmed in, more fully identified as a disciple of Jesus, and likely to be recognized as having resisted the process of law by force. John wrote this account probably after Peter's death. He suppresses nothing essential to his purpose, but brings out Peter's guilt much less strongly than Mark, who is supposed to have written his Gospel under Peter's own direction; and John alone relates the recognition by the relative of Malchus which terrified Peter and unnerved him most of all. This tenderness is very touching and suggestive. The full story was on record in the three other Gospels, and John passes over it as lightly as he can without mutilating the history.

27. **Peter then denied again.** John simply names the fact. See last remarks on vers. 26. We learn from Matthew and Mark that *he began to invoke curses* on himself if he told not the truth, *and to swear* in confirmation of the denial. In this lowest point of Peter's fall, terrified, confounded, shorn of all moral strength by previous failures, he broke out into profanity; perhaps an old, forsaken habit. Orientals use the name of God and appeal to him continually on the most trivial occasions. In his second denial he swore a single oath; now a volley, for he was beside himself with fear and anger. **And immediately the cock crew.** This was the second occurrence of the sign foretold by Jesus. It was about the opening of the morning watch, three o'clock. As Peter heard the sound he remembered and his heart smote him. At this point, also, the Lord, in the apartment of Caiaphas, perhaps while being mocked and abused (Mark 14 : 65), turned and looked out and upon Peter, Luke 22 : 61. The whole enormity of his conduct broke upon him; overwhelmed with shame, sorrow, and anguish, he "went out and wept bitterly." In spite of his great sin, Peter was a true Christian. Jesus had prayed for him that his strength fail not (Luke 22 : 32); and John 17 : 15), and had declared of his true disciples "they shall never perish," John 10 : 28. Hence Peter was speedily brought to unfeigned repentance, learning by his fall to know better both himself and his Saviour.

28–40. JESUS BEFORE PILATE, WHO

of judgment. ^a And it was early; ^b and they themselves went not into the judgment hall, lest they should be defiled; but that they might eat the passover.

^a Prov. 1. 16; 4. 16, Luke 22. 66.
^b Matt. 23. 23-28; Acts 10. 28; 11. 3.

PRONOUNCES HIM INNOCENT, AND SEEKS TO RELEASE HIM; THE JEWS PREFER BARABBAS. Matt. 27 : 1-26; Mark 15 : 1-15; Luke 22 : 66-71; 23 : 1-25. Here occurs one of the most remarkable omissions in John's account. He condenses the preliminary examination before Caiaphas and the formal trial and condemnation of Jesus by the Sanhedrim—events occupying several hours—into the two statements, *Annas sent him bound to Caiaphas* (ver. 24), and this in vers. 28, that *they led Jesus* to Pilate. But the discipleship were in possession of full accounts by the other evangelists. Besides, "with the fact of Annas sending the Lord bound to Caiaphas everything further . . . was decided."—LANGE. Concerning the formal session of the Sanhedrim after daylight, held, no doubt, in Caiaphas' apartments (see Matt. 27 : 1; Mark 15 : 1; Luke 22 : 66-71), Luke gives the full account. The examination at this session was the result of the previous informal examination. The questions asked were those which Jesus had then answered, and he answered them again. His statement that he was the Son of God awakened no violent demonstrations, being taken as a matter of course and a ground of condemnation. Hence they needed and examined no witnesses. They also consulted as to the best means of securing his death, and fixed upon two charges—viz. blasphemy and treason against the Roman emperor. It seems that the whole Sanhedrim went with their prisoner to Pilate. Joseph of Arimathea and Nicodemus (ch. 19 : 39 and Luke 23 : 50) alone, so far as we know, courageously dissented from the condemnation, and had no part in their evil counsels and accusations of the Lord before Pilate. Farrar suggests also the possible exception of Gamaliel. Compare Acts 5 : 34-39.

28. **Then led they Jesus** (bound, Matt. 27 : 2) **unto the hall of judgment;** rather, *into the governor's palace*. The governor's palace, or Prætorium, was on Mount Zion, in the western part of the city. The governors generally resided in Cæsarea, but came to Jerusalem during the great festivals to keep order and to exercise judicial functions. **It was early**—early in the day, not long after sunrise. In Syria business is done very early, not in the heat of the day. The appearance of the whole Sanhedrim with a bound prisoner at the earliest proper hour would impress the governor with the idea that Jesus was a great criminal. This important hour was the morning of Friday, the 15th Nisan, April 7th, in the year 783 from the founding of Rome. **They themselves went not into the** *palace*, but stood in front of it. This gave them a better opportunity of overawing the governor by the clamor of the multitude. They assigned, however—and perhaps in part sincerely—another reason—viz. **lest they should be defiled; but that they might eat the passover.** No law of God, but the glosses and additions of Jewish tradition, had taught that a Jew became ceremonially unclean by entering the house of a Gentile. Hence the Sanhedrim refused to go into the governor's palace to attend the trial in the "judgment hall." **Eat the passover.** Not eat the paschal supper, for that had been eaten the evening before; besides, the uncleanness they wished to avoid would have expired at sunset. The expression is a general one, and is equivalent to *observe the passover festival*, which lasted eight days. They did not wish to be ceremonially defiled, and so disqualified for its observance, during any part of it. On a misunderstanding of this and other passages some have imagined a discrepancy between John and the other evangelists concerning this last passover. Such eminent authorities as Robinson, Lightfoot, Luthardt, Lange, and Schaff declare that none exists. See *Author's Harmony*, pp. 295-301. This reason was, probably, in part sincere. Like many other formalists, they cared more for ceremonies than for justice and righteousness. Hence their scrupulousness on this point while carrying forward the judicial murder of the Son of God.

At this point Matthew relates the re-

29 Pilate then went out unto them, and said, ᵉ What
30 accusation bring ye against this man? They answered and said unto him, If he were not a malefactor, we would not have delivered him up unto
31 thee. Then said Pilate unto them, Take ye him, and judge him according to your law. The Jews therefore said unto him, ᵈ It is not lawful for us to

• Acts 25. 16.

ᵈ ch. 19. 15.

morse, confession, and suicide of Judas. Matt. 27 : 3–10; Acts 1 : 18–19.

29. **Pilate.** After Archelaus (Matt. 2 : 22) was deposed, Judæa and Samaria were annexed to the Roman province of Syria and governed by procurators, the sixth of whom was Pontius Pilate. He was appointed A. D. 25, and held his office ten years, during the reign of the emperor Tiberius. He was noted for his severity and cruelty, and by several massacres, to one of which Luke refers (Luke 13 : 1), he rendered himself odious to both Jews and Samaritans. At the time of the trial of Jesus, Pilate showed himself not incapable of feeling impulses of justice and mercy, but also revealed his character as " a selfish, unprincipled, worldly Roman politician, sceptical, or rather utterly indifferent to truth, cruel, weak, and mean; and so he sacrificed innocence itself to the fear of losing place and power."—SCHAFF. Pilate is called, in general terms, governor. This term belonged more properly to the rulers of provinces. The office of procurator pertained rather to the revenue, but sometimes extended to every department of government in a portion of a large province where the proconsul or legate (senatorial or imperial governor) of the province could not reside. Such was the case with Pilate, Felix, Festus. Hence Pilate could, with propriety, be called "governor." **Went out unto them,** conceding so much to their scruples. Foreign rulers were obliged to pay some regard to the religious customs of the Jews, to avoid exasperating them and producing a fierce explosion of dangerous fanaticism. The same thing is true in regard to Muslims at the East now. The Sepoy rebellion of India, it is said, arose from disregard of such a policy. **What accusation.** He had a right to inquire before passing judgment or allowing them to execute it. " Besides this, however, Pilate immediately observed, doubtless, that they came to him purposing by a pompous and boisterous procession to move him to confirm their sentence of death without more ado."—LANGE. He thwarts them at the start. **This man,** of whom Pilate must have heard, but whom, as yet, he regarded with supreme indifference

30. **Malefactor,** a criminal, one who has violated the laws by some grave offence. **Delivered.** The same word elsewhere translated " betrayed." As Judas betrayed or delivered up his Lord to the Jewish rulers, so they, the representatives of Israel, betrayed or delivered up their Messiah, whom God had given them according to his promise, into the hands of the heathen. They thus unconsciously uttered their own condemnation. Compare Acts 2 : 23. Their answer was intended to carry matters with a high hand. They demanded that the Roman governor should confirm the sentence of the Sanhedrim without re-examination. They hoped thus to compass the death of Jesus without the troublesome attempt to make good their accusations at a Roman seat of justice. If Pilate had yielded to this impudent demand, they would have stoned Jesus as a blasphemer, according to the law of Moses (Lev. 24 : 16), as they had unlawfully repeatedly attempted to do (8 : 59 ; 10 : 31), and as they actually did without legal right in the case of Stephen, Acts 7.

31. **Take ye him,** etc. A bitter sarcasm on their subjection to Roman power. Pilate knew that the Roman law demanded for one accused a fair trial before the Roman authorities. His answer amounts, then, to this: Since ye are such competent and independent judges, who will brook no review of your decisions, take him, condemn him under your law, and execute him if you dare! **It is not lawful,** etc. The Jews lost the power of executing a death-sentence when Archelaus was deposed, A. D. 6. The Sanhe-

A. D. 30. JOHN XVIII. 289

32 put any man to death: *that the saying of Jesus might be fulfilled, which he spake, signifying what death he should die.
33 ᶠThen Pilate entered into the judgment hall again, and called Jesus, and said unto him, ᵍArt thou the
34 King of the Jews? Jesus answered him, Sayest thou this thing of thyself, or did others tell it thee of me?

* ch. 12. 32, 33; Matt. 20. 19.
ᶠ Matt. 27. 11.
ᵍ ch. 1. 49; Matt. 2. 2.

drim were obliged either to abandon their full purpose or to take a lower tone and acknowledge their subjection —a thing ever exasperating and humiliating to them. They chose the latter. Pilate delighted to mock and harass them, as far as he could with safety to himself.

We learn from Luke 23 : 2 that they now accused Jesus of fomenting sedition among the people, of interfering with the tribute paid to Cæsar, and of treasonably giving himself out as Christ, a king,—all of which they knew to be false. The first charge had been met before Annas. As to the second, they knew that Jesus commanded to pay tribute to Cæsar, Matt. 22 : 15-22. As to the last, they knew that the Saviour's claim of Messianic royalty had no tendency to treason; he had himself refused a popular call to become a temporal king, John 6 : 15. Whatever they might fear in the future, they knew that Jesus had not as yet committed any act of treason. Note the depth of their infamy! Chafing under the hated dominion of Rome, they falsely accuse their own God-given Messiah, the King of Israel, the Son of David, of treason against the heathen conqueror! Yet this charge was cunningly chosen. On no other point would a Roman governor be so sensitive.

32. **That the saying of Jesus might be fulfilled,** etc. It was in the divine counsel that Jesus should be crucified. Jesus had repeatedly preannounced **what death he should die.** If the Jews had had the power of life and death, or if Pilate had yielded to their first demand, Jesus would have been stoned, not crucified. The cruel and shameful "death of the cross" was the severest form of capital punishment among the Romans. God so ordered matters that his own predestined counsel should stand. Nor does all this in the least interfere with human freedom or responsibility, Acts 2 : 23.

33. **Into the judgment hall;** rather, *into the palace*, the proper place for administering justice. Pilate wished to examine Jesus privately, therefore he **called** him into the palace, where he, as one accused, "stood before the governor," Matt. 27 : 11. Pilate, following out the accusation of the Jews, asks, **Art thou the King of the Jews?** This had a touch of sarcasm. Jesus, poor, plainly dressed, and bearing the marks of recent abuse, looked like anything but a king to the proud Roman. But Pilate wished to draw from Jesus what his pretensions might be, and why his countrymen so hated him. The governor could hardly have been utterly ignorant concerning Jesus. Some accounts of his great popularity and miracles must, it would seem, have reached the ears even of the scoffing pagan procurator. Compare Mark 15 : 10.

34. **Sayest thou this thing of thyself,**—Hast thou, as governor, any information that leads thee to suspect me of rebellion against the Roman authority?—**or did others tell it thee of me?** Dost thou simply base the question on the charge of the Sanhedrim, that I claim to be "Christ, a king"? This is substantially equivalent to inquiring in what sense the question is asked. Did Pilate use the phrase "King of the Jews" as a Roman would use it, in reference to common secular dominion or aspiration thereto, or as a Jew would use it, in reference to the Messianic hope of the nation, and the claim of Jesus that he was the promised One—"Christ, a king"? This claim of Messianic royalty did not interfere with submission to the authority of the Roman government, Matt. 22 : 20. Hence our Saviour's answering question was admirably adapted to expose the deception which the Sanhedrim were endeavoring to impose upon

35 Pilate answered, Am I a Jew? ᵇThine own nation and the chief priests have delivered thee unto me: 36 what hast thou done? ʲJesus answered, ᵏMy kingdom is not of this world: if my kingdom were of this world, then would my servants fight, that I should not be delivered to the Jews: but now is my kingdom not from hence. Pilate therefore said unto him, 37 Art thou a king then? Jesus answered, ˡThou sayest that I am a king. ᵐTo this end was I born, and for this cause came I into the world, that I should bear

ᵇ ch. 1. 11; Acts 3. 13.
ʲ 1 Tim. 6. 13.
ᵏ ch. 6. 15; 8 15; Dan. 2. 44; 7. 14; Luke 12. 14; 17. 20, 21; Rom. 14. 17; Col. 1. 13.
ˡ Matt. 26. 64; 27. 11.
ᵐ ch. 3. 11, 12; 8. 14; 14. 6; 1 Tim. 6. 13; Rev. 1. 5.

the governor in order to secure the death of Jesus.

35. **Am I a Jew?** Pilate asks this question in scorn and indignation. He despised the Messianic hopes of the Jews and their claim to be the people of God as fanatical superstition; it was impossible that he should speak or think as a Jew. **Thine own nation and the chief priests have delivered thee unto me.** Here Pilate disclaims any ground of suspicion or complaint against Jesus except the accusation of the Sanhedrim. He had framed his question in accordance with that, but not with the views of a Jew. Then he bluntly puts the question, in true Roman style, **what hast thou done?**—anything to justify such hatred and such accusations?

36. Instead of directly answering Pilate's last question, Jesus pursues the idea suggested by his question in verse 34. Tacitly acknowledging that he is a king, and thus virtually answering the first question of Pilate in ver. 33 in the affirmative, he proceeds to define the nature of his kingdom—first negatively: **My kingdom is not of this world**, not a political, secular, temporal kingdom. It is not within the sphere of the world, which is fallen and carnal. The Jews generally expected their Messiah to be a religio-political king, mingling the spiritual and the temporal, and subduing the whole earth by military or supernatural power. But Jesus had never given any countenance to these crude ideas; on the contrary, he had discouraged them. Disavowing everything political and secular as to the nature of his kingdom, Jesus would show Pilate that his claim of royal dignity could not be treason against Cæsar. **If . . . then would my servants fight.** Earthly kings and pretenders rely upon force. But Jesus had forbidden his disciples to defend him by force from arrest by the Jews. This circumstance conclusively showed the unworldly and spiritual nature of his kingdom, and it was an argument which Pilate could not but feel. **But now (as it is) is my kingdom not from hence.** It is not worldly, political, secular in its origin; of course the same is true of its aims and methods. There is no need of collision with secular government. Compare Matt. 26 : 52, and remarks on it under verse 11 of this chapter.

37. To Pilate, of course, all this was strange and new. He seems to have been puzzled, and to have begun to feel the influence of that wonderful personality. Hence the question, **Art thou a king then?** betokening, perhaps, a mingling of scorn, awe, and curiosity in Pilate's mind. **Thou sayest that I am a king** (see Matt. 27 : 11; Mark 15 : 2; Luke 23 : 3); rather, *Thou sayest it, because I am a king*—that is, "It is as thou sayest;" an affirmative assent, "for indeed I am a king," though not in an earthly, political sense. Compare Matt. 26 : 25. There may be a hint, also, that this kinghood is real, notwithstanding the lowly appearance of Jesus, which seems to have inclined Pilate at first to make sport of his claims. Jesus then proceeds to give the positive statement of the nature of his kingdom. The negative is in ver. 36. But how could this religious and spiritual conception be even suggested to the dark mind of a proud, worldly, sensual, and sceptical Roman? The Lord, with divine skill, seizes upon the only avenue of approach. Greek and Roman philosophers had speculated much concerning *truth*, moral and re

witness unto the truth. Every one that ⁿis of the ᵃch. 8. 47; 10. 26,
38 truth heareth my voice. Pilate saith unto him, What 27; 1 John 3. 19; 4. 6.
is truth? ᵒch. 19. 4, 6; Isa.
And when he had said this, he went out again unto 53. 9; Matt. 27.
the Jews, and saith unto them, ᵒI find in him no fault 18, 19, 24; Luke 23. 4.
39 *at all.* ᵖBut ye have a custom, that I should release ᵖMatt. 27. 15–17;
Mark 15. 6–9; Luke 23. 17–19.

ligious. The idea was not wholly foreign to this civilized and educated pagan. **To this end was I born, and for this cause came I into the world,** etc.; that is, I have been born and have come into the world in order to bear witness to the truth. **Born.** Christ was born for this purpose; it was the divinely-appointed mission of his life, or a great part of it. This alone would not prove him more than a man, but he adds **came I into the world,** thus distinctly involving his pre-existence. He had come from another state of being **into** this by a supernatural birth, in order to bear witness to the truth. Thus the great fact of the incarnation is affirmed and presented in the manner most likely to be received. **Bear witness.** Jesus did not come to teach human wisdom or discover truth or reason about it. He was a witness, declaring with authority what he knew, Rev. 3 : 14; ch. 14 : 10; ch. 3 : 31–36—the truth concerning God and man, sin and salvation and human destiny—the highest truth, all that mankind is supremely concerned to know, and which men could learn only by a "teacher sent from God." **Every one that is of the truth,** every one who loves it and is in moral harmony with it. A partial revelation had been made by the Son, through the prophets, before his incarnation. Whoever had received this, in the love of it, would recognize the great Teacher, ch. 7 : 17; ch. 8 : 47. So would any devout Gentile, though before without the light of revelation, if any such had existed; we have no reason to suppose this was the case. **Heareth my voice;** recognizes and accepts me and my teaching, ch. 10 : 26, 27. And so, as to Pilate, if he had really cared for truth, he would have attended to the words of Jesus and found the truth.

In this wonderful conversation, which demands the most exhaustive study, recorded only by John, Jesus accomplishes these three things : (1) He makes his own innocence clear to the governor. Pilate perceives that Jesus has no political aspirations. Notice, that when a fair hearing would be had Jesus was ready to defend himself from false charges. He was silent only when justice was turned into a mockery. (2) He brings out in a strong light the true nature of his kingdom for the benefit of all men in all time. (3) He opens the door of salvation to Pilate. If Pilate had been candid and earnest, he would have sincerely inquired further. It was probably the crisis of his fate.

38. **What is truth?** If this question had been asked with a desire to obtain the true answer, Jesus would undoubtedly have instructed Pilate in the doctrine taught in ch. 17 : 3 and 1 John 5 : 19, 20. But the fact that **when he had said this, he went out,** waiting for no answer, shows that the question was asked in a flippant and sceptical spirit, and that no answer was desired. "It expresses, not without scoff and irony, that truth can never be found, and is an apt representative of the state of the polite Gentile mind at the time of the Lord's coming." It expresses the contemptuous scepticism of one who believes in nothing. **Unto the Jews,** who were waiting in the court, **I find in him no fault.** (Omit **at all,** not in the original, which only weakens.) This was the just and emphatic decision of the governor. He probably regarded Jesus as a harmless visionary, with some undefined misgivings that he might be something more. These, however, he suppressed, but declares the result of his examination—no fault in Jesus.

39, 40. Just here John omits several events not necessary to his special picture of Christ before Pilate. When Pilate came forth to announce the innocence of Jesus he brought the prisoner with him or quickly sent for him. The Jews accused him of many things, but to Pilate's surprise he answered nothing. Their malignant charges

unto you one at the passover: will ye therefore that
40 I release unto you the King of the Jews? ⁋ Then
cried they all again, saying, Not this man, but Barabbas. ʳ Now Barabbas was a robber.

⁋ Matt. 27. 16-21;
Acts 3. 14.
ʳ Luke 23. 19.

---

were unworthy of an answer. He had stated the facts concerning his kingdom to Pilate, and had nothing more to add. It was the governor's plain duty to release him, but he hesitates. At this time, partly to evade responsibility and partly to conciliate Herod, Pilate sends Jesus to him. The Saviour there maintained perfect silence, both when questioned and when mocked—the second time of abuse. Herod probably had no lawful jurisdiction in his case, nor did he care for justice, Matt. 27 : 12-14; Mark 15 : 3-5; Luke 23 : 4-12. When Herod had sent Jesus back to Pilate, the latter called together the Jewish rulers again in the open space before the palace, a crowd gathering with them. Pilate, stating that neither Herod nor himself had found any fault in the prisoner, proposed to "chastise and release him," Luke 23 : 13-17. A singular way to treat an innocent man! But Pilate hoped this indignity would satisfy the rage of his enemies. It here comes plainly to light that Pilate, though despising the Jews and liking to thwart them, was afraid of them. They might complain of him to the emperor, and by this means endanger the loss of his place, or worse. Besides, his corrupt and cruel administration would not bear investigation. His self-interest, therefore, prevented him from doing simple justice, while he shrank from the monstrous crime of condemning an innocent man to death. He therefore stooped to reason with and strive to pacify the rulers and populace—conduct inexpressibly base in a judge.

39. **Jesus before Pilate the second time. But ye have a custom.** The origin of this practice is unknown. The custom was probably established by the Romans—possibly by Pilate himself—to conciliate the Jews, since persons would often be in prison whom the Jews would desire to liberate from the Roman law. **Will ye ... the King of the Jews?** Matthew states that he said, "Barabbas or Jesus, who is called Christ." Combining the two gives the whole. Pilate knew that the rulers had delivered Jesus to him "for envy" (Mark 15 : 10), on account of his popularity with the multitude, and because they regarded him as a formidable rival. He had heard, no doubt, of Jesus' late triumphant entry into the city. He hoped that the multitude would demand the release of their favorite, especially when contrasted with a vile criminal. Another wretched expedient, and one that defeated itself, though Pilate appealed to what he considered a popular superstition by calling Jesus "King of the Jews." But the friends of Jesus, through fear, were not in the crowd, and the fickle populace, who had cried "Hosanna!" one day, are diligently wrought upon by the rulers (Mark 15 : 11) to call for Barabbas.

40. **Then cried they all again;** loud cries were again heard, this time not accusing him, but **saying, Not this man, but Barabbas.** We learn from Matthew that Pilate, made more anxious by a message from his wife, repeated the appeal. The rulers and the populace made the same answer. "What will ye then that I shall do with him whom ye call King of the Jews?" The answer comes, instigated by the priests and scribes, "Crucify him!" "Why, what evil hath he done?" persists Pilate. The mob, increasing in violence, respond by loud cries of "Crucify him!" Here Pilate, seeming to yield, but hoping to produce a reaction, washes his hands, and renounces, though vainly, responsibility for this judicial murder. And the dreadful reply is made, "His blood be on us and on our children" Having gone so far, Pilate is obliged to release Barabbas to them, and he sends Jesus, as if condemned, to be scourged, but not without the intention to save him from the cross if he can without endangering himself. By this time we see just what Pilate is. Knowing the right, but lacking the courage to do it, by every concession and artifice he en-

tangles himself more and more, till he is pushed into the murder of the Prince of Life. **Now Barabbas was a robber.** Luke informs us that "for a certain sedition made in the city and for murder [he] was cast into prison." Thus the Jewish rulers and people, wickedly rejecting their Messiah, were led to choose formally a plundering rioter and murderous rebel in place of the holy Jesus. If Barabbas had not escaped thus, he would undoubtedly have been crucified. The guilt of the persecutors of Jesus appears of the deepest dye—wilful, against light, almost devilish. The calm manner of John is worthy of special notice. No remarks on the wickedness of either Pilate or the Jews, no coloring or expressions of a just indignation, even like Luke's (23 : 25) temperate statement. John gives a colorless narrative of facts. This manner, in general, characterizes all the biblical writers of history, and is a strong sign of their perfect trustworthiness.

The parallels to verses 39, 40 are Matt. 27 : 15-26; Mark 15 : 6-15; Luke 23 : 13-25. These evangelists omit Pilate's futile effort to save Jesus after his scourging. They speak of Jesus as scourged and then crucified. When Pilate yielded in seeming, he had really yielded for good.

PRACTICAL REMARKS.

1. One traitor can effect more evil than many open enemies, ver. 2; Matt. 26 : 5; Ps. 41 : 9; Prov. 27 : 6. And it is a remarkable thing that here came Jews and Gentiles led by an apostle of Christ. All classes of the world and traitors in the church unite to assail or betray the Saviour's cause, 2 Tim. 4 : 10; Heb. 6 : 6; 1 Cor. 11 : 27; Gal. 1 : 7 and 5 : 12; Matt. 13 : 41.
2. How awful is the goodness and the presence of God with his servants! vers. 4-6; Deut. 32 : 30; 1 Kings 18 : 17-20; 21 : 20-29; Acts 4 : 21.
3. The sufferings and death of Christ were voluntary on his part, vers. 4-6; Matt. 26 : 53; John 10 : 18; 19 : 11.
4. Christ ever watches over his own. In that care those who are "in him" may repose. Both soul and body are safe in his hands, ver. 9; ch. 17 : 12; Ps. 23; 2 Tim. 1 : 12; 4 : 8, 17, 18.
5. Prayer made Jesus ready for "the cross." So by it we may attain to submission to the will of God, ver. 11; Matt. 26 : 39; 2 Cor. 12 : 8, 9.
6. Religious leaders and hierarchs are often the deadliest enemies of Christ and of his truth, vers. 13, 14. Witness the persecutions instigated by the Romish and Anglican clergies!
7. Those who boast beforehand of their strength generally fail in trial, vers. 15-18, 25-27; Mark 14 : 29-31; 1 Cor. 10 : 12; Prov. 16 : 18.
8. A soul unprepared is apt to fall into rashness, ver. 10.
9. A soul unprepared is apt to pass from rashness to cowardice, vers. 15-18, 25-27.
10. Only God's help can prepare us for peril and temptation, vers. 25-27; 1 Cor. 10 : 13.
11. The inconsistent Christian must expect to be recognized and put to shame by the worldly, vers. 17, 26.
12. Sin is progressive. Beware of the very first step, vers. 15-18, 25-27; James 1 : 15.
13. A true Christian may fall, but not perish, because God will bring him back, vers. 25-27; ch. 10 : 27-30; Luke 22 : 31, 32.
14. Peter's humble sincerity, as shown in the full statement of his sin by Mark, who wrote under his direction and by his authority, should teach us that open sin should be as openly acknowledged, without attempt to extenuate or apologize, Job 31 : 33; Prov. 28 : 13.
15. John's tender reticence concerning Peter's sin should teach us not to dwell upon or unnecessarily detail a brother's fault, beyond what duty may absolutely require, vers. 15-18, 25-27; 1 Cor. 13 : 6.
16. Formalists and fanatics, committing the greatest crimes, are often scrupulous in minor matters or human traditions, ver. 28; Matt. 23 : 13-33.
17. God forsakes to judicial blindness those who long reject his truth, ver. 28; 2 Thess. 2 : 11, 12; 1 Kings 22; Ex. 9 : 12, etc.
18. When men reject Christ, they are forced to choose instead some unworthy object, really Satan, ver. 40.
19. The death of Christ was eternally foreordained of God, even the manner of it, ver. 32; Luke 24 : 44; Acts 2 : 23; 1 Pet. 1 : 11, 20; Heb. 13 : 20.

Jesus scourged and mocked; Pilate seeks again to release him, but finally delivers him to be crucified.

XIX. THEN *ᵃ Pilate therefore took Jesus, and scourged 2 him. And the soldiers platted a crown of thorns, and

ᵃ Matt. 27. 26–30;
Mark 15. 15–19;
Matt. 20. 19;
Luke 18. 33.

20. The wicked act with perfect freedom and are justly responsible, even though unintentionally they fulfil the divine purpose, ver. 32; Acts 4 : 25–28.
21. Jesus was ever ready to "seek to save" in the most skilful way all whom he met, vers. 36, 37; ch. 4.
22. Coming in close contact with Christ is the crisis of a man's fate, vers. 33–37.
23. Christ taught with authority. He came out of the invisible world from the Father. It is the part of wisdom implicitly to receive his testimony, ver. 37; Matt. 7 : 29; 17 : 5.
24. Perfect candor and love of truth are essential to discipleship, ver. 37 : Acts 17 : 11.
25. One of the worst possible frames of mind is a scornful, indifferent, and supercilious materialism and scepticism. This marks many scientific men to-day, and their followers. It is as fatal to true philosophy as to religion, ver. 38 ; 2 Pet. 3 : 3–7 ; Rom. 1 : 22.
26. Jesus taught, as Baptists now do, that his kingdom is purely spiritual. This, our great fundamental principle, carries with it reliance on spiritual, not on carnal means, separation of church and state, a regenerate church membership, and similar truths, ver. 36; 1 Pet. 2 : 1–10 ; Eph. 4 : 4–6; Acts 2 : 47; 2 Cor. 10 : 4; John 1 : 13.
27. "Conscience does make cowards of us all." Pilate's oppressions and maladministration made him the more afraid of the Jews. Wickedness is weakness, ver. 39; Prov. 28 : 1.
28. If any one means to do justice at all, let him stand squarely from the first, and "dare to do right, dare to be true." All compromise or evasion is likely to end in surrender and shame, vers. 38–40; Matt. 6 : 24.
29. Jesus was absolutely innocent, ver. 38 ; ch. 8 : 46.
30. Wicked men often utter great truths unintentionally, as Caiaphas in ch. 11 : 49, 50, Pilate in ver. 39.
31. The conduct of Jesus during his **trial** is worthy of profound study. It **teaches** valuable lessons.

CHAPTER XIX.

This chapter continues the account of the sufferings and death of Christ. See note at the beginning of chapter 18.
1–16. JESUS SCOURGED AND MOCKED. PILATE AGAIN SEEKS TO RELEASE HIM, BUT FINALLY DELIVERS HIM UP TO BE CRUCIFIED. Most of this (except the scourging) is particularly narrated by John only.
1. **Scourged.** The Roman mode is meant, much severer than the Jewish. The number of the stripes was not limited to forty, as it was by the Mosaic law, Deut. 25 : 3. "The body was stripped, tied in a stooping posture to a low block or pillar, and the bare back lacerated by an unlimited number of lashes with rods or twisted thongs of leather, so that the poor sufferer sometimes fainted or died on the spot."—SCHAFF. Roman citizens could not be thus tortured — only foreigners and slaves, whose lives were held worthless. The object was either to extort confession or to suitably "prepare" the victim for crucifixion, according to the cruel method of dealing with criminals then in vogue. It is dreadful to think of our Lord as undergoing such an infliction!
Pilate seemed to be proceeding in the manner usual when persons were to be crucified, but he secretly hoped that this scourging, so terribly severe, would satiate the rage of the Jews, or else that it would so degrade Jesus in the eyes of the rulers that they would no longer fear and "envy" him. He was still inwardly resolved not to crucify him, if he could avoid it without incurring the dangerous ill-will of the Jews. Jesus was undoubtedly scourged by soldiers whom Pilate appointed for the purpose. It took place outside of the palace, in sight of the people, and was a fulfilment of prophecy, Isa. 50 : 6; 53 : 5.
2, 3. JESUS MOCKED BY THE ROMAN SOLDIERS, Matt. 27 : 27–30 ; Mark 15 : 16–19. This was the third time our Lord had been subjected to abuse and

A. D. 30.   JOHN XIX.   295

put *it* on his head, and they put on him a purple
3 robe, and said, Hail, King of the Jews! and they
smote him with their hands.
4 · Pilate therefore went forth again, and saith unto

mockery: first, by certain elders and officers after the hearing before Caiaphas, Matt. 26 : 67, 68; Mark 14 : 65; Luke 22 : 63-65; second, by Herod and his body-guard, Luke 23 : 11, 12; third, by the soldiers who had just scourged him. These took Jesus into the court of the palace and gathered together the whole cohort, Mark 15 : 16.
2. **Platted,** wove; **crown of thorns,** to imitate the crowns and triumphal wreaths of emperors, kings, and conquerors. The principal object was mockery; a secondary one to give pain. Both ends were well subserved by a rudely-wrought crown made of so mean and common a plant as the thorn. What species of thorn was used is not known. Tradition says the *Spina Christi*. It may have been some other. Thorns and thorny shrubs abound in Palestine. The thorns would lacerate the head of Jesus. This crown may possibly have remained on his head during the crucifixion, since Matthew and Mark relate the removal of the purple robe, but not of the crown of thorns. **A purple robe,** having first "stripped him" of his outer garment, Matt. 27 : 28. Matthew calls it a "scarlet robe." These colors intermingled, and their names in popular language were often interchanged, so that there is here no discrepancy. Purple-red was the color worn by the Roman emperors. It was doubtless a Roman officer's crimson military cloak which the soldiers took; perhaps an old and cast-off garment. Matthew further says that they put "a reed in his right hand" as a mock sceptre.
3. **And said;** read, according to the highest critical authorities, *And they came to him and said.* The soldiers (compare Matt. and Mark) drew near to Jesus as if in solemn procession, bowing the knee as if to a king. **Hail, King of the Jews!** A salute as to a king, like "Long live the king!" A mocking allusion to his royal claim and to the accusation of the Jews, uttered in bitter contempt. **And they smote him with their hands.** Properly, *gave him blows on the face.* See ch. 18 : 22. Also they struck him over the head with the reed, which his fettered hand perhaps could not hold, and they spat upon him, Matt. and Mark. The pain of the blows with the reed would be increased by the presence of the sharp thorns. Thus their mockery was turned into the grossest insult and violence. This treatment was not required by the law. It was the lawless sport (compare Acts 2 : 23, which should read "crucifying him by the hands of lawless ones") of a coarse and brutal soldiery, who knew little of Jesus except what they had heard from the Jews, and who doubtless regarded him as a rebel or religious fanatic. "The low, vile soldiery of the Prætorium—not Romans, but mostly the mere mercenary scum and dregs of the provinces—led him, etc. . . . It added keenness to their enjoyment to have in their power one who was of Jewish birth, of innocent life, of noblest bearing. The opportunity broke so agreeably the coarse monotony of their lives that they summoned all of the cohort who were disengaged to witness their brutal sport. In sight of these hardened ruffians they went through the whole heartless ceremony of a mock coronation, a mock investiture, a mock homage."—FARRAR. It added to the horror of this scene that Jesus was fresh from the scourge and covered with stripes and blood. The silent patience of the Son of God was wonderful. He bore all meekly, submissively, without a word, Isa. 53 : 7.
4-16. JESUS BEFORE PILATE FOR THE LAST TIME. Six times was our Saviour tried and examined—before Annas, before Caiaphas, before the Sanhedrim in formal session, before Pilate, before Herod, being returned to Pilate, and now before Pilate for the third and last time. The first (before Annas) and this last are narrated only by John. The other evangelists omit the last, perhaps because the death of Jesus was already assured by the cowardly yielding of Pilate to the Jews. But it is too im-

them, Behold, I bring him forth to you, 'that ye may
5 know that I find no fault in him. Then came Jesus
forth, wearing the crown of thorns, and the purple
robe. And *Pilate* saith unto them, Behold the man!
6 ⁿ When the chief priests therefore and officers saw
him, they cried out, saying, ˣ Crucify *him*, crucify
him. Pilate saith unto them, ʸ Take ye him, and
7 crucify *him:* for I find no fault in him. The Jews

ᵗ ver. 6; ch. 18. 38
Heb. 7. 26.

ⁿ Acts 3. 13.

ˣ ver. 15.

ʸ ch. 18. 31.

portant, as bearing on the divinity of Christ and the conduct of the Jews, to be altogether omitted. John naturally supplies "the missing link."

4. **Pilate went forth again,** after the scourging and mocking of Jesus, to the Jews outside. **Behold, I bring him forth to you.** A formal statement. Pilate will bring Jesus out from the Prætorium, or palace, where he has been mocked. **That ye may know that I find no fault in him.** This was the object of "bringing him forth." "The Jews not possessing the right of capital punishment, the return of the person of Jesus to them was a declaration that he was free from the offence with which they charged him." — LANGE. Pilate, moreover, had bethought him of a new expedient. He will assume that the scourging was not preparatory to crucifixion, but by way of examination; and nothing has been extorted from the sufferer. Pilate therefore judicially and unconditionally declares Jesus innocent. Why does he not at last do his plain duty and release him? Through selfish fear. But he is anxious to do so, and will, if he dare. This solemn declaration of the innocence of Jesus by such a governor is important. Also the trial becomes now rather a trial of Pilate than of Jesus. The prisoner is acquitted. Will the judge perpetrate a judicial murder?

5. **Then came Jesus forth,**—*i. e.* at the command of Pilate—**wearing the crown of thorns, and the purple robe,** bleeding and lacerated by the scourging, fresh from mockery, insult, and violence, an object of pity to any humane eye, yet calm in majestic silence and patience. Pilate hoped that the sight would awaken contempt or compassion, or both, and that the Jews would consent to his release. **Behold the man!** See him for yourselves—an object not for wrath or envy, but for pity! Take him from me and release him. He is innocent and harmless. Pilate seems himself to have felt an emotion of pity; but his words, like many other words and acts concerning Christ, have a significance far beyond the intention. "Behold the man!" Truly, Jesus is the most wonderful being ever seen by mortal eyes or spoken of in human history!

6. **Chief priests** are specially named as leaders in the conspiracy against Jesus. They were the heads of the twenty-four courses into which the priesthood was divided. **Officers**—that is, of the temple, who acted under their influence. Compare ch. 18 : 3. **Saw him.** No pity in their malignant hearts. They were only inflamed with greater rage, and filled with fear lest their plot should fail. **They cried out,** the chief priests, etc. But the populace, excited by their arts, doubtless joined. **Crucify him,** or simply, *Crucify, crucify.* This fearful cry had been uttered before, at the time of the choice of Barabbas, Mark 15 : 13. Now it swells as the frenzied demand of an Oriental mob. **Take ye him, and crucify him.** Pilate is enraged at this inhuman and infamous demand that he shall basely crucify an innocent man; hence he adds, **for I find no fault in him.** If they wish Jesus crucified, they must do it themselves. Pilate, baffled and angry, mocks the Jews in this reply, for he well knew that they had lost the power to inflict capital punishment. Yet Pilate is contemplating the selfish necessity of doing that the demand for which enrages and disgusts him. Notice this renewed solemn testimony of Pilate to the innocence of Jesus, and the mingled scorn and fear with which he regarded the Jews.

7. Pilate having repeatedly declared Jesus innocent of the political charge, the Jews fear the prisoner's release; but the governor's hesitation to act on his own judgment of right emboldens them

A. D. 30. JOHN XIX. 297

answered him, *We have a law, and by our law he ought to die, because ᵃ he made himself the Son of God.
8 When Pilate therefore heard that saying, he was
9 the more afraid; and went again into the judgment hall and saith unto Jesus, Whence art thou? ᵇ But
10 Jesus gave him no answer. Then saith Pilate unto

* Lev. 24. 16.
ᵃ ch. 5. 13; 10. 30–33; Matt. 26. 65.

ᵇ Isa. 53. 7; Matt. 27. 12, 14.

now to bring forward the religious accusation on which Jesus had been condemned by the Sanhedrim. **We have a law,** the law of Moses, which their foreign rulers were often obliged by policy to respect. The Roman government, indeed, protected the Jewish worship. **By our law he ought to die.** This statement was true to this extent—namely, that by the law a blasphemer must die; also a false prophet, Lev. 24 : 16; Deut. 18 : 20. And Jesus had been condemned by the Sanhedrim as a blasphemer. It was false, in that the Innocent One had been falsely, illegally, and wickedly convicted. They oppose it to Pilate's declaration of the innocence of Jesus. "*You* may find no fault with him politically, but *we* know that he is guilty by our law of a capital crime. We are judges on that point, and demand that our sentence be carried out." **Because he made himself,** assumed and claimed to be, **the Son of God.** See Luke 22 : 70, 71. Their words imply that his claim was false. If this had been the case, the sentence of the Sanhedrim would have been just. But, being a true claim, their sentence was blasphemous, and made them guilty of the murder of God's Son. It is noteworthy that God so ordered events that Jesus should not be condemned on any side-issue, but solely on the ground of his claim to the Messiahship and to the divine nature—convicted on his own true confession of his nature and mission. Thus the rejection and crucifixion of Jesus result from the deliberate and blasphemous act of the rulers of Israel, and without the possibility of imputing any fault to him. And Pilate is forced to sentence him unjustly, with the full consciousness of it. **The Son of God;** not merely the Messiah, but the eternal Son, "the only-begotten and well-beloved Son," and hence a partaker in the divine nature and attributes, ch. 5 : 17–23;

ch. 10 : 30, 36; ch. 14 : 9, 10, 23. Believing Jesus to be the Son of God in any other sense is not the faith required in the gospel.
8. **The more afraid.** Already Pilate had been filled with fear and horror of the great crime of condemning Jesus to death—a very unusual scrupulousness on his part. On his callous heart the bearing and words of Jesus and the warning of his wife had made a deep impression. Hence the effect of the words of the Jews was opposite to what they intended. In the Roman and Greek mythology "immortal gods" were represented as having human sons. Pilate in times of quietness may have had little belief in any religion, but now his soul was haunted by fears, superstitious in the form they assumed, yet having, after all, a solid ground. What if Jehovah, God of the Jews, were a real divinity, and this remarkable person his Son, as Hercules was said to be the son of Jupiter? If Pilate should condemn him unjustly, would not celestial vengeance come upon him?
9. Pilate, disturbed by this new fear, **went again into the** *palace*, summoning Jesus to another private examination. **Whence art thou?** What is thy lineage and origin? Framed, too, no doubt, in remembrance of the words of Jesus, ch. 18 : 37. **No answer.** Pilate needed no more facts in order to know what justice required. The present examination was suggested by selfish fears. Jesus will not answer, but leaves the governor to do justice or injustice as he pleases. Yet, comparing it with 18 : 37, this very silence seems a renewed testimony to his superhuman origin.
10. **Speakest thou not unto me?** *Unto me* is emphatic. **Knowest thou not,** etc. According to the best authorities, **crucify thee** and **release thee** should exchange places. Pilate is irritated by the silence of

13 *

him, Speakest thou not unto me? Knowest thou not that I have power to crucify thee, and have
11 power to release thee? Jesus answered, ᵃThou couldest have no power *at all* against me, except it were given thee from above: therefore he that delivered me unto thee hath the greater sin.
12 And from thenceforth Pilate sought to release him. But the Jews cried out, saying, ᵈ If thou let this man

ᵃ ch. 7. 30; 1 Chron. 29. 11, 12; Jer. 27. 5; Matt. 26. 53; Luke 22. 53 Rom. 13. 1.

ᵈ Luke 23. 2.

Jesus, and appeals to the motive of fear. He boasts of his power, while he is a slave by reason of conscious guilt and moral cowardice.

11. **Thou couldest** (rather, *wouldst*) **have no power** (omit **at all**, a weakening addition of the translators) **against me,** to do me harm, **except it were given thee from above**—that is, from God. Christ does not say *from my Father;* he uses a general term more intelligible to a heathen. The power of the civil magistrate is from God (Rom. 13 : 1-5), and should be exercised in his fear. Power for evil, as well as for good, is a gift from God. Pilate had these powers only by gift of divine Providence. **He that delivered,** a general expression equivalent to *those who deliver.* Specifically, the Sanhedrim. **Hath the greater sin,** greater than thine, as the principal is guiltier than the accomplice; the malicious act blacker than the cowardly; the Jew instructed in God's word and heir of the promises of Messiah infinitely more sinful, in the murder of the Promised One, than the heathen Roman governor. **Therefore** seems to point to the fact that the privileges and powers of all were "given," and the more given the more required. "Thou art indeed committing a great crime; but Judas, Annas, Caiaphas, these priests and Jews, are more to blame than thou. Thus with infinite dignity, and yet with infinite tenderness, did Jesus judge his judge." —FARRAR.

12. **Thenceforth,** properly, *therefore, upon this.* "In the very depths of his inmost soul Pilate felt the truth of the words."—FARRAR. This saying "cast a bright, accidental light upon his obscure, fateful, perilous situation, that for an instant marked the path of duty as the path of deliverance."—LANGE. Shrinking from the great guilt of condemning the wonderful prisoner, and tortured with a dreadful fear of celestial vengeance, he then anew **sought to release him**—not releasing him, as duty demanded, but attempting to do it without danger to himself. It is probable that he came out to the Jews, and by some word or act seemed to them to be upon the point of releasing the prisoner. **But the Jews,** a term used in John's Gospel to denote the official representatives of the nation, who, with two or three exceptions, appear to have been united in rejecting Christ and conspiring against him, **cried out.** It was probably some of the chief priests who raised this furious outcry. The mob, perhaps, re-echoed it. Oriental mobs were, and are, fierce and terrible. When excited the Jewish populace did not hesitate to break forth in insult, or even violence. **If thou let this man go,** release Jesus, **thou art not Cæsar's friend.** The title "friend of Cæsar" was bestowed on prefects, legates, and allies. It may have been conferred on Pilate. Thus was the speech of the Jews moulded into this form, but the main idea is simply, *loyal to Cæsar.* **Whosoever maketh himself a king**—that is, lays claim to royalty—**speaketh** (or *declareth*) **against Cæsar,** derogates from his majesty, is a traitor. The Jews and Pilate well knew that Jesus was not a political offender. Pilate had repeatedly declared him innocent. But the imperial government was very jealous of its supremacy, and an accusation of disloyalty was full of peril. The emperor himself, Tiberius, was a sensual and jealous tyrant, old, diseased, and malignant. He had just been made more suspicious and revengeful by the discovery of the "falsity and treason of his only friend and minister, Sejanus; and it was to Sejanus himself that Pilate is said to have owed his position." This cry, then, really meant, If you do not condemn this innocent

go, thou art not Cæsar's friend; *whosoever maketh himself a king speaketh against Cæsar. *When Pi-
13 late therefore heard that saying, he brought Jesus forth, and sat down in the judgment seat in a place that is called the Pavement, but in the Hebrew, Gab-
14 batha. And *it was the preparation of the passover, and about the sixth hour. And he saith unto the

*Luke 23. 2; Acts 17. 7.
*Prov. 29. 25.

*Matt. 27. 62· Mark 15. 42.

man, you will expose yourself to be denounced as a traitor to the emperor; with the implied threat that the Jews would so complain of him. Before the vision of loss of place and favor, and perhaps punishment for treason, Pilate was completely cowed. Earthly fear overcame the fear of celestial vengeance.

13. **When Pilate therefore heard that saying** (rather, according to the approved text, *these words*), moved by this threat and yielding utterly his manhood and conscience, **he brought Jesus forth,** from the palace where he had just left him, **and sat down in** (properly *on*), **the judgment seat,** an elevated, movable seat, probably placed upon a floor of tessellated work. Such a "pavement" Julius Cæsar carried about with him. Upon this he seated himself to give formal sentence. The judgment-seat was placed in the open air, to accommodate the Jews (ch. 18 : 28), **in a place called the Pavement.** Why "pavement" we do not know, unless the reference be to the "pavement" on which Pilate's judgment-seat was placed. **In Hebrew, Gabbatha.** The etymology of this word is uncertain; probably it means *ridge* or *hump*—*i. e.* an elevated spot of ground. It was close to the palace. By Hebrew is meant the vernacular Aramaic or Aramæan, a dialect composed of a mixture of Hebrew, Chaldaic, Syriac, etc. *Gabbatha* does not mean "pavement." The name was given from some other cause.

14. **Preparation of the passover.** *Passover* here means the whole paschal festival. *Preparation* means the day before the Jewish Sabbath, Friday, the day on which men should prepare for the day of rest. "Preparation of the passover," then, simply means the Friday which occurred during the passover week, something as a Catholic or Anglican speaks of Easter-Friday, the Friday of the (so-called) Easter festival. This is a most important mark of time; it fixes the day of our Lord's crucifixion as Friday, 15th Nisan, the first day of the passover festival. It shows that Jesus and his disciples "ate the passover" at the right time, the evening of 14th Nisan. And it shows that John's account agrees with that of the other evangelists. See *Author's Harmony of the Gospels,* note on ⸹ 159. **And about the sixth hour.** Thus John definitely marks not only the day, but, approximately, the time of day. Mark says (15 : 25) *It was the third hour* of the day, nine o'clock in the morning, when they arrived at Golgotha and fastened Jesus to the cross. The discrepancy can be explained by supposing that some early transcriber mistook the sign for three for that for six, the two resembling each other. Indeed, some MSS. of John read *third hour,* but none of the oldest and best. This supposition, therefore, is hazardous. Or, that the time of crucifixion was somewhere between the two broad divisions, the third and sixth hours, Mark designating by the beginning, John by the ending, of the period. The ancients were not as precise in regard to exact time as we are. John says *about.* Or John may have used the Roman mode of reckoning, from midnight to midnight. He had long resided beyond the bounds of Palestine when he wrote his Gospel. His readers were largely Gentiles, and the Jews were no longer a nation. To use the Jewish mode of reckoning might have misled his readers. Josephus, the Jewish historian, in his autobiography uses the Roman method. *About the sixth hour* may here mean that it was between six and seven o'clock when Jesus stood before Pilate at Gabbatha. This agrees with the fact that "it was early" (ch. 18 : 28) when the Jewish rulers led away Jesus to the governor, Matt. 27 : 1. Thus the time in John is when the trial is in progress—in Mark, when the sentence was put into execution. The

Jews, Behold your King! But they cried out, Away
15 with *him!* Away with *him!* crucify him. Pilate
saith unto them, Shall I crucify your King? The
chief priests answered, ʰ We have no king but Cæsar.   ʰ Gen. 49. 10.
16 Then delivered he him therefore unto them to be
crucified.

---

intervening time could easily have been occupied with the close of the trial, the preparation for crucifixion, and the going forth to Golgotha. Not only at this time, but on other occasions, does John appear to use the Roman reckoning. Thus, concerning his own first interview with Jesus, he says "it was about the tenth hour"—*i. e.* ten o'clock A. M., ch. 1 : 39. It was not a late and hurried visit, but one extending through the day, for the two disciples "abode with him that day." So also in ch. 4 : 6, 52. Compare *Author's Harmony*, note on § 181. **And he saith unto the Jews,** Pilate, as he thus sat on the judgment-seat, Jesus standing before him, **Behold your King!** Farrar thinks this was said "as with a flash of genuine conviction." It sounds rather like the outbreak of passion combined with weakness. Pilate dared not to release Jesus, lest he should be accused before Cæsar, but he could safely mock the Jews. He knew that their pretended regard for Cæsar's authority was transparent hypocrisy. They would gladly throw off the yoke if they could. He seems to have vented the bitterness of his spirit in this taunt: Here is your King, this man insulted, scourged, and about to be crucified! 15. **Away with him! Away with him!** A furious outcry of hate, in which the mob joined heartily with the members of the Sanhedrim. It was called forth by the taunt, "Behold your King!" "To the Jews it sounded like shameful scorn to call that beaten, insulted sufferer their king."—FARRAR. **Crucify him.** They renew the demand with loud voices and riotous demonstrations as before, Matt. 27 : 24. **Shall I crucify your King?** This question marks the last moment of hesitation on Pilate's part, and in it he gave expression to the bitter anger he felt at being compelled by his selfish fears to commit an outrage from which even his callous heart shrank, angry with the Jews, with the circumstances, and probably with himself, but too great a moral coward to do right. **We have no king but Cæsar.** Goaded to madness, the rulers and people of Israel renounce Messianic hopes and promises and acknowledge the hated heathen tyrant as their lawful king. Their degradation could not well go further. God ordered it so that in denying his Son they should renounce all hope of the kingdom of David. They declared themselves unworthy of it by word and deed. Yet this loyalty was a mere pretence, intended to shame and terrify Pilate, for they all hated Cæsar and his rule, and some of them afterward perished miserably in rebellion against the emperor. Thus malice, impiety, and hypocrisy were united in these wicked men, especially in the leaders. 16. **Then delivered he him therefore unto them**—*i. e.* to their will. It is not meant that Pilate delivered him into the custody of the Sanhedrim for crucifixion, which would have been unlawful; besides, we know that Pilate directed the details of the crucifixion. The meaning is simply that he sentenced Jesus to death according to their will, so that at one and the same time the Jews wickedly delivered up their Messiah "to the Gentiles to be put to death," and Pilate, in despite of his conscience, basely delivered up Jesus to the Jews—*i. e.* to the fate they demanded. It is proper here to note the fate of the murderers of Jesus. Judas died by his own hand. Pilate was soon recalled, degraded, banished to Gaul, where he committed suicide. The tower from which he is said to have precipitated himself is still standing. Herod died in infamy and exile; Caiaphas was deposed the next year. "The house of Annas was destroyed a generation later by an infuriated mob, and his son was dragged through the streets and scourged and beaten to his place of murder." — FARRAR. Some of the

A. D. 30. JOHN XIX. 301

The crucifixion.

17 And they took Jesus, and led *him* away. ¹And he, bearing his cross, ᵏ went forth into a place called *The*

Matt. 27. 31-33
Mark 15. 20-22
Luke 23. 26, 33.

ᵏ Lev. 16. 21, 22; 24. 14; Num. 15. 35, 36; 1 Kings 21. 13; Acts 7. 58; Heb. 13. 11-13.

wicked rulers and raging populace who that day cried "Crucify him!" and thousands of their children, shared in the unparalleled horrors of the destruction of Jerusalem. "They had forced the Romans to crucify their Christ, and . . . they and their children were themselves crucified in myriads by the Romans outside their own walls."—FARRAR. Surely in vain did Pilate wash his hands! And from that day to this has been fulfilled the horrible imprecation of the Jews—"His blood be on us and on our children." **To be crucified.** Pilate sentenced an innocent man to this dreadful death knowingly, through selfishness and cowardice. The final order was probably in words like these: "I, miles, expedi crucem"— *i. e.* "Go, soldier, make ready the cross."

Crucifixion was the severest and most ignominious punishment among the ancients. To a proud Roman the cross was a symbol of infamy, and crucifixion an unspeakable disgrace. The cross was generally first driven into the ground, and then the criminal was lifted up and fastened to it by nails through the hands and feet, the latter being separate or united and from one to two feet above the ground. Sometimes the victim was first fastened to the cross, and then it was sunk into its place with a sudden shock, causing horrible torture. Whether a single nail was driven through the feet of Jesus or each was nailed separately cannot be determined; but they were nailed, not tied, Luke 24 : 39. See HACKETT'S *Smith's Dict. of the Bible*, art. "Crucifixion." In order that the hands might not be torn away, a large wooden pin was commonly inserted in the upright timber, passing between the legs, to support the weight of the body. The unnatural position and tension of the body, the laceration of the hands and feet, which are full of nerves and tendons, and the resulting inflammation; the pressure of the blood to the head and stomach, causing severe pain, terrible anxiety, and thirst burning and raging,—all these, with no vital part wounded, made crucifixion a most lingering and excruciating death. Sometimes the wretched victim would hang three days before death came to his relief. The unusual quickness of death in our Saviour's case can be accounted for by remembering his previous exhausting agonies, wearisome trials and insults, and deep mental anguish on the cross. Crucifixion was abolished by Constantine, the first Christian emperor.

There were several forms of the cross. The one used for the crucifixion of our Saviour was the form preserved by tradition and familiar to us—viz. †. This is certain from the fact that a written title was affixed to the cross over his head, which would be impossible with the other forms—viz. T and X.

16-30. THE CRUCIFIXION AND DEATH OF JESUS. John's account is brief and comprehensive, but supplies important particulars not in the other Gospels. The day of the crucifixion was Friday, 15th Nisan, the first day of the passover festival. The hour was about nine o'clock A. M. Parallels, Matt. 27 : 31-56; Mark 15 : 20-41; Luke 23 : 26-49.

16. **And they took Jesus**—the centurion and his men—**and led him away,** from the palace. Matt. 27 : 27, 31. The last clause, however, is now generally regarded as an interpolation.

17. **And he, bearing his cross,** having been stripped of the military robe and invested with his own garments, Matt. 27 : 31, etc. It was usual for the condemned to bear his own cross. The general custom was not to alleviate, but to increase, the sufferings of capital punishment. Thus, Jesus carried the rough and heavy symbol of his present pain and ignominy, of his future glory and victory, and of our salvation. **Went forth,** on foot, out of the city, Heb. 13 : 12. The traditional route, by the street of Jerusalem called Via Dolorosa, is

26

place of a skull, which is called in the Hebrew, Gol-
18 gotha; ¹where they crucified him, and two others
with him, on either side one, and Jesus in the midst.
19 ᵐAnd Pilate wrote a title, and put *it* on the cross.
And the writing was, JESUS OF NAZARETH THE KING

¹ Matt. 27. 35-38
Mark 15. 24-28
Luke 23. 33, 34, 38.
ᵐ Matt. 27. 37;
Mark 15. 26;
Luke 23. 38.

not authenticated. The sad procession was followed by a great crowd, including many women, who bewailed and lamented him, Luke 23 : 27-31. We learn from Matthew that just at the city-gate, meeting Simon of Cyrene, the centurion impressed him to bear the cross, from which it is inferred either that Jesus fainted under the burden or gave evidence of inability to go on unaided. He was exhausted by suffering and loss of blood. Simon probably aided him in bearing the cross. Compare Luke 23 : 26.
Place of a skull ... Golgotha. "Golgotha" is Hebrew (Aramæan) for *place of a skull.* "Calvary" in Luke should be *a skull.* Some suppose that it was so called from the skulls of criminals executed there. This is not well supported. More probably because it was a slight knoll, rounded and skull-like, but not a hill. *"Mount* Calvary" is a pure invention. Tradition places it north-west of the temple, where the church of the Sepulchre now stands; but this is impossible, since Golgotha was without the gate. Its sight must probably remain undetermined, and it is perhaps better so. Identification of the spot would serve no important spiritual ends, and would probably minister to superstition. J. L. Porter, in *Alexander's Kitto's Cyclopædia,* thinks it was just outside the gate now called St. Stephen's, in the eastern wall Dr. J. P. Newman would place it near the north-east corner of the city-wall, in a place desolate and secluded. More probably it was at the grotto of Jeremiah, north of Jerusalem, near the Damascus gate. Compare Jer. 31 : 39. On reaching the place of execution "wine mingled with myrrh" was offered to him, according to a usage not Roman, but Jewish. Probably there were other drugs in it. The object was to stupefy and deaden the pain. Compare Prov. 31 : 6. But he refused to drink, since he would retain perfect consciousness and all his powers unimpaired to the end, and so finish perfectly his atoning sacrifice. It might be allowable for others, but not for the Lamb of God "for sinners slain."
18. **Where they crucified him.** Nailed him to the cross, either before or after its erection, thus unconsciously fulfilling prophecy, Ps. 22 : 16. They had previously stripped him of his clothes. It was probably just as this dreadful process was completed that he uttered his *first dying word*—a prayer for his murderers: "FATHER, FORGIVE THEM ; FOR THEY KNOW NOT WHAT THEY DO," Luke 23 : 34. **Two others with him.** Robbers ("thieves" is a mistranslation), very likely companions of Barabbas, who suffered justly (Luke). They were Jews. **Jesus in the midst,** as if he were the greatest criminal of the three. This would gratify his enemies and fulfil the Scriptures, Isa. 53 : 12. This was Pilate's own arrangement. See next verse.
19. **Pilate** *also* (this is the proper rendering) **wrote.** In addition to commanding what is recorded in verse 18 he *also* wrote, very likely with his own hand, **a title,** or inscription. It was customary to publish in some way the crime for which a person was crucified. Sometimes a public crier announced it; sometimes it was written on a tablet and hung about the neck of the criminal as he was led to execution; and very commonly, as here, it was inscribed on a white tablet and affixed to the cross above the criminal's head, Luke 23 : 38. **And the writing was,** JESUS THE NAZARENE (better than *of Nazareth*) THE KING OF THE JEWS. Mark gives it "The King of the Jews;" Luke, "This is the King of the Jews;" Matthew, "This is Jesus, the King of the Jews." The difference may be explained : (1) Some or even all the evangelists may have given the sense instead of the exact words ; exact words were not so important to the Oriental mind as to the European, provided the meaning be truthfully given, or (2), as the title was written in three languages, the expression, and so a

20 OF THE JEWS. This title then read many of the Jews: for the place where Jesus was crucified was nigh to the city: and it was written in Hebrew, and
21 Greek, and Latin. Then said the chief priests of the Jews to Pilate, Write not, The King of the Jews; but
22 that he said, I am King of the Jews. Pilate answered, What I have written, I have written.
23 ᵃ Then the soldiers, when they had crucified Jesus, took his garments, and made four parts, to every

ᵃ Matt. 27. 35; Mark 15. 24; Luke 23. 34.

translation of it, would be likely to vary. Latin was the official language of the empire; Greek the language of culture and of international communication, and very common in Palestine; Hebrew—i. e. Aramæan—the vernacular language of the Jews. It is likely that John's version of the inscription, containing the contemptuous phrase "the Nazarene," was the one in "Hebrew." Pilate purposely wrote this sarcastic title, purporting that the Jews were crucifying their king and that he was a Nazarene. His object was to revenge himself on the Jews, but he wrote more wisely than he knew.

20. Jews, members of the Sanhedrim, according to John's general usage, or perhaps including the populace, since they had identified themselves with the hostile rulers. Nigh to the city, not very far from the wall. A great crowd collected to gaze. Many, both of the populace and of the rulers, brutally and shamefully insulted and derided the patient sufferer, Matt. 27 : 39–43; Mark 15:29–32; Luke 23:35–37. Hebrew, and Greek, and Latin. See remarks under the last verse. It is a pleasant fancy, if no more, which sees in this a coincidence reminding us of the universal value and import of Christ's atoning death.

21. The chief priests, perceiving the implication and vexed exceedingly, applied to Pilate to change the title into he said, I am King of the Jews— i. e. his offence is being a traitor and rebel against Cæsar. It was intolerable that it should remain as written. Their king, hanging between two robbers, the inscription legible to all!

22. What I have written, I have written. Pilate had written the title in bitter scorn and anger, and was delighted to "revenge himself on his detested subjects," who had forced him, as it were, to violate his own wishes and sense of right, "by an act of public insolence." He was not unwilling also to honor Jesus after a fashion. He had ordered the manner of his crucifixion, not from a wish to disgrace him, but to mortify the Jews. "Pilate's courage, which had oozed away so rapidly at the name of Cæsar, had now revived. He was glad in any and every way to browbeat and thwart the men whose seditious clamor had forced him in the morning" to condemn Jesus. "Without deigning any justification of what he had done, Pilate summarily dismissed these solemn hierarchs with [this] curt and contemptuous reply." But it was the spite and poor revenge of a man who would "browbeat" when he dared, yet would yield all manhood to craven fear. (The quotations on this verse are from Farrar.) The Jews were forced to content themselves with this insult and mortification.

23. The soldiers. To prevent any possible rescue and ensure the completion of the execution, a quaternion (band of four) of Roman soldiers, under command of the centurion in charge, were left upon the ground. No doubt a large guard attended the prisoner to Golgotha and remained till he was crucified. Then the four, who probably did the actual work of crucifixion, kept watch while their comrades were relieved. These four soldiers doubtless sat down upon the ground, close to the crosses, and passed the time in drinking and gambling. We learn from Luke (23 : 36, 37) that they joined in mocking Jesus, also tantalizing his thirst, already aggravated by the continual sight of their jar of wine, by offering or pretending to offer him of their drink. Took his garments, outer garments. The garments of the crucified were the perquisites of the soldiers having charge of the execution. It is possible, though not cer-

soldier a part; and also *his* coat: now the coat was
24 without seam, ᵒ woven from the top throughout. They   ᵒ Ex. 39. 22, 23.
said therefore among themselves, Let us not rend it,
but cast lots for it, whose it shall be: that the Scripture might be fulfilled, which saith, ᵖ They parted my   ᵖ Ps. 22. 18.
raiment among them, and for my vesture they did
cast lots. These things therefore the soldiers did.

tain, that a linen cloth was bound about the Saviour's loins. His clothes they divided into four parts, one for each, probably ripping to pieces his mantle or outer garment. The cloth was of some value even in pieces. **Coat,** properly *tunic,* a garment worn next the skin like a shirt, commonly without sleeves, usually reaching to the knees. **Without seam,** etc. Altogether woven in one piece, not sewed at all. Torn to pieces, it would have been of no value. The Saviour's garments were undoubtedly simple and plain, such, perhaps, as were commonly worn in Galilee. But this tunic seems to have been an attractive piece of workmanship. It was probably an offering of love to the Great Teacher from some believing woman.

24. **Cast lots.** Deciding matters not easily determined otherwise by the lot was very common in ancient times. It is occasionally practised among us, as when men draw lots for a longer or shorter term of office. The soldiers agreed not to spoil the tunic by tearing it, but to decide by lot **whose it shall be: that the Scripture might be fulfilled.** This cardinal necessity is often recognized by the Saviour and the apostles. Yet it is not simply that God must bring these things to pass because he has caused them to be predicted, though, indeed, his veracity is unchangeable and his word sure, but rather thus: These things form a part of his eternal counsel. They are foreordained for the best of reasons. They had been foreshadowed in ancient prophecy, because God condescended in many cases dimly to indicate his purposes. As the counsel of God they must come to pass, and the Scripture must be fulfilled because it announced things eternally purposed by him. **They parted my raiment,** etc. Quoted from Ps. 22 : 18, *Septuagint Version.* In this psalm David doubtless had some reference to his own experience, but even if he speaks of himself, yet he was a type of Christ; and what is said of the type is more perfectly true of the antitype, and was so intended by the Holy Spirit. It would thus be a typical prophecy. This is not the dogma of an arbitrary "double sense," which is an absurdity, but a rational and necessary principle of interpretation, applicable to many quotations from the Old Testament in the New, and justified by many analogies and obvious instances. We must hold fast to the idea of a true prophecy, even if we should concede that here it has the typical form. Compare note on Matt. 1 : 23. **These things therefore.** Therefore—*i. e.* because they were embraced in the divine plan. Here, as often, this was done by the voluntary acts of free agents, who knew nothing of the will of God and cared nothing for it. **The soldiers did.** These words emphasize the minute and wonderful fulfilment of the ancient prophecy by heathen soldiers who knew nothing of the Scriptures, but their actions fulfilled them as perfectly as if their sole object had been to carry out the divine decrees. Thus God's purposes are always accomplished, and what he has predicted is always made good.

Not very long after this one of the robbers who was crucified with Jesus, exercising sublime faith, recognizing the Lord Messiah in the sufferer by his side, uttered the prayer, "Lord, remember me when thou comest in thy kingdom!" It is not credible that the same man an hour before reviled the Lord, as did his fellow. It is better to understand Matthew and Mark as speaking in general terms concerning the insults endured by our Lord, and Luke as giving us the full particulars concerning the two robbers. To him Jesus, silent through all pain and mockery, instantly replied (*the second dying saying*), VERILY, I SAY UNTO

25 ⁋ Now there stood by the cross of Jesus his mother, and his mother's sister, Mary the *wife* of ʳ Cleophas,
26 and ˢ Mary Magdalene. When Jesus therefore saw his mother, and ᵗ the disciple standing by, whom he loved, he saith unto his mother, ᵘ Woman, behold thy son! Then saith he to the disciple, Behold thy
27 mother! And from that hour that disciple took her ˣ unto his own *home*.

ᑫ Matt. 27. 55; Mark 15. 40; Luke 23. 49.
ʳ Luke 24. 18.
ˢ Mark 16. 9.
ᵗ ch. 13. 23; 20. 2; 21. 7, 20, 24.
ᵘ ch. 2. 4.

ˣ ch. 1. 11; 16. 32.

THEE, TO-DAY SHALT THOU BE WITH ME IN PARADISE, Luke 23 : 43.

25. **There stood**; better, *were standing*. At first, probably, they were unable to get near, on account of the tumult, but after a time, greater quiet prevailing, they ventured to approach, and were standing, in faithful love, **by the cross of Jesus**. Afterward all but the mother of Jesus are found looking on, again at a distance, Matt. 27 : 55, 56; Mark 15 : 40, 41. **His mother.** Here she finds fulfilled the prediction recorded in Luke 2 : 35. **His mother's sister, Mary the wife of Cleophas** (*Clopas*). Some suppose these words to describe one person, but it is exceedingly improbable that Mary had a sister named also Mary, and equally so that John should omit to mention his own mother, who was one of these faithful women (Matt., Mark). Probably the punctuation is wrong, and John means to name four women — viz. Mary and her sister (Salome, mother of John, thus modestly introduced; then John was first cousin of Jesus), Mary, the wife of Clopas, and Mary the Magdalene. **Magdalene,** not a proper name, but a female inhabitant of Magdala. Mary the Magdalene had been a demoniac of the worst kind (Luke 8 : 2), and her love to her deliverer was stronger than fear or death itself.

26. **When . . . therefore**—*i. e.* in view of the facts in the case, especially the fact that John and Mary were now standing near the cross. **The disciple . . . whom he loved.** John's favorite designation of himself in this his Gospel. He, too, was now faithfully watching by his Master's cross. It seems he was the only apostle courageous and self-possessed enough to do so. **Woman, behold thy son!** indicating John by a glance. The use of *woman* as a term of address was respectful, though it might not be with us. As on a former occasion (ch. 2 : 4; compare Matt. 12 : 50), so now, the Saviour seems thus to indicate that Mary, though his own dear mother according to the flesh, was but a woman— one who, like all his other disciples, was dependent upon him for the pardon of sin and for eternal life, and that this relation was of much greater importance than any mere earthly one. Nothing could be more irreconcilable with Romish Mariolatry. Besides, woman is an honorable title.

27. **Behold thy mother!** addressed to John, who, of course, understood the Saviour's meaning. Here we have the *third dying saying:* WOMAN, BEHOLD THY SON! and BEHOLD THY MOTHER! Jesus was about to die, then to rise and ascend to the Father. He could no more act the part of a son, but, a tender son to the last, he commits his beloved mother to the dearest friend he had upon earth. If it be asked why this was necessary when Jesus had "brothers," in all probability children of Joseph and Mary, the answer seems to lie in the fact that they did not yet believe in him, John 7 : 5. The only man living at all fit to take the place of Jesus as a son and to care for the sorrowful mother was the beloved disciple. By this, however, no filial obligation on the part of her children was annulled. We are not in full possession of all the facts, but the above view seems to be the natural conclusion from all that we do know. Evidently, Joseph was now dead and Mary a widow. This incident, related by John alone, is exceedingly beautiful and touching, and the trust reposed in John was a precious token of his Lord's confidence and affection. **And from that hour,** at once, with no delay—to be understood literally. Jesus probably perceived that the scene was too dreadful for his mother longer to endure, and spoke at

28 ⁷ After this, Jesus ᶻ knowing that all things were now accomplished, ᵃ that the Scripture might be fulfilled, saith, I thirst. Now there was set a vessel full
29 of vinegar: and ᵇ they filled a sponge with vinegar, and put it upon ᶜ hyssop, and put it to his mouth.

ᶜ Ex. 12. 22; Num. 19. 18.

⁷ Matt. 27. 45–50; Mark 15. 33–37; Luke 23. 46.
ᶻ ch. 13. 1.
ᵃ Ps. 22. 15; 69. 21.
ᵇ Matt. 27. 34, 48.

---

the moment he did in order to spare her anguish too great to be borne. It was probably past eleven o'clock, and the Saviour had been hanging on the cross two hours or more. **Unto his own home,** in Jerusalem, no doubt. It is not certain that he owned a house in the city, but at this time he had a home there. Thither he led Mary, and she probably was henceforth a member of his family. John appears to have held greater relations with the city than his brethren. Compare ch. 18 : 15. The idea that the apostles were indigent men, almost paupers, is not sustained by the New Testament. After conducting Mary to his home John returned, for we find him with his Master at the end.

28. **After this,** what is related in vers. 25–27. But John omits much that is recorded by the other evangelists. At about noon a supernatural darkness covered the land, a visible token of God's displeasure at the crime of crimes, and an outward symbol of the soul-darkness in which the Saviour was whelmed. This alarming phenomenon apparently filled all with awe and dread, and put an end to all mockery. It lasted about three hours. During this time Jesus, so far as we know, uttered not a word. He was enduring the hidings of his Father's countenance and bearing our sins in his own body on the tree. Into the mysterious agonies of those hours no mind on earth is permitted to penetrate, but here was the very crisis of the work of redemption by which alone human salvation is made possible. At the close of this period, as the darkness rolls away from the land and from his soul, Jesus cries aloud (*the fourth dying saying*), MY GOD, MY GOD, WHY HAST THOU FORSAKEN ME? Matt. 27 : 46; Mark 15 : 34. **Jesus knowing . . . accomplished,** knowing that he had completed all that was appointed for him to do and suffer for human salvation, except the mere fact of dying—perceiving that the end had come, **that the Scripture might be fulfilled.** Some connect this with the preceding clause, but its more natural connection seems to be with what follows. It is not meant that Jesus cried "I thirst" just for the sake of fulfilling Scripture, but that this cry, extorted by sore need, was a divinely-ordered fulfilment. The passage referred to is Ps. 69 : 21. Compare Ps. 22 : 15. On this impressive phrase, and on these typical prophecies in the Psalms as referred to in the New Testament, see note on verse 24. It seems impossible to regard Ps. 69 as directly and exclusively Messianic, as Ps. 16, *e. g.*, appears to be, on account of verse 5. **I thirst.** The crucified were tormented by a fevered thirst, burning and intolerable, similar to that of men lying wounded on the field of battle. This thirst was so great that it forced from the lips of Jesus his only word concerning his physical sufferings—his *fifth dying saying:* I THIRST. He could hardly die in composure unless this intolerable thirst could be assuaged. He was no stoic—did not teach us stoicism.

29. **A vessel;** some think a jar from which the soldiers had been drinking or dipping out to drink; others, that it was placed there to supply the want of the sufferers. **Vinegar** (rather, *sour wine*), the cheap, sour, inferior wine in common use by the lower classes. **Full.** It would seem that it had been once emptied, and that the soldiers had just replenished it. **They.** By comparing Matthew and Mark it appears that certain bystanders misunderstood his former cry, mistaking "Eloi" (My God) for "Elia" (Elijah). Wrought up to dread expectancy by the darkness, they imagined he was calling for Elijah, so prominent in all Jewish ideas of Messianic times. As one, perhaps a soldier, prepared to relieve the sufferer, some in their excitement cried out to forbear and see if Elijah would come and take him down from

30 When Jesus therefore had received the vinegar, he said, ᵈ It is finished: ᵉ and he bowed his head, and gave up the ghost.

ᵈ ver. 28; ch. 4. 3; 17. 4; Isa. 53. 12; Col. 2. 14, 15; Heb. 9. 11-14, 22

28; 10. 1-14.   ᵉ Matt. 27. 50.

the cross. But he replied that they should let him alone, and for the same purpose—desiring to prolong the life of Jesus, so as to see if Elijah would come. The word *they* may indicate that more than one participated in this act of mercy, or may in general terms declare that this proceeded from a group of several persons, one or more favoring, others remonstrating, as we have seen. A **sponge**, used probably to close the mouth of the jar. **Filled,** saturated by being dipped in the wine and put upon **hyssop**; rather, a *hyssop-stalk*, which was from one to two feet long. Thus could they conveniently convey the wine to the parched lips of Jesus. This fact shows that persons crucified were elevated to no such height above the earth as pictures and popular imagination represent; the mouth was only a little beyond a man's reach.

30. **Received the vinegar,** *the sour wine.* He had at the first refused the stupefying draught of drugged wine, nor did he receive the sour wine afterward tendered to him in mockery; perhaps it was not really offered to him. But now he accepts the few swallows absorbed by the sponge, the inferior beverage, all that the world had to offer her King to quench his dying thirst, Ps. 69 : 21. But the relief was sorely needed and welcome; besides, his sinking energies were probably thus sustained for a moment, enabling him to utter the last words: **It is finished.** These few words are of unutterable significance. Jesus glances, as the dying do, back over his whole life. He sees all his work perfectly done, every temptation resisted, the atonement completed. It only remained to breathe out his life. It was a cry of unspeakable joy to him and to us. The doctrinal and practical importance of these words is infinite. The Saviour perfectly finished his redemptive work. By it he (1) removed every obstacle to the salvation of man which lay in the holiness and government of God, satisfying at once the sense of justice in God and in man, Rom. 3 : 24-26; 1 John 2 : 2. (2) He secured the eternal salvation of the elect given to him by the Father, Heb. 13 : 20; John 17 : 2, 9, 24; Eph. 1 : 4; Heb. 12 : 2. Having identified himself with us, he honored the law we had broken, and bore the weight of our guilt and shame. His finished work is the sole ground on which God can justly pardon or man rightly hope; and the words of Jesus, confirmed by his resurrection and glorification, assure us that the foundation he has laid for human salvation is perfect and will stand the test of divine scrutiny and of the "great storms that will shake down earth and skies." The gospel of salvation is compressed into these three words. Luke informs us that he " cried with a loud voice "—no doubt referring to this, *the sixth dying saying:* IT IS FINISHED! and that he then said, *the seventh dying saying:* FATHER, INTO THY HANDS I COMMEND (better, *commit*, as in Ps. 31 : 5) MY SPIRIT. John alone records the *third*, the *fifth*, and the *sixth;* the latter perhaps the most important of all. The *fourth* and the *sixth* were loud cries—one of mental anguish, the other of victory. Each of these was followed by words uttered probably in a lower tone—one a plaint of bodily distress, the other a committal of his spirit to his Father. The *fourth* and *seventh* were quotations from that Old Testament which Jesus so perfectly knew, and, now as ever, honored and fulfilled. In adopting as his own the words of the ancient psalmist, he not only manifested their character as typical prophecies, but the more identified himself with his people, expressing his own anguish and his own trust, in words which had expressed the anguish and the trust of one of his ancient saints. **Bowed his head.** No longer having strength to sustain it in an upright position, he permitted it to sink upon his breast. **Gave up the ghost;** better, *gave up his spirit* —*i. e.* to God. These expressions, being active, possibly imply the voluntariness

The burial.

31 The Jews therefore, ᶠbecause it was the preparation, ᵍthat the bodies should not remain upon the cross on the sabbath day (for ʰthat sabbath day was an high day), besought Pilate that their legs might be broken, 32 and *that* they might be taken away. Then came the soldiers, and brake the legs of ⁱthe first, and of the

ᶠ vers. 14, 42; Mark 15. 42.
ᵍ Deut. 21. 22, 23.
ʰ Lev. 23. 7, 8.

ⁱ ver. 18; Luke 23. 39-43.

of the Saviour's death, John 10 : 18. When he had power to deliver himself (Matt. 26 : 53) he yielded himself meekly to suffering and death of his own free will, in order to complete the work of redemption according to the will of God. Compare Matt. 26 : 42; Heb. 12 : 2. This is his meaning in John 10 : 18. The supposition of some that he terminated his own life by an act or exertion of his own will is unscriptural, for he was "slain," and wicked men are charged with murdering him, Acts 2 : 23; 3 : 15, etc.; and absurd, for that would resemble suicide. Jesus died as we do, because the powers of life were exhausted. Not, however, because he was helpless, but because he submitted to undergo conditions in which his physical life was naturally and necessarily destroyed.

That Jesus should have died in six hours (ver. 33; Mark 15 : 44), instead of lingering two or even three days, as the crucified often did, was owing to previous exhaustion, and still more to the unfathomable mental anguish endured on the cross during the hours of darkness. The only wonder is that a mortal frame, however perfect in health, could have held out even so long.

As Jesus expired there was an earthquake, the rocks were rent, and the veil of the temple was rent in twain from the top to the bottom. The effect of these scenes was very great on all beholders. The centurion in charge was convinced that Jesus was a righteous or innocent man—nay, more, a divine Being. He openly avowed it. The multitude, in fear, perplexity, remorse, and vague apprehension, returned to their homes beating their breasts, Matt. 27 : 54; Mark 15 : 39; Luke 23 : 47-49.

31-42. THE BURIAL OF JESUS. John's account is the fullest, Matt. 27 : 57-66; Mark 15 : 42-47; Luke 23 : 50-56.

31. **The Jews**, as usual, the rulers. **Preparation**, our Friday, the day before the Jewish Sabbath. **That the bodies . . . sabbath** (omit *day*). The Romans were accustomed to let the bodies rot on the cross and be devoured by birds. But the Jews were very careful to have the bodies of those executed taken down and buried before sunset, Deut. 21 : 23. "So great care did the Jews take respecting the burial of men that even the bodies of those condemned to be crucified they took down and buried before the going down of the sun."—JOSEPHUS, *Jewish War*, iv. 5, 2. The murderers of Jesus were scrupulous and zealous concerning the ceremonial law. **An high day;** better, *a great day*—not only the Sabbath, but the Sabbath of the passover-week; therefore doubly important and sacred. **Besought Pilate**, etc. The Jewish rulers urgently requested that the death of the victims should be hastened, so as not to have the sanctity of the Sabbath infringed by the hanging of dead bodies upon the crosses; or, if the men should survive till then, so as to avoid the marring of the festival by a public spectacle of horror. They besought Pilate probably at least two hours before sunset; evidently, they did not know that Jesus was already dead. Thus they were preparing, in their own view, a new torture of a horrible kind for their rejected King. But he was beyond their reach.

32. Pilate gave the desired orders, after the common Roman policy of respecting the religious scruples of subject nations. **The soldiers** in charge, glad to be released the sooner from their watch, which, on peril of their lives, must be vigilant until the death of the crucified, obeyed with alacrity. They **brake the legs of the first, and of the other**—*i. e.* of the two robbers. This was effected by blows with a wooden mallet, and the uniform result was to kill those crucified outright or cause their speedy death. This custom was as cruel and

33 other which was crucified with him. But when they came to Jesus, and saw that he was dead already, 34 they brake not his legs: but one of the soldiers with a spear pierced his side, and forthwith ᵏ came thereout blood and water.

ᵏ Heb. 9. 13, 14, 22. 1 John 1. 7; 5 6, 8.

barbarous as crucifixion itself. Thus the penitent robber was released in a savage but speedy manner from his misery, and so the Lord's promise was exactly fulfilled: "*To-day* shalt thou be with me in paradise."

33. **They came to Jesus, and saw that he was dead already.** Perhaps they had not understood his very last word, or examined to see whether he was positively dead or had fainted. They now examine and find him dead, therefore **they brake not his legs.** His sacred body was spared that further outrage.

34. Still, men had been known to fall into syncope on the cross, and, being taken down, to revive. The soldiers were responsible for fulfilling their trust with their lives, and they wished to make "assurance doubly sure." Therefore **one of the soldiers with a spear pierced his side.** He aimed at the heart and no doubt reached his aim. The **spear**, the Roman *hasta*, a lance or pike with a sharp-pointed iron head, a weapon used by the Roman soldiery somewhat as the bayonet is now used. **Forthwith came thereout** (on the withdrawal of the spear there flowed forth) **blood and water.** This act of the soldier is of value in establishing beyond the possibility of question the reality of the Saviour's death as against all opposers and all heretics. He was, indeed, already dead. The opinion of some that the spear-thrust caused his death contradicts the plain and positive statement of John and of all the evangelists. But if he had not been dead the spear-thrust must inevitably have killed him. The flowing forth of the *blood and water* is evidently regarded by John as a remarkable circumstance, ver. 35. Some have regarded it as miraculous, but there seems to be no sufficient ground for this assumption. Others strangely imagine that it betokened a change already begun in the body of Jesus—incipient glorification. But to say nothing of the fact that this is utterly unsupported, it is far from certain that Jesus had a glorified body before he ascended the heavens, and that he did not rise with his very same earthly body. Compare ch. 20: 27 and Luke 24: 39. See J. W. WILLMARTH on "Translation" in *Baptist Quarterly*, Oct., 1868, especially pages 424-427. It is better to regard the flowing of blood and water as a natural phenomenon, susceptible of a physiological explanation. Dr. William Stroud (*The Physical Cause of the Death of Christ*, 2d ed., London, 1871) maintains that Jesus died of a broken or ruptured heart produced by the agony he endured on the cross for sinners. It has been found that under violent and intensely-excited emotion the heart is sometimes ruptured by the violence of its own action. The blood pours out into the pericardium, the sac which encloses the heart, fills it, and by pressure gradually stops the beating of the heart. The blood, sometimes a quart or more, thus in the pericardium quickly separates into its solid and liquid constituents, *crassamentum* and *serum*, popularly *blood* and *water*. The spear opening the pericardium from below, its contents would be instantly discharged, a stream of clear, watery liquid mixed with clotted blood. It is not at all needful to suppose, as many do, that the blood was liquid and the water pure. This harmonizes admirably with John's description and with the predictions in Ps. 22: 14; 69: 20. It gives additional prominence to the blood of Christ, as his death was then literally caused by the flowing forth of his blood from the heart when ruptured, not by flowing of blood and water from the spearthrust; and this rupture was caused by the agony endured on our behalf. This theory is well worthy of consideration, and if be not the exact explanation it indicates in what direction we are to look for it.

35 And ¹he that saw *it* bare record, and his record is true: and he knoweth that he saith true, ᵐ that ye 36 might believe. For these things were done, ⁿ that the Scripture should be fulfilled, A bone of him shall 37 not be broken. And again another Scripture saith, ᵒ They shall look on him whom they pierced.

ˡ ver. 26; ch. 21. 24.
ᵐ ch. 20. 31; 1 John 5. 13.
ⁿ Num. 9. 12; Ps. 34. 20.
ᵒ Ps. 22. 16, 17; Rev. 1. 7.

---

35. **He that saw**, etc.; better, *He that has seen has borne witness.* John, the writer, was present to the last, and beheld that of which he testifies. His **record** (*testimony*) **is true,** *is genuine;* **and he knoweth that** *what* **he saith is true,** *is exactly so.* John seems to feel that the thing was important as a fulfilment of prophecy, and also very strange. It is not necessary to suppose that he understood the cause, but marvellous as it was, he asserts the fact in the strongest terms of his own personal knowledge as an eye-witness who could not possibly be mistaken. **That ye might believe**, not merely what he says, but, as the *for* in the next verse shows, that the faith of believers in Christ may be strengthened by the occurrence of so strange yet so certain a phenomenon, in which the prophecies of Scripture were so remarkably fulfilled.

36. **For** (see note on last verse) **these things,** just related, and which are found in John's Gospel alone—probably the flow of blood and water was only noticed by the few close by—**were done,** *came to pass* in the providence of God, **that the Scripture should be** (*might be*) **fulfilled**—that God's purpose, revealed in the Old Testament, should be carried out in every particular, however unlikely it might seem. **A bone of him shall not be broken,** Ex. 12 : 46. Spoken of the paschal lamb—a conspicuous type of the Lamb of God slain for sinners—and must be fulfilled in the case of the great Antitype. The solemn earnestness with which John quotes and emphasizes this and other typical prophecies shows that they are real prophecies fulfilled, and not mere coincidences, however striking. Much of the Old Testament records acts, events, and words which are typical prophecies, because these things were ordered so as to be types and object-lessons. But caution is needed in applying the principle. We are absolutely sure only in cases where the New Testament furnishes the explanation, and safe only when we follow strictly the analogy of these precedents. From want of caution here much folly has been spoken and written.

37. John refers to **another Scripture,** Zech. 12:10: **They shall look on him whom they pierced.** This is not a typical but a direct prophecy, yet not without its bearing on the events of the prophet's own day. Compare Matt. 23 : 31. Jehovah Revealed (the Father) in the old dispensation was known to Israel through Jehovah Revealing (the Son). See John 1 : 18. He (the Son) was the Shepherd of Israel. Compare Ex. 32 : 34; Deut. 1 : 31; Josh. 5 : 13-6 : 2. They rebelled continually against him, killed his prophets, treated him as nearly as they could as their descendants did. The Holy Spirit foresaw that when he should become incarnate and come to them as their Messiah, he would not only be rejected, but slain, and literally *pierced* by a spear when delivered up by "his own people" to the Gentiles. Therefore the Spirit moved the prophet—perhaps he did not fully understand, 1 Pet. 1 : 10-12—to compress into this one word Jewish rebellion then and to come; and more—the world's rejection of Christ. It is a wonderfully pregnant Messianic prophecy. The world, both Jewish and Gentile, rejected their Saviour, slew him, pierced his very heart. The "looking upon him" is the terrible discovery by the wicked, too late, of who he is and what they have done when they shall see the Son of man in his glory (Rev. 1 : 7; compare Matt. 27 : 64), though it may have many partial fulfilments previously. It embraces in its scope the whole world of unbelievers in all ages; since the murder of the Son of God, summed up in the word *pierced,* is but the culmination and typical embodiment of the common disposition of all unconverted men toward Christ and his truth. Hence all such must yet *look upon him* and "wail because of

38 ʳAnd after this Joseph of Arimathea (being a disciple of Jesus, but secretly ᑫfor fear of the Jews), besought Pilate that he might take away the body of Jesus: and Pilate gave *him* leave. He came therefore, and took the body of Jesus. And there came also ʳNicodemus (which at the first came to Jesus by night), and brought ˢa mixture of myrrh and aloes,

ᵖ Matt. 27. 57-61
Mark 15. 42-47;
Luke 23. 50-56.
ᑫ ch. 9. 22; 12. 42.

ʳ ch. 3. 1, 2, etc.; 7. 50-52.
ˢ 2 Chron. 16. 14.

---

him." In order to the complete fulfilment of all this Jesus must be literally *pierced.* Hence the stroke given by the Roman soldier was a divinely-ordered and wonderful fulfilment of prophecy.

38. **After this,** "When the even was come" (Matt., Mark)—*i. e.* the "first evening," extending from three o'clock to sunset. This may have occurred at four o'clock or later. **Joseph,** a man of high rank, a member of the Sanhedrim, a "good and just man" (Luke 24 : 50), who was "waiting for the kingdom of God," Mark, Luke. He had not consented to the condemnation of Jesus. **A disciple of Jesus,** a believer in him, **but secretly for fear of the Jews**—*i. e.* the rulers. He had not gained sufficient courage to avow his faith openly at the risk of persecution and disgrace (ch. 9 : 22); compare ch. 12 : 42, which hardly includes Joseph, though his weakness was sinful. But when open disciples were terrified and scattered this secret but real believer is emboldened to show his love for Jesus and see that he has an honorable burial. And this is recorded by all of the four evangelists. Honor to Joseph of Arimathea! Criminals were usually huddled into a common grave, but Joseph will not have Jesus buried so. Matthew tells he was "a rich man ;" so was Nicodemus, ver. 39. Thus was fulfilled Isa. 53 : 9, which may be translated, "And his grave was appointed with the wicked, but he was with the rich in his death." **Arimathea,** probably Ramah, called Ramahthaim-Zophim, the birthplace of Samuel, 1 Sam. 1 : 1, 20. It has generally been located at the modern Lydda, about twenty-four miles north-west of Jerusalem. Its location, however, is uncertain. From 1 Sam. 9 : 4-6; 10 : 2 it is inferred that it lay south or southwest of Bethlehem. **Besought Pilate,** probably at the palace. It required some courage, chiefly with reference to the Jews. Mark says that he "went in boldly." Faith and love, timid but true, are apt to grow bold in time of real peril. Joseph knew that Jesus was dead, and was aware of all that had occurred, which indicates that he was among the multitude who looked on. Pilate had given orders to hasten the death of those crucified. He was now surprised to hear that Jesus was "already dead ;" but having learned the facts of the centurion, he **gave Joseph leave.** Mark's language indicates that he gave him the body freely —not for money, as was often the case. Joseph was a man of rank and of the Sanhedrim ; besides, Pilate was probably not sorry that Jesus should be honorably buried. **He came therefore** to the place of crucifixion, **and took the body.** From Luke it appears that he arrived just in time to aid in taking the body down.

39. **Nicodemus,** another rich, honorable man, a member of the Sanhedrim, who had not consented to the condemnation of Jesus. **He at the first,** in the early Judæan ministry of Jesus, **came to Jesus by night.** See ch. 3 ; compare ch. 7 : 50, 51. Evidently he too had since become a believer, though perhaps a secret one. The death of Jesus, filling him with sorrow, inspired him also with courage. The two men felt that Jesus was a prophet basely murdered, whom in this very public and perhaps dangerous manner they would openly honor and tenderly bury. As to his Messiahship, of which they had been convinced, they possibly were in confusion of mind, like the other disciples. Nicodemus may have called to mind the words of Jesus, ch. 3 : 14, 15. **Myrrh and aloes,** costly spices, **about an hundred pound weight**—in great profusion, regardless of expense. It was an offering of love.

40 about an hundred pound *weight*. Then took they the body of Jesus, and 'wound it in linen clothes with the spices, as the manner of the Jews is to bury.

41 Now in the place where he was crucified there was a garden; and in the garden ᵘ a new sepulchre, wherein

42 was never man yet laid. ˣ There laid they Jesus therefore, ʸ because of the Jews' preparation *day;* for the sepulchre was nigh at hand.

* Acts 5. 6.

ᵘ Matt. 27. 60.
ˣ Isa. 53. 9; Matt. 12. 40.
ʸ ver. 31.

40. **They wound** the body round and round **in linen clothes** — the mummy-cloths of the Egyptians were always linen—**with the spices,** so as to enclose the spices next to the body, **as the manner of the Jews.** This was not to mutilate the body and mummy it, but so to anoint the body as to make it fragrant and pleasant in burial, and to form, so to speak, a "consecrated and beautiful transition of the corpse from death to corruption."—LANGE. It was a good "manner," in striking contrast with the horrible and ghastly "manner" of the Egyptians. Yet this wrapping and anointing of the body of Jesus was but temporary—hurriedly done on account of the approach of the Sabbath, which began at sunset, and on which, according to the law, such work would be forbidden. Their object was to preserve and prepare the body for a more formal and careful embalming, which, as we learn from Luke, "the women" intended to perform on the first day of the week, as soon as the Sabbath should be past.

41. **In the place,** in the district or vicinity; **a garden.** Close to Golgotha was a garden, walled of course, which Matthew informs us belonged to Joseph. He had no doubt a city residence in Jerusalem, hence provided himself with this garden as a place of beauty, valuable as a place of resort as well as for its productions. Here he had hewn out of the solid rock a **new sepulchre,** doubtless for a family vault. It was providential and fitting that Jesus, whose body "saw no corruption," should be laid in a tomb **wherein was never man yet laid,** where a human body had never decayed. Besides, it could never be asserted that some one else besides Jesus had risen.

42. **Because of the Jews' preparation day,** *on account of the preparation of the Jews—i. e.* because it was Friday and very near the Sabbath.

Here is an intimation that if there had been more time they would have given to the body of Jesus what seemed to them a more honorable burial in another place. "The very haste of the preparation-day was providential. Jesus should be interred in a new grave in a manner the most extraordinary."—LANGE. **For the sepulchre was nigh at hand,** near Golgotha. It is well known that the church of the Holy Sepulchre is built over the traditional site of this tomb. But the tradition must be false, for the place where this church stands could never have been "without the walls," as Golgotha and Joseph's garden were. It was contrary to Jewish custom to bury the body of one not belonging to the family in a family vault; but Joseph's love was so great that in this emergency he gladly opened his own "new tomb." But there is no reason to suppose that he intended later to remove the body.

We learn from the other evangelists that the women who had watched the crucifixion to the end were present. They sat over against the tomb while the burial was going on, and after the stone had been rolled to the door and Joseph and his companions had departed, they lingered in the same spot, as if to watch the body of their beloved Master. This was the act of desponding but faithful love. A very different guard was soon after stationed there through Pilate's tart and scornful order. issued in compliance with the request of the Jews, who were haunted by guilty fears, Matt. 27 : 62-66.

Jesus must, however, have been buried an hour or two before sunset, as the women at length "returned and prepared spices and ointments" for the more careful embalming of the body, "and rested on the Sabbath day according to the commandment," Luke 23 : 56. "The pious observance of the

Sabbath on the part of Jesus' friends on the occasion of their burial of him [was] a testimony against those who, with the charge of Sabbath-breaking, introduced his persecution unto death."—LANGE.

This memorable day was Friday, 15th Nisan—April 7, A. D. 30. It is commemorated by a large part of the Christian world naturally, though not by any command or example of Scripture, on the day called "Good Friday." (Concerning the vain attempt to show that the day of the crucifixion was Thursday see *Author's Notes on Mark*, pp. 311-313.)

PRACTICAL REMARKS.

1. The willingness of Jesus to be scourged, mocked, and crucified in shame and agony shows his love for his people, and should awaken tender contrition and fervent love in us, the whole chapter; Isa. 53; Phil. 2 : 5-8, 9, 10; Gal. 2 : 20.

2. That Jesus should be scourged like a slave, insulted, beaten, and even vilely spit upon, illustrates at once the horrible depravity of man and the amazing forbearance and persevering goodness of God, ver. 1, etc.; Jer. 17 : 9; 2 Pet. 3 : 9.

3. Human depravity is illustrated by the fact that the vilest men delight in mocking the innocent and the suffering and in giving pain, vers. 2, 3; Ps. 35 : 15; 74 : 20.

4. The depravity shown by Jews and Gentiles in their treatment of the Lord is not exceptional, but the natural development of our common corrupt human nature. What one has become another might in the same circumstances. Hence we should be filled with penitence and self-loathing, Ps. 51 : 5-7; Rom. 3 : 9, 20; Eph. 2 : 3; Rom. 7 : 18; 1 Cor. 4 : 7.

5. What an example is Christ to us of calmness, fortitude, and patience! the whole chapter; Isa. 53 : 7; 1 Pet. 2 : 21-25; 4 : 1, 12-19.

6. After a sixfold trial no fault in Jesus could be shown. Pilate repeatedly and solemnly pronounced him innocent. He was condemned only for his own truthful words. So, and in all respects, he was a blameless sacrifice, ver. 6; Heb. 9 : 14; 1 Pet. 1 : 19.

7. Unitarianism is self-stultifying. If Jesus is not divine he was justly condemned. If he had not been the Son of God, but only the best of men or of created beings, he would not have declared himself divine and died for it, ver. 7; ch. 10 : 33-39.

8. Those who deny the divinity of Christ do virtually range themselves with the impious Jews and justify the murderers of the Lord, for they condemned him for his claim of divinity, ver. 7; 1 Cor. 1 : 23; 2 John 7.

9. The enemies of Christ and his church can go no further than God permits, ver. 11; 2 Kings 19 : 28, 33; Acts 4 : 31; Rom. 9 : 17; 2 Tim. 4 : 17; Rev. 19 : 16.

10. There are degrees in sin and in punishment, ver. 11; Rev. 20 : 13; Rom. 2 : 12; Luke 12 : 47, 48.

11. Men of great religious professions have sometimes urged the grossest wickedness by the most hypocritical and lying reasons, vers. 7 and 12; *e. g.* the cruel inquisition pretended to burn and torture in obedience to God.

12. When a man turns away from special light he is prepared for the most dreadful and fatal sins, vers. 12, 16; Ahab in 1 Kings 22; John 12 : 35.

13. Natural men are more afraid of men and of temporal evils than of God and his eternal wrath, ver. 12; ch. 12 : 42; Rom. 8 : 5.

14. Assumptions of dignity and mocking and browbeating others may only cover a mean and cowardly spirit and deeds of craven fear and shame, vers. 10, 14, 15, 22.

15. See what human nature is, and what sin is in the cry, "Crucify him!" ver. 15; 1 Cor. 16 : 22.

16. God permitted the Jews, in reject ing his Son, to disavow their hopes and heritage. They were not sincere, but God held them to their word. So sinners who reject Christ now reject all hope here and hereafter, ver. 15; Acts 4 : 12; 13 : 46.

17. He who condemns the servants or the word of God only passes sentence upon himself, vers. 11, 18.

18. Jesus changed the cross to a symbol of glory, victory, and eternal life. So will it be for us when he comes if we are called to "bear the cross for him," to show fidelity unto shame or agony or death, John 12 : 25, 26; Luke 14 : 27; Rom. 8 : 17.

19. The three men crucified at Calvary are types of the three deaths possible to man: 1. *Innocent and holy*—Jesus. Also the sin-bearer and Saviour. And the possibility of so dying is forfeited by sin. 2. *A penitent and believing sinner*, dying in peace. 3. *An impenitent and unbelieving sinner*, dying in despair. We must choose one of the two last, ver. 18.

20. Wicked men writhe when their shame is written for all to read. But "what is written [is] written." Sin can never be undone, ver. 21; Dan. 12 : 2.

21. Every purpose of God and prediction of Scripture will surely be fulfilled, vers. 24, 28, 35-37, etc.; Isa. 46 : 10; John 10 : 35.

22. God fulfils his purposes by all agencies, including the free and wicked deeds of his enemies. What supreme folly to rebel against such a being or to distrust him! Eph. 1 : 11; Rom. 8 : 28.

23. One man and four women stood beside the cross. Thus a far greater number of women than men have believed in Jesus in all ages and now. Women have always had a great part in the service of Christ, but only in a womanly capacity, vers. 25-27; Acts 1 : 14; 16 : 14, 15; Rom. 16 : 5, 12; Phil. 4 : 3; Acts 9 : 36; Col. 3 : 18; 1 Tim. 2 : 11-15; 5 : 5-15; Eph. 5 : 22-33.

24. Christianity sanctions and glorifies natural affection. Also it sanctions and elevates personal friendship. All affection of every kind not so hallowed cannot pass over into eternity, but must utterly perish, vers. 25-27; Matt. 25 : 46.

25. Though earthly relationships cease at death; yet if in Christ, those who have loved on earth will love hereafter in a purer and holier manner, Matt. 22 : 30; 12 : 48-50; Phil. 4 : 1; 1 Thess. 2 : 19; Col. 1 : 28.

26. Romish doctrine as to the Virgin Mary has no scriptural sanction. The doctrine of her "perpetual virginity" is false, Matt. 1 : 25; 13 : 55, 56. Her "immaculate conception" is a preposterous fable. To give her divine honor and to pray to her is idolatry. She is named only once after the crucifixion (Acts 1 : 14), and, like us all, was a sinner saved by grace (Luke 1 : 47), but highly honored in being the mother of the Lord (Luke 1 : 28, 48), and eminently pious, Luke 1.

27. Pure wine is useful for medical purposes, and was set apart by Jesus himself in the Lord's Supper, ver. 29; Matt. 11 : 19; 1 Cor. 11 : 25 (*cf.* ver. 21); 1 Tim. 5 : 23; Ps. 104 : 15; John 2 : 1-11.

28. Wine (as also liquors and drugged beverages) should never be used to stupefy (unless medically necessary), nor where it can interfere with our work or usefulness or injure others, Matt. 27 : 34; Isa. 5 : 11, 12; 28 : 1; 1 Cor. 6 : 20; Eph. 5 : 18; Rom. 14 : 21.

29. Our Saviour had a true humanity and true human experiences, ver. 28; ch. 4 : 6; Heb. 2 : 14; 4 : 15, 16.

30. Sin and physical misery are connected. All pain may not be caused by sin, but all misery and anguish are directly or indirectly by our own sin or the sin of others. Because man sinned Jesus thirsted. Let us beware lest we thirst for ever on account of impenitence in sin, ver. 28; Rom. 2 : 8, 9; Luke 16 : 24; Rev. 21 : 8.

31. The finished work of Jesus is the only and all-sufficient ground of hope to sinners, ver. 30; Acts 4 : 12; Rom. 4 : 24, 25; Gal. 2 : 16, 20.

32. To trust in anything else, in whole or in part, is presumption and ruin, ver. 30; Acts 13 : 38-41; Rom. 3 : 28; 10 : 3; Gal. 2 : 16-18.

33. To deny or explain away the atonement destroys Christianity, ver. 30; Gal. 1 : 8, 9; Heb 9 : 22; 2 Pet. 2 : 1, 2.

34. By fidelity we should seek to be able at the close of life, in humble imitation of Christ, to say of our own work, "It is finished," ver. 30; Matt. 25 : 23; 2 Tim. 4 : 5-8; Rev. 2 : 10; 3 : 21.

35. The worst of men are sometimes bigoted formalists devoid of common humanity, ver. 31; ch. 16 : 2; Acts 18 : 13; 23 : 12; 1 Thess. 2 : 15, 16.

36. Death, even in its most dreadful form, is safe and blessed to the believer, ver. 32; Acts 7 : 59 60; Rom. 8 : 35-39; Phil. 1 : 21.

37. If the heart of Jesus was broken by our sins, ought not our hearts to melt in penitence and gratitude? ver. 34; Gal. 2 : 20.

38. The New Testament was written primarily for the church. One object is to confirm the faith of believers, ver. 35; ch. 20 : 30, 31; 1 John 5 : 13.

39. Men who reject Christ here must

Jesus' appearance to Mary Magdalene.

XX. THE ᶻfirst day of the week cometh Mary Magda- ᵃMatt. 28. 1; Mark 16. 1; Luke 24. 1.

look on him with terror and remorse in the hopeless Hereafter, ver. 37; 1 Cor. 16 : 22; Rev. 1 : 7.
40. Care for the tender and decent burial of our dead is in accordance with true piety, vers. 38–42; Acts 8 : 2; 9 : 37; Gen. ch. 23.
41. The way to honor Jesus now with riches is to devote them to his cause, the support of his ministers, and the relief of the poor, especially of his needy disciples. This principle also applies to the smaller offerings of those not rich, ver. 42; Acts 4 : 32, 34, 35; Phil. 4 : 15, 18; 1 Cor. 9 : 11, 14; Luke 19 : 8; Matt. 25 : 40; 1 John 3 : 17; Gal. 6 : 6, 10; 2 Cor. chs. 8 and 9.
42. Love is ready to offer its most precious and sacred things to Christ, ver. 41; ch. 12 : 3; Acts 21 : 13.

CHAPTER XX.

If we examine the different accounts given by the four evangelists concerning the resurrection of Jesus and the events which followed on that first day of the week, we find difficulties in the way of harmonizing them. Yet it cannot be shown that the evangelists contradict one another even in a single statement; and if we knew more of the incidents in detail, we might be able to harmonize their accounts completely on a basis of known facts. But in the absence of such detail and in the light of the facts we have, the following is the probable order in which the events occurred:

The resurrection takes place at the early dawn, about the time the women start for the sepulchre. On their way the women inquire among themselves who shall remove the stone from the door. They approach the sepulchre just after the guard of Roman soldiers have recovered from their fright at the angel's appearance (Matt. 28 : 4) sufficiently to flee from the scene. At their first view of the sepulchre the women see that the stone has already been rolled away. Mary Magdalene runs back to the city, and reports the matter to Peter and John; and they both run in excitement to the tomb. After she has left for the city the other women view the rolled-away stone, enter the sepulchre, and not finding the body of Jesus they are greatly perplexed. While in this state of mind they behold the two angels and hear the announcement of Jesus' resurrection and the charge that they go and make it known to his disciples. They flee from the tomb to bear the glad tidings. Soon after they leave, John and Peter come to the sepulchre, followed by Mary Magdalene. They do not find the body of Jesus; and the orderly arrangement of the grave-clothes and the napkin convinces John that the body has not been stolen, but the prediction of Jesus that he should rise on the third day has been miraculously fulfilled. They immediately return to the city. But just after they leave, Mary Magdalene comes up, looks into the sepulchre and sees the two angels there, and then turns round and *beholds Jesus.* The other women are hastening toward the city, and *Jesus appears to them.* Mary Magdalene also returns to the city, and both she and they tell the disciples what they have seen. Some of the guard likewise go into the city, and report to the chief priests what has occurred. Afterward *Jesus appears to Peter,* and, subsequently, *to the two disciples* going to Emmaus. In the evening he appears to *ten of the apostles* in Jerusalem, and other disciples with them. See the *Author's Harmony of the Gospels,* rem. ⅔ 187, pp. 310, 311.

This twentieth chapter gives an account of the first (vers. 1–18) and the fifth of these appearances (vers. 19–25), and also of the *sixth appearance,* which occurred one week later, 26–29. It then states why the inspired writer was led to record his choice-selection of facts respecting Jesus the Christ, 30, 31.

1–18. JESUS APPEARS TO MARY MAGDALENE AT THE SEPULCHRE, Mark 16 : 9. The full account is found only here.
1. **The first day;** rather, *But on the first day,* expressing a contrast to "the preparation" of the verse preceding, and to the implied rest from

lene early, when it was yet dark, unto the sepulchre, and seeth ᵃthe stone taken away from the sepulchre. 2 Then she runneth, and cometh to Simon Peter, and to the ᵇother disciple, whom Jesus loved, and saith unto them, They have taken away the Lord out of the sepulchre, and we know not where they have laid him.

3 ᶜPeter therefore went forth, and that other disciple, 4 and came to the sepulchre. So they ran both together: and the other disciple did outrun Peter, and came first 5 to the sepulchre. And he stooping down, *and looking in*, saw ᵈthe linen clothes lying; yet went he not in.

ᵃ Matt. 27. 60, 66; 28. 2; Mark 16. 3, 4.
ᵇ ch. 13. 23; 19. 26; 21. 7, 20, 24.

ᶜ Luke 24. 12.

ᵈ ch. 19. 40.

labor during the intervening Sabbath. **First day of the week,** Sunday, the Lord's Day, Rev. 1 : 10. This day, on which Jesus rose from the dead, was ever afterward observed by the disciples as the day of Christian rest and worship. It comes down to us sanctioned by the example of Christ himself, and by the example and manifest oral teaching of his inspired apostles, vers. 19, 26; Acts 20 : 7; 1 Cor. 16 : 2; Rev. 1 : 10. Not only did Jesus twice meet his assembled disciples on that day, but he further hallowed it by sending the Holy Spirit on the day of Pentecost, which that year occurred on the first day of the week. See Lev. 23 : 15, 16; Acts 2 : 1-4. **Mary Magdalene.** See on ch. 19 : 25. She was not alone, but with the other women, Mark 16 : 1. She is singled out because of the interesting narrative which follows. **Seeth the stone taken away;** better, *sees the stone has been taken away.* The act of its removal she did not see, but she saw the stone after it had been removed, as the Greek clearly signifies. The stone is mentioned in Matt. 27 : 60; Mark 15 : 46. **From the**—more exactly, *out of the*—**sepulchre,** because "the stone had been fitted *into* the mouth of the tomb, which was hewn in a rocky elevation."—DR. P. SCHAFF. See Mark 16 : 3, 4.

2. **Then she runneth;** in her haste to seek counsel and help in the perplexing difficulty which so deeply interested her. **The other disciple**—see ver. 8; ch. 1 : 35-40; 18 : 15, 16—**whom Jesus loved;** properly, *loved as a friend*, honored with his particular friendship (derived from a word which means *a friend*), meaning the writer, John himself. **They have taken . . . they have laid;** more exactly, *They took . . . they laid*, showing that she had in her mind some particular time when she feared his body was either stolen or taken away by his enemies. **We know not,** probably intending to speak in the name of the other women in connection with herself. In verse 13 she speaks simply in her own name.

3. **And that other disciple, and came to the sepulchre.** Impulsive Peter started at once, being closely followed by John, and the two were thus making progress toward the tomb. The word used for "sepulchre" from John 19 : 41 onward is different from the one used six times by Matthew, and properly translated "sepulchre." The latter is *taphos*, a sepulchre or place of burial; the former is *mnēmeion*, a memorial, remembrance, or record, a monument. So our word *sepulchre* means a burial-place; and *tomb* originally signified a mound of earth raised over the dead to commemorate them or preserve them in memory.

4. **So they ran both together.** They not only "were going," but were running because they were in haste. **The other disciple did outrun Peter,** or, *ran on faster than Peter*, being younger and more elastic, so that he came first to the tomb.

5. **And he stooping down, and looking in, saw;** or, *And stooping to look, he sees.* The change of the tenses, aorist, imperfect, and present, the characteristic details, the liveliness, circumstantiality, and inner truth of the narrative in vers. 3-8, betray unmistakably an eye-witness and participator in the scene. **Yet went he not in.** John's pace had been more winged than that of Peter. But on reaching the tomb he seems fettered

6 Then cometh Simon Peter following him, and went into the sepulchre, and seeth the linen clothes lie,
7 and ᵉthe napkin, that was about his head, not lying with the linen clothes, but wrapped together in a place
8 by itself. Then went in also that other disciple, which came first to the sepulchre, and he saw, and believed.
9 For as yet ᶠthey knew not the Scripture, ᵍthat he must
10 rise again from the dead. Then the disciples went away again unto their own home.
11 ʰBut Mary stood without at the sepulchre weeping.

ᵉ ch. 11. 44.

ᶠ Matt. 16. 21, 22; Luke 18. 33, 34.
ᵍ Ps. 16. 10; Acts 2. 25–31; 13. 34, 35.
ʰ Mark 16. 5.

---

by the fear of a sad discovery, by awe, by astonishment at the orderly appearance of the linen clothes.

6. Then cometh Simon Peter, while John is delaying outside the tomb, **and went into the sepulchre.** While the contemplative John stands meditating on the new signs, the more decided and practical Peter goes before him into the sepulchre. **And seeth the linen clothes lie.** Peter does not merely get a distant and indistinct or a momentary sight, as John may have done, but he goes near and *beholds* directly and attentively the things within the sepulchre, so as to learn what is there and in what condition.

7. Wrapped together in a place by itself. It may seem strange to us that this orderly condition of the grave-clothes and the napkin did not make a deeper impression on Peter, and immediately remind him of Jesus' repeated prediction that on the third day he should rise from the dead. But this dulness on his part may doubtless be accounted for by his being so absorbed with the objects on which he was looking and with his usual ideas of the state of the dead that for the time he could not well go beyond that customary range of mental view.

8. Then went in also that other disciple, because Peter had gone before him. John is encouraged by the boldness of Peter, so that he wakes from his meditation, rises above his fear, and also himself goes in. **And he saw** the order of the grave-clothes, and the napkin neatly folded up and laid away by itself, as if Jesus had risen from sleep and leisurely adjusted his lodging-room before leaving it. There was no evidence of the hurry and confusion which must have existed had the body been stolen or taken away by either friends or enemies, and therefore it dawned upon his mind that the Lord whom he loved might be again alive. He probably also called up the predictions of the resurrection which had been given the disciples during the last few months, and he *believed* that Jesus had fulfilled those pledges and risen from the dead.

9. For as yet they knew not the Scripture; such passages as Ps. 16 : 10; 110; Isa. 26 : 19; 53 : 10–12; Zech. 6 : 12, 13. After they received the Holy Spirit on the day of Pentecost, the apostles understood the Old Testament *Scripture* and its accomplishment in the Lord Jesus as they never had before. See Acts 2 : 25–31. And in the light thus shed upon the Old Testament they were enabled to recall the sayings of Jesus, perceive their application, and feel their force. See ch. 2 : 22.

10. Then the disciples went away again unto their own home. The apostles had only a temporary home in Jerusalem among their friends. It was prudent for Peter and John to retire soon from the sepulchre, lest they should be questioned by the rulers or be accused of a design to steal the body of Jesus, and because, not knowing what further they could do, they desired to hasten back and report to their brethren. But while Peter retired "wondering at that which had come to pass" (Luke 24 : 12), John retired *believing* and enjoying a calm satisfaction of heart. Yet, later in that very day, Jesus' special appearance to Peter, after his recent denial and subsequent tears and bitter repentance, served also to tranquillize his mind, and prepare him to "strengthen his brethren," Luke 22 : 32.

11. But Mary stood without at

And as she wept, she stooped down, *and looked* into
12 the sepulchre, and seeth two angels in white sitting,
the one at the head, and the other at the feet, where
13 the body of Jesus had lain. And they say unto her,
Woman, why weepest thou? She saith unto them,
Because they have taken away my Lord, and I know
14 not where they have laid him. ¹And when she had
thus said, she turned herself back, and saw Jesus
15 standing, and ᵏ knew not that it was Jesus. Jesus

¹ Mark 16. 9-11
Matt. 28. 9.
ᵏ ch. 21. 4; Luke 24. 16, 31.

the sepulchre, because she had returned from the city to the sepulchre, and come up to it probably just after Peter and John left; **weeping,** on account of her sincere love to him who had done so great things for her, and her deep grief for him as dead and his corpse missing, perhaps fallen into the hands of unfeeling and abusive enemies. **And as she wept, she stooped down, and looked into the sepulchre,** because she was anxious to see whether she might not, after all, be mistaken about the absence of the body. She *stooped* because the top of the entrance was so low that she could not otherwise get a near view of the inside of the tomb.

12. **And seeth two angels in white** *garments,* the word being plural. No angels had appeared to Peter and John, although they both went inside the tomb only a short time before. **Sitting;** when the other women saw the two angels in the sepulchre after Mary Magdalene had left in haste for the city, Luke mentions the fact by saying, "Behold, two men *stood* by them in shining garments," Luke 24 : 4. Also, Mark says in ch. 16 : 5, "Entering into the sepulchre, they saw a young man *sitting* on the right side, clothed in a long white garment." This angel on the right-hand side is particularly mentioned by Mark, probably because he spoke to the women, and thus received their special attention. When he began to speak he was most likely *sitting;* but as he proceeded he rose and *stood,* as declared by Luke. **The one at the head, and the other at the feet.** Comparing these expressions with that of Mark, "on the right side"—more literally, "in the right-hand parts"—it would seem that the body of Jesus, lying in a niche or cell cut into the inner wall

of the sepulchre, would, to persons facing it, present the head at their right hand and the feet at their left.

13. **And they** (or *they also*) **say unto her.** This form of the sentence gives prominence to the pronoun *they,* which is expressed in the Greek, and is therefore emphatic. **Woman, why weepest thou?** Angels are concerned on beholding the griefs of God's people. **They have taken . . . they have laid.** See on ver. 2. **Taken away my Lord, and I know not where they have laid him.** These expressions clearly show the idea had not then entered her mind that Jesus had risen from the dead.

14. **And when she had thus said, she turned herself back.** After replying to the angels she may have turned away her face from them to give free vent to her tears; or, as Doddridge suggests, she may have heard a sudden noise behind her, and turned round to see whence it came. **And saw** (or *beholds*) **Jesus standing,** the present tense giving a vivid description; and she does not merely catch a glance, but she continuously *beholds* him. **And knew not that it was Jesus.** She had her eyes dimmed with tears and her mind occupied and excited, so that she did not recognize Jesus. Besides, she was not at all expecting to see him alive; and if she raised her eyes upward, she probably did not see his face and his garments presenting their usual appearance. It was therefore no strange thing that she did not at first sight know him. Dräseke, as quoted by Schaff, beautifully expresses it: She knew not, "because her tears wove a veil, and because the seeking after the dead prevents us from seeing the living." She was wholly absorbed in the thought of the absent Lord.

15. **Woman, why weepest thou?**

A. D. 30.   JOHN XX.   319

saith unto her, Woman, why weepest thou? Whom seekest thou? She, supposing him to be the gardener, saith unto him, Sir, if thou have borne him hence, tell me where thou hast laid him, and I will take him away.
16 Jesus saith unto her, ˡMary! She turned herself, and saith unto him, Rabboni! (which is to say, Master!).
17 Jesus saith unto her, ᵐTouch me not; for I am not yet ascended to my Father: but go to ⁿmy brethren,

ˡ ch. 10. 3; Ex. 33. 17.
ᵐ Matt. 28. 7, 9, 10.
ⁿ Ps. 22. 22; Rom. 8. 29; Heb. 2. 11.

Whom seekest thou? These words were probably spoken in a tone somewhat different from that which Mary had been accustomed to hear from Jesus, and therefore she did not recognize him as the speaker. **She, supposing him to be the gardener, saith unto him.** Mary, supposing no other man except the guard of Roman soldiers would be likely to be there at that early hour, concluded he must be the garden-keeper, and must consequently well know what had there occurred; and thinking he was not pleased to have the body of Jesus in Joseph's new tomb, she also concludes he must have moved it to some less honorable place. She therefore respectfully addresses him in the very natural language, **Sir, if thou have** (rather, *hast*) **borne him hence, tell me where thou hast laid him, and I will take him away.** Her heart and thoughts are so full of this Jesus who was crucified and buried in Joseph's tomb that she supposes the gardener will readily understand whom she means by *him*—borne *him* hence, laid *him*. Like the spouse in Solomon's Song, she would inquire, "Saw ye him whom my soul loveth?" Cant. 3 : 3. And so strong and sincere is her affection that, wherever he has been laid, she will undertake to remove him to a more suitable place, not considering that the body, with a hundred pounds of spices bound about it, is much more than she can carry. "But," says Henry, referring to this over-estimate of her own strength, "true love makes nothing of difficulties."

16. **Jesus saith unto her, Mary!** It was spoken in her own native Aramæan or later Hebrew, then used by the Jews in Palestine, and doubtless in a tone so familiar that she recognized it at once and knew the speaker was Jesus himself. **She turned herself, and saith unto him** (the best critical authorities say *in Hebrew*), **Rabboni!** or *Rabbouni* (**which is to say, Master!**), or *Teacher*. She recognized Jesus not through the eye, but through the ear. She knew the voice that had bidden the demons depart from her, Mark 16 : 9. After addressing the supposed gardener, she probably assumed a posture as if to hurry away in some direction and get the body; but on hearing the familiar voice calling "Mary!" she instantly turned toward the speaker and exclaimed "Rabbouni!" In the Jewish schools, *rab*, a great or learned man, master, teacher, was a title of respect; *rabbi*, my teacher, was a higher title; and *rabbouni*, my great teacher, was the highest of all, and was given to only seven of their most celebrated rabbis. This title Mary spontaneously applies to Jesus. In Mark 10 : 51 the same word is translated *Lord*.

17. **Touch me not; for I am not yet ascended to my Father.** Few passages in the New Testament have perplexed commentators more than this. No interpretation can be satisfactory which does not harmonize with the two declarations, "I have not ascended" and "Go, tell my brethren that I ascend." Dr. A. C. Kendrick thus defends an interpretation set forth at length in the *Bibliotheca Sacra*: "We will not vouch for its correctness, but it seems attended by no inherent difficulty, and to have the merit of giving a simple and coherent meaning to the entire passage. Its fundamental assumption is—and it finds in this passage its chief authority—that Christ's ascension to his Father *followed close upon his resurrection;* that thenceforth his abode was heaven, whence he came to make his appearance to his disciples; and that his ascension from Mount Olivet was only the last formal, public withdrawal from earth until his second coming. Our Saviour then meets Mary at the sepulchre; they exchange greet-

and say unto them, °I ascend unto my Father, and ᵖ your Father; and *to* ᑫmy God, and your God. • ch. 13. 1, 3; 14. 2; 16. 28; Eph
1. 17-23; 1 Pet. 1. 3. ᵖ Rom. 8. 14-17; Gal. 4. 6, 7; 1 John 3. 2. ᑫ Gen. 17. 7, 8; Jer. 31. 33; Heb. 1. 9; 11. 16; Rev. 21. 3.

ings; but as she clings to him in her joy he reminds her that he has a high and solemn act immediately awaiting him which must suspend this interview: 'Cling not to me, for I have not yet, since I rose, ascended to my Father. But go and inform my brethren that I ascend (at once) to my and their God and Father.' Mary departs, and Jesus, according to his declaration, ascends to heaven. . . . This interpretation harmonizes with all the facts following our Lord's resurrection. He no longer dwelt with them. He only occasionally *appeared* to them. His coming among them was felt by them to be mysterious and startling, as of a visitor from the invisible world. 'They were terrified,' says Luke, 'and affrighted, and supposed that they had seen a spirit.' So Paul puts the appearance of Christ to the disciples in the same category with his manifestation to himself. 'He was seen of Cephas, then of the twelve, and last of all he was seen of me also.' We can scarcely resist the conviction, then, that after our Saviour's resurrection he was no longer a dweller upon earth. With his spiritual body he became an inhabitant of the spiritual world; and where did he dwell except in heaven? Whither did he go except where he told Mary to inform the disciples that he was going —to his and their God and Father?"

In regard to this interpretation it may be said: The rendering of the original, *Cling not to me*, is not sustained by other passages in the New Testament. It occurs thirty-five times, and is properly translated *touch* in each instance; as, touching the hand, garment, body, etc. Compare Matt. 8 : 3; 9 : 20; Luke 22 : 51; 1 John 5 : 18. It is more natural also to regard the ascending to his Father to have taken place at the end of the forty days. Compare ver. 27; Luke 24 : 39, 51; Acts 1 : 3, 9-12.

Rather to be preferred is the view defended by Dr. Hackett, as follows: "She had already, it is true, exclaimed in the ecstasy of her joy, 'Rabboni!' but she may not have been certain of the precise form or nature of body in which she beheld her Lord. It is he, the Great Master, verily, she is assured; but is he corporeal, having really come out of the grave, or is it his glorified spirit, having already gone up to God, but now having descended to her in his spiritual investiture? In this state of uncertainty she extends her hand to assure herself of the truth. . . . The Saviour knows her thoughts and arrests the act. The act is unnecessary; his words are a sufficient proof of what she would know. He 'had not ascended to the Father,' as she half believed, and consequently has not the spiritual body which she supposed he might possibly have. . . . Her case was like Thomas', and yet unlike his—she wished, like him, to touch the object of her vision, but, unlike him, was not prompted by unbelief." — Article "Mary Magdalene," SMITH'S *Bible Dictionary*, Amer. edition.

But go to my brethren; hasten to do this, and let them know that I have risen, for they are *my brethren* still, though they all forsook me and fled. How cheering these words, indicating their Lord's sympathy, forgiveness, and love! **I ascend unto my Father;** let them therefore no longer expect me to set up a temporal Messianic kingdom on the earth. *I ascend*, therefore let them be comforted with the thought that I go to plead their cause and to send forth to them the Holy Spirit. I go that I may prepare a place for them, and may come again and receive them to myself, that where I am they also may be. **My Father, and your Father; and to my God, and your God.** Do thou tell them that I ascend, and let them know that while he is *my* Father in the eternal relations of the Godhead, he is also *their* Father by adopting them into his spiritual family; and while he is *my* God in my official character as Mediator, he is also *their* God by regenerating and sanctifying them and giving them the indwelling of his Spirit. "*My God and your God*—mine that he may be yours; the God of the Redeemer (Ps. 89 : 26) that he may be the God of

18 ʳMary Magdalene came and told the disciples that ʳMatt. 28. 10; Luke 24. 10.
she had seen the Lord, and *that* he had spoken these
things unto her.

Jesus appears to the Apostles, Thomas being absent.

19 ˢThen the same day at evening, being the first *day* ˢMark 16. 14–18; Luke 24. 36–49; 1 Cor. 15. 5.
of the week, when the doors were shut where the dis-

the redeemed. The summary of the new covenant is, God *will be to us a God*, and therefore, Christ being the Head of the covenant, who is primarily dealt with, and believers only through him, this covenant relation fastens first upon him. *God becomes his God*, and so *ours;* Christ's *Father* is *our Father;* and he partaking of the human nature, *our God* is *his God*."—M. HENRY.

18. **Mary Magdalene came and told** (or, *comes telling*) **the disciples** (the animated present tense, showing also her love and prompt obedience to Christ) **that she had seen the Lord, and that he had spoken these things unto her.** She first expresses her joy that she has seen the Lord, and then she delivers her particular message from the Lord to them. Thus, as the woman of Samaria announced to her countrymen Jesus as the Christ, so Mary Magdalene announced to the disciples Jesus as the risen Redeemer.

19–25. JESUS APPEARS TO THE APOSTLES IN JERUSALEM, THOMAS BEING ABSENT, Mark 16 : 14; Luke 24 : 36–49.

19. **Then the same day at evening, being the first day of the week.** John does not attempt to describe *all* the appearances of Jesus to the disciples after his resurrection, but selects a few, and gives interesting particulars respecting them, especially such as afford clear proof of the fact that he has truly risen. Two of these occurred on the very day of his resurrection. **When the doors were shut where the disciples were assembled for** (rather, with the critical editors, *on account of their*) **fear of the Jews, came Jesus and stood in the midst;** more accurately, *came into the midst and stood.* The fact that the doors were shut is emphasized both here and in ver. 26, indicating how wonderful these appearances were. Jesus himself had been so maltreated by the Jewish officials that his disciples felt there was occasion for *them* to fear; and if they had then heard the absurd story put into the mouths of the Roman soldiers, " His disciples came by night and stole him away while we slept, ' (Matt. 28 : 13), they may have thought the officers would be watching, and seeking to apprehend them on that pretence. They therefore closed the doors, probably fastening them on the inside, as a matter of safety. But how did Jesus come into their midst when the doors were thus closed? Most likely by quietly opening the doors, passing in, and closing them after him, as the angel by night opened the prison-doors for the apostles to go out, Acts 5 : 19, and as afterward an angel similarly opened the prison-door for Peter to pass out, Acts 12 : 7–9. This required superhuman power. The doors seem to have been opened and closed so quietly as to be unnoticed by the disciples; and the first they observed, *Jesus came into the midst and stood*, so that " they were terrified and affrighted, and supposed they had seen a spirit," Luke 24 : 37. Henry remarks: "Though the doors were shut, he knew how to open them without noise, as formerly he had walked on the water and yet had a true body." Luke's account, however, looks more as if Jesus entered without opening the doors: "Jesus himself *stood in the midst of them.*" ᶠ While the disciples were talking Jesus was there, standing in the midst of them, Luke 24 : 36. The language implies that the manner of his entering was at least extraordinary. The question whether Jesus had his glorified body at his resurrection or at his ascension naturally arises here. The following from Tholuck is worth noting : "In the opinion of the Fathers and the theologians of the Lutheran Church, it is a just inference from the text that Jesus passed through the closed doors, and conse-

14 *

ciples were assembled for fear of the Jews, ᵗcame Jesus and stood in the midst, and saith unto them, Peace be 20 unto you. And when he had so said, ᵘhe showed unto them *his* hands and his side. Then were the disciples 21 glad, when they saw the Lord. Then said Jesus to

ᵗ ch. 16. 22; Matt. 18. 20.
ᵘ Luke 24. 39, 40; Acts 1. 3; 1 John 1. 1.

quently must have risen in a glorified body. This view seems to be favored by the fact that the disciples did not recognize him (ver. 14; 21 : 4; Luke 24 : 13); by the express declaration (Mark 16 : 12); the sudden appearing (John 21 : 1); and the vanishing (Luke 24 : 31); to which is to be added the doctrinal argument that the resurrection of Christians in glory is designated as a repetition or continuation of the resurrection of Christ, 1 Cor. 15 : 20; Col. 1 : 18. . . . The fact, indeed, that Christ after his resurrection partook of earthly nourishment (Luke 24 : 42; John 21 : 13) may be set aside by the distinction that the *capacity* to assimilate food does not necessarily presuppose its *necessity;* but when the risen Lord attributes to himself flesh and bones (Luke 24 : 39), can this body be the *body of his glory* which is ascribed to him in his present condition? Phil. 3 : 21. Can this be harmonized with the fact that according to 1 Cor. 6 : 13 there shall be in the glorified state no questions about *meats* and the *stomach*, and that 'flesh and blood' are excluded from the perfected kingdom of God? 1 Cor. 15 : 50. On the other hand, were there no analogy between the risen Christ and Christians when they shall rise, how could Paul run a parallel between them? Again, if Christ remained subject to all the earlier conditions of his earthly being, how, during the forty days that followed his resurrection, could he keep aloof from the circle of his disciples, when he must, on this supposition, have been impelled to seek in it to allay their agitation? We consequently find ourselves compelled to take an intermediate view, to suppose an essential change potentially in bodily organism, which did not, however, come to its completion until the act of ascension." Compare an able article on "Translation" by J. W. Willmarth in *Baptist Quarterly*, Oct., 1868, pp. 424-427, in which he maintains that Christ did not have his glorified body till he ascended to heaven. While I incline to the latter view, I cannot suppose that the body of our Lord underwent a gradual and progressive change between his resurrection and ascension. Whatever change or changes occurred, either at the one time or the other, it was doubtless instantaneous, similar to that which shall take place with believers who shall be living at his second coming, who "shall be changed at the last trump in a moment, in the twinkling of an eye," 1 Cor. 15 : 51, 52; comp. 1 Thess. 4 : 17. **Peace be unto you;** though the disciples had deserted him in the hour of trial, he knew their integrity of heart and the strength of the temptation, and he now speaks to them the words of pardon and peace. See ch. 14 : 27.

20. **And when he had so said** (rather, *having said this*), **he showed unto them his hands and his side.** He has allowed them to recognize him, at least in part, by his general aspect and his voice, and now he will confirm the impression and assure them by showing them his wounded hands and side. The scars of his wounds, newly yet perfectly healed, remain in his body after his resurrection, that they may demonstrate the truth of it. Earthly conquerors glory in the scars of their wounds. "Christ's wounds were to speak on earth that it was *he himself;* and therefore he rose with them; they were to speak in the intercession he must ever live to make, and therefore he ascended with them, and appeared in the midst of the throne, 'a Lamb as if it had been slain,' Rev. 5 : 6. He will come again with his scars, that they may 'look on him whom they pierced,' ch. 19 : 37." — M. HENRY. **Then were the disciples glad** (or, *rejoiced*), **when they saw the Lord,** and were assured it was he. This indeed was the first-fruits of the joy promised in ch. 16 : 22.

21. **Then said Jesus to them**

them again, Peace *be* unto you: ˣ as *my* Father hath
22 sent me, even so send I you. And when he had said
this, ʸ he breathed on *them*, and saith unto them, ᶻ Re-
23 ceive ye the Holy Ghost: ᵃ whosesoever sins ye remit,
they are remitted unto them: *and whosesoever sins ye
retain, they are retained.*
24 But Thomas, one of the twelve, ᵇ called Didymus,
25 was not with them when Jesus came. The other
disciples therefore said unto him, We have seen the

ˣ ch. 17. 18, 19;
Isa. 61. 1-3;
Matt. 28. 18; 2
Tim. 2. 2; Heb.
3. 1.
ʸ Gen. 2. 7; Job 33.
4; Ezek. 37. 9.
ᶻ ch. 14. 16; 15. 26.
ᵃ Matt. 16. 19; 18.
18; Acts 10. 43;
1 Cor. 5. 3-5; 2
Cor. 2. 6-10; 1
Tim. 1. 20.   ᵇ ch. 11. 16.

---

again, Peace be unto you. He
does not upbraid them with their past
delinquencies, but now repeats this
salutation to comfort them with the
assurance of his love. As my Father
hath sent me, even so send I you.
With the same divine authority with
which he acted in sending me forth I
also act in sending you. But how could
he say this if he was not God? See Isa.
42 : 8; 45 : 21, 22. And according as
the Father gave me all needful power
and every requisite gift and grace for
my work as Mediator, I also give you
every needed qualification as my apostles. Moreover, as he sent me forth to
be his ambassador of peace and life to
sinful and perishing men, I also send
you to be my ambassadors of pardon,
peace, and life to them.
22. **And when he had said this,
he breathed on them.** As in Gen.
2 : 7 it is said, "The Lord God . . .
breathed [Septuagint, *inbreathed*] into
his nostrils the breath of life, and the
man became a living soul," so here the
risen Redeemer *inbreathes*, or breathes
within them symbolically, the breath
of his resurrection-life, to fit them to
live and act in their new and important
sphere, into which he sends them. Compare Ezek. 37 : 9-14. **Receive ye the
Holy Ghost.** This would be to them
indeed the spirit " of life," and would
qualify them for their new sphere as
nothing else could, and enable them to
act in it according to his will. And
while this inbreathing was sufficient
for the present, it may be regarded as
a first-fruit and pledge of the more
abundant imparting of the Holy Spirit to
the disciples on the day of Pentecost.
23. **They are remitted** (or, with
the best critical authorities, *have been
remitted*) **unto them,** already in the
plan and purpose of God and by the
decision of the Spirit. **And whosesoever sins ye retain,** or pronounce
unforgiven, **they are retained**; rather, *have been retained* already in the
plan of redemption, on the principles
of justice and truth and by the decision of the Holy Spirit. The *have been
remitted* and *have been retained* are cor-
relative terms. Compare Matt. 16 : 19;
18 : 18. The apostles should be so
guided by the Holy Spirit as to be able
to declare authoritatively *the principles*
on which men's sins are forgiven and
those on which they cannot be forgiv-
en; also to announce the Spirit's decision in regard to individual cases that
would arise. See, for examples of the
first class, Acts 2 : 38; 3 : 19; 11 : 17,
18; 16 : 31; 20 : 21; 26 : 20; and of the
second class, Acts 1 : 25; 5 : 3, 9; 8 :
21-23. They were to feel the assurance
that they were thus guided by the Spirit
into all the truth, John 16 : 13.
24. The Greek word **Didymus,** meaning a *twin*, is intended to define the Syriac word **Thomas,** and the expression
in this verse and in ch. 11 : 16 may be
translated, *Thomas, which means Twin*.
One of the twelve, this being the
number of the apostolic body as originally constituted, and by which it had
been generally known. **Was not with
them when Jesus came.** We are
not told why Thomas was not with the
other disciples at this time. It may
have been through his own fault, and
in consequence he lost the early blessing which he might otherwise have enjoyed.
25. **We have seen the Lord**—that
is, we have seen him alive since he was
crucified and buried. How speedily and
joyfully they make this announcement
to their fellow-disciple! **Except I
shall see in his hands the print
(or, *the mark*), . . . and thrust** (better

Lord. But he said unto them, *Except I shall see in his hands the print of the nails, and put my finger into the print of the nails, and thrust my hand into his side, I will not believe.

* ch. 6. 30; Ps. 106. 21; Heb. 3. 12.

He appears to the Apostles again, Thomas being present.

26 And after eight days again his disciples were within, and Thomas with them: *then* came Jesus, the doors being shut, and stood in the midst, and said, Peace be 27 unto you. Then saith he to Thomas, ᵈReach hither thy finger, and behold my hands; and reach hither

ᵈ Ps. 78. 38; 103 13, 14; 1 Tim. 1 16; 1 John 1. 1.

put, as in the preceding clause, since the Greek word is the same) **my hand into his side, I will not believe;** more accurately, on account of the double negative, *I shall not at all believe. The mark of the nails,* showing that Jesus' hands were *nailed* to the cross when he was crucified. In Luke 24 : 39 we also read: "Behold my *hands* and my *feet*, that it is I myself," implying that both the hands and the feet exhibited marks of the wounds made by the nails. Thomas had a warm, affectionate heart, as is shown by his language to his fellow-disciples when he perceived Jesus was resolved to go into Judæa again, and by so doing expose his life: "Let us also go, that we may die with him," ch. 11 : 16. He has been called Doubting Thomas; but though doubting until he had satisfactory evidence, he was not disbelieving. True, he was not satisfied to take evidence at second-hand in so important a matter as the resurrection of Jesus. He wished sensible proof of the Lord's resurrection similar to that which his fellow-disciples had received—to see with his own eyes, and thus become assured there was no mistake in the case; and not only this, but to feel with his own hand, and thus have the evidence of *touch*.

26-31. JESUS AGAIN APPEARS TO THE APOSTLES, THOMAS BEING PRESENT. Found only here. Also, WHY JOHN HAS WRITTEN OF JESUS' MIRACLES, AND OF HIS APPEARING TO THE DISCIPLES AFTER HIS RESURRECTION.

26. **And after eight days,** or one week, both the first and the last days being counted, as in Matt. 12 : 40 and 27 : 63, compared with 16 : 21. Whether the disciples met every day of the intervening week, we are not informed; but when the first day of the week again came round, they were careful to be together, **and Thomas this time with them.** Jesus thus honored the first day of the week by his second appearance to the assembled apostles. **Then came Jesus** (rather, without *then, Jesus comes*), the animated present tense. **The doors being shut** (see above, in ver. 19), Jesus comes *into the midst,* **and stood . . . and said, Peace be unto you.** Thus a second time by his own example Jesus sanctions the disciples' meeting for religious worship on the first day of the week in commemoration of his resurrection. See ver. 19 and note on ver. 1. *Peace be to you!* This repeated salutation, as it comes from Jesus' lips, is full of meaning, and adapted to quiet the fears and encourage the hearts of his anxious disciples. "Peace be to you!" was the common salutation of a man to his friends, and it implied his wishing them prosperity and every needed blessing. See 1 Sam. 25 : 6; Luke 10 : 5, 6. Hence that saying of the rabbins: "Great is peace; for all other blessings are included in it." —DR. A. CLARKE.

27. **Then saith he to Thomas.** He speaks to Thomas in particular, who, having been absent from the former meeting, was incredulous about the reported resurrection. **Reach** (or, *bring*) **hither thy finger, and behold my hands; and reach hither thy hand, and thrust** (too violent; better, as in ch. 5 : 7; 13 : 2, *put*), **it into my side.** It would seem that the spear-wound was large enough to admit the hand. Jesus responds exactly to the desire Thomas has expressed in ver. 25, and thereby proves that he is the One who searches the heart and knows all the words and

A. D. 30. JOHN XX. 325

thy hand, and thrust it into my side: and be not
28 faithless, but believing. And Thomas answered and
29 said unto him, *My Lord and my God! Jesus saith *ch. 9. 38; Rom.
unto him, Thomas, because thou hast seen me, thou 9. 5.

actions of men. Thomas perceives this, and as he beholds the scarred hands and the pierced side of his risen Lord, the same body in which he suffered, prompted by his reason and his feelings, he exclaims: "My Lord and my God!" **And be not faithless** (better, *not unbelieving*), **but believing**, the first word in the original being the same as the last, with the negative particle prefixed.

28. **And Thomas** (rather, with the critical authorities — omitting *and — Thomas*) **answered and said,** making the language concise and forcible. He was evidently a man of decided convictions as well as strong feelings. Although he could not believe without evidence, yet whenever he had evidence that he deemed appropriate and sufficient, the conviction which it produced in his mind was of a positive character, and influenced his conduct accordingly. On this occasion he is satisfied that none but God can thus know the thoughts and feelings which he has cherished in his heart—no stranger can be so acquainted with the very words he has spoken to his brethren; and the marks of the wounds which Jesus received on the cross are so manifest before his eyes that he cannot but express his conviction in the earnest and decided words, **My Lord and my God!** Thus Thomas recognized not only the Messiahship of Jesus, but also his Deity. He at once grasped the great truth which John enunciates in opening his Gospel (ch. 1 : 1)—that the Word was God—and was the first, so far as we are informed, to make this direct and explicit confession. The confession is in full harmony.

29. **Thomas.** Omit this word, with the critical authorities, and read, **because thou hast seen me, thou hast believed.** He had not previously given sufficient credit to the intelligence and testimony of his brethren. But now with his own eyes he has seen such proofs of the living person before him being really Jesus that he can no longer doubt. **Blessed are they that have not seen, and yet have believed;** more exactly, *Happy they who saw not and yet believed*—who, when they heard the glorious truths of the gospel, including the resurrection, believed them on the adequate testimony of the preachers, the Scriptures, and the first disciples. Compare also ver. 8.

Thomas was favored with a conviction from the evidence of his own senses of sight and hearing and of touch. But the evidence given us from the *combined testimony* of the first disciples is still more reliable and conclusive. Besides the six appearances enumerated in the prefatory note to this chapter, Jesus appeared (7) to seven disciples at the Sea of Galilee, ch. 21 : 4–22; (8) to the apostles and five hundred brethren on a mountain in Galilee, Matt. 28 : 16-20; (9) to James, probably at Jerusalem, 1 Cor. 15 : 7; (10) to the apostles at Jerusalem and on the Mount of Olives just before his ascension, Luke 24 : 50, 51. He seems also to have appeared to his apostles at some other times. See Acts 1 : 3, compared with ch. 20 : 30, 31. It is thus manifest that he appeared at least ten, and probably more, times during the forty days after his resurrection, to so great a number of witnesses, at so many different times and places, and in such various circumstances, that fraud in regard to the fact of his resurrection was impossible, because it could not have escaped detection. These witnesses all tested the thing with their senses of sight and hearing, and the apostles with the sense of feeling (ver. 27; Luke 24:39; 1 John 1:1), and they were harmonious in their testimony. They were honest and competent, and would not deceive others. They were not enthusiastic, but were in their calm, sober senses, and not at first expecting the event; yet so fully convinced were they that to the end of their lives, even in the face of persecution and of death itself, they continued to bear the same unwavering testimony to the fact of Jesus' resurrection. This they never would have done to falsify a fact. Men may, indeed, endure per-

hast believed: ᶠblessed *are* they that have not seen, and *yet* have believed.

30 ᵍAnd many other signs truly did Jesus in the presence of his disciples, which are not written in this
31 book: ʰbut these are written, that ye might believe that Jesus is ⁱthe Christ, the Son of God; ᵏand that believing ye might have life ˡthrough his name.

ᶠ 2 Cor. 5. 7; Heb. 11. 1; 1 Pet. 1. 8.
ᵍ ch. 21. 25; 1 Cor. 10. 11.
ʰ ch. 5. 39; Luke 1. 4; Rom. 15. 4; 2 Tim. 3. 15.
ⁱ ch. 1.41,45; Matt. 16. 20; 1 John 2. 22.
ᵏ ch. 3. 15, 16; 5. 24; 10. 10; 1 Pet. 1. 8, 9.
ˡ Luke 24. 47; Acts 3. 16; 10. 13.

---

secution, and even death, for their *opinions*, because they hold them so dear, but they will not thus expose themselves to falsify a known *fact* relating to others. Christ's resurrection is therefore in this way established with the certainty of moral evidence, besides being confirmed from other sources.

30. And many other signs truly did Jesus, rather, *Many other signs, therefore, Jesus also indeed wrought,* expressing each point with great minuteness and accuracy. Compare ch. 21 : 25. **In the presence of his disciples,** and not in some dark corner or concealed place; *his disciples,* who, as servants of the God of truth, are competent and faithful witnesses.

31. But these are written, that ye might (rather, *may*) **believe that Jesus is the Christ, . . . might** (or *may*) **have life through** (rather, *in*) **his name,** being united to him by a living faith, and thus on the ground of the promises entitled to *life in his name.* Compare ch. 6 : 47, 57; 15 : 5, 16. The writer's object here is especially to strengthen the faith of believers. Compare 1 John 5 : 13.

Some make the *signs* of vers. 30 and 31 refer to the whole Gospel of John, while others restrict them to this chapter and the supplementary chapter which follows. The latter view appears to be the correct one, because (1) The signs here spoken of seem to have been wrought by the *risen* Redeemer, and those described have been written as specimens, to confirm the faith of believers in him as risen and divine—**the Son of God.** (2) They were performed *in the presence of his disciples.* After his resurrection Jesus appeared only to his disciples, and with each appearance some *wonderful deed* of his seems to have been connected, such as his sudden appearance and disappearance; his recognition by Mary the moment her name was spoken; his coming suddenly into the midst of the assembled disciples and standing when the doors had been shut; his showing them his wounded hands and side; his omniscience, manifested to Thomas; his bidding the disciples cast the net on the right-hand side of the ship, where they should find fishes; his providing a fire of coals, with a fish and bread; his threefold inquiry and charge to Peter; and, while checking Peter's curiosity, his intimation respecting the protracted life of John. All these were *signs* to his disciples indicating who and what he was. (3) This view renders consistent the three forms of expression, ch. 12 : 37, "done so many miracles before them"—the Jewish multitude; here, those *wrought in the presence of his disciples;* and ch. 21 : 24, 25, "things which Jesus did," of which John has not written.

PRACTICAL REMARKS.

1. Mary Magdalene early at the sepulchre, a pattern of love and devotion to Jesus. The fragrance of her affection was far sweeter than the most precious spices which she and the women had brought to embalm him, ver. 1; Mark 16 : 1, 2; Song Sol. 8 : 6, 7.

2. On the first day of the week we seek not a dead but a living Saviour, vers. 1, 16, 19, 26; Ps. 118 : 24; Heb. 4 : 14-16; 12 : 2; Rev. 1 : 10.

3. Christians, in the weakness of their faith and in their ignorance of God's plans, often make that a cause of fear and sorrow which should be to them a ground of hope and an occasion of joy, ver. 2.

4. In the darkest hour we should not forsake Christ and his people, but strive, like Peter and John, to be active to help and ready to encourage others who may be in sorrow with us, ver. 3.

5. The warmest affection is often attended with the greatest humility, calmness, and deference to others. John modestly stoops down and looks into the sepulchre, and with deference allows Peter first to enter in, vers. 4, 5.

6. In Peter and John we have an illustration of how God dispenses his gifts differently. Some are quicker, others more daring, vers. 5, 6.

7. How slow were the disciples to believe, when we find Peter leaving the sepulchre, as Luke tells us, "wondering"! We need often to suspect ourselves and be patient with the weak faith of others, ver. 7; Luke 24 : 12.

8. "John saw and believed; a mind disposed to contemplation may perhaps sooner receive the evidence of divine truth than a mind disposed to action" (M. HENRY), ver. 8.

9. Ignorance of the Scriptures is often the cause of a weak faith, vers. 9, 10; Luke 24 : 25-27.

10. We must wait God's time for revealing himself or his mercies to us. Peter and John must wait before seeing their Lord, vers. 10, 19; Luke 24 : 34; 1 Cor. 15 : 5; Ps. 40 : 1.

11. True love to Christ is connected with a tender heart. There is beauty in every tear of affection for Jesus, ver. 11.

12. They who, weeping, would find Jesus must seek for him. Mary not only wept, but *stooped down* to look into the sepulchre, vers. 11, 12; Luke 2 : 48.

13. Angels are ministering spirits to God's people. They were at the sepulchre not so much as guardians as consolers and directors of the heart-burdened women who came hither, ver. 13.

14. We are often distressed and weep at that which springs from infinite love, and which is for God's glory and the good of men, ver. 14.

15. Jesus is often nearer his sorrowing people than they suppose, ver. 15; Mark 6 : 48-50.

16. How often is Jesus seen through tears of penitence and love! vers. 14-16.

17. "Jesus first showed himself to Mary Magdalene, out of whom he had cast seven devils, not to Mary his mother. He would not by word or deed do anything to countenance the superstitious reverence and idolatrous worship which has since been offered to the Virgin," ver. 16; Mark 16 : 9.

18. Our first business in this world is duty, not enjoyment nor the satisfying of an unnecessary curiosity. There will be time enough for joy and the solving of mysteries in heaven, vers. 16-18.

19. Though Jesus is in glory, he is still identified with his people in nature, in sympathy, and in relation to the Father, ver. 17; Heb. 2 : 11, 17, 18; John 17 : 21-24.

20. The first day of the week was honored by repeated appearances of our Lord. How often from that day to this has he manifested himself on that day to his disciples, gathered for public worship! vers. 19, 26; Acts 20 : 7.

21. The manifestation of Christ's presence to his disciples is attended with joy. And he asks none to believe without the clearest evidence. Hence he showed himself to many witnesses, inviting the most careful scrutiny, vers. 20, 27.

22. Jesus calls his ministers and sends them into the world, and he will furnish them with needed grace and with his Spirit for the performance of their duties, vers. 21, 22.

23. The apostles, as inspired men, spoke and taught with authority. It will be soon enough for ministers to resort to the confessional when they can show by apostolic works, by miracles and prophecy, that they possess apostolic gifts, ver. 23.

24. Absentees from the prayer-meeting, and from other assemblies of God's people, know not how much they lose, ver. 24; Heb. 10 : 25.

25. We should encourage and help others by telling them of our spiritual joys and striving to make them sharers of the same, ver. 25; Phil. 2 : 18, 21; 2 Cor. 11 : 2.

26. How does Christ condescend to the weakness of his disciples! Luke 24 : 15-18. But "observe that Christ did not appear to Thomas for his satisfaction till he found him in society with the rest of his disciples" (M. HENRY), ver. 26.

27. Jesus suffered Thomas and the rest of the apostles to go to the full length of their unbelief, in order that all his followers after them might believe. All reason for doubt was for ever taken away, ver. 27.

28. In true, saving faith we take hold

Our Lord's appearance to seven disciples at the Sea of Galilee.—Conclusion.

XXI. AFTER these things ᵐ Jesus showed himself again ᵐ Matt. 26 32.
to the disciples at the sea of Tiberias; and on this

of Christ as a personal Saviour. "*My Lord and my God!*" ver. 28; Song Sol. 2:16.

29. We are permitted to receive a blessing and a joy which even the apostles were not privileged to share. *Not having seen*, we have believed, ver. 29.

30. The sum of Christ's history and teaching is his mission as the Saviour of men; and the object is salvation through faith in him, ver. 30; see marginal references.

31. As God's word was given so that men might believe and be saved, it should be taught and read by all, ver. 31; ch. 5:39; 2 Tim. 3:16.

CHAPTER XXI.

This chapter contains an important and instructive interview of the Saviour with seven of his disciples, recorded here only. The Gospel comes to a fitting close at the end of ch. 20. This chapter is usually considered supplementary, but none the less genuine and inspired. Alford says: "I believe it to have been written some years probably after the completion of the Gospel, to meet the error which was becoming prevalent concerning himself," ver. 23. Tholuck also: "We are inclined to think that the occasion of this appendix was furnished by the current saying concerning him, that he would not die. A lowly, child-like man would be the very one to feel a hearty desire to repel an expectation of that sort; and it is our opinion that, partly to give a vivid picture of the circumstances under which this last expression was uttered by our Lord, partly to link it with the appearings after his resurrection, which had been previously detailed, he gives the *complete* account of this delightful interview in Galilee." It is a chapter that bears the marks of an eye-witness, is full of minute details, and presents precious words of Jesus. It begins with the miraculous draught of fishes, followed by a social meal (vers. 1-14), after which Jesus draws from Peter a threefold though humble avowal of sincere and fervent love, and foretells his martyrdom (vers. 15-19), rebukes Peter's curiosity, and intimates John's long service on earth, 20-23. The book closes with the fact that much might be added. Compare *Author's Harmony*, ½ 198.

1-8. THE MIRACULOUS DRAUGHT OF FISHES, Matt. 28:16.

1. **After these things,** after the appearances of Jesus in Jerusalem by which the faith of the disciple had been established. The disciples remained in Jerusalem until after the Lord's Day following the resurrection, 20:26. They were now in Galilee, in accordance with the Saviour's directions, Matt. 28:10. Several days must have intervened since our Lord's appearance recorded in ch. 20:26-29. **Showed himself.** The expression implies that there was in his appearing something wonderful—*manifested himself*, Mark 16:12. After the resurrection Jesus did not abide with his disciples as before, but only at intervals revealed himself to them. **Again.** John records two previous appearances, ch. 20:19, 26. **To the disciples,** apostles without doubt, ch. 20:19, 25, 26. **Sea of Tiberias,** so called from a city built on the south-west shore, and named in honor of the emperor Tiberius. Also called Sea of Galilee (ch. 6:1), Lake of Gennesaret (Luke 5:1), and in the Old Testament Sea of Chinnereth, Num. 34:11. It still abounds in fish. "As I once rode out into the lake as far as I could force my horse, and then stood still, I could see swarms of fishes gathering around, about the size of the American trout."—DR. FISH, *Bible Lands Illustrated*, p. 566. On its shores a large part of our Saviour's ministry had been passed. Tiberias, Bethsaida, Capernaum, Chorazin, and other populous towns crowded around the sea on every side. See further on ch. 6:1. **On this wise**—that is, *in this manner.* Described in the following verses.

2 wise showed he *himself.* There were together Simon Peter, and Thomas called Didymus, and ⁿNathanael of Cana in Galilee, and °the *sons* of Zebedee, and two
3 other of his disciples. Simon Peter saith unto them, ᴾI go a fishing. They say unto him, We also go with thee. They went forth, and entered into a ship immediately; and that night they caught nothing.
4 But when the morning was now come, Jesus stood on the shore: but the disciples ᑫknew not that it was
5 Jesus. Then ʳJesus saith unto them, Children, have
6 ye any meat? They answered him, No. And he said unto them, ˢCast the net on the right side of the ship,

ⁿ ch. 1. 45.
° Matt. 4. 21.

ᴾ Matt. 4. 18.

ᑫ ch. 20. 14; Luke 24. 15, 16.
ʳ Luke 24. 41.
ˢ Matt. 17. 27; Luke 5. 4, 6, 7.

2. Simon Peter. Simon is contracted from Simeon, and means *hearkening*. Peter, signifying a *rock*, was given by our Lord to Simon, ch. 1: 42. His name always stands first in the lists of the apostles. He had a primacy of leadership and enthusiasm. **Thomas called Didymus,** *The Twin*, a surname of Thomas used only by John. See ch. 20:24. **Nathanael,** probably the same as Bartholomew of the first three Gospels. For his first meeting with Jesus see ch. 1 : 45-51. **Sons of Zebedee,** James and John, Luke 5 : 10. John always alludes to himself in an indirect manner. **Two.** That they were apostles seems evident from vers. 1, 13. It is generally supposed that they were Andrew, the brother of Peter, and Philip, the friend of Nathanael. Seven were present in all. This may have embraced all the fishermen of the apostolic group. Matthew, we know, was a tax-collector. Matt. 9 : 9.
3. I go a fishing. The disciples now resume their occupation of fishing, probably as a means of livelihood during the time which the Lord had appointed them in Galilee between the feasts of the passover and Pentecost. They cannot take up the great commission (Matt. 28 : 19), which was probably given later than this (Matt. 28 : 16), and preach of the atonement and the risen Saviour, until endued with power from on high, Acts 1 : 8. This seems to be the first proposal to resume their old calling. The decisive words of Peter influence all the rest, and straightway they accompany him. **Ship;** rather, *the small fishing-boat*, ver. 8; **immediately** should be omitted, according to the highest critical authorities.

That night; night was the most favorable time for catching fish (Luke 5 : 5), yet there were nights like this— unsuccessful. Their complete failure without Christ was now to be turned into complete success with Christ.
4. Morning was now come (according to another reading, *now about dawning*), Jesus stood upon the beach, but the disciples knew him not. The early morning, the despondency in their hearts, and the sudden appearance when not looking for him may partially account for their not recognizing him. A deeper reason perhaps lies in a mysterious change in the resurrection-body of Jesus. Mary did not recognize her risen Saviour (ch. 20:14); "Their eyes were holden," Luke 24 : 16.
5. Children; a word that might be used equally by a stranger to inferiors and by a teacher to his disciples. Jesus, wishing not to be known at once, addresses them in this general way. **Meat;** literally, *something to eat*. Chrysostom, whose native language was Greek, says that he addressed them just as one who wished to buy fish might have addressed them. Jesus, though omniscient, would bring them to confession of their emptiness, that so he may help them, ch. 6 : 5.
6. Cast the net on the right side, the command implying that they should have success in its obedience. The divine purpose works through human agencies. Dispirited with their fruitless work, they perhaps have drawn the net into the boat. In Luke 5 : 4 Jesus bids them launch into the deep, here, to cast the net on the right side. The *right* side showed his sovereign choice and his knowledge of the results, Matt. 17 : 27. **Able to draw;** a dif

JOHN XXI. A. D. 30

and ye shall find. They cast therefore, and now they were not able to draw it for the multitude of fishes.
7 Therefore ¹ that disciple whom Jesus loved saith unto Peter, It is the Lord. Now when Simon Peter heard that it was the Lord, he girt *his* fisher's coat *unto him* (for he was naked), and did cast himself into the sea.
8 And the other disciples came in a little ship (for they were not far from land, but as it were two hundred cubits), dragging the net with fishes.
9 As soon then as they were come to land, ⁿ they saw

¹ ch. 13. 23; 20. 2.

ⁿ 1 Kings 19. 5, 6; Matt. 4. 11.

ferent word from that used in verse 8. They could not draw it up over the water, perhaps to themselves, in order to empty the fish into the boat (Luke 5 : 7), but they could drag it through the water, which was a much easier feat.

7. **Therefore,** because of the multitude of fishes, which evidently indicated the presence of divine power. (See below.) **Whom Jesus loved.** John employs the same expression concerning himself in ch. 13 : 23; 20 : 2. It is an expression fragrant with the memory of the tender intimacy that existed between John and his Saviour. **It is the Lord.** The remembrance of a former miracle upon this same sea (Luke 5 : 6), when, after a fruitless night of toil, their empty nets were filled at the word of Christ, brings to the mind of John the thought—*It is the Lord!* The beloved disciple sees in the stranger the form of Jesus, and hears in the "*children*" (ver. 5) the voice of the Saviour. **Fisher's coat;** the upper garment, without sleeves and extending to the knees. **Naked;** having thrown off the outer garment for work. He probably had on his under-garment. The word in the original does not always mean complete nakedness. He **girded** the garment that it might not impede him in swimming. **Cast himself into the sea.** The characteristic mark of Peter stands out distinctly. His zeal has no patience with the slow moving of the boat. "John, the more thoughtful, is first to *perceive;* Peter, the more ardent, is the first to *act.*"

8. **In a little ship;** literally, *in the boat,* before spoken of, ver. 3. **Two hundred cubits,** about three hundred feet. Peter swam or waded while they made use of the boat. They now come to the shore, dragging the over-loaded net. **With fishes;** rather, full of fishes, which they had caught.

The similarities and contrasts between this miracle and that recorded in Luke 5 : 1–11 are striking. In that the net began to tear; in this it did not, ver. 11. Hence some have supposed that to symbolize the gathering of men into the visible church on earth, from which some may be lost; but this the elect, a definite number, who are members of Christ's spiritual kingdom, of whom none will be lost. Thus there is an advance on the former miracle. See further on ver. 11, last paragraph.

9–14. THE MEAL UPON THE SEA-SHORE.

9. **As soon as they were come to land;** rather, *when therefore they went out upon the land,* disembarked upon the shore. **Saw . . . fish;** rather, *see.* The Bible Union version renders *a fish,* which accords well with the original, and with the fact that Jesus commands the disciples to bring of their fish. Were the bread and fish miraculously provided? Lange thinks they were furnished by the agency of the friends of Jesus living along the shore. Compare Matt. 19 : 30; Luke 22 : 10. Most interpreters refer them to the ministry of angels or the creative word of Jesus. Compare 1 Kings 19 : 6. The impression made upon the mind of the reader is that it was a miraculous provision. Surely he who filled their net with fishes could provide the fish, and he who fed the multitudes on the north-eastern shore of this same sea could provide the bread without human hands. **A fire of coals,** perhaps of charcoal. It is much used in Bible lands at the present day. "Charcoal is so much esteemed for cooking purposes that travellers generally man-

A. D. 30.   JOHN XXI.   331

a fire of coals there, and fish laid thereon, and bread.
10 Jesus saith unto them, Bring of the fish which ye have
11 now caught. Simon Peter went up, and drew the net
to land full of great fishes, an hundred and fifty and
three: and for all there were so many, yet was not
the net broken.
12 Jesus saith unto them, ˣ Come *and* dine. And none   ˣ Acts 10. 41.
of the disciples durst ask him, Who art thou? know-
13 ing that it was the Lord. Jesus then cometh, and
taketh bread, and giveth them, and fish likewise.

age to carry some of it along with them on their journeys packed in a bag or basket, and a fire of coals is not an uncommon sight in the open country."— VAN LENNEP, *Bible Lands*, p. 465.
10. **Bring of the fish;** rather, *the fishes.* A double supply, his and theirs. Although the fish were caught in accordance with his directions alone, yet Jesus graciously attributes the result to them. He will sup with them and have them sup with him.
11. **Simon Peter.** Peter, having greeted his Lord, now takes the leadership of the work in hand. **Went up,** that is, *went on board* of the boat now at the shore, with the net probably fastened to it. **Full of great fishes.** They were all large; in this consisted part of the miracle. No mystical significance attaches to the number *one hundred and fifty-three.* It indicates the careful counting which took place after the event, and in which John the narrator took a part. Every minute detail of this occurrence made a deep and lifelong impression upon the mind of the beloved disciple. **Not broken.** It was a marvel to the fishermen that the net was not rent. Herein this miracle differs from that recorded in Luke 5 : 5, when the net began to break.
This whole narrative has much richness and depth of meaning, typifying the work of the apostles and their source of success. When Simon, Andrew, James, and John were called to the work of the ministry (Matt. 4 : 18, 19), Jesus said, "Follow me and I will make you fishers of men." At the miraculous draught of fishes (Luke 5 : 1-11), when their nets were full, Jesus said, "Fear not; from henceforth thou shalt catch men." This miracle revealed not only the omniscience of Jesus, his wondrous love for them in the supply of their wants, but also contained a prophecy of the wondrous success of the apostles in their work of saving men. "Toiling alone, though at the most favorable time, they toil in vain; but when at the command of Jesus, however unpropitious the hour, they cast in the net, many fishes are taken. And the repetition of this lesson illustrates the wisdom of Christ. When required to forsake all that they might prepare for their great mission, and again when about to assume the full responsibility and toil of that mission, they need to have its character brought distinctly before their minds." —DR. HOVEY, *Miracles of Christ*, p. 43. See on ver. 8, last paragraph.
12. **Come and dine;** rather, *come break your fast,* or *come lunch.* That it was the early morning meal is evident from vers. 3, 4. "Breakfast took place in the morning on ordinary days not before nine o'clock, which was the first hour of prayer. The more prolonged and substantial meal took place in the evening."—SMITH's *Dictionary.* **Durst ask him.** They did not presume to do it. Tholuck says: "The disciples, far from the familiarity which had been their wont, refrained from expressing the joy they felt at beholding their Lord again." The *durst not* sprang from reverence for the Saviour. They were admitted into his fellowship as friends (John 15 : 15), but in their case familiarity did not breed contempt, but rather awe of him as the Son of God. Compare ch. 4 : 27. **Knowing.** The appearances of Jesus after the resurrection were attended with such incontestable proofs of the reality of his presence that doubt became faith, and faith was attended with positive knowledge, Acts 1 : 3.
13. **Jesus then cometh,** from the

14 This is now ʸ the third time that Jesus showed himself to his disciples, after that he was risen from the dead.

15 So when they had dined, Jesus saith to Simon Peter, Simon, *son* of Jonas, lovest thou me ᶻ more than these? He saith unto him, Yea, Lord; ᵃ thou knowest that I love thee. He saith unto him, Feed my ᵇ lambs. He saith to him again ᶜ the second time, Simon, *son* of

ʸ ch. 20. 19, 26.

ᶻ Matt. 26. 33.
ᵃ Heb. 4. 13.
ᵇ Isa. 40. 11; Matt. 18. 10, 11.
ᶜ Matt. 26. 72.

spot where they had seen him standing to the fire of coals. **Taketh bread.** Jesus acts as host. "He took bread and blessed it, and brake, and gave to them," Luke 24 : 30. It is probable that in this case Jesus pronounced the customary blessing. It is probable, too, that the Saviour partook with them of this meal, Luke 24 : 42, 43.

14. **The third time,** the third appearance to the disciples or apostles in a group. It is also the *third* recorded by John. The two previous appearances are recorded ch. 20 : 19, 26. This is the *seventh* manifestation of Jesus after the resurrection, if we enumerate *all* his appearances. The following is the order as given in the *Author's Harmony of the Gospels*, p. 312 : To Mary Magdalene; to the other women returning from the sepulchre; to Peter; to two disciples going to Emmaus; to the apostles, Thomas being absent; to the apostles, Thomas being present; to seven disciples or apostles at the Sea of Galilee.

15-23. PETER'S THREEFOLD CONFESSION OF LOVE; HIS MARTYRDOM PREDICTED. Jesus, before this, appeared to Peter alone, Luke 24 : 34. In the presence of his fellow-disciples Jesus now lays bare the shame of his fall, and graciously grants forgiveness. Peter once made a noble confession of Christ's Messiahship (Matt. 16 : 16); he now makes a noble protestation of his deep personal love for his Saviour.

15. **Had dined,** or, *taken their morning meal.* The meal appears to have passed in silence. Alford says: "Surely every word would have been recorded." **Simon.** Notice that Jesus addresses him not as Peter, the name which he had given him, but by his former name, perhaps to remind him of his frailty, Mark 14 : 37; Luke 22 : 31. **Son of Jonas.** *John* is here the true reading Also in vers. 16, 17, ch.

1 : 42, Jona in Bar-jona (Matt. 16 : 17) is an abridged form of the word for John. He thrice calls him by his original name, Simon, not by his new and official name, Peter. Compare Luke 22 : 31. The apostolic name of honor gives way for a time to the old name indicative of natural descent and weakness exhibited in his fall. **Lovest thou me more than these?** more than these, thy fellow-disciples? This question springs from Peter's boastful expression, "Although all shall be offended, yet will not I," Mark 14 : 29; compare Matt. 26 : 33. Peter had boasted in the presence of all; he must now make public confession of his weakness. **Thou knowest that I love thee.** He appeals to the heart-searching knowledge of Jesus. Compare ch. 1 : 48. The spirit of boastfulness has passed away. He no longer compares himself with others, but simply expresses his own personal attachment to Christ. The word used by Peter in his reply, rendered *love*, is not the same as that used by Jesus in his question, though both are translated alike. Peter chooses a word denoting deep personal attachment as a friend. His answer may be rendered, *"I love thee dearly* as a personal friend." **Feed** refers to the spiritual sustenance required by the flock of Christ. Instruction concerning Christ's person, work, and promises would be food for the soul. Compare ch. 4 : 32. **Lambs.** This designates a distinct class of the spiritual flock—the young and tender disciples, whether in age or Christian standing. Compare Isa. 40 : 11; Heb. 5 : 13; 1 John 2 : 12, 13.

16. Jesus now repeats his question: **Lovest thou me?** He omits the *more than these* contained in his first question. Christ was a tender physician, "breaking not the bruised reed." The absence of a boastful spirit in Peter's reply was a sufficient confession

Jonas, lovest thou me? He saith unto him, Yea, Lord; thou knowest that I love thee. [d] He saith unto 17 him, Feed my sheep. He saith unto him [e] the third time, Simon, *son* of Jonas, lovest thou me? Peter was grieved because he said unto him the third time, Lovest thou me? and he said unto him, Lord, [f] thou knowest all things; thou knowest that I love thee. 18 Jesus saith unto him, Feed my sheep. [g] Verily, verily, I say unto thee, When thou wast young, thou girdedst thyself, and walkedst whither thou wouldest: but when

[d] ch. 10. 11, 16; Matt. 25. 33; Acts 20. 28; Heb. 13. 20; 1 Pet. 2. 25; 5. 2, 4.
[e] ch. 13. 38.
[f] ch. 2. 24, 25; 16. 30.
[g] ch. 13. 36; Acts 12. 3, 4.

of his folly and sin. To this question Peter makes the same reply as at first. No questioning can drive him from a consciousness of his love for Christ and the confession of it. **Feed;** a different word from that used in verse 15, and one more difficult to translate into English in this connection. It means *tend*. Perhaps the full force of the original is best expressed by the paraphrase, *Be a shepherd of my sheep*. Upon the second confession of Peter's love the Saviour rises higher in the manifestation of his restoring grace. Be a shepherd; let the love of the Shepherd, who tends and feeds, leads and guards, and lays down his life for the flock, abide in you. Alford says: "The shepherding the sheep refers to the government of the church, as shown forth in the early part of the Acts." If so, yet that no exclusive primacy, as the Romanists teach, was here conferred upon Peter is evident. There was an entire equality in all powers and rights among the apostles, Matt. 19 : 28; Acts 15 : 6, 21; Gal. 2 : 11. Yet there is not necessarily implied in the expression anything more than what belongs to any overseer or pastor, Acts 20 : 28. Peter may have had this in mind when he wrote to "elders" or pastors (1 Pet. 5 : 2–4), "Feed" (rather, *tend*) "the flock of God."

17. A third time Jesus puts to Peter the question—**Lovest thou me?** The Saviour now uses the same word for "love" that Peter had used in his replies. **Peter was grieved because he said unto him the third time.** The threefold denial of Christ, with all its guilt and shame, overwhelmed Peter with grief. The thrice-repeated question brought before his mind the "thrice denying that he knew him," Matt. 26 : 75. Then a look of Christ made him weep bitterly, Luke 22 : 62. Now the words of Christ grieved his heart sorely. He was grieved also because in this third inquiry Jesus took the very word from his mouth and put it into the question, "Dost thou love me dearly?" as though it could fairly be doubted, and thus even more keenly reminding him of his denial. **Thou knowest all things.** He appeals to the Saviour's omniscience for the reality of his love. The first two replies *imply* his omniscience; this reply clearly expresses it. Compare ch. 16 : 30; Acts 1 : 2. **Feed my sheep;** *feed* here is the same as in ver. 15. Again Jesus bids him provide nourishment for the flock. Wordsworth says: "To provide wholesome food for Christ's sheep and lambs is the first and last thing." The word used for *sheep*, according to the majority of critics, is different from that used in ver. 16, denoting the preciousness of the flock, and may be rendered *sheeplings*. The command of Christ "to watch over the flock" cannot properly be said to reinstate Peter in his office, for he had not been displaced. But in view of his sad fall, the stain left upon his character, the damage done to his standing among the brethren and his own rest of mind, Jesus encourages him, and gives him assurance that he still has a place in feeding the flock and guiding the church.

18. The end of his pastoral office is now announced to him. Before this Peter had denied his Saviour; hereafter he should bear witness for him even by dying for him. **Verily, verily,** calling attention to some important announcement. Compare ch. 3 : 3 ; 5 : 24. **Wast young;** literally, *wast younger*, embracing the whole period of life to the verge of old age. **Girdedst thy-**

thou shalt be old, thou shalt stretch forth thy hands, and another shall gird thee, and carry *thee* whither
19 thou wouldest not. This spake he, signifying ʰ by
what death he should glorify God. And when he
had spoken this, he saith unto him, Follow me.
20 Then Peter, turning about, seeth the disciple ᵏ whom
Jesus loved, following; which also leaned on his breast
at supper, and said, Lord, which is he that betrayeth
21 thee? Peter seeing him saith to Jesus, Lord, and
22 what *shall* this man *do?* Jesus saith unto him, If I

ʰ 2 Pet. 1. 14.

ⁱ ch. 13. 36; 1 Sam. 12. 20.

ᵏ ch.13. 23–26; 20. 2.

self. In ver. 7 he girded himself and cast himself into the sea. Girding the raiment about the body was preparatory to journeying, Acts 12 : 8; 1 Pet. 1 : 13. By the use of a familiar figure Jesus meant to say that Peter went hither and thither as it pleased him. **Shalt be old;** literally, *gray.* In his old age different treatment awaits him. Peter doubtless alluded to this prophecy in 2 Pet. 1:14. **Stretch forth thy hands.** These terms must all be explained in the light of ver. 19, which makes them explanatory of a definite *mode* of dying. The allusion here is to stretching forth the hands on the transverse beam of the cross. **Another shall gird.** The mastery over his own movements had passed away. The executioner shall bind him to the cross with cords. **Carry;** rather, *lead*: by a figure of speech that is put last in narration which lies first in order of time. The prominent thought in the Saviour's prophecy is the aged Peter with outstretched hands bound to the cross. **Wouldest not** does not imply an unwillingness on Peter's part to suffer martyrdom, but indicates that his life would be in the power of others.

19. **Signifying by what death** (*what manner of death*) **he should glorify God.** Jesus used the words "signifying by what manner of death" (ch. 12 : 33), concerning his own death on the cross. According to Tertullian, who lived about A. D. 200, and Eusebius, the first church historian, Peter was crucified at Rome A. D. 67 or 68. When John wrote his Gospel the crucifixion of Peter must have been well known in the Christian churches. Peter by his fall had dishonored God; by his witnessing for Christ, even unto death, he glorified God. The full depth of the meaning of the Saviour's prophecy to Peter doubtless came to the minds of the disciples only gradually in the light of subsequent events. This prediction not only revealed the omniscience of Jesus, but also showed the honor conferred upon Peter that he was counted worthy to walk in the footsteps of his Master. **Follow me.** Alford understands this as a following Christ through the cross to glory. Compare ch. 13 : 36. The allusion (ver. 20) to John following shows that it was a literal following. The preceding conversation took place in the presence of the disciples, ver. 15. Jesus now rose in order to speak aside with Peter, whom he commands to follow him. The *literal* following of Jesus may have had in it a *symbolic* meaning, Matt. 4 : 19.

20. The **turning about** indicates that Peter at once followed Christ. The words **whom Jesus loved,** designating John, occur elsewhere, ch. 13 : 23; 20 : 2; 21 : 7. The tender relationship existing between Jesus and John, illustrated by leaning on his breast at *the* Supper, furnishes the reason for John following. His love begot a holy boldness. The question, **Lord, which is he that betrayeth thee?** put to the Saviour by John at the instigation of Peter (ch. 13 : 24, 25), may perhaps account for Peter's question to the Lord concerning John.

21. Seeing John following Jesus, Peter says, **Lord, and what shall this man do?**—meaning, *how shall it fare with this man?* Knowing that serious trials awaited himself, there springs up in his mind a desire, compounded of curiosity and love, to know whether a like destiny awaited the beloved disciple.

22. In the words **If I will** appears the absolute supremacy of Jesus over human life. If he were a mere man

A. D. 30. JOHN XXI. 335

will that he tarry ¹till I come, what *is that* to thee? 23 Follow thou me. Then went this saying abroad among the brethren, that that disciple should not die. Yet Jesus said not unto him, He shall not die; but, If I will that he tarry till I come, ᵐ what *is that* to thee?

24 This is the disciple which testifieth of these things, and wrote these things: and ⁿ we know that his testimony is true.

25 ° And there are also many other things which Jesus did, the which, if they should be written every one, ᵖ I suppose that even the world itself could not contain the books that should be written. Amen.

¹ Matt. 16. 27, 28; 25. 31; 1 Cor. 4. 5; 11. 26; Rev. 2. 25; 3. 11; 22. 7. 20.
ᵐ Deut. 29. 29; Job 33. 13.
ⁿ ch. 19. 35; 1 John 1. 1, 2; 3 John 12.
° ch. 20. 30, 31; Job 26. 14; Ps. 40. 5
ᵖ Amos 7. 10.

the claim would be absurd. They show that he claims to be "God blessed for evermore." **That he tarry** (*remain* in this life, Phil. 1 : 24, 25) **till I come.** Our Lord had already spoken of his coming to his disciples, ch. 14 : 18. In this use of the term it included his coming by the Spirit, his coming in judgment, and his coming personally at the close of this dispensation. Compare Mark 9 : 1; Matt. 26 : 64. "It is generally referred here to that notable coming at the destruction of Jerusalem which John alone lived to see, and which was the opening of that series of events that looked forward to the final coming to judgment, as in Matt. 25."—JACOBUS. John also had revealed to him on Patmos the whole series of events connected with Christ's kingdom and final coming. It is doubtful whether Christ intended to fix any specific time or give any definite indication of John's fate. His life was entirely in Christ's hands. If he so willed, he would live until he should come "the second time without sin unto salvation," Heb. 9 : 28. Jesus administers a rebuke to Peter in his reply, **what is that to thee?** He wishes that Peter should, in rigid earnestness, keep before his eye his own calling alone. "Every one of us shall give account of himself to God," Rom. 14 : 12. **Follow thou me.** The word *thou* is emphatic.—*Do thou follow me.* "*His* appointed lot is no element in *thy* appointed course; it is *me* that *thou* must follow."—ALFORD.

23. **Brethren,** the beautiful name by which Christ's followers were designated. The heathen writers ridiculed their love for each other. **That disciple should not die.** They inferred if Christ's coming meant his final coming to judgment, then John, remaining until that time, could not see death, 1 Cor. 15 : 51; 1 Thess. 4 : 17. The prevalence of this saying shows that they did not expect the coming of Christ in the near future. **Yet Jesus said not.** Jealous for the Saviour's honor, John removes the occasion of misunderstanding, and gives the Saviour's words. Patiently awaiting the revelation of the Master's will, John abides by the conditional "if I will." "This saying" had a wonderful vitality in the minds of many for several centuries, creating the belief that John had not really died.

24, 25. JOHN'S AUTHORSHIP ASSERTED, AND CONCLUSION.

24. **This is the disciple.** Some have regarded these verses as a later addition. But the manuscript authority is so great in their favor as to leave no reasonable doubt of their genuineness. The disciple just referred to is the author not of this chapter alone, but of the entire Gospel. John writes his name at the end of it, and bears witness to the truth of it. His *testifying* continues through all the ages; "Being dead, he yet speaketh." **We know.** Lange and others think the plural refers to the added testimony of the Ephesian church. But it is John's style to associate himself with his readers. See ch. 1 : 14; 1 John 4 : 14, 16. **Testimony is true.** See ch. 19 : 35.

25. John's Gospel was written last, with the design, in part, to fill up the gaps left by the other evangelists. But with this fourfold view of Christ his life is presented only in fragments

Yet this was to be the last inspired record of Jesus. Curiosity was now to be repressed, and all attempts to add to the gospel testimony were to be discountenanced. **Many other things** might have been written which Jesus did and said. See ch. 20 : 30. To describe the fulness of the acts and utterances of Jesus he employs a popular hyperbole (compare ch. 12 : 19), intimating the impossibility of recording all. There would be no room for all the riches of this divine life if the events of it were written out one by one. It will be part of the bliss of the glorified life to be the companions of the evangelists and learn more fully of Jesus, but infinitely more blessed to be with Jesus and learn from him. **Amen,** So let it be. The word, however, should be omitted, according to the highest critical authorities.

PRACTICAL REMARKS.

1. The resurrection of Jesus from the dead is established by repeated appearances to his disciples and by many infallible proofs, ver. 1 ; Acts 1 : 3 ; 1 Cor. 15 : 20.

2. Physical labor is not degrading; even the apostles of Christ shrank not from it, nor regarded it as inconsistent with waiting for the Lord, ver. 3 ; Acts 20 : 34 ; 1 Thess. 4 : 11.

3. Fruitless toil without Christ's presence becomes successful when Christ comes, ver. 3; John 15 : 5; Phil. 4 : 13.

4. In times of deepest darkness and need Jesus will reveal his presence, ver. 4 ; Ps. 40 : 6, 10, 15.

5. The daily wants of God's children are borne in mind by our heavenly Father, ver. 5 ; Matt. 6 : 11, 32.

6. God's sovereign purpose is in entire harmony with the use of means, ver. 6; Acts 27 : 24, 31.

7. Obedience to God's word, even if we walk in the dark, will cause God's face to shine upon us, ver. 6; John 7 : 17 ; 9 : 8.

8. Reverence for God is a fitting spirit with which to come into his presence, ver. 7 ; Ex. 3 : 5 ; Isa. 6 : 2.

9. At the end of this gospel age the net full of souls shall be drawn to the shore, ver. 11 ; Matt. 13 : 47, 48.

10. The gospel of the Saviour offers a continual feast for those who are hungry, ver. 12; Matt. 22 : 1-11; Rev. 3 : 20.

11. Personal love for Christ is the best preparation for pastoral work and for leading souls to salvation, ver. 15 ; 2 Cor. 5 : 14.

12. There are gradations in the Christian life—lambs and sheep; there is also the law of growth by which babes become men, ver. 16; Heb. 5 : 12-14; 1 John 2 : 12, 13.

13. The omniscience of God is a terror to the impenitent, but a delight and a refuge to the redeemed soul, ver. 17 ; Ps. 139 : 1-17.

14. Deep grief should follow the revelation of great sins, ver. 17 ; Ps. 51 : 3 ; 2 Cor. 7 : 10.

14. Life and death may equally glorify God, ver. 19; Ps. 116 : 15; Rom. 14 : 8.

15. We may still follow Jesus, walking in his footsteps, and become imitators of God, ver 19; Eph. 5 : 1 ; 1 Pet. 2 : 21.

16. It is better for us to ask, "What wilt thou have me to do?" than, "What shall this man do?" ver. 21; Acts 9 : 6; 2 Cor. 5 : 10.

17. It should be the first concern of every one to attend to his own proper business, ver. 22.

18. Our last appeal in religious controversy must be to the Scriptures of divine truth. "To the law and to the testimony" must be our cry, ver. 23; Isa. 8 : 20.

19. The disposal of all life rests in Jesus, ver. 23 ; Matt. 28 : 18.

20. The disciples, sealing their testimony with their blood, had no other object than to bear witness for the truth, ver. 24 ; 2 Cor. 4 : 2.

21. It is not the amount we write, but its fitness and propriety, ver. 24 ; Prov. 25 : 11.

22. An unwritten history of Jesus is reserved for us in heaven, and there will be time and space for the whole of it. Happy and blessed are they who shall be permitted to peruse it! ver. 25.

INDEX.

Abiding in Christ.......................... 246
Abraham and the Jews, 156–158;
 and Jesus........................163, 164
Ænon... 70
Andrew, 41; findeth Simon, 42;
 and Philip................................. 214
Angels ascending and descending. 47
Annas, 280; examination of Jesus
 before.. 283
Anointing at Bethany.................. 210
Apostles, inspired, 256, 257;
 Christ's witness-bearers............ 257
Appearances of Jesus to Mary
 Magdalene, 319; to the apostles,
 Thomas absent, 321; Thomas
 present, 524; to the seven at the
 Sea of Tiberias........................... 329

Baptism, 36; in water, 36; Holy
 Spirit, 39; nature of Christ's,
 69; and purifying....................... 71
Barabbas, 293; preferred to Jesus. 293
Baptizing, John, 36, 70, 76; Jesus
 not baptizing, but his disciples.. 76
Baskets, twelve........................... 112
Bethany, 195, 198, cave or tomb
 of Lazarus................................. 202
Bethesda, pool of....................94, 95
Bethsaida, its meaning and prob-
 able location............................. 44
"Bless" and "give thanks"....... 112
Blind man's eyes opened, 170;
 when and where, 168; on the
 Sabbath, 172; his parents fear
 to defend him, 174; the rulers
 examine and condemn him, 172,
 176, 177; put him out of the
 synagogue, 179; his interview
 with Jesus, 179; who rebukes
 the Pharisees............................. 180
Born of God, 31; again or from
 above......................................63–65
Born of water and the Spirit....... 64
Brothers of Jesus, 128; did not
 believe on him.......................... 129
Burial of Jesus, 311-313; where,
 312; time of.............................. 313

Caiaphas, 205, 280; his prophecy,
 205, 206; influences the people
 to put Jesus to death, 207; examination of Jesus before......... 284

Cana of Galilee, 49; marriage at,
 50; and Capernaum.................. 90
Capernaum, its probable site, 55,
 56; Jesus preaching in the synagogue of................................114ff
Casting the first stone................. 147
Christ, the bread of life, 117;
 from heaven, 119; the sustenance of believers, 120–122; a
 hard saying............................... 123
Christ a king, 289; concerning
 the truth.................................... 291
Christ's knowledge of what was
 in man, 60, 123; of himself...150–158
Christ, the light of the world..... 149
Christ's ministry, three stages of,
 58; early Judean....................... 74
Christ, the Messiah..................32, 84
Christ's opinion concerning an
 adulteress.................................. 146
Christ praying.................203, 215, 264
Christ's record of himself true,
 145ff; his Father, where........... 151
Christ, whence he is........135, 152, 153
Christ's withdrawal from the
 world, 258; its effect, 259; his
 help... 260
Christians kept by Christ's power,
 269; Christ glorified in them,
 268; belonging equally to the
 Father and the Son................... 268
Cleansing the temple, Jesus first... 56
Cleopas....................................... 305
Condemned unheard................... 141
Confession of the Twelve........... 124
Convicting of sin, righteousness,
 and judgment....................255, 256
Cross, of Jesus, 301; the super-
 scription over the, 302; attendants at the, 305; his death upon, 307; pierced, 309; taken
 down and buried, 312; Gol-
 gotha... 302
Crown of thorns.......................... 295
Crucifixion.................................. 301
Crucifixion of Jesus intimated,
 154; robbers crucified with him,
 303; the soldiers, 303; casting
 lots, 304; Scripture fulfilled,
 304, 306, 310
Crucifixion, a pre-judgment of
 the world................................... 216

INDEX.

Day, high, 308; preparation........ 299
Death, a sleep, 197; believers shall not see, 161, 162; preceding life, the dying seed germinating life, 215; Christ first intimates his, 59; his crucifixion, 67, 154; Christ's, would glorify the Father, 215, 216; of Jesus, 307; a broken or ruptured heart, 300; and resurrection of Jesus evidences of his Messiahship......... 154
Dedication, feast of..................... 188
Devil, his existence, 125, 150; the father of liars and murderers... 161
Disciple whom Jesus loved........... 218
Discipleship.............155, 231, 247, 248
Discourses of Christ, their relation to miracles in John, 108; of Jesus, 16, 61; to Nicodemus, 62; to a Samaritan woman, 78; vindicates himself in regard to the cure of the blind man on the Sabbath, 99; at Capernaum on the bread of life, 114; analyzed, 108; in the temple at the Feast of Tabernacles, 130; further teaching in the temple, representing himself as the light of the world, 148; the good shepherd, 183; at the last passover to his disciples, 230; valedictory discourse...............233–262
Dispersion, Jews of....................... 137
Divinity of Christ, 28, 313; remarks............................... 7, 8

" Eat the passover "....................... 287
Enon.. 70
Eternal life.................................. 67

Faith, imperfect, 90; answered, 91, 93; remarks, 42, 43; and eternal life, 102; and miracles... 91
Fall of Peter foretold............230, 231
Father and Sonship, 264, 107; remarks.................................13–20
Feast, of tabernacles, 127, 128; Jesus goes up privately, 130; the last great day of, 137; wedding, 51; governor of....................... 52
Feeding the five thousand, 110ff; place where, 111; attempts to explain away the miracle......... 112
First day of the week, 316, 327; remarks................................... 23
Flock or fold, Christ's, its extent.. 187
Food, perishable and imperishable.. 116
Four months and then the harvest... 86

Fountain of life............................ 138
Freedom, true, 155; freedom or bondage not of natural descent. 155, 156
Galilee, 43, 141; prophets of........ 142
Genuineness of ch. 7 : 53 to 8 : 11, 142; of 5 : 3, 4......................... 95
God a Spirit, 84; only begotten, or only begotten Son, 33; taking upon himself our nature, 47; remark................................ 2
Good Shepherd, 183; character of, 186; laying down his life for his sheep, 186; none shall be lost... 189
Gospel, the fourth, 7; when and where written, 10; its sources, 11; its design, 11; compared with the synoptic Gospels, 13, 15, 25; its peculiarities, 15; arrangement and analysis, 17; characteristics, 13, 14; object, 326; authorship..................3, 335
Gospels, the four, 4; synoptical view of.................................... 21
"Greater works"......................... 236
Greeks who would see Jesus, 213; when this occurred.................. 213
Groaning or indignant................. 201
Glorifying Christ, 264, 266; the Father..................................... 265
Glory, Christ's and the Christian's....................................... 273

Heart... 234
Hireling..................................... 185
"Holy of holies of evangelical history"................................... 233
Holy Spirit, the Comforter or Helper, 237, 251, 255; the source of consolation, 238; indwelling, gives spiritual light and life, 238; his instruction, 240; his guidance, 257; his mission and work, 254–256; the time of his coming, 254; see also remarks 15 and 17, p. 245; remarks 5, 6, and 7, p. 262; given to Jesus, 73; work of, 74; remarks........10, 17
Hosanna..................................... 212

Incarnation, at the foundation of the Gospel.............................47, 48
Intercessory prayer, Christ's, 264; prayer for himself, 264–266; for the apostles, 267–271; for believers...............................272–275
Impotent man, healing of............ 96

Jacob's well................................ 77

INDEX.

Jerusalem.................................. 34
Jesus, 38, 171; arrest of, 276; gives himself up, 277, 278; contact with those outside of Israel, 88; the door, 184; the way, 235; the good shepherd, 185; and the Father, 100-102, 105, 189; the Lamb of God, 38; and the Sabbath, 98-100; his defence against the charge of breaking, 107; remarks, 13-20; triumphal entry into Jerusalem, 212; Jesus receiving Messianic honors....... 212
Jews, whom in this Gospel, 33; and Abraham, 155-158; and the devil, 158, 159; Christ's reflections on their unbelief............... 218
John the Baptist, 29; his testimony to Jesus, 31, 32, 34, 38, 40, 71; his baptism, 36; why he came baptizing, 39; who he was, 34, 35; at Ænon, 70; his humility, 72; a burning and shining light, 104; and Jesus compared.. 192
John, the writer of this Gospel, 8; the son of thunder, 9; the one whom Jesus loved, 9, 228; in the book of the Acts, 10; at Ephesus, 10; tradition regarding his writing this Gospel, 4; evidences that he wrote it.........................7, 20
Jordan, Jesus beyond..................... 191
Joseph of Arimathea, 311; begging the body of Jesus............... 311
Judas Iscariot, 125; a thief and the betrayer, 210, 228; and Satan, 223, 229; pointed out as the traitor, 229; going out before the Lord's Supper, 230; treachery of.. 277
Judea.. 69
Judean ministry, early................74, 76
Judgment hall............................. 287

King, Jesus a............................. 290
Kingdom of God, 63; how and what Jesus taught, 64, 294; remarks, 26; how being born of water and the Spirit is necessary..............................64, 65
Kingdom, Christ's............290, 289, 291
Knowledge and faith..................... 265

Lamb of God............................. 38
Lazarus, meaning of, 194; the miracle of, 193; its design, 195, 203; its effect, 204, 205, 213; Jesus' love for........................... 201
Light of the world....................... 149
Life, 73; everlasting, 67; eternal.. 265

Letters, Jesus not knowing, 131; unlettered people accursed........ 141
Levites....................................... 34
Life, fountain of.......................... 138
Living water..........................79-81
Logos, the Word.......................... 38
Love, discourse on, 230, 233; remarks, 24, 26; of the brethren, 248; of Christ......................223, 268
Loving, his own to the end, 222, 223; the praise of men, 219, 221; remarks.................................... 31
"Lovest thou me"...................... 332

Malchus, right ear cut off, 279; healed by Jesus....................... 279
Malefactor................................ 288
Manna, and Moses, and Christ..... 117
Many mansions.......................... 234
Martha............................195, 198, 210
Mary Magdalene........................ 305
Mary, the three, 195; the sister of Lazarus, 195, 201, 210; anointing Jesus, 210; mother of Jesus...... 305
Messiah, the Christ, 32, 42, 84, 124; the Son of God, Jesus reveals himself................................84, 180
Miracles, 53, 54; credibility of, 55; Christ's first miracles, 53, 54; and faith, 91; second in Galilee, 92; and his discourses, 108; of Jesus, 54, 55; of turning water into wine, 49; heals a nobleman's son, 89; heals the impotent man at the pool of Bethesda, 94; feeds the five thousand, 109; walks upon the waters and stills the tempest, 113; heals a blind man on the Sabbath, 168-171; raising of Lazarus, 202; unrecorded 60, 326
Miraculous draught of fishes, 328; its meaning to the apostles....... 331
Money changers.......................... 57
Mother of Jesus and John at the cross....................................... 305
Mount Gerizim and Ebal.............. 82
"Much water," 70, 75; remark.... 23

Nathanael, 44; his conversion, 46; one of the seven to whom Jesus appears after his resurrection.... 329
Nazareth, its meaning, place, and characters................................ 45
New birth................................... 63
Nicodemus, 62; Christ's discourse to, 61ff; and the law, 141; at the burial of Jesus............................ 311
Nobleman's son healed................. 90

Passover, 60, 222; the first of Christ's ministry, 57; the second, 94; the third, 110; the fourth and last, 222; no discrepancy between John and the synoptics respecting the last passover, 222, 287; preparation of.. 299
Peace, Christ's............................... 240
Persecution foretold, 254; overcoming opposition............251, 262
Peter, 42, 43; cutting off the ear of Malchus, 278; denying his Lord, 281, 285, 286; at the sepulchre, 317; threefold confession of love, 332; his martyrdom predicted........................ 334
Pilate, 288; Jesus before, 287ff, 295–300; and the Jews, 288, 292, 296, 300, 303; and Jesus, 289–291, 298; and Cæsar................298, 299
Pharisees, 35, 140; John's testimony to.. 36
Prayer to be answered..........237, 250
Pre-existence of Christ............... 164
Philip, 43; and Nathanael, 44; and certain Greeks, 214; his request 235
Porter... 183
Priests.. 33
Prince of the world....................... 241
Promise of extraordinary powers, 236; of answers of prayers, 237, 250; of the Comforter, 237, 251, 255; to endure............................ 257
Prophet, 174; without honor in his own country.......................... 89
Prophets out of Galilee................ 142
Purple robe................................... 295

Regeneration, 63; Holy Spirit in, 74; remarks.................................. 10
Resurrection, of Jesus, 315; John's account and those of the other Gospels, 315; and Peter and John, 316; and Mary Magdalene, 318–320; and the apostles, 321–326; the apostles competent witnesses of, 325; body of Jesus, 321; of life and of judgment..... 103

Sabbath, its proper observance, 93; circumcising a man on the.. 134
Salvation....................................... 83
Samaria... 76
Samaritans, 79, 160; and Jews, 78, 79; the Saviour and salvation... 88
Samaritan woman....................... 76ff
Sanctification, 271; Christ's....271, 272
Sanhedrin, the letter.................... 172

Scribes.. 146
Scriptures, the, testifying to Christ...................................105, 106
Scourge, the................................. 294
Seal, on documents...................... 73
Sepulchre of Jesus, 312; place of.. 312
Sheep, 183; other sheep, 186; shall not perish................................. 189
Sheepfold...................................... 183
Shepherd and his sheep.............. 183
Siloam, pool of............................. 170
Sin and suffering, of parents and children, 168, 169, 181; remark... 3
Sinlessness of Christ................... 160
Sinner.....................................178, 176
Sins retained, or remitted........... 323
Sixth hour, in ch. 19 : 4, 299; Roman reckoning........................ 299
Son, of God, 40; of man, 47; only begotten, 33; of perdition......... 269
Sop, a... 229
Spirit and life, Christ's words are. 123
Spiritual worshipers true worshipers.. 83
Stone, attempting to stone Jesus, 164, 189
Supper at Bethany.................209–211
Supper being ended, served........ 223
Synagogue, its meaning and application, 122; casting out of, 176; the healed man cast out, 179; three degrees of excommunication from.......................... 176

Tabernacles, feast of................... 128
Teaching of Jesus, how to know it, 132; agreeable to God's will.. 132
Temple....................................57, 59
Tiberias, and lake of, 109, 115; Jesus never entered, 115; showed himself at the sea of................. 328
Thomas, 197; his question and Christ's answer, 235; doubting, 323, 324; believing, 325; at the sea of Tiberias............................ 325
" Touch me not "........................... 319
Treasury, the................................ 151
Trial of Jesus, first examination before Annas, 280, 283; before Caiaphas, 284, 287; the three before Pilate..............287, 294, 297
Truth, God's word is, 271; Pilate's question, what is? 291; making freemen................................155, 157

Unity, of the Father and Son, 189; of Christ and his disciples....272, 273

Valedictory discourse..............233–263

Vine, Christ, the true, 244; pruning, 245; and the branches....... 247
Walking on the water.................. 114
Washing his disciples' feet, 224, 225; Peter's refusal and assent, 225; significance of, 226, 232; remark, 9; the command, how obeyed..................226, 227
Water, living..................79, 80
Water pots.................... 51
"What have I to do with thee?". 51
Wine, 50; the good wine, 53; water turned into..................... 52
Works of God, which Christ did.. 169
World, the, 152; who are of the... 152
World's hatred of Christ and his disciples, 249; sinfulness of...... 250
Worshiping Jesus.................... 107
Writing on the ground.................. 147

www.ingramcontent.com/pod-product-compliance
Lightning Source LLC
Chambersburg PA
CBHW030007240426
43672CB00007B/853